Doing Business with Saudi Arabia

GLOBAL MARKET BRIEFINGS

Doing Business with Saudi Arabia

Third Edition

Consultant Editor:
Anthony Shoult
Middle East Series Editor:
Anthony Shoult

Forewords from:
Prince Turki Al-Faisal Al-Saud,
Saudi Ambassador to the United States of America

Sir Sherard Cowper-Coles,
British Ambassador to the Kingdom of Saudi Arabia

GMB

Saudi Basic Industries Corporation (SABIC)

Founded in 1976, Saudi Basic Industries Corporation – SABIC – is the largest and most profitable publicly traded company in the Middle East, the seventh largest petrochemical company in the world (in annual revenues), and ranks 22nd in the Financial Times 500.

The company is headquartered in Riyadh and has assets of US$33 billion, market capitalization of US$175 billion, annual production of more than 42 million metric tons, and product exports to more than 100 countries.

SABIC is the world's second largest producer of ethylene glycol, methanol and MTBE; third largest producer of polyethylene; and sixth largest producer of polypropylene.

Overall, SABIC is the world's fourth largest polyolefin producer. The company operates 18 industrial complexes in Saudi Arabia, two in Europe and three joint ventures based in Bahrain.

Publisher's note

Every possible effort has been made to ensure that the information contained in this book is accurate at the time of going to press, and the publishers and authors cannot accept responsibility for any errors or omissions, however caused. No responsibility for loss or damage occasioned to any person acting, or refraining from action, as a result of the material in this publication can be accepted by the editor, the publisher or any of the authors.

This third edition first published in Great Britain and the United States in 2006 by GMB Publishing Limited

120 Pentonville Road
London N1 9JN
UK
www.gmbpublishing.com

525 South 4th Street
#241 Philadelphia, PA 191471573
USA

ISBN 1-905050-06-2

British Library Cataloguing-in-Publication Data

A CIP record for this book is available from the British Library

---

Library of Congress Cataloguing-in Publication Data

Doing business with Saudi Arabia / consultant editor, Anthony Shoult.– 3rd ed.

p. cm.

ISBN 1-905050-06-2

1. Saudi Arabia–Foreign economic relations. 2. Investments, Foreign–Saudi Arabia. 3. Business etiquette–Saudi Arabia. 4. Saudi Arabia–Economic conditions. I. Title: Saudi Arabia. II. Shoult, Anthony.

HF1584.7.D65 2006

330.9538–dc22 2005029828

Typeset by Digital Publishing Solutions

Printed and bound in Great Britain

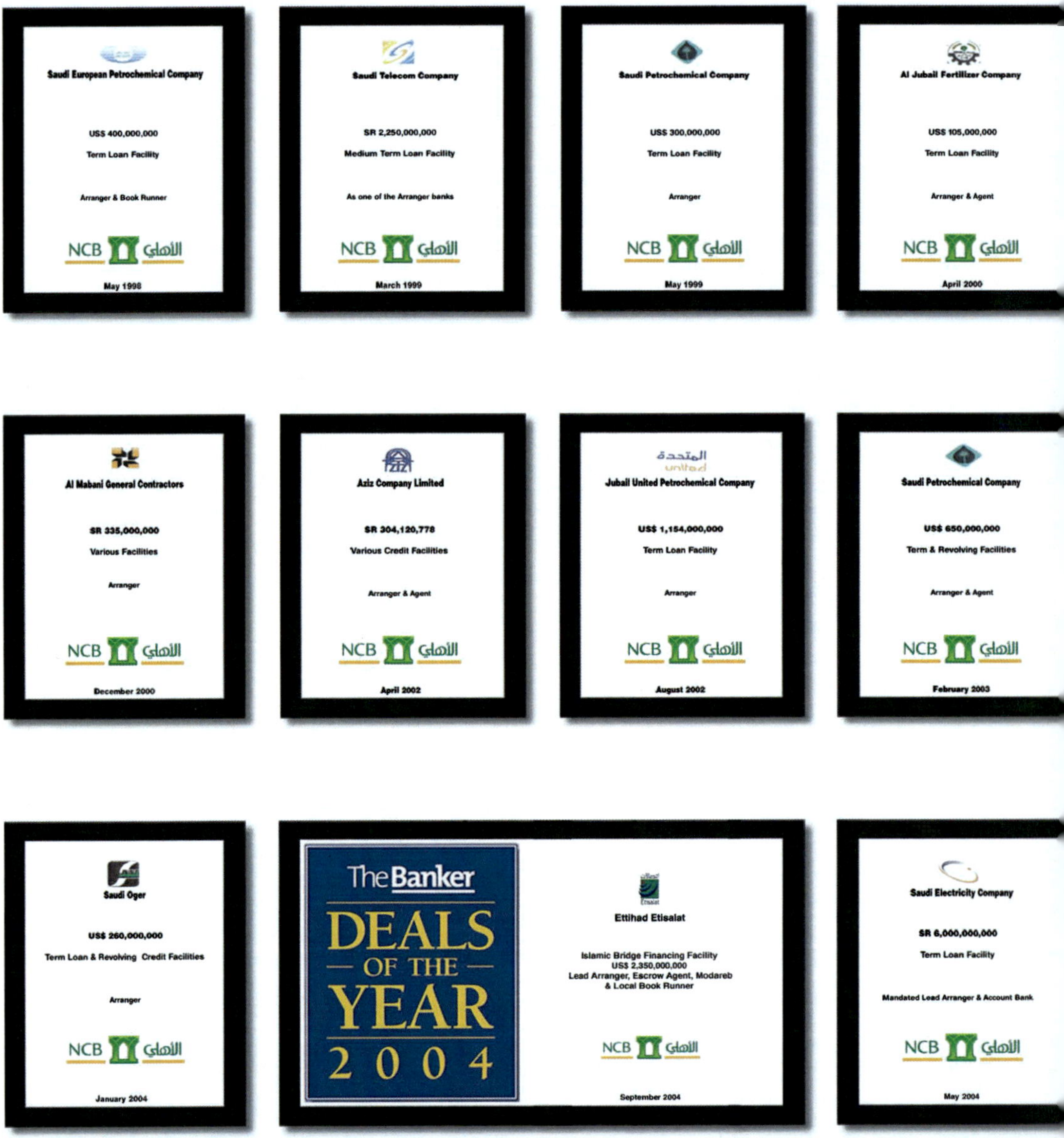
Saudi European Petrochemical Company
US$ 400,000,000
Term Loan Facility
Arranger & Book Runner
NCB الأهلي
May 1998
Saudi Telecom Company
SR 2,250,000,000
Medium Term Loan Facility
As one of the Arranger banks
NCB الأهلي
March 1999
Saudi Petrochemical Company
US$ 300,000,000
Term Loan Facility
Arranger
NCB الأهلي
May 1999
Al Jubail Fertilizer Company
US$ 105,000,000
Term Loan Facility
Arranger & Agent
NCB الأهلي
April 2000
Al Mabani General Contractors
SR 335,000,000
Various Facilities
Arranger
NCB الأهلي
December 2000
Aziz Company Limited
SR 304,120,778
Various Credit Facilities
Arranger & Agent
NCB الأهلي
April 2002
المتحدة
united
Jubail United Petrochemical Company
US$ 1,154,000,000
Term Loan Facility
Arranger
NCB الأهلي
August 2002
Saudi Petrochemical Company
US$ 650,000,000
Term & Revolving Facilities
Arranger & Agent
NCB الأهلي
February 2003
Saudi Oger
US$ 260,000,000
Term Loan & Revolving Credit Facilities
Arranger
NCB الأهلي
January 2004
The Banker
DEALS OF THE YEAR 2004
Ettihad Etisalat
Islamic Bridge Financing Facility
US$ 2,350,000,000
Lead Arranger, Escrow Agent, Modareb & Local Book Runner
NCB الأهلي
September 2004
Saudi Electricity Company
SR 6,000,000,000
Term Loan Facility
Mandated Lead Arranger & Account Bank
NCB الأهلي
May 2004

Contents

Part Three: Legal Framework and Business Regulation

Part Four: Finance, Accountancy and Taxation

Part Five: Marketing and Promotion

Part Six: The Business Environment

Part Seven: Key Sectors of Trade and Investment

It's easier to think outside the box when you're not staying in one.
Welcome to the 'new' InterContinental Jeddah.

Foreword

The Kingdom of Saudi Arabia is experiencing exciting and challenging times.

In the past three decades, Saudi Arabian economic development has been broadly governed by Five Year Development Plans. Our Eighth Development Plan is due to be published soon and is expected to continue to further liberalize and reform the economy as we look forward towards our accession to the World Trade Organization.

Saudi Arabia remains the main economic powerhouse of the entire Middle East, with the largest banking sector and stock market, as well as being the largest exporter, importer of goods. It holds the world's largest proven oil reserves, and gas reserves are increasing rapidly as new discoveries are made. The modern infrastructure equals that of major industrialized countries. We have developed state-of-the-art industries, hospitals, educational institutions, communications, transport facilities and other services.

Today we have a world class petrochemical industry, operated by the Saudi Arabian Basic Industries Corporation (SABIC), which is the largest non-oil >industrial producer. As a result we have two major industrial cities: Jubail on the Arabian Gulf and Yanbu on the Red Sea. These prosperous economic enclaves have not only been a success story for Saudi Arabia, but have become the model on which other world petrochemical enterprises have been based.

We have mega projects on the drawing board forecasting their worth at US $624 billion open to local, regional and international investors. The past year has seen unprecedented high rates of growth in the Kingdom, fuelled by the economic reforms and current demand for oil. The opportunities are great and the future is bright.

I trust that this edition of 'Doing Business with Saudi Arabia' will provide companies seeking to conduct business in the Kingdom with valuable information to encourage them in pursing their business interests.

H.R.H Prince Turki Al-Faisal Al Saud
Ambassador to the United States of America

Foreword

Saudi Arabia continues to see steady growth and offers tremendous business potential, driven by high oil prices and production levels, as well as a construction boom. The underlying economic fundamentals are staggering.

Saudi Arabia holds the world's largest proven reserves of oil. Its known gas reserves are increasing rapidly as new discoveries are made. It is planning to raise oil and gas production by some 30 per cent in the next few years, with infrastructure to match, and the Kingdom accounts for 25 per cent of the Arab world's GDP.

The real estate market is buoyant, local banks have performed exceptionally well, and the stock market grew by 83 per cent in 2004. Real GDP growth for 2004 is estimated at 5.3 per cent. Assuming oil prices hold up, the outlook for 2005 is equally promising.

Reaping a windfall from record prices for its crude exports, Saudi Arabia announced, in December, a 2004 budget surplus of SR98 billion (US$26.1 billion) and set a balanced budget for 2005 with revenue and expenditure projected at SR280 billion (about US$74.5 billion). This reflects an increase over 2004 expenditure of SR50 billion (about US$13.3 billion).

Saudi Arabia is also facing up to its demographic challenges: a population of some 25 million, growing at three per cent per annum and expected to reach 47 million by 2020, while 60 per cent of Saudis are under 20 years old. Government spending plans focus sensibly on developing social infrastructure to keep pace with this rapid growth. The budget for the 2005 financial year provides for a SR70.1 billion investment in education, with a focus on building capacity in the vocational and technical education sector. This figure includes SR14.65 billion for new schools, technical colleges and universities. A further SR27.1 billion will be invested in health services and social development, including building and renovating 420 primary healthcare centres and 23 new hospitals.

Efforts are also being made to create a better environment for foreign direct investment. The new Foreign Investment Law has come into force, new sectors are being opened up to foreign investors, and the regulatory framework is being revised and simplified.

Saudi Arabia remains the UK's largest trade and investment partner in the Middle East. The healthy growth in two-way trade continues, with commercial partnerships flourishing and visible exports again set to exceed £1.4 billion for 2004. There are over 150 UK/Saudi joint ventures, with a total investment of around US$3.5 billion. New ventures are in the pipeline.

At the same time, Saudi Arabia has had to tackle a serious terrorist threat, which may take time to eradicate. The Saudi security authorities have made real progress, but would be the first to admit that there is still some way to go. In the meantime, those who want to do business in, and with, the most important economy in the Middle East need to keep a sense of proportion about the dangers of terrorism.

All of this sends out a strong positive message. UK business should feel encouraged to explore what are real and significant opportunities. This third edition of *Doing Business with Saudi Arabia* is an important and up-to-date reference point for anyone approaching the market. It includes contributions from authorities on diverse business topics, and provides genuine insights into the Saudi market and business culture.

I would also strongly encourage companies to contact the UK Trade & Investment teams in Saudi Arabia (in Riyadh, Jeddah and Al Khobar), who are able to advise on market entry and help Saudi companies looking for British partners. We are also able to help companies and individual business representatives to address any security worries they may have.

Sir Sherard Cowper-Coles KCMG, LVO
British Ambassador to Saudi Arabia

List of Contributors

Al Harithy Company for Exhibitions is one of Saudi Arabia's three principal exhibition organizers that are able to provide world-class facilities in purpose-built exhibition halls in the heart of the Kingdom's major business locations.

Al Harithy is a specialist exhibitions organizer for Jeddah-based exhibitions.

Al Yaqoub Legal Advisers (ALA) is a leading Saudi law firm and member of Ernst & Young International. Al Yaqoub Legal Advisers are established as corporate, commercial and business lawyers throughout the Kingdom of Saudi Arabia, with law offices in the Kingdom's major cities, Riyadh, Jeddah and Al Khobar.

Kamal K Mahjoub is a Legal Counsel with Al Yaqoub Legal Advisers.

ASA Consulting is a UK-based independent marketing-focused consultancy specializing in the Middle East region. The firm provides a wide range of consultancy services across industrial sectors, either directly or through affiliated organizations, to both international and Saudi public and private sector agencies and organizations. The services provided include assistance to investors in specific areas such as market research and investigations for technical and industrial products and services and techno-economic feasibility studies to the standard required by Saudi Industrial Development Fund (SIDF).

Examples of the work undertaken by ASA Consulting are as follows:

- power and water industry – market study for gas turbine filters in Saudi Arabia and feasibility study for water treatment plant and installations facility;
- minerals and mining industry – world market study for barite used in the oil and gas drilling mud and other industrial applications and study of the GCC market for basalt wool;

- agriculture – review of the marketing operation of a major Saudi agricultural products producer and a feasibility study for a food processing plant;
- manufacturing industry – ASA Consulting has conducted a large number of manufacturing industry-related market and techno-economic feasibility studies in Saudi Arabia and other Middle East countries including the following:
  - market study for industrial polyurethane products manufacturing in Saudi Arabia (2004);
  - feasibility study for industrial valve refurbishment services in Saudi Arabia (2004);
  - market study for a specialist vehicle manufacturing plant in Saudi Arabia (2003);
  - feasibility study for steel industrial flooring manufacturing plant in Saudi Arabia (2001);
- construction industry – study of utilization of thermal energy storage air conditioning systems in the Saudi construction industry (2005);
- medical and healthcare – market, techno-economic and financial feasibility study for the establishment of an intravenous solutions manufacturing facility in Saudi Arabia (2001);
- travel and tourism – market study for the establishment of an integrated travel and tourism centre in Riyadh.

Anthony Shoult is a Director and Principal Consultant of ASA Consulting. He is also Consultant Editor for *Doing Business with Saudi Arabia* and Series Editor for the GMB Publishing Middle East business book series.

As a result of the Al-Yamamah project, the **British Offset Office** was established to help encourage greater investment and assist the transfer of new technology into Saudi Arabia. It comprises personnel from the UK Ministry of Defence and BAE Systems (BAES) and is responsible for planning, coordinating and administering the UK's involvement in the offset programme. It actively looks for ways to assist technology-holding companies to identify new business opportunities in Saudi Arabia. Experience of Saudi Arabia and the special arrangements of the Al-Yamamah Economic Offset Programme make it possible for the Offset Office to offer companies detailed and confidential guidance on the development of project ideas.

The British Offset Office has offices in the UK and Saudi Arabia and, with its merchant bank advisers, can provide an unparalleled level of knowledge and experience on business in the Kingdom. Furthermore, UK companies working through the offset programme benefit from the status derived from their proposals being administered on a government-to-government basis.

Further information concerning the Al-Yamamah Economic Offset Programme and the new project financing facility can be obtained from the British Offset Office via their website at www.britishoffset.com.

Colin Clarke, Executive General Manager of **Yusuf Bin Ahmed Kanoo**, contributed information that has been incorporated into chapters 7.2 and 7.3. Yusuf Bin Ahmed Kanoo is a diverse group, with corporate offices based in Dammam. Activities include shipping, travel, freight forwarding, oil field supplies, machinery, power and industrial projects and chemicals.

Formed in 1765, **Cluttons** is one of the leading firms of Chartered Surveyors and Property Consultants in the UK, with its head office in central London. Since 1976 Cluttons has established a strong real estate presence within the Middle East through its growing and integrated network of offices throughout the Arabian Gulf with branches in Jeddah, Bahrain, Dubai, Sharjah and Oman.

The services provided by Cluttons in Saudi Arabia and throughout the Middle East include international valuations and appraisals, development consultancy and feasibility reports, project coordination, market reports, property and portfolio management, marketing and letting, facilities management, international sales and investment advice.

In Saudi Arabia, Cluttons has a joint venture with Project Management and Development Company (PMDC). Operating as PMDC Cluttons, the team has advised on the management of the Lotus Residential Compounds, beach resorts, various office buildings, the Madinah Mall and other property projects across Saudi Arabia. In addition, PMDC Cluttons operate, manage and lease the prestigious Abraj Al-Bait Shopping Centre in Makkah, the fifth tallest building in the world.

Together with its partners SYRA House, a Jeddah-based market research company, **ERAS** has worked on a wide range of studies and business development projects for consumer products and services, real estate and industrial products. While focusing on Saudi Arabia, ERAS' market research work has covered all the Arabian Gulf states as well as much of the Middle East.

David Green is a Senior Consultant with ERAS Limited, a UK-based business development and market research company, having strong links with the Middle East.

Ernst & Young is a leading Saudi professional services firm and member of Ernst & Young International. Ernst & Young offers a full range of audit and accounting, taxation, corporate finance and business advisory services to private enterprises and government agencies in Saudi Arabia.

Green Vista Agriculture is a firm of management consultants specializing in the agricultural sector of Saudi Arabia. **John Lawton** is a Director of Green Vista Agriculture Specialists.

Gulf International Bank (GIB) is a leading merchant bank in the Middle East, with its principal focus on the Gulf Cooperation (GCC) states. With a proven track record spanning more than 28 years, GIB provides client-led, innovative financial products and services. Its client base includes major private sector corporations, Gulf-based financial institutions, multinational companies active in the region and the governments of the GCC states.

GIB is now one of the most respected banks in the Arab world, with total assets of US$19.1 billion and shareholders' equity of US$1.53 billion at the end of December 2004. GIB currently has branches in London, New York and Riyadh, in addition to representative offices in Beirut and Abu Dhabi.

Michael J Parkhouse was Head of Investment Banking at Gulf International Bank in Riyadh from 1993 until March 2005. From April 2005, Salman M Al-Deghaither has succeeded him in this position.

The **Islamic Development Bank** is an international financial institution established to foster economic development and social progress of member countries and Muslim communities in non-member countries individually as well as jointly in accordance with the principles of *Shari'a*, (Islamic law). The present membership of the Bank consists of 54 countries.

The bank participates in equity capital and grants loans for productive projects and enterprises, providing financial assistance to member countries in other forms for economic and social development. The Bank is also required to establish and operate special funds for specific purposes, including a fund for assistance to Muslim communities in non-member countries, in addition to setting up trust funds. The Bank is authorized to accept deposits and to mobilize financial resources through *Shari'a* compatible modes. It is also charged with the responsibility of assisting in the promotion of foreign trade, especially in capital goods, among member countries and in providing technical assistance and training.

Dr Bashir Fadlalla is a senior officer with the Islamic Development Bank of Jeddah, which offers a range of Islamic banking products. These include profit sharing contracts for equity financing such as Al-Mudarabah and Al-Musharakah.

Saleh Hejailan established the **Law Firm of Al-Saleh Hejailan (LSFH)** in Riyadh in 1967. Since then, LSFH has become the largest law practice in the Kingdom of Saudi Arabia and is regarded as the pre-eminent law firm in the region. The firm is staffed by seven Western lawyers who are qualified to practise in the US and the UK, as well as 15 local attorneys from various jurisdictions in the Middle East. LFSH, which has offices in Riyadh and Jeddah, is a full service law firm with particular expertise in the areas of corporate and commercial law, banking and finance, commercial litigation and government contracting.

Jean-Benoît Zegers, a UK-qualified solicitor who holds an LLB (Hons) from the University of Auckland, is on temporary secondment from the Paris office of Freshfields Bruckhaus Deringer, where he works in the international commercial arbitration department.

Dr Yahya Al Salman, who holds a PhD from the University of Dundee, is an assistant Professor of Law and International Arbitration at the Institute of Diplomatic Studies at King Saud University and has acted as legal adviser to the Ministry of Foreign Affairs and the Council of Ministers.

Legal Advisors, in association with **Baker & McKenzie Limited**, is a leading law firm in Saudi Arabia and is a member of Baker & McKenzie International a Swiss Verein, which has member offices worldwide.

Riyadh Bank was established in 1957 as the Kingdom's first Saudi joint stock banking company. It has 193 branches in addition to

ERNST & YOUNG OFFICES AND CONTACTS IN SAUDI ARABIA

Riyadh

Telephone No. +966 1 273 4740 Fax No. +966 1 273 4730

Contacts	Service Line	E-mail
Abdulaziz Al-Sowailim	Audit	Abdulaziz.Al-Sowailim@sa.ey.com
Paul Bevan	Audit	Paul.Bevan@sa.ey.com
Gordon Bennie	Risk Management (Internal Audit)	Gordon.Bennie@sa.ey.com
Gaafar M Eisa	Tax and Zakat	Gaafar.Eisa@sa.ey.com
Kevin C O'Brien	Tax and Zakat	Kevin.Obrien@sa.ey.com
Phil Gandier	Business Advisory	Phil.Gandier@sa.ey.com
Meraj Ahmed	Technology and Security	Meraj.Ahmed@sa.ey.com

Jeddah

Telephone No. +966 2 667 1040 Fax No. +966 2 667 2129

Contacts	Service Line	E-mail
Dr. Abdullah A Baeshen	Audit	Abdullah.Baeshen@sa.ey.com
Richard Chatwin	Audit	Richard.Chatwin@sa.ey.com
Mohammed Saleem Desin	Tax and Zakat	Mohammed.Desin@sa.ey.com

Al Khobar

Telephone No. +966 3 882 5414 Fax No. +966 3 882 7224

Contacts	Service Line	E-mail
Riad Shafik Feddah	Audit	Riad.Feddah@sa.ey.com
Abdulaziz S. AlShubaibi	Audit	Abdulaziz.Shubaibi@sa.ey.com
Naveed Ahmed Jeddy	Tax and Zakat	Naveed.Jeddy@sa.ey.com

* Time Zone: GMT +3

ey.com/me & eyonline.com

ERNST & YOUNG
Quality In Everything We Do

ladies' banking sections and a network of more than 450 Automated Teller Machines throughout the Kingdom. The Bank enjoys an international presence through its London Branch, Houston Agency and Singapore Representative Office, in addition to its global correspondent banking relationships.

Dr Khan Zahid is Chief Economist and Vice President of Riyadh Bank, Riyadh.

The Saudi Arabian Business Information and Economic Research Centre (SABIERC) of which John Presley is the founding director, was established in 1994 primarily to promote trade and business relations between Saudi Arabia and Britain. Professor Presley has written 15 books on various topics including the Saudi Arabian economy, banking in the Arab Gulf and Islamic finance, and has contributed over 150 articles to academic and popular journals and magazines.

Professor John Presley was Professor of Economics at Loughborough University, UK between 1984 until his retirement in 2004. He has also been chief economic adviser to The Saudi British Bank since 1980 and continues in this role.

The primary objective of the **Saudi Arabian General Investment Authority (SAGIA)** is to oversee investment affairs in Saudi Arabia, including foreign investment. In fulfilling this role, SAGIA has responsibility for proposing and implementing policies that encourage both local and foreign investment and for issuing investment licences and other documents required by foreign investors to enable the obtaining of visas and other permits.

Other functions of SAGIA include the development of policies that promote investment in Saudi Arabia; making recommendations for the improvement of the Kingdom's investment environment; evaluating and following up investment opportunities of perceived potential and subsequently promoting them both domestically and internationally; working closely with government agencies directly related to foreign and local investment; undertaking research and developing databases; and participating in conferences, exhibitions, seminars and symposia on investment, both at home and overseas.

Trilaterial Training Solutions is a specialist firm involved in the field of intercultural management training services for multinational companies and organizations. **Dr Jehad Al-Omari**, who manages Trilaterial Training Solutions, is a management consultant with over 16 years' experience in the field of inter-cultural management. He has worked with a wide range of multinational companies both as an adviser and trainer. Much of his work focuses on 'doing business in the Arab world' and 'multicultural teams'. This involves considerable work on a variety of disciplines including communication and negotiation skills. He has, on many occasions, trained potential trainers for large multinational companies.

Part One

Country Background

1.1

Country Overview

Anthony Shoult, ASA Consulting[1]

Introduction

With an economy of first-world proportions, a developed infrastructure and some examples of quite startling modern infrastructure, it is easy to forget how far Saudi Arabia has come in just three generations.

The discovery of huge quantities of oil in the 1930s – the Kingdom has around one quarter of the world's proven oil reserves – and more recently gas, has propelled the country from an underdeveloped, disparate state to a modern, first-world economy.

It is the largest Arab economy, formed in 1932 when Abdul Aziz bin Abdul Rahman Al-Saud (known as Ibn Saud) united different regions of the Arabian Peninsula into one nation. It was King Abdul Aziz who laid the foundations for the modernization of his country. He began to develop its infrastructure, improve education, healthcare and agriculture, and introduced modern technology.

The current ruler, King Abdullah bin Abdul Aziz Al-Saud, succeeded to the throne in August 2005, following the death of King Fahd bin Abdul Aziz Al-Saud, who, in 1986, had stopped using the title 'His Majesty', having taken the title 'Custodian of the Two Holy Mosques'.

Geography

Saudi Arabia is about 2.2 million square kilometres in area, bordered by the Gulf to the east, the United Arab Emirates and Oman to the south east and Yemen to the south, the Red Sea to the west and Iraq, Jordan and Kuwait to the north.

Most of the country consists of desert. The Rub'al-Khali (Empty Quarter) in the south occupies about half the country. In the north, is Arabia's second great sand desert, the Nafud.

[1] Sources of information include UK Trade & Investment.

Mountains on the western side of the Kingdom run parallel with the Red Sea coast. The Eastern Province is generally low lying and flat, with a number of salt flats or *sabkhas*.

Daytime temperatures can rise to over 45°C between May and September, with high humidity in the coastal regions. Summer night-time temperatures give little relief, falling to only 28°C.

Winter temperatures (December to February) in the main cities drop to around 20°C during the day and may fall to below 10°C at night, particularly in the central deserts.

Riyadh is the capital city, with an estimated population of over 4.7 million. All the main Saudi government offices are located here. Jeddah, with a population of approximately two million, is the other main business centre and the largest harbour on the Red Sea.

Dammam and Al Khobar on the Gulf coast, are the two main towns in the Eastern province, which has a population of 2.9 million, and serves Saudi Aramco, the world's largest oil producer.

Makkah has around 1.5 million inhabitants. It is the most sacred city in Islam and closed to non-Muslims. Madinah has a population of 1.1 million and is Islam's second holiest city, as the prophet Mohammed and a number of his disciples are buried here. Only the centre of the city is closed to non-Muslims.

The central region

The central region is dominated by the capital city, Riyadh. Riyadh is the seat of government and home to the various ministries that still do much to direct and guide the economic life of Saudi Arabia.

As a capital of a conservative Islamic state, Riyadh is rather formal and the more traditional elements of business and social etiquette are more in evidence here than in some other cities. A short drive out of the sprawling city, however, reveals a stunning escarpment and ancient landscape dotted with camel trails – a reminder that trade here is nothing new.

The central region is considered to be the heartland of Saudi Arabia, both physically and culturally. It is a vast eroded plateau, consisting of areas of uplands, broad valleys and dry rivers.

There are also a number of marshes in the area, believed to be the remnants of inland seas that existed in ancient geological times. Most of the central region is arid, with some oases in the north around Qasim, 300 miles to the north of Riyadh.

The area south of Riyadh around Kharj is a major source of wheat, and part of the Kingdom's burgeoning agricultural industry; while the area around Qasim is an even larger farming area that spearheads the Kingdom's self-sufficiency in wheat and poultry.

The western region (the Hijaz)

Jeddah, the 'Pearl of the Red Sea', is the country's main port and the centre of commercial activity. It is brisk and business-like, a thriving commercial centre for hundreds of years.

Jeddah is the main commercial centre of the western region, or the Hijaz, which comprises the west coast of the Kingdom, north of Asir. The Hijaz contains a north–south mountain chain (up to 3,000 metres in height), decreasing gradually in elevation as it moves northward, and the coastal plain bordering the Red Sea.

The western region is also home to the holiest cities of Islam, Makkah and Madinah, which are visited by some two million Muslims annually. Every year, over two million Muslims make the *Hajj*, or major pilgrimage, to the holy city of Makkah. Hundreds of thousands more make the *Umrah*, or minor pilgrimage. The entire city of Makkah is closed to non-Muslims.

The Eastern Province

The third major region of Saudi Arabia is the Eastern Province, centred around the two conurbations of Dammam and Al Khobar, and where Western influence is more apparent than in other parts of the Kingdom.

The Eastern Province, which sits on a quarter of the world's oil reserves, regards itself as the industrial heartland of Saudi Arabia. It is the home of Saudi Aramco, the world's largest fully-integrated oil and gas company; Saudi Basic Industries Corporation (SABIC), the Middle East's largest petrochemical producer; the rapidly expanding Jubail industrial complex; the Kingdom's premier university, King Fahd University of Petroleum and Minerals (KFUPM); and the town of Hofuf centred in the middle of the world's largest oasis. In addition, Dammam has a huge commercial port.

The Eastern Province is linked to Bahrain by the 25 kilometre King Fahd Causeway, making downtown Bahrain and its airport about one hour's drive from Al Khobar.

The American influence that is present all over the country is particularly apparent here in the oil and gas dominated east, where the cities are low-rise and more informal.

The south-western region (the Asir)

The south-western region, or the Asir, is the relatively fertile area of coastal mountains in the extreme south-west of Saudi Arabia, near Yemen.

Mountains peaks rise to 3,000 metres and there is ample rainfall to support natural vegetation and cultivation. With some juniper trees, wild olive trees and even some larger trees, Asir is the only part of the Kingdom to support woodland.

Due to its attractive climate and the fertility of the land, the south-western region has always been relatively densely populated. With the implementation of government irrigation schemes, the effective exploitation of the region's agricultural potential is a key objective.

Religion and the role of Islam

As home to the two holiest places in Islam, Makkah and Madinah, Saudi Arabia is the centre of the Islamic world.

Unsurprisingly, it conducts its affairs in an Islamic way. Thus, no alcohol or pork products can be imported and there is no live entertainment, although definitions of entertainment are being stretched.

Public executions are not uncommon for offences such as murder and drug trafficking. There are restrictions on what women may do in public and everything stops five times during the day for prayers.

This combination of strict application of rules and laws and what some see in the West as a different mindset has given Saudi Arabia the reputation of being a difficult place in which to do business, but it need not be so.

The industrial cities

The industrial cities of Jubail on the Gulf and Yanbu on the Red Sea have been an integral part of Saudi Arabia's drive to develop hydrocarbon-based and energy-intensive industries. The basic infrastructure for the two cities, often described as the jewels in the Kingdom's industrial crown, was formulated in 1975 by Royal Decree.

Jubail is the larger of the two cities, but both have large and modern deep-water ports, from which products manufactured locally and in other areas of the Kingdom are exported. They both have export terminals for crude oil and liquefied natural gas.

The two cities constitute a unique experiment in development that has so far proved outstandingly successful. They were conceived on the drawing board and were planned to provide a purpose-built and highly-efficient environment for modern petrochemical and industrial production.

The massive investment centred on the cities is designed to achieve a significant reduction in the Kingdom's dependence on oil revenues by gaining access to the world's petrochemical markets, thereby exploiting Saudi Arabia's natural advantages of cheap energy and cheap raw materials for petrochemical manufacture.

Both Yanbu and Jubail offer sites at low rents and low-cost utilities, as well as a wide range of industrial facilities, for healthcare, education, telecommunications, transport and recreation.

New developments

In December 2005, Saudi Arabia announced its intention to create a new commercial and industrial city to be called King Abdullah Economic City, at Rabigh on the Red Sea, north of Jeddah. At an investment cost of SR100 billion (US$26.6 billion), this will be the single largest private sector investment in Saudi Arabia. It will involve the development of a greenfield site of 55 million square metres, with a 35 kilometre shoreline including a world-class seaport covering an area of 2.6 million square metres. It will also include an industrial district covering eight million square metres for the development of both heavy and light industries and a financial and commercial centre that will provide employment for some 60,000 professionals.

1.2

People, History and Culture

Anthony Shoult, ASA Consulting[1]

Geographical location

Saudi Arabia is located at the heart of the Arabian Peninsula in a region of great cultural and geographical significance due to its central location between the continents of Asia, Europe and Africa. Its major strategic significance is due to the fact that Saudi Arabia is bounded by the Arabian Gulf to the east, the Red Sea to the west and the Arabian Sea to the south. Saudi Arabia is bordered by the Arab countries of Kuwait, Iraq, Syria and Jordan to the north and to the south by Yemen and Oman, all ancient civilizations steeped in cultural heritage. Caravans have connected these centres of civilization since ancient times, and it was the seafaring traders of Syria and the southern Arabian Peninsula who originally carried the religion of Islam to the peoples of south-east Asia and Africa.

The Kingdom of Saudi Arabia forms the major part of the Arabian Peninsula that comprises the Arab-speaking peoples. The Kingdom's relations with its neighbouring countries have been good, and natural barriers have not obstructed direct ties. Sea, land and air transportation have all helped to facilitate the Kingdom's increasing economic access to the wider international community. Saudi's access to the Mediterranean countries through the Red Sea has encouraged trading links with the Arab countries of North Africa as well as with southern European countries bordering the Mediterranean. The Red Sea also connects the Kingdom with the eastern side of the African continent, giving access to Egypt, Sudan, Somalia, Djibouti and Ethiopia, while the Arabian Gulf provides the Kingdom with access to the important economic market countries of east and south Asia.

---

[1] Based on information provided by Sami T Salman of Arabian Services Group.

International significance

The location of Saudi Arabia at the very heart of the Islamic world gives it enormous international significance for all Muslims. This is because all Muslims, whether in the east or the west, turn to the Holy Shrines or the Holy Kaabah to perform their prayers five times a day. It is at the Prophet's Mosque in Madinah that millions of Muslim pilgrims congregate each year during the pilgrimage season. It was from this country that Arabs went out more than 1,400 years ago to preach the message of Islam to the world. This noble enterprise gave rise to the distinguished position held by the Kingdom of Saudi Arabia in the Muslim world today. This is because the Kingdom has been bestowed as the custodian of Islam's Holy Shrines and protector of the land in which God's message of adherence to Islam as a religion, law and constitution was revealed.

Population and lifestyles

The population of Saudi Arabia consists of a number of tribes, each occupying a region with which they are traditionally associated. The late King Abdul Aziz Al-Saud (better known as Ibn Saud) reigned for three decades and, being known for his great wisdom and sense of justice, is acknowledged to have played a major role in uniting the scattered tribes of Saudi Arabia.

The lifestyles of the Kingdom's inhabitants of the various regions, namely the modes and patterns of life of those living in the Western, Central, Eastern and Southern Provinces of Saudi Arabia, are dealt with in the following four sections.

Inhabitants of the Western Province

The Hijaz, widely referred to as the Western Province, is the native land of those referred to as Hijazis. Since ancient times, fishermen and farmers of this region have inhabited settled communities alongside other groups leading a nomadic life. The people of Hijaz were distinguished by their trading activities. Every year, the Quraysh tribe of Makkah used to assemble trade caravans, dispatching them to the north and south of the country. In the Surah of Quraysh, the Holy *Qur'an* referred to the journeys of this tribe more than fourteen centuries ago in the following verse:

> *.....by winter and summer, let them adore the Lord of this House, who provides them with food against hunger, and with security against fear.*

With the advent of Islam and its onset in this region, particularly in Makkah, later to become the prime source of Muslim inspiration, commerce and trade prospered spectacularly. Caravans and merchant vessels owned by Muslims used to frequent all parts of the then-known ancient world, carrying goods and products needed by the Islamic countries. In their travels to other non-Islamic countries, tradesmen of this region acted not only as 'businessmen' but also as preachers of the religion of Islam, spreading the religion to the remotest corners of the world. These tradesmen are credited for being the early pioneers in laying down the foundations of the Islamic civilization.

The region of Hijaz has, today, become the spiritual focal point for all Muslims of the world, who visit in flocks both as performers of the duty of pilgrimage and as visitors.

Sound moral values, an aptitude for trade and a sense of adventure have combined to give this region of Saudi Arabia its unique nature.

Inhabitants of the Central Province

The Najdis are the inhabitants of the Central Province of Najd that stands at the heart of the Arabian Peninsula. The urban population of this region, which outnumber nomadic Bedouins, are still strongly attached to traditional patterns and modes of life.

Saudi Arabia's capital, Riyadh, is located in the Central Province. During the first century of Islam, the people of Najd worked to promote the cause of Islam by acting as religious missionaries or *Mujahideen* (strugglers in the cause of Islam), travelling as far east as China and as far west as Spain, many never returning to their native country. Thus, along with their brethren in the Western Province, they are credited with having played a major role in spreading the Islamic religion throughout the world.

Najdis were also known for their animal breeding and agriculture, and they developed close relations with the peoples of the Eastern and Western Provinces through trading in agriculture and fisheries.

Inhabitants of the Eastern Province

Settlement in the Eastern Province of Saudi Arabia dates back to the most ancient of times. The original inhabitants lived in vast palm tree oases, such as Hofuf, known for its abundant water and fertile soil, or along the numerous sea ports of the Arabian Gulf, such as Al Khobar, where people earned their living from fishing and trade.

Nomadic Bedouins, who settled in the northern fringes of the Empty Quarter (Rub'al-Khali), were in the habit of moving with all their belongings from place to place in search of pastures for their animals, staying nowhere for more than a few days. There was a steady movement of the inhabitants of the region in the direction of the coast, where sea trade routes could be established. Thus, the population of the region became mixed with non-tribal elements as the coastal centres prospered.

In this particular region of Saudi Arabia, an American geological mission discovered oil for the first time in 1938. The first tanker was loaded in 1939, laden with Saudi crude oil for international markets.

Inhabitants of the Southern Province

Inhabitants of this region, known for the high mountains of Asir, enjoy rainfall throughout the year. They lead a stable life, based on agriculture and animal breeding. The traditional veil is not popular among the women of this region, who are fond of wearing brightly coloured clothes. The lowlands of Tihamah are located to the west. The African impact on dwellings is particularly noticeable in the cone-like huts along the southern coast, although these are now being replaced by permanent homes in housing compounds provided with mosques, schools and social facilities.

The growth of modern Saudi cities

Before the signs of prosperity emerged in the 1960s, the Kingdom's towns were no more than desert communities characterized by mud and brick buildings and other structures. Roads were non-existent between these towns, while the principal centres of population, Riyadh, Jeddah and Dammam, were little more than small conurbations surrounded by huge mud walls several metres high.

Viewed from inside, the typical Saudi town resembled a labyrinth of narrow alleyways, with the market place at the centre being the only open area. In 1940, Riyadh had a population of only 30,000 people, all of whom lived in an area of 8.5 square kilometres. In 1947, the year in which its city walls were dismantled, Jeddah had a population of about 40,000 people living in an enclosed area of 1.5 square kilometres.

After a period of rapid urban development and population growth, the Kingdom's cities were transformed from desert towns with their old mud buildings into large and cosmopolitan cities with complex infrastructural developments, high-rise buildings and sophisticated commercial centres. A very small number of the original mud built structures have escaped the overall programme of urban renewal and modernization that began in the early 1970s. Those buildings that remain, stand as a testimony to the tumultuous changes that have been experienced by Saudi urban society over the last three decades.

Bearing in mind that public utility projects in Saudi towns and villages have been undertaken at an overall cost of some SR266 billion

(US$60 billion) over the course of the last four development plan periods, the enormous degree of achievement in a period of just 20 years becomes fully evident.

Historical and cultural background

Some knowledge of the history leading to the formation of the Kingdom of Saudi Arabia and of its cultural background is essential to gaining a full understanding of the principles that have guided the Kingdom's development.

A brief history of the Saudi Royal Family

The name of 'Al-Sa'ud', which means 'Family of Sa'ud' or 'House of Sa'ud', comes from the name of Sa'ud bin Muhammad bin Mugrin, who lived in the early 18th century. The first ruler of the First House of Sa'ud was Muhammad bin Sa'ud, the forebear of the present rulers. Initially ruler of Ad-Dir'iyah, he joined forces with Sheikh Muhammad bin Abdul Wahhab, an eminent religious leader, in what was to become the first political alliance in the formation of Saudi Arabia.

Imam Muhammad bin Wahhab was born in the town of Uyaina in Najd of a highly respected and religious family. Showing a keen interest in religion and being dismayed by contemporary deviations from Islamic teachings, the Sheikh started to preach the revival of Islam. He stripped away the heresies and abuses that had grown up around Islam and preached the faith in its original simplicity. For this he was prosecuted by the authorities and forced to leave his hometown. He took refuge at Ad-Dir'iyah, the home of Al Sa'ud, under the protection of Amir Muhammad bin Sa'ud.

Perceiving the value of Imam Muhammad bin Abdul Wahhab, Muhammad bin Sa'ud reached a pact with him that together they would bring the Arabs of the Peninsula back to the true faith of the Islamic religion. They confirmed this agreement with an oath in AH1157 (1744). Their alliance was to prove successful and Muhammad bin Sa'ud's son, Abdul Aziz bin Muhammad bin Sa'ud, ruled from 1765 to 1803, retaining the association with Imam Muhammad bin Abdul Wahhab in the same capacity as his father and continuing to reform Islam in the Peninsula.

Abdul Aziz bin Muhammad bin Sa'ud successfully captured the city of Riyadh in 1773. The combination of a deeply held theological conviction and military success proved irresistible to many. As a result, the Saudi state began to spread rapidly and within 15 years had extended its authority throughout the Najd. After the death of Abdul Aziz, his son, Sa'ud, ruled from 1803 to 1814.

In 1803, Sa'ud, provoked by the Sharif of the Holy City of Makkah, marched on the Holy City and captured it. There, he and his followers performed *Hajj*. The Saudi Kingdom now stretched from Najd to Hasa in the west, and south towards Najran.

Such an increase in authority was not to pass unchallenged. The Ottoman Empire concluded that action must be taken and invited Muhammad Ali, the Viceroy of Egypt (which at that time came within the Ottoman sphere of influence), to dismantle the work of Muhammad bin Sa'ud, his son and grandson, and to put an end to the emerging nation. Before Sa'ud died in 1814, Muhammad Ali was to retake the Hijaz. Sa'ud's successor, his son Abdullah (who ruled until 1818), was unable to halt the Egyptian advance. Ad Dir'iyah was taken and Abdullah removed to Istanbul, where his captors executed him. Riyadh was captured in 1818.

From 1818 to 1824, the Ottoman Empire maintained a number of garrisons in Najd, as a gesture of their dominance. Thus, the first temporary decline in the House of Sa'ud occurred. However, within a few years, the fortunes of the House of Sa'ud were to revive. In 1824, Turki bin Sa'ud, a cousin of Sa'ud bin Sa'ud, assumed the amirship of Najd. During his rule, which spanned from 1824 to 1834, Turki bin Sa'ud reoccupied the city of Riyadh. While continuing the Saudi drive for consolidation of the area, he recognized the symbolic sovereignty of the Viceroy of Egypt, Muhammad Ali.

In 1834, Turki bin Sa'ud was assassinated and his eldest son, Faisal, became Imam. Faisal bin Sa'ud refused to acknowledge the Viceroy of Egypt. Muhammad Ali was not prepared to see his earlier victories so quickly reversed, and in 1838, Egyptian forces defeated Faisal, retaking the Najd. Faisal was taken captive and sent to Cairo. Later, when Muhammad Ali declared Egypt's independence from the Ottoman Empire, he was forced to withdraw the troops stationed in Najd in order to support his own position in Egypt.

After five years of captivity, Faisal bin Sa'ud escaped from Cairo and returned home, where he was able to resume his reign that was to last until 1865. By this time, the House of Sa'ud once more controlled most of Najd and Hasa. However, on Faisal's death, Saudi fortunes declined once more as disagreements between the sons of Faisal weakened the House of Sa'ud. At the same time, the tribal leader of the Shammer, Muhammad bin Raschid, based in Hail, created a strong political body that rapidly covered the greater part of Najd. By 1871, after concluding a pact with Turkey, Muhammad bin Raschid captured Al-Hasa.

In 1889, the third son of Faisal, Abdul-Rahman bin Faisal, managed to consolidate the rule of the Saudi dynasty by assuming leadership of the family. At that time, the authority of the Saudi family centred on Riyadh but, in 1891, the House of Sa'ud faced a further setback. Muhammad bin Raschid consolidated his control of Najd by capturing

Riyadh, the citadel of the House of Sa'ud. Abdul Rahman was forced to leave the city. He settled for months with the Murra tribes at the Great Waste, in the outskirts of the Rub'al-Khali, the Empty Quarter, accompanied by his son, Abdul Aziz, the future king of Arabia. Eventually he departed for Bahrain, to gather his family, before leaving for Kuwait where he was to live in exile.

From exile in Kuwait, Abdul Aziz, son of Abdul Rahman, was deeply preoccupied with thoughts of his home territory, Najd, the land of his ancestors. He anticipated that he would someday go back and once again regain control of that part of Arabia. In 1902, King Abdul Aziz Al Sa'ud recaptured the city of Riyadh to re-establish his family's rule over the area. From 1902 to 1926, King Abdul Aziz vigorously and brilliantly extended his authority over most of the Arabian Peninsula. In September 1932, the territory he ruled acquired its official name, The Kingdom of Saudi Arabia.

From the first Saudi ruler, Muhammad bin Sa'ud in 1744 until 1902, the succession process had been from father to son. Accordingly, on the death of King Abdul Aziz in 1953, his son Sa'ud assumed leadership. However, in 1964, his brother, Faisal, succeeded King Sa'ud and since then there has been no father to son succession.

In 1975, King Khalid succeeded his brother King Faisal, and in 1982, King Fahd succeeded his brother King Khalid. Thus, a new process of succession to the leadership of the Kingdom had been established, namely a process of succession among the sons of King Abdul Aziz Al-Sa'ud in order of their ages. There are over 35 sons of Ibn Saud. Another new and equally important political factor is the majestic size of the Kingdom founded by Ibn Saud. Currently, members of the Royal Family hold positions in the government at all levels throughout the Kingdom.

The importance of Islam as a unifying force

In any account of the development of the Kingdom of Saudi Arabia, the thread that binds all the parts together is Islam. Throughout the history of the Arabian Peninsula, from the time of the Prophet Muhammad, Islam has largely determined the history of the region. Indeed, it was Islam that led to the emergence of the Arabian Empire, and unified the Arabs not only in the Arabian Peninsula, but also from Asia to the Atlantic Ocean during the 7th and 8th centuries. Again, in the early years of the 20th century, King Abdul Aziz Al Sa'ud consolidated his control over the major parts of the Arabian Peninsula ('by the name of God and the force of his right hand') until Saudi Arabia was officially proclaimed fully sovereign on 22 September 1932.

In unifying the Arab states into one cohesive nation, it was Islam that was to weave the various Arab peoples together to form a fabric of nations. It was the strength of faith, rather than other factors, which was to enable King Abdul Aziz to found the Kingdom. Therefore, it must be emphasized that behind all the remarkable statistics that indicate the extraordinary development and growth of the Kingdom of Saudi Arabia in all areas, Islam remains the spirit that drives and pervades all, and is the guidance that has ensured that the available resources have been wisely utilized.

Values, cultural framework and heritage of Saudi society

The importance of Islam

The origin of values and culture in Saudi Arabia comes from the values, virtues and moralities contained in the Holy *Qur'an*. Thus, the most important characteristic that distinguishes Saudi society from other world societies is the strict adherence to Islamic laws (*Shari'a*) as a solid basis for all aspects of life within Saudi Arabia. The *Shari'a* contemplates the building of an ideal society, emancipated from all the social ills ravaging today's world. At the same time, it preaches honesty, truthfulness and straightforwardness in any day-to-day dealings. This has allowed rapid economic change to take place in Saudi Arabia without adverse social effects.

Moreover, the principle of social commitment to the fair and equitable distribution of the returns of the socio-economic development plans among all parts of the Kingdom has contributed to the country's sustained social and political stability. This factor is considered by local and international investors to be of key importance when comparing worldwide investment environments.

The country's traditional cultural and social values have remained intact and deeply entrenched, despite the great strides of growth witnessed by the Kingdom during the past two decades. The Kingdom's heritage has remained unchanged. This lasting heritage is demonstrated by a large annual exhibition known as the 'Al-Jinadriyyah Exhibition', organized by the Saudi government, in an attempt to communicate to a wider audience the ancient and deeply rooted traditions, history and cultural heritage of the Saudi people.

Traditional pastimes

Bedouins and urban people share traditional values such as generosity and hospitality. These virtues are still observed by the Saudis in their individual and collective dealings and between citizens and the government. A traditional and ceremonial demonstration of this quality is the picturesque style in which thick Arabic coffee is prepared and sipped. The coffee boy grinds the roasted grains of coffee in a mortar, which is rhythmically tapped by his hand, as though he is inviting and welcoming all listeners in the neighbourhood to join them while coffee is being served.

The use of incense has been practised in the Kingdom since ancient times and this is still an essential, ceremonial part of Saudi society; the practice is intended to aromatize houses and clothes. Incense is customarily burnt after food is served, especially in the presence of guests. The sensor is placed near to the guest, who leans forward and draws it near his headgear. With a forward and backward movement of his hand, the guest acquires as much as he desires from the fragrance.

Poetic tradition inculcating Bedouin life is another fine art known to, and practised by, the Saudis. The tribe's virtues and characteristics, including respect of social values, are highlighted through poetry.

Horseback riding has been, and still is, a popular exercise in the Bedouin society of Saudi Arabia. Horses are cherished and occupy a special place in Bedouins' hearts. Bedouins always go out in groups to chase animals and hunt. Horses are trained to engage in popular dance routines such as 'Al-Aradah' and 'Al-Samer and the Pipe', which are performed on special occasions. In the course of these dances and rhythmic movements, folkloric songs and odes are chanted. Their theme is usually an expression of genuine Arab traditions, still rooted in the heart of Saudi Arabia's communities.

Local dress codes

As to men's attire, the popular dress consists of a gown and a headscarf with most men preferring to wear white. The local environment may have prompted them to choose white as it reflects the sunlight and thus diminishes the heat's impact on the body. Furthermore, white denotes purity, transparency and clarity. Employees in government and private organizations characteristically wear a headband (*uqal*) on top of the white headgear or thread scarf. Religious men are distinguished by wearing a cloak and headscarf, but without the headband.

Saudi women, who wear a veil, cover their long gowns with a black silk cloak and cover their faces with a thin black and transparent shawl when they venture out in public. By doing so, they observe the prevailing Islamic traditions.

Further reading

The Saudis: Inside the Desert Kingdom, Sandra Mackey, WW Norton & Company Limited (January 2003).

A History of Saudi Arabia, Madawi Al-Rasheed, Cambridge University Press. (September 2002).

The Kingdom of Saudi Arabia, David E Long, University Press of Florida (February 1998).

Personal Narrative of a Pilgrimage to Al-Madinah and Mecca: Volumes 1 and 2., Richard F Burton, Dover Publications (1964).

1.3

Economic and Political Background

Anthony Shoult, ASA Consulting[1]

Introduction

The Saudi government recognizes that both economic and political challenges lie ahead if its wealth and economic growth are to be maintained. The economy is still largely dependent on oil, which accounts for 85 per cent of its exports, and the national unemployment figure is officially acknowledged at four per cent.

The Saudi government is pursuing a policy of generating sustainable growth by economic diversification and increasing the role of the private sector.

New political challenges to have arisen since the 9/11 attacks on the United States, with pressure on the government to crack down on Islamic charities, change the school curriculum and democratize political life, particularly in respect of the role of women.

Recent acts of terrorism inside the Kingdom have led to strong and concerted action by the government to apprehend the perpetrators of bombings and other atrocities.

The economy

Main drivers of economic activity

With one quarter of the world's proven oil reserves, the Kingdom is expected to retain its position as the world's largest oil producer for the foreseeable future, with crude oil representing around 40 per cent of the country's GDP. In addition, it has around four per cent of the

1 Sources of information include UK Trade & Investment, BBC News (UK Edition) and Times Newspapers Limited.

world's gas reserves as well as a variety of other natural resources, such as gold, iron ore and copper.

It is oil and gas that dominate the country's economy though. Saudi Arabia estimates its crude reserves at about 260 billion barrels. With vast areas of the Kingdom yet to be thoroughly explored, Saudi Aramco expects to add at least 150 billion barrels to proven reserves by 2025. In any given year, 75–90 per cent of Saudi export revenues are derived from sales of crude oil, natural gas and refined products.

Recently, investment in petrochemicals has increased. It is not a new sector but it has benefited from initiatives to reduce the country's dependence on oil and gas.

The Saudi Basic Industries Corporation (SABIC) was formed in 1976 and is 70 per cent owned by the state and 30 per cent by private Saudi investors. It now accounts for about five per cent of world petrochemical production and is the main non-oil industrial enterprise in the country.

The national oil producing company, Saudi Aramco, is continuing to invest heavily in new production and is increasing the productivity of existing facilities. The estimated day-to-day running costs of Saudi Aramco exceed US$2 billion per year. This does not take account of its expenditure on major new projects, which include some US$50 billion over the next 20 years on gas projects.

Saudi's proven gas reserves are estimated at over 220 trillion cubic feet and Saudi Aramco plans to increase annual natural gas production from three to five trillion cubic feet.

A number of new gas fields have already been discovered and the recently completed and ongoing Hawiyah and Haradh projects will necessitate an expanded gas network, including an additional 3,000km of pipeline by 2006.

The Kingdom has reached agreement with Shell on an oil exploration initiative and is in discussion with other international oil companies about other projects.

Foreign investment

The Saudi Arabian General Investment Authority (SAGIA), established in April 2000 under Prince Abdullah ibn Faisal ibn Turki Al-Saud, has established overall responsibility for expediting investment applications, liberalizing investment laws and attracting new international investors.

Since the formation of SAGIA, licences for over US$1.6 million of new investment in the Kingdom have been issued to foreign investors. However, both the private sector and investors will have to conform to the government's 'Saudiization' programme, aimed at creating jobs for its rapidly expanding population.

The public sector

Public sector purchasing still largely drives the economy as a whole and ministries such as health and education are investing heavily each year into facilities and supplies.

Since the mid-1990s, the government has attempted to reduce state involvement and increase that of the private sector, to enhance foreign investment and to gradually reduce state subsidies and the imbalance in public employment, while at the same time preserving jobs in the public sector.

Both the public sector and the private sector are involved in numerous construction projects, bringing potential contracts in areas ranging from design, through building materials to contract furnishing. In recent years, Saudi Arabia has also been the world's largest (non-OECD) buyer of defence equipment.

Growth in demand

The Saudi market, which constitutes 60 per cent of the Gulf's GDP, has enormous potential for international investors.

Its population is growing at around 3.5 per cent each year, with 60 per cent of the population under 20 years old and 100,000 of them entering the workforce each year. This far exceeds the rate of job creation and it has accelerated the need to diversify the economy and attract far greater levels of foreign direct investment.

The demand for power, water, communications, healthcare, education/training, housing and consumer goods is expanding dramatically. Power and water alone will need US$200 billion of investment by 2020, while around US$10 billion is required to increase mobile phone penetration to 50 per cent of the population. The government also plans to build 900 new schools and 65 new hospitals by 2005.

Economic reforms

Political sensitivities largely preclude any significant broadening of the tax base, which means that growing consumer demand must be met by private, largely foreign, investment. To encourage this, the government has embarked on a programme of gradual reform.

Foreigners can now wholly own joint ventures in most sectors. Laws enacted in May 2001 provide for a competitive, independently regulated telecoms market, and new insurance and capital market laws have paved the way for reform of the stock market.

The government has also approved a massive expansion of the rail network and the basic customs tariff has been reduced from 12.5 to five per cent, in line with other GCC states.

Political background

Historical context

The history of Saudi Arabia is entwined with the fortunes of the House of Saud, which traces its origins back to the 18th century. By the middle of the 18th century, the clan had become members of the Wahhabi sect, which was then a militantly puritanical branch of Sunni Islam. Wahhabism was the catalyst for the emergence of the Saud dynasty and the foundation on which the Kingdom was built.

The role of religion

Today Wahhabism is practised with less rigour than in the 18th and 19th centuries, but Wahhabi doctrine still ensures that life in the Kingdom is more constrained than in other Arab states. Not only is alcohol forbidden, but shops are required to close five times daily for prayers, women are not allowed to drive or be active in public life, cinemas are banned and non-Islamic worship is proscribed.

The power of decision making

Ultimate power in Saudi Arabia rests with the King. From 1996, when King Fahd suffered a stroke, Crown Prince Abdullah had handled the day-to-day affairs of state until his eventual accession to the throne in August 2005.

Although the King can be seen on television attending cabinet meetings in his *ex officio* role as prime minister, he appears to play little part in proceedings.

Decision making within the royal family is discreet, with senior princes discussing issues in private in a bid to reach consensus. Disagreements are never aired in public. Serious rifts often see the offended party withdraw from public view, rather than openly voice grievances.

The informal consultation process appeared to gain a firmer structure in June 2000, when a family council chaired by the then Crown Prince Abdullah and comprised of 18 princes was set up. However, Prince Nayef, not a member himself, has denied that the council has a broader political role.

The role of the cabinet or Council of Ministers

The Council of Ministers, or cabinet, takes decisions affecting daily life in Saudi Arabia. One of the cabinet's roles is to enact legislation. Here again, the royal family is strongly represented. Prince Sultan serves as deputy prime minister and other senior princes hold the foreign affairs, defence and interior portfolios.

While other cabinet members would be expected to defer to the royal family on major issues, they are not without influence in their own sectors. For example, Oil Minister, Ali Al-Naimi, supported the state oil company against a scheme proposed in 1998 by the then Crown Prince Abdullah to allow foreign consortia to search for gas.

The role of the Shura Council (Consultative Council)

Draft laws first require the approval of the Majlis al-Shura, or Consultative Council. This was established, initially with 60 members appointed by the King, in 1992. Its membership was increased to 90 appointees in 1997. Each council serves for four years.

As well as approving proposed legislation, the Shura Council has the power to summon and question government ministers.

In March 2004, Second Deputy Prime Minister and Defence Minister, Prince Sultan, said there would not be elections to the Shura Council in the foreseeable future, although he did not rule this out completely.

The King and senior princes maintain the ancient tradition of holding *majlises*, or open assemblies, in their palaces so that citizens can present petitions or air grievances.

Saudis have no voting rights and political parties are banned. However, in October 2003, the government announced its intention to establish municipal councils within a year, with half the members voted into office.

The succession

The accession to the throne of King Abdullah bin Abdul Aziz Al Saud, following the death of King Fahd bin Abdul Aziz Al Saud in August 2005, followed much Western speculation about uncertainty surrounding the succession. While it is clear that the current defence minister, Prince Sultan bin Abdul Aziz will succeed King Abdullah, after that the succession is less certain.

Following the death of King Fahd, Prince Sultan has five surviving full brothers of the seven known as the Sudayri seven. This is because they are the offspring of Hassa bin Ahmad al-Sudayri, the fifth wife of King Abdul Aziz Al-Saud, who proclaimed himself King of Saudi Arabia in 1932. King Abdullah is a half brother to the seven.

While the Saudi constitution states simply that the monarch must be a male heir of King Abdul Aziz, the seven have believed that they had a stronger claim on the throne than other senior princes.

However, others might stake a claim in the future. All the sons of King Abdul Aziz are elderly. At some point the issue of handing power to the second generation will have to be faced. Figure 1.3.1 shows the House of Saud.

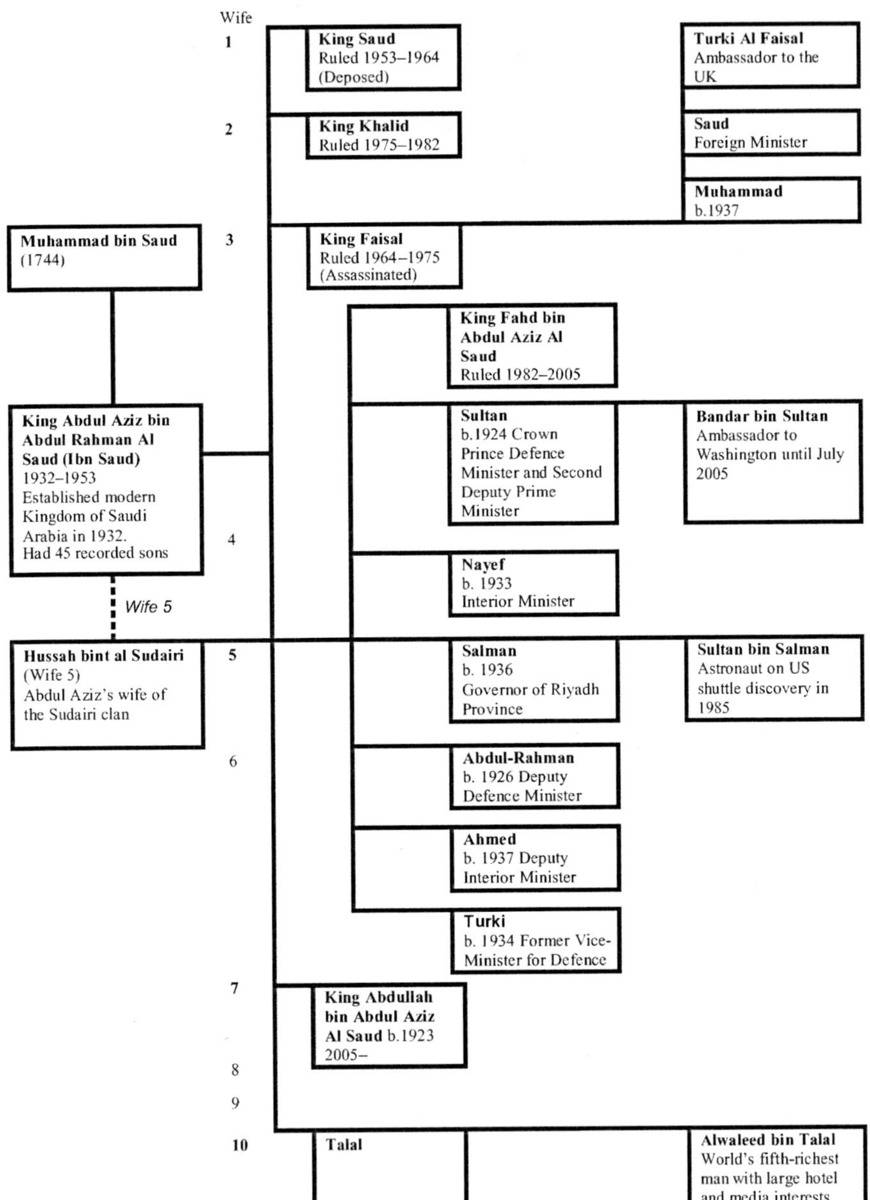

Figure 1.3.1 The House of Saud

Future of the House of Saud

While much is written in the West about splits within the ruling family, as well as challenges from reformers and fundamentalists, talk of collapse of the House of Saud seems premature. It is after all a huge structure, with an estimated 7,000 princes.

Although differences exist over relations with the West, or political and economic liberalization, the family is united in its desire to maintain control. It would be wrong to overlook the fact that the family has many loyal supporters within the Kingdom.

The outlook for reform

After the 9/11 attacks, Saudi Arabia came in for harsh criticism from the United States for allowing a milieu where perpetrators of bombings could live unchecked. American pressure on the Saudi government to crack down on Islamic charities, change the school curriculum and democratize political life increased.

The leadership was initially reluctant to act, but a series of suicide bomb attacks appeared to convince the government that action was needed on two fronts – a crackdown on militants and the first tentative reforms.

King Abdullah has chaired two meetings of a National Dialogue forum, attended by 60 men and women comprising clergy, academics and leading opinion-formers. The forum tackled sensitive issues such as school curriculum reform and the role of women. The process is still in its early stages.

King Abdullah, when Crown Prince, wasted no opportunity to stress that the Kingdom has no choice but to proceed with dialogue and introduce change. However, the arrest in March 2004 of a number of reformists demonstrated the fragility and sensitivity of the process.

Part Two

The Economy and Investment

2.1

Economic Performance and Outlook

Professor John R Presley, Saudi British Bank

Introduction

This review of the Saudi economy, in 2005, looks at both the background to economic policies within the Kingdom and current economic developments. This approach is intended to provide a broad picture of the Saudi economy, while emphasizing the consistency of policies over time and the stability of the economic environment.

Background to the economic framework

The Saudi economy, having achieved the completion of most infrastructural development, is now focused on public sector to private sector activity. The development process, to date, has emphasized four central goals as the key to future progress:

- to maintain the religious values of Islam;
- to assure the defence of the religion and the country and to maintain internal security and social stability within the Kingdom;
- to promote balanced growth by using the country's resources so as to increase oil income in the long term without depleting resources too quickly;
- to reduce the dependence upon crude oil as the primary source of national income.

The key to understanding the Saudi economy rests in the appreciation of the links between the government, the development process and religion. The Kingdom has embarked upon a process of industrialization that has brought rapid growth since the early 1970s and significant structural change. This has involved a major input from the government and a very high level of public sector activity. Even today, annual government spending of some SR280 billion represents less than one-third of Saudi gross domestic product.

The provision of basic infrastructure by the public sector not only relates to social (education, health) and physical (roads, airports etc) infrastructure. It also extends to the supply of basic materials on which secondary industry can develop. Through the Saudi Arabian Basic Industries Corporation (SABIC), the government has established world-class petrochemical industries, supplying basic commodities and raw materials to a domestic manufacturing sector and for export markets. This activity stemmed from the recognition that the private sector alone could not undertake the large-scale investment required, nor was it prepared to carry the high risks involved in such industrial development. The ultimate objective has always been, when such projects are seen to be viable, to transfer them to the private sector.

The public sector emphasis of the 1970s and 1980s was very much an economic necessity to create the infrastructure to enable industrialization to take place. The intention is now to move away from this emphasis towards a free enterprise, free market economy in which the private sector dominates. This also embraces the objective of free trade and Saudi Arabia is in the final stages of negotiating to join the World Trade Organization (WTO). It has also created a common external tariff system within the GCC countries.

Economic performance and structure

Past achievements in economic performance

Over the last 25 years of economic development, Saudi Arabia has witnessed a major transformation in its economy. This has been possible through the financial advantage offered by oil revenues and by the consistent and determined economic policies – geared to industrialization – followed by the Saudi government. The Saudi economy has seen its physical and social infrastructure revolutionized, and the non-oil sector, including agriculture, yielding an increasing and significant proportion of total output.

This rapid progress has required economic management that has involved the creation of an institutional structure to support development, and the recognition that social costs attached to the high growth rates must be controlled if sustainable and balanced growth is to be achieved. Financial surplus, particularly in the 1970s, has put pressure on other resources in short supply – notably labour and technology.

While the short-term solution has been to import both, the long-term desire is to become more self-dependent. More recently, labour shortage has been replaced by labour surplus, as the rapid growth of the Saudi population has now resulted in large numbers of young, educated Saudis seeking employment.

Table 2.1.1 Key economic indicators, 1999–2004

	1999	2000	2001	2002	2003	2004
Nominal GDP (SR billion)	535.8	708.5	688.3	708.9	806.2	932.0
Real GDP growth (%)	5.5	4.9	0.5	0.1	6.4	5.3
Oil production (million b/d)	8.7	9.3	9.0	8.7	8.8	8.8
Oil price (US$/barrel average WTI Crude)	19.25	30.30	25.92	26.10	31.14	41.45
Real private sector growth (%)					4.0	5.7
Nominal private sector growth (%)	3.9	3.8	3.9	3.9	4.4	6.7
Total government revenues (SR billion)	147.0	157.0	228.2	213.0	293.0	393.0
Total government expenditure (SR billion)	183.8	235.3	255.1	233.5	257.0	295.0
Annual inflation rate (%)	-1.3	-0.6	-0.8	-0.6	0.5	0.2
Population (million)	21.5	22.2	22.8	23.5	24.2	25.0
Total exports (SR billion)	190.08	290.5	254.9	268.4	356.3	426.2
Total imports (SR billion)	96.5	113.2	107.8	111.2	138.4	132.2
Fiscal out-turn – overall deficit/surplus (SR billion)	-34.0	-28.0	-29.9	-20.5	36.0	98.0
Balance of payments – current account balance (SR billion)	1.5	53.7	35.0	44.5	105.2	193.0

Sources: IMF Economic Outlook; SAMA Statistical Bulletin (2004)

Whereas growth in the last two decades depended upon the initiatives and spending of the government and the public sector, the future will be less dependent, and it is the desire and expectation that the private sector will exert more influence in dictating the pace of development. This is the natural consequence of the development process embarked upon and also an economic necessity as oil revenues fluctuate and their real value trend diminishes. Quite simply, despite recent improvements in oil revenues, the government has much less real purchasing power than it had 20 years ago. Financial necessity and economic desirability have continued to put more of a burden on the private sector.

It became evident in 2004 that, as in the 1970s, the trends in oil sector nominal growth and overall economic activity still remain inextricably linked. Variations in oil revenues dictate potential government spending levels that then determine the volume and value of public sector activity; this, in turn, has multiplier effects on private sector activity. Hence, prospects, both short and long term, for the Saudi economy will still be highly dependent on developments in the oil market.

Current economic performance

Despite the political and military problems in neighbouring Iraq, in late 2004 and early 2005 the Saudi economy is currently witnessing a period of relatively high growth and economic progress. This is based upon a very strong oil sector that is furnishing the government with record oil revenues and is allowing the Kingdom to increase its spending and to grow its infrastructure and welfare spending to match the increased needs of the Saudi population.

In turn, the non-oil private sector is feeding off this activity in the public sector. Government debt is falling, allowing greater liquidity for the private sector. Business and consumer confidence is flourishing, and the stock market remains on a strong upward trend as corporate profits continue to record high double-digit increases.

Therefore, while psychology is damaged by the military and terrorist activity within the region, this appears to be more than counteracted by the positive economic signals in the Kingdom allowing foreign investment to grow, aided also by the very pro-active measures of the Supreme Economic Council (SEC). This is making the Kingdom a much more attractive country in which to invest. This has come about through tax changes, drastically reformed property ownership laws and more incentives for business activity. Hence, the current prospects in both oil and non-oil sectors are considered to be very upbeat.

In 2004, the following key features were evident:

- recent national accounting figures show nominal growth of GDP in 2004 at 16.9 per cent (this was boosted by a 28.1 per cent growth in the oil sector) – this is a nominal growth rate that has only been surpassed in 2000 and during the Gulf War period (1990);
- the non-oil sector (now about 60 per cent of total GDP) is sustaining historically high growth rates alongside the buoyant oil sector – in 2004 real non-oil industrial growth was 6.4 per cent;

- the fiscal situation improved almost beyond recognition during 2004, with the government announcing revenues of SR393 billion (almost double the initial government projections and SR100 billion higher than the record level of SR293 billion achieved in 2003) and a budget surplus of SR98 billion, and setting a balanced budget for the 2005 fiscal year with revenues and expenditures projected at SR280 billion;
- the strength of the oil sector translates into a very favourable trading position for the Kingdom. The balance of payments surplus of SR101.5 billion in 2003 on the current account has been followed by an even bigger surplus of SR193 billion in 2004. One of the main beneficiaries has been the Riyal exchange rate that was subjected to huge devaluation pressures in the 1990s that no longer exist;
- Saudi Arabia is almost in a unique position worldwide, as prices have actually fallen since 1995 – by June 2004, the general cost of living index for all cities was down 1.4 per cent on its 1999 level.

These factors contributed to a very healthy economy in 2004, with oil revenues and government spending at robust levels, the non-oil sector enjoying a period of relatively rapid growth, the fiscal situation as impressive as it has ever been, inflation continuing at record lows and the current account surplus approaching SR200 billion a year.

These are the kind of fundamentals that any economy would be delighted to witness. The only downside, which the government is tackling, is the level of unemployment, which for the Saudi workforce has grown from 8.1 per cent in 1999 to 9.7 per cent by end-2002, out of a total labour force of 6.2 million. Non-Saudi unemployment is only 0.8 per cent.

The oil sector

Whilst the Kingdom now has a non-oil sector that contributes up to 60 per cent of GDP, the oil sector value-added in 2003 was SR331 billion from a GDP of SR806 billion. This is of key importance as the non-oil sector still 'feeds off' the oil sector. Not only does it provide 75 per cent or more of total government revenues from oil exports that, in turn, determines the buoyancy of government spending, but also both business and consumer confidence, in large part, reflect the strength of the oil market. Also, government funding ability largely determines the level of public sector contracts offered to the private sector.

Despite oil production of over eight million barrels per day (mbd), Saudi oil reserves remain at 260 billion barrels. Even if no new oil discoveries emerge, reserves are sufficient to produce eight mbd for the next 90 years.

The year 2004 was an exceptional one for the oil market and brought in a new era, with average crude oil prices of above US$40 per barrel and Saudi oil production close to 8.8 mbd becoming the norm (see Table 2.1.2).

Table 2.1.2 Oil sector performance, current prices (SR billion)

Year	Total nominal GDP	Total oil sector	Nominal oil sector growth (%)	Oil % total GDP	Oil Production (mbd)	Oil price (US$/barrel average WTI crude)
1999	535.8	193.5	31.3	36.1	8.7	19.25
2000	708.5	283.5	46.5	40.1	9.3	30.30
2001	688.3	249.6	-13.5	36.3	9.0	25.92
2002	708.9	257.4	3.1	36.3	8.7	26.10
2003	806.2	331.1	28.6	41.1	8.8	31.14
2004	932.0	453.0	28.2	48.1	8.8	41.45

Source: SAMA Report 2004

The industrial (non-oil) sector

Despite volatile growth rates in the oil sector between 1999 and 2003, the industrial (non-oil) private sector has been able to achieve annual nominal growth rates within the range of 3.8 to 4.4 per cent. These are very high figures by international standards and indicate that private sector growth is now becoming less dependent on oil sector activity than would have been the case 20 years ago. In 2003, the private sector was not only buoyed by business confidence, high levels of liquidity in the economy and high oil revenues but also by government spending and policies to encourage private sector activity. In 2004, the private sector grew by 6.7 per cent in nominal terms and 5.7 per cent in real terms, reflecting buoyant government spending, high profitability levels and a strong oil market.

Government industrial (non-oil) activity also increased in 2003 above recent trends, recording a nominal growth of 6.3 per cent. Typically since 1997, non-oil sector government growth has been less than one half this rate as the government has endeavoured to switch resources from public to private sector (Table 2.1.3).

Table 2.1.3 Industrial (non-oil) sector performance, current prices (SR billion)

Year	Private sector	Private sector growth (%)	Govern-ment sector	Govern-ment sector growth (%)	Total industrial (non-oil) sector	Total indus-trial (non-oil) sector growth (%)	Industrial (non-oil) % total GDP*
1999	255.2	3.9	139.8	1.2	395.0	2.9	73.8
2000	264.9	3.8	143.0	2.3	407.8	3.2	57.6
2001	275.1	3.9	148.5	3.8	423.6	3.9	61.5
2002	285.7	3.9	150.5	1.3	436.2	3.0	61.5
2003	298.3	4.4	159.9	6.3	458.2	5.0	56.8
2004	311.4	6.7	169.8	6.4	481.2	6.4	51.6

* includes import duties

Source: SAMA Report 2004

In 2003, growth of the manufacturing sector was 11.7 per cent, well in excess of the targeted 7.16 per cent. Growth rates were relatively high in most other sectors compared to recent years, and the utilities sector in particular achieved relatively high growth at 6.1 per cent (see Table 2.1.4).

Table 2.1.4 Industrial (non-oil) sector 2002–2003, current prices (SR billion)

Sector	2002	2003	Growth (%)	Seventh development plan target
Agriculture	36.1	36.5	1.0	3.05
Manufacturing	73.0	81.5	11.7	7.16
Electricity, gas, water	9.3	9.9	6.1	4.62
Construction	44.7	46.3	3.4	6.17
Wholesale/retail trade	51.7	53.8	4.1	4.21
Transport, storage and communications	31.9	33.2	4.0	3.75
Finance and insurance	82.1	85.8	4.6	7.68
Community, social and personal services	24.1	25.1	4.1	4.17

Source: SAMA Report 2004

In 2004, the industrial (non-oil) sector grew in real terms at 6.4 per cent, due to strong performance by the construction sector (7.5 per cent) and the transport and communications sector (7.8 per cent).

Economic outlook

Given the state of government oil revenues, the related level of government spending, the fiscal surplus and current account surplus, there is every reason to believe that the growth out-turn in 2005 will be on the high side. Business and consumer confidence continues to be strong and this confidence is reflected in the stock market, where share prices grew to extremely high levels during 2004. This is partly a reflection of the strong growth in corporate profits, up by over 50 per cent on average in 2003, with some reported profits growing to unprecedented levels in 2004.

Supporting this confidence and high profitability is the level of liquidity in the economy. The commercial banks now have to lend less to the government to finance fiscal deficits, allowing more funds to flow to the private sector. SAMA figures indicate that between January and July 2004, bank claims in the private sector grew by over 16 per cent to SR273 billion, while the cost of credit remains historically very low, making bank credit very attractive to corporate clients.

Initial indications are that 2005 will be impressive in its out-turn due to the following factors:

- in 2004 the oil sector increased its value-added by some 28 per cent over 2003, with average crude oil prices above US$40/barrel. On current trends, these price levels are expected to be maintained or slightly abated in 2005/06, perhaps heralding in a period of oil prices between US$30 and US$40/barrel. Oil production also, which averaged 8.8 mbd in 2003 and was raised to 9.5 mbd in late 2004, may decline slightly in 2005, depending upon actual world economic growth, currently forecast to be above four per cent;
- the government sector maintained high levels of spending in 2004, with oil revenues soaring to SR393 billion and this will tend to set a benchmark for 2005;
- the 'knock-on' effects for the industrial (non-oil) sector have been very positive, with real growth of 6.4 per cent in 2004 and all sectors with construction and transport and communications performing even better with growth rates of 7.5 per cent and 7.8 per cent respectively;
- there is every possibility that inflation rates will continue to be below one per cent in 2005.

Bringing together all of these factors for 2005, while a small fall in oil sector activity may be anticipated, at best overall GDP growth will probably come out at around 2.5 per cent as export revenues accrued in 2004 continue to feed into the non-oil sector.

Foreign investment policy

The strength of the Saudi economy and recent changes in the environment for foreign investment in the Kingdom make Saudi Arabia a more attractive place for foreign investment. The downside has been the trouble in its neighbouring country, Iraq, which tends to damage the 'political' will to invest in the region. Despite this, recent figures on foreign investment from the Saudi Arabian General Investment Authority (SAGIA) have been reassuring, as the value of industrial licences approved in terms of capital to be invested continues to increase (see Table 2.1.5).

Table 2.1.5 Number of licences issued by SAGIA (2003–2004)

Activities	**2003***		**2004****		**Change (%)**	
	Number	Value (SR billion)	Number	Value (SR billion)	Number	Value (SR billion)
Industrial	692	27.6	928	33.0	236 (34%)	5.40 (20%)
Non-industrial	898	22.7	1,347	24.5	449 (50%)	1.80 (8%)
Agriculture	5	0.1	5	0.15	–	–
Total	1,595	50.4	2,280	57.6	685 (43%)	7.20 (14%)

* at February 2003

** at May 2004

Source: SAGIA July 2004

Foreign investors are involved in over 80 per cent of all industrial licences awarded. The United States continues to hold the lead in terms of foreign investment, with Japan ranked second. Other important investing nations include France, UK and Canada (see Table 2.1.6).

Table 2.1.6 Leading investing countries in Saudi Arabia (April 2000 to May 2004)

Country	Investment value (SR billion)
USA	15.56
Japan	11.22
France	3.86
UK	2.68
Canada	2.01
Syria	1.85
India	1.31
Germany	1.10
Jordan	0.92
Palestine	0.85
Total:	41.36

Source: SAGIA July 2004

Foreign investors accounted for in excess of 80 per cent of the financial share of the 2,280 licensed joint ventures in Saudi Arabia in 2004 (see Table 2.1.7).

Table 2.1.7 Licensed joint venture projects in Saudi Arabia, 2004

Activities	Number of projects	Saudi share in projects		Foreign share in projects		Total project finance
		%	SR billion	%	SR Billion	SR billion
Industrial	928	25.4	8.37	74.6	24.60	32.97
Service	1,347	6.4	1.57	93.6	22.90	24.47
Agriculture	5	22.2	0.04	77.8	0.13	0.17
Total	2,280	–	9.98	–	47.63	57.61

Source: SAGIA July 2004

Trade and the balance of payments

Background to balance of payments policy

It is evident from the development process that trade is very important to the Kingdom. Export values of SR368 billion in 1980 represented 71 per cent of the Kingdom's GDP. Although this proportion has diminished since, it still stands at over 40 per cent of GDP. Import values peaked at SR230 billion in 1984, which at that time represented 65 per cent of the value of GDP; visible and invisible imports together now stand at around SR132 billion, or approximately 14 per cent of GDP (2004). Therefore, trade is less dominant than it was, but remains central to economic activity in the Kingdom.

Essentially, there is a mutual dependence between Saudi Arabia and the rest of the world, especially Western economies. Saudi Arabia still requires capital goods and managerial and technical expertise, while other countries need Saudi Arabia's oil. The Kingdom also needs those consumer goods that cannot yet be produced domestically to support a rapidly growing population. In simple terms, the structure and pace of development has been dependent upon the revenue derived largely from oil exports. This, in turn, has affected the ability to import goods and services necessary for development to take place. With the growth of the private sector and domestic production and the growth in the domestic workforce and skill levels, this relationship has weakened, but nevertheless even today it exerts a significant influence on the rate of economic progress.

Balance of payments – the current position

One major beneficiary of strong oil exports is the current account of the balance of payments. SAMA figures for 2004 show a current account surplus of SR193 billion, following on from a surplus of SR105.2 billion in 2003 (see Table 2.1.8).

Table 2.1.8 Balance of payments: the value of merchandise exports, merchandise imports and current account balance (SR billion)

	1980	1990	1995	2000	2001	2002	2003
Merchandise exports (FOB)	335.1	165.7	40.6	289.7	254.2	271.0	348.7
Merchandise imports	85.0	80.6	96.0	103.9	107.3	111.1	127.0
Current account balance	142.2	-15.5	-19.9	53.7	35.0	44.5	105.2

Sources: IMF statistics; SAMA Annual Report, 2003

Current account surpluses have rarely reached such high levels, the exception being the Gulf War period (the current account deficit rose to over US$20 billion in 1991). Even during the height of the oil price adjustments in the 1970s, surpluses remained consistently below SR100 billion a year.

However, foreign trade developments continue to be very dynamic. After a period of relatively slow import growth averaging only 2.1 per cent a year between 1996 and 2002, growth accelerated alongside the increase in government spending, private sector activity and record oil exports. Hence, in 2003 visible imports rose by over 14 per cent, from SR121 billion to SR138 billion.

Trade – the current position

Alongside oil exports, which increased from SR315 billion in 2003 to SR338 billion in 2004, non-oil exports have been very buoyant, having doubled in value between 1999 and 2004. In 2003, non-oil exports grew by 28 per cent to a figure in excess of SR41 billion, while in 2004 they grew by a further 24 per cent to SR51 billion, accounting for 11 per cent of total exports.

There is an interesting change taking place in the Kingdom's sources of imports – it is increasingly looking east. While the United States remains the main source of imports, its share of exports to the Kingdom fell, yet again, to 15 per cent in 2003. In contrast, China's exports to the Kingdom have more than doubled since 1998 and reached SR8.2 billion in 2003, a growth rate of 27 per cent in one year.

Western Europe is also suffering in terms of exports to the Kingdom, with the notable exception of Germany. All of this is, in part, indicative of the changing composition of Saudi imports, with an 84 per cent increase in imports of transport equipment between 1996 and 2003 to over SR29 billion a year. By 2003, it was second only to the import of machinery and electrical and mechanical appliances in value terms (22 per cent of total visible imports).

These trends have been present over several years and there is no expectation that this picture will change in the short term. The United States and Western Europe, in particular, need to be more proactive in the Saudi market if they are not to lose market share to China, South Korea and India.

Control of inflation

Background to inflation policy

Certainly one of the major successes of government policy over the last 15 years has been the control over the rate of inflation. Although always a central objective of the Saudi government, the inflationary experiences of the 1970s hardened its resolve to bring inflation under control and to achieve relatively low inflationary levels by world standards.

The lessons of the 1970s, when excess demand caused inflation rates of over 10 per cent per annum, demonstrated that high inflation could jeopardize the development process, even when there was an abundance of finance for capital formation.

As production capacity in the economy has grown and government spending levels have moderated, so the problem of inflation has diminished significantly. Between 1979 and 2004, the annual rise in the cost of living has always been less than five per cent per annum, while in some years it was negative, such that the average rise in the cost of living was less than two per cent per annum between 1990 and 2004. Similarly with wholesale prices, the increases between 1985 and 2004 were less than two per cent per annum over the entire period.

Inflation – the current position

Price stability remains a key government objective so as to generate a predictable business environment for investment and to guard against the income redistribution effects of inflation.

Inflation rates have been minimal, if not negative, over recent years, with reductions particularly in costs of fabrics, housing, entertainment and education. With inflation at 0.2 per cent for 2004, there is every possibility that the inflation rate will continue to be below one per cent in 2005, as the government, through SAMA, exerts strict control over money supply growth and the cost of credit – the economy is very competitive and further moves towards WTO membership will work to enhance efficiency and competitiveness, leading to a beneficial effect on domestic prices.

Fiscal budget

Background to fiscal policy

It has been a difficult period for fiscal policy over the last 15 years as the fiscal surpluses of the 1970s have been followed by a series of fiscal deficits, which peaked at SR89 billion in 1991 as the costs of the Gulf War heightened government spending. Since then there has been a steady improvement in the fiscal position.

The volatility of oil revenues has had a significant impact upon the fiscal out-turn since 1973. Government revenues fell as low as SR77 billion in 1986 as oil prices dropped, but increased to SR172 billion in 1991 as the Gulf War forced up oil prices. In 1996, revenues peaked at SR177 billion.

Oil-related revenues in recent years have normally accounted for approximately 80 per cent of total government revenues. Investment income has fallen from over SR15 billion in 1989 to less than SR10 billion in 2003. Government fees, charges and customs duties normally represent only approximately one-fifth of revenues generated via oil, while income taxes and other taxes are minimal in their revenue raising capacity.

On the expenditure side, the government has been faced with increasing wage and salary expenditure on public sector employees. The emphasis upon capital project expenditure has given way to a higher proportion of spending being devoted to recurrent spending.

Public debt has grown in recent years, with interest payments now accounting for over SR30 billion annually. By 2000, the public debt in Saudi Arabia stood at over SR600 billion, in excess of GDP. Concern with public debt as a proportion of GDP is now much reduced. Public debt by 2004 fell to some SR614 billion (less than 66 per cent of GDP). HRH Crown Prince Abdullah announced that the fiscal surplus in 2004 will be used to bring public debt down in future.

There were clear objectives laid down for fiscal policy over the period of the Seventh Development Plan (2000–04). Government spending was to be used to achieve a 'positive GDP growth rate', and by so doing, to create job opportunities for the growing Saudi workforce. It was also to be used in the control of inflation and to create a diversified economy alongside improvements in public services.

In essence, these policies have been followed already over recent years. The Gulf War left a major financial burden upon Saudi Arabia; the fiscal deficit for 1990–91 (two-year period) is estimated at SR140 billion, an average of 17 per cent of GDP.

As a consequence, the Saudi government has, over recent years, been following a prudent approach, bringing down the fiscal deficit through a dual policy of lowering government spending alongside reduced subsidization expenditures and price support on agricultural produce and utilities (electricity, telephones, petrol).

Fiscal budget 2005

The fiscal situation in Saudi Arabia in early 2005 is healthier than it has been for over 20 years. The windfall of oil revenues from both high oil prices and export levels combined to generate a fiscal surplus in 2004 well above expected levels (see Table 2.1.9).

Table 2.1.9 Fiscal out-turn and forecasts 2001–2005* (SR billion)

	2001	2002	2003	2004	2005*
Revenue					
Oil	183.9	166.1	231.0	n/a	n/a
Non-oil	44.2	46.9	62.0	n/a	n/a
Total revenue	228.2	213.0	293.0	393.0	280.0
Expenditure					
Current	223.5	203.5	223.5	n/a	204.5
Capital (project)	31.6	30.0	33.4	n/a	75.5
Total expenditure	255.1	233.5	257.0	295.0	280.0
Overall deficit/surplus	-26.9	-20.5	36.0	98.0	–

* Fiscal statement end 2004 (Finance Ministry)

Source: Ministry of Finance, SAMA Annual Report, SABB estimates

In 2004, government spending exceeded the budgeted figure of SR230 billion, reaching the level of SR295 billion. In September 2004, HRH Crown Prince Abdullah announced an additional spending package alongside the Eighth Development Plan (2005–2010) amounting to SR41 billion, with an emphasis on 'projects that will have direct and considerable impact on the welfare and prosperity of citizens'. Key areas to be targeted include water and sewage, roads and expressways, primary healthcare, school buildings and technical and vocational education. This is consistent with the trends in the breakdown of government spending as well as the priorities of the Seventh Development Plan (2000–04) and the current Eighth Development Plan (2005–10). Clearly, human resource development and healthcare have been a focus over recent years and this emphasis will undoubtedly continue (see Table 2.1.10).

The strength of the fiscal budget in 2005 allows the Kingdom to implement some of the fiscal reforms identified in the Seventh Development Plan and recommended on a regular basis by the annual IMF reports on the state of the Saudi economy.

First, as the series of fiscal deficits previously recorded have been replaced by surpluses, the target of a balanced budget over the medium term is now achievable. Second, concern with public debt as a proportion of GDP is much reduced. Public debt by 2004 stood at SR614 billion (less than 66 per cent of GDP), while in 1999 it would have exceeded GDP.

Table 2.1.10 Fiscal budget: breakdown of projected expenditures (SR billion)

	1997	2001	2004
Human resource development	41.6	53.0	55.8
Transport and communications	6.9	5.7	6.4
Economic resource development	4.7	5.6	7.0
Health and social development	14.4	18.0	17.8
Infrastructure development	1.6	2.6	2.6
Municipal services	5.4	7.3	6.3
Defence and security	68.0	78.9	78.4
Public administration and other government spending	30.8	37.3	50.0
Government lending institutions*	0.5	0.4	0.4
Local subsidies	7.1	6.2	5.3
Total	181.0	215.0	230.0

* includes transfers to SFD

Source: Ministry of Finance

As previously mentioned, the fiscal budget for 2005 does indicate that the SR41 billion from the fiscal surplus in 2004 will go to additional development projects; SR30 billion of this will go to extra social and infrastructure projects, with both the Saudi Credit Bank and Real Estate Development Bank receiving a boost of SR11 billion in their capital in order to widen their lending programmes. The budget anticipates that all specialized development funding institutions will see their lending expand by SR10 billion in 2005.

In 2005, spending policy is expected to remain consistent, with 25 per cent of spending allocated to education and manpower development (SR70.1 billion); health and social affairs receives SR27.1 billion, transport and communications SR8.9 billion and municipality services SR10.7 billion.

New educational projects totalling SR14.7 billion for 2005 include 1,420 new schools, 10 new technical colleges and 32 vocational training centres, while all universities will receive increased budgets, representing increases on 2004 of up to 28 per cent.

Health and social development projects will include 420 new primary care centres and 23 new hospitals providing 3,150 extra beds.

The transport and telecommunications sector expects SR8.4 billion to be assigned to new capital projects including 6,700km of new roads, railroad and airport development including the first phase of the King Abdulaziz Airport in Jeddah.

The Ministry of Finance is very conservative in its plans and projections for 2005. Accordingly, given that the government is proposing a balanced budget of SR280 billion, it is expected that in 2005, actual government levels for revenue raising and spending could well exceed those put forward in the budget statement.

2.2

Foreign Investment Regime

Saudi Arabian General Investment Authority (SAGIA)

Introduction

In just a few decades, the Kingdom of Saudi Arabia has made immense strides in national economic development. Since the early 1970s, national revenues have been used to fund a series of five-year plans, which have ensured the Kingdom's development from a rural community to an advanced industrial society.

Throughout this period of growth, the government has sought always to ensure diversification of the economy while encouraging private sector and foreign participation and investment.

In the more recent past, the government has recognized the need for major economic reform to take the country forward into the early decades of the 21st century. Thus, the Supreme Economic Council (SEC) was formed and has become a true driving force for that economic change. Integral to the reform package has been the new Foreign Investment Law, of which the Saudi Arabian General Investment Authority (SAGIA) is the implementing authority. Yet more recently, the government has moved to privatize more public undertakings and to welcome foreign investment.

This further opening up of the Saudi economy has created many opportunities for local and foreign investors to participate in the Kingdom's growth in the coming years.

Why invest in Saudi Arabia?

The Kingdom of Saudi Arabia is located at the heart of the Arab and Islamic worlds and bridges the major air routes between North America and Europe in the West and Asia in the East. Within three hours flying time live 1.4 billion people, with a further 1.6 billion within just seven hours flying time. The Kingdom is the largest Arab economy and the world's largest oil producer, with one quarter of all proven oil reserves. It is also blessed with vast quantities of natural gas, which is used as fuel for domestic power generation and industry and as feedstock for the country's burgeoning petrochemicals industry.

The substantial revenues earned over the years have been wisely invested in a comprehensive infrastructure that has enabled development of the country into a modern, industrialized society in just 60 years. Wholly integral to that development has been comprehensive diversification of the economy away from dependence on oil to encompass agriculture, fishing, banking, financial services, industry, manufacturing, construction, mining, tourism and a highly-developed trading sector, offering quality goods and services from every corner of the world.

But why invest in Saudi Arabia today? Because Saudi Arabia offers:

- political and economic stability;
- a well established infrastructure;
- readily available primary and secondary raw materials;
- well-defined open-market trade policies;
- a strong banking sector;
- a competitive commercial culture;
- a friendly tax regime;
- ready access to a skilled and affordable work force;
- a recent Foreign Investment Law that has considerably liberalized inward investment;
- a major programme privatizing public sector assets and services;
- simplified market entry through the 'one stop shop' SAGIA Investment Service Centres;
- a constantly improving investment environment;
- a safe and secure family environment;
- excellent residential and educational facilities.

The Saudi political system, socio-political structure and social fabric have evolved from within over many years through a close adherence to the tenets of Islam. This has endowed the nation and its people with an inherent strength that has enabled rapid, indeed unprecedented, social and economic progress in just a few decades.

Although revenues from oil remain integral to national economic progress, ongoing diversification of the economy, supported by a rapidly growing population and readily available raw materials, has proven highly rewarding and continues to provide numerous opportunities for investment. The privatization of a number of wholly or partially government-owned entities provide substantial opportunities for local and foreign investors. So do the major projects planned under the Gas Initiative and the recent gas deals, which foresee the participation of international oil companies in up- and down-stream gas-based activities and in the power generation and water desalination sectors that will provide major enhancements to the already well-developed infrastructure.

Throughout its history, the Kingdom has maintained a free market economy and avoided the imposition of exchange controls and barriers to the free transfer of capital and income. This situation, allied to close trading links with international partners, has ensured strong business practices among Saudi businessmen and has prepared them for globalization following the anticipated accession of Saudi Arabia to the World Trade Organization (WTO).

Entering the Saudi marketplace has been simplified for foreign investors through the establishment of the Saudi Arabian General Investment Authority (SAGIA) and the opening of Investment Service Centres under its aegis. Never has it been easier for foreign companies to enter the Saudi market since these 'one stop shops' were introduced to ensure rapid issuance of investment licences and all other necessary documentation.

Local banks, together with government funding agencies for agriculture and industry, provide ready access to finance for viable projects, often at preferential rates and on extended terms. Also, the Foreign Investment Law has reduced the tax ceiling from 45 per cent to 20 per cent.

Together with Saudi Arabia's and the wider Middle East's high population growth rates, and the anticipated commensurate growth in the region's markets, these attributes provide a highly conducive environment for investment which, together with the support of SAGIA in cutting through the red tape and ensuring the constant applicability of the Kingdom's investment criteria, place Saudi Arabia well to the fore as a destination of real opportunity for international investors.

Investing in Saudi Arabia

Foreign direct investment

Saudi Arabia has been most successful in attracting foreign direct investment over many years, due in large part to the Kingdom's open-market, private enterprise policies and also to the absence of both foreign exchange controls and restrictions on the repatriation of capital and profits.

A major innovation occurred in April 2000 with the introduction of a new Foreign Investment Law to spur potential investors. This allows 100 per cent foreign ownership of projects and the associated real estate for both factory and staff accommodation.

Subsequently, in late 2002 and early 2003, further major decisions were made of marked benefit to potential foreign investors when the Council of Ministers formally decided to privatize many public sector utilities and services and to open up a number of sectors that earlier had been included on the excluded list.

From its inception in April 2000 up to May 2004, SAGIA has licensed 2,280 projects with total finance of US$15.4 billion, 928 of which were industrial, 1,347 services or non-industrial and five agricultural. Of the total investment since the formation of SAGIA, almost 83 per cent has been from foreign investors. These figures compare with 1,753 joint venture projects with foreign investment up to 2000.

Countries from which Saudi Arabia has received foreign investment proposals, and for which licences have been issued, have included the United States, Japan, the UK, Germany, France, Switzerland, Finland, India, Italy and a number of countries within the Arab World.

The introduction of the new Foreign Investment Law has received a markedly positive response and expectations are high in the Kingdom that many further projects, both large and small, will be implemented in the coming years.

The Foreign Investment Law (FIL)

The FIL of April 2000 has opened a new chapter in the history of foreign investment in Saudi Arabia. Today, under the Law, international companies may own up to 100 per cent of their projects and the associated real estate, while enjoying the same general benefits offered to local companies. Thus, they are eligible for loans from the Saudi Industrial Development Fund (SIDF) in addition to other facilities offered by other institutions (government and non-government). Investors are permitted to hold investment licences for more than one activity. Changes have been made also with regard to sponsorship arrangements, as now foreign investors and their non-Saudi management and employees may be sponsored by their licensed venture.

Corporate taxation has also changed such that foreign companies will now be subject to lower levels of taxation and will be allowed to carry forward losses for an unspecified number of years until the company starts making profits.

The FIL also seeks to ensure faster licensing approvals and initiation of projects through SAGIA than was the case in the past. Thus, all licensing approvals must be made within 30 days, given that all documentation is in order, and the overall processing time for new investments has been markedly reduced.

Sectors to be privatized

In late 2002, the Council of Ministers issued a decision to privatize a number of formerly public sector activities. The method, size and timing of the privatization processes will be determined according to the privatization strategy defined by the supreme Economic Council.

The utilities, economic activities and services to be privatized comprise:

- water and sewerage facilities;
- desalination of sea water;
- telecommunication services;
- aviation and allied services;
- railways;
- roads – the management and maintenance of existing highways and the construction and operation of new highways;
- airport services;
- postal services;
- flour mills and grain silos;
- seaport services;
- industrial zones and cities services.

Also to be privatized are the following:

- Saudi government shares in companies such as banks, the Saudi Basic Industries Corporation (SABIC), the Saudi Electricity company, the Saudi Arabian Mining Company (Ma'aden), the Saudi Telecommunications Company (STC) and the local refineries;

- Saudi government shares in the capital of Arab and Islamic investment joint venture companies;
- government-owned hotels and sports clubs;
- municipal services, including the building, operation and maintenance of slaughterhouses, shopping malls, public markets and parks, public transportation, cleaning services and garbage collection and disposal;
- educational services (primary, secondary and adult education), including the building and maintenance of educational buildings, printing of textbooks, transportation of students, building of student housing etc.
- social services, including management and operation of welfare institutes and Saudi employment office services;
- agricultural services, including quarantine centres, laboratories and veterinary clinics;
- health services, including the establishment and operation of health facilities and the provision of patient transportation services.

Activities to be excluded from foreign investment

Integral to the FIL are a number of activities from which foreign investment has been excluded. As of the beginning of 2003, excluded activities comprised the following:

- the industrial sector:
  - oil exploration, drilling and production (except services related to mining);
  - manufacture of military equipment, devices and uniforms;
  - manufacture of civilian explosives.
- the services sector:
  - military catering services;
  - security and detective services;
  - real estate investment in Makkah and Madinah;

- Haj and Umrah (pilgrimages) tour guide services;
- real estate brokerage;
- recruitment and employment services, including local recruitment offices;
- printing and publishing;
- audiovisual services;
- distribution services, including wholesale and retail trade involving medical retail services such as private pharmacies and commercial agencies other than patients' rights services;
- land and air transportation;
- satellite transmission services;
- specified telecommunications services;
- space projects;
- services rendered by midwives, nurses, natural therapists and paramedics;
- blood banks, poison centres and quarantine centres;
- fisheries.

It should be noted that SAGIA seeks to reduce the number of activities presently excluded and the Supreme Economic Council has undertaken to review the list annually. Thus, over time, certain of the above sectors may be opened up to foreign investment and contact should therefore be maintained with SAGIA directly or through its website (www.sagia.gov.sa) to ensure receipt of the most up-to-date information.

Priority areas for investment

All industrial sectors are open for investment with the specific exclusion of those mentioned above, and no specific areas have been defined as primary areas for investment.

However, the government has expressed a desire to see further private sector investment in mining, water desalination, power generation, and high technology projects, although these should not be looked upon as all inclusive.

The role and activities of SAGIA

SAGIA was formed concurrently with the announcement of the FIL and is leading the way in drawing the world business community's attention to the opportunities available in the Kingdom for foreign investors and to the benefits that may be derived by investors.

The primary objective of SAGIA is to oversee investment affairs in Saudi Arabia, including foreign investment. In fulfilling this role, SAGIA has responsibility for proposing and implementing policies that encourage both local and foreign investment and for issuing investment licences and other documents required by foreign investors to enable the obtaining of visas and other permits.

Other functions of SAGIA include the development of policies that promote investment in Saudi Arabia; making recommendations for the improvement of the Kingdom's investment environment; evaluating and following up investment opportunities of perceived potential and subsequently promoting them both domestically and internationally; working closely with government agencies directly related to foreign and local investment; undertaking research and developing databases; and participating in conferences, exhibitions, seminars and symposia on investment, both at home and overseas.

Key to SAGIA's success to date has been the simplification of the procedure for obtaining investment licences. An important move in this regard has been the setting up of Investment Service Centres in Riyadh, Jeddah and Dammam. In effect, these are 'one stop shops' for would-be investors, from pre-investment assistance through to initiation of a project.

Incentives offered to foreign investors

Foreign investment projects generally enjoy the same benefits, incentives and guarantees extended to locally-owned projects. These include:

- pre-investment assistance through SAGIA;
- the incentives stipulated under the Protection and Promotion of National Industries Act, which include authorized duty-free import of goods and equipment used in industry; duty-free export; and some preferential treatment for national products in government procurement;
- availability of land in industrial cities at nominal charges;
- the ownership of real estate directly connected to a project, including employee residences and accommodation;

- the benefits of all bilateral and multilateral agreements related to taxation and investment;
- guaranteed private property ownership subject to applicable laws;
- the repatriation of capital and profits;
- freedom of movement of shares between partners;
- sponsorship of the licensed project of the foreign investor and his/her non-Saudi staff;
- the availability of utilities at existing reduced prices;
- the availability of loans from the Saudi Industrial Development Fund;
- the carrying forward of losses into later years for tax purposes.

The Economic Offset Programme

Initiated in 1984 the Saudi Economic Offset Programme (SEOP) sought to ensure that the Kingdom's economy as a whole would benefit from major defence procurements; ten years later the SEOP was expanded to include major civil contracts.

A fundamental objective of the SEOP is to facilitate the formation of Saudi–foreign joint ventures and thereby to encourage local investment and employment opportunities.

Under the terms of the SEOP, a defined element of a defence procurement or civil contract is to be reinvested into Saudi Arabia. To date, the United States, the UK and France have committed to participation in the SEOP and have made substantial investments in Saudi Arabia approximating to 30 to 35 per cent of the value of relevant contracts won. All project proposals made under the SEOP are evaluated and agreed upon by the Saudi Economic Offset Committee and the Ministry of Defence and Aviation.

The Saudi Industrial Development Fund (SIDF)

The SIDF provides medium- and long-term loans to industrial projects for up to 50 per cent of total project costs. It also provides marketing and financial consultancy, technical advice and ongoing monitoring of projects.

The policies and lending criteria of the SIDF are:

- to support local and foreign entities possessing an industrial licence by extending medium- and long-term loans;

- all projects to be financed must be shown to be viable from all technical, financial and marketing points of view;
- the maximum loan term is 15 years and is connected to a project's projected cash flow;
- the financing of used equipment and machinery is proscribed;
- the promoters' equity of any project must represent a minimum of 25 per cent of the total project cost;
- security must be provided in the form of a mortgage over the fixed assets financed and of personal guarantees from the shareholders of limited liability companies;
- loan disbursement is subject to actual expenditure and progress made on the project, supported by appropriate documentation;
- all repayments must be made according to a defined schedule following a specific period of grace;
- the maximum loan granted is SR400 million (US$106.7 million) but that figure is made available only to joint stock companies or companies in which a joint stock company is a shareholder.

The full text of the Foreign Investment Law of April 2000 can be found on website: www.sagia.gov.sa.

2.3

The Al-Yamamah Economic Offset Programme

British Offset Office, London

Introduction

The Al-Yamamah project was set up by the Saudi and British governments in 1985. As part of this project, Saudi Arabia agreed to purchase Tornado, Hawk and PC-9 aircraft with related equipment and support facilities, as well as specialized naval vessels. The UK government's prime contractor for the project was British Aerospace.

The agreement between the two governments also established an economic offset programme (the Al-Yamamah Economic Offset Programme) with the primary purpose of encouraging and assisting the transfer of technology to Saudi companies through joint ventures or licensing agreements. The value of the investment under the programme is expected to be at least £1 billion, thus it will constitute a vital part of the continuing commercial relations between the UK and Saudi Arabia.

The British Offset Office

As a result of the Al-Yamamah project, the British Offset Office was established to help encourage greater investment and assist the transfer of new technology into Saudi Arabia. It comprises personnel from the UK Ministry of Defence and BAE Systems (BAES) and is responsible for planning, coordinating and administering the UK's involvement in the offset programme. It actively looks for ways to assist technology-holding companies to identify new business opportunities in Saudi Arabia. Experience of Saudi Arabia and the special arrangements of the Al-Yamamah Economic Offset Programme make it possible for the Offset Office to offer companies detailed and confidential guidance on the development of project ideas. The Offset Office also extends advice and assistance to companies on available UK government support, including the Export Credit Guarantee Department's discretionary overseas investment insurance scheme.

The British Offset Office has offices in the UK and Saudi Arabia and, with its merchant bank advisers, can provide an unparalleled level of knowledge and experience on business in the Kingdom. Furthermore, UK companies working through the offset programme benefit from the status derived from their proposals being administered on a government-to-government basis.

Eligibility for participation in offset

Both governments fully recognize that for the offset programme to succeed in its objectives, it must be as flexible and as broadly based as possible to provide maximum benefit to all concerned. Participation is therefore open to companies from most countries in both the civil and defence sectors, and includes ventures in both manufacturing and service industries.

The only projects that are specifically excluded from the programme are the primary extraction, processing and marketing of crude oil and gas.

The Saudi Arabian Economic Offset Committee

Although there is a general procedure for developing investment ideas under the offset programme, this can be tailored to meet the nature and needs of a particular project. For this reason, it is essential to discuss project ideas at the earliest possible stage. Once the project has been fully conceived, the British Offset Office will, with the company's approval, outline the proposal to the Saudi Arabian Economic Offset Committee, which will frequently contribute constructive suggestions as to how project proposals can be improved.

From these early discussions, an initial proposal is prepared that sets out in broad terms the aims, structure and principal features of the project to be presented to the Saudi Arabian Economic Offset Committee for confirmation that the venture accords with offset programme criteria.

With the approval of the Saudi Arabian Economic Offset Committee, the partner companies are invited to complete their studies and prepare a business plan similar to that which a company would present to its own board of directors for approval, or to a bank for project financing. The groundwork undertaken before each submission has ensured that the British Offset Office has an excellent record in obtaining approval for proposed ventures from the Saudi Arabian Economic Offset Committee.

Projects implemented under the Al-Yamamah Economic Offset Programme

Because of the offset programme and the unique investment opportunities available in the Kingdom, a variety of blue chip companies from the UK have already been attracted to the setting up of joint ventures in Saudi Arabia to the value of over £1 billion.

Projects that have been brought to Saudi Arabia as a result of the offset programme include:

- the Jeddah-based Glaxo pharmaceuticals plant;
- a major sugar refinery at Jeddah port;
- an aircraft gas turbine maintenance and overhaul facility located at King Khaled International Airport, Riyadh;
- the establishment of a training company to introduce state-of-the-art techniques in job analysis, employee assessment, training needs analysis and training package delivery, in formats appropriate to the Saudi environment;
- two important petrochemical projects using Cyclar, a new process developed by UOP and BP to produce aromatics from liquid petroleum gas;
- a joint venture between the UK company HARCO and Dhahran Chemical Industries (DCI) for the production of polymer dispersion products;
- an export-orientated petrochemical joint venture developed to take advantage of leading technology and competitively-priced feedstocks available at Jubail on the Kingdom's east coast.
- a joint venture to produce polypropylene in the Eastern Province.

Glaxo pharmaceuticals project, Jeddah

In May 1992, Glaxo secured approval to build an advanced pharmaceuticals plant at Jeddah Industrial City. This US$26 million plant commenced operations in 1995; its products include such well-known medicines as Zantac and Ventolin.

United Sugar Company (USC) refinery, Jeddah

Work on this world-scale sugar refinery in Jeddah commenced in 1995. This project is a joint venture between Tate & Lyle of the UK and the Savola Group. The plant began full production in 1997, with one-fifth of production earmarked for export markets. USC announced that it planned to raise production at the refinery from 500,000 to 885,000 tonnes annually by end 2002.

Middle East Propulsion Company (MEPC), Riyadh

This is a joint venture between Rolls-Royce of the UK, Pratt and Whitney of the United States and their Saudi partners that repairs and maintains a range of air propulsion units.

Saudi Development and Training Company (SDT), Dammam and Riyadh

This company, a joint venture between BAES and Al Gosaibi, provides tailored development and training packages.

SABIC Cyclar process aromatics plant, Yanbu

Saudi Arabian Basic Industries Corporation (SABIC) has adopted the British Cyclar technology for its 730,000 tonne aromatics plant at Yanbu. This process enables the conversion of locally available liquid petroleum gas into benzene, paraxylene and other aromatic products. The Cyclar process was developed jointly by BP and UOP. The plant is the first petrochemical project to be implemented under the Al-Yamamah Economic Offset Programme.

Project for polymer dispersions, Dammam

In March 1996, a joint venture was formed between Harlow Chemical Company (HARCO) and Dhahran Chemical Industries Limited (DCI) to produce a range of polymer dispersions used in the paint, adhesive and textile industries.

MA/BDO, Jubail

This US$200 million joint venture involving Kvaerner (UK), Huntsman (US) and GACIC (Saudi Arabia) will produce 50,000 tonnes of butanediol and 10,000 tonnes of malaeic anhydride per year for use in the manufacture of a wide range of plastic products.

Saudi Polyolefins Company, Eastern Province

This is a joint venture in the Eastern Province between the Saudi partner National Petrochemical Industries Company (NPIC) and Europe's Basell to produce 450,000 tonnes per annum of polypropylene.

Project finance initiative

In addition to the existing range of investment incentives for companies setting up industrial projects in Saudi Arabia, BAES has developed the project finance initiative, a joint venture financing facility that will offer significant financial incentives for foreign technology companies to invest in Saudi Arabia through the Al-Yamamah Economic Offset Programme.

Under the project finance initiative, a bank facility may be arranged by BAES to provide technology holders with non-recourse loans for up to 50 per cent of their equity stake in an offset joint venture. In addition, BAES may also arrange a portion of the 'parent company' guarantee required to support the joint venture's commercial debt financing. This would also be on a non-recourse basis.

Through this arrangement, BAES is effectively sharing the risk of business investment with the technology holder, while at the same time allowing management freedom and an enhanced return potential. It is intended that this initiative will lead to greater investment and technology transfer in Saudi Arabia through the Al-Yamamah Economic Offset Programme.

Advantages of the project finance initiative

The advantages of the project finance initiative are:

- each equity loan and commercial debt guarantee is supported by BAES without recourse to the technology company;
- the loan is made at an attractive interest rate (SIBOR + 0.375 per cent, an increase to 0.8 per cent is under consideration);
- loan repayment is linked to the returns paid by the joint venture company to the technology company – the loan repayment schedule is based on the financial projections in a business plan agreed by BAES, its bank and the technology company;
- coupled with current incentives in Saudi Arabia, the technology company can achieve a 50 per cent shareholding through an investment equal to 6.25 per cent of the joint venture's initial capitalized value.

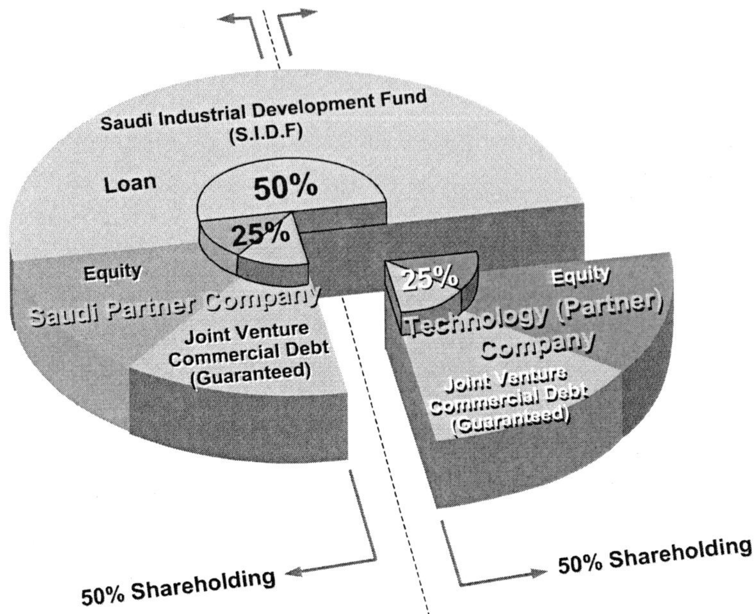

Figure 2.3.1 Typical funding structure for a Saudi joint venture

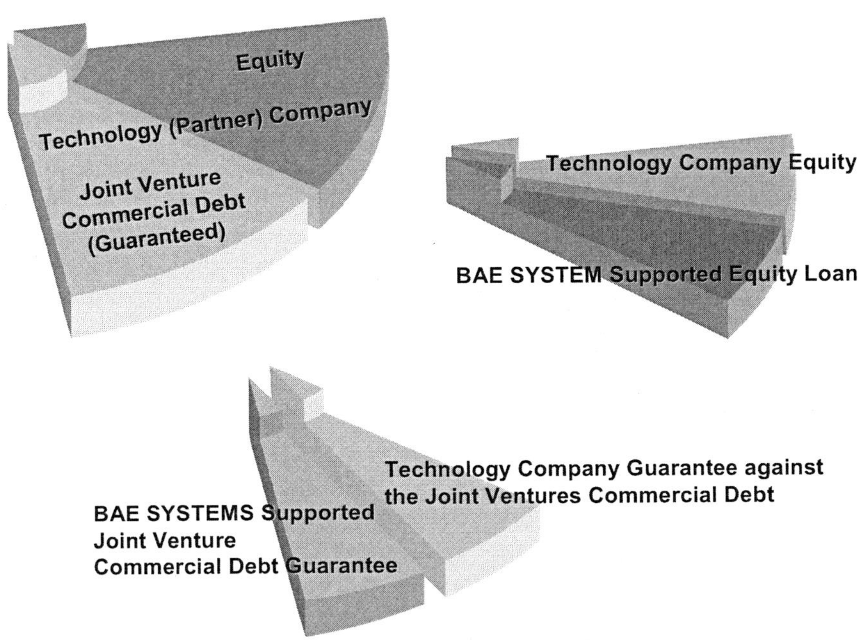

Figure 2.3.2 Typical commercial partner commercial dept and equity structure

Basic conditions for accessing the project finance initiative facility

The following basic conditions for accessing the project finance initiative facility apply:

- the joint venture must be developed under the Al-Yamamah Economic Offset Programme and may only be accessed through the British Offset Office;
- the proposed joint venture must be commercially viable;
- BAES support will be arranged at an amount equal to the technology company's cash equity investment and commercial debt guarantee, and issued under agreed conditions;
- the maximum total amount of loan and guarantee support for an individual joint venture is SR37.5 million (US$10 million);
- the joint venture company should have a minimum initial capitalized value of SR60 million (US$16 million), although each case is considered on its merits.

Target sectors for new investments under Offset

The British Offset Office is particularly interested in hearing from technology companies in the following sectors:

- downstream petrochemicals;
- chemicals and process industry;
- pharmaceuticals, healthcare and medical products;
- food processing and agro-technology;
- education and training;
- environmental technology;
- utilities;
- engineering.

Further information

Further information concerning the Al-Yamamah Economic Offset Programme and the new project financing facility can be obtained from the British Offset Office via their website at www.britishoffset.com or from either of the following:

- London: The British Offset Office, Castlewood House, 77–91 New Oxford Street, London WC1A 1DT. Tel: +44 (0) 20 7829 8556, Fax: +44 (0) 20 7829 8116, Email: AYOffset@aol.com;
- Riyadh: The British Offset Office, UK MoD Team, PO Box 1003, Riyadh 11431, Saudi Arabia. Tel: +966 1 419 5957 ext 4210, Fax: +966 1 419 5957 ext 4214.

2.4

Foreign Trade Relations

Anthony Shoult, ASA Consulting[1]

Introduction

This review of Saudi foreign trade relations seeks to offer both present and potential exporters to Saudi Arabia an analysis of the current nature of imports into the Kingdom and to identify the changes taking place in relation to exports from the Kingdom.

Saudi Arabia is increasingly diversifying its export base as industrialization occurs and is no longer entirely dependent upon oil exports as a wide range of non-oil related goods in a variety of sectors are beginning to appear on the list of exported products.

Saudi Arabia remains a key market for most countries in the Western Hemisphere. In most cases, it is the largest export market in the Middle East despite a relatively small population compared with some of its neighbours. With visible imports at around the level of US$37 billion annually, it is a particularly important market for the United States, Japan, Germany and the UK.

The composition of imports

The most significant imports to Saudi Arabia since 1995 have been machinery, mechanical appliances including electrical machinery and equipment, foodstuffs and transport equipment comprising mainly of automobiles and spare parts. In 2003, machinery including electrical machinery and equipment constituted 22 per cent of total visible imports, with transport equipment representing 21 per cent and foodstuffs representing around 16 per cent of the total (see Table 2.4.1).

---

[1] Sources of information include The Saudi British Bank, Saudi Industrial Development Fund (SIDF) and UK Trade & Investment.

Table 2.4.1 Composition of imports, 1996, 2000, 2003 (SR millions)

Category of import	1996	2000	2003	% increase 1996–2003
Live animals and animal products	5,071	5,675	7,181	41.6
Vegetable products	7,674	8,268	7,779	1.4
Animal and vegetable fats, oils and their products	800	784	789	-1.4
Prepared foodstuffs, vinegar and tobacco	4,411	5,531	6,710	52.1
Mineral products	1,159	1,062	1,013	-12.6
Products of chemical and allied industries	8,382	9,512	12,652	50.9
Artificial resins/plastics, rubber/synthetic rubber etc	3,777	4,141	5,334	41.2
Raw hides and skins, furs and leather articles	355	394	401	12.9
Wood and articles of wood, charcoal, cork etc	1,463	1,444	1,439	-1.6
Paper-making materials, paper, cardboard etc	2,295	2,356	2,702	17.7
Textiles and textile articles	7,589	6,674	7,513	-1.0
Footwear, headgear, umbrellas etc	1,120	899	967	-13.7
Articles of stone, plaster, asbestos, ceramics, glass etc	1,749	1,931	2,890	65.2
Pearls, precious/semi-precious stones/ metals and jewellery	4,399	4,574	1,395	-68.3
Base metals and articles of base metals	10,396	8,895	12,544	20.7
Machinery, mechanical appliances, electrical equipment/parts	21,848	24,982	30,210	38.3
Transport equipment	15,903	19,995	29,299	84.2
Optical, photographic, measuring, precision instruments etc	2,897	3,048	4,291	48.1
Arms, ammunition and parts etc	411	788	762	85.4
Miscellaneous manufactured articles	1,935	2,264	2,542	31.4
Works of art and antiques	345	23	22	-93.6
Total imports	*103,980*	*113,240*	*138,435*	*33.1*

Source: Central Department of Statistics, Ministry of Economy and Planning

There has been some change in the structure of imports over the longer term. In 1981, for example, foodstuffs accounted for only 11 per cent of total imports, while electrical and transport equipment combined represented around 40 per cent of imports compared with 43 per cent in 2003.

Major fluctuations occur in the case of some types of import from year to year and this is particularly the case in respect of some categories of capital goods. In contrast, there is much less volatility in imports of consumer goods, particularly in certain categories of foodstuffs.

Import substitution

Visible import values in 1983 represented almost 50 per cent of the value of Saudi Gross National Expenditure. By 2004, this proportion had fallen below 15 per cent, with visible imports at SR132 million and GDP estimated at some SR932 billion. As a consequence, over the last 20 years imports have become much less important to the Saudi economy. One reason for this has been a growing self-sufficiency as import substitution has taken place.

The manufacturing sector, comprising over 3,400 licensed factories in the Kingdom in 2001, now contributes almost 10 per cent of GDP. Exporters to Saudi Arabia now need to consider competition from local producers, including that from the increasing number of joint ventures with foreign companies that are being established.

The level of import substitution that has been achieved varies from sector to sector. Cement production in the Kingdom, for example, now fulfils almost all of domestic demand, while in 1977 there was a 70 per cent dependence upon imports. During 2002, the eight cement plants in the Kingdom produced 23.3 million tonnes of Portland cement, of which over 10 per cent was exported. Other examples of successful import substitution are to be found in the consumer and household market sectors, for example in vegetable oils and disinfectants.

The trend towards increased import substitution has not necessarily led to the total closure of markets to outsiders. It often facilitates new areas of demand such as raw materials, intermediate goods and support services. For example, in spite of the marked decline of demand for foreign agricultural products due to import substitution, the rapid growth of dairy and poultry farming has necessitated massive imports of barley into the Kingdom.

There will be considerable opportunity for exporters to Saudi Arabia arising from membership of the WTO, which, in 2005, is imminent.

This will involve the gradual elimination of trade barriers that will result in a net benefit to exporters.

Finance ministers of Gulf Cooperation Council (GCC) states launched their own customs union on 1 January 2003. The union between Bahrain, Kuwait, Oman, Qatar, Saudi Arabia and the United Arab Emirates means a unified customs tariff of five per cent is charged on goods and services across the trade block. The GCC, which covers over 31 million people with a GDP of US$341 billion, is also considering ongoing plans to establish a common market by 2005 and a single currency by 2010.

Sources of imports

Saudi Arabia is dependent upon relatively few countries for the vast majority of its import requirements. Historically, the leading exporter to the Kingdom has been the United States and it still exports more than any other country to Saudi Arabia.

Over the years 1984 to 1998, the importance of the United States as an exporter to the Kingdom increased, with its share of the Kingdom's imports rising from 18 per cent in 1984 to 21 per cent in 1998. Since 1998, the importance of the United States as an exporter has declined, with its share of the Kingdom's imports falling to 15 per cent in 2003 (see Table 2.4.2).

Japan occupies second ranking for import sources, with its share of the Kingdom's imports rising from 8.6 per cent in 1998 to 10.3 per cent in 2003.

The greatest improvements in import values has been recorded by China and South Korea. China saw exports to the Kingdom rise from SR6.4 billion to almost SR8.2 billion in 2003, a growth of over 27 per cent and more than twice its level in 1998. South Korea reversed a drop in exports to the Kingdom in 2002, to record a growth of almost 28 per cent, taking exports to over SR5 billion. India also saw its exports to the Kingdom increase to almost SR4.1 billion, representing a 25 per cent increase.

From these changes in trade patterns, it would appear that Saudi Arabia is increasingly pointing towards the East in its trading relations, with its older trading partners, particularly the United States and Western Europe being superseded by the new industrial economies of China, South Korea and India.

Table 2.4.2 Imports by main trading countries, 1998, 2002, 2003 (SR million)

Rank *(2002)*	Country	1998 SR million	1998 % total	2002 SR million	2002 % total	2003 SR million	2003 % total
1	United States	23,984	21.3	19,737	16.3	20,777	15.0
2	Japan	9,666	8.6	13,405	11.1	14,316	10.3
3	Germany	7,052	6.3	10,217	8.4	12,377	8.9
4	UK	9,535	8.5	7,240	6.0	8,120	5.9
5	China	3,593	3.2	6,441	5.3	8,199	5.9
6	Italy	4,667	4.1	5,203	4.3	5,508	4.0
7	France	5,862	5.2	4,350	3.6	5,062	3.6
8	Australia	1.978	1.8	4,194	3.5	3,708	2.7
9	South Korea	3,884	3.5	3,989	3.3	5,099	3.7
10	India	3,057	2.7	3,307	2.7	4,093	3.0
	Other countries	39,119	34.8	42,917	35.5	51,176	37.0
Total		*112,397*	*100.0*	*121,000*	*100.0*	*138,435*	*100.0*

Source: Central Department of Statistics, Ministry of Economy and Planning

The top six exporters to the Kingdom account for over 50 per cent of total exports, valued at some SR69.3 billion in 2003. The next four countries account for almost SR18 billion or 13 per cent of the Kingdom's imports. This tends to indicate that Saudi Arabia's trade relations at present are very country specific by international standards.

Exports from Saudi Arabia

Despite the major industrial growth now taking place in the Kingdom, exports are still dominated by crude and refined oil. Exports of crude and refined oil were at the level of SR168.3 billion in 1999, representing over 88 per cent of total exports of SR190.1 billion. By 2003, the value of exports of crude and refined oil had risen to almost SR315 billion, still representing over 88 per cent of total exports of SR356.3 billion (see Table 2.4.3).

Table 2.4.3 Exports by product category,# 1999, 2001, 2003 (SR million)

Sector	1999		2001		2003*	
	SR million	% total	SR million	% total	SR million	% total
Oil exports						
Crude oil	136,321	71.7	190,557	74.8	n/a	-
Refined oil	31,977	16.8	33,648	13.1	n/a	-
Total oil exports:	*168,298*	*88.5*	*224,205*	*87.9*	*314,933*	*88.4*
Non-oil exports						
Petrochemicals	9,189	4.8	13,451	5.3	16,331	4.6
Construction materials	2,808	1.5	2,779	1.1	4,632	1.3
Agriculture, animal and food products	1,768	0.9	1,541	0.6	3,324	0.9
Other exports	8,021	4.3	12,922	5.1	17,149	4.8
Total non-oil exports	*21,786*	*11.5*	*30,693*	*12.1*	*41,436*	*11.60*
Total all exports:	*190,084*	*100.0*	*254,898*	*100.0*	*356,369*	*100.0*

includes re-exports

* preliminary

Source: Central Department of Statistics, Ministry of Economy and Planning

Given substantial increases in oil prices in 2004, with export prices averaging US$45/barrel and with export volume increases as well, oil export values should exceed SR530 billion.

Petrochemicals dominate Saudi Arabia's non-oil exports and their value continues to fluctuate with changes in world petrochemical prices. Other exports, for example construction materials, have not been subjected to depressed world prices in recent years and have seen rising values.

Whilst the GCC countries are relatively unimportant in terms of overall exports, they do figure strongly in relation to non-oil exports, with over SR10 billion non-oil exports to the GCC in 2003 (see Table 2.4.4).

Table 2.4.4 Non-oil exports by destination, 2003 (SR million)

Region	SR million
Africa (non-Arab)	700
Oceania	719
North America	2,345
South America	76
Western Europe	4,983
Eastern Europe	27
GCC	10,333
Other Arab League	4,035
Islamic countries (non-Arab)	2,307
Asian countries	9,503
Other countries	23
Total	*35,051*

Note: excludes re-exports

Source: Saudi Arabian Monetary Agency (SAMA)

The regions buying Saudi oil are largely in Asia, accounting for almost SR122 billion or almost 45 per cent of the total in 2002. Asia is followed by North America with just over 20 per cent and Western Europe with 15 per cent (see Table 2.4.5).

Over the period 1996 to 2002, there was a major growth in exports to Asian countries, whilst exports to Western Europe fell over the period. Exports to North America increased by SR14 billion over the period, reflecting their growing need for oil.

Table 2.4.5 Oil exports by destination, 1996, 2002 (SR million)

Region	1996		2002	
	SR million	% total	SR million	% total
GCC	16,283	7.2	16,734	6.2
Other Arab League	6,106	2.7	8,936	3.3
Islamic countries (non-Arab)	11,808	5.2	14,702	5.4
Asia (non-Arab)	96,156	42.3	121,897	44.9
Africa	2,750	1.2	7,187	2.6
Oceania	3,483	1.5	2,335	0.9
North America	41,607	18.3	55,310	20.4
South America	5,844	2.6	3,512	1.3
Western Europe	43,235	19.0	41,008	15.0
Eastern Europe	50	-	37	-
Other countries	104	-	83	-
Total	*227,426*	*100.00*	*271,741*	*100.00*

Source: Central Department of Statistics, Ministry of Economy and Planning

2.5

Privatization and Economic Reforms

Anthony Shoult, ASA Consulting[1]

Introduction

At the end of 2002, Saudi Arabia announced plans to privatize many of its vital economic sectors including telecommunications, civil aviation, desalination, highway management, railways, sports clubs, municipal services, health services and government hotels.

For Saudi Arabia, privatization is seen as a tool to attract local private and foreign investment. It is hoped that the success of the Saudi privatization programme will help to speed up economic reform and eventually create a more attractive investment environment. The aim is to follow the global model, in which privatization programmes are an integral part of public policies associated with economic reform, liberalization, monopoly control and the achievement of improved competitiveness.

The Saudi government has adopted privatization to achieve sustainable and higher productivity and economic and budgetary efficiency. Other specific reasons for privatization in Saudi Arabia include the need to increase private sector contribution to GDP and meet the growing demand for services (in particular electricity, water and telecommunications services) resulting from population growth and improved economic activity.

The privatization programme is seen as a means to assist the government to deal with the economic challenges facing the Saudi economy over forthcoming years. These include the need to increase the level of foreign direct investment (FDI), as well as those challenges arising as a result of structural and demographic changes in the

---

[1] * Sources of information include The Saudi British Bank, National Commercial Bank (NCB), Saudi Industrial Development Fund (SIDF) and UK Trade & Investment.

Kingdom, including the need to upgrade productivity rates and increase employment opportunities.

To support privatization and the huge investment programmes taking place in the key sectors of the economy, the Saudi government is implementing a continuing programme of economic reforms.

Objectives of privatization

In November 2002, Saudi Arabia announced plans to privatize many of its vital economic sectors. The Supreme Economic Council (SEC) has taken overall charge of the programme, specifying the sectors to be privatized and setting out the strategic plan and timetable for the privatization programme.

Sectors open to privatization include telecommunications, civil aviation, desalination, highway management, railways, sports clubs, health services, government hotels, municipal services, education services, operation and management of social service centres, Saudi employment services, agricultural services, construction and management of abattoirs, public parks and recreation centres and cleaning and waste collection.

The principal objectives of the Saudi privatization programme are to:

- improve the efficiency of the national economy and enhance its competitive ability to meet the challenges of regional and international competition;
- encourage private sector investment and effective participation in the national economy, and increase its share of domestic production to achieve growth in the national economy;
- enlarge the ownership of productive assets by Saudi citizens;
- encourage domestic and foreign capital to invest locally;
- increase employment opportunities, optimize the use of the national workforce, and ensure the continued equitable increase of individual income;
- provide services to citizens and investors in a timely and cost-efficient manner;
- rationalize public expenditure and reduce the burden on the government budget by giving the private sector opportunities to finance, operate, and maintain certain services that it is able to provide;

- increase government revenues from returns on participation in activities to be transferred to the private sector, and from financing compensation obtained, for example, from granting concessions and from proceeds of the sale of part of the government's share.

Methods of privatization

The approach to the privatization process that is being adopted in Saudi Arabia comprises a number of tools that can be used to privatize public enterprises, projects, and services.

These methods include contracting for management and operation, leasing, financing, either from sale through public subscription, or sale to a principal investor and the transfer of ownership. Each of these methods has its own consequences, regulations, and factors that contribute to its success or failure.

The various methods of privatization contract that are under consideration in Saudi Arabia are as follows:

- *management contracts:* the responsibility for managing, operating and developing an entity is transferred to a contractor or investor from the private sector for period of time and an amount of money to be agreed upon;
- *leasing contracts:* agreements between the government and the private sector whereby the latter provides administrative and technical expertise for a specific period of time in exchange for an agreed-upon financial remuneration;
- *financing contracts:* the investor assumes responsibility for providing the capital, operating, and investment expenditure. There are several kinds of financing contracts, including:
  - lease-build-operate (LBO);
  - build-transfer-operate (BT and BTO);
  - build-own-operate-transfer (BOT and BOOT);
  - buy-build-operate (BBO) and build-own-operate (BOO).
- *sale contracts:* these can comprise either:
  - direct sale to the private sector through public subscription; or
  - sale to a principal investor.

Progress of privatization

Apart from the privatization of 30 per cent of the government stake in SABIC in the early 1980s, the Saudi government's intention to roll out a privatization programme did not become apparent until 1994, when the government announced its interest in expanding the role and contribution of the private sector to the ownership and management of state-owned projects.

A ministerial committee was formed in 1997 to coordinate and oversee privatization programmes, review the sectors proposed to be transferred to the private sector and define the overall objectives and principles of privatization.

The establishment of the Supreme Economic Council (SEC) in 1999 followed this. The SEC was later empowered to supervise the privatization programme and monitor its implementation in coordination with competent government agencies. It was also empowered to finalize the activities to be privatized, and draft a strategy and timeframe to manage the process.

Although the privatization process commenced in 1994, little early progress was made other than the initial moves to proceed with the privatization of the telecommunications and power sectors by establishing the Saudi Telecom Company and the consolidation of the electricity companies.

Oil and gas

Agreements valued at more than US$7 billion have been reached with international oil companies for investments in the Saudi energy sector, including a project with Royal Dutch shell and Total FinaElf, to develop upstream gas operations in the southern part of the Empty Quarter (Rub'al-Khali). These are the first of what is expected to be a total of more than US$25 billion of investments over the period 2005–2010.

Water and electricity

The Saudi government issued a decree in 1997 redefining power generation as an industrial activity to encourage private sector investment in power generation. As the new classification brought power generation under the authority of the foreign investment code, both domestic and foreign investors are now allowed freely to invest in power generation.

In 2003 and 2004, the Saudi government took further steps to liberalize the electricity sector through offering to the private sector a total of 11 power generation and desalination projects worth US$2.2 billion. The amount of investment required in power generation during the period from 2006 to 2010 has been estimated at about US$3.5 billion.

Minerals and mining

In May 2004, the SEC approved the privatization of the Saudi Arabian Mining Company (Ma'aden), which is wholly owned by the ministry of Petroleum and Mineral Resources. As an initial step towards privatization, Ma'aden set up a unit, in early 2005, to study and evaluate the precious and base metals sector.

Telecommunications

The privatization process for the telecommunications industry commenced in 1998 when the government passed control of telecommunications services to a joint stock company called the Saudi Telecom Company (STC).

STC was formed as a major holding company with a starting capital of over SR12 billion and with the aim that it will eventually consist of several subsidiaries.

In January 2003, STC sold 60 million shares or 30 per cent of the company through an initial public offering (IPO), raising nearly US$4 billion for the Saudi government.

Postal services

In 2002, the Saudi government approved the transfer of the responsibilities of the state-run postal services from the Ministry of Posts, Telegraphs and Telephones (PTT) to the private sector.

In January 2003, the newly-named Ministry of Telecommunications and Information Technology reported that the privatization of postal services had been successful, with about 100 new agencies established by the private sector.

Healthcare

The Ministry of Health supports the privatization of some state-run hospitals. In 2003, a private company was employed to promote its pre- and post-natal healthcare education programme, with the programme introduced in more than 85 per cent of the Kingdom's hospitals.

In 2003, the Ministry of Commerce and Industry approved the formation of a joint stock company for medical care that will establish, own and manage health facilities, including hospitals.

Insurance

In May 2004, the SEC approved the sale of government shares in the Arab world's largest insurance company, the National Company for Cooperative Insurance (NCCI). The sale of government shares in NCCI is intended to assist in the opening of the Kingdom's insurance market, which is estimated to be worth more than US$2.5 billion. NCCI has assets of about US$0.5 billion and is the only insurance company officially licensed in Saudi Arabia.

Airlines

In 2004, it was reported that research has begun for the partial privatization of Saudi Arabian Airlines (SAA). This is the largest airline in the Middle East, with a fleet of 117 aircraft carrying more than 16 million passengers every year to over 50 cities around the world.

Also, in 2003, the SEC approved the opening of the Saudi aviation sector to private enterprise, giving private companies the opportunity to provide domestic airline services.

Airports

The Kingdom will privatize the management and operation of both local and international airports. However, airport security will remain in the hands of the government. The privatization programme will involve all 24 domestic airports and the three international airports at Riyadh, Jeddah and Dammam.

Railways

In 2004, the Saudi Railways Organization (SRO) confirmed that three major rail projects had been approved by the Supreme Economic Council (SEC) for immediate implementation by the private sector.

The first project will extend the existing Dammam–Riyadh line to Jeddah. The second will connect Makkah with Madinah through Jeddah. The third will link Riyadh with the phosphate and bauxite mines in the provinces of Qasim and Northern Borders.

Urban transportation

In 2003, the transportation ministry announced plans to privatize and reorganize Saudi Arabia's urban transportation system.

Ports

The Ports Authority has assigned several projects to the private sector to expedite the handling of goods and maritime services at the Kingdom's eight seaports. For example, at Jeddah Islamic Port and King Abdul Aziz Port, Dammam, the King Fahd Repair Yard and two areas for processing re-exports are now leased to the private sector.

Economic reforms

Introduction

In recent years the government of Saudi Arabia has implemented a number of economic reforms to promote economic growth, increase foreign investment and expand employment opportunities.

In particular, the Kingdom is promoting its free market economy by privatizing 20 major state enterprises, establishing 14 regulatory authorities to carry out reforms, improving the foreign investment laws and revising a broad range of commercial laws as well as implementing intellectual property rights to foster innovation. It is also becoming a more significant player in international trade by seeking membership of the World Trade Organization (WTO).

Major new economic initiatives

Key current reforms are being implemented by the Saudi government that are providing positive benefits to the Saudi economy by expediting the privatization process. The key new economic initiatives and legislation are summarized as follows:

- accession to the World Trade Organization (WTO) (2005);
- the Gulf Cooperation Council (GCC) Customs Union agreement and economic integration (2030);
- the GCC common currency (2010).

Saudi Arabia was one of the largest economies outside the WTO. Following recent steps towards privatization and market liberalization, Saudi Arabia became the 149th member of the WTO in December 2005.

In the accession process, the Kingdom negotiated bilateral agreements with current WTO members while adopting the organization's various trade rules. Saudi Arabia and the European Union signed a bilateral agreement in August 2003, guaranteeing free access to goods and services. Moreover, Saudi Arabia has already signed 35 bilateral trade agreements with other WTO members, including China, Japan, Canada, Brazil, Argentina and Australia. Talks between Saudi Arabia and the United States were ongoing at the end of 2004.

The GCC Customs Union was established in January 2003 to standardize customs duties in the six member countries. In accordance with the Customs Union, Saudi Arabia approved the reduction to five per cent for goods formerly charged at between seven and 12 per cent. In addition, the GCC agreed to the principle of a single port of entry. Most related laws and regulations will be standardized by the end of 2005.

New regulatory framework

The Saudi government has sought to update the regulations and procedures related to investments to create a suitable environment in which the private sector can operate effectively to meet the challenges of regional and international competition. These are:

- a new capital markets law and the liberalization of the financial markets;
- a new foreign investment law, including a review of the list of exclusions for foreign investment and reduction in capital gains tax for foreign investors;
- new labour laws and structural reforms in the labour market;
- the establishment of independent regulatory authorities;
- modernization of the trade regulatory framework and new laws for business such as those related to copyright and patents and insurance.

The need to develop the capital markets in Saudi Arabia is one of the most important aspects of policy being pursued to achieve the goals of the privatization process. This includes expanding the scope for participation by Saudi citizens in the ownership of productive assets and public enterprises and projects, as well as encouraging local investments of domestic and foreign capital.

In June 2003, the Council of Ministers passed the Saudi Arabian Capital Markets Law. The aims are to stimulate and strengthen the Saudi economy and increase the participation of Saudi citizens in the capital markets. The law provides for the establishment of the following institutions:

- the Saudi Arabian Securities and Exchange Commission (SASEC) to protect investor interests, ensure fair business, promote and develop capital markets, license brokers and offer securities to the public, and
- the Saudi Arabian Stock Exchange (SASE), which incorporates the national securities depository centre.

The Foreign Investment Law, enacted by the Saudi Arabian General Investment Authority (SAGIA), was set up to allow foreign investors to own property, transfer capital and profits, claim full ownership of their projects and enjoy a reduction in tax rates. The law protects foreign investors from confiscation of property without a court order, or expropriation of property, except for public interest, against an equitable level of compensation. In 2002, the law was strengthened to allow foreigners to own land and avoid double taxation.

Structural reform of the Saudi labour market is a further key area of economic reform. The existence of a well-developed, highly productive pool of well-trained and experienced manpower is seen to be a critical factor in the success of the privatization programme. Many Saudis currently face difficulties in finding employment owing to lack of skills and competition from foreign workers in addition to the problem of excess labour in some enterprises that are targeted for privatization.

In order to develop manpower and enhance skills and competitiveness, enterprises targeted for privatization will be required to develop appropriate training programmes to retrain their workers, develop their skills, and help keep their jobs or find employment with other companies or enterprises.

The Saudi government is seeking to create job opportunities through a series of reforms and initiatives including:

- *The National Programme for Training and Employment* – this helps Saudi citizens find jobs in both the public and private sectors through the creation of job opportunities, training and Saudiization.
- *Saudiization* – this applies limitations to the number of foreign workers employed in order to increase dependency on Saudi workers over time.
- the *Centennial Fund* – set up in 2004, this provides assistance to Saudi citizens in setting up small business enterprises and helps entrepreneurs develop project concepts.
- *Employment of Women* – the establishment of accounting, banking and computer training centres to create more job opportunities for women.

New agencies to promote economic reform

The new agencies being established by the Saudi government to assist with the process of economic reform include the following:

- the Supreme Economic Council (SEC);
- the Saudi Arabian General Investment Authority (SAGIA);
- the Saudi Communication Commission (SCC);
- the Supreme Council for Petroleum and Minerals (SCPM);
- the Supreme Commission for Tourism (SCT);
- the Food and Drugs Authority (FDA).

Supreme Economic Council (SEC)

A ministerial committee was formed in 1997 to coordinate and oversee Saudi Arabia's privatization programme, review the sectors proposed to be transferred to the private sector and define the overall objectives and principles of privatization.

The establishment of the Supreme Economic Council (SEC) followed in 1999. The SEC was later empowered to supervise the privatization programme and monitor its implementation in coordination with competent government agencies. It was also empowered to finalize the activities to be privatized, as well as to draft a strategy and timeframe to manage the process.

In 2002, the SEC endorsed a privatization strategy in Saudi Arabia and spelled out the objectives, policies, methods, controls and the main issues that needed to be resolved during the implementation phase. The strategy also defined the parameters for prioritization as well as procedures to be adopted to carry out the privatization programme. Later, in 2002, the Saudi Council of Ministers issued Resolution 219 listing the sectors and services to be privatized. The resolution also indicated the type, extent and timeframe of private sector involvement in these sectors.

Saudi Arabian General Investment Authority (SAGIA)

In April 2000, the Saudi Arabian General Investment Authority (SAGIA) was set up to further promote foreign investment and serve the business community as a 'one stop shop' for licences, permits, and other business paperwork. By the end of 2004, SAGIA had licensed more than 2,000 projects worth around US$15 billion.

Saudi Communication Commission (SCC)

The Saudi Communication Commission (SCC) was established in December 2001 to open up the market and enable foreign companies to invest in telecommunications. In August 2004, the Council of Ministers licensed UAE's Etisalat to establish and operate the second mobile phone network to include the GSM service.

Supreme Council for Petroleum and Minerals (SCPM)

Saudi Arabia established the Supreme Council for Petroleum and Minerals (SCPM) in January 2000 as a body responsible for policymaking on the exploitation of petroleum, gas and other hydrocarbon materials. The SCPM passed the Gas Initiative to develop natural gas fields, transmission pipelines and petrochemical projects, in cooperation with international and national companies.

Supreme Commission for Tourism (SCT)

The Supreme Commission for Tourism (SCT) was established in April 2000 to help the tourism sector grow and encourage investment from the private sector. In March 2004, the government approved a strategy for the development of the Kingdom's tourism industry, which is to be implemented by the SCT.

Food and Drugs Authority (FDA)

In March 2003, the Food and Drugs Authority (FDA) was established to provide consumer protection and ensure the safe utilization of all foodstuffs, pharmaceuticals, medical devices and electronic products.

Need for further reforms

Building on the current reforms, the future reform process will require a further strengthening of the political will to restructure the Saudi economy in support of the privatization process.

The process of further reform needs to encompass:

- the development of a regional economic strategy with key targets;
- an acceleration of privatization, including the development of public-private partnerships;
- further development of the industrial sector;

- further development of the country's capital markets and further measures to improve the investment climate;
- applying the principle of good corporate governance to Saudi organizations;
- implementing mergers and acquisitions in the face of international competition;
- improving the legal framework and ensuring the enforcement of new business regulations;
- further developing the country's human capital by:
  - streamlining the educational system according to the requirements of the business community, and
  - encouraging more extensive female participation in the workforce.

Part Three

Legal Framework and Business Regulation

3.1

The Legal Framework in Saudi Arabia

Jean-Benoît Zegers (with the assistance of Dr Yahya Al-Samaan), The Law Firm of Salah Al-Hejailan

Sources and nature of the laws of Saudi Arabia

Introduction

Islam is both a religion and a way of life in Saudi Arabia. More than anywhere else in the Muslim world, Islamic law underpins every aspect of life, from the administration of justice to the formulation of government policy, from social convention to commercial relations. The tenets of Islamic law are enshrined in the Holy Book (*Qur'an*)[1], as well as in the deeds and sayings (*Sunna*)[2] of the prophet Mohammed. The *Qur'an* and the *Sunna* are considered to be primary sources of Islamic law, while the opinions of Islamic scholars reached by consensus (*idjima*)[3] and reasoning by analogy (*qiyas*)[4] are its secondary sources.

---

[1] Muslims believe that the *Qur'an* is the sacred will of God as expressed to the Prophet Mohammed. The precepts and tenets of the *Qur'an* are to be followed strictly in all the affairs of Muslims, whether of a legal or moral nature.

[2] *Sunna* (literally, 'tradition'), the body of deeds and utterances (*hadith*) of the Prophet Mohammed, is a code of universal rules of conduct and acceptable views. Compilation of the *hadith* was completed approximately in the 10th century, some three centuries after the emergence of Islam. The number of *hadith* was enormous.

[3] Islam has adapted to the changing conditions of life through the religious sanctification of new traditions and the demonstration of their correspondence with the *Sunna*. Thus, when faced with issues not addressed in the *Qur'an* or *Sunna*, early Islamic jurists arrived at *idjima* (a consensus of individual opinions). When *idjima* was reached among the theologians (*ulema*), it became a rule of law.

[4] Where none of the above sources related to the matter in question, decisions were reached by analogy (*qiyas*) to matters dealt with in the *Qur'an* or *Sunna*. The process of

Together, they are known as the *Shari'a*.[5] In addition, a number of Royal Decrees and implementing regulations have come into force over the past few decades in order to address matters not specifically covered by the *Shari'a*. This growing body of legislation, together with the *Shari'a*, form the nation's legal system.

The four orthodox schools of Sunni jurisprudence

The *Shari'a* was largely developed between the 7th and 10th centuries AD by the early Islamic theologians (*ulema*) who established the four orthodox schools of *Sunni* jurisprudence (as opposed to the Shiite branch whose adherents reject the first three successors to the Prophet Mohammed in favour of his son-in-law Ali), known as the *Hanbali*, *Hanafi*, *Shafi'i* and *Maliki* schools of jurisprudence. Broadly speaking, these four schools are distinguished by the degree of flexibility in their interpretation of the primary sources of Islamic law. The *Hanafi* School is considered to be the most flexible and tolerant school in this regard, while the *Hanbali* School, which is predominant in Saudi Arabia, is the most rigid and rejects any deviation from the *Sunna* outright.[6]

The fundamental law

Traditionally, Saudi Arabia has been seen as an absolute monarchy, where the ruling monarch exercises supreme executive, legislative and judicial power. However, in 1992 King Fahd bin Abdulaziz Al-Saud, issued a 'fundamental law' in a bid to organize power in the Kingdom. The fundamental law provides, amongst other things that:

- the Constitution of the Kingdom is the *Qur'an* and the *Sunna* of the Prophet;[7]
- power in Saudi Arabia is based on justice, consultation (*al shura*) and equality in accordance with the *Shari'a*;[8]
- power is given to the sons of King Abdulaziz bin Abdulrahman Al-Saud and to the sons of his sons, subject to the following rules: (i) allegiance shall be pledged to the best amongst the sons or sons of sons of King Abdulaziz, (ii) the King shall choose the Crown

legal reasoning by analogy has been encouraged in recent times, so as to adapt the *Shari'a* to the requirements of modern life.

[5] Literally 'the laid down path to salvation'.

[6] Alexei Vassiliev, *The History of Saudi Arabia*, page 67.

[7] Article 1 of the Fundamental Law.

[8] Article 5 of the Fundamental Law.

Prince: however, he may also revoke him and (iii) citizens shall pledge allegiance to the King;[9]

- the judiciary is independent[10] and when exercising their functions, judges are only subject to the authority of the *Shari'a* without restricting it to the *Hanbali* doctrine.[11]

Recent developments in Saudi law

While the legislative provisions of the *Qur'an* are deemed to satisfy all aspects of Muslim society, in reality these are complimented by Royal Decrees and implementing regulations to address situations where the *Qur'an* is silent. Thus, when a regulatory need is perceived, the Council of Ministers undertakes the approval of draft principles leading to the issuance of a Royal Decree or a resolution, which normally becomes effective after promulgation in the *Official Gazette* (*Umm al-Qura*). Another means of regulation is through the issuance of ministerial circulars or instructions. Technically, resolutions, circulars and instructions are not laws and are considered valid only to the extent that they do not contradict the *Shari'a*. However, this recent legislative regime provides a reasonably adequate legal framework for many modern commercial transactions through the growing body of regulations that apply to such transactions. This is the theory underlying the interaction of the *Shari'a* and the regulatory regime.

General contractual principles under the Shari'a

The *Shari'a* firmly upholds the binding force of contract, the freedom to negotiate terms (provided such terms do not violate divine law)[12] and the independent settlement of disputes. The principle that a contract embodies the 'sacred law' of the relationship between the parties is central to the *Shari'a* and is most typically expressed in the maxim 'the contract is the law of the parties'.[13] No distinction is drawn between treaties, state contracts and private contracts. Indeed, early Islamic scholars considered that such contracts had equal validity and should be performed in good faith.

---

[9] *Ibid.*

[10] Article 44 of the Fundamental Law.

[11] Article 46 of the Fundamental Law.

[12] The *Shari'a* forbids usury and gambling, as well as trading in certain goods, including alcohol and pork items.

[13] Dr Yahya Al-Samaan, *The Legal Protection of Foreign Investment in the Kingdom of Saudi Arabia*, Dar Al Andalus for Pub. & Dist., 1st Edition, 2000, page 113.

Moreover, the respect and inviolability of private property is a fundamental principle under the *Shari'a*.[14] In accordance with Chapter IV, Verse 29 of the Holy *Qur'an*, it is stated: 'O ye who believe! Eat not up your property amongst yourselves in vanities, but let there be amongst ye traffic and trade by mutual goodwill'. Classical Islamic jurists have interpreted this verse to mean, 'One is not allowed to take another's property without legal cause'.[15]

The inviolability of private property has also been asserted in the teachings of the jurists of the four schools of Islamic jurisprudence. According to Ibn Taimyya, a pre-eminent jurist of the *Hanbali* School, 'the first duty of the State is scrupulously to respect private property'.[16]

The *Shari'a* guarantees the protection of rights and property of Muslims and non-Muslims living within an Islamic state. However, it should be noted that there exist two exceptions to the principle of inviolability of private property under the *Shari'a*, namely, expropriation by the state and the enforcement of a final judgement against a debtor's property.

With respect to the former, the *Shari'a* only admits expropriation if the public interest in doing so outweighs the prejudice to the owner of foregoing his rights of private ownership, subject always to the payment of just compensation, and Saudi Arabia has shown strict adherence to such doctrine. It should also be noted that compensation for the loss of future profits is prohibited under the *Shari'a* on the grounds that such claim would be tantamount to the payment of unearned profits, hence speculative in nature. In relation to the latter exception, foreign investors are strongly advised to insist on the inclusion in the contract of a clause specifying payment of liquidated damages or delay penalties as a means of compensation in the event of delay.

Thus, Saudi courts (namely the *Shari'a* courts and the Board of Grievances) have declined to award compensation to parties claiming loss of future profits or to approve the payment of interest on overdue amounts (regardless of the reason for the delay), on the grounds that both are unenforceable under the *Shari'a*.[17]

In principle, therefore, the *Shari'a* respects the rights of contracting parties to fix the terms of their relationship. Generally, this means when doing business in Saudi Arabia the foreign businessman may make such contractual arrangements as he can succeed in negotiating, provided that he observes the principles of good faith and fair dealing enshrined in the *Shari'a* and refrains from violating the provisions of any applicable regulations and decrees.[18] From a practical

[14] *Ibid*, page 57.
[15] *Ibid*.
[16] *Ibid*.
[17] Dr. Yahya Al-Samaan, *The Legal Protection of Foreign Investment in the Kingdom of Saudi Arabia*, page 57.
[18] Dennis Campbell, *Legal Aspects of Doing Business in Saudi Arabia*, Volume V,

standpoint, specificity and thoroughness are particularly essential to a workable contract under Saudi law, although it would probably be fair to say that highly detailed contracts have, historically, often been viewed an unnecessary by Saudi businessmen.

Saudi law does not generally recognize the prescription of rights by the passage of time. This is because the *Shari'a* (according to some interpretations) considers it unjust to deprive a claimant of his rights. Various statutes, such as the Labour and Workmen's Regulations, the Negotiable Instruments Regulations and the Rules of Civil Procedure before the Board of Grievances (1989), however, contain limitation periods for the bringing of actions.

Litigation before the Saudi courts

Introduction

As a general rule, disputes arising out of an investment agreement entered into by a foreign investor and a private Saudi entity would be subject to adjudication by a competent Saudi judicial authority, unless otherwise provided in such agreement or in the articles of association of the Saudi joint venture or the limited liability company. However, investment agreements between the Saudi government (or any of its agencies) and foreign investors are subject to Saudi law and any dispute arising thereunder would be heard by the Saudi courts. Accordingly, a foreign investor seeking to bid for a government tender should be aware that the ensuing contract would be governed by Saudi law and subject to adjudication by a competent Saudi judicial authority, in the event of a dispute between the parties.

Shari'a courts

Shari'a courts have general jurisdiction over all matters and will not decline jurisdiction unless other judicial bodies have been granted specific jurisdiction. Article 26 of the Judiciary Law of 1975 stipulates:

> 'The courts shall have jurisdiction to decide all disputes and offences except those which are excluded pursuant to a law... Specialized courts may be established by Royal Decree made upon a motion of the Supreme Judiciary Council.'[19]

Kluwer Law 1986, page 160.

[19] Examples of such specialized courts include the Commercial Papers Committee and the Committee for the Resolution of Banking Disputes.

Shari'a courts, which are divided into Summary Courts, General Courts and the Court of Appeal, are administered by the Ministry of Justice in accordance with civil and criminal procedural rules, as amended and promulgated in April and October 2001, respectively. There is a presumption that the *Shari'a* courts have jurisdiction over all matters and it is unlikely that they will decline jurisdiction to hear a dispute unless another judicial authority has been granted exclusive jurisdiction. In practice, we have noted conflicting approaches by certain *Shari'a* judges.

Labour disputes, commercial disputes and all disputes involving the Saudi government or any of its agencies are excluded from the *Shari'a* courts.

The Board of Grievances (diwan al-mazalim)

Commercial disputes in Saudi Arabia have always had, at least potentially, a separate forum from that appropriate to other disputes. The Commercial Court Regulations (Royal Decree M/32) of 1931 (much of which remains in effect) make provision for procedural rules, the effect of judgements and enforcement in matters concerning the Commercial Court. The Commercial Court was superseded in 1967 by the Committee for the Settlement of Commercial Disputes, which was in turn superseded in 1988 by the expansion of the jurisdiction of the Board of Grievances.

The Board of Grievances deals with a broad range of matters of a commercial nature (other than those involving banks, negotiable instruments or employee rights) involving government or any of its agencies, foreign investors and private Saudi entities. The Board of Grievances has two functions: a judicial function in ensuring equitable treatment of those persons and companies that deal with government, and a prosecutorial function relative to the acts of government officials and civil servants. Its jurisdiction has been expanded to include:

- compensation claims filed by interested parties against the Saudi government or its agencies by reason of an administrative agency's actions;
- disciplinary cases brought by the supervision and investigation authority;
- criminal cases arising under the anti-corruption and anti-forgery laws;
- commercial disputes that were adjudicated by the commercial disputes committees prior to their abolishment in 1987; and

- enforcement and execution of foreign judgements and arbitral awards, as discussed in more detail below.[20]

The 'Rules of Civil Procedure before the Board of Grievances', promulgated in July 1989, codified the Board of Grievances' procedures and extended the limitation period for claims against governmental agencies from three to five years. There is no limitation period in relation to claims not involving governmental agencies.

The Board of Grievances consists of administrative circuits, a commercial division and a penal division, all of whose judges must be *Shari'a*-trained. There are scrutinizing committees that act as appeal courts; each committee is made up of three senior judges. Unlike the *Shari'a* courts, legal consultants, as well as other experts, professionals and academics assist the judges. All decisions are made by a majority vote and then reviewed by a scrutinizing committee, which can affirm, reverse or remand the decision. Any appeals against the final decision must be made to the King.

One characteristic of the Board of Grievances is that, because its judges can consult both legal and technical experts, they are able to consider cases that are far more complex than those in *Shari'a* courts. In the past, the Board of Grievances published its decisions from time to time. However, this practice has now been discontinued.

Although the Board of Grievances is generally considered to be a fair and independent forum for hearing disputes and has the advantage of being better equipped to hear more complex cases, one of the major disadvantages is the length of time it takes to reach a final judgement. The length of time between hearings is very long and frequent adjournments and the large volume of cases brought to the Board of Grievances mean that it can take a number of years before a final decision is reached in relation to a dispute.

Quasi-judicial committees

Besides the *Shari'a* courts and the Board of Grievances, there are several quasi-judicial committees with limited jurisdiction. These committees follow judicial procedures similar to those of other courts in Saudi Arabia and render binding awards.[21] The most important of these committees that foreign investors are likely to encounter, include the Commercial Papers Committee and the Committee for the Resolution of Banking Disputes.

---

[20] Article 8(g) of the Rules of Civil Procedure before the Board of Grievances of 1983.

[21] Dr. Yahya Al-Samaan, *Dispute Resolution in Saudi Arabia*, Kluwer Law International 2002, Yearbook of Islamic and Middle Eastern Law, Volume 7, page 75.

Commercial Papers Committee
The intention of this committee is to provide an expeditious forum where matters relating to debts evidenced by 'commercial papers' (for example, cheques and promissory notes) may be heard. In practice, the caseload faced by the Commercial Papers Committee has been heavy and the hearings can be subject to delays. Delaying tactics used by defendants, such as requesting further information, changing lawyers and failing to appear before the panel, slow the process further. In addition, there are limitation periods that must be observed, but should these have expired, it is always possible to resort to the *Shari'a* courts or the Board of Grievances, although the negotiable instrument will be available only as evidence of a debt, rather than as a negotiable instrument in its own right.

Committee for the Settlement of Banking Disputes
Disputes relating to banking matters, other than matters relating to negotiable instruments, are heard by a special committee under the auspices of the Saudi Arabian Monetary Agency (SAMA), which is the central bank of Saudi Arabia. The SAMA Committee (as it is known) performs a valuable role by providing a more specialized forum that is acquainted with the business of banking, and may generally be relied upon to resolve disputes by reference to the contractual arrangements involved. More particularly, it does not appear to apply *Shari'a* principles as strictly as, for example, the Board of Grievances. For example, in relation to defaulted loan agreements, the SAMA Committee has been known to award lenders compensation calculated by reference to some of the interest (interest is unenforceable as a matter of *Shari'a* law) that would have been payable under the applicable loan agreement.

Decisions of the SAMA Committee cannot be appealed and are enforceable (there used to be some doubt as to whether the SAMA Committee's decisions were directly enforceable).

Points to bear in mind when commencing litigation in Saudi Arabia

Foreign investors should bear the following in mind before commencing legal proceedings against a Saudi entity or when defending a claim before the Saudi courts.

No binding precedent
The doctrine of binding precedent is only applicable in a very limited range of cases. However, previous favourable court judgements may be of persuasive value. Decisions in any judicial forum must conform, at least in theory, to the *Shari'a*. Moreover, case law (that is, judicial

judgements) is not systematically reported. Therefore, an understanding of Saudi law and practice, particularly as regards interpretation of the implementing regulations and also enforcement practices, is based, for the most part, on anecdotes current in the legal profession and experience in the field. Although the *Hanbali* School of Islamic law is applied in Saudi Arabia, one should not expect direct guidance on the issues under consideration from that source or from classical Islamic law generally, except in the most abstract sense.

No retroactivity

It should be noted that the principle of non-retroactivity is an established principle of law in Saudi Arabia. In other words, laws and regulations come into effect as of the date of their promulgation in the *Official Gazette*, without retroactive effect.

No juries

Jury trials in either civil or criminal matters are unknown. There is no strict rule against hearsay evidence and cross-examination is not normally permitted. Proceedings are more in the style of a committee than that of conventional courts in common or civil jurisdictions. Saudi courts observe few formalities in case presentation; the judge considers the evidence, renders a decision, dictates it to the court clerk, and the parties collect a copy.

Burden of proof

In civil matters, the burden of proof generally rests with the claimant. A claimant who lacks proof may require the defendant to take an oath. The procedures are basically inquisitorial and judges may make their own investigation of the facts where they consider that these have not been sufficiently well presented and may raise issues not raised by the parties.

Legal representation

Only a qualified person holding a licence issued by the Ministry of Justice to practice law in Saudi Arabia may represent any person or company before all judicial authorities (ie *Shari'a* courts and the Board of Grievances) and quasi-judicial committees. Non-Saudi lawyers are not permitted to represent a party alone, but may join a licensed Saudi lawyer as an adviser. In theory, any person involved in legal proceedings may represent himself. Proceedings before Saudi courts are in Arabic and documents submitted in support of a claim or case must also be in the Arabic language. If a person does not speak Arabic, a translator will be required.

If one has to sue on a contract in a Saudi court, only Arabic documents or Arabic translations of non-Arabic language documents are admissible. Where contracts are complicated, obtaining accurate translations can be very difficult, not only because translators can be of variable quality, but also because it is sometimes difficult or impossible to find the proper Arabic equivalent of certain foreign legal concepts. For example, if one were to refer to an 'option' in an English document, all of the legal incidents of an option should be carefully spelled out, because the nearest translation of option in Arabic has entirely different legal effects.

3.2

Foreign Investment Protection in Saudi Arabia

Jean-Benoît Zegers, The Law Firm of Salah Al-Hejailan

Background

In late 1943, American geologist Everette Lee DeGoyler, who had spent a considerable amount of time prospecting for oil in Saudi Arabia, recognized that he was investigating something for which no precedent existed in history. Indeed, the following year one of the members of DeGoyler's exploratory mission was to inform the US State Department, 'The oil in this region is the single greatest prize in all history'.[1]

Saudi Arabia has long since become one of the world's primary oil exporting nations and is currently the biggest producer of petrochemical by-products. Throughout the mid-1970s and early 1980s, the Saudi economy benefited enormously from the influx of petrol dollars, which reached a high point in 1981 with earnings from oil alone estimated at US$119 billion,[2] attracting vast foreign interest as the Saudi government embarked on ambitious infrastructure projects. However, with the discovery of oil reserves elsewhere and increased production by other oil-producing countries, combined most recently with the US-led war on Iraq and uncertainty about the future stability of the region, the price of crude oil has fluctuated unpredictably and, until the oil price rises of 2004/2005, Saudi Arabia had seen its average earnings

---

1 Daniel Yergin, *The Prize – the Epic Quest for Oil, Money and Power*, Simon & Schuster Ltd, 1991, page 393.

2 *Ibid*, page 747.

from the sale of crude oil plummet over the past two decades. Until the substantial oil price rises of 2004/2005, government spending had been curtailed and lucrative government contracts had appeared to be a thing of the past.

As a result of diminished government expenditure, recently the focus of investment opportunity has shifted to the private sector to meet the needs of Saudi Arabia's steadily rising population and increased consumer demand.[3] In turn, these factors have led to a surge in the demand for electricity, water, communications, transport, healthcare, education, training and consumer goods.

The response of the Saudi government has been to drive through reforms aimed at liberalizing those sectors of the Saudi economy previously controlled by the state and reserved for Saudi nationals. Pursuant to the new Foreign Capital Investment Law, which came into effect in April 2000, foreign companies can now establish wholly foreign-owned subsidiaries or branch offices in Saudi Arabia, thus benefiting from all the privileges hitherto enjoyed only by Saudi companies, including the right to transfer funds and profits, to own and dispose of real estate and to sponsor foreign employees. In February 2003, the Supreme Economic Council approved the revision of the so-called 'negative list', thus signalling the Saudi government's intention to open up to foreign investors certain sectors of the Saudi economy previously excluded from foreign investment, including parts of the telecommunications sector, insurance, educational services, publishing and distribution services (including wholesale and retail trade).[4]

Perhaps one of the most ambitious projects to date involves the expansion of the nation's gas sector to ensure that there is sufficient gas for the next generation of power, desalination and petrochemical projects. The Saudi 'Gas Initiative', as it has been dubbed, is estimated to be worth at least US$25 billion and is the Middle East's biggest project of the decade.[5] Other major initiatives and infrastructure projects include the consolidation, in April 2000, of the country's 10 regional power companies into a single joint stock company, now known as the Saudi Electricity Company (SEC); followed by the recent creation of the Saudi Electricity Regulatory Authority, which will act

---

[3] In fact, the Saudi population is growing at a rate of 2–3 per cent per annum, with 60 per cent of Saudis under the age of 20. Unemployment among Saudi males is conservatively estimated at 14 per cent and every year 100,000 graduates flood the job market, prompting the Saudi government to implement tougher rules requiring local and foreign employers rapidly to reach target figures of at least 75 per cent Saudi employees in all sectors.

[4] Reported in an article titled 'Kingdom opens up new sectors to foreign investors', *Saudi Gazette*, 3 February 2003.

[5] Angus McDowall, 'Seizing the initiative', *MEED*, 15 February 2002, page 4.

as the regulatory body in connection with the restructuring and reorganization of the Saudi electricity sector; the joint initiative by the Saudi Water Conversion Corporation and SEC to commission up to four independent water and power projects[6] (including the construction of four desalination plants) throughout the country by January 2008; and the proposed expansion by the Saudi Railway Organization[7] of its existing railway network.[8]

Given the significant capital expenditure involved in such projects, coupled with concerns over the future stability of the Saudi market, not to mention the region as a whole, one of the primary concerns of foreign companies seeking to invest in these expanding sectors of the Saudi economy will be the degree of protection such investors are likely to be afforded under Saudi law. Typically, foreign investors will want to know how a Saudi court would treat them in the event of a contractual dispute with a Saudi entity, the effectiveness of contractual and legal remedies under Saudi law, including recourse to litigation before the Saudi courts or arbitration, as well as alternative means of recourse through foreign institutional arbitration or under various international treaties to which Saudi Arabia is a signatory (and, where appropriate, the recognition and enforcement of foreign arbitral awards).

Introduction

In addressing such issues, this chapter seeks to outline the degree of protection available to and the risks facing foreign investors seeking to rely on existing means of legal recourse in Saudi Arabia. Accordingly, in Chapter 3.1 we presented an overview of the sources and nature of Saudi law, with particular emphasis on general contractual

---

[6] It is intended that the Saudi Government will have a 32 per cent stake in each project, with SWCC and SEC holding 60 per cent and 8 per cent, respectively.

[7] On 27 February 2003, *MEED* reported that the French railways operator, Société Nationale des Chemins de Fer (SNCF), was awarded the mandate to provide technical advisory services to the Saudi Railway Organization (SRO), in conjunction with a financial team comprising National Commercial Bank and UBS Warburg. At the time of writing, SRO has yet to appoint a legal adviser, which will be mandated, *inter alia*, to make recommendations on changes to the legal and regulatory environment to allow private sector involvement in the railways sector. We understand that the legal adviser will also advise SRO on its merger with the future concessionaire of the so-called east-west link. Following such merger, SRO will effectively cease to exist and become fully integrated in the private concession holding company.

[8] This project includes the construction of over 1,600km of new railway lines throughout the country, including from Riyadh to Jeddah (about 950km) and from Dammam to Jubail (about 115km), as well as a rail link connecting Jeddah to Makkah and beyond to Madinah and Yanbu (about 570km).

principles under Islamic law (*Shari'a*). Against this background, we focused on the Saudi judicial system itself, with particular emphasis on some of the advantages and pitfalls commonly encountered by practitioners in Saudi Arabia.

In this chapter we look at current Saudi legislation applicable to foreign investors focusing, in particular, on the advantages and shortcomings of the Foreign Capital Investment Regulations, which came into effect in April 2000. This includes a discussion of the role of arbitration as an alternative means of recourse available to foreign investors in Saudi Arabia, including domestic and foreign institutional arbitration, as well as the implications of arbitration under various bilateral and multilateral treaties to which Saudi Arabia is a signatory.

Investor protection under Saudi law

The Foreign Capital Investment Law

As previously mentioned, in recent years expanded commercial contacts between Saudi Arabia and foreign investors have led to the promulgation of a number of laws and implementing regulations, many of which contain provisions that reflect generally accepted commercial and civil law influences.

One such law is the Foreign Capital Investment Law, which came into force in April 2000, and which provides a regulatory framework for foreign investors seeking to invest foreign capital in one or more licensed activities in Saudi Arabia. In this section we propose to assess some of the advantages and shortcomings of the new law as far as foreign investors are concerned.

What is a 'foreign investor' and 'foreign capital'?

Pursuant to Article 1 of the Foreign Capital Investment Law, the term 'foreign investor' means:

> 'A natural person of non-Saudi nationality or otherwise the body corporate, in which all partners are not exclusively Saudi nationals.'

The term 'foreign capital' as defined in the Foreign Capital Investment Law includes:

> 'The following property and rights, as may be owned by the foreign investor namely:
>
> (i) banknotes, securities and negotiable instruments;

(ii) profits realized from foreign investment if used to increase capital, expand existing projects or establish new projects;

(iii) machinery, equipment, instruments, spare parts, means of transportation and production requirements related to such investment;

(iv) intangible rights such as licences, intellectual property rights, technical know-how, administrative skills and production techniques.'

What is a 'licensed activity'?

Article 3 of the Foreign Capital Investment Law stipulates:

> 'The Supreme Economic Council Licensed shall issue a list specifying the types of activities from which foreign investors are excluded.'

Thus, in accordance with Resolution No.11/21 dated 17/11/1421H (equivalent to 11/02/2001 AD), the Supreme Economic Council published a list of 22 investment activities from which foreigners are excluded. Such list includes exploration, drilling and production of oil and gas, road, air and pipeline transport, as well as insurance and telecommunications services.[9]

However, in keeping with the Saudi government's recent policy of opening up certain sectors of the economy to foreign investment to meet increasing local demand for improved services in such sectors, the Supreme Economic Council has recently approved a revised list of investment activities by removing, fully or partially, from the previous so-called 'negative list' certain parts of the telecommunications, insurance, educational and publishing sectors hitherto reserved for Saudi companies, in order to encourage foreign investment in these sectors.[10]

Guarantees afforded to foreign investors under the Foreign Capital Investment Law

Of primary concern to any investor seeking to do business in a foreign country is protection of its investment. Other than foreseeable commercial risks facing a foreign venture, foreign investors also fear that a host country may arbitrarily exercise its sovereign powers, for

---

[9] A complete list of excluded activities is set out in Appendix A at the end of this chapter.

[10] 'Kingdom opens up new sectors to foreign investors' reported in the *Saudi Gazette* on 3 February 2003.

example, through expropriation or nationalization of the venture or restrictions on the transfer or repatriation of investment capital or profits.

Saudi Arabia has sought to allay such fears by providing various guarantees to foreign investors in the form of equitable treatment under Saudi law. Article 6 of the Foreign Capital Investment Law stipulates:

> 'A project that has been licensed pursuant to these regulations shall enjoy all rights, incentives and guarantees available in respect of a national project in accordance with Saudi law.'

Such guarantees include the right to: (i) transfer the profits or proceeds of the sale of the foreign-owned entity or dispose of the same by any other lawful means (Article 7), (ii) own real estate as may be necessary for the conduct of the licensed activity or accommodation of its employees (Article 8), (iii) sponsor non-Saudi employees (Article 9), and most significantly (iv) protection of the foreign investment from arbitrary expropriation, other than pursuant to a judicial decision or in the public interest and subject to fair compensation (Article 10).

Dispute resolution under the Foreign Capital Investment Law

In addition to protection of their investments, foreign investors seeking to do business in Saudi Arabia, want to be assured of the existence of adequate and impartial dispute resolution mechanisms to which they can have recourse in the event that their rights have been infringed by the Saudi government, its agencies or a private Saudi partner.

The Foreign Capital Investment Law contemplates two possible scenarios, namely: (i) a dispute between the foreign investor and the Saudi government (or any of its agencies), or (ii) a dispute between the foreign investor and its Saudi partner. Article 13 of the Foreign Capital Investment Law stipulates:

> 'Without prejudice to the agreements to which Saudi Arabia is a party:
>
> (1) Disputes that may arise between the government and a foreign investor in relation to foreign investments that are licensed pursuant to this law shall, as far as possible, be settled amicably, failing which the dispute shall be resolved in accordance with the relevant laws.
>
> (2) Disputes that may arise between a foreign investor and its Saudi partners in relation to foreign investments that are licensed pursuant to this law shall, as far as

> possible, be settled amicably, failing which the dispute shall be resolved in accordance with the relevant laws.'

As previously mentioned, the Board of Grievances is the competent judicial authority in cases involving investment disputes between the Saudi government (or any of its agencies) and foreign investors, whereas disputes between foreign investors and a private Saudi entities may be subject to a competent Saudi judicial authority, unless otherwise provided by the parties in the investment contract.

Notwithstanding the well-established authority of the Board of Grievances to intervene in disputes involving the Saudi government, arguably Article 13 may not necessarily limit such disputes to the jurisdiction of Saudi courts alone. Under Article 13, the Arabic term '*ittifaqiyat*' (إتفاقيات) is rendered in English as 'agreements'. However, the Arabic meaning is very broad and includes concepts such as treaties or conventions, as well as contracts or agreements. Moreover, as previously stated, under general *Shari'a* principles no distinction is drawn between treaties, state contracts and private contracts. In addition, in sub-paragraphs (1) and (2) the Arabic term '*nízam*' (نظام), which means 'law', is a specific reference to the Foreign Capital Investment Law, whereas the term '*anzima*' (أنظمة), which is the plural of '*nízam*', appears to be a more general reference to the laws and regulations of Saudi Arabia.

Moreover, due to the fact that the Saudi government could, in theory, unilaterally amend or abrogate its domestic legislation, foreign investors may consider the guarantees and assurances embodied in the Foreign Capital Investment Law to be of limited value.[11] Accordingly, foreign investors may seek redress directly against the Saudi government or Saudi entities under various bilateral and multilateral treaties to which Saudi Arabia is a party, as discussed below.

Alternative means of recourse available to foreign investors

Introduction

Notwithstanding the relative protection afforded to foreign investors under the *Shari'a* and the guarantees extended to foreign investments under the Foreign Capital Investment Law, foreign investors may

---

[11] Dr Yahya Al-Samaan, *The Legal Protection of Foreign Investment in the Kingdom of Saudi Arabia*, Dar Al Andalus for Pub. & Dist., 1st Edition, 2000, page 51.

nevertheless feel uncomfortable about commencing litigation before the Saudi courts for several reasons.

Typically, litigation in Saudi Arabia (as elsewhere) can be protracted and expensive and the outcome uncertain, pending a final judgement. In addition, many foreign investors may perceive that Saudi courts are not sufficiently experienced in, or knowledgeable about, potentially complex legal issues that may arise out of specialized contracts such as design-build, turnkey or EPC contracts, or sophisticated infrastructure finance schemes involving multi-jurisdictional syndicated loans, bond issues etc. Moreover, as previously mentioned, Saudi courts have declined to award compensation to parties claiming loss of future profits or to approve the payment of interest on overdue amounts (regardless of the reason for the delay), on the grounds that both are unenforceable under the *Shari'a*. Furthermore, foreign investors are understandably keen to avoid any adverse publicity generated by media interest in their dispute, as such publicity could have a detrimental effect on the parent company or its share value if such company is listed on a stock exchange. Lastly, yet perhaps most importantly, foreign investors generally have limited confidence in the impartiality of the national courts of certain host countries.

For these and other reasons, many foreign investors readily seek alternative means of dispute resolution. To that end, one of the most common approaches adopted by foreign investors is to include an arbitration clause in the investment agreement. In this section, we propose to examine the role of arbitration as an alternative means of recourse available to foreign investors in Saudi Arabia, including domestic and foreign arbitration, as well as enforcement procedures under Saudi law, including under various bilateral and multilateral treaties to which Saudi Arabia is a signatory.

Arbitration under the Shari'a

Generally speaking, Saudi law regards both mediation and arbitration as a valid means of resolving commercial disputes within the private sector and, subject to certain limitations, disputes between the Saudi government and private parties.[12]

According to the *Hanbali* School, which is predominant in Saudi Arabia, an arbitral award is deemed to have the same binding effect as a court judgement. Nevertheless, there is no legal requirement for the courts to renounce their jurisdiction to hear an arbitrated case on the merits. Concomitantly, arbitral awards will not be automatically

---

12 A. Lerrick and Q.J. Mian, *Saudi Business and Labor Law: Its Interpretation and Application*, 1982, page 176.

enforced. *Hanbali* jurists insist that an arbitrator be qualified in the *Shari'a*.[13] In addition, parties to arbitration may revoke an arbitrator at any time before the arbitrator renders the award, unless the arbitration agreement contains a provision expressly prohibiting revocation or if a judge has appointed the arbitrator. In the latter case, the arbitrator is deemed to be the representative of the judge, and his mandate cannot be revoked during the arbitral proceedings.

Domestic arbitration and enforcement of awards under the Arbitration Law of 1983

Prior to the enactment of the new Saudi Arbitration Law in 1983, the Saudi arbitration system was based on various texts, including certain provisions of the Commercial Courts Regulations, the Chamber of Commerce Regulations, the Labour and Workmen's Regulations and the Commercial Agencies Regulations, which authorized recourse to arbitration, subject to certain restrictions. The new Arbitration Law of 1983[14] and the implementing regulations of 1985[15] (the Arbitration Law) superseded the piecemeal provisions contained in such regulations and constituted an attempt to harmonize such texts and provisions in a single body of legislation.

The Arbitration Law distinguishes between arbitrations arising out of (i) an agreement by the parties to arbitrate a specific existing dispute and (ii) an arbitration clause that may be invoked by the parties in the event of a dispute resulting from the performance of a specific contract.

Article 1 stipulates:

> 'The parties may agree to arbitrate a specific existing dispute; a prior agreement to arbitrate may also be made in respect of any dispute resulting from the performance of a specific contract.'

Article 1 is to be read in conjunction with Articles 5 and 7.

In the former case, the parties to a dispute are obliged to file their agreement to arbitrate with the authority originally competent to hear

---

[13] Dr. Yahya Al-Samaan, *The Legal Protection of Foreign Investment in the Kingdom of Saudi Arabia*, Dar Al Andalus for Pub. & Dist., 1st Edition, 2000, page 250.

[14] The Saudi Arbitration Law came into effect by Royal Decree M/46 on 12.07.1403 (equivalent to 25 April 1983).

[15] The implementing regulations, which came into effect by Decree No. 7120211M dated 08.09.1405 (27 May 1985), were subsequently promulgated in the *Official Gazette* on 10/10/1405 (28 June 1985).

such dispute.[16] In addition, such agreement has to be signed by the parties or their authorized attorneys, as well as by the arbitrators, and it must state the details of the dispute, the names of the arbitrators and their agreement to hear such dispute.[17] In the latter case, if the parties have agreed to arbitrate before the occurrence of the dispute, or if the agreement to arbitrate relating to a specific existing dispute has been approved by the relevant authority, then the subject matter of the dispute shall be heard only in accordance with the provision of the Arbitration Law.[18]

These new provisions appear to address the vexed question of the validity of arbitration clauses in contracts before a dispute arose, in that *Shari'a* courts generally refused to implement such clauses and only parties to an existing dispute were authorized to submit such dispute to arbitration, provided that they entered into a separate arbitration agreement, which was subject to formal rules and had to be executed before a notary public. According to certain commentators, the new law acknowledges that arbitration clauses are binding on the parties and recognizes arbitration stemming from such clauses without the necessity to enter into a new arbitration agreement (which would then have to be confirmed by the authority originally having jurisdiction).[19] In other words, arguably there is now official acknowledgement of the validity and binding nature of arbitral clauses in contracts.

It should be noted that the Arbitration Law precludes the Saudi government or its agencies from resorting to arbitration for settlement of their disputes with third parties, except by leave of the President of the Council of Ministers, although such prohibition is subject to amendment by resolution of the Council of Ministers.[20]

Article 3 reflects a decision taken by the Saudi Council of Ministers over two decades prior to the enactment of the Arbitration Law and adopted by Royal Decree,[21] following an unfavourable arbitral award made against the Saudi government in the Aramco case.[22] In essence, Decree No. 58 prohibited recourse to arbitration in the event of a dispute between the Saudi government or any ministry, administration, directorate or agency thereof and a private individual or legal entity.

---

[16] For domestic arbitration, depending on the object of the dispute, such authority includes (i) the *Shari'a* courts, (ii) the Board of Grievances and (iii) the Committee for the Settlement of Labour Disputes.

[17] Article 5 of the Arbitration Law.

[18] Article 7 of the Arbitration Law.

[19] Abdul Hamid El-Ahdab, *Arbitration with the Arab Countries*, Second Edition, Kluwer Law International, 1999, Part III, at page 569.

[20] Article 3 of the Arbitration Law.

[21] Decree No. 58 of 25 June 1963.

[22] Saudi Arabia *v.* Arabian American Oil Company (Aramco), 23 August 1958, reported in 27 I.L.R. (1963).

No distinction was made between national or international arbitration. The Decree contained two exceptions, namely (i) if the contract related to a concession, which was deemed to be of 'vital interest' to the state (the state alone determining what constituted such vital interest), or (ii) if a dispute arising under a government contract was technical in nature. Although the significance of Decree No. 58 has diminished over time, it should nevertheless be noted that the Arbitration Law makes no distinction between national or international arbitration.

Article 10 of the Arbitration Law stipulates:

> 'If the parties have not appointed the arbitrators, or if either of the parties fails to appoint its own arbitrator(s), or if one or more of the arbitrators is unable or refuses to assume his mission or withdraws, or if he is dismissed, and there is no special agreement between the parties, the Authority originally competent to hear the dispute shall appoint the required arbitrators upon request of the party who is interested in expediting the arbitration...'

However, it should be stressed that under Article 18 of the Arbitration Law, either party may appeal the arbitration award within 15 days of receiving notification of the award being rendered. Thus, under the Arbitration Law, the Saudi courts are deemed to be the competent authority having jurisdiction over the dispute and control over all stages of the proceedings, including in particular, the power to hear an appeal filed by either party against an award. In other words, under Saudi law a domestic arbitral award is not deemed to be final and binding until the Saudi courts have settled any appeal against the award, thus rendering such award enforceable.

Foreign arbitration and enforcement under the 'New York Arbitration Convention'

Increasingly, foreign investors are seeking to include foreign arbitration clauses in agreements entered into with Saudi counterparties, in particular in relation to major infrastructure or construction projects or agreements for the supply, delivery, installation and commissioning of expensive plant or equipment. In so doing, the intention is to waive Saudi judicial jurisdiction in favour of private justice, on the assumption that should a dispute arise between the parties and result in an arbitral award in favour of a foreign investor, such award would be final and enforceable against the assets of the Saudi counterparty in Saudi Arabia, as the case may be.

Foreign investors wishing to include foreign arbitration clauses in their agreements should bear in mind that a key problem of arbitration is the enforcement of an arbitral award, a problem which often becomes more complicated in the case of foreign arbitral awards. The enforcement of a foreign arbitral award may be hindered by the claim of sovereign immunity where the respondent is a state or one of its constituent sub-divisions or agencies.[23] In order to address this issue, the Saudi government has entered into a number of bilateral and multilateral conventions for the purpose of regulating the enforcement of foreign arbitral awards. One such multilateral convention is the Convention on the Recognition and Enforcement of Foreign Arbitral Awards[24] to which Saudi Arabia acceded in 1994.[25] Generally referred to as the New York Arbitration Convention, this multilateral treaty (which has been adhered to by over 120 jurisdictions) provides for recognition of both the arbitration clause and the resulting award.[26] In this section, we propose to analyse the degree of protection afforded by the New York Arbitration Convention to foreign investors in Saudi Arabia.

Generally speaking, the legal basis for the enforcement of foreign arbitral awards is expected to be found in the domestic legislation of the state in which enforcement is sought, although in Saudi Arabia there is no specific legislation on the enforcement of foreign arbitral awards. However, the Board of Grievances is empowered to consider applications for the enforcement of foreign judgements (and arguably foreign arbitral awards) pursuant to the Rules of Civil Procedure before the Board of Grievances of 1989, which specify, *inter alia*, the manner in which applications for the enforcement of foreign judgements should be made and the procedures to be followed by the Board of Grievances in this regard.[27]

It is important to note that while there is no restriction under the Arbitration Law against an arbitration being held inside or outside Saudi Arabia, an arbitral award that is rendered outside Saudi Arabia is deemed to be foreign only if it is rendered according to substantive and procedural foreign law.

From a practical standpoint, the procedure for enforcement of the foreign arbitral award is initiated by a petition, which is submitted to the Board of Grievances by the relevant party (usually the party in

---

[23] Dr. Yahya Al-Samaan, Dispute Resolution in Saudi Arabia, Kluwer Law International 2002, *Yearbook of Islamic and Middle Eastern Law*, Volume 7, 81.

[24] 330 U.N.T.S 38, 21 U.S.T 2517, T.I.A.S. No. 6997 (1958).

[25] Saudi Arabia did so by Royal Decree No. 7-11 dated 29 December 1993, which was promulgated in the *Umm Al-Qura* (*Official Gazette*) on 21 January 1994.

[26] Craig, Park and Paulsson, *International Chamber of Commerce Arbitration*, 3rd Edition, p.679.

[27] Dr. Yahya Al-Samaan, *Dispute Resolution in Saudi Arabia*, Kluwer Law International 2002, Yearbook of Islamic and Middle Eastern Law, Volume 7, 81.

whose favour the award has been rendered). After ensuring that the award does not contravene the mandatory principles of *Shari'a* law,[28] the Board of Grievances may invite the parties to present oral submissions. If the Board of Grievances is satisfied that the award should be recognized, it will grant an enforcement order.

If the arbitral award has been rendered in a state that is not a party to the New York Arbitration Convention, the Board of Grievances may nevertheless agree to enforce such award on the basis of reciprocity. In accordance with Article 6 of the Rules of Civil Procedure before the Board of Grievances, the Board of Grievances may issue an order for enforcement of a foreign judgement if the foreign state in which such judgement is rendered affords reciprocal treatment to judgements rendered by the Saudi courts, provided that nothing in the foreign judgement contravenes the mandatory principles of *Shari'a* law.

Notwithstanding the above, the author is not aware of the existence of any previous instances where a party has sought to petition the Board of Grievances to have a foreign arbitral award enforced in Saudi Arabia under the New York Arbitration Convention.[29]

Bilateral investment treaties

Introduction

In the previous section, we touched upon how the Saudi government sought to prevent foreign investors from seeking recourse to arbitration in the event of a dispute arising under a contract between the Saudi government (and any of its agencics) pursuant to Decree No. 58. Since the promulgation of that Decree in 1963, Saudi Arabia has come under increasing pressure from foreign governments and, in particular, the United States to modify its stance. This led to the signing by the Saudi government of a bilateral investment treaty with the United States, as well as bilateral treaties with several other states, as discussed below, as a means of allaying the fears of foreign investors about political risk, and encouraging investment in Saudi Arabia.

---

[28] An example of an award that would contravene such principles would include cases where the foreign arbitral award contained an order requiring the payment of interest, which is strictly forbidden under *Shari'a* law. The Board of Grievances would also reject an application for the enforcement of a foreign arbitral award on public policy grounds, for example, where the dispute arose under an agreement for the provision of forbidden goods or services, or contractual dealings with the State of Israel, which is the subject of a boycott by the Saudi government.

[29] However, at the time of writing the author understands that a petition may soon be filed before the Board of Grievances by a foreign party seeking the enforcement of such an award, which may result in the first test case in Saudi Arabia. Depending on whether or not such petition is filed and subject to confidentiality requirements, the author proposes to discuss the outcome of this case in a future article.

OPIC Convention

On 26 April 1975, Saudi Arabia and the United States, under the aegis of the Overseas Private Investment Corporation (OPIC),[30] entered into a convention (the OPIC Convention), which contained a clause authorizing recourse to arbitration in the event of a dispute between the Saudi government (or any of its agencies) and an American investor guaranteed by OPIC. The OPIC Convention stipulates that the parties to a dispute arising in connection with an investment guaranteed by virtue of the OPIC Convention must first attempt to resolve such dispute by negotiation,[31] failing which either government may refer the matter to arbitration.[32] The arbitral tribunal is to consist of three arbitrators, one to be appointed by each contracting state and the chairman, who is to be neither Saudi nor American, by mutual agreement of the parties.[33] If one of the parties should fail to appoint an arbitrator, the other party may request that the President of the International Court of Justice do so in lieu of the defaulting party.[34] However, the OPIC Convention is silent as to the steps to be taken in the event that the parties fail mutually to agree a chairman. The award is rendered by majority vote and is final and binding. It should be noted that under the OPIC Convention, the arbitral tribunal is obliged to apply the principles and rules of international law.[35] In addition, the arbitral tribunal is authorized to determine its own procedural rules, which it deems appropriate to the subject matter of the dispute.[36]

Other bilateral investment treaties

In addition, Saudi Arabia is a party to five other bilateral investment treaties, namely with China, Egypt, Germany, Italy and the Philippines.[37] Recent reports in the Saudi press suggest that the Saudi government is currently negotiating or has signed several new bilateral treaties with an undisclosed number of other states.

Multilateral conventions

In addition to acceding to the New York Arbitration Convention, Saudi Arabia is also a signatory to multilateral conventions that provide

---

[30] OPIC is a state-owned agency that guarantees American foreign investment against political risks.

[31] OPIC Convention, Article 3(a).

[32] *Ibid*, Article 39.

[33] *Ibid*, Article 3(c)(i).

[34] *Ibid*, Article 3(c)(ii).

[35] OPIC Convention, Article 3(c)(ii).

[36] *Ibid*, Article 3(c)(iv).

[37] See Appendix B at the end of this chapter for more details.

foreign investors with a means of dispute resolution through foreign arbitration, and the enforcement of resulting judgements or awards. In this section, we propose to look briefly at the Convention on the Settlement of Investment Disputes and the Convention on Judicial Cooperation between states of the Arab League.

Convention on the Settlement of Investment Disputes

In 1980, Saudi Arabia acceded to the Convention on the Settlement of Investment Disputes between States and Nationals of Other States (the Convention)[38] providing for a means of resolution of investment disputes between member states and nationals of other states who are parties to such Convention, under the aegis of the International Centre for the Settlement of Investment Disputes (the Centre or ICSID).

In accordance with Article 1 of the Convention, the Centre is intended to encourage private foreign investment in developing countries by providing facilities for conciliation and arbitration of investment disputes between a contracting state and a national of another contracting state.

Under Article 25 of the Convention, the jurisdiction of the Centre is limited to legal disputes arising directly from an investment between a contracting state (or one of its constituent subdivisions or agencies designed by it) and a national of another contracting state.

The preamble to the Convention emphasizes the use of the Centre's arbitration facilities. It states that a contracting state, by the mere fact of its ratification of the Convention and without its consent, is under no obligation to submit any particular dispute to conciliation or arbitration. This rule is also confirmed by Article 25(1), which provides that the disputing parties must consent in writing to submit to ICSID.

The Convention does not specify the form of instrument in which the consent may be expressed. Consent can be expressed in an exchange of letters or in the investment contract. Alternatively, a contracting state may give its consent in advance to submit investment disputes to ICSID arbitration by providing for that in the domestic investment law or in an investment treaty.[39]

To date, the Arbitration Law contains no provisions in this regard and Saudi Arabia has not concluded an investment agreement referring investment disputes to ICSID arbitration. At the time of writing, no dispute arising out of investment in Saudi Arabia has been submitted to the Centre.[40]

---

[38] The ICSID Convention entered into force on 14 October 1966.

[39] Dr. Yahya Al-Samaan, *The Legal Protection of Foreign Investment in the Kingdom of Saudi Arabia*, Dar Al Andalus for Pub. and Dist., pages 301–302.

[40] Ibid p. 302.

According to Article 25(4) of the Convention, a contracting state may notify ICSID of the categories of disputes that it would not submit to ICSID arbitration. At the time of ratification, the Saudi government reserved the right of not submitting 'all questions pertaining to oil and to acts of sovereignty to ICSID, whether by way of conciliation or arbitration'.[41] With respect to the latter reservation, there is no official interpretation of the term 'acts of sovereignty' under Saudi law. However, as a general proposition some scholars have interpreted this as a reference to those discretionary executive actions that are not subject to judicial review, corresponding to the so-called 'act of state' doctrine.[42] This doctrine bars the adjudication of claims or enforcement of awards resulting from an act carried out by a sovereign power, within its territory, of a governmental rather than a commercial nature, a quintessential 'act of state' being the nationalization of foreign-owned property by legislative decree.[43]

There are a number of advantages to using ICSID arbitration. First, it is regarded as a flexible and impartial mechanism for the resolution of investment disputes because it seeks to maintain a balance between the parties' interests. Second, it meets the desire of most foreign investors not to have their disputes publicized because, according to Article 48(5) of the Convention, an arbitral award rendered under the auspices of ICSID cannot be published unless the parties to the dispute agree thereto. Third, ICSID arbitration does not raise the problem of sovereign immunity of a state party to the dispute preventing it from being subjected to foreign jurisdiction. In other words, under ICSID arbitration, the defence of sovereign immunity of a disputing state from the Centre's jurisdiction cannot be invoked as long as the state has given its prior consent to submit to ICSID arbitration. Thus, ICSID arbitration offers foreign investors a guarantee against the possible refusal of the host state to submit a dispute to arbitration. Lastly, so far as enforcement of arbitral awards is concerned, ICSID arbitration is deemed by many to be the most effective dispute settlement mechanism. The Convention provides in Article 54(1) that each contracting state is obliged to recognize an award rendered pursuant to this Convention as binding and enforce it within its territories as if it were a final judgement of its court.[44]

---

41 Ratified on 16 April 1980. The Saudi ratification entered into force in Saudi Arabia on 7 June 1980.

42 A. Lerrick and Q.J. Mian, *op cit*, page 181.

43 Craig, Park and Paulsson, *International Chamber of Commerce Arbitration*, Third Edition, 2000, page 671.

44 Dr. Yahya Al-Samaan, *The Legal Protection of Foreign Investment in the Kingdom of Saudi Arabia*, Dar Al Andalus for Pub. and Dist., pages 304–305.

Convention on Judicial Cooperation between States of the Arab League
On 6 April 1983, Saudi Arabia signed the Convention on Judicial Cooperation between States of the Arab League in Riyadh. Articles 25 and 37 of the 1983 Convention deal with the recognition and enforcement of foreign judgements and arbitral awards, without reviewing the subject matter of the underlying dispute, provided that such judgements or arbitral awards do not violate public order, morality or the constitution of the state in which enforcement is being sought, or the overriding principles of *Shari'a* law.

Thus, the enforcement of an arbitral award that has been rendered in a member state and that awards the claimant interest, can be rejected in Saudi Arabia on the ground that it violates the prohibition on the payment of interest under *Shari'a* law.

The 1983 Convention distinguishes between public order and morality on the one hand and *Shari'a* law on the other. It seems that the distinction is due to the fact that the mandatory principles applicable in certain Arab League states (such as Saudi Arabia) are not regarded as matters of public order in other states (such as Egypt).

Appendix A: List of investment activities excluded to foreigners

Industrial sector

- exploration, drilling and production of oil and gas;[45]
- manufacturing of military equipment;
- manufacturing of explosives for civil use.

Services sector

- catering for military personnel;
- investigation and security;
- all insurance and insurance-related services;[*]
- real estate investment in Makkah Al-Mokaramah and Al-Madinah Al-Munawarah;

[45] Excluding mining services internationally classified under No. 883 and 5115.

- travel agencies, tour operators and tourist guides services related to Hajj and Omrah;
- placement and supply services of personnel including labour recruitment and commercial employment offices;
- real estate commission services;
- printing and publishing;*
- distribution services (wholesale trade, retailing[46] and commission agents);[47]
- audio-visual services;
- educational services (primary education, secondary education and adult education);*
- telecommunications services;*
- road and air transport;
- services incidental to electrical energy distribution;
- space transport;
- pipeline transport;
- services provided by midwives, nurses, physiotherapists and paramedical personnel;
- services incidental to fishing;
- poison centres, blood banks and quarantine services.

* Sectors recently approved by the Supreme Economic Council for investment by foreign investors.

---

[46] Including medical retail trade (pharmacies) internationally classified under No. 631, 632, 6111, 6112 and 6121.

[47] Excluding franchise services internationally classified under No. 8929, provided that foreign ownership is not more than 49% on the basis of one license for each region.

Appendix B: Bilateral investment treaties entered into by Saudi Arabia[48]

Counterparties	Signature	Entry into force
China	29 February 1996	1 May 1997
Egypt	13 March 1990	15 September 1992
Germany	29 October 1996	9 January 1999
Italy	10 September 1996	22 May 1998
Philippines	17 October 1994	11 November 1996

[48] At the time of writing, the author understands that Saudi government is currently negotiating or has signed several new bilateral treaties with an undisclosed number of other states.

3.3

Business Structures

Ernst & Young, Riyadh

Regulations for companies

The Regulations for Companies (the Regulations), issued by Royal Decree on 20 July 1965 with subsequent amendments, contain the rules and procedures for several types of business organizations permitted in Saudi Arabia. Limited liability partnerships are of particular interest to foreign investors. Other business organizations specifically covered by the Regulations include the following:

- general partnerships;
- limited partnerships;
- registered branches of foreign companies;
- joint ventures (temporary associations for carrying out specific projects);
- joint stock companies;
- partnerships limited by shares;
- companies with variable capital;
- cooperatives.

Foreign investors may also be interested in establishing branches of foreign companies, liaison offices, or technical and scientific services offices, all of which are subject to the Regulations, although not specifically described in them.

A company registered under the Regulations is defined as a joint undertaking to participate in an enterprise with a view to profit. A company has the following characteristics:

- it is deemed to be a commercial company, regardless of its objectives;
- it acquires a legal identity of its own after the registration formalities are completed, unless it is a joint venture;
- its statutes must include certain mandatory information, such as the type of company, its duration, its objectives, the location of its head office, the amount of capital, etc;
- its contractual conditions, which are established by the partners or shareholders, must be consistent with the Regulations;
- it is dissolved if one individual owns all of the shares or interests, because sole proprietorships cannot be registered companies;
- it may not enjoy certain rights if it is not 100 per cent owned by Saudis, but it would still be considered a Saudi company.

Commercial registration

Foreign entities that wish to carry on business inside Saudi Arabia are required to create a formal legal presence for themselves – whether this is by way of a branch, representative or technical and scientific services offices or through a limited liability partnership company with or without Saudi partners – and obtain the appropriate commercial registration or licences from the Saudi Ministry of Commerce and Industry (MOCI) or other appropriate agencies.

It is against the law for a foreign company to do business in Saudi Arabia without a commercial registration or licence. The MOCI may impose penalties on foreign companies doing business in the Kingdom without the proper legal registration.

Structure of business entities

There are various options available to the foreign investor wishing to do business in Saudi Arabia. The limited liability partnership is the most common for foreign investors intending to establish ongoing business activities. The following structures are commonly encountered.

Limited liability partnerships

A limited liability partnership (LLP) is a privately held company that can be used to establish an industrial, agricultural, contracting or services project that may have either both Saudi and foreign partners or be owned 100 per cent by foreign partners. All LLPs with foreign participation are required to obtain a foreign capital investment licence from the Saudi Arabian General Investment Authority (SAGIA) and are subject to the Regulations for Companies and Foreign Capital Investment Regulations (FCIR). The FCIR permit the foreign investor to invest in any investment activity in the Kingdom, on a permanent or a temporary basis, except for those activities that are specifically excluded by SAGIA, as set out in the negative list provided by SAGIA (see Chapter 2.2).

An LLP is often referred to as a Saudi limited company because all partners have limited liability subject to certain conditions. An LLP cannot offer a subscription to the public to raise or increase its capital, and cannot conduct insurance, savings or banking operations.

The Saudi government may grant various incentives to approved projects with a foreign capital investment licence that transfer technological expertise and provide training opportunities for Saudis. These incentives include:

- *financing assistance*: low-cost financing through the Saudi Industrial Development Fund (SIDF);
- *industrial facilities*: nominal rent on building sites and reduced fees for water and electricity;
- *protective tariffs*: tariff protection once the local product achieves an approved standard.

SAGIA requires a minimum capital of SR25 million for agricultural projects, SR5 million for industrial projects and SR2 million for other projects. According to company regulations, an LLP can be formed with a minimum capital of SR500,000, which will now be applicable to a company that is wholly owned by Saudi nationals.

The requirements for audits, annual general meetings, legal reserves, filing returns and loss situations are similar to those of a joint stock company.

Joint stock companies

A joint stock company has the following characteristics:

- it is owned by five or more individuals or entities;
- its capital is divided into negotiable shares of an equal amount and shareholders are liable only to the extent of the value of their shares;
- its capital cannot be less than SR2 million, or less than SR10 million if its shares are offered for public subscription;

- the par value of each share cannot be less than SR50;
- at incorporation, its paid-up capital cannot be less than one-half of the authorized capital, and the amount payable on subscription not less than one-quarter of the authorized capital.

A recent change to the Regulations allows joint stock companies to issue preferred shares in an amount not to exceed 50 per cent of its capital.

Joint stock companies being established to conduct certain businesses, primarily in the mining, utility and banking sectors, can be incorporated only after authorization by a Royal Decree based on the approval of the Council of Ministers.

Other joint stock companies are required to obtain a licence issued by the Minister of Commerce and Industry, and to announce in the *Official Gazette* that the licence has been issued. If an invitation for subscription is made to the public, it should generally be done within one month of the date that the Royal Decree or licence authorizing incorporation is published in the *Official Gazette*. The offering must be in the form of a prospectus and subscriptions must be received through banks designated by the MOCI. If the capital includes contributions in-kind, the MOCI appoints experts to ascertain their correct valuation.

Management consists of a board of directors that has at least three members and is appointed by the shareholders. A director must own at least 200 shares of the joint stock company. Those shares are set aside as a guarantee against the director's liability.

Each year the board of directors must set aside 10 per cent of the joint stock company's (other than banks) net profit to establish a legal reserve. This is done until the reserve is equal to one-half of the capital. The legal reserve is not available for distribution.

Auditors of a joint stock company, appointed at the annual general meeting, are selected from among the Kingdom's licensed auditors. A general shareholders' meeting must be held at least once a year to approve the audited financial statements. The meeting should be held within six months of the closing of operations for the calendar year.

The audited financial statements of a joint stock company must be filed with the Department of Zakat and Income Tax (DZIT), at the MOCI.

If the losses of a joint company equal 75 per cent of its capital, the directors must call an extraordinary general meeting to consider whether the joint stock company should continue or be dissolved.

Branches of foreign companies

Permanent branch of foreign company

Foreign companies can establish a permanent branch in Saudi Arabia by obtaining a licence issued by the SAGIA under the FCIR. Once a foreign capital investment licence has been issued it is necessary to obtain a Commercial Registration (CR) from the MOCI. The SAGIA specifies a minimum capital of SR2 million for a branch.

Temporary branch of foreign company

A foreign contractor operating solely for a government contract can set up a branch of a foreign company by obtaining a temporary licence from the SAGIA under the new FCIR. The temporary licence issued is restricted to the specific contract and is valid only for the duration of the contract.

Liaison offices

Foreign companies that have contracts with departments or agencies of the Saudi Arabian government can establish a liaison office to facilitate coordination with the head office, supervise their activities in Saudi Arabia and cooperate with the government departments or agencies involved.

Under the new FCIR, liaison offices are established by obtaining a licence from the SAGIA. Once a licence is issued, the liaison office is required to obtain commercial registration from the MOCI. The SAGIA requires minimum capital of SR2 million before issuing a licence to establish a liaison office. Such offices are specifically prohibited from engaging in any commercial activity, and the licence for the office indicates the maximum number of employees it is permitted to hire. Liaison offices are required by the MOCI to file annual statements showing expenses funded by head office and a detailed annual report of the liaison office's activities. In practice, it is understood that the MOCI discourages liaison offices, preferring the establishment of permanent branches instead.

Technical and scientific services offices

Foreign companies with commercial agents in Saudi Arabia may apply to the SAGIA for permission to open a technical and scientific services office (TSSO) in order to provide technical, scientific, advisory and consulting services to commercial agents and customers who purchase the company's products. The office may not engage in commercial activity, and its expenses must be funded by the head office. Audited statements of expenses and a report of the office's activities must be filed annually with the MOCI. Generally, TSSOs are entitled to employ a limited number of foreign experts, but may hire any number of Saudi nationals.

Joint adventures

A joint adventure is a business arrangement created by a contract between two or more persons that is unknown to third parties. It does not enjoy corporate status and is not subject to public formalities. Third parties have recourse only against the partner who carried out business with them. If the partners perform any act that reveals the existence of a 'company' to a third party, the company will be considered a de facto general partnership as far as the third party is concerned. This type of business organization is different from the 'joint venture' loosely referred to by the business community in Saudi Arabia, which is usually a limited liability partnership with foreign participation.

Consortia

Consortia, which are business arrangements between two or more legal entities, are commonly formed to complete large projects. Consortia are not separate legal entities.

Trading operations

Saudi commercial regulations do not permit foreign entities to carry out trading activities in Saudi Arabia. Trading is strictly reserved for Saudi individuals, 100 per cent Saudi-owned companies and, in certain cases, Gulf Cooperation Council (GCC) nationals. There are strict penalties for both Saudis and foreigners involved in 'cover-up operations' where the Saudi is deemed to be sheltering a foreigner doing business in the Kingdom for which he should obtain proper legal registration. Foreigners wishing to sell goods in Saudi Arabia must do so through a Saudi commercial agent.

A Royal Decree restricts the appointment of commercial agents and distributors for foreign firms in Saudi Arabia to Saudi nationals and companies that are 100 per cent owned by Saudi nationals. Trading organizations must therefore sell their products to Saudi Arabian concerns, which then market them locally. A foreign organization's profit comes only from supplying goods to the Saudi commercial agent.

Partnerships

General partnerships
A general partnership is an association of two or more persons that are liable jointly for partnership debts to the extent of their entire personal wealth. It is a separate legal entity and can transact business in its own name. Partners may not transfer partnership interests without unanimous consent. There is no minimum capital requirement. Contribution terms are set out in the partnership agreement, which must be registered with the MOCI. The general partnership is a common form of business organization used by Saudi nationals.

Limited partnerships
A limited partnership is composed of general and limited partners. General partners are liable to the entire extent of their personal wealth and limited partners are liable to the extent of their investment in the partnership. A limited partnership is registered in the same way as a general partnership.

Professional partnerships
Regulations relating to professional partnerships that enable foreign professional firms and individuals to form joint practices in Saudi Arabia with locally licensed partners were issued in 1991. Approval for forming a joint partnership must be obtained from the MOCI; conditions for approval include:

- the foreign firm must have a distinguished international reputation;
- 10 years must have elapsed since the founding of the foreign firm;
- the foreign firm must transfer expertise and train Saudis;
- a permanent representative of the foreign firm must be resident in Saudi Arabia for at least nine months per year; and
- the Saudi partners must own at least 25 per cent of the capital.

Legal advice

It is very important to consult a Saudi law firm before taking any action that would require a legal presence in Saudi Arabia or that would require an agreement such as an agency agreement. Furthermore, it is important to have current information, as legal requirements change from time to time.

Note: The information in this chapter concerning business structures is current as of February 2005.

3.4

Agency and Distribution Agreements

Legal Advisors in Association with Baker & McKenzie Limited

Introduction

Setting up agency and distribution agreements in Saudi Arabia comes under the broad heading of 'commercial agencies', a term that includes commission agencies, distributorships and franchise arrangements.

Some of the main factors to take into consideration when entering into a commercial agency arrangement in the Kingdom are:

- seek an agent of good standing and reputation when establishing a trading business or exporting products to the Kingdom;
- seek a local representative with premises located in all of the main urban centres of Saudi Arabia;
- negotiate a contract of agency or distributorship acceptable from the foreign supplier's point of view and which has been reviewed by legal counsel in Saudi Arabia;
- make early contact with the Saudi Chamber of Commerce and Industry, which has branches located in the major urban centres of the Kingdom and use them as necessary to locate a representative, distributor, partner or agent and obtain the names of Saudi importers handling relevant products.

In general, it is always advisable to establish direct contact with the Saudi business community by making a personal visit to the Kingdom.

Setting up commercial agencies

When setting up trading links with Saudi Arabia, it is first necessary to establish whether an agent is a necessary requirement or not. According to the requirements under the so-called 'Negative List' published by the Supreme Economic Council (as amended from time to time) and the Commercial Agency Regulations (defined below), only Saudi nationals and entities 100 per cent owned by Saudi nationals may conduct importation and sales and marketing activities and be appointed as commercial agents for foreign firms in Saudi Arabia. Foreigners who wish to sell goods inside Saudi Arabia must do so through a Saudi commercial agent that markets the goods locally.

Another restriction that should be noted is provided for under Council of Ministers Decision No. 1275 dated 12/9/1395H (corresponding to 18/9/1975G), which prohibits the payment of any commission to any intermediary, sales agent, representative or broker in connection with armaments contracts (including equipment and installations necessary thereto).

Sales to the private and public sectors

There is no legal requirement for foreign companies that wish to sell goods from outside of Saudi Arabia to appoint a Saudi commercial agent. Therefore, sales may be made directly to purchasers from outside the country, having the Saudi purchaser arrange for the importation itself. In practice, however, if a firm wishes to make more than the occasional sale, or if it wants someone to market and sell its goods from within the Kingdom, a Saudi agent or distributor will most likely be necessary.

The majority of government purchasing is conducted by local tender, and a foreign supplier's Saudi commercial agent would typically participate in the tendering process for the supply of goods to governmental ministries, agencies and instruments. Many governmental bodies often require that the Saudi commercial agent be 'registered' in the Commercial Agent Registry at the Ministry of Commerce and Industry (MOCI), although that is not always the case and it has been possible for unregistered commercial agents to successfully market goods to the Saudi government. In the case of pharmaceutical and certain other products that must be registered with, for example, the Ministry of Health, it is generally necessary for the foreign supplier to have a distributor that is registered with the MOCI before the supplier's products can be registered with the relevant Ministry and imported into the Kingdom.

Companies that are wholly owned by the Saudi government, for example, the Saudi Electricity Company (SEC) or the Saudi Arabian Oil Company (Saudi Aramco), may have their own sets of detailed purchasing procedures. Companies wholly owned by the Saudi government are not covered by governmental tendering procedures, although those entities sometimes adopt similar procedures and contractual language.

Selection of an agent

For companies seeking agents, there are several possible sources to consult. Foreign trade desks of national embassies can normally provide advice on obtaining lists of companies dealing in particular product lines. For example, such lists are prepared by the commercial department of the British Embassy in Riyadh, whose staff can provide more background and possibly recent leads as to local business interests.

There are several commercial banks whose staff are aware of their customers' interests, and in over a dozen cities and towns there are Chamber of Commerce and Industry offices, some of which publish magazines containing brief details of foreign companies seeking local contacts. A visit to the market with a trade mission is also extremely useful in establishing contacts, as is participation in trade exhibitions that are held from time to time in Jeddah, Riyadh or the Eastern Province.

Foreign companies are often approached by Saudi companies interested in taking up their agency. While this is most encouraging, the foreign company should always try to visit a potential agent on his home ground before concluding any agreement.

Before entering into a written agreement, companies will need to assess the following commercial considerations carefully:

- the Saudi company's reputation, status and financial position;
- the storage facilities that are available for equipment and spare parts;
- the back-up and servicing facilities, including qualified personnel that the company has (and that the new official format of agency agreement requires the principal to develop as necessary);
- the territory is covered effectively – few agents are able to operate in all three main trading centres, Riyadh, Jeddah and the Eastern Province;
- the management's knowledge of local laws, regulations and customs that affect business;

- the company's willingness to take care of the routine arrangements (such as visas, airline reservations, local transport and accommodation, appointments, etc).

The foreign supplier should ensure that any proposed agreement suits its needs and should consult with a Saudi legal adviser in order to obtain detailed advice on the provisions of the agreement, including (but not limited to) comments on duration; exclusivity; termination (eg non-payment of damages or compensation, etc); registration and governing law and jurisdiction.

One cannot be too careful when selecting and entering into an agreement with a commercial agent in Saudi Arabia. Potential agents sometimes suggest that the parties use the MOCI's standard commercial agency agreement form, although nothing would oblige the parties to use that form. The Ministry's standard form contains provisions that are rather favourable to the Saudi commercial agent, in particular the provisions that protect the commercial agent in the event of termination or non-renewal of the contract by the foreign supplier. For that reason, foreign suppliers tend to avoid using the Ministry's standard form and prefer to use their own form, amending it as needed following consultation with a Saudi legal adviser.

It should be emphasized that for the success of any business venture, it is essential to select a reliable Saudi business partner. Initial contacts between prospective business partners are not difficult to arrange and these can generally be facilitated through either commercial attachés or the Saudi Chamber of Commerce and Industry (SCCI).

Exclusivity

Given the vast physical size of the country and the difference between regions, few agents offer effective coverage of the whole of the Kingdom. It is permissible under Saudi law and the current practices of the Saudi authorities to appoint agents on a regional basis, and for particular products. A principal wishing to restrict the coverage of an agency must, therefore, make this explicit in the agreement by defining the territory and range of commodities to be covered.

Commercial agency regulations

Commercial agencies are governed by the Commercial Agencies Regulations issued under Royal Decree M/11 dated 20/2/1382H (corresponding to 22/7/1962G), as amended by Royal Decrees M/5 dated 11/6/1389H (corresponding to 24/8/1969G), M/8 dated 20/3/1393H (corresponding to 23/4/1973G), and M/32 dated 10/8/1400H (corresponding to 24/6/1980G) (the 'Commercial Agency Regulations').

Some of the key features of the Commercial Agency Regulations are as follows:

- non-Saudis are not permitted to act as commercial agents in Saudi Arabia;
- Saudis appointed as commercial agents are obliged to register the appointment with the Commercial Agents Register at the MOCI and pay a one-time fee of SR500; and
- the Saudi commercial agent is required to guarantee the quality of the products and (where appropriate given the type of product) supply necessary maintenance and spare parts to consumers during the term of the agency and for up to a year after its termination.

Registration

A threshold concern before entering into an agency or distributorship agreement with a Saudi commercial agent will be to consider if the agreement between the parties is to be registered with the MOCI.

The Commercial Agency Regulations require that any commercial agency agreement be registered at MOCI by the Saudi commercial agent within three months of its commencement. The Ministry reviews commercial agency agreements submitted to it for compliance with the Commercial Agency Regulations and the policies and practices of the Ministry. For an agreement to be accepted by the Ministry for registration, it must be notarized before a notary public, legalized by the Saudi Consulate in the country where the supplier is located and, upon arrival in the Kingdom, be officially translated into Arabic. A supplier would not need to fulfil the foregoing process if the agreement is not to be registered.

One requirement, which derives from the definition of 'commercial agent' in the Commercial Agency Regulations, is that the agreement be entered into either directly with the manufacturer of the products subject to the agency or the manufacturer's representative in the manufacturer's own country. Other requirements have varied a good deal over the years. At one time, the Ministry used to insist that agreements submitted for registration adhere fairly closely to a model form agreement prepared by the Ministry, but for many years now it has accepted for registration agreements that differ very significantly from the 'model form' in both form and substance. A 1998 MOCI circular states that commercial agency agreements submitted for registration should include provisions requiring (a) a warranty by the foreign party as to the good quality of the products and their compliance with applicable standards set by the Saudi Arabian Standards Organization (SASO), if any; (b) the foreign party to supply spare parts for the products (if applicable) during the term of the agency and for up to a year after its termination and the commercial agent to provide spare parts and maintenance service to customers in all regions of Saudi Arabia and not just in the major cities; (c) the foreign supplier to provide a certificate of origin of the products; (d) the parties to announce any defects in the products and to withdraw the defective products from the market for repair or replacement at the manufacturer's expense; (e) the agent to provide technical and managerial training to Saudis; and (f) disputes relating to the agency relationship to be resolved by arbitration or litigation in Saudi Arabia. The MOCI tends to be fairly flexible about these requirements. The last requirement, for example, has been interpreted to mean simply that the agent should try to convince the foreign supplier to agree to resolve disputes in Saudi Arabia. However, agreements providing for foreign dispute resolution and foreign governing law continue to be registered.

Both the responsibility for registering a commercial agency agreement with the Ministry and the penalties for non-compliance fall upon the Saudi commercial agent rather than the foreign party. Such penalties are seldom (if ever) imposed in practice, and non-registration does not seem to prevent commercial agents from operating effectively, for the most part, in Saudi Arabia. For this reason, and because registration is not a prerequisite to enforceability of an agreement in Saudi Arabia, foreign suppliers sometimes take the position that effecting the registration is entirely the problem of the Saudi party. Registration does confer a certain status on the commercial agent that it would not otherwise have and that makes it easier for the agent to deal with government agencies with respect to matters such as compliance with SASO or other government requirements (software, for example, is subject to censorship by the Ministry of Information), infringement of trademarks and other intellectual property rights and government bids.

Between the parties, the rights and responsibilities under a commercial agency are contractual and need to be precisely defined in the agreement. Foreign principals should take legal advice to the extent it is possible, or desirable, to depart from the MOCI standard form and generally before taking any action that would require entering into a formal commercial agency agreement. It is also important to receive current advice, as legal requirements do change from time to time.

After selection of the agent

Frequent visits by experienced sales staff (preferably the same people) are most desirable. Such visits are needed to cultivate a good relationship with the agent, and also to help him/her to market the goods.

If the goods are of a technical nature, it may be very useful to provide short training visits to Europe for sales and maintenance personnel appointed from within the agent's staff.

There are often short deadlines for bidding in Saudi Arabia and it is therefore essential that the agent is kept up to date with technical and price information on all products, and that the need to respond quickly to questions on these matters is appreciated.

There are more foreign firms chasing business than there are well-established agents to go round. Therefore, certain foreign principals have made arrangements whereby a representative will accept employment with the commercial agent for a period. Technically speaking, secondment arrangements could be problematic under the Saudi regulations and the appointment would be as an employee of the commercial agent. It is also reasonably common for suppliers to provide ad hoc support to their commercial agents by having company representatives visit Saudi Arabia from time to time.

Termination

A commercial agency is not easily terminated without the mutual agreement of both parties, especially if the agency agreement has been formally registered.

Unlike the situation in many other Middle Eastern countries, there is, at present, no regulation in Saudi Arabia that entitles a commercial agent to any sort of indemnity upon the non-renewal or termination of a commercial agency. Even in those cases where Saudi courts have awarded compensation to the commercial agent, the awards have historically been limited to direct, actual and easily quantifiable damages and have not included compensation for lost profits or other consequential damages, which typically form the bulk of a termination compensation claim. Broader compensation claims may, however, be available to the extent that the commercial agency agreement provides for the right to termination compensation, such as in the MOCI's 'model form', or the termination violated the terms of the agreement or involved a serious abuse of rights. Since, however, Saudi courts are not bound by any formal system of binding precedent and there is no case reporting system, the courts have considerable discretion in reviewing termination disputes, which they do on a case-by-case basis.

Agency disputes committee

Termination of an agreement would not constitute automatic deregistration however, and once an agreement is registered with a commercial agent for a given line of products and territory, it has historically been difficult to register a new commercial agent in its place. The MOCI has reportedly reaffirmed its policy that no new commercial agent may be registered pending resolution of any outstanding dispute with the previously registered commercial agent for the line of products and territory specified in the agreement with the principal. In addition, if the parting is not settled amicably, it may prove difficult to get another Saudi company to take on the agency. If a new agent is appointed and attempts to register its agreement, the Commercial Agencies Department would typically refer the new agent to the Committee for Settlement of Commercial Agency Disputes (the Committee), if there was a pre-existing registration.

The MOCI created the Committee, which is constituted of officials from the Ministry and members of the Chamber of Commerce Industry. The Committee's role is to mediate between parties to promote an amicable settlement between them, failing which it is supposed to make a recommendation to the MOCI as to whether a new Saudi agent may be registered with them. The Committee is not a court and has no authority to award damages. Although it has been possible to convince the Committee to recommend in favour of transferring the registration, the process can be very prolonged as the Committee is only a part-time body. In some cases, it has taken years to make a recommendation one way or the other. In the meantime, the terminated commercial agent would remain the only registered agent for the products.

In view of the new policy permitting the registration of multiple non-exclusive agreements, it seems reasonable to expect that a non-exclusive registered agent would have much greater difficulty impeding the registration of any new non-exclusive agents, whether through the Committee or otherwise, than exclusive registered agents have had historically. The policies and practices of the MOCI and the Committee can always change in this regard, however.

Repeal of service agencies requirement

Saudi Arabia previously had a requirement pursuant to Royal Decree No. M/2 dated 21/1/1398H (corresponding to 1 January 1978G) that a foreign company contracting with a Saudi governmental body must appoint a Saudi service agent in connection with that contract. The foregoing requirement was repealed, however, by Royal Decree No.M/22 dated 16/5/1422H (corresponding to 6/8/2001G) and foreign parties are no longer obliged to appoint a service agent in order to perform a contract for the Saudi government.

Foreign (and local) parties that desire to contract with the Saudi government should, however, be cognizant of the requirements under the Tender Regulations issued under Royal Decree No. M/14 dated 7/4/1397H (corresponding to 27/3/1977G) and its Rules of Implementation, which apply to all government contracts, regardless of whether or not they are specifically incorporated by reference. The Tender Regulations cover all stages of the government contracting process and outline the bid process, specify the manner in which delay penalties are to be assessed, lay down the basic rules for government procurement activities and generally regulate and control how government agencies can contract with third parties.

Concluding comments

Investing in Saudi Arabia by foreign organizations through commercial agency arrangements based on a comprehensive business agreement can bring considerable rewards to the foreign company where there is a valid business need in the Kingdom. However, the investor must be prepared to spend time in understanding the workings of the internal market and be sympathetic in attempting to understand the aspirations of the government and the potential partner.

The key qualities that the foreign investor needs are patience and the ability to undertake realistic planning, coupled with strong determination to ensure that the venture is a complete success for both the foreign organization and the Saudi commercial agent.

3.5

Employment Law

Legal Advisors in Association with Baker & McKenzie Limited

Introduction

During the first half of the 20th century, the economic development of Saudi Arabia was, to a large extent, pre-industrial, and the role of labour relations was rather limited. However, rapid industrialization and the economic advancement of Saudi Arabia increased the need to regulate labour relations and these were addressed by the passage of regulations to govern such relationships. The current Saudi Labour and Workmen Regulations were issued pursuant to Royal Decree No. M/21 dated 6/9/1389H (corresponding to 16/11/1969G) and became effective on 19/9/1389H, corresponding to 28/11/1969G, as amended (the 'Labour Regulations').

The Labour Regulations is considered to be a reasonably well-conceived piece of legislation, providing rights and obligations on both the employer and the employee. The Labour Regulations generally aim to create a good atmosphere and a desire for cooperation between the employer and the employee, and provide for the scheme that governs the settlement of disputes when these arise.

Ministry of Labour

The development and use of the Kingdom's human resources is one of the main concerns of the Ministry of Labour. It is the ministry's responsibility to develop and prepare annual and long-range plans on manpower requirements and labour relations, as well as to monitor and prepare periodic reports on matters relating to employment and social security. For instance, the ministry is generally responsible for administering the Labour Regulations that provide, in relevant parts, for the need to employ disabled and rehabilitated employees.

The Labour Regulations

Labour contracts

The Saudi Labour Regulations provide that the employer and the employee should enter into a contract for employment, whereby the employee works under the direction and control of the employer for a specified or unspecified period of time (or a specific project) in consideration for a wage. The Labour Regulations provide that the labour contract should be in writing, drawn up in Arabic and in duplicate; however, contracts drafted in another language would be binding. If the labour contract is prepared in Arabic and another language, the Arabic version shall prevail, while contracts prepared in a foreign language only will not be reviewed by the Labour Courts in the event of a dispute, and a certified translation must be submitted. Moreover, the absence of writing does not mean that a labour contract does not exist and the existence of a contract can be proved by all evidentiary means, including oral testimony.

Termination of service

The Labour Regulations imposes certain restrictions on an employer's right to dismiss an employee; however, governmental approval is not required. In general, certain changes made by the employer to essential elements of the relationship (such as responsibilities, place of performance and compensation) without the consent of the employee, may be treated by the Labour Courts as a constructive termination of the employment relationship, thereby entitling the employee to indemnification.

The manner in which the employment may be terminated would depend on an employee's employment contract. Generally speaking, definite term contracts for a specified period of time are generally terminable only for 'cause' prior to the expiration of the defined term, whilst indefinite term contacts, for an unspecified period of time, may be terminated for 'cause' or for a 'valid reason' at any time during the employment relationship. The Labour Regulations provide that a definite term contract becomes indefinite if the parties continue to observe it after the completion of its term.

Termination by employer for cause

Pursuant to Article 83 of the Labour Regulations, an employer may terminate a definite or indefinite term employee without notice or liability for an end-of-service award or termination indemnity if the employee commits an egregious for 'cause' act. Article 83 lists the for 'cause' bases for termination. Any termination under Article 83 requires the employer to give the employee a 'show cause notice' permitting the latter to present his defence. The employer has to prove that any discharge was for cause and the employee has the right to appeal the dismissal to the local Labour Office.

Termination by employer for valid reason

Indefinite term employment contracts may also be terminated for a 'valid reason', without liability for the payment of a termination indemnity; however, the employee would be entitled to notice and the payment of an end-of-service award. What constitutes a 'valid reason' for terminating an indefinite term employee is not explicitly delineated under the Labour Regulations; however, the standard is clearly less stringent than 'cause'. A Saudi Labour Court on a case-by-case basis would, therefore, consider the determination of whether a termination was made for a 'valid reason'. Arguably, the employer's contractual obligations, impossibility or frustration of purpose, business considerations, or the employee's incompetence all constitute a 'valid reason'. Employment contracts sometimes cite specific examples of 'valid reasons' for termination but a Labour Court will not necessarily consider these binding.

Termination indemnity / reinstatement

If a definite term contract is terminated prior to the expiration of its term in a manner that does not comply with the Labour Regulations, the employee may be able to successfully argue for payment of the remainder of the contract period. If the employer without 'cause' or a 'valid reason' terminates an indefinite term employment contract, a terminated employee could be entitled to a termination indemnity as provided for under the Labour Regulations. (This termination indemnity is separate from the end-of-service award, which is commented on below.) The traditional practice of the Labour Courts has been to award (in average cases) the aggrieved employee an indemnity of three month's pay, but this can vary a good deal as the Labour Courts have considerable discretion in this regard.

The Labour Regulations provide that a Labour Court may oblige an employer to reinstate a wrongfully terminated employee, pay his wages in arrears and consider the employee's service as 'uninterrupted'. Reinstatement, however, is rarely granted in practice, particularly with respect to non-Saudi employees.

The Labour Regulations also provide that claims made by an aggrieved employee could, in principle, be time barred if it is not brought within 12 months from the termination of the employee's contract.

End-of-service award

Upon termination other than for 'cause', an employee is ordinarily entitled to an end-of-service award equal to half a month's 'wage' for each year of employment for the first five years, and a full month's 'wage' for each subsequent year. 'Wage' is broadly defined to include not just base salary but also the value of every cash or in-kind allowance or benefit payable to the employee on a regular basis pursuant to his contract or as an 'acquired right', arising from the conduct of the parties. The calculation is based on the last wage being paid at the time of termination and is pro-rated for fractions of a year. The only elements of the 'wage' that can be excluded by contract from the end-of-service award calculation are, under Article 87 of the Labour Regulations, commissions 'and similar elements of the wage that by their nature are subject to increase and decrease'. For instance, housing allowances that are paid in cash or in-kind, air travel tickets granted to an employee, as well as the payment of bonuses that are made on a regular basis are ordinarily included as part of the wage.

If the employment relationship ends due to the employee's resignation, the end-of-service award is generally reduced or eliminated. If an employee resigns for 'cause'[1] under either a definite or indefinite term labour contract, he is entitled to full severance benefits. An employee who resigns prior to completing a definite term contract or within the first two years of an indefinite term contract would not ordinarily be entitled to an end-of-service award. If an employee under an indefinite term contract resigns, having served at least two years but less than five, he is entitled to one third of the normal end-of-service award. If he has served at least five years but less than 10, he is entitled to two thirds of the normal award. If he resigns after serving at least 10 years, he is entitled to the full end-of-service award.

Employees are also entitled upon termination to compensation for accrued holiday.

Organization of work penalties and rewards

Establishments employing 20 employees or more are required under the Labour Regulations to adopt a set of internal workplace rules that apply to the organization of the workplace and the penalties and rewards system implemented by the employer. The employer's

[1] 'Cause' in this case is defined by Article 84 of the Labour Law as the employer's breach of the labour contract, assault against the employee, unfair treatment of the employee, the employer's misrepresentation of the contract's terms at the time of employment and jeopardizing the employee's health or safety.

workplace rules must be approved and registered with the Ministry of Labour. The workplace rules would provide, *inter alia*, for the work hours, official holidays, annual leave, weekly days off, dates of wage payment, rules ensuring regular attendance and penalties for delay and absence. Procedures for admission into, and departure from, work sites are also specified, as well as procedures for periodic inspections and other matters warranted by work needs. The workplace rules would also contain the employer's benefits and rewards procedures for its employees, namely, governing penalties and rewards for offences listed in the workplace rules. The Ministry of Labour has issued its own 'standard' set of rules in relation to employee penalties and rewards that acts as a guideline. However, it is permissible for an entity to issue work rules that differ from the Ministry of Labour's standard and the ministry would exercise its discretion when accepting or commenting on an entity's proposed work rules.

No employer may apply a penalty in respect of an offence mentioned in its internal work rules nor may he apply more than one penalty or fines in excess of five days' pay for a single offence. The Labour Regulations require that notice to the employee of an offence must be issued within 15 days from the date the act of misconduct occurred and be provided with an opportunity to rebut any allegations of wrongdoing against him.

Protection against hazards

The Labour Regulations generally require an employer to take precautionary measures for the protection of employees from hazards and disease and to provide its employees with a safe work environment. Furthermore, the Labour Regulations provide that employers are also required to take all necessary precautions to guard against employees being exposed to dangerous moving parts of machines or being exposed to diseases and emissions caused by gas, smoke and any other exhausts emanating from the operation. Adequate fire prevention policies, as well as fire fighting equipment and contingency planning, are also mandatory for employers. The employer may not charge its employees or withhold from their remuneration the costs of providing for the protection of the health of its employees.

Healthcare

Medical coverage for occupational hazards is provided by virtue of the Social Insurance Regulations issued by Royal Decree M/33 dated 3/9/1421H (corresponding to 29/11/2000G), and the Implementing Rules of which were issued by Ministerial Resolution No. 128 dated 25/10/1421H (corresponding to 20/1/2001G) of the Minister of Labour.

Under these regulations, an employer must contribute two per cent of an employee's wage, calculated based on his basic salary and housing allowance, to the General Organization for Social Insurance (GOSI). GOSI is responsible for providing medical treatment and other benefits to an insured employee suffering from a work-related injury. In addition, employers must provide certain medical services, as discussed below.

The Labour Regulations provide that an employer that employs over 50 employees in a single location (or within a 15 kilometre radius), must employ a full-time nurse for the provision of first-aid services. The employer must also assign a physician to treat the employees and provide all the necessary medications. If an employer employs over 100 employees, he must, in addition to providing the foregoing services, provide the means for specialized medical treatment and surgical operations where necessary. All services are provided at no cost to the employees. The foregoing obligations do not apply to an employer who employs less than 50 employees, but the employer must, in this case, properly maintain a medical aid cabinet containing bandages, medicines and antiseptics in compliance with the relevant specifications.

An employer's obligations with respect to its non-Saudi employees were broadened by the Cooperative Health Insurance Regulations (CHIR), which were issued under Royal Decree No. M/10 dated 1/5/1420H (corresponding to 13/8/1999G) but implemented only in 2002G. The CHIR requires that an employer provide medical insurance coverage to its non-Saudi employees and their families. Failure to take out such insurance could result in an obligation to pay a penalty. An employee's family, as defined under the CHIR Implementing Rules enacted pursuant to Ministry of Health Resolution 23/460 dated 27/3/1423H (corresponding to 9/6/2002G), would include his wife, children up to the age of 18 and (unless covered by their own insurance) the employee's unmarried daughters, provided they are in possession of residence permits in Saudi Arabia.

The CHIR Implementing Rules provide that it shall be applied in stages and all employers would be required to be in compliance with CHIR within three years from the CHIR Implementing Rules' issuance.

Working hours

The Labour Regulations set out the general rules for determining daily working hours, the number of working days per week and official and ordinary holidays and annual leave. The Labour Regulations provide that a work day consists of eight work hours, exclusive of the intervals reserved for prayer, rest and meals. Subject to certain limited exceptions, an employee may not be required to work more than eight hours per day. For certain categories of employee or in certain industries where employees do not work continuously, such as seasonal establishments, hotels and restaurants, the employer may increase the working day to nine work hours but the total numbers of work hours may not exceed 48 hours per week. An employee may not be required to work more than five consecutive hours without an interval for rest, prayer and a meal. Each interval must consist of at least half an hour. Alternatively, the total interval time should be at least one and a half hours per day. An employee may not be required to remain at the place of work more than 11 hours in any one day.

The Labour Regulations further provide that Friday is the official weekly day of rest, with full pay. An employer may designate another day as the official rest day for some of his employees with the approval of the Labour Office.

Employees are entitled to additional pay for overtime hours in excess of normal hours of actual work. The overtime pay is one and a half times the hourly base salary with respect to overtime hours worked during a regular work day, and twice the hourly base salary with respect to overtime hours worked during the official rest day or official holidays. It is also worth noting that the Labour Regulations do not differentiate between employees having managerial status and others, so managers and other high-level employees may, in theory at least, claim overtime compensation.

Holidays and sick leave

The Labour Regulations provide that an employee would be entitled to 15 days of paid annual leave, provided he has completed a full year of service. If an employee completes 10 continuous years of service, he is entitled to 21 days of paid annual leave. It is worth noting that an employee may not renounce his right for paid annual leave and that an employee is entitled to receive pay for unused leave days *pro rata*. The employer has the right to determine the timing of the paid annual leave. An employer may also approve employee leave without pay for up to 10 days per year. Furthermore, an employee is entitled to three days of leave with full pay for marriage and one day with full pay in the event of childbirth or the death of his or her spouse, parent or child.

In addition to the paid annual leave, an employee is entitled to Saudi official holidays designated as such by the Minister of Labour, provided that such holidays do not exceed 10 days per year.

The Labour Regulations provide, with respect to employees employed by an employer who employs 20 or more employees, that such employees are, if their sickness is confirmed by an accredited physician, entitled to sick leave with full pay for the first 30 days and with three-quarters pay for the next 60 days, during the course of any one year, starting from the first day of employment. The Regulations are silent with respect to the sick leave entitlements of employees employed by an employer employing less than 20 employees, but as a practical matter the same benefits would apply.

Official holidays

Saudi Arabia provides official holidays and weekly days off that are observed under Islamic tenets. Friday, the weekly day for prayer, is the weekly day off, during which people rest and perform their prayers. Thursdays and Fridays are the weekend for government offices and some members of the private sector. The Muslim Hijrah calendar year, which is followed in Saudi Arabia, consists of 12 lunar months and the official calendar is approximately 10 to 11 days shorter than the Gregorian calendar year.

Office hours for government agencies and instrumentalities are typically from 7:30am and to 2:30pm from Saturday to Wednesday. The hours of the private sector vary a great deal depending on the industry, with many employers providing a break during midday to their employees. Industrial manufacturing operations may implement shift timings in accordance with their operational needs.

Government offices and schools and many private sector businesses close for the two official holidays each year of *Eid Al-Fitr* and *Eid Al-Adha*. Three days holiday are observed for *Eid Al-Fitr*, in which Muslims celebrate the ending of the holy fasting month of Ramadan. It should be remembered that during Ramadan a Muslim employee must abstain from ingesting anything orally (ie food, drink, cigarettes) between sunrise and sunset. Non-Muslims should be careful not to cause offence to Muslims and they should not eat, drink and smoke in public during the fasting hours, since penalties can be imposed on offenders who are apprehended. Four days of holiday are observed for the *Eid Al-Adha* holiday, which occurs approximately two months after *Eid Al-Fitr*. The *Eid Al-Adha* holiday marks the *Hajj* pilgrimage to Makkah by Muslims to perform their religious duty, often also visiting the Prophet's mosque in Madinah. Private sector employers may, of course, provide additional days off to coincide with the *Eid Al-Fitr* and *Eid Al-Adha* holidays, and Saudi government employees are typically granted days off in excess of those holidays.

As mentioned above, only Islamic holidays are officially observed in Saudi Arabia and other holidays, namely Christmas and Boxing Day, are not officially observed, although some employers provide their employees with those days off.

Additional services

Employers may be obliged under the Labour Regulations to provide additional services to their employees. For instance, employers with 50 or more employees should establish a thrift and savings scheme for its employees that is approved by the Ministry of Labour. The scheme would be optional to the employees and in practice is not always established. For employers having 500 or more employees, the Ministry of Labour is required to examine the nature and circumstances of the work and the number of employees, and then decide whether the employer may, at his own cost and expense, provide in whole or in part the following facilities:

- parks and playgrounds adjacent to the place of work and a library;
- facilities for the sale of food, clothing and other necessary commodities at moderate prices;
- school facilities for educating the children of employees in the event that no suitable schools are available in the region;
- mosques in the place of work.

The Ministry of Labour would be responsible for administering these requirements and the enforcement practices tend to vary.

In addition to the foregoing, employers are required to provide a means for transporting employees from their housing areas, or appropriate gathering points nearby, to their work sites and to provide for their return if their work locations cannot be accessed by ordinary, regular means of transportation. In respect of employees working in remote locations, such as employees in mines, quarries or oilfields, the employer is required to provide appropriate housing facilities, three meals a day, as well as medical, social and cultural services, in accordance with the guidelines determined by the Ministry of Labour.

Settlement of labour disputes

The Labour Regulations established Primary and Supreme Commissions for the Settlement of Disputes, which have jurisdiction over labour disputes. There is one Primary Commission for the Settlement of Disputes in each of the cities of Riyadh, Jeddah and Dammam. Each of the Primary Commissions is composed of three members, who must be 'experienced in legal matters'. The chairman of each Primary Commission must hold a degree in *Shari'a* and at least one of the other two members must hold a degree in either *Shari'a*, administrative or 'civil' law.

The Primary Commissions have exclusive and final jurisdiction over labour disputes relating to:

- claims not exceeding SR10,000;
- requests to stay the termination of employees; and
- the imposition of fines on employees.

The Primary Commissions also have jurisdiction in the first instance over labour disputes relating to:

- claims exceeding SR10,000;
- termination; and
- labour injuries regardless of the amount involved.

The Supreme Commission for the Settlement of Disputes is located in Riyadh. It is composed of five members, of whom three represent the Ministry of Labour, one the Ministry of Commerce and Industry, and one the Ministry of Petroleum and Mineral Resources. The members of the Supreme Commission must be 'experienced in legal matters'.

The Supreme Commission has exclusive jurisdiction to render final decisions on appeal of decisions rendered by the Primary Commissions in the first instance. The Supreme Commission is also competent to sanction violations of the Labour Regulations.

It is also worth mentioning that the Labour Regulations take the view that any attempt by employees (or by employers for that matter) to organize a collective bargaining mechanism (such as a union) or to otherwise devise an organized structure in order to 'pressure' the other side, would encroach on the jurisdiction of the authorities specifically set up for resolving labour disputes. Therefore, there is no collective bargaining mechanism under Saudi law. Similarly, there are no provisions regarding employee participation in management.

Social security

The Social Insurance Regulations, which were enacted pursuant to Royal Decree M/33 dated 3/9/1421H (corresponding to 29/11/2000G) and the Implementing Rules of which were issued by Ministerial Resolution No. 128 dated 25/10/1421H (corresponding to 20/1/2001G) of the Minister of Labour, provide a regime in relation to occupational hazards (industrial injuries and occupational diseases), and pensions (disability, old age and death). The occupational hazards branch, which applies to Saudi and non-Saudi employees, is concerned with temporary and permanent disabilities and injuries arising from workplace occupation hazards. The annuities/pensions branch, however, only applies to Saudi nationals, and foreign nationals are not authorized to participate in the scheme. The General Organization for Social Insurance (GOSI) is the body responsible for administering the schemes under the Social Insurance Regulations.

Employers must contribute an amount equal to two per cent of an employee's (whether Saudi or foreigner) wage to the occupational hazards branch of GOSI. No contribution is required from the employee. Employers must, in addition, contribute an amount equal to nine per cent of a Saudi employee's wage to the annuities/pensions branch of GOSI to fund the retirement benefit. A Saudi employee must, as of 1/4/2003G, contribute a further nine per cent of his salary to that branch. These contributions must be deducted by the employer and paid by the employer to GOSI.

Categories of employees that are exempt from the Social Insurance Regulations include state public officers, and members of the armed forces and the police. The Civil Service Regulations and the Retirement Regulations cover these categories of employee. Foreign employees in diplomatic missions are also exempt.

Employment of expatriates

The Labour Regulations provide that employment is a right of the Saudi national and may not be exercised by others unless certain conditions provided in the Regulations have been fulfilled. Pursuant to the Labour Regulations, the percentage of Saudi employees should not be less than 75 per cent of the overall workforce of any employer and their wages should not be less than 51 per cent of the total salaries value. This requirement, although in the Labour Regulations from its inception, was seldom enforced. In 1996, however, the Saudi government became more focused on the issue and Council of Ministers Decision No. 50 dated 21/4/1415H (corresponding to 27/9/1994G) was issued requiring all employers with 20 or more employees to increase the percentage of Saudis among their workforce by five per cent annually, and restricting certain activities (eg personnel recruitment positions, receptionist, government relations officer, security guard) to Saudi employees only. The applicable minimum percentage reached 30 per cent in 2001, and has not since been increased, although this must be checked periodically to confirm the level at any given time.

In light of the above, foreigners may not enter Saudi Arabia to work unless the approval of the Ministry of Labour has been obtained and a work permit has been issued in accordance with the procedures established by the Ministry of Labour. The employer acts as the employee's sponsor for residency purposes and would be responsible for obtaining both work and residence permits. The employer/sponsor would also assist in obtaining the necessary exit and re-entry visas that must be stamped into the employee's passport in order to enable him to depart and re-enter the Kingdom. For instance, the re-entry visa would be required to enable a non-Saudi employee to take holidays outside of Saudi Arabia. An exit-only visa would be issued to an employee intending to depart from the Kingdom due to completion of a contract, resignation or termination, mutual or otherwise. If an employee transfers to another employer/sponsor in the Kingdom, he is required to obtain the consent of his previous employer to complete the transfer.

Conclusion

As mentioned above, the Labour Regulations are considered to be reasonably well conceived and provide broad coverage of labour matters in Saudi Arabia. Labour relations between employers and employees in the Kingdom tend to be amicable, although the treatment of labour affairs differs considerably from the norms in Western jurisdictions. It is, therefore, always advisable to consult with legal counsel in Saudi Arabia in order to obtain specific advice on labour matters.

3.6

Intellectual Property Rights

Kamal Khalifa Mahjoub, Al Yaqoub Legal Advisers

Introduction

Various forms of intellectual property, as defined by the relevant international treaties and conventions, have been recognized in the Kingdom of Saudi Arabia. In this respect, a number of laws and regulations have been passed in Saudi Arabia to govern and lay down the rules that organize the recognition and enforcement of these forms of intellectual property within the local jurisdiction. They are as follows:

- Trade Marks Regulations governed by Royal Decree M/21 of AH 1423 (2003) replacing previous regulations governed by Royal Decree No. M/5 of AH 1404 (1984);
- Patents Regulations governed by Royal Decree No. M/38 of AH1409 (1989);
- Copyright Regulations governed by Royal Decree No. M/11 of AH 1410 (1989).

In addition, the Kingdom has ratified and acceded to some of the international treaties and conventions governing and regulating various forms of intellectual property. Furthermore, some positive additional steps have recently been taken by the Saudi Arabian authorities in order to make the local laws and regulations relating to these recognized forms more effective. These include the enforcement of certain measures such as prevention of the merchandizing of fake products and the use of misleading labelling. The aim is to accord more protection to lawful and registered owners as well as providing protection to local consumers against specious products or services that are illegally marketed under forged marks, designs, patents and copyrights.

Trade/service marks regulation

Introduction

The previously prevailing Saudi Trade Marks Regulations of 1404 H (1984) have now been abrogated and replaced by the now prevailing Trade Marks Regulations promulgated on 28.5.1423 H (2003) by the Royal Decree No M/21. (It should be noted that the term 'Regulations' is locally adopted by the Saudi authorities to denote any law, legislation, act, or statute. It is formally established that the term 'Law' refers only to the Supreme Law of Allah 'the *Qur'an*'. All other types of law in the Kingdom, which are basically statutes, are termed 'Regulations').

The new Regulations differ very slightly from the previous regulations. However, the substantive provisions remain basically the same, including the effects of registration of trade marks and the protection accorded to them; the licensing of use and the assignment or transfer of title; defence against infringement and the like; and the provisions dealing with procedures, especially the requirements of registration, the official processing of applications, objections and appeal, period of protection and the relevant fees.

In Saudi Arabia, trade mark protection is based on registration with the Ministry of Commerce. Both trade marks and service marks are recognized. The trade and service marks classification follows the International Classification of Goods and Services. (It should be noted that the registration of trade/service marks in the area of alcoholic drinks, Classes 32 and 33, would not be acceptable.)

The registration of trade/service marks is for a period of 10 years (based on the *Hejira* calendar), subject to renewal for similar periods with no grace period being allowed. If a trade/service mark is used continuously for two years from the date of registration, the owner has an incontestable right to use the mark for a 10-year period. Registration enables a Saudi licensee to enforce the ownership of a trade/service mark on behalf of its foreign owner. A trade/service mark can be assigned with or without the goodwill of the business. Priority claims can be registered on the basis of an application for registration in another country.

It is also possible to register control marks. These are trade/service marks used by producers of the same type of products who coordinate their production and sale.

It should be noted that if the application for registration of the mark meets all the conditions and requirements and is accepted by the Trade Mark Department of the Saudi Arabian Ministry of Commerce, then a notice of application must be published in the Saudi *Official Gazette* to notify the public at large. When such notice is published, any interested party has the right to object to the application being accepted. Such objection must be made within 90 days of the date of publication of the notice of registration in the *Official Gazette*. The objection must be filed on the basis that the acceptance of the mark is being granted in violation of any of the provisions of the Trade Marks Regulations or the associated Rules of Implementation. If no objection arises, the registration process will be completed within a few days following expiration of the 90-day notice period. Registration of the mark warrants protection for a period of 10 years and is renewable on application.

Modifications to trade mark regulations

The modifications made by the new Trade Mark Regulations of 1423 H (2003) are summarized as follows:

- The period for lodging an appeal to the Minister of Commerce against rejection of an application, is increased to 60 days instead of the 30 days prescribed by Section 14 of the repealed Regulations.
- A trade mark may be charged or attached with or without the commercial premises or the project on and for which the said trade mark is used. The repealed Regulations dictate that a charge on or attachment of the trade mark shall extend to the commercial premises or the project for which purpose the said trade mark is used (Sec. 35 of the repealed Regulations).
- The pecuniary penalties (fines) for offences relating to trade marks are stiffened, as follows:
  - for forging or counterfeiting a trade mark, dishonestly using a trade mark owned by others and for offering for sale or selling products with fake or counterfeit trade marks, the new Regulations impose a discretionary fine of no less than SR50,000 and no more than SR1 million, in addition, of course, to the discretionary penalty of imprisonment, the term of which remains unchanged (the fine under Section 49 of the previous Regulations was up to a maximum limit of SR50,000);
  - for particular uses of unregistered marks or for making any false inscription or print on the offender's marks or commercial documents to insinuate the registration thereof, the new

Regulations impose a fine of no less than SR20,000 and no more than SR250,000. The imprisonment term is unchanged (Sec. 50 of the repealed Regulations).

- The period of limitation of the action for Public Right in increased in the new Regulations from three years to five years (Sec. 53 of the repealed Regulations).
- The new Regulations vested the power of prosecution in criminal actions and the defence of the Public Right in the Bureau of Investigation and Public Prosecution. In the repealed Regulations it was left to the Minister of Commerce to decide in whom to vest this power (Sec. 60 of the repealed Regulations).

Requirements for trade/service marks

Registration
The present requirements for registration of a trade/service mark are as follows:

- copy of the Certificate of Incorporation or Registration of the applicant in the country of origin;
- Power of Attorney (or letter of authorization) duly certified by the relevant bodies and then authenticated by the Saudi Arabian Consulate;
- an undertaking by the applicant that the mark is an original one and is not a copy of any other mark owned by an entity other than the applicant;
- ten 6 × 8 cm photographs of the trade mark;
- a list of the goods and/or services for which the trade mark will be used;
- full particulars of the applicant, ie name, address, nationality, etc.

Renewal
The present requirements for renewal of a trade/service mark are as follows:

- Power of Attorney (or Letter of Authorization) duly certified by the relevant bodies and then authenticated by the Saudi Arabian Consulate;
- six 6 × 8 cm photographs of the trade/service mark;

- original Saudi Arabian Certificate of Registration of the mark.

Assignment
The present requirements for the assignment of a trade/service mark are as follows:

- Power of Attorney or Letter of Authorization (certified and authenticated by the Saudi Arabian Consulate as above);
- Deed of Assignment or Home Certificate of Assignment (also certified and authenticated by the Saudi Arabian Consulate as above);
- original Saudi Arabian Certificate of Registration of the trade/service mark;
- six 6 × 8 cm prints of the mark.

Change of name and address
The following requirements relate to a change of name and address:

- Power of Attorney or Letter of Authorization (certified and authenticated by the Saudi Arabian Consulate as above);
- Certificate of Change of Name (certified and authenticated by the Saudi Arabian Consulate as above);
- original Saudi Arabian Certificate of Registration of the trade/service mark;
- six 6 × 8 cm prints of the mark.

Fees for trade/service marks

Registration
The present fees for registration of a trade/service mark are as follows:

- SR1,000 application fee for each mark in each class;
- SR3,000 registration fee for each mark in each class;
- SR500 to SR1,000 for the publication notice in the *Official Gazette* (depending on the size of the notice).

Renewal
The present fee for renewal of a trade/service mark is SR3,000, which covers the renewal of registration of each mark in each class.

Assignment
The present fee for the assignment of a trade/service mark is SR1,000, which covers the assignment of each mark in each class.

Change of name and address
The present fee for changes to name and address in relation to a trade/service mark is SR1,000 in respect of each change or addition to each mark in each class.

Patents regulation

Introduction

The registration and protection of patents in the Kingdom of Saudi Arabia is governed by the provisions of Royal Decree No. M/38 of AH 1409 (1989). Under these regulations, patents denote only *patents of inventions*. New products, processes and improvements to existing products and processes may be patented provided they fulfil certain criteria regarding novelty, involve an incentive and have an industrial application that provides a practical solution to a defined technological problem.

The following categories may not be patented:

- methods for the treatment and medical diagnosis of human beings and animals (products used in connection with these methods may, however, be patented);
- varieties of plants, species of animals, biological processes used to produce plants or animals, with the exception of microbiological processes and products;
- methods of doing business, engaging in purely mental activities or playing games;
- discoveries, scientific theories and mathematical formulae.

Applications for patents must be submitted to King Abdulaziz City for Science and Technology (KACST) and must include the name and other information relating to the applicant or owner, the name of the inventor if the applicant is not the inventor and the name of the local agent if the applicant is not a resident of the Kingdom of Saudi Arabia. The application must also contain a comprehensive description of the patent and particulars of the protection requested.

Application fees ranging from SR200 to SR8,000 are payable. Patents are valid for 15 years from the date on which they were granted. A five-year extension may be granted provided that an application is made during the last year of the original term and at least 60 days before the patent expires. Patents must be exploited on a full industrial scale within two years from the date of grant.

The Patents Regulations also provide for the licensing of patents. Licenses must be in writing, signed by both parties, authenticated and registered with KACST. If a patent is not used in an industrial application within two years of being issued, a licence to use the patent can be granted to any person who can show that the invention can be utilized or exploited.

Registration requirements for patents

KACST is the local entity that is officially responsible for and authorized to accept registration of patent rights inside the Kingdom of Saudi Arabia.

To register a patent with KACST, the applicant should provide the following information and documents:

- Power of Attorney (or Letter of Authorization) by the applicant, duly certified by the relevant bodies and then authenticated by the Saudi Arabian Consulate;
- Deed of Assignment from the inventor to the applicant (certified and authenticated by the Saudi Arabian Consulate as above);
- special KACST forms, to be filled out locally in Arabic and signed and stamped by the applicant;
- name, residence and profession of the patent inventor and of the applicant who submits the registration application on behalf of the inventor;
- certificate of registration evidencing that the said patent is owned by and registered in the name of the inventor at its country of origin – this certificate must be certified by the local authorities and then authenticated by the Saudi Arabian consulate as above.

Copies of the complete specification in both English and Arabic must be prepared according to the following order of information:

- background to the invention;
- summary description of the invention;
- summary description of the drawings;

- detailed description of the invention;
- claims for the invention.

Copies of the abstract in English and Arabic not exceeding one page should be provided. This should be accompanied by any drawings that would provide further elaboration on the invention and on its implementation. Also required are:

- full particulars regarding any foreign patent and/or patent application;
- full particulars of the inventor(s);
- full particulars of the of the applicant.

Patent registration fees

The registration fees to be paid to KACST where the owner of the patent is an individual are as follows:

- SR400 application fee;
- SR500 for publication and registration;
- SR400 as an annual fee through the protection term (15 years renewable for five years);
- SR100 for the certificate of registration;
- SR50 for any additional copy of the certificate of registration.

Copyright regulation

Copyright protection in the Kingdom of Saudi Arabia is governed by the Copyright Regulations No. M/11 of AH 1410 (December 1989), and are enforced by the Ministry of Information. Under these regulations, original works belonging to Saudis are accorded protection if they are published, displayed or performed for the first time, whether inside or outside Saudi Arabia. Original works belonging to foreigners are accorded protection under the regulations only if they are published, displayed or performed for the first time inside Saudi Arabia. The protection covers artistic, literary and musical works. The protection also extends to include computer software.

In 2005, new and more comprehensive Copyrights Regulations have been passed by the Legislature (The Consultative Council), but these have yet to receive Royal approval.

Designs regulation

The Kingdom of Saudi Arabia has not yet issued legislation that governs the protection of industrial designs. Therefore, the only available method of protection of such designs is through publication of a cautionary notice in the Saudi *Official Gazette*. In this regard, it has to be noted that publication in the *Official Gazette* does not yield the same effects as those to be acquired by registration. In other words, the act of publication *per se* does constitute conclusive evidence of ownership of the published design, but it is regarded merely as prima facie evidence of ownership that gives the publishing owner the right to sue against any infringement of the design. Considering the local business environment and in order to attain a higher degree of publicity, it is recommended that any such cautionary notice is published in both the Arabic and English versions.

Requirements for cautionary notice

The present requirements in relation to publication of a cautionary notice for the protection of designs are as follows:

- title of the design;
- summary description of the design;
- full particulars of the applicant;
- full particulars of home application and/or any foreign registration.

3.7

Joint Venture Formation

Anthony Shoult, ASA Consulting[1]

Introduction

Saudi Arabia is the giant of the six countries of the Arabian Gulf. It is the Arab world's largest economy, the nominal GDP of which is now over twice the combined total of its nearest two rivals. Saudi Arabia, like the other Gulf Cooperation Council (GCC) countries, Kuwait, the United Arab Emirates, Qatar, Oman and Bahrain, has, since 2002, entered upon a new and unprecedented phase of prosperity and national development, financed by the windfall of a huge surge in the prices of both oil and gas. It has benefited too from the fact that, with the removal of Saddam Hussein's regime in Iraq and the moderation in Iran's revolutionary zeal, it need no longer feel under physical threat from powerful neighbours. While there are certainly new challenges to the stability and security of the country, these are domestic in character and should be managed without serious upheaval.

The buoyancy of Saudi Arabia's present economic performance can be seen in Table 3.7.1. This has been reinforced by economic cooperation within the GCC, including the introduction of a unified external tariff, the advancement of plans for a single currency and a regional power grid. With policies over recent years designed to diversify production away from hydrocarbons, Saudi Arabia can, today, point to a rapidly growing industrial sector, which although concentrated upon oil products and petrochemicals, now encompasses aluminium products, electronics, domestic equipment, foodstuffs and, most

---

[1] Sources of information include Arab-British Chamber of Commerce, Saudi Arabian General Investment Authority (SAGIA), Graham Flack Bilingual Occupational Testing and Guidance Consultancy and Ernst & Young.

recently, mineral extraction. Service industries are also becoming established on a broad front.

The Saudi private sector has made major advances in recent years and contributed nearly half of national GDP in 2004. This now includes investment in national infrastructure projects such as power, water and transport. This is, today, being funded with domestic capital, although given the huge scale of the investment programmes, there remains a strong demand for financing and technology from overseas.

Table 3.7.1 Saudi Arabian economic performance indicators, 2001 and 2003 (SR billion)

	2001	2003	Change (%)
GDP in market prices	SR686.3 billion	SR804.2 billion	+17.2
Non-oil sector share of GDP	SR430.9 billion	SR494.6 billion	+14.8
Government revenue	SR228.2 billion	SR295.0 billion	+29.3
Government expenditure	SR255.0 billion	SR250.0 billion	-1.98
Population (estimated)	22.8 million	24.2 million	+6.14
Balance of trade	SR148.02 billion	SR230.77 billion	+55.90
Oil production	7.89mb/d	8.41mb/d	+6.61
Average price per barrel	US$22.81	US$26.78	+17.4
Tadawul All Share Index (TASI)#	2,430	4,438	+82.63

February 1985 = 1,000 (formerly known as the NCFEI Index)

Source: Arab-British Chamber of Commerce

Choice of joint venture location

International organizations wishing to establish a joint venture in the Gulf will wish to consider the merits of Saudi Arabia in comparison with other locations in neighbouring GCC states.

The case for Saudi Arabia is underpinned by Saudi oil production. This is running at its highest level since the crisis of the Gulf War, at 9.5 mb/d, producing revenues in excess of US$100 billion and a forecast growth in real GDP in 2005 of over six per cent.

Saudi Arabia, with its rapidly growing population, is the dominant economy in the Gulf region (see Table 3.7.2). Population has increased from less than five million in 1960 to the current estimated level of

23 million. According to United Nations' projections, the Saudi population can be expected to grow to over 45 million by 2030.

The Saudi economy is being well managed and structural reforms designed to facilitate growth and new investment continue to take shape, albeit at a cautious pace. Local business confidence is high and there is great liquidity in the market with corporate profits, particularly in the banking and petrochemical sectors, currently at record levels.

In 2005, new project work, estimated to total some US$1.3 trillion over the next two decades, includes power and water, minerals, telecommunications and transport, including the world's largest railway construction programme. There are huge plans for natural gas development, with Saudi Aramco's annual capital expenditure estimated at some US$34 billion. There are also ambitious plans to build a complete new industrial city on the Gulf at Ras al Zor, north of Al Jubail.

Table 3.7.2 Saudi Arabia and other Gulf investment locations

	Population '000	GDP $bn	Containers '000 TEU	Factories	Oil '000b/d
Abu Dhabi	950	24	250	290	1,775
Dubai	675	10	4,200	45	310
Sharjah	400	3	650	53	0
Saudi Arabia	*23,000*	*140*	*1,800*	*3,120*	*8,400*

Attracting foreign technology to Saudi Arabia

Provision in Saudi Arabia's regulations for the establishment of 'joint ventures' between national and foreign firms has existed since the 1960s, but, outside the oil sector, the country probably had little to attract the foreign investor. In the late 1970s, therefore, the Saudi Arabian government decided to adopt a 'carrot and stick' strategy to induce foreign enterprises to 'transfer technology' into the national economy.

The Foreign Capital Investment Regulation (FCIR) issued in 1979, was a 'carrot' measure designed to attract foreign companies to form partnerships with, primarily, the Saudi private sector. The aim was to establish industrial, agricultural and maintenance projects that would help to introduce new and profitable technologies into the Kingdom's economy, reduce its dependence on oil exploration and development, and provide the growing national labour force with new employment opportunities. In 1983, the government produced a 'stick' in that foreign contractors engaged on public sector projects were obliged to subcontract 30 per cent of the works involved to Saudi Arabian companies.

The new Foreign Investment Law (FIL) of 2000 provides a range of new incentives to overseas technology companies wishing to establish business ventures in Saudi Arabia. As part of this new approach, it is no longer mandatory to have Saudi participation to take advantage of the range of financial incentives available. (See also Chapter 2.3: The Foreign Investment Regime.)

Under the FIL of 2000, 100 per cent foreign ownership of projects and the associated real estate is permitted, together with advantages such as eligibility for soft loans from the Saudi Industrial Development Fund (SIDF). Also under the FIL, the tax ceiling for corporate tax on the foreign investor's share of profits has been reduced from 45 to 20 per cent. However, the foreign partner is no longer granted a 10-year 'tax holiday' (exemption from corporate tax on their share of the profits for 10 years) as under the provisions of the previous FCIR.

A key advantage is the availability of project funding on favourable terms from the SIDF. This is an experienced credit institution controlled by the Ministry of Industry and Electricity, which may provide a low cost loan for up to 50 per cent of the capital of an industrial enterprise, although it does not normally make such loans to 'maintenance' or non-industrial enterprises. The Saudi Arabian Agricultural Bank (SAAB), controlled by the Ministry of Agriculture and Water, plays a similar role in relation to agricultural projects.

Site rentals in the industrial estates established outside the major cities and towns are low, in some cases even nominal, while water, electricity and other utilities in these areas are supplied at subsidized rates.

Up to 2001, the Saudi Arabian Investment Authority (SAGIA) estimated that over 470 joint venture factories involving foreign participation had been established in Saudi Arabia, with a combined value of SR132.4 billion. This represents some 55 per cent in value terms of all factories established at that time (see Table 3.7.3).

Table 3.7.3 Joint venture projects in Saudi Arabia by sector up to 2001 (SR million)

Industry sector	Number of joint venture factories	Value of joint venture factories	Average factory value
Food and beverages	37	3,057	82.6
Textiles and clothing	19	463	24.4
Wood products	19	324	17.1
Paper products	20	1,542	77.1
Petroleum and chemicals	133	113,416	852.8
Construction materials	58	6,448	111.2
Basic metals	0	0	0
Machinery and equipment	181	6,755	37.3
Other manufacturing	8	433	54.1
Transport and storage	0	0	0
Total joint ventures:	*475*	*132,478*	*278.9*
Total non-joint ventures:	*2,943*	*107,601*	*36.6*
Total factories:	*3,418*	*240,079*	*70.2*

Source: Saudi Arabian General Investment Authority (SAGIA)

Relevant regulations and laws concerning foreign investment

Although Saudi Arabia has a capitalist economy, its society is culturally averse to ambiguity or uncertainty. This propensity probably accounts for the system of licences and permissions that the foreign investor has to negotiate before he can establish a business in the Kingdom. However, although the procedures can be time-consuming, the rules governing them are certainly not complex and require relatively little in the way of specialist interpretation. Moreover, the SAGIA, set up in 2000, has established a number of Investment Promotion Centres located in the main cities of the Kingdom to provide a 'one stop shop' to assist the foreign investor in overcoming any bureaucratic hurdles.

Regulations in Saudi Arabia mean laws elsewhere. The only Law in Saudi Arabia is the *Shari'a*, of which the two primary sources are the *Qur'an* (the Word of God as revealed to the Prophet Muhammad) and the *Sunnah* (which embodies the *Ahadith*, ie the sayings and actions of the Prophet). All regulations are drafted and construed in line with these two sources.

The FIL delegates to the Ministry of Industry and Electricity (MIE) the responsibility of scrutinizing the applications of foreign organizations to establish enterprises in the Kingdom and of issuing a 'licence' – a ministerial resolution – to do so where the Kingdom's criteria are met. Since 2000, the evaluating body is SAGIA, chaired by a deputy minister of the MIE and with members drawn from the MIE itself and other agencies concerned with national economic development. The Governor of SAGIA reports directly to the President of the Supreme Economic Council.

The regulation of companies operating in Saudi Arabia

The Companies Regulation

This specifies the form that Saudi Arabian companies must take and the manner in which their affairs are to be run. The Ministry of Commerce is responsible for ensuring that companies meet its provisions.

The Company Income Tax Regulations

The Zakat and Income Tax Department of the Ministry of Finance and National Economy applies these provisions. Zakat, in origin a charitable donation and one of the principal obligations of Islam, is levied on the income only of the Saudi partners in a joint venture enterprise. Corporate income tax is levied on the profits only of the foreign partners.

The new investment and tax regulations issued in April 2000 eliminated tax holidays for new foreign investment, irrespective of the proportion of Saudi participation in the new project (joint venture company). However, five- and 10-year tax holidays for foreign investors existing at April 2000 continue to be honoured through to their expiry dates. Accordingly, in the absence of a specific tax exemption (very rare and generally requiring a Royal Decree), all new foreign investment is subject to the normal corporate tax at 20 per cent, based on the foreign investor's share of the joint venture company's tax adjusted net profit.

The Chambers of Commerce Regulations

There are 18 chambers of commerce and industry established in the main cities and towns. Each is financed by compulsory subscription from the companies in its area. The chambers act as the interface between the government and the private sector, provide services to business, provide businessmen with a forum in which to air common concerns, and authenticate official submissions, returns, and other documents.

The Labour and Workmen Regulation

The Labour and Workmen Regulations, based on an International Labour Organization model, govern employment conditions and relations between employer and employed. Labour unions do not exist, and strikes are illegal. A system of labour dispute settlement tribunals under the aegis of the Ministry of Labour and Social Affairs exists to arbitrate in disputes between employers and employees. Tribunals are inclined to favour the employee over the employer, to counterbalance the prohibition on unions and strikes.

Also, the Regulation has, for many years, formally required that Saudi Arabian citizens comprise 75 per cent of the workforce of every company and establishment and that 50 per cent of its wage bill be for the benefit of its Saudi workers. However, the Minister of Labour and Social Affairs has the discretion to vary these proportions where nationals with the requisite expertise or skills are not available. In the past, this discretion has been quite freely exercised in the interest of projects held to serve the Kingdom's economic development. Foreign workers, consequently, constitute at least half of the private sector workforce and, indeed, a substantial proportion of the public sector. In recent years, however, the numbers of young Saudis reaching working age have raised the prospect of widespread national unemployment and the social instability to which such a phenomenon might give rise. The government has passed legislation designed to head off a contingency of this sort. Every company and establishment is now obliged to increase the proportion of Saudis in its workforce by five per cent per year. Although there are exceptions, companies who fail to 'Saudiize' their labour force at an appropriate rate are increasingly finding that the Ministry of Labour's offices reject their applications to bring in foreign workers.

Foreign Labour Import (Istiàqdam) Regulations

The Ministry of Labour and Social Affairs and the Aliens Control branch of the Ministry of Interior cooperate over the implementation of regulations issued from time to time governing the grant of work permits and resident status to foreign workers.

Forms of enterprise

The principal types of entity in the Kingdom in which a foreign organization may participate are summarized as follows.

The joint venture

The type of entity in which foreign companies had been accustomed to invest under the FCIR was, until 2000, the mixed-capital (ie Saudi and foreign) limited liability partnership or company, popularly termed (in English) a 'joint venture'. This is a closely held affair governed by a board of partners (investors or their representatives) that usually delegated certain powers to a committee or board of registered managers or a general manager. Saudis had to own over half the shares if the venture was to qualify for a FCIR licence and a tax holiday. Since the new FCIR of 2000, it is no longer mandatory to have Saudi participation to take advantage of the range of financial incentives granted by the FCIR.

The FCIR permits the foreign investor to invest in any investment activity in the Kingdom, on a permanent or temporary basis, except for activities specifically excluded by SAGIA.

Liaison offices

The Ministry of Commerce may also permit foreign public sector contractors to establish a 'liaison office', under licence from SAGIA, to coordinate their activities in the Kingdom and to facilitate communications with their head office abroad. The liaison office is prohibited from engaging in any commercial activity outside the scope of the contract.

Technical and scientific services offices

Companies that have sold products into the Kingdom through commercial agents, whether into the public or private sector, may be licensed by the Ministry of Commerce to set up a technical and scientific services office (TSSO). Foreign specialists may staff these to provide advice and assistance to commercial agents or clients who have bought their companies' products. Like the public sector contractor's liaison office, the technical and scientific services office is prohibited from commercial activity.

Permanent and temporary branches

These entities lie outside the purview of the FCIR and attract none of the associated incentives. The permanent branch is a type of enterprise that does not involve partnership with a Saudi citizen or organization. Hitherto, permission to set up permanent branches has generally been confined to foreign companies with unique or rare expertise, of which the Kingdom stands in real need. There are, consequently, relatively few of them. Although the permanent branch is constitutionally much like a Saudi company, albeit without a Saudi partner, the commercial activities in which it can engage may be circumscribed to a degree that gives it little commercial advantage over a liaison or technical and scientific office. Under the new FCIR, foreign contractors operating on government contracts can set up a temporary branch and operate under a temporary licence from SAGIA.

Assistance under the economic offset programmes

A foreign investor will wish to consider whether any of the 'economic offset' programmes that have been established by foreign governments or agencies over the past 15 years or so might be of assistance to them in establishing a joint venture enterprise in Saudi Arabia.

Background to offset

In the early 1980s, the Saudi government introduced a system whereby defence equipment or services supply contractors would be obliged to reinvest a proportion of the value of the goods or services supplied to the Kingdom in the form of 'commercially viable' businesses in partnership with its private sector.

The initial economic offset scheme was signed in 1984 in connection with the US$2 billion Peace Shield I Command and Control Programme for the supply of an air-defence system, including ground support for airborne warning and control systems (AWACS) aircraft. A US consortium, led by the Boeing Company and including General Electric (GE), AT&T (now Lucent Technologies) and Westinghouse Electric Corporation, was required to reinvest 35 per cent of the technical value of the contract in economically useful and viable joint ventures in the field of aircraft repair, overhaul and logistics, to form a series of viable private companies.

The second scheme arose out of the supply of aircraft, weapons and other equipment between 1986 and 1992 under what became known as the Al-Yamamah Project. The British government undertook to establish an economic offset programme in the Kingdom whereby the British private sector would be encouraged to invest in commercially viable projects in partnership with the Saudi private sector. The investment target was set at 25 per cent of the value of the hardware supplied under the Al-Yamamah Project. This programme has resulted in a number of successful projects, including the Jeddah sugar refinery involving Tate & Lyle, which has, in 10 years, expanded to become the second largest in the world. The Al Yamamah Economic Offset Programme has now been expanded to include non-British investors.

The third programme, the Al-Sawari Economic Offset Programme, was linked to the US$3.5 billion sales by Thomson-CSF of France of frigates and associated weapons systems to the Royal Saudi Naval Forces. The Franco–Saudi agreement that covers it requires contractors 'benefiting' from (ie being paid for) the supply of ships or their equipment to invest some 35 per cent of the price of the hardware involved in viable joint ventures.

The first non-military offset agreement was entered into in 1994. This was in connection with a US$6 billion expansion of the Saudi telecommunications network, with AT&T International as the main contractor.

Offset and the prospective investor in the Kingdom

Investing under the economic offset programmes offers the independent foreign investor a number of advantages. The intergovernmental agreements provide for foreign shareholdings in ventures formed under the offset programmes to equal or exceed those of the Saudi partners and still to attract the full range of investment incentives. Moreover, the Saudi Economic Offset Office, the British and French governments and BAe Systems retain advisers that are most willing to give advice and help to prospective investors, particularly over the choice of suitable partners for their enterprises.

BAe Systems operates a scheme that provides non-recourse loans to assist in offsetting risk associated with equity investment by the overseas technology partner. There is always the possibility, too, that one of the 'beneficiary' companies of the defence supply projects might itself be willing to invest in a venture that is related to its business objectives and is seen to have good prospects.

On the downside, the programmes add a further layer of bureaucracy – that of the Saudi–British or Saudi–French economic offset committees – to an already bureaucratic system.

Preliminaries in business venture formation

Preparatory work

The official procedures involved in forming a business venture take, on average, about six months to complete. However, it is unwise to assume that this is the real time-scale. The prospective foreign investor and then his Saudi partner have a fair amount of preparatory work to do before they will be in a position to make a formal application for licensing. From first discussions to establishment of a substantial venture may take 18 months to two years, and three years is not uncommon. Some ventures involving multiple Saudi and foreign partners have taken as long as six years to incorporate officially.

The prospective foreign partner's first consideration must be the advantage to the business that setting up a joint venture in Saudi Arabia will bring. The second issue is what it is about the business that will appeal to a Saudi Arabian partner, to the SAGIA, and to the Saudi Industrial Development Fund (SIDF).

Avoiding no-go areas

In February 2001, the Supreme Economic Council (SEC) announced the approval of a list of economic sectors to which the new foreign investment regulations will not apply. The list covers a number of important sectors, namely oil exploration and production, military-related business, air and land transportation and retail and wholesale distribution (see Table 3.7.4).

Foreign investment is not completely prohibited in the listed sectors, but existing or separate regulations will apply and foreign companies may not make 100 per cent foreign owned investment otherwise permitted by the new law. Consistent with future membership of the WTO, the Saudi government is seeking to reduce the number of sectors where foreign investment is not allowed. In particular, SAGIA recently successfully promoted the removal of general telecommunications, education and insurance services from the exclusion list.

In general, importation of goods and their distribution in the Kingdom and trading are the prerogatives of Saudi citizens and wholly Saudi-owned companies and establishments, as are service and commercial agencies. A foreign partner who has already invested in a joint venture working in a particular field or activity is not permitted to invest – at least not while the original venture exists – in another in the same or similar fields.

Table 3.7.4 Saudi Arabia's exclusion list

Industry	
1.	Oil exploration, drilling and production
2.	Manufacture of military equipment, devices and uniforms
3.	Manufacture of civilian explosives
Services	
4.	Military catering services
5.	Security and detective services
6.	Real estate in Makkah and Madinah
7.	Tourism services related to the pilgrimages
8.	Real estate brokerage
9.	Recruitment and employment services
10.	Printing and publishing
11.	Audio-visual services
12.	Distribution services (wholesale and retail trade) including pharmaceuticals and medical goods
13.	Land and air transportation
14.	Satellite transmission services
15.	Specified telecommunications services
16.	Space projects
17.	Services provided by midwives, nurses, natural therapists and paramedics
18.	Blood banks, poison centres and quarantine facilities
19.	Fisheries

Source: Saudi Arabian Investment Authority (SAGIA) 2003

Understanding Saudi Arabian concerns

The Saudis are primarily interested in the ideas, technology and knowledge of foreign markets that a foreign organization will bring to a Saudi Arabian enterprise. SAGIA is looking for projects that clearly contribute to the economic development of the Kingdom. Until a few years ago, it was conventionally accepted that capital intensive projects would be favoured over those that were labour intensive, because of the relative scarcity of skilled Saudi labour.

Awareness of the rate at which young Saudis are reaching working age is causing this attitude to be modified to some extent: ventures that hold out a real prospect of employing Saudis in appropriate and gainful ways also have a reasonable prospect of being sanctioned. However, a venture that involves importing large numbers of foreigners, especially tradesmen and operatives, is unlikely to find favour.

Locating suitable business partners

In general, having a reliable Saudi Arabian partner willing to play his full part is essential to the success of any venture. Initial contacts are not usually difficult to make. In the Kingdom itself, commercial attachés and chambers of commerce and industry can usually effect introductions, and taking part in 'inward business missions' can put the prospective foreign partner in touch with suitable Saudi businessmen. However, finding the Saudi partner willing to take the time to understand the nature of a proposed venture, the risks involved as well as the prospective rewards, is not quite so easy.

Understanding Saudi business culture

An important section of the influential business community comprises families with diverse business interests. While the acumen of members of such family groups is not be doubted, they may be subject to numerous approaches from aspirant foreign partners and their attention can sometimes be hard to retain. For example, one particular international organization that was making a critical and costly demonstration of a product around which it had proposed to establish a joint venture, was inconvenienced to find that the prospective partner had suddenly chosen to take a holiday abroad over the period in question.

Moreover, it is not unknown for a new venture that has been established with ostensibly interested partners drawn from a leading business group to find itself without effective support. Indeed, if its performance has failed quickly to reach the Saudi partners' expectations, it may even find itself treated as a distressed department of their own establishment.

Establishing a rapport and mutual understanding

Saudis set considerable store by personal relationships in business as elsewhere and such relationships are rarely forged overnight. Many of the more successful ventures have their roots in successful commercial agency relationships. The parties have had time to size each other up and to understand and accommodate each other's business approach. Where there is no pre-existing relationship of this sort, then a good deal of time may need to be spent in building up a rapport with the prospective partner, seeking to inform him of the nature of the venture, and reaching a sympathetic understanding of his inclinations, strengths and weaknesses.

At this stage, the foreign investor may wish to appoint a project manager who is committed to concentrate more or less exclusively upon developing a relationship with the Saudi partner. He should be equipped with a power of attorney, empowered to negotiate within appropriate limits with the prospective partner, and represent the foreign partner before the Saudi Arabian authorities.

Entering into shareholder agreements

Once the two parties have reached a firm understanding of what they propose to do, then the next step should be to set down a shareholders' agreement. Agreements of this sort should be in plain Arabic and English setting out the duties, obligations and rights of each party in relation to the venture.

Long, complex, or ambiguous preliminary memoranda of understanding, shareholders' agreements, or, later, articles of association will not only make negotiations with partners difficult and lengthy, they also run the risk of being ignored by Saudi arbitration agencies if a serious dispute arises. The temptation to have an agreement only in English or in the foreign partner's first language should also be resisted. The official language of Saudi Arabia is Arabic and a document only in a foreign language may be dismissed as invalid by official bodies.

Taking timely legal advice

The prospective foreign investor will need to take timely legal advice. *Shari'a* lawyers do exist in the Kingdom, but they are not, in general, concerned with commercial matters. The usual source of legal advice (really advice over regulations and procedures) is a legal consultant. It is probable that the foreign investor's Saudi partner will already have retained, or have access to, one.

Commercial law in Saudi Arabia is not particularly complex; indeed, the regulations are drafted so that lay people can easily interpret them. Legal consultants do not really have the same standing in Saudi Arabia as they do elsewhere. Before the judiciary and the courts, which are religious in character, they carry no greater weight than an ordinary citizen or resident. They generally have the advantage, however, of experience of the processes of venture formation and drafting the necessary documents. The chambers of commerce and industry retain legal consultants who are quite prepared to give preliminary or general legal advice and even exemplar documents as models for the more common forms of commercial agreement. In the interest of commercial confidentiality, however, the foreign investor would be advised to retain his own legal consultant.

Many legal consultancies in the Kingdom are professional partnerships between international and local legal firms. Only the Saudi principals are permitted to appear before the courts; the 'international' lawyers simply act as advisers, and charges are comparable with those prevailing in Europe. The foreign investor's corporate legal department or representative should act in support of the nominated project manager, who is in the best position to monitor and direct the local legal consultant's efforts at first hand.

Securing approval in principle

Once the partners have agreed upon the nature of the venture, it is for the Saudi partner, theoretically, to ask the Governor of SAGIA for the MIE's approval 'in principle' to the venture and its objectives. This initial letter is no formality, since if there is no approval in principle, there is no point in proceeding further. It needs, therefore, to be the result of a cooperative effort between the Saudi and the foreign partner and truly to reflect their joint intentions.

Carrying out a feasibility study

Once the MIE's preliminary approval has been secured, the partners will then need to carry out a detailed feasibility study to submit with their formal application for their venture to be licensed by SAGIA. Meeting the requirements set out in the formal application form for licensing can be demanding. However modest the venture, a convincing and detailed feasibility study is essential.

The foreign partner, who is, in effect, the party that is being licensed, has to produce proof, officially authenticated by the 'relevant authorities' in his own country, that he has the necessary technology and experience in the field in which he is proposing to invest. In support of this, he has to detail the relevant projects that he has executed outside (and, if applicable, inside) the Kingdom, along with an inventory of relevant material and facilities that he owns and the number and grade of appropriately qualified staff that he employs. His board of management has to have formally resolved upon participation in the venture. He has to include a formal undertaking to the Saudi authorities and to his prospective partner that he will provide all the technical and administrative support that the venture requires.

A number of professional organizations exist to help in the research for and preparation of feasibility studies. However, at the feasibility study stage, one issue that needs particular attention is staffing the venture. The Minister of Labour and Social Affairs has, in the past, exercised discretion to vary the proportions of Saudi and foreign staff in company workforces; pressure to 'Saudiize' means that his representatives will be less and less likely to do so in the future. If the venture is likely to need foreign specialists in any number, then, at the feasibility study stage, it is worth establishing whether or not the foreign investor will be able to secure the necessary work permits and residence visas for them. Moreover, in view of the obligation to increase the Saudi Arabian proportion of the workforce by five per cent a year, the foreign investor will need to include planning provision for training Saudis to take over from expatriates in an effective fashion and to fill new jobs that may be needed.

Procedures for joint venture formation

Submission to SAGIA

SAGIA will study the completed application for licensing and make its recommendations to the Minister of Industry and Electricity. While SAGIA is considering the application, the prospective partners can expect to have to answer queries and incorporate any adjustments that SAGIA requires or suggests. However, provided that SAGIA's recommendations are favourable, the Minister will sign a resolution approving the grant of a foreign capital investment licence. The terms of the licence form the basis for the joint venture's articles of association.

Company 'objects' or 'purposes'

A striking difference between articles of association drawn up under, say, the English Companies' Acts and those drawn up under their Saudi Arabian equivalents lies in the statement of the venture's 'purposes'. In England, the statement can purport to permit the company to engage in the widest range of activities conceivable. In Saudi Arabia, the purposes statements have to be much more specifically drafted. The venture's freedom of action is consequently – formally at least – fairly closely circumscribed.

Approval of articles of association

The Ministry of Commerce needs to approve the venture's articles of association before they are notarized and published in the *Umm al Qura*, the official state gazette.

Notarization

Once the Ministry of Commerce has assented to the articles of association, the partners or their authorized representatives need to make an appointment with a Notary Public before whom they sign the articles in token of the legally binding agreement that they have made. This takes about a month to arrange, but it is not wise to start the arrangements until the Ministry of Commerce has actually approved the articles. The partners' representatives should insist on examining any papers that their legal consultant (who will normally accompany them to the Notary Public) proposes to produce for notarization purposes, to ensure that all details are actually correct.

Publication

The legal consultant can usually be trusted to arrange for an extract from the articles of association to be published in the *Umm al Qura*. At this stage, the important issue is not the actual publication, which may not take place for some months, but securing an official receipt from the *Umm al Qura* for submission, along with the application to have the venture entered in the commercial register.

Deposit of capital

The partners need to arrange for the venture's capital to be deposited and secure a certificate from the bank confirming that they have done so.

Commercial registration

The final step is to arrange for the venture to be entered in the commercial register. The application should contain the details of each office to be registered, the name of the manager responsible for each, and a precise description of the activities to be undertaken. It should enclose proof that the articles of association have been accepted for official promulgation and that the venture's capital has been deposited with a Saudi Arabian bank.

Only when it has been entered in the commercial register can a business legally begin operations.

Registration with the Department of Zakat and Income Tax

The venture must register with the Department of Zakat and Income Tax (DZIT) in order to obtain a file number for the business and a 'certificate of commencement'. A venture needs a certificate of commencement before it can bid for government contracts, obtain release of progress payments on contracts, or – most importantly – apply for work permits and residency visas for essential foreign staff.

Application for SIDF financing

Once all the licensing and commercial registration formalities have been completed, the partners in an industrial venture may apply to the SIDF for a soft loan. It is here that a careful and detailed feasibility study will be of the greatest value to them. SIDF assessors are experienced and cautious, but not unprepared to put their expertise at the disposal of borrowers. However, they will only recommend that a loan be made if the business prospects of the venture are demonstrably favourable.

Conclusion

It is clear that investing in Saudi Arabia can bring considerable rewards to the foreign company in a line of business that the Kingdom feels that it needs. However, the prudent investor must be prepared to spend time in reconnaissance, understanding the internal market and reaching a sympathetic understanding of the aspirations of the government and the potential partner. The key qualities that the intending foreign investor needs are patience, persuasiveness and a capacity for detailed, realistic planning allied to a determination, where a Saudi Arabian partner is involved, to ensure that the venture is truly a 'joint' enterprise.

3.8

Review of Business Regulations

Anthony Shoult, ASA Consulting[1]

Introduction

Investor's and other business people wishing to do business in the Saudi market will need to acquaint themselves with the economy, markets and the relevant business laws.

Saudi Arabia, due to its strategic location within the Gulf region, is full of potential business and investment opportunities. However, a detailed knowledge of the country's open market approach is recommended in order to develop appropriate strategies in dealing with the highly competitive business environment and the rigid business transaction requirements in terms of quality, reliability, cost and timeliness.

To obtain a full understanding of the key local regulations that govern the conduct of business affairs in Saudi Arabia, it is wise to take independent specialist local advice. The key areas of foreign investment law, taxation and zakat, company structures, intellectual property and accountancy and audit requirements are addressed in detail in individual chapters of this publication. Other areas of current regulation that will be interest to those wishing to do business with Saudi Arabia are reviewed in outline in this section.

Laws effecting industrial investment

Encouragement of national industries legislation

The National Industries Protection and Encouragement Act was introduced by Royal Decree in the early 1960s. In short, the legislation

[1] Based on information from Saudi Arabian General Investment Authority (SAGIA).

provides for authorized exemption from customs duty for all imports for industrial projects. It also provides for the provision of land and employee housing at a nominal rent, the availability of financial aid through such organizations as the Saudi Industrial Development Fund (SIDF), the exemption of local products from export duties and other taxes (see also website: www.sagia.gov.sa).

Mining code

All activities involving the extraction of minerals are subject to the regulations enshrined in the Mining Code. The existing code is undergoing revision with the aims of increasing investment in the mining sector, enhancing transparency of the code and increasing efficiency and the ease of administration of all mineral-related activities.

The new code is expected to liberalize investment procedures in the mining sector, such that they are friendlier to private sector investors, including foreign investors who are entitled to invest in mining under the Foreign Investment Law (FIL).

The Mining Code covers all permissions and authorizations for exploration, excavation and mining and quarrying activities. It also covers authorizations to build and operate refineries, mines, treatment plants and related transportation matters.

Under the Mining code, all licensing is made through the ministry of Petroleum and Minerals Resources (see also website: www.mopm.gov.sa).

Employment regulations

Labour Law

All labour regulations in Saudi Arabia are subject to the requirements of the Labour Law, which calls for the preferential employment of Saudi nationals. Foreign and local labour are equally protected under the law.

All employment contracts offered by companies must comply fully with the Labour Law and must contain full details of the terms and conditions of employment, including wages and salaries, working hours, end-of-service awards, indemnities and healthcare, settlement of disputes and payment of social insurance, as applicable (see also website: www.commerce.gov.sa).

Social Insurance Law

The Social Insurance Law defines benefits applicable in two circumstances, namely, as a result of occupational hazards and for non-occupational disability, old age and death.

The payment of benefits as a result of occupational hazards is applicable to all workers irrespective of sex, nationality or age. Annuities paid for non-occupational disability, old age and death are applicable only to Saudi nationals, while expatriates employees receive end-of-service benefits instead.

At present, contributions for occupational hazards are two per cent of an employee's income, payable by the employer. Contributions for annuities are 18 per cent of an employee's income, payable equally at nine per cent by the employer and the employee.

All registered entities operating in Saudi Arabia and with 10 or more employees are subject to social insurance contributions. The responsible authority for social insurance in the private sector is the General Organization for Social Insurance (GOSI) (see also website: www.gosi.com.sa).

Health insurance law

A newly-introduced health or medical insurance law is intended to cover all expatriate and Saudi employees. Cover under the law will be compulsory, initially for larger companies, and all policies will be issued in-Kingdom. (All Saudis are eligible for free treatment at government hospitals.)

Saudi Arabian Capital Markets Law

A new Saudi Arabian Capital Markets Law, issued by Royal Decree in July 2003, set out the framework for the capital market including:

- the establishment of the Saudi Arabian Securities and Exchange Commission (SEC), with the objectives of protecting investor interests, ensuring orderly and equitable dealings in the securities business and promoting and developing the capital market;
- vesting the Commission with the powers to license non-bank financial intermediaries and to authorize the offering of securities to the public;
- the establishment of the Saudi Arabian Stock Exchange (SASE), incorporating the national securities depository centre.

Intellectual property regulations

Trade marks

Under existing legislation, all letters, names, drawings or other distinguishing marks may be protected through registration at the Trade Marks Bureau of the Ministry of Commerce and Industry.

For the protection to be effective, an applicant must be a Saudi citizen or a resident of a country that provides reciprocal protection to Saudi marks. Once registered, a trade mark is protected for renewable 10-year periods.

Trade mark legislation is being increasingly rigorously enforced and will be subject to upgrading when a new bill, already passed by the Consultative Council, has been signed into law by Royal Decree. (See also website: www.commerce.gov.sa.)

Commercial agencies law

Under the terms of the current agencies legislation, any agent in Saudi Arabia must be registered in the commercial agents' register at the Ministry of Commerce and Industry and any agency agreement must be registered within three months of its coming into effect.

The registration of agencies with the Ministry is especially important where sales to the government are anticipated, as a foreign supplier must have a registered service agent in the Kingdom.

New commercial agencies legislation is under discussion (2003) and is due for implementation in due course.

Tender regulations and rules

There is no central tender board in Saudi Arabia and every government agency is empowered to enter into contracts. The Kingdom supplemented the existing tendering regulations through Royal Decree M/14 of 1977. This contains a number of articles that govern submission bids, methods of procurement and performance, the award of contracts, contract conditions, advance payments, fines in the event of delay, contract forms, etc.

The Council of Ministers Resolution 124 of 1983 specifies that at least 30 per cent of public works contracts that are awarded to foreign contractors or any Saudi/foreign joint venture prime contractor (with less than 51 per cent Saudi capital), must be subcontracted to contractors who are at least 51 per cent Saudi owned and sponsor their own workers.

Business regulations governing trade

Saudi Arabia pursues a liberal trade policy and no quantitative or price restrictions are imposed on importers. However, there are a number of regulations and procedures governing business and trade in the Kingdom and adherence could be very helpful to those intending to do business there.

Compliance with the Saudi Arabian Standards Organization (SASO)

Imported goods should comply with the norms established by the Saudi Arabian Standards Organization (SASO). This is the Kingdom's standardization body, entrusted with all activities related to standards and measurements, including:

- formulation and approval of national standards for all commodities and products, as well as standards concerned with metrology, calibration, marking and identification of commodities and products, methods of sampling and inspection and testing;
- the publishing of all Saudi standards;
- promoting standardization awareness by publicity and other means and coordinating all activities relating to standards and measurements in the Kingdom;
- setting the rules for granting certificates of conformity and quality marks and regulating their issuance and use.

Documentation

Imported goods must have a certificate of origin in order to enter the country, an invoice or shipping documents, a full description of goods and, if applicable, a health certificate and a level of radiation certificate. All documents must be translated into Arabic. Commercial invoices and certificates of origin must be certified by the foreign chamber of commerce and by the Saudi Consular Office. Importers must be registered by the Ministry of Commerce and must consult the appropriate ministry about goods and materials to be imported.

Saudi commercial regulations do not permit foreign entities to carry out trading activities in Saudi Arabia. Trading is strictly reserved for Saudi individuals, 100 per cent Saudi-owned companies, and in certain cases, Gulf Cooperation Council (GCC) nationals.

There are strict penalties for both Saudis and foreigners involved in 'cover-up operations', where the Saudi is deemed to be sheltering a foreigner in doing business in the Kingdom for which proper legal registration should be obtained. Foreigners wishing to sell goods in Saudi Arabia must do so through a Saudi commercial agent.

Customs and customs exemptions

All goods imported into Saudi Arabia are subject to customs inspection and the application of well-defined rates of customs duty, unless otherwise exempted. A majority of goods are now subject to five per cent duty as part of the Kingdom's move to a uniform tariff within the GCC, effective 2003. However, some imports continue to be subject to a 12 per cent tariff and yet others have 20 per cent imposed to protect local industry.

Customs duty exemption applies on all authorized imports for industrial establishments, be they equipment, machinery, tools, spare parts and raw materials (whether primary or semi-manufactured or packaging materials). (See also website: www.mof.gov.sa.)

Environmental law

Comprehensive environmental legislation known as the General Environmental Regulation, covering air, water, waste, hazardous materials and noise, came into effect in October 2001.

Under the General Environmental Regulation, the Meteorological and Environmental Protection Authority (MEPA), an agency of the Ministry of Defence and Aviation, was appointed the supervisory authority.

Prior to the introduction of the new regulations, MEPA had introduced a set of general environmental protection standards that covered air quality standards, air pollution source standards and various water and sewage related guidelines. Additionally, the Royal Commission for Jubail and Yanbu enforces its own environmental regulations for the two industrial cities for which it is responsible. These cover air, water, hazardous materials, waste management, dredging and noise pollution.

Marine pollution is also covered by separate legislation, specifically addressing oil contamination and oil pollution; this also comes under the aegis of MEPA. (See also website: www.mepa.org.sa.)

Part Four

Finance, Accountancy and Taxation

4.1

The Saudi Monetary System

Dr Khan H Zahid, Chief Economist and Vice President, Riyadh Bank, Saudi Arabia

Introduction

While analysts forecast that the year 2004 was going to be one of the 'best ever' in economic terms, full year data released by the Saudi Arabian Monetary Authority (SAMA) and the government show that, in fact, 2004 was the second best ever in Saudi economic history, after 1982, the peak of its second 'oil boom' era (1978–85). It is widely expected that the year 2005 will be even better, given strong oil prices and Saudi crude production. During the current or third 'oil boom' of Saudi Arabia (2003 onwards), the Saudi stock market has more than quadrupled its value. It has been making new, all-time records almost on a weekly or monthly basis recently. The level of Initial Public Offering (IPO) activity has picked up to a frenzy. In a liquidity-driven economy, liquidity and bank credit are at all-time highs, so much so that the banking sector's loan-to-deposit ratio has reached a record level. Economic analysts have been busily revising up their forecasts for Saudi economic growth throughout the year. The government has announced the highest private sector growth (5.7 per cent in real terms) ever in the last two decades, and the second highest ever budget surplus of SR98 billion in 2004.

The Saudi banking system is on a roll. Liquidity, as measured by broad money supply (M3), is at an all-time high of over US$130 billion (53 per cent of last year's estimated GDP). Total bank lending stands at an all-time high of US$91.5 billion, which is 79 per cent of total system deposits. Bank lending to the private sector (which includes consumer banking) has reached a record US$79.7 billion (87 per cent of total lending). The Saudi stock market has also been breaking records almost on a weekly basis, with the Tadawul All Shares Index briefly crossing the 12,000 mark recently, a staggering 377 per cent gain over its end-2002 level of 2,518. As a result, the 10 listed Saudi banks' profits soared 35.2 per cent to US$4.5 billion in 2004 from US$3.3 billion in 2003.

Regulatory reforms are changing the boundaries of the Kingdom's banking and financial markets. Five overseas banks have been granted licences to operate in the Kingdom in the last two years, including the three latest – Deutsche Bank of Germany, BNP Paribas Bank of France and J.P. Morgan Chase Bank of the United States. A brand new local bank, Al Bilad Bank, was established recently through the merger of eight money changers and listed on the Saudi stock market through an IPO. Three other major IPOs, managed and conducted by local banks – the Saudi Telecom Company (STC), Etihad Etisalat, the second telecoms company, and the National Company for Cooperative Insurance (NCCI) – have been carried out since 2003, and a number of others are in the pipeline.

The most important changes in the financial system have been the introduction of a new Capital Markets Law in 2003, the establishment of a securities market regulator, the Securities and Exchange Commission (SEC), and an insurance market regulator. The new Capital Markets Law is intended to open up the financial system to a whole new range of market players and new financial instruments that will increase the breadth and depth of the Saudi financial system. As an emblem of the changes being heralded by the new law, the Kingdom has seen, for the first time ever, the issuance of medium-term fixed income debt instruments by the private sector. The first was Saudi Hollandi Bank that issued a US$187 million seven-year domestic subordinated debt issue in January 2004, which was priced at 81 basis points over Sibor, and was oversubscribed. This was quickly followed by the Kingdom's first private sector Eurobond issue, a US$600 million five-year floating rate note by the Saudi British Bank, priced at a remarkably low 41 basis points over Libor. Its size was increased from US$300 to US$400 million after it was oversubscribed at US$1 billion. A number of similar deals from banks, and notably the Saudi Arabian Basic Industries Corporation (SABIC), in the pipeline will change the landscape of asset/liability management and medium-term funding for private corporates and banks. In recognition of the Kingdom's financial and economic strength, Standard & Poor's, the international ratings agency, assigned Saudi Arabia its first ever solicited rating of A+/A in local/foreign currency in July 2004.

The banking and financial sector: Latest developments

The country is awash with liquidity from oil revenues, leading to record numbers in the stock market, banking and the real estate market.

Bank lending has grown so much in recent months that banks find themselves facing a liquidity crunch. Banks are also facing another challenge, namely, the reduced availability of government development bonds (GDBs) to invest surplus funds long term. GDBs have traditionally provided banks with fixed income, safety of principle and ample liquidity. Long-term fixed income assets do not exist in the Kingdom except in GDBs.

Thus, this is the only safe and risk-free long-term investment vehicle available to banks. The new capital market regulations are designed to address this and other shortcomings. The supply of GDBs has declined in recent months as the government racks up a large budget surplus. Recently, SAMA has also changed the rules for auctioning GDBs among banks.

Liquidity

The broadest measure of liquidity, M3, which includes currency in circulation, demand deposits, time and savings deposits and quasi-monetary deposits, stood at US$130.5 billion in February 2005, the highest level ever recorded. It is up 16 per cent from its 2004 February level of US$112 billion. Thus, US$18.5 billion in new money was pumped into the Saudi banking system in the 12 months to February 2005 (see Table 4.1.1).

Table 4.1.1 Liquidity trend

End of period	February 2005	February 2004
Broad money, M3 (US$ billion)	130.5	112.0
Cumulative volume growth over preceding 12 months (US$ billion)	18.5	+10.0
Percentage change from one year ago	16.2	9.8

Bank deposits

Consistent with the liquidity growth, bank deposits and lending are also at record levels. As of February 2005, total banking sector deposits stood at a record high of US$115 billion (see Table 4.1.2). Total deposits include non-interest bearing demand deposits, time and savings deposits, and quasi-monetary deposits (which consist of foreign currency deposits in local banks, deposits backing letters of credit and credit guarantees). On a year-over-year basis, total deposits grew

18.2 per cent in February 2005, compared to 10.7 per cent in the twelve months ending on February 2004.

Table 4.1.2 Total bank deposits

End of period	February 2005	February 2004
Total bank deposits (US$ billion)	115.0	97.3
Cumulative volume growth over preceding 12 months (US$ billion)	+17.7	+9.4
Percentage change from one year ago	18.2	10.7

Table 4.1.3 shows the breakdown of total deposits by type and their share of the total. Interest-free demand deposits grew a staggering US$9.1 billion in the 12 months ending February 2005, and comprise 48 percent of total bank deposits. Time and savings deposits grew US$6.1 billion during the same period and comprise 32 per cent of total bank deposits. Finally, quasi-monetary deposits grew only US$2.5 billion during the period and its share of total deposits fell from 21 to 20 per cent. The bulk of the fall in quasi-money deposits is foreign currency deposits. It should be noted that demand deposits, which form the core of banking sector deposits in the Kingdom, have been growing at double-digit annualized rates going back to early 2001. Time and savings deposits have also been growing at double-digit levels since October 2002, except for a period of single-digit growth between October 2003 and June 2004.

Table 4.1.3 Composition of bank deposits

In US$ billion *(% of total in brackets)*	February 2005	February 2004
Total bank deposits (US$ billion)	115	97.3
of which:		
Demand deposits (US$ billion)	55.7 *(48%)*	46.6 *(48%)*
Time and savings deposits (US$ billion)	36.5 *(32%)*	30.4 *(31%)*
Quasi-monetary deposits (US$ billion)	22.8 *(20%)*	20.3 *(21%)*

Bank lending

Bank lending is also at an all-time high. Total bank lending hit a record US$91.5 billion in February 2005, a remarkable US$24 billion rise during the preceding 12 months, compared to US$9.8 billion in the prior 12-month period ending on February 2004. Loan growth has outstripped deposit growth (see Tables 4.1.2 and 4.1.4) by a total of US$6.4 billion during the 12 months ending on February 2005. As a result, the banking system's loan-to-deposit ratio increased from 69 per cent to 80 per cent during the period.

Table 4.1.4 breaks down bank lending into two categories, firstly by original maturity (short, medium and long term), and secondly by public and private sector. The bulk of the recent growth in bank lending has been to the private sector and in the long-term category (defined by SAMA as loans with original maturity of three years or more).

Table 4.1.4 Total bank lending in US$ billions (percentage of total in brackets)

Category	February 2005	February 2004
Total bank lending	91.5	67.4
of which:		
Short-term	53 *(58%)*	39.9 *(59%)*
Medium-term	11.8 *(13%)*	10.4 *(15%)*
Long-term	26.7 *(29%)*	17.0 *(25%)*
of which:		
Loans to private sector	83.4 *(91%)*	60.6 *(90%)*
Public sector	8.1 *(9%)*	6.8 *(10%)*

The Saudi stock market

The Saudi stock market has recorded an outstanding bull-run since the end of 2002 (see Table 4.1.5). Following a 76.3 per cent gain in the market in 2003, the Tadawul All Shares Index has risen 85 per cent in 2004 and another 38 per cent in 2005 (up to 16 April 2005). Cumulatively, the gain in the entire period since 2002 (year-end) has been a whopping 351 per cent.

Compared to major global equity markets, the Saudi market's performance is nothing less than stellar. Since 2002, the US blue chip Dow Jones Index has gained 20 per cent in value; the technology-laden NASDAQ has gained 41 per cent; Germany's Dax, 38 per cent; the UK's FTSE 100, 16 per cent; and Japan's Nikkei, 27 per cent.

Table 4.1.5 The Saudi stock market

End of period	2005 (to16 April)	2004	2003	2002
All Shares Index (Tadawul)	11,348	8,206	4,438	2,518
% gain in 2005 year to date	38			
% gain in 2004	85			
% gain in 2003	76			
% gain since 2002	351			

Structure and evolution of the Saudi financial and monetary system

Saudi Arabia has an unbroken successful record of achieving the long-standing and consistent goals of its core monetary policies for:

- maintaining price stability;
- preserving the strength and stability of the Saudi riyal; and
- fostering a sound, growing and state-of-the-art banking and financial system.

Since the mid-1990s, increasing importance has been attached to developing the local and regional capital markets – to add greater breadth, depth, and diversity. In scope and quality, the products and services on offer to Saudi investors rival any on offer by the money boutiques of Europe or Asia. Reflecting years of careful preparation, the Kingdom appears on the doorstep of major capital markets reform that will greatly enhance the local and regional investment opportunities open to Saudi and global investors.

Regulatory restrictions and oversight

In banking, there are no restrictions on payments and transfers for international current and capital transactions. The only exceptions are those notified by the International Monetary Fund with regard to Iraq, and in accordance with IMF, UN, and Basel Committee for Banking Supervision resolutions, the global Financial Action Task Force and Interpol cooperation, and the Arabian Gulf Cooperation Council (GCC) and other Arab multi-lateral resolutions for combating illegal money laundering and support for terrorism.

Conservative rules govern Saudi Arabia's stock market, where share lending and short-selling are prohibited. Any foreign portfolio investor may own shares in Saudi mutual funds, including those that invest in local Saudi shares. Investors from the other GCC countries may invest directly in Saudi shares, except in the banking and other sectors deemed strategic.

Currency peg

The Saudi Arabian riyal is formally pegged to the SDR[1] at the rate of SR4.28255 = SDR1, within margins of 7.25 per cent. Since 1981, however, these margins have been suspended. In practice, the riyal is pegged to the US dollar. Since 1986, the riyal has been fixed to the dollar at an exchange rate of SR3.7450 = US$1 (mid-rate). The parity offer rate is usually referenced at SR3.7500 = US$1.

By law, the Saudi riyal currency is fully backed by hard currencies or monetary gold. As of January 2005, SAMA – the central bank – maintained official reserves totalling US$25 billion for this purpose (including a large amount of gold valued at US$32/oz.). Currency in circulation, as at the end of February 2005, amounted to about US$16 billion. From SAMA's February 2005 balance sheet, the identifiable foreign assets (foreign currencies, gold, deposits abroad and foreign securities) totalled around US$95 billion. The independent government organizations (primarily the two private sector and public sector pension organizations) had a further US$40 billion. Thus, gross official foreign assets amounted to about US$135 billion. In contrast, gross official foreign assets at end-2001 totalled US$82 billion, showing an increase of US$53 billion during the last three years. In its national monetary survey, SAMA posts its net foreign assets at about US$93 billion and private bank net foreign assets at US$12 billion, giving a total national net foreign assets position of US$105 billion. The Kingdom's M3 (broad) money supply amounted to US$131 billion as of February 2005, 71 per cent of which represents very stable demand, savings, and time deposits. With such a high ratio of M2 to M3, the system has very little 'hot money' as would be found in the 'other quasi money' categories, for example for residents' foreign currency deposits held by Saudi banks (money that could easily move). No currency peg is bullet-proof, and as the Saudi economy becomes more diversified and

---

[1] The SDR is an international reserve asset, created by the IMF in 1969 to supplement the existing official reserves of member countries. SDRs are allocated to member countries in proportion to their IMF quotas. The SDR also serves as the unit of account of the IMF and some other international organizations. Its value is based on a basket of key international currencies.

regionally integrated, the benefits of moving to a more responsive and broadly based exchange system will become evident. For now, the Saudi riyal appears exceptionally well-supported and structurally very sound.

SAMA's unswerving support for the riyal is presently paying dividends. The Saudi riyal's strength, the large growth in the domestic equity markets and confidence bred from economic reforms have contributed to a clear post-September 11 trend for greater financial assets repatriation and retention within the Kingdom. As reflected in rising local deposits and money market fund holdings, the Saudis, who are now more worried about their offshore portfolios, feel confident enough in the Kingdom to invest more of their money at home.

Money market rates

With a pegged currency, Saudi riyal money market rates will tend to fluctuate around US dollar rates, generally within a range of less than one per cent. For comparison, the money market rate differentials for other pegged currencies, such as the Hong Kong dollar, range above six per cent.

Given Saudi Arabia's low inflation rate, the stability of its currency and the large and mobile foreign assets of its banks and individuals, the difference between riyal and dollar money market rates (the rate 'differentials') will tend to reflect differences in the relative liquidity of the Saudi and American economies. From mid-1991 to mid-1993, riyal deposit rates hovered below dollar rates, as liquidity generated by Gulf war spending washed through the economy. Oil prices fell during the last half of 1993, and government payments slowed, tightening local liquidity. Aggravated by speculation from offshore, riyal rates rose briefly to as much as 180 basis points (180 bp) above dollar rates. The rate differential receded to less than 50 bp for most of 1994, but widened to about 120 bp again at year-end on another brief round of speculation. Oil prices recovered in 1995, then rose steeply in 1996 and stayed high into 1997. Throughout this period, actual oil export revenues exceeded the levels planned in government budgets. Payments accelerated and outlays exceeded planned levels. The difference between riyal and dollar deposit rates narrowed to less than 20 bp – at times turning slightly negative.

During 1998, new pressures developed in Saudi riyal money markets as a reaction to the drop in oil prices, and to reflect a general rise in speculation against 'emerging market' rates and currencies in the wake of Asia's financial turmoil. In 1998, the rate differential averaged nearly 80 bp, at times spiking much higher. These pressures subsided as oil prices and revenues rose in late 1999 and 2000, and the differential dropped to 20 bp or less for most of 2000 and 2001. Insecurities in the wake of September 11 pushed the differential out beyond 60 bp.

In the last two years (2003 and 2004), ever-rising oil prices and production have greatly increased liquidity in the Kingdom and reduced the riyal-dollar spread from 50 bp in 2003 to 10 bp in February 2005.

Saudi government debt

SAMA is the government's bank. As a fundamental protection for the soundness of the currency and the monetary system, SAMA is prohibited by its charter from lending directly to the government. Rather, it acts effectively as a secured agent to issue debt securities or arrange loans for the government and some quasi-government companies. Generally speaking, the government is averse to international borrowing. Since the 1960s, there have been only a few international loans involving SAMA and these have long-since been fully repaid. From time to time, SAMA does enter into off-balance sheet transactions, for example currency swaps to generate short-term liquidity in particular foreign currencies. The usual buyers of official domestic debt are the official autonomous government institutions (AGIs), such as the General Office of Social Insurance and Government Pension Funds, and specialized credit institutions (SCIs), such as the Public Investment Fund or the Saudi Fund for Development, and the local commercial banks.

Private companies came into the market on the back of programmes during the late 1990s that enabled government suppliers and contractors to exchange long-standing government receivables for government debt securities. This led to the creation of a rediscount market for Saudi government bonds, funded particularly by the banks. Although the company bond sales created many real bargains in the market, few, if any, individual investors sought to participate. There are no restrictions on foreign ownership of Saudi government bonds. The instruments exist electronically with SAMA and can be held by individuals in unrestricted custody accounts offered by most Saudi banks. In addition to the rediscount market, there is a deep and well-developed market in Saudi government bond repurchase agreements. Thus, an investor has several liquidity options.

Inasmuch as SAMA acts as the government's formal debt placement agent and manager, the whole stock of Saudi government bonds outstanding is carried under SAMA's contra accounts. As of February 2005, the contra accounts totalled US$53 billion. Two years of government budget surpluses have resulted in a drop in the contra account from US$58 billion at the end of 2002.

Only a fraction of the total bonds outstanding are held by the Saudi commercial banks or by private investors (directly or through Saudi mutual funds). As of February 2005, the banks' holdings of bonds amounted to US$38.6 billion, down from a peak of US$42.5 billion in March 2004, reflecting the strong government budget position. From 1995 to 1999, a number of the local mutual funds held up to US$0.6 billion in bonds, but these positions were liquidated at the end of 2000 and have not been rebuilt.

The remaining US$20 billion balance in bonds outstanding is believed to be held by the independent government organizations (IGOs), whose accounts also appear on the SAMA balance sheet. The IGOs report a total of around US$89 billion in local securities, which includes their bond holdings (about US$20 billion) and their Saudi share portfolios (presumably the remaining US$69 billion).

The banks also hold about US$8 billion in direct loans to government entities, up from about US$6 billion in the mid-1990s. Thus, the banks' gross total credit to the government amounts to US$47 billion, or 26.5 per cent of total assets, up from about 22 per cent in 1995. However, the banks also hold some US$37 billion in government deposits. Their net credit to the government amounts to only US$10 billion, or scarcely six per cent of their balance sheets.

Over the last 22 years since the Saudi Government Development Bonds were first introduced, Saudi Arabia has made strides to develop its public funding programme. To appreciate the scope and nature of this task, it is important to recall that the first official financial structures to be established were to handle large surpluses. Thus, the view of markets was that of the investor rather than the borrower. The revenue surpluses accumulated for a decade, beginning in 1973.

Since inception, the Kingdom's debt programme has performed flawlessly. All debt issues have been serviced and repaid fully and on time. By virtue of Saudi Arabia's participation in the IMF's General Agreements to Borrow and its formal Observer status with the Basle Committee for International Banking Supervision, its debt instruments deservedly carry a zero risk weighting under the old Capital Accord's bank capital adequacy calculations.

Confident of its strong fiscal position, backed by solid oil reserves, the Kingdom solicited its first ever financial ratings last year with Standard and Poor's, and obtained a A+/A (local currency/foreign currency) rating on May 2004.

The types of debt instruments offered by the Saudi government have evolved in line with its budget needs and in view of changing conditions in world securities markets. Attention has also been paid to insuring the liquidity of bond holdings through the availability of official and private repurchase agreements (repos), as well as through encouragement for the development of a secondary market operated on a local basis. The various classes of Saudi government securities are described below.

Saudi Government Development Bonds (GDBs)

These first appeared in June 1988. They are closely patterned after US Treasury Bills with maturities of two, three, five, seven and 10 years. Denominations are in multiples of SR1 million (US$266,667) wholesale and SR50,000 (US$13,333) for retail investors through the secondary market. In 1997, in order to satisfy market demand and broaden the secondary market, GDBs came to be offered once a month in amounts of SR1 billion for maturities of two, three, four and five years. The issues are available for up to three months on a 'tap' basis, or until exhausted. They would pay a coupon pegged to the prevailing Treasury coupon plus a 'liquidity premium' of 20–50 bp (more for longer tenures).

Since March 2004, SAMA has changed the bond issue system slightly to make it more competitive, in its desire to wean banks away from GDBs given the government's strong fiscal position, and, hence, a lesser need for borrowing. In the current system, SAMA issues GDBs worth SR1 billion in each of the five tenures (two, three, five, seven, and 10 years) at the start of each quarter, a total of SR5 billion. Banks submit bids specifying the price (yield) and quantity by tenure they desire. SAMA takes in all the banks' bids and then selects the best bid price, based on its reading of the market. Then the banks that match the best bid are awarded the quantity up to the maximum amount they bid. Each SR1 billion issue is made on a 'tap' basis, ie any amount that is not auctioned off at the start of the quarter will be made available for re-bidding in the subsequent two months. SAMA, of course, has the discretion to issue no amount at any bid – something, it has been doing more and more during the last year because of the reduced need for government borrowing. Banks may repo up to 25 per cent of the face value of their GDB holdings with SAMA at any time to meet short-term liquidity needs. In extreme circumstances, as followed Iraq's invasion of Kuwait for example, the banks may request to repo 50 per cent or more of their GDBs.

SAMA 'T-Bills'

These were introduced in November 1991, to provide a short-term investment option in order to supplement the funding raised by GDBs after the Gulf War. Like US Treasury Bills, these are offered in tenures of one, four, 13, 26 and 52 weeks. SAMA T-Bills pay prevailing Saudi riyal deposit rates and are repo-able like GDBs. Up to 75 per cent of bank T-Bill holdings are repo-able to SAMA.

Saudi riyal-FRNs

In 1997, SAMA introduced Saudi riyal-FRNs. These are offered in maturities of up to seven years. They pay a coupon, the rate of which is tied to local money market rates and carry a fixed liquidity premium. Depending on the rate trends, Saudi riyal-FRNs have been very popular and, at times, issues are oversubscribed.

Money supply, inflation and growth

The trends in Saudi Arabia's monetary aggregates reflect that the monetary system is increasingly well developed and that the economy, as a whole, is diversifying. Demand and quasi-money deposits represent a rising share of the total money supply. Since 1991, the ratio of currency in circulation has declined from about 24 per cent to about 12 per cent in 2005. The banks' local deposits (demand, time, and savings) now represent 71 per cent of the total money supply (M3). The more volatile other quasi-monetary deposits represent only about 17 per cent of money.

Both passive and active factors help to regulate the Saudi money supply. Given the openness of the financial system, the fixed peg with the dollar and that the Saudi private sector remains a net creditor to the world, the difference between Saudi riyal and dollar interest rates will set into motion large capital movements. Thus, when local liquidity rises and local rate differentials drop, investors will tend to expatriate funds in search of higher yields offshore. Conversely, when local liquidity tightens, the attraction of higher local rates will prompt capital repatriation. From time to time, often in view of short-term factors, SAMA will enter the market directly to add or drain liquidity. This is accomplished through its sales of government securities (to drain liquidity) and its guaranteed repurchase agreement facilities ('repo window') for Saudi government bonds and bills. Following September 11, the banks' portfolios of SAMA securities rose to a peak of US$42 billion in March 2004, reflecting a draining of excess liquidity prompted by a modest surge of Saudi depositors bringing their money home. This number has since fallen to US$39 billion as a result of two years of government budget surpluses.

The result of the Saudi riyal peg to the dollar, the resulting limited manoeuvrability of domestic interest rates and SAMA's tight control of domestic liquidity, has been a remarkably benign inflation environment in the Kingdom. Despite massive swings in oil prices and oil revenues, consumer price inflation has averaged between one and two per cent in recent years.

4.2

Banking, Credit and Financial Institutions

Dr Khan H Zahid, Chief Economist and Vice President, Riyadh Bank, Saudi Arabia

Introduction

As elsewhere, Saudi Arabia's financial and capital markets play essential roles to convert national savings accumulated by the government, businesses and individuals into productive investments.

While Saudi commercial banks are taking the lead in many areas, Saudi Arabian official financial institutions and foreign banks and financial services providers remain important. Whether government or private, all of these institutions are called upon to contribute to the high priority national goals of accelerating the pace of national economic diversification and expanding employment opportunities for Saudis. Throughout the Kingdom, for the growing middle class and the proliferating small, medium-sized and large businesses, demand is growing for a widening array of financial products and services. There is greater awareness that Saudi Arabia's financial and capital markets are large, well regulated and increasingly sophisticated. Steps to open up these markets to greater foreign direct participation are attracting increasing attention – within the Kingdom, regionally and globally.

Large shares of the oil revenue surpluses that were amassed during the first oil boom decade of 1973–83 were used to capitalize a number of official financial institutions. The official specialized credit institutions (SCIs) continue to lend under concessionary terms to support industry, agriculture, housing, the professions and individuals. While in 2004 they received the first substantial infusion of new capital from Saudi budgets since the mid-1980s, their missions are changing in step with changing national priorities. Unlike other countries where national pension schemes start with small balances or require continual budget support, Saudi Arabia's Retirement Pension Agency for government employees and the General Organization for Social Insurance (GOSI) for the private sector benefited from very large infusions of official capital during the first oil boom.

That was even before these autonomous government institutions (AGIs) began to accumulate employee contributions. The potential for massive accumulations of funds by the two pension agencies is evident from the fact that the Kingdom has a very rapidly growing labour force (over four per cent annual growth rate) and a small and decreasing dependency ratio (the ratio of retirees to workers).

The roles of foreign financial institutions have also evolved. During the first oil boom era, the foreign institutions operated through Saudi branches or from offshore to provide banking, investment, and insurance products and services. In effect, they filled gaps left open between what was provided by the still young official institutions and the few wholly Saudi banks and exchange companies. Some of the relationships established during that era continue today in the form of dealings with Saudi ministries, companies and individuals. In recent years, moreover, the major Saudi companies and to a lesser extent the government, have used internationally syndicated loans to manage their liquidity or to raise capital for expansions.

During 1981–82, the foreign bank branches operating in the Kingdom were 'Saudiized', meaning that they were given the option to depart or reincorporate as domestic banking joint ventures with majority Saudi ownership. Later in the 1980s, the Kingdom's largest exchange house was reconstituted under a banking charter. More recently, one of the joint ventures was merged with a local bank and later on, the bank was fully Saudiized. In addition, a number of new foreign banks have been granted a licence by the Saudi Arabian Monetary Agency (SAMA) to operate in the Kingdom and a group of eight money changers were, together, incorporated into a new bank.

Since the Gulf War, the balance sheets and capabilities of Saudi Arabia's 11 domestic banks have expanded dramatically. This growth benefits from a strong and stable monetary system, and exceptionally broad regulatory mandates that call upon the banks not only to play the central role in local finance and transaction services, but also to generate and develop local capital markets.

Maturity of the banking sector in Saudi Arabia

Of the 13 registered commercial banks, all but three are listed on the stock exchange. One is the Bahrain-based Gulf International Bank (GIB), and the other is the UAE-based Emirates Bank. The third, the National Commercial Bank (NCB) is a 'closed joint stock' company, having reconstituted from being a limited partnership where, in reflection of SAMA's hands-on prudential supervision during 1999 and 2000, 100 per cent of the partnership shares are now in the hands of the central bank.

Of the 10 publicly owned banks, four are wholly Saudi (Riyad Bank, Al-Rajhi Company for Banking and Exchange, SAMBA Financial Group and the new Al Bilad Bank). Six have some foreign shareholding, although in the case of the Saudi Investment Bank (SAIB) and Bank Al Zajira, the proportions of foreign ownership are small. There are four foreign joint venture banks with substantial foreign ownership. These are Saudi British Bank (SBB): 40 per cent HSBC; Arab National Bank (ANB): 40 per cent Arab Bank; Saudi French Bank (SFB): 40 per cent Credit Agricole/Indosuez); and Saudi Hollandi Bank (SHB): 40 per cent ABN-Amro. Recently, the fifth joint venture bank, Saudi American Bank (SAMBA), which was 20 per cent owned by Citigroup of the United States, became a fully Saudi-owned bank after Citigroup divested its share and relinquished its management contract with the bank.

Saudi Arabia is becoming increasingly 'banked' as both companies and individuals move away from what had been a largely cash-based approach to business. The government is borrowing less, and it is also a large depositor. Thus, its claim on banking resources is still far away from 'crowding out' the banks' abilities to support other sorts of economic activity. The Saudi banks are also becoming increasingly 'Saudi' in all that they do. The principal problem for Saudi banking is the general lack of availability of longer-term Saudi assets. The new Capital Markets Law, passed in 2003, is set to make a sea change in this area. It is expected to enable banks and other institutions to issue medium- to long-term securities and create a secondary market for them, thus opening up a whole new class of local assets for the banks. At present, other than the shrinking supply of Government Development Bonds (GDBs), the main type of local assets available for the banks are private and government sector borrowing from the banking sector. Over the period of 24 months ending in February 2005, private sector borrowing from local banks increased by about US$31 billion, while government and quasi-government borrowing from banks increased by US$1.4 billion. Banks also hold net foreign assets totalling US$12 billion, reflecting that government borrowing demands are not crowding out local lending.

The banks' funding is largely local; local customer deposits were up by almost US$27 billion in the same 24-month period. By contrast, foreign liabilities rose by only US$1.3 billion over the two years. As a general note about asset quality, it is important to note that from 1996, the government went a very long way toward catching up on payments to suppliers and contractors. Further, as a consequence of the progress toward privatizing the electric power and telecommunications sectors, and toward reorganizing water, many of the past ambiguities associated with giving credit to these sectors of the economy have been resolved.

Balance sheets

Since 2002, the consolidated balance sheet of Saudi Arabia's banking sector has grown 30 per cent, from US$135.5 billion to US$176.5 billion. During the same period, the banking sector's capital accounts grew 16 per cent, from US$15.4 billion to US$17.8 billion. Under the prevailing BIS standard for calculating capital adequacy, the Saudi banks' average capital adequacy ratio is consistently over 20 per cent, more than twice the BIS's eight per cent minimum.

Customer deposits

Deposits have grown since 2002 by over 31 per cent, from US$87.5 billion to US$115 billion. In the 12 months ending on February 2005, deposits grew more rapidly than the long-term trend – increasing by 18.2 per cent.

Foreign liabilities

From the end of 1991 to end-2001, foreign liabilities grew at an average annual rate of 7.9 per cent. In the 12 months ending on February 2005, foreign liabilities rose by US$1.1 billion. The banks have a large net foreign assets position (see 'Foreign position' below).

Assets – Private sector loans

On the assets side of the balance sheet, the fastest rising asset class has been loans to the private sector. In the 12 months ending on February 2005, bank loans to the private sector rose US$21.9 billion. In contrast, in the five years from 1999 to 2004, it grew by an annual average of US$7.4 billion. As of February 2005, total bank loans to the private sector stood at US$79.5 billion.

In the past few years, Saudi banks have 'discovered' consumer credit. They have developed credit and risk management systems and a credit rating agency to monitor retail borrowers. As a result, consumer loans have exploded in the banks' balance sheet. Consumer loans have almost tripled, from US$6.6 billion in 2000 to US$23 billion as of September 2004, in the areas of real estate financing, automobiles and other consumer credit. This is up from almost nothing in the mid-1990s. This growth also reflects the banks' increasing success at offering acceptable Islamic alternatives to the sorts of consumer credit options that are available in the West. Also contributing to such rapid growth is the success banks are having at structuring securities around and making markets in an increasing variety of categories of consumer credit, for example, the receivables accumulated by automobile or furniture showrooms, or the banks' credit card debt. Credit card loans have not grown as fast – from US$0.8 billion in 2002 to US$1 billion as of Q3 2004, reflecting the conservative criteria banks put over these accounts.

Table 4.2.1 Consolidated balance sheet of Saudi banks* (US$ billions)

	1991	1995	1999	2000	2002	Feb '05
Total deposits	45.7	52.5	65.6	70.3	87.5	115
Foreign liabilities	7.4	10.6	13.6	17.2	11.5	12.4
Unclassified	10.8	17.4	18.5	19.4	21.0	31.3
Capital accounts	5.0	10.5	13.0	14.0	15.4	17.8
Total liabilities	68.9	91.0	110.7	120.9	135.5	176.5
Loans to government entities	4.2	6.5	3.8	3.3	3.2	8.0
Government bonds	6.6	13.9	27.3	29.9	35.0	38.7
Cash	3.4	3.0	4.4	5.0	na	na
Loans to private sector	19.6	32.3	43.3	45.9	51.0	79.7
Foreign assets	31.7	26.1	24.4	27.0	25.4	24.5
Other	3.3	9.1	7.6	9.7	7.3	10.8
Total assets	68.9	91.0	100.7	120.9	135.5	176.5
Banks net foreign assets	24.3	15.7	10.8	9.5	14.0	12.2
Saudi Banks' position to government						
Gross credit to government	10.9	20.5	31.1	33.3	40.2	46.7
Government deposits	n/a	8.4	11.6	12.4	13.8	38.3
Net credit to government	n/a	12.1	19.5	20.9	26.4	8.4
Bank credit exposure ratios (% of total assets)						
Net government debt	n/a	13.3%	17.6%	17.3%	19.5%	4.8%
Gross government debt	15.8%	22.5%	28.1%	27.5%	29.7%	26.5%
Private loans	28.5%	35.5%	39.1%	38.0%	37.6%	45.2%
Total foreign assets	46.0%	28.7%	22.0%	22.3%	18.7%	13.9%

	1991	1995	1999	2000	2002	Feb '05
Net foreign assets	35.2%	17.3%	9.7%	7.9%	10.3%	6.9%
Bank credit exposure ratios (% of GDP)						
GDP (US$ billion)	118	125	143	176	188	248
Net government debt	n/a	9.6%	13.7%	11.9%	14.0%	3.4%
Gross government debt	9.2%	16.4%	21.8%	18.9%	21.4%	18.8%
Private loans	16.7%	25.8%	30.3%	26.1%	27.0%	32.0%
Money supply (M2), *US$ billion*	44.0	49.5	64.5	68.4	82.7	107.7
Share market indicators, *US$ billion*						
Average monthly trading volume	0.2	0.5	1.3	1.5	2.3	43.7
Market capitalization	5.8	40.8	61.1	68.0	75.0	438.0
All shares index ('85=1,000)	1,765	1,367	2,028	2,258	2,518	9,096

*** Treats foreign branches as foreign entities**

Government loans and overall position

Direct loans to the government and quasi-government companies stand at US$8 billion as of February 2005, reflecting increased project and infrastructure financing. That is up from US$3.2 billion in 2002. While gross credits to the government (bonds and loans) have increased, so have the deposits with local banks by government entities. As of February 2005, total government deposits with the banks were US$38.3 billion, up from US$13.8 billion as recently as 2002, reflecting the strong fiscal position of the government flush with oil revenues. The figure was US$9.4 billion at the end of 1996. Thus, the bank's net credit to the government stands at about US$8.4 billion compared to US$26.4 billion in 2002. Thus, net credit is only about 18 per cent of gross credits (US$46.7 billion) to the government and government companies. Gross credits to the government now represent 26.5 per cent of total bank assets (down from 29.7 per cent at the end of 2002), while net credits represent 4.8 per cent of total assets (down from 19.5 per cent in 2002). For comparison, loans to the private sector represent 45.2 per cent of total assets.

Foreign position

Between 1991 and 2001, the banks' total foreign assets have declined about 20 per cent from US$31.7 billion at the end of 1991 to US$25.4 billion at end-2002. As a result of some repatriation of overseas assets and the local retaining of oil revenues, foreign assets of the banking system have declined further to US$24.5 billion in February 2005. Nevertheless, the large foreign securities portfolios remain an important source of strength for the individual banks that hold them, and the system as a whole.

Profitability and non-performing loans

The banks accumulated some US$4.4 billion in retained earnings during 2004, up by 36 percent from US$3.2 billion during 2003 (see Table 4.2.2). For comparison, the banks' capital and reserves (excluding retained earnings) amounted to US$13.9 billion, indicating an overall return on capital for the sector averaging 32 per cent. For most of the banks, assets quality is not an issue and the write-offs will be small.

Table 4.2.2 Saudi banks' consolidated assets, capital and reserves and cumulative annual profits (US$ billion)

	Assets	Capital	Cumulative annual profits	Return on assets %	Return on capital
1995	91.0	9.3	1.2	1.3	15.0
2000	120.9	11.6	2.4	2.0	25.5
2003	145.4	12.5	3.2	2.2	25.6
2004	174.8	13.9	4.4	2.5	31.6

Non-asset businesses

It is noteworthy that much of the growth in bank profitability has been from fee-generating activities – not simply the growth of non-interest bearing accounts (NIBs) or credit. A good indication of this is the growth of ATM and point of sale transactions, which increased to about 464 million in 2004, up over ninefold from about 50 million in 1996.

The banks also run all the brokerage accounts for the local exchange, where daily transactions topped 26 million shares in 2005 year-to-date (mid-2005) compared to only 1.5 million in 2001. Banks also administer the some 175 investment funds they offer (up from about 80 in 1995), and in most cases, manage the more than US$14 billion that these funds have under management.

Transaction banking is a growth business – whether for company and ministry payrolls, remittances or other sorts of business account (eg travel agency ticketing). Similarly, the banks' brokerage and fiduciary businesses are expanding, and we see whole ranges of new opportunities for insurance-based products.

The Saudi bank clearing system – the Saudi Arabian Riyal Interbank Express (SARIE) – is among the most advanced in the world. It handled over US$1.9 trillion in annual transactions in 2003 (personal and interbank) on a 'real-time online' basis, where all of the flows through the system are completely transparent by payee, beneficiary, and amount to the regulator. For SAMA, finding the payments to anyone who might support terrorism can be done, virtually, at the touch of a button.

Foreign banks and brokers

Finally, it is important to touch on the role of foreign financial institutions. During the boom years, foreign banks played a large role, particularly in the areas of trade finance, investment services and foreign exchange. With the Saudiization of the banking system in 1980–81, and the subsequent growth of local capabilities, the role of foreign banks declined. While many continued to visit clients in the Kingdom, particularly the large official and private investors, the local banks were quick to pick up much of the liabilities and asset-based business. As a consequence, the overseas banking unit (OBU) centres shrank.

More recently, however, the foreign banks have renewed activities in the market to participate in the numerous major international syndications associated with ongoing petrochemical expansions and infrastructure projects. It is estimated that the country will need over US$830 billion to finance these types of projects in the next 20 to 25 years. Local banks do not have the capacity or appetite to handle such a huge volume, and foreign banks are certainly expected to participate in these lucrative projects.

The activities of foreign banks, brokers and insurance companies to garner private investor money is coming under increasing scrutiny from the central bank. A new Insurance Law has been passed and SAMA has been designated as the insurance regulator. SAMA has recently licensed 13 insurance companies, including local, foreign and joint ventures, to conduct insurance business in the Kingdom; another 20 licences are expected to be granted soon. Several SAMA directives have been issued to warn that unlicensed or unauthorized banking, insurance and charitable activities are prohibited. In part, this reflects the desire to protect local investors against unscrupulous activities. There is also a desire to bring the same degree of regulatory supervision to the activities of foreign entities that already applies to local banks.

The 1997 decision by the Gulf Cooperation Council (GCC) to permit branching by GCC banks across the region has resulted in competition mainly on the assets side of the business, where GIB is a player in almost all the major syndications. The net effect now appears to be for the large and diverse Saudi banks to seek branches and affiliates in the other GCC countries.

Access to Saudi Arabia's financial markets is an important topic under discussion in the context of the Kingdom's application to become a member of the World Trade Organization (WTO). There is every indication that the Kingdom may become a member of the WTO by the end of 2005. Saudi Arabia's remarkable ability to generate low cost customer deposits is very appealing to foreign financial institutions. On the other hand, those banks that want to open new activities in the Kingdom could be expected to meet the same requirements as local banks, for example in the area of staffing by Saudis. Local bank staff already have a proportion of Saudis – exceeding 75 per cent of total staff in most instances.

Specialized credit institutions and pension funds

The Saudi official specialized credit institutions (SCIs) remain important for credit formation and savings generation across broad sectors of the economy, and continue to hold upwards of US$41 billion in loans and investments in the local economy, representing about 73 per cent of total bank lending to the private sector in 2003.

The SCIs in Saudi Arabia are:

- Saudi Agricultural Bank (SAB);
- Saudi Credit Bank (SCB);
- Public Investment Fund (PIF);
- Saudi Industrial Development Fund (SIDF);
- Real Estate Development Fund (REDF).

These institutions help to finance growth and development across the economy. The SAB, established in 1965, and the SCB and PIF, both established in 1971, have played important social as well as economic roles. The SIDF and REDF were established after the first big increases in oil prices in 1974.

The SAB's agricultural loans and subsidies helped to settle nomadic bedouin populations and fostered national self-sufficiency in basic food products, particularly cereal grains. Since 1995, the subsidies for grains have been substantially reduced. The focus of new SAB lending has shifted increasingly to support non-subsidized produce and water conserving agricultural technologies. As of 2003, SAB's lending totalled US$2.5 billion.

The SCB has recently been totally reorganized to lend to Saudi individuals who want to establish small- and medium-sized businesses (SMEs). Previously, it used to lend to individuals, for example to help a young bridegroom pay a dowry before marriage. The SCB's total loans outstanding at the end of 2003 stood at US$256 million. In the latest 2005 budget, the government has promised to allocate an additional US$534 million capital to the SCB.

The PIF provides concessionary medium- and long-term loans to commercially orientated public corporations, such as the national airlines and the domestic refineries. It has provided considerable capital to the Saudi Arabian Basic Industries Corporation (SABIC), which operates on an entirely commercial basis. SABIC – the largest publicly traded company in the Middle East – is listed on the Saudi stock exchange where private investors own a 30 per cent share. The PIF is the nominal owner of the government's 70 per cent interest. The government intends to sell down its share ownership in the future.

For other private sector manufacturing industries, the SIDF provides long-term soft loans and offers technical advice and marketing services. The SIDF will finance up to half of the capital cost of wholly Saudi or wholly foreign enterprises. It aims to build Saudi industries to compete with imports, develop non-oil exports and expand job opportunities for young Saudis. As of 2003, its total loans outstanding stood at US$2.45 billion.

The REDF was established to finance home building by Saudis on concessionary terms. As of 2003, its total loans outstanding stood at US$18.5 billion. The 2005 budget also promised to allocate an additional US$2.4 billion capital to REDF to expand its activities. The PIF's total loans were US$7 billion.

The importance of the SCIs is evident from their sheer size. The consolidated balance sheet of the SCIs amounted to US$65.2 billion at the end of 2003 (converted at the prevailing exchange rate). The SCIs had not grown substantially since the early 1980s, until the new capital infusion in the 2005 budget. Paid-in capital amounted to US$50.7 billion – also unchanged in 16 years. In a very real sense, the SCIs husband a considerable share of the 'national patrimony' of the Kingdom.

Needless to say, the growth and development of Saudi Arabia's banking system and capital market have been broadly affected by the activities of the SCIs. Similarly, the evolving roles and increasing limitations faced by the government financial institutions clearly create opportunities for private sector banking and finance. The SCIs still represent a significantly large supplier of credit to Saudi Arabia's private sector and quasi-government companies compared to Saudi Arabia's commercial banks.

However, the influence of the SCIs is starting to wane in several important respects. Because the great bulk of lending by the SCIs is for the medium or long term, the opportunities for banks to build longer maturities into their loan portfolios had been constrained. As recently at 1995, more than 86 per cent of bank loans were for maturities of less than one year. By 2005, however, the short-term portion had declined to 58 per cent. The medium-term portion had tripled to 13 per cent, and the long-term portion was up more than eightfold to 29 per cent. Whether for agriculture, housing, personal loans or industry, the role of the SCIs is declining and Saudi banks are coming into their own to play expanding roles to meet marginal new credit needs.

The Saudi share market

The Saudi stock exchange is the largest in the Middle East, with total capitalization of US$427 billion and with market turnover averaging about US$22 billion per day. In early 1998, the Saudi share market was accepted for inclusion in the International Finance Corporation's (IFC's) 'Global Index'. The IFC is an affiliate of the World Bank (the IBRD) that is responsible for supporting the growth and development of capital markets around the world.

At end-2004, 74 companies were listed on the exchange, including the Saudi Arabian Basic Industries Corporation (SABIC), a world-scale petrochemicals and industrial conglomerate.

The largest sector in the market is banks, which account for about 27 per cent of market capitalization, followed by industry at about 43 per cent. Respectively, the electricity, cement, telecoms and services sectors represent about six, four, 16 and 2.5 per cent of total market capitalization, with smaller shares for insurance and agriculture. Ownership of the market is more than half in the hands of private individuals. Through their shares in local banking joint ventures, foreign banks own about eight per cent of the market. The government, through the PIF's 70 per cent holding of SABIC and the holdings of the pension funds, owns roughly one-third of the market.

These familiar ratios are likely to change substantially very soon as a result of the Kingdom's privatization and IPO activities. For now, however, the cost of equity capital remains relatively low. By international comparisons, the share values seen in the Saudi market reflect investor calculations that are largely 'yield based,' rather than 'growth based' as seen in markets elsewhere. Comparatively, dividend yields are low (1.7 per cent) and the prevailing price-to-earnings ratios are high at 31.4 (vs. the historic average of 16.8).

At the most basic level, one of the main aims of the new Capital Markets Law is to bring on a re-rating of the market, which has the potential to make raising equity capital more attractive. By opening up the market to more direct GCC participation, and by making it generally easier to list shares, the new law will make it easier for the world of investors to bring and deploy their capital. The law also provides for regional market integration, the privatization of the stock market, and for a regulatory structure patterned after the US Securities and Exchange Commission and the UK's Financial Regulatory Agency.

Since 1985, the share market itself has been electronic or 'dematerialized,' and any need for paper custody was disposed of in mid-1995. Share trading is conducted through the Tadawul Electronic Securities Information System (ESIS). Tadawul/ESIS is a floorless, continuous, order-driven market with up-to-the-minute price, volume and company information dissemination. It processes buy and sell orders from order entry to transfer of ownership. Using central computers within SAMA and terminal workstations within the banks, a high-speed telecommunications network links the system.

Tadawul/ESIS offers the market a number of important attributes. It provides a high level of transparency, with instantaneous dissemination of bids and offers, executed volumes, and prices to all market participants. It is a fair system, providing equal access to all market information across the network. Share price spreads are narrow, and the trading cycle is brief and efficient. The system operates with a high degree of accuracy. About 95 per cent of all transactions are settled on the day of execution (T), and are delivered the following business day (T+1). These attributes help to insure that the market is liquid for the great bulk of listed shares. The system itself is user friendly. The fact that transaction terminals reside at banks provides for smooth interfacing between a customer's share trading brokerage accounts and their customer accounts with the bank.

4.3

Capital Markets and Investment Banking

Michael J Parkhouse, Gulf International Bank

The Saudi Arabian stock market

The Saudi Stock Market is the largest and most liquid in the Middle East, with a market capitalization of SR1.15 trillion (US$306.3 billion) at the end of 2004.

The resurgence in the Saudi market, following the first government privatization through an initial public offering (IPO) of shares in Saudi Telecom in January 2003, has been sustained, outperforming most, if not all, of the major stock markets in the West.

Over the 12-month period to January 2005, four companies were listed on the Stock Market, and many more are expected over the 12-month period to January 2006, as the new Capital Market Authority becomes fully operational. Also during this period, the Tadawul All Share Index (TASI) increased 84.93 per cent over the previous year, closing on 30 December 2004 at 8,206.23 (see Figure 4.3.1). Since then, activity has spurred the TASI above 10,000, with market practitioners suggesting that it could reach anywhere from 11,000 to 15,000 by 2005 year-end.

The principal reasons ascribed to this growth include:

- a buoyant economy with worldwide oil prices reaching new highs in 2004 and 2005;
- a marked preference in the past three to four years by both Saudi and other regional investors to invest in their domestic markets;
- strong results from many of the listed Saudi companies;
- some repatriation, together with less expatriation, of funds from the region.

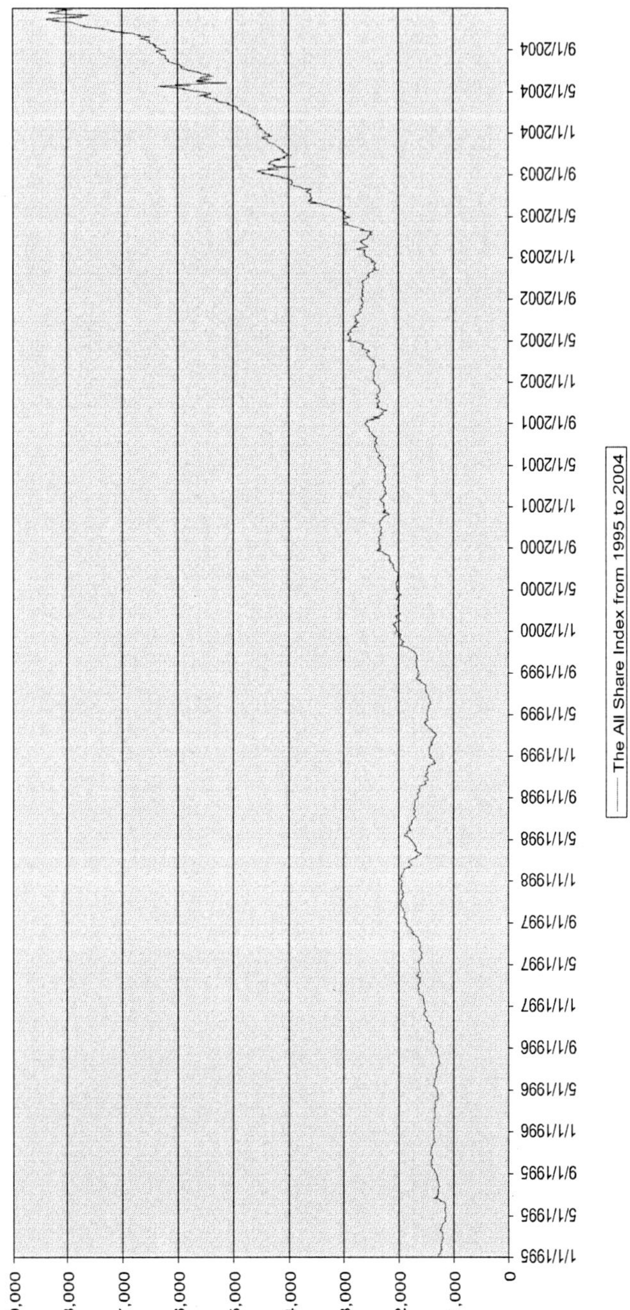

Figure 4.3.1 Saudi Arabia's Tadawul All Share Index (TASI) from 1995 to 2004

Currently there are 74 listed companies, broken down into generic sectors as shown in Table 4.3.1

Table 4.3.1 Saudi Arabia's Tadawul All Share Index (TASI) from 1995 to 2004, by sector

Sector	No of companies	Sector capitalization (US$ million)
Agriculture	9	1,455
Banking	9*	92,746
Cement	8	15,629
Electricity	1	29,666
Industry	26	94,666
Insurance	1**	
Services	18	10,940
Telecommunications	2***	60,866

* Bank Al-Bilad is due to be listed in April 2005

** NCCI first listed in February 2005. Around 13 to 15 new insurance companies are expected to be licensed and listed during 2005

*** Etihad Etisalat was first listed in January 2005

The Capital Market Authority

One of the most encouraging features of 2004 was the establishment of the Capital Market Authority (CMA), a vital link between the Kingdom's economic well-being and its capital market development. The Capital Market Law was issued under Royal Decree No. M/30 on 2/6/1424H (equivalent to 31 July 2003).

The Law provided for the establishment of the CMA, with an executive board comprising a full-time Chairman and four Commissioners, who were appointed in July 2004. The CMA, which reports directly to the President of the Council of Ministers, is a government organization with financial, legal and administrative independence.

The CMA's functions are to regulate and develop the Saudi Arabian Capital Market. It issues the required rules and regulations for the implementation of the provisions of the Capital Market Law, aimed at creating an appropriate investment environment.

The CMA has the authority to *inter alia*:

- regulate and develop the capital market including issues such as IPOs and private placements of equity and debt (including bonds), as well as regulating and monitoring trading;
- protect investors and the general public from unfair and unsound practices;
- regulate and monitor full disclosure of information related to securities and their issuers;
- regulate and monitor the activities of entities and persons subject to the control of the CMA.

For the first time in Saudi Arabia there are established and transparent guidelines on which companies can list, with a defined process to achieve this.

Since inception, the CMA has been involved in four heavily oversubscribed IPOs that have come to market under the new Law, thus quickly winning on-the-job experience. It has also developed the necessary infrastructure, which includes a full professional team in the regulatory areas of authorization, licensing, supervision, corporate finance and enforcement.

The CMA's vision

The CMA has developed a four-part vision to guide its stewardship of the Kingdom's capital markets. As a regulator, the CMA will:

- facilitate the government's drive to deliver sustained, diversified economic growth and increase employment in the Kingdom;
- foster the continuous development of the capital market to ensure its position as the largest and most liquid market in the Middle East;
- protect investors by promoting fair, open, and efficient markets as well as by ensuring the full and timely disclosure of material information; and
- maintain the stability of the financial system through worldclass, efficient, transparent and predictable regulation, licensing and supervision of all market participants jointly with the Saudi Arabian Monetary Agency.

Investment banking

The investment banking arena in the Kingdom was relatively small until 2004. Prior to that year, few public M&A transactions were consummated, although there were more private deals concluded, many of which not involving external professionals. There was one IPO between the mid-1980s and 2003, when Saudi Telelcom was privatized, and no more than 10 private placements of mature businesses. There are numerous reasons behind the latter, including the lack of a regulatory framework, the two-stage process required to make the transition from limited liability company to a listing, and a lack of perceived incentives to merge or list.

From the mid-1990s into the new millennium, the market for investment banking has been essentially dominated by Saudi International Bank (now Gulf International Bank) and, in the case of M&A transactions, by the accounting firms. With the advent of the Capital Markets Law this is undergoing radical change, with a number of the local banks establishing corporate finance capabilities to complement their existing brokerage and asset management arms. For example, the Saudi British Bank is establishing a joint venture with HSBC to provide such services. Other Saudi banks appear to be seeking to compete through selective recruitment from external markets, combined with internal talent. One further development in 2004 has been the granting of licences to international banks such as J P Morgan Chase, BNP Paribas and Deutsche Bank, although the suite of services they will offer, as yet, remains unclear. Nevertheless, the expectation is that such international banks will spur growth in the development of the corporate bond market (as yet untested, apart from government issuance), although intense competition can be expected from the domestic banks.

The CMA will require that any intermediaries in the market be authorized, with each applicant having to convince the authority that it is fit and proper to conduct the various areas of activity that it applies to undertake and that it has the requisite managerial expertise, financial and other systems, appropriate policies and procedures to fulfil the various legal, operational and regulatory obligations. This process will be exhaustive and will also include the authorizing of persons engaged in the business, along the lines established in the UK by the FSA. Market conduct conditions are also being implemented and the bywords and phrases of many markets, including 'integrity', 'due care', 'Chinese Walls' and 'conflicts of interest', will all eventually become enforceable in setting the standards for the participants in the largest regional market.

The opportunities for the new players appear to be emerging. Many family and other limited liability companies are, for the first time, considering the implications of a listing; the government will continue with its privatization programme; foreign joint venture partners in Saudi companies are now offered an exit route through an IPO; and owners of private companies are able to work by a set of Takeover Regulations when approached by a listed predator, thus ensuring transparency and fairness when dealing with the other party and the regulator.

The Listing Rules and Takeover Regulations set out, for the first time in this market, the process to be followed, the disclosure requirements and the information to be provided to investors. The latter will now be considerably more comprehensive than ever before, thus encouraging more investors to participate. This seems to be bearing fruit already, increasing the number of subscribers from just over 900,000 for the Saudi Telecom IPO to in excess of nine million for the Bank Al-Bilad IPO in 2005. It has to be said, however, that the latter was also influenced by the general exuberance of the market and also by the pricing of a number of issues at par. For example, the Bank Al-Bilad IPO was priced at par (SR50 or US$13.3) due to its start-up nature.

The outlook, therefore, is very positive from many perspectives. There are opportunities for banks and other authorized firms to engage in investment banking activities, either offering a comprehensive or selective set of services. In addition, a transparent set of rules and regulations is available for all potential issuers of public equity and debt instruments and for those contemplating a merger with, or takeover of, a listed company. The present liquidity in the market should also ensure that new issues are subscribed for, although issuers will also have the back-up of the underwriting of any new share offering by the investment banks.

4.4

Islamic Banking Practices

Dr Bashir O M Fadlalla, Islamic Development Bank

Introduction

This chapter discusses various Islamic banking products that are currently available to business people, both investors and traders. In the context of a perspective of the history of Islamic banking, a working definition is provided to the reader. There is also an explanation of the religious basis of Islamic banking, which has its origin and foundation in the teachings of Islam – a subject often not very well comprehended in the West.

Also provided are definitions, features and applications of some of the Islamic modes of finance that are currently utilized for resource mobilization and for the financing of investment and trade. While this review of Islamic banking practices is in no way comprehensive, it does cover the major modes of finance available.

Background to Islamic banking

For a number of years now Islamic banking and finance has grown as a distinctive field of business and of study throughout the Islamic and non-Islamic world. Indeed, its rate of growth has been encouraging, given the short span of time it has been in existence.

The first quasi-Islamic banks were established in Malaysia and Egypt in the early 1960s, in the form of the Pilgrims Fund in Malaysia (1968) and in the form of a savings bank in Egypt (1963). But the very first fully-fledged Islamic bank was Dubai Islamic Bank, chartered in the UAE in 1975. The Islamic Development Bank commenced operations in the same year, although it was formally set up in 1973.

Today, there is a confirmed Islamic banking presence in more than 30 countries, notably in Africa, the Middle East, the Far East, Europe and the United States. Three countries, Iran, Pakistan and Sudan, have an Islamic banking system, while Malaysia has a parallel banking system where Islamic financial institutions operate side by side with conventional financial institutions.

The growth of Islamic banks indicates that there is a growing demand for their services and products. In addition, major conventional banks have also opened Islamic banking windows to cater to the financial needs of Muslims.

It is worth noting that after only three decades or so, Islamic banking has come to be accepted as an integral part of the world financial order and, together with other financial systems, is helping through the globalization process in integrating the world economy. This chapter seeks to answer the following questions:

- What is Islamic banking?
- What are the objectives of Islamic finance and in what way does it differ from conventional finance rendered by conventional banks and other conventional financial institutions?
- What is the underlying philosophy and what are the governing principles of Islamic banking, and what are its operational characteristics?
- What are some of the most important services/products that are currently being utilized as modes of financing for production and trade, and how available are those services to the ordinary investor or consumer?

The answers to these questions as presented here are designed in such a way as to indicate the theoretical foundation and the sphere of application in today's business environment. Notwithstanding this, the chapter seeks to provide a practical guide to those wishing to know more about Islamic banking and finance.

A working definition of Islamic banking

Islamic banking may be defined as the practice of banking business in conformity with *Shari'a* (Islamic law). The main differentiating factor between conventional banking and Islamic banking is that in the latter the payment and the receipt of interest (*riba*) is not allowed. Islamic banking derives its inspirations and guidance from the religious edicts of Islam and has to conduct its operations strictly in accordance with the directives of *Shari'a*. That is why Islamic banks often need to institute a *Shari'a* Board to be responsible for screening and scrutinizing their operations. Over and above this, as may be expected, an Islamic bank also has to comply with the law of the land (jurisdiction). As such, it may also find itself in need of the counsel of traditional lawyers.

However, Islamic banking should not be perceived merely in the narrow context of the prohibition of the payment of interest, as is often the case. Rather, it is a financial system that focuses on mobilizing and organizing resources for the betterment of not only the individual, but society as a whole. This is well within the framework of the overall Islamic economic system, which strives to build a society based on social justice, equity, moderation and balanced relationships – a society in which exploitation, deceit and irrationality in the use of resources are very much abhorred. In such a system, the individual Muslim is constantly reminded of the Islamic aspiration that all resources available to human beings 'must always be put to optimum use, and no one has the right to hoard them or to keep them idle, or to squander them, or to use them for conspicuous consumption or wanton display, be it the individual, the community or the state'.[1]

The religious basis of Islamic banking

Islamic banking is primarily based on the *Shari'a*, often referred to in the writings of Western scholars as Islamic jurisprudence. As such, it is part of the overall teachings of Islam, which encompasses all aspects of the life and activities of the individual, family, society, state and the *Ummah* (all the Muslim community as a whole).

The *Shari'a* is divided into:

- *Ibadat*, which describes man's relationship with God, reflected in worshipping; and
- *Mua'malat*, which describes men's interacting activities among themselves.

A significant part of *Mua'malat* is the daily conduct of economic activities under which umbrella lie financial and banking activities. Islamic banking, therefore, has its direct origin in *Shari'a* law.

---

[1] Adapted from Muzzam Ali, 'Reflections on Islamic Banking' (forthcoming), The Institution of Islamic Banking and Insurance.

However, *Shari'a* itself is derived from two primary sources, namely:

- the *Qur'an*, which is the ultimate word of God;
- the *Sunnah*, which is the sayings, teachings and the deeds of the Holy Prophet Muhammad (peace be upon him).

All the laws derived from the above two sources are then categorized into five levels indicating the degree of enforcement of that law. These levels are:

- *Fard* or *Wajib*: an obligatory duty, the omission of which is punishable;
- *Mandoub* or *Mustahab*: an action that is rewarded, but its omission is not punishable;
- *Jaiz* or *Mubah*: an action that is permitted, and the law is indifferent;
- *Makruh*: an action that is disliked yet not punishable, but its omission is rewarded;
- *Haraam*: an action that is absolutely forbidden and is punishable.

Accordingly, banking and financial activities being part of *Shari'a* law and of *Mua'malat* are themselves subject to the above categorization. In conducting his/her daily business activities, a Muslim would screen his/her deeds in the light of these guiding principles and would subsequently make decisions. It is, therefore, not only material satisfaction (be it profit maximization, cost minimization, attainment of high quality of product or whatever) that guides his/her decision-making process, but also, and perhaps more so, religious abidance and spiritual satisfaction that are of the essence.

Islamic banking services

Islam allows both equity financing and debt financing. Equity financing is normally effected through profit-sharing contracts, while debt financing is effected through deferred contracts of exchange. The most distinguishing features of Islamic modes include financing of real transactions and rescheduling of financing without interest. A chart highlighting the Islamic equity and debt financing modes can be found in Figure 4.4.1.

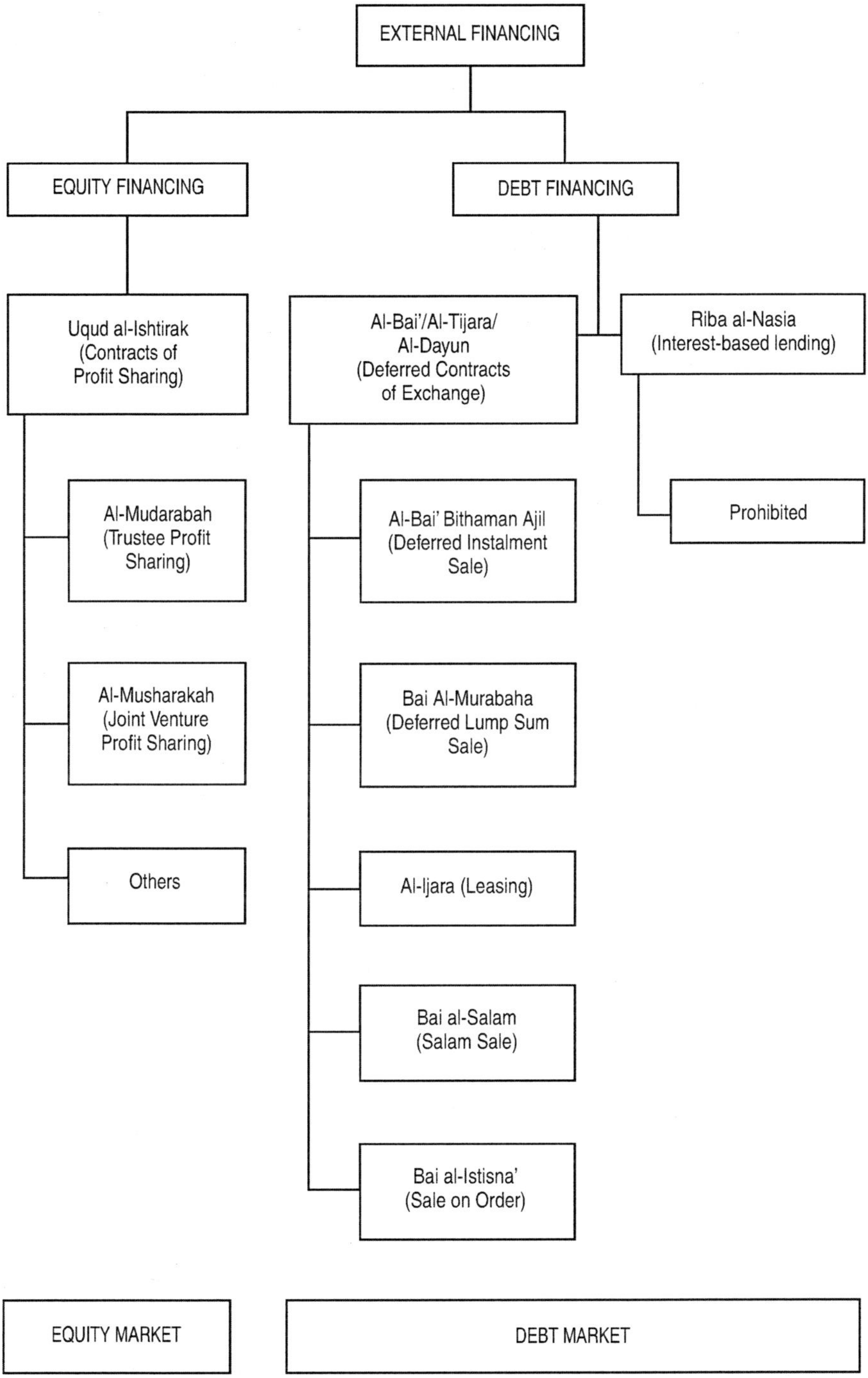

Source: Adapted from Bank Malaysia Berhad (BIMB), 1994

Figure 4.4.1 Equity financing and debt financing in Islam

Equity financing

Keeping in mind the five levels of *Shari'a* law discussed earlier, there are no major differences between Islamic finance and conventional finance in as far as equity financing is concerned. However, some schools of thought are of the view that equity investment in an enterprise that has even a small portion of conventional debt is not '*halal*' (permissible). The contract of *al-musharakah* (joint venture profit sharing) is, in essence, similar to the conventional concept of a joint stock company.[2] Therefore, to finance projects through equity participation, float a company on the stock exchange, organizse a venture capital company, or form an equity unit trust would generally be the same under Islamic equity financing as under conventional equity financing. However, there is an important qualification in that considering the case of equity alternatives, the given equity stocks must meet some additional criteria to conform to Islamic norms. All business activities of the company issuing the stocks should be *halal*. Given this requirement, stocks of companies belonging to breweries, entertainment industries or interest-based (ie financed through conventional sources) businesses where the major product is '*haraam*' (forbidden), will fall under the forbidden category.

Al-mudarabah (trustee profit sharing)

This instrument may be utilized for project financing whereby the Islamic bank becomes the 'provider of capital' and may provide 100 per cent of the capital requirement. The sponsor of the project or the 'entrepreneur' will undertake to manage the project and, as such, the bank normally does not interfere in the management details but has the right to conduct follow-up and supervision. The two parties agree *a priori* through negotiations on the distribution of the realized profits. Should the project incur a loss, the bank bears all the losses. However, it should be made clear that this is true only when no neglect or misconduct on the part of the capital user is ascertained. It thus becomes clear that the proven viability of the project, the tested managerial capability of the sponsor, and the degree to which the Islamic bank is capable of follow-up and supervision are key elements in the successful implementation of the project and the avoidance of losses for the bank and its shareholders.

Using this device, the bank may utilize shareholders' funds and customers' deposits to set up wholly-owned subsidiaries, take up equity in (*Shari'a* compatible) quoted or unquoted companies or other types of

---

[2] BIMB (1994), p. 22.

portfolio investment. The ability of the Islamic bank to identify, appraise, analyse the risk of, and manage that portfolio must therefore be ascertained.

Al-musharakah (joint venture profit sharing)

This instrument may also be utilized to finance acceptable projects, whereby the Islamic bank together with the sponsor(s) of the project agree *a priori* on the proportions of the project's capital each will shoulder. While each party has the right to be involved in the project management, the decision to do so or not is voluntary. As in the case of *al-mudarabah*, the ratio of profit distribution is fixed in advance through negotiations, and this may not necessarily tally with the ratio of participation in capital. However, unlike *al-mudarabah*, should the project make a loss, all parties bear the loss proportionately.

Islamic (equity) funds

A good example of the *musharakah* concept is Islamic equity funds, which though a new phenomenon, have already grown into an important source of funds and investment. As such, they are expected to play a central role in the future of Islamic finance.

Islamic funds have grown substantially over the past 18 years or so, with an estimated annual growth of 10 to 15 per cent. It is widely believed that by 2008/9 this market will be responsible for managing at least 40 to 50 per cent of the total savings of Muslims worldwide.

The Gulf region is growing into a centre of financial intermediation, with Bahrain being the industry's favourite offshore centre where key players have established themselves. Neighbouring Kuwait and Saudi Arabia command sizeable market shares in terms of managed fund levels. However, the Malaysia experience figures prominently in terms of product blending and financial engineering within the confines of *Shari'a*, particularly to arrange deals that can provide limited or full equity participation for an agreed period of investment on a clearly-defined, profit-sharing basis.

However, as mentioned earlier, some of the Islamic schools of thought hold the view that investment in equity of an enterprise that has any conventional debt is not in accordance with *Shari'a*. This makes it difficult to find suitable equity investments and much more difficult to set up equity-based unit trusts/mutual funds.

The current most popular Islamic funds are open-ended unit trusts or mutual funds with the underlying investments in stocks and shares that are listed on one or more stock markets. This becomes all the more important since there is ample evidence that in the medium and long term, a diversified portfolio of equities in developed markets produces a higher total rate of return than most other types of assets. Given good diversification across markets and sectors and reliable stock markets, the major risk relating to higher price volatility[3] can be greatly reduced. Even though there are still some differences among *Shari'a* scholars on the eligibility of companies for equity investments, the following general criteria are acceptable to most:

- the company should carry on its business in a manner compatible with *Shari'a*;
- investments should not be made in companies involved in *riba*-based businesses – thus conventional banking, insurance, finance and securities will not qualify;
- the company should not engage in the manufacture, distribution and trading of either alcoholic beverages, pork, or armaments and ammunitions;
- it should not deal in gambling and games of chance;
- debts and cash should not constitute more than 50 per cent of the company's overall assets.

Quasi-equities

In addition to the above, new modes of financing are evolving such as 'declining participation', which can be classified as quasi-equity.

Debt financing

Debt financing is the area where Islamic financing differs a great deal from conventional financing. In the latter, debt financing is almost entirely interest-based, while this contract is totally forbidden in Islam (ie *haraam*).[4] On the other hand, Islamic debt financing instruments of deferred contracts of exchange are not used very frequently in the conventional financial system. An exception will be the contracts of '*al-ijara*' (leasing) and '*al-murabahah*' (deferred lump sum), which are often practised in the conventional system.

---

[3] Loosely defined to be the percentage movement of prices from an average price base.

[4] Reference here is to *Riba al-Nasia*, which involves an increment on the principal of a loan to be paid by the borrower. The arrangement is that one party would lend money to another on the understanding that the latter would return the money at the end of an agreed period, the sum of which will comprise the original sum of money borrowed plus an increment in consideration of the former having granted the borrower time to pay.

Al-bai bithaman ajil (instalment) for financing the acquisition of assets
It is permissible for the Islamic bank to finance a customer who wishes to acquire a given asset and to pay by instalment or to defer the payment altogether for an agreed period of time. Under this mode of financing, and to comply with the requirements of *Shari'a*, the bank first purchases the asset concerned and then sells it to the customer at the actual cost of purchase plus a mark-up. The mark-up is meant to reflect the cost of administration plus a profit margin.

Al-ijara (leasing) for financing the use of services of assets
All categories of enterprises (from large scale to small and medium) require the services of a given asset to help them in conducting their normal business. Here also, the bank purchases the asset desired by the customer and leases it to him for a fixed period. Lease rentals and all other terms and conditions are agreed with the customer in advance through business negotiations. Both the rental payment and the lease period are usually determined in light of the projected profitability and cash flow of the project. Although the asset will need to be insured by the customer, the mark-up will always be designed to reflect various risks. These risks can be spread between a number of banks/financial institutions through a syndication arrangement. The bank retains the ownership of the leased assets throughout the entire lease period. After the end of the lease and full payment of the rentals by the lessee, the bank transfers the ownership of the equipment to the lessee as a 'gift'.

Istisna' financing
Istisna' is a contract for manufacturing/construction and sale or supply of goods (capital goods or other assets).[5] It is a contract where the manufacturer (seller) undertakes to supply the buyer with goods of an agreed technical specification, within an agreed time frame and at an agreed price.

Istisna' is also an instrument of pre-shipment financing. Unlike in the case of *murahabah*, *istisna'* is binding on both parties upon signing the contract. The buyer (beneficiary) is obliged to take delivery of the goods manufactured within the stipulated time and specifications. As a medium- and long-term financing mode, *istisna'* can effectively enhance the manufacturing capabilities of the economy, while availing needed goods and assets for further production. The role of the Islamic bank is to finance the contract reached between the beneficiary and the manufacturer through a separate contract with the beneficiary.

Moreover, *istisna'* can be utilized for the financing of infrastructure projects and trade in the private sector and also for intangible assets

---

[5] IDB (1996).

like gas and electricity. By being suitable for both project and trade finance, *istisna'* helps in creating linkages between various sectors of the economy in the framework of pre-shipment financing that would include financing of working capital, which is not otherwise possible under leasing or instalment.

Al murabaha (deferred lump-sum) letter of credit for trade financing
While the previous modes cover both medium- and long-term 'project' finance, the bank may also finance trade, mostly on a short-term basis, including the financing of working capital. This includes the whole range of import/export (or purchase/sale) of goods and machinery, the acquisition and holding of stock and inventories, raw materials and semi-finished goods.

In this context, and under an *al-murabaha* contract, the customer approaches the bank with certain letter-of-credit requirements. The bank agrees to purchase/import the goods on the understanding that the client would subsequently purchase the goods from the bank on an *al-murabaha* basis. The Islamic bank establishes the letter of credit and pays from its own funds to the requiring bank. The Islamic bank then sells the goods to the client at a sale price covering the cost plus a profit margin. The settlement is deferred to an agreed date.

Conclusion

In this review of Islamic banking practices, Islamic banking, for the purpose of simplicity, has been defined as 'the practice of banking business in conformity with *Shari'a* (Islamic law)'. As such, Islamic banking and finance derives its origins from Islamic jurisprudence whose axioms are the *Qur'an* and the *Sunnah*. Islamic banking is not merely the prohibition of *riba* (interest), as it is sometimes mistakenly interpreted. It is rather a financial system that focuses on mobilizing and organizing resources for the betterment of not only the individual but also society as a whole.

It has been pointed out that Islam allows both equity financing and debt financing. Equity financing is normally effected through profit-sharing contracts like *al-mudarabah* (trustee profit sharing) and *al-musharakah* (joint venture profit sharing) and equity funds, while debt financing comprises a whole list of products. Examples of such products are deferred instalment, leasing, *istisna'*, and deferred lump sum. Therefore, there are a number of financial products pioneered by Islamic banking for resource mobilization, project and trade financing and investment in general. Current efforts in the area of financial engineering are likely to expand Islamic banking products to new frontiers in the foreseeable future.

Further reading

Al-Najjar, A (1993) *The Movement of Islamic Banking*, (in Arabic) Harakat Al-Benook Al-Islamia, Cairo, Sprint Co.

Ausaf Ahmed and Khan Tariqullah (eds) (1997) *Islamic Financial Instruments for Public Sector Resource Mobilization*, Islamic Research and Training Institute (IRTI) – Islamic Development Bank (IDB), Jeddah, K.S.A., Seminar Proceedings No. 39.

Bank Islam Malaysia Berhad (1994) *Islamic Banking Practice – From the Practitioner's Perspective,* BIMB, Malaysia.

Fuad al-Omar Abdal-Haq Mohamed (1996) *Islamic Banking Theory, Practices and Challenges*, Zed Books, Oxford University Press, Karachi.

Hassanuzzaman, S M (1997) 'Defining Islamic Economics', *Journal of Islamic Banking and Finance*, Vol. 14 (Jan) No. 1 Karachi.

Imamuddin, S M (1982) 'A Historical Background of Modern Islamic Banking' in *Thoughts on Islamic Banking*, Islamic Economic Research Bureau, Dacca.

Iqbal, Zamir (1997) 'Islamic Financial Systems' in *Finance & Development*, Vol. 34 (June).

Islamic Development Bank (1996) 'Istisna's Mode of Financing', IDB, Jeddah.

Islamic Development Bank, Annual Reports 1990–1998.

Qayum, K (1998) 'The Scope and Challenges of Islamic Banking', *New Horizon, No. 78,* August 1998, London.

Qureshi, A I (1957) 'Usury and Interest', in *Islamic Review*.

Wilson, R and D Baldwin (1985) 'Islamic Finance in Principle and Practice', in *Islamic Finance*, Graham and Trotman, London.

Fadlallah, B O M (1998) 'Some thoughts on The Financial Crisis in South East Asia' – a discussion paper presented to the FINANCE Professional Group of the Islamic Development Bank (IDB), May 1998, Jeddah and published in '*Al Manar*', IDB Information Bulletin, No. 72, Nov. 1998.

4.5

Accounting Standards and Financial Reporting Requirements

Ernst & Young, Riyadh

Accounting books and records

The Ministry of Commerce and Industry (MOCI) requires that all companies and establishments (with capital that exceeds SR100,000) should keep the following books of account in Arabic within the Kingdom:

- daily journal;
- general ledger;
- inventory book – this is a comprehensive trial balance of all assets, liabilities and results for the year, which should be comparable to a detailed balance sheet and income statement.

These requirements were enforced by Royal Decree in July 1989. Taxpayers must maintain Arabic accounting records within the Kingdom, and field inspections are frequently carried out by the Department of Zakat and Income Tax (DZIT). Computerized accounting systems are allowed, provided that they comply with the requirements of the MOCI and that Arabic printouts of the accounts are generated on a regular basis. A penalty of SR5,000 is imposed where a company does not comply with the requirements for Arabization. There are also tax implications if no Arabic books are properly maintained. To help English speaking taxpayers, some companies have computerized English and Arabic translation services.

The Ministry of Finance controls the enforcement of these requirements by having the DZIT report to the MOCI those cases where companies do not comply with Arabization rules.

Accounting standards

Companies registered in Saudi Arabia are required to comply with the accounting standards issued by the Saudi Organization of Certified Public Accountants (SOCPA). In case no SOCPA accounting standard exists, International Financial Reporting Standards (IFRS) are to be used as a guide.

The major accounting and auditing regulations are contained in the following:

- Regulations for Companies;
- Income Tax Regulations;
- Saudi Arabian accounting and auditing standards issued by SOCPA;
- additional accounting standards issued for financial institutions by the Saudi Arabian Monetary Agency (SAMA);
- IFRS.

The regulations require that financial statements should include auditor's report, balance sheet, statements of income, cash flows and changes in the shareholders' equity and notes to the financial statements.

Auditors are required to be licensed by SOCPA in Saudi Arabia, which functions under the auspices of the MOCI. It has been vested with the responsibility of monitoring and guiding the auditing profession, issuing auditing standards and accounting principles and enforcing the rules and regulations relating to the licensing of auditors and reporting violations.

Specific standards and regulations

Certain accounting standards and regulations for financial statements presentation include the following:

- in cases where the losses of a limited liability company reach three-quarters of its share capital, the partners must convene a meeting to determine whether the company shall continue to exist or be dissolved before the expiry of the term specified in its articles of association. Such decision should be published in the *Official Gazette*;
- limited liability companies are not allowed to lend money to their partners because lending transactions are considered to be a banking activity and a means of repaying capital, and therefore a violation of the Banking Control Law and the Regulations for Companies;
- companies' assets cannot be revalued except in cases of reorganization or liquidation. This is intended to prevent abuse by fictitiously overstating the value of property, plant and equipment;
- income tax for a wholly-owned foreign company is charged to the income statement;
- zakat for companies wholly owned by Saudi or GCC nationals is charged to the income statement;
- income tax and zakat on mixed ownership companies is charged to retained earnings and may be deducted from dividends.

Financial reporting

Filing with MOCI

All publicly-held and limited liability companies are required to file copies of the board of directors' report and audited financial statements with the MOCI within six months after their financial year-end. In addition, manufacturing entities are required to file a performance report including financial and operational ratios.

Filing with the DZIT

All incorporated entities operating within Saudi Arabia, regardless of ownership, are required to file a tax and zakat return at the DZIT and pay any taxes/zakat due. For detailed information in respect of filing with the DZIT please refer to Chapter 4.6.

Audit requirements

Companies are required to have annual independent audits. Joint stock companies and limited liability partnerships must appoint at least one independent auditor, and banks are required to have two independent joint auditors. The auditor must be a licensed accountant. Banks' and joint stock companies' auditors must have been registered for more than five years.

4.6

Business Taxation

Ernst & Young, Riyadh

Introduction

The government of the Kingdom of Saudi Arabia levies all taxes in the Kingdom, and the Department of Zakat and Income Tax (DZIT), which is part of the Ministry of Finance and National Economy, administers the tax system. The Saudi Arabian government issued a new income tax law promulgated through Ministerial Resolution No. 278 dated 20/11/1424H (12/01/2004) and published in the *Official Gazette* on 11/3/1425H (30/04/2004), which has superseded the income tax regulations of 1951 and subsequent amendments and clarifications issued through Royal Decrees, Ministerial Resolutions and circulars. The new tax law came into effect on 30 July 2004. It is applicable to taxpayers in respect of accounting periods beginning on or after the effective date. The withholding tax provisions of the new tax law became applicable from 30 July 2004.

Principal taxes

Income tax

Income tax is assessed on the foreign ownership interest in the taxable income of joint stock companies, limited liability partnerships, partnerships and other Saudi legal entities and on the taxable income of branches of foreign companies, contractors and independent professionals.

Foreign entities (except Gulf Cooperation Council (GCC) nationals) and their interests are not subject to zakat (see 'zakat' section below). The Saudi Arabian branches of GCC companies are subject to income tax.

Individuals are not taxed on salaries or wages.

Zakat

Zakat is a religious wealth tax payable by Saudis and GCC nationals on their ownership interest in Saudi joint stock companies, limited liability partnerships, partnerships and other Saudi legal entities. Saudis and GCC nationals are not subject to income tax on their shares of profit in such Saudi entities.

The zakat rate is 2.5 per cent of capital employed that is not invested in fixed assets, long-term investments and pre-incorporation expenses deferred, as adjusted by net results for the year. Complex rules apply to the calculation of zakat liabilities.

If companies or partnerships are owned by Saudi or GCC nationals or both, as well as by other foreigners, zakat is assessed in proportion to the equity interest of Saudi and GCC nationals in the entity.

Natural Gas Investment Tax (NGIT)

NGIT is applicable to every natural or juristic person (including GCC nationals and entities) engaged in natural gas, natural gas liquids and gas condensates investment activities in the Kingdom of Saudi Arabia. NGIT is not applicable to a company engaged in the production of petroleum or both petroleum and natural gas.

The Natural Gas Investment Tax Rate (NGITR) is determined on the basis of the Internal Rate of Return (IRR) on cumulative annual cash flows.

Withholding tax

Withholding tax is a tax deducted at source from payments made to non-residents not having a legal registration or a Permanent Establishment in Saudi Arabia in respect of income earned from a source in the Kingdom. A Saudi resident entity, whether or not such entity is a taxpayer under the tax regulations, is responsible for withholding the tax and settling with the DZIT. Non-resident Saudi/GCC nationals and entities are also subject to withholding tax on income earned from business activity undertaken in Saudi Arabia rather than the previously applicable withholding zakat.

Capital gains tax

Capital gains on the sale of business assets and business interests are treated as ordinary business income. Complex rules apply to the computation of capital gains on the sale of business interests by non-Saudi investors. However, the following gains are exempt from income tax:

- capital gains on sales by non-Saudi shareholders of securities in a Saudi joint stock company traded on the Saudi stock exchange, provided that the securities were acquired after the effective date of the new tax law (ie 30 July 2004);
- gains on the disposal of property other than assets used in the business activity.

Indirect taxes

Indirect taxes consist of customs duties levied on imported goods. Saudi Arabia does not impose sales tax, value added tax, estate tax or gift tax.

Rates of tax

The various tax rates are shown in Table 4.6.1.

Table 4.6.1 Tax rates as at February 2005

Nature of tax	Tax rate (%)
NGIT on entities engaged in only natural gas investment fields	30–85
Tax on entities engaged in oil and other hydrocarbons production	85
Income tax applicable to entities engaged in activities other than above	20
Tax on capital gains	20

Withholding tax rates are as follows	
Management fees	20
Royalties; payments made to head office or an affiliated company for services	15
Rent; payments made for technical and consulting services; payments made for air tickets, freight or marine shipping; international phone calls; dividend payments; loan interest; and insurance or reinsurance premiums	5
Payments for any other services	15

Taxable income and deductible expenses

Taxable income

Tax liabilities are assessed by the DZIT on the basis of audited financial statements, as adjusted for tax purposes. Foreign airlines and foreign freight, land and marine transport companies operating in the Kingdom may be assessed for tax under the 'presumptive basis'. Under the presumptive basis, no financial statements are presented, and the tax liability is assessed on a deemed profit, calculated at rates specified in the tax regulations.

Dividends received from profits previously taxed in Saudi Arabia are excluded from the income of the recipient. Foreign source income of Saudi resident business entities is assessed in the same manner as income derived from within the Kingdom.

Deductible expenses

In general, normal business expenses are deductible provided they can be substantiated by appropriate documentation. Deductions are restricted with respect to the expenses described below.

Head office expenses
Allocations of general or administrative costs of the head office are not deductible. Only certified technical costs of the head office that are directly related to Saudi Arabian operations are tax deductible. Irrespective of whether these costs are tax deductible or not, such charges are subject to a 15 per cent withholding tax if paid by the branch.

Technical expenses
Technical expenses incurred outside Saudi Arabia in connection with engineering or other technical services directly related to a project undertaken in Saudi Arabia are deductible if the main contractor has approved the performance of the technical work and if the taxpayer produces specific detailed statements supported by an overseas auditor's certificate. Payments for technical and consultancy services rendered by third parties (including foreign shareholders), irrespective of the place of performance of services, are subject to withholding tax (see sections above 'Withholding tax' and 'Rates of tax').

Depreciation

Depreciation is calculated for each group of fixed assets by applying the prescribed depreciation rate to the remaining value of each group at the fiscal year-end.

The remaining value for each group at the fiscal year-end is the total remaining value of the group at the end of previous fiscal year after deduction of the depreciation charge for the previous year *plus* 50 per cent of the cost of assets added during the current year and the previous year *minus* 50 per cent of the proceeds from assets disposed of during the current year and the previous year, provided that the balance is not negative.

Assets acquired under BOT or BOOT contracts should be depreciated over the period of the contract or the remaining period of contract if acquired or renewed during that period.

Cost of repairs or improvements of fixed assets are deductible on condition that the deductible expense for each year may not exceed four per cent of the remaining value of the related asset group at year-end. Amounts in excess should be added to the remaining value of the asset group and depreciated.

Social insurance

Contributions to foreign social insurance, foreign pensions and foreign trust plans, and contributions to Saudi Arabian social insurance that exceed the stipulated employer's share, are not deductible. However, trust and pension fund plans managed and maintained in accordance with Saudi Arabian regulations are deductible, subject to certain restrictions.

Provisions and termination benefits

Provisions for doubtful debts, slow moving inventories, termination benefits and other similar items are not deductible. Specific write-offs and actual employment termination benefit payments that comply with Saudi Arabian labour laws are deductible.

Agency fees

During 2001, the Council of Ministers issued a decision cancelling the regulations governing the relationship between foreign contractors and Saudi agents. Accordingly, except for agency fees paid by a foreign insurance company to its Saudi agent, any agency fees paid in respect of a contract signed after the issuance of the council decision may not be allowed by the DZIT. Agency fees paid to a Saudi agent by a foreign contractor engaged in contracts with government entities entered into by them prior to the issuance of the aforesaid decision are deductible provided:

- the required agency agreement is entered into before signing the contract;
- the foreign contractor is a main contractor, not a subcontractor;
- the fee does not exceed five per cent of the contract value or five per cent of the contract revenues reported in any one year;
- the agent's name was disclosed in the offer or bid documents or in the contract.

Losses

Losses may be carried forward indefinitely. However, the maximum loss that can be adjusted against a year's profit is 25 per cent of the tax adjusted profit for that year. Saudi tax regulations do not provide for the carry back of losses.

Non-deductible expenses

No deduction is allowed for the following:

- expenses not connected with the earning of income subject to tax;
- any payments or benefits to a shareholder, a partner or their relatives that constitute salaries and wages or bonuses and like items or that do not represent an 'arm's length' payment for property or services;
- entertainment expenses;
- expenses of a natural person for personal consumption;
- income tax paid in the Kingdom or another country;
- financial penalties and fines paid or payable to any party in the Kingdom, except those paid for breach of contractual terms and obligations;
- any bribes or similar payments that are considered a criminal offence under the laws of the Kingdom, even if paid abroad;
- any amount paid to the head office abroad by branches of foreign companies in respect of royalties, commission, interest or indirect

administrative and general overheads allocated on an estimated basis.

Treatment of groups of companies

According to the tax regulations, each company within a group is considered an independent entity and should file a separate tax return directly with the DZIT. Consolidation is not acceptable to the DZIT.

Partnerships

In the case of a personal (partnership) company, individual partners are subject to tax rather than the personal company. However, the personal company is required to file an information declaration within 60 days following the end of the taxable year.

Consortiums

Each member of a consortium is required to file its own tax return and to report the revenues and expenses arising from its share of the scope of work of the consortium, together with any other activities in the Kingdom.

Taxation of individuals

Foreign employees are not taxed on their wages or salaries received from employment. Self-employed foreign professionals resident in Saudi Arabia are taxed on the taxable profits from all of their activities in the Kingdom. Taxable profits are computed in a manner similar to that described above and the profits are taxed at 20 per cent. Non-resident professionals are subject to withholding tax on their Saudi source income.

Tax treaties

Saudi Arabia's only double tax treaty is with France, although European tax authorities generally allow a credit for Saudi Arabian income taxes paid. Saudi Arabian income taxes paid by Saudi Arabian registered companies in which a US company has an interest, may generally be taken as a foreign tax credit in the US company's US tax return.

However, the US tax authorities may, under certain circumstances, limit the amount of Saudi income tax creditable to the US company's percentage of ownership in the entity, even though the tax is based on the US company's share of the profit.

Filing of tax returns and administration of tax

Registration with the DZIT

All persons subject to tax, excluding non-resident taxpayers subject to withholding tax, are required to register with the DZIT before the end of the first fiscal year.

Income tax/zakat filing

The following entities must file their annual tax declaration with the DZIT based on their annual audited financial statements within 120 days following the end of the taxable year and pay the income tax due with the tax declaration:

- a resident capital company;
- a non-resident with a permanent establishment in Saudi Arabia;
- a resident non-Saudi natural person carrying out business activity in Saudi Arabia.

In the case of a personal company, partners are subject to tax rather than the personal company. However, the personal company is required to file an information declaration within 60 days following the end of the taxable year.

Entities wholly owned by Saudis and GCC nationals are required to file zakat returns.

Withholding tax filing

The withholder of tax is required to register with the DZIT prior to the settlement of the first tax payment. The withholder of tax is under obligation to settle the tax withheld with the DZIT within the first 10 days of the month following the month in which the taxable payment is made and file a withholding tax return in the prescribed form. An annual withholding tax return is due within 120 days following the end of the taxable year.

Advance payment of tax

An advance payment on account of tax for the year is payable in three instalments, ie by the end of the sixth, ninth and 12 months. Each instalment of advance payment of tax is calculated in accordance with the following formula:

$$25\% \times (A - B)$$

where A is equal to the taxpayer's liability as per the tax declaration for the preceding year; and B is equal to tax suffered by the taxpayer at source (ie withholding tax) in the preceding year.

A taxpayer is not required to make an advance payment if the amount of each instalment calculated above would be less than SR500,000.

Review procedure

After reviewing the final tax return, the DZIT sends the taxpayer either a letter requesting additional information or a notice of assessment that states the tax and zakat liability for the year and requests payment of the amount still due, if any. The DZIT may conduct a field audit of the taxpayer's books and records at the taxpayer's premises, either with or without notice.

Normally, the review procedure occurs within one year of submission of the final tax return and finalization occurs within two years. Final clearance will take longer if a tax assessment is appealed.

Restricted tax clearance certificate

After filing the tax declaration and paying any tax and zakat due, the taxpayer may request a restricted tax/zakat clearance certificate. This certificate enables the taxpayer to:

- collect progress payments due on contracts (other than the final instalment);
- bid on government contracts;
- apply for work visas;
- renew commercial registration.

Final tax clearance certificates

The final tax clearance certificate (FTCC) is issued by the DZIT if no tax/zakat is outstanding from the tax/zakat payer. In case an assessment is appealed, the FTCC is issued when a bank guarantee has been provided to the DZIT for the amount of tax or zakat under appeal. The FTCC enables the taxpayer to obtain progress payments and final instalments due under contracts completed during the period covered by the certificate.

Fines

The following fines are imposed. Failure to register with the DZIT results in the imposition of a fine ranging from SR1,000 to SR10,000.

Fines for non-submission of tax declarations within the statutory period are payable at one per cent of the total revenue, subject to a maximum delay fine of SR20,000. However, if the fine calculated as set out below is higher, the higher amount is payable:

- five per cent of the underpaid tax if the delay is up to 30 days from the due date;
- 10 per cent of the underpaid tax if the delay is more than 30 and not more than 90 days from the due date;
- 20 per cent of the underpaid tax if the delay is more than 90 and not more than 365 days from the due date;
- 25 per cent of the underpaid tax if the delay is more than 365 days from the due date.

Failure to settle the advance tax and withholding tax within the stipulated period results in imposition of a delay fine of one per cent for each 30 days of delay. The delay fine is computed from the due date of tax until the time the tax is paid.

Evasion fines at 25 per cent of the difference in tax resulting from misrepresentation or fraud committed by the taxpayer may be imposed.

Appeals

A tax/zakat payer may appeal against a final assessment issued by the DZIT. A formal appeal must be filed within 60 days of the date of the assessment letter.

The tax/zakat payer is formally notified of the appeal hearing date. The appeal is heard by the Preliminary Tax Appeal Committee (PTAC) in the presence of both the DZIT and the taxpayer or the taxpayer's representatives. Only Saudi nationals may represent the taxpayer at the appeal hearing, which is conducted in Arabic. The PTAC notifies the taxpayer of its decision in writing. A taxpayer may either accept the PTAC decision or appeal to the Higher Appeal Committee (HAC) for a final decision. The DZIT also has the right to appeal a decision of the PTAC. The DZIT issues an amended assessment based on the PTAC's decision.

The appeal of a PTAC decision to the HAC must be filed within 60 days of receipt of the PTAC's decision and may only be filed after settlement of the taxes due or submission of a bank guarantee for the amount of additional liabilities due based on the PTAC's decision. The decision of the HAC is final unless an appeal is filed with the Grievance Board.

Tax advice

This chapter contains information current as of February 2005 and is based on the present understanding of the new tax regulations. Companies and individuals planning to do business with, or in, Saudi Arabia should seek specific tax advice from their professional advisers before taking any action.

4.7

Insurance Services

Anthony Shoult, ASA Consulting[1]

Introduction

Following recent changes in legislation, Saudi Arabia's underdeveloped insurance sector has undergone a major boost that has opened the sector to increased competition from major foreign insurance companies. It is expected that this will lead to improvements in the performance of the Saudi insurance industry, with the addition of new products, services and the introduction of higher levels of professionalism.

Until recently, the National Company for Cooperative Insurance (NCCI) was the only organization that was legally allowed to offer insurance products within Saudi Arabia, although the authorities had turned a blind eye to the many other international firms selling insurance under local agency agreements.

In 2003, the Saudi Council of Ministers approved, as per resolution No. 125 dated 14/7/2003, the Law of Cooperative Insurance Supervision. The Saudi Monetary Agency (SAMA), the body that will regulate the industry, has formulated the executive regulations to activate the law, which became effective in 2004. The sector should benefit from an improved regulatory framework. However, the regulation of the insurance market will be a major challenge for SAMA, not only in terms of the acceptability and cost of the products and their premiums, but also whether they are being sold ethically and adequately articulated to a nascent insurance market.

New legislation reflects the desire of the Saudi authorities to have a fully functioning insurance industry with proper regulation and controls on unauthorized companies. Policy-makers also intend to make the holding of certain types of insurance a requirement, once they have taken the necessary steps to boost public confidence in the industry.

---

[1] Sources of Information include *Arab News*, Saudi Economic Survey and National Company for Cooperative Insurance (NCCI).

NCCI will continue to be the industry's flagship firm but as a publicly listed company with audited accounts.

The government took two important policy decisions in 2002 concerning health and automobile insurance prior to the introduction of the new regulatory framework. The new health insurance and automobile insurance requirements in Saudi Arabia have created favourable opportunities for investment in the Saudi market by foreign firms.

The pace of development of the Saudi insurance sector will depend on the type and acceptability of the insurance schemes that are introduced and adopted in a country where large sections of the population are still sceptical about the efficacy and ethical basis of the very concept of insurance.

Structure of the market

National Company for Cooperative Insurance (NCCI)

The National Company for Cooperative Insurance (NCCI), incorporated in 1986, is one of the largest insurance companies in the Middle East. In 2004, NCCI claimed to be the market leader in the Saudi insurance sector, with a market share of over 30 per cent. NCCI's market coverage includes aviation, energy, marine hull, engineering and medical, as well as property, motor and accident insurance.

NCCI was floated on the Saudi stock exchange in January 2005 when the government sold seven million NCCI shares, or about 70 per cent of the company's total capital. The issue was 12 times over subscribed, with more than 800,000 applicants each receiving nine shares valued at SR205. NCCI had previously amended its Articles of Association to be consistent with the new Cooperative Insurance Companies Supervision Act.

Changes in legislation leading to an influx of international companies will make the insurance sector far more competitive. Consequently, it is likely that NCCI will lose some business and market share to these companies.

Establishment of new insurance firms

In March 2005, Saudi Arabia opened up its insurance sector for local and foreign investments. The new regulations are aimed at regulating the Kingdom's insurance market as well as attracting foreign capital to this sector. This was one of the steps taken by the government to attract more capital into this sector in order to fulfil the requirements associated with Saudi Arabia gaining accession to the World Trade Organization.

The new regulations allow insurance companies, in addition to NCCI, to become established in Saudi Arabia. This will provide equal opportunity for both local and international investors to establish new companies, provided that these companies fulfil the necessary prerequisites related to capital and technical reserves and practise their insurance business in accordance with the cooperative concept, as defined in the executive regulations.

According to the new law, the capital of an insurance company shall not be less than SR100 million and it will be turned into a joint stock company with floating of at least 25 per cent of its stocks. Earlier, SAMA had notified the insurance companies that were seeking a licence, to implement at least 30 per cent Saudiization as a prerequisite for the grant of a licence.

The Saudi insurance and reinsurance sector has gained a significant boost from the granting of licences to 13 new insurance companies under the new insurance and foreign investment laws. These include well-known insurance companies from the UK, Germany, Switzerland, Japan, India, the Netherlands, the United States, Bahrain, Jordan, Lebanon and France, with a combined paid-up capital of some SR2.5 billion.

The licensing has opened the Saudi insurance market to foreign companies by ending the monopoly of the NCCI. Earlier, foreign insurance companies were allowed to operate in the Kingdom only through their agents.

Of the new insurance companies to become established, the largest include Mediterranean and Gulf Insurance and Reinsurance (MedGulf), BUPA Arabia, Al-Alamiya Insurance, United Cooperative Assurance, Arabian Shield Insurance and Saudi United Cooperative Insurance. Other smaller companies include the Saudi-Indian Insurance, Tokyo Marine and Nichido, Saudi National Insurance, AXA Insurance, Saab Takaful, Saudi-French Insurance and National Takaful.

The introduction of competition to the sector will greatly improve the performance of the Saudi insurance market, as it will add new products, services and levels of professionalism.

The new regulations are likely to drive unqualified companies out of the market, making insurance more reliable and secure. It is likely that the number of insurance companies in the Kingdom will be reduced from over 100 in 2004 to just 10 to 20 players that will dominate the market. As a result, the Saudi market is expected to witness mergers between companies.

Size of the Saudi insurance market

The NCCI estimated the insurance market in the Kingdom in 1999 at SR2.8 billion, in terms of gross written insurance premiums. According to a study conducted by the Insurance Ombudsman Bureau, the Saudi insurance market had risen to a recorded SR3.4 billion as gross written premiums in 2002.

The per capita insurance premium in Saudi Arabia is, therefore, relatively low at around US$41 per annum, representing just 0.6 per cent of Gross Domestic Product (GDP). This is primarily caused by low insurance awareness as a result of various factors, religion being one of them. Growth is expected with the application of compulsory motor and medical insurances. Also, the reorganization of the industry with the entry of new players will prompt campaigns to expand insurance awareness and to promote it as a necessity rather than a luxury.

In terms of potential, industry sources expect personal product lines, such as medical, motor, accident and life insurance, will increase as these account for only 30 per cent of customers at present.

To put the potential volume of insurance business in Saudi Arabia into context, the Kingdom currently has a ratio of 0.01 per cent for Life Insurance Premium Income to GDP. This compares with a world average of five per cent and 10 per cent for the UK. It is worth noting that a one per cent increase in this ratio in the Kingdom would create a life insurance market of in excess of SR300 billion. The health segment alone is believed to have the potential to generate an additional SR20 billion in premiums as a result of the Cooperative Health Insurance Law for expatriates and the opening up of the market to foreign firms.

Health insurance

In June 2002, the Cooperative Health Insurance Council issued the new mandatory Cooperative Health Insurance Law for expatriates. This law, which applies to some seven million expatriates and their families working and living in the Kingdom, is to be implemented gradually over a period of up to three years, depending upon the number of employees.

The scheme covers most medical conditions but excludes AIDS treatment, mental disorders (except chronic cases), organ transplants and unnecessary cosmetic surgery. The law requires employers to pay for insurance coverage of foreign workers and dependant family members.

The scheme is to be implemented in three phases. The first phase became effective in September 2002, when the Health Ministry instructed that any company with a workforce of 500 or more expatriate employees must provide them with medical insurance coverage before the expatriates will be issued an *Iqama* (residence permit).

The second phase will involve companies with a non-Saudi workforce of 100 to 500, and the third stage companies with a non-Saudi workforce of less then 100.

Up to 200 hospitals across the Kingdom were expected to take part in the cooperative health insurance programme. The new law, which established an industry oversight mechanism and clearly authorized foreign participation in the market, was introduced to boost a market with the potential to generate an additional US$5 billion in premiums.

It remains to be seen what impact the mandatory health insurance for expatriates will have on the foreign direct investment (FDI) flows into the Kingdom. Some potential foreign investors have stressed that the provisions of the health insurance scheme would play a part in their investment decisions as an additional cost factor.

Although medical coverage it is now mandatory for expatriates, it is expected that medical insurance would eventually be compulsory for all Saudi citizens. It will be interesting to see how the major Western health insurance providers, such as BUPA, take up the challenge of implementing a *Shari'a* compliant health insurance product.

Motor insurance

Saudi Arabia has long been notorious for its high rate of motor vehicle accidents. Largely as a result, second and third party motor vehicle insurance has now become compulsory.

In November 2002, driving licence insurance was made mandatory for the first time in the Kingdom as part of the implementation of the Royal Decree No. 222 dated 30/10/2001.

There are more than 10 million cars registered in Saudi Arabia, and approximately 1.2 million cars enter the Kingdom every year. The Saudi Ministry of Interior prohibits any car entering the borders of Saudi Arabia without insurance coverage. There are currently around 75 car insurance companies in the Kingdom.

Islamic insurance (*Takaful*)

Takaful is an Arabic word meaning 'guaranteeing each other' or joint guarantee. The basic fundamentals underlying the Takaful concept are very similar to cooperative and mutual principles, to the extent that the cooperative and mutual model is one that is accepted under Islamic Law. Under Takaful, members contribute a certain sum of money to a common pool. The purpose of this system is not profit but to uphold the principle of 'bear ye one another's burden'. The principles of Takaful insurance are as follows:

- policyholders cooperate among themselves for their common good;
- every policyholder pays his subscription to help those that need assistance;
- losses are divided and liabilities spread according to the community pooling system;
- uncertainty is eliminated in respect of subscription and compensation;
- no advantage is derived at the cost of others.

Companies at the forefront of pioneering Takaful products in the Kingdom include Bank Al-Jazira, Islamic Insurance and Reinsurance Company (IIRCO), the Bahrain-based insurance holding company of Jeddah-based Dallah Al Baraka Group (DBG), Arab-Eastern Insurance Company (AEIC), a joint venture involving Tokyo Marine and Fire Insurance and Takaful International of Bahrain, in which Kuwait's International Investment Group (IIG) and DBG are shareholders.

Bank Al-Jazira, for example, has introduced its Takaful Ta'awuni Programme, an Islamic life insurance product, which is a *Shari'a* compliant insurance programme that has been approved by SAMA for distribution in the Kingdom. This was the first Takaful programme to adopt the *Wakala* contract concept. Takaful Ta'awuni is a full suite of products for individuals, families and businesses that includes savings and protection plans for education, marriage expenses, a ladies' savings plan and capital savings plans. There are also plans to launch a corporate product called group market retirement plan.

AEIC has also launched a Family Takaful Programme comprising a range of products including life insurance and a Children's Takaful Plan. AEIC has also launched a Group Term Takaful for consumer loans and financings, such as Murabaha, aimed at private companies (on behalf of their employees) and Islamic financial institutions (on behalf of their borrowers).

As far as health insurance is concerned, Saudi Arabia is expected to follow the lead taken by Malaysia in the development of health Takaful products that include a Takaful Wiladeh Plan launched by Syarikat Takaful Malaysia (STM), the largest Islamic insurance provider in the country, which covers childbirth costs and provides benefits in the event of pregnancy complications, congenital birth defects, and a cash benefit in the event of the death of the mother or infant during or immediately after childbirth.

Part Five

Marketing and Promotion

5.1

Marketing Information for Business Planning

Anthony Shoult, ASA Consulting

Introduction

The first requirement for any company wishing to establish new business interests in Saudi Arabia is to ascertain the nature of market demand for the products or services that they wish to promote and sell. This involves the gathering and interpretation of information obtained from various sources, which is generally characterized by lack of consistency and often exhibits varying degrees of accuracy and reliability.

With many new industrial undertakings relying on the availability of financing on favourable terms by the Saudi Industrial Development Fund (SIDF), the standard for the nature and quality of information required in the marketplace tends, increasingly, to be influenced by the requirements of this organization.

Specialist management consulting companies with strong links to Saudi Arabia and the neighbouring Gulf and other Middle East markets, increasingly undertake the work of obtaining and interpreting information. Such companies have often been exposed to numerous project opportunities, including those that have floundered in the planning stages for a wide variety of reasons.

The issues as outlined above that are covered in this chapter, may be summarized as follows:

- the requirements for information for purposes of business planning;
- sources and availability of information;
- the means of obtaining reliable information.

Requirements for information

The SIDF has fairly stringent requirements in respect of the content and presentation of information to be provided by potential investors in support of an application for project funding. The viability of the project will need to be demonstrated but any financial analysis must be based on a comprehensive analysis of the market and on a sound techno-economic evaluation.

Market studies

In order to satisfy the current SIDF requirements, a number of aspects concerning the market for the products to be manufactured in-Kingdom need to be covered. These may be summarized as follows:

- product demand;
- end user demand;
- competition – both local and foreign;
- market size, characteristics and growth trends;
- pricing and distribution;
- level of market penetration;
- marketing strategy considerations.

Product demand
It will be important to know what the broad nature of market demand is for the products in question in Saudi Arabia. Typically this includes information concerning product type and specification and possibly packaging requirements. For example, in the case of uPVC windows and door frames, a potential investor wished to know full details of the specification of products currently on the market, including dimensions, composition, performance characteristics under Saudi climatic conditions and so on. Similarly, a potential investor in a food product processing facility was very concerned to obtain an accurate breakdown of the range of packaging sizes and types for a variety of food products as required in the market.

Where existing markets are served by both locally-produced and imported products it will be important to ascertain whether any apparent preference for imported products is solely on the grounds of product quality or is based on other criteria. Also important is the nature of the

Saudi regulatory framework covering the manufacture and use of the products in question.

End user demand

For industrial or business-to-business products, it is necessary to identify the key end users of the product in question. Typically, these may comprise either a relatively small number of intermediate processors or a large number of very small-scale businesses. However, in the case of industrial and technological products, it is often necessary to obtain accurate end user information from a relatively small number of key players in the market.

In industrial product markets, it is important to ascertain the underlying drivers of end user demand, for example the relative importance of perceived quality or specification differences between the products of competing manufacturers versus price differentials. It is true to say that in Saudi Arabia, other things being equal, price is almost always the key determinant in the choice of supplier.

In the case of consumer products, a demographic analysis of the Saudi population with conclusions regarding consumption of the products in question is required. However, it is also important to categorize consumers; for example, food product producers will wish to confirm exactly what the main categories of consumer of their products are. These could include not only households, but also restaurants and commercial caterers.

It is important to identify end user or consumer trends, and in particular to provide details of changes in consumer taste, and any new product types or technology changes that are affecting the underlying or established pattern of market demand. Similarly, it is important to ascertain which manufacturers' brands are preferred by consumers and why, and what factors affect the purchase decision, including the extent to which the consumer is influenced by product advertising, in-store promotions or other sales promotional activities.

Competition from local production

It is necessary to identify the key Saudi and other GCC producers of competitive products and to provide estimates of both national and regional production capacity. Also required are individual company profiles for competitors with details of products produced, outputs, market share estimates, strategies and distribution policies. The new investor should also know whether there are any new local or regional players about to enter the market. In the case of Saudi Arabia, it is relevant to ascertain the extent to which new manufacturing licences have been issued by the Ministry of Industry and Electricity and are still current for the products in question.

Competition from imported products

The investor wishing to set up production facilities in the Kingdom is usually intending to manufacture products that will act as substitutes for similar imported goods. It is therefore necessary to ascertain the key international manufacturing companies supplying the market, together with details about their local representation, market share of competitive brands and overall strengths and weaknesses in the marketplace.

Reference should be made to international and national trade statistics to verify the extent and nature of trade volumes over the preceding five-year period. The investor will also wish to know what the prevailing rates of import duties levied on the products in question are.

Market size and characteristics

It will be necessary to provide an estimate of the size of the Saudi market in terms of both volume and value. Market value estimates are usually best expressed in terms of local manufacturers' selling prices or landed (c&f, duty paid) prices for imported equivalent products.

This will need to be qualified by reference to factors such as the volume of imports, the level of local production, any exports or re-exports that may be relevant and the rate of utilization by key end user organizations for industrial products (or rates of household/individual consumption for consumer products).

Market segmentation

Estimates of the way in which the market is segmented will be required, generally with reference to segmentation as follows:

- product type and specification;
- end user category;
- geographical breakdown, usually as between:
  - regions of Saudi Arabia (central/north, eastern, western/south);
  - other GCC countries (where export sales are expected).

Market growth and trends

Also required is a five-year growth projection for the growth in demand for the products in Saudi Arabia by volume and value. Such projections will need to be qualified by reference to the key factors that are responsible for determining the rate of growth in demand. This analysis should indicate whether product consumption in Saudi Arabia and the wider GCC has been increasing or declining over the period in question.

Market trends should be identified including, in particular, the importance of new technology on product design or specification, the extent to which new producers are entering the market and the extent to which end user/consumer preferences and requirements are changing over time.

Pricing and distribution

Examples should be given of prevailing Saudi pricing levels for a range of locally-produced and imported products. These prices should generally be expressed in terms of SR per unit of volume (tonne, m^2 etc) ex local manufacturer. The pricing of imported goods should be at local received levels, ie duty paid and delivered to the end user or primary distributor's warehouse. Where complex distribution is involved, for example in the case of automotive components or consumer products, it will be necessary to identify the value chain from the local or foreign manufacturers, through importers and distributors to retailers and then on to customers.

One particular investor establishing a food processing plant needed to know whether producers generally self-delivered their products or used the services of independent distribution companies. Also important were the extent to which the sales were spread between the different types of retail outlet in the Kingdom, the relative importance of the big supermarket chains and the extent to which the food products retailers would welcome a new supplier to the market.

Market penetration projection

Based on the market size and market growth projections, it will be necessary to produce a 10-year market penetration scenario in terms of volume for each product group to be marketed. This may involve the development of separate market penetration scenarios in respect of each product group for the Saudi market and if exports are planned, also for the five GCC export markets – namely the United Arab Emirates, Kuwait, Oman, Qatar and Bahrain.

Marketing strategy considerations

The main elements of the investor's proposed marketing strategy will need to be defined during the project feasibility stage. The principal aspects to be covered are summarized as follows:

- product range – a preliminary product range breakdown for each product group to be marketed;
- product pricing – preliminary product pricing estimates and associated pricing policy covering the main products to be marketed and indicating the level of trade discount to be made available to large

direct end users (factories) and wholesalers/distributors covering both Saudi and export markets;

- sales support – an associated policy covering the terms of business to be adopted, including technical support to manufacturers and after sales support;
- distribution strategy (routes to market) – the options for distribution of the company's products should be considered in turn and a preferred route to market identified; typical of the options that are available for manufactured products are:
  - setting up a comprehensive distribution structure, with a large number of branches located throughout the Kingdom of Saudi Arabia and in other GCC countries;
  - setting up stocking points or distribution centres at strategic sites close to the main centres of population;
  - a policy of direct distribution from factory to customers, both end users and distributors;
- sales promotion, advertising and publicity – an outline of the need for company sales literature and other sales promotional information and material, together with advertising and other promotional sales support activities;
- preliminary organizational planning – a preliminary plan for the organization of sales and marketing, covering all necessary management, sales and support staff;
- programme for implementation – this should include the key marketing planning activities including the establishment of the necessary sales and marketing organization, including:
  - recruitment of sales and marketing personnel;
  - appointment of distributors in Saudi Arabia and export markets;
  - preparation of sales support material, publicity and advertising activities.

Sources of information

For companies examining business opportunities in Saudi Arabia there are a number of important sources of key information. These can be classified as follows:

- primary sources – industry insiders involved in the business or industry or allied businesses or industries with involvement in the Saudi and/or other GCC markets;
- secondary sources – published information, international trade data, industry or country/region specific trade associations, the internet.

Primary sources of information

The primary sources of information concerning the market are generally to be found through local investigation on the ground in Saudi Arabia or elsewhere in the Gulf. Important sources of primary information include:

- senior management in industrial manufacturing companies, many of which are to be found at the industrial city locations in Riyadh, Jeddah or Dammam;
- oil and petrochemical industry executives, particularly Saudi Aramco (Industrial Development Division) at Dhahran, SABIC (Marketing) at Riyadh and SABIC affiliate operating companies at both Al Jubail and Yanbu;
- senior management of trading companies, commercial agencies and marketing and distribution companies;
- senior partners in firms of architects and engineering consultants and managers of building and engineering contracting companies;
- senior management in retailing establishments, particularly the big supermarket chains;
- owners and managers of small-scale workshops and repair shops located in the old industrial areas or 'souk' locations;
- senior managers and project officers in banks and financial institutions, particularly the Saudi Industrial Development Fund (SIDF) in Riyadh;
- foreign embassy and consular commercial personnel;
- technical, engineering and projects personnel at:
  - key government ministries such as Ministry of Industry and Electricity and the Ministry of Municipal and Rural Affairs;

  - important quasi-government organizsations such as Saudi Consolidated Electric Company (SCECO) and Saline Water Conversion Company (SWCC);

- information services supervisory staff of the chambers of commerce and industry at Riyadh, Jeddah and Dammam.

Secondary sources of information

Secondary sources of information can be accessed from both within Saudi Arabia and internationally. The major sources of secondary information available internationally may be summarized as:

- published material in specialist Middle East technical publications* such as:
  - *Middle East Economic Digest* (MEED);
  - *Gulf Marketing Review* (GMR);
  - *Gulf Business*;
  - *Gulf Construction*;
  - *Saudi Economic Survey*;
  - *Middle East Economic Survey* (MEES).
- international trade statistics, particularly Eurostat and World Trade Atlas (these are available in London at the Export Marketing Information Centre (EMIC) at the Department of Trade and Industry);
- the internet – some useful sites are as follows:
  - www.saudinf.com (The Saudi Arabian Information Resource);
  - www.meed.com (Middle East Economic Digest – MEED);
  - www.gmr-online.com (Gulf Marketing Review);
  - www.gulfbusiness.com (Gulf Business);
  - www.gulfconstructiononline.com (Gulf Construction);
  - www.saudieconomicsurvey.com (Saudi Economic Survey);
  - www.mees.com (Middle East Economic Survey);
  - www.sama-ksa.org (Saudi Arabian Monetary Agency).

Information centres in London

The key centres of information located in London are as follows:

- Saudi Arabian Business Information and Economic Research Centre (SABIERC);
- Export Marketing Information Centre (EMIC) at the Department of Trade and Industry;
- the Middle East Association (MEA).

Means of obtaining reliable information

The need for the collection and accurate interpretation of reliable information usually results in the investor obtaining the services of an experienced marketing consultant with a good working knowledge of Saudi Arabia and the wider Gulf region. These consultants will be required to conduct assignments that require the collection of complex information, and so it is necessary to have an approach that ensures the information obtained is reliable. This approach generally includes the following principal steps:

- a full client briefing, covering the company's present marketing strategy as well as the aims and objectives of the investor wishing to establish a business in Saudi Arabia;
- market research deskwork and fieldwork preparation;
- market research fieldwork in Saudi Arabia and possibly other GCC and Middle East countries;
- data analysis, and the reporting and presentation of results.

Comprehensive client briefing

It is always very important to fully appreciate the client company's current marketing and sales resources, product range, distribution strategy and customer profile. A good initial briefing allows the consultant to discuss a field research interview programme, a survey sample with the client and reach an agreement on the marketing strategy to be followed. This stage is often inadequately addressed in Saudi Arabia, with the result that there is not a sufficiently clear mutual understanding of the scope of work to be undertaken by the consultant. This inevitably leads to disagreement at a later stage.

Desk research and fieldwork preparation

The consultant will always undertake preliminary desk research with the objective of building up background information. This is done by referring to trade statistics, trade periodicals, directories and internet searches.

It is important that the fieldwork planning activities are carried out with sufficient care to ensure that adequate provision is made for the inclusion of all key respondents in the market research fieldwork stage. It is also important to fully ensure that any questionnaires to be used during the market research fieldwork fully reflect the terms of reference as agreed between the consultant and the client organization.

Market research fieldwork

The market research fieldwork will generally be divided between face-to-face and telephone interviews. In general, the preferred method of investigation is a face-to-face interview programme with key respondents, although cost considerations sometimes limit the scope of such types of investigation.

The aim of the fieldwork research will be to obtain both reliable qualitative and quantitative information regarding consumption levels, product specifications, market position of key competitors, as well as end user or consumer preferences.

The consultants will also generally discuss salient points with key government institutions, in particular the Saudi Industrial Development Fund (SIDF) and Saudi Arabian Standards Organization (SASO).

For research in Saudi Arabia, consultants generally use a semi-structured questionnaire in order to provide a consistent framework of information from each interview, while allowing particular issues to be researched in-depth when they arise. Subject to cost constraints, the aim is to undertake a comprehensive interview programme in an attempt to cover an adequate sample size that will give substance and validity to the consultancy's analyses and conclusions.

In consumer markets where there is a need to evaluate the perceptions held by Saudi individuals who purchase and use products for private and business use, consultants will typically carry out a sample survey of purchasers. This work would usually be carried out by telephone, covering a representative sample of sufficient size to reliably indicate the major preferences and grievances of typical consumers for the purposes of market planning.

Prior to such consumer research, the consultants will prepare a questionnaire that will enable the understanding of preferences, prejudices, the purchase decision-making process, levels of after sales support received and other key perceptions.

Data analysis and reporting

Following the data collection and fieldwork stages, the consultants will analyse the material to form an opinion of the level of current and future market demand, market trends, consumer perceptions and preferences and pricing and distribution policies. This information will often be presented in both matrix and report format. Following the data analysis stage, the consultants will generally be required to prepare a draft report for submission to the client. After discussions with the client, the final version of the report will be prepared and submitted. In Saudi Arabia, senior executives will not wish to read a long report and so a well-prepared executive summary is essential if the consultant's views are to be adequately conveyed to decision-makers within the client organization. In addition, clients in Saudi Arabia generally require a full oral presentation with visual aids.

Publications recommended for regular reading

Publications recommended for regular reading by executives in organizations planning business investments in Saudi Arabia include the following:

Middle East Economic Digest (MEED)
33-39 Bowling Green Lane
London EC1R 0DA, UK
Tel: +44 (0) 20 7470 6200
Fax: +44 (0) 20 7470 6641
or MEED Regional Office
Dubai Media City
PO Box 25960 Dubai, UAE
Tel: +9714 390 0045
Fax: +9714 390 4560
Email: edmundosullivan@meed-dubai.com (Editor-in-Chief)

Gulf Marketing Review
Gray Business Communications
PO Box 7260 Dubai, UAE

Tel: +971 4 349 6663
Fax: +971 4 349 9552
Email: barryg@GatewayGBC.net (Publisher)

Gulf Business
Motivate Publishing
PO Box 2331 Dubai, UAE
Tel: +971 4 282 4060
Fax: +971 4 282 4436/282 7593
Email: gb@motivate.ae

Gulf Construction
Al Hilal Publishing and Marketing Group
PO Box 224 Manama, Bahrain
Tel: +973 1729 3131
Fax: +973 1729 3400
Tel: +44 208 943 3630 (London)
Email: info@gulfconstructionworldwide.com

Saudi Economic Survey
PO Box 1989, Jeddah 21441
Saudi Arabia
Tel: +966 2 651 4952/652 9120
Fax: +966 2 652 2680
Email: info@saudieconomicsurvey.com

Middle East Economic Survey
MEPEP (Cyprus)
PO Box 24940
1355 Nicosia, Cyprus
Tel: +357 22 665 431
Fax: +357 22 671 988
Email: info@mees.com

Opportunity Middle East
The Middle East Association
Bury House, 33 Bury Street
London SW1Y 6AX, UK
Tel: +44 (0) 20 7839 2137
Fax: +44 (0) 20 7839 6121
Email: mail@the-mea.co.uk

5.2

The Advertising Industry in Saudi Arabia

Anthony Shoult, ASA Consulting[1]

Introduction

Saudi Arabia is by far the most important advertising market in the Gulf Cooperation Council (GCC) region. This is because of the country's geographical size, the preponderance of youth, the high spending power of its population and its overall influence as a country that dominates the entire Gulf region.

Until the late 1990s, the Saudi advertising market was essentially served by local branches of international agencies that handled almost exclusively multinational accounts, like Ford or McDonald's.

These agencies were all based in Jeddah, the country's bustling commercial capital, which was generally viewed by outsiders as the point of entry to Saudi Arabia. Therefore, Jeddah, a cosmopolitan city and a gateway to Makkah, was where the advertising industry initially became established.

In contrast, Riyadh, the traditionally more conservative home to the government as well as a capital for big business, was nearly entirely passed over when the advertising industry first blossomed in the Kingdom. However, in recent years, the Saudi advertising business has changed as a significant geographic shift has taken place. Today, most major agencies have offices in both Jeddah and Riyadh, while in the future, Riyadh is likely to replace Jeddah as the Kingdom's true advertising hub.

GCC regional advertising expenditure stood at US$1.7 billion in 2002. Saudi Arabia with a population of 24 million and with an average age of 18, is the biggest spender and is now clearly a highly attractive market for the multinational advertising agencies. Despite the blips

---

[1] Sources of information include International Marketing Communications and AME Info-Middle East Finance and Economy.

caused by the SARS outbreak and the conflict in Iraq, the growth of Saudi Arabia's advertising sector shows little sign of slackening. Behind this boom in advertising expenditure is the rise of pan-Arab media and the consolidation of the national media, with a top tier in both print and television taking the lion's share of budgets.

The Saudi advertising industry is now looking outwards towards the commercial opportunities presented by the GCC and wider Middle East region, in terms of a need for the communication of clear, effective advertising messages to a vast population. The key difference is that advertising spend in other GCC markets tends to be driven by foreign clients, while Saudi Arabia has its many of its own high-spending local brands such as Saudi Arabian Airlines (SAUDIA).

The boom in advertising expenditure is most evident in Riyadh, increasingly home to the Kingdom's biggest firms, which is now extremely well-covered by forward-thinking international agencies. Paradoxically, the city's conservative inclinations have set it on a close par with global advertising trends. Today, advertising is about branding and image-building for the long term. This approach suits producers of goods and services, who are more interested in the big picture than in the sales figures for the last 24 hours. Saudi firms have been quick to embrace the shift towards pan-Arab media, since this has been viewed as an opportunity to further build a brand. While the trend has been particularly noticable in Riyadh, Jeddah, too, has witnessed growth in the advertising sector. However, Jeddah-based agencies tend to serve more local clients whose focus is on immediate distribution and short-term sales rather than long-term strategic considerations.

Until the late 1990s, in Saudi the advertising spend was mostly limited to the local media. Since the media were local, companies saw little need for advertising agencies. As companies knew the market, they tended to set up their own in-house creative departments to sell their products and services to local customers by way of the local media. This approach to marketing, which proved cheap and seemingly efficient, was the status quo in Saudi Arabia for decades.

Saudi Arabia presents agencies with its own particular set of challenges. One of the difficulties facing the advertising industry is a perceived lack of centralization. This is because the country is divided into three distinct regions, namely the east, centered on Dammam; the west, on Jeddah; and the central area on Riyadh. The advertising industry is aware that each region has its own particular culture and its likes and dislikes. The most effective advertising campaigns are those that take advantage of these regional differences.

Another key challenge, as in most of the region, is a lack of investment in research, so the profile of the typical Saudi consumer remains blurred. Cultural notions of privacy have also hampered researchers. Consumer market studies that have been carried out lack detail but tend to confirm that the typical Saudi consumer is young and high-spending. Also, agencies realize that consumers are demanding ever more sophisticated advertising messages. While the basic content of advertisements has not changed, production values have improved beyond all recognition in recent years, as the audience will no longer put up with anything that is old-fashioned or cheap.

The Saudi advertising industry is largely managed by non-Saudis, with a strong representation of Lebanese, British and Asian managers. This is because, although Saudis are responsive to advertising and regard it as part of popular culture, they have only very recently began considering it as a career option. Traditionally, local agencies have also relied on foreigners for their creative work, with the result that cultural differences created barriers between advertisers and consumers. More recently, agencies are attempting to use more local expertise for creative work on the basis that the best way to deliver an effective campaign is to understand the target audience.

Advertising fmcg brands

Much of the work carried out by Saudi-based advertising agencies is related to the promotion of international and local fast moving consumer goods (fmcgs) brands. However, the facts are that for an affluent market with a relatively high per capita disposable income, the expenditure in Saudi Arabia on advertising for both durable and fmcgs is relatively low.

The majority of multinational fmcg advertisers adopt a regional approach to media planning and as a proportion of their advertising investment is placed in pan-Arab or pan-Gulf media, the figures for communications directed towards the Saudi consumer tend to be understated.

There are obviously a number of factors responsible for this situation. In the case of fmcg brands, an understanding of the retail structure in the Kingdom is as important as understanding the consumers and the media available for reaching them. As those fmcg companies venturing into the retail market for the first time and wishing to establish a new brand will quickly become aware, the dominance of the wholesaler in the Saudi retail chain is an important factor. It is a factor that impacts on the nature and direction of any promotional activities to be undertaken.

Although the Saudi market has a growing number of sophisticated supermarket and self-service outlets, this retail sector (which numbers around 1,000 outlets) generally accounts for less than 25 per cent of sales in most fmcg categories. The wholesale market is responsible for providing distribution of the balance of product to 15,000 small grocery outlets, otherwise known as the *bakalas*. There are, in addition, as many as 70,000 sales points Kingdom-wide through very small *bakalas* and kiosks.

The wholesalers tend to stock brands that can be rapidly turned over, while providing a collection point for product rather than physical distribution into the down-market sector. Operating on extremely low margins, the Saudi wholesaler stocks brands that are demanded by the *bakala* customers, usually the brand leader plus one or two competing lines at the most.

A high proportion of sales of many staple brands find their way into the Saudi home direct from the wholesalers. Bulk buying (taking advantage of trade prices for product bought by the case) is a traditional and still common feature of the market.

In Saudi Arabia, brand loyalty is particularly strong and the consumer is not easily swayed from established, trusted brands unless given a very good reason to switch. The brand leaders, which have built up the trade and consumer franchise over a number of years in the market, are difficult to displace at wholesaler level. This is because brand leaders have built market share and critical mass, while establishing a category price point. It is difficult for brands with a much smaller market share to compete on price, build volume in the retail sector and still have funds available to advertise, to communicate the brand, build awareness and generate sales demand at consumer level.

Communicating to the target market

The population structure of Saudi Arabia, where around 45 per cent of the local settled population is under the age of 15, will appear attractive to companies investing for the longer term. While the Saudi market does provide a consumer base with inherent natural growth, the problems in reaching the adult market are exacerbated by a number of factors, namely:

- a shortage of local media providing coverage of a target market composed of local Arabs;
- the general lack of availability of reliable media data to facilitate planning;
- constraints on creativity imposed by social and cultural aspects of Saudi society;
- the absence of a creative culture within the local market in comparison with that found in more developed and sophisticated advertising markets;

- the availability locally of creative talent to develop or adapt concepts that communicate across cultural boundaries.

In those markets where media choices exist in abundance, the issue is not one of opportunity but of evaluation. However, reaching and converting the Saudi housewife, who is basically house-bound, makes shopping trips only with male members of the family and has been imbued with a trust in only a small number of staple brands, would be a challenge even in a market with a sophisticated media infrastructure.

In Saudi, the communication problem begins at point of sale in the stores themselves. Packaging that communicates clearly that 'this product, this brand is for me – the Saudi consumer – is vitally important. Too much emphasis has been placed in recent years on conveying the image of a 'quality, imported international' product.

More recently, the grocery brands that have achieved greatest penetration in the consumer market from scratch, have been brands communicated as local products – either brands manufactured locally or developed as product ranges from a local stable, such as Afia Corn Oil, Al Marai dairy products and the Al Alali range of distributor own-brand products.

The choice of media

Press media

In terms of the number of press titles available, there appears to be a good choice, but, in effect, good coverage of what can be regarded as the mass market is confined to very few titles. If we were to compare the press media with that of a sophisticated, developed market of roughly the same population, Australia, this supports five women's magazines with a circulation of over 250,000 and 12 with a circulation of over 100,000. By comparison in Saudi Arabia, *Sayidaty* is the only women's magazine with a circulation of over 100,000.

Television

As in any market, the proliferation of satellite channels is now confusing the television media scene. While Saudi TV offers advertising on both its local and 'international' channels, it does not purport to be an entertainment medium and its position with regard to advertising is basically to extend a service to manufacturers to provide information on their products to local consumers.

Advertising spots on Saudi TV are transmitted in blocks at set times, and prior to the advent of satellite television, the main evening break used to be as long as a programme. The station, itself, does not provide the advertisers with any data on viewership. Advertisers have turned to the major satellite channels to carry their advertisements, as local consumers have tended to turn to the Arabic language satellite channels for entertainment and news coverage.

Currently, satellite dish ownership amongst local and expatriate Arabs in Saudi averages over 70 per cent of homes. In the main cities, ownership runs at 80 per cent, while in rural areas ownership currently runs at around half this figure.

Radio

A more recent addition to the entertainment and information scene in Saudi Arabia has been the first commercial radio channel to offer good coverage of the country as a whole, MBC FM. MBC, arguably the leading satellite TV channel, launched an FM radio service in 1998, which provides a means of communicating to both women at home or men on the move. The station recognizes the different gender trends, where men generally work and women do not, and provides an effective means of covering both audiences.

In-store promotions

For grocery and consumer products, in-store promotions, in-store sampling activities and expenditure to secure a brand's position on the shelf generates below-the-line expenditure in excess of that spent in above-the-line media.

These activities are not just additional promotional support for a brand but, to a large degree, a substitute for media whose impact and efficiency cannot be measured as easily as in-store promotions.

Outdoor advertising

Outdoor advertising has become a dynamic medium in the Kingdom and over recent years contractors have established circuits to provide campaign possibilities similar to those that advertisers will be accustomed to in more developed markets.

Media research

Although it is possible to buy into post-campaign research as a measure of effectiveness, media planners currently have to rely on somewhat scant historical data combined with an empirical feel for which programmes are most popular with their target viewers. Media sources do recognize the need for an improved database, and a consortium has now been formed to provide regular, affordable research conducted along developed market lines by the consumer research company, Taylor Nelson Sofres (TNS).

The TNS household panel for Saudi Arabia was launched in May 2002 with 600 households (Saudi nationals and Arab expatriates). In August 2004, the sample was increased to 1,300 after adding on 700 more Saudi nationals to the sample. (TNS also operates an all-female research centre based in Jeddah, with all-Arab researchers that can provide a direct link to the Saudi female consumer).

The creative process

Finding the right message, generating an idea that captures attention and sets one brand apart from its competition is the job of advertising agencies, and is their very reason for existence in any market, whether developed or developing.

In the Saudi market, the cultural constraints placed on the process of creative execution by the advertising industry have often been cited as a straitjacket for those responsible for creative development. In any market one has, above all, to take into consideration the sensibilities of the consumer, as ignoring these sensibilities only results in communications that are irrelevant in consumer terms. For example, a Saudi TV requirement that women should be presented with their heads covered should be seen as an executional requirement rather than a bar to producing creative advertising.

There are two main issues in the Kingdom with regard to the creative process in advertising, and both revolve around local market attitudes to creative work. The first is that as advertising has developed in a market where budgets are relatively small, the tendency has been for local clients to expect to get 'free creative work'. Agency remuneration has been expected to come from placing advertising, and the price the agency pays for its profit is from giving its clients the ideas.

It has not been helped by some media owners who have pursued a strategy of selling to clients direct, while offering them the same discount structure as given to agencies and including 'creative work' in the cost of a page of booked advertising. For this reason, the agencies in the local market have had to find a way of adding value to their product by way of service provided in order to attract and keep clients, rather than simply to provide creative concepts, to be judged by the strength of their creative work and to be paid accordingly.

Secondly, in producing good creative work for the market, there is neither the pool of local Saudi talent available to execute concepts on the basis of a creative brief, nor a day-to-day environment that actually inspires creativity, as we know it in developed markets. The market does not offer the thousands of opportunities to see good advertising daily that creative people need to provide the initial and continued stimulus. Grafted on to this is the prospect of creative people trained outside of the market having to translate ideas conceived in one culture into relevant concepts for the traditional and conservative Saudi consumer market.

There has been some improvement in this situation in recent years as more Arab people have entered the industry, and advertisements are evolving that are less forced and more in tune with the local population. There has also been a change in the way the advertisements are made. Previously, the entire crew would be foreign, and the advertisement may have even been shot in Europe. Although advertisements cannot be shot in the Kingdom due to the red tape involved, there are now very good production facilities in both Dubai and Beirut where there is good access to local talent.

The rise of satellite television has made advertising more liberal and yet, at the same time, more fragmented. The strongest channel remains Saudi-owned MBC, but stations like Orbit and Showtime from Lebanon are also popular, and they show unrestricted, uncensored, Western-style programming. In fact, the average viewer has access to between 30–50 channels from all over the world. This has made it harder to target the Saudi viewer efficiently.

It is not surprising that what may be regarded as the best press advertising in the market is concept adaptation, stylised and nicely photographed to appeal to the local market. The greater freedom offered by satellite television makes this and other international media more attractive vehicles for the consumer message, but the risk is that the message misses the point and, with it, the heart of the Saudi consumer.

The multinational agencies and some local agencies are well aware of these pitfalls. In the final analysis, it is the client's awareness of these facets of the market that will determine whether the advertising for his/her brand will be relevant and effective. When budgets are tight, there is a tendency to buy advertising cheaply rather than cost-effectively.

Further information

For information concerning the services of the leading advertising agencies located in Saudi Arabia contact the following:

Intermarkets Advertising
PO Box 4635 Jeddah
Tel: +966 2 652 3344/643 8482
Fax: +966 2 643 6690
PO Box 61 Riyadh
Tel: +966 1 466 0695
Fax: +966 1 466 0705

Focus DMB & B Advertising
PO Box 15 Jeddah
Tel: +966 2 667 4447

Akeel Saatchi & Saatchi Advertising
PO Box 26532 Riyadh
Tel: +966 1 473 1413
Fax: +966 1 478 2657
Website: www.saatchi-saatchi.com

Target Leo Burnett Advertising
PO Box 295797 Riyadh
Tel: +966 1 273 7070
Fax: +966 1 273 7071
PO Box 6093 Jeddah
Tel: +966 2 651 1272
Website: www.leoburnett.com

Impact BBDO
PO Box 7242 Jeddah
Tel: +966 2 651 5013/4901
Fax: +966 2 651 6602
Website: www.impactbbdo.com

Memac Ogilvy & Mather
PO Box 54062 Riyadh
Tel: +966 1 460 4484/460 3499
Fax: +966 1 460 4474
PO Box 7868 Jeddah
Tel: +966 2 651 4269/651 5269
Fax: +966 2 653 3800
Website: www.ogilvy.co.ae

For further information on media research in Saudi Arabia contact:

Taylor Nelson Sofres (TNS)
4th Floor, Emirates Industries Building
PO Box 60662, Dubai, UAE
Tel: +971 4 282 2688
Fax: +971 4 282 2711
Website: www.tns-global.com

5.3

The Media

Anthony Shoult, ASA Consulting

Introduction

Advertising spending in Saudi Arabia reached the level of US$497 million in 2003. According to the Pan Arab Research Centre (PARC) analysis of media expenditure in the Middle East, the total Saudi advertising media spend has grown to this level from only US$10 million in 1975.

The print media dominates in Saudi Arabia, with newspapers and magazines together accounting for a share of 84 per cent of the total in-Kingdom advertising spend in 2003. Newspapers are by far the most popular medium in Saudi Arabia, accounting for 74 per cent of the Kingdom's total advertising spend worth some US$370 million in 2003 and having risen from the level of only just over US$140 million in 1993.

The advertising spend in relation to the press is mainly concentrated on the three leading Arabic daily newspapers, namely *Asharq Al Awsat*, *Al Riyadh* and *Okaz*, although an estimated 20 per cent of this spend is in the Saudi English language daily press. A lower level of advertising spend is allocated to the other main regional titles, *Al Yaum* and *Al Madinah*, with *Al-Jazirah*, *Al Bilad* and *Al Nadwaa* much less significant in agency media planning. However, many well-educated newspaper readers in Saudi Arabia read more than one title, typically subscribing to a local pan-Arab title, such as *Al Hayat*, and perhaps a business and economics daily, such as *Al Alam Al Youm*. Local custom and practice in Saudi Arabia is for daily newspapers to be purchased on a single copy basis via newsstand sales, rather than on a multiple issue basis by subscription.

In general, advertisers see little to choose between the main Arabic daily titles other than their particular regional orientation. Therefore, budgets are mainly directed towards the three leading titles unless there is a strong regional bias to the campaign. Much of the advertising placed in the Saudi daily newspapers is non-local, ie imported and multi-market brands, although many of these advertisers have local representation with branch offices located in the Kingdom.

Only seven per cent of the total advertising spend in Saudi Arabia in 2003 was devoted to visual media and radio broadcasting. However, the advent of new satellite channels and improved programme content by pan-Arab broadcasters is likely to result in increased utilization of television and radio media by advertisers in the future. The balance of nine per cent of media spend in Saudi Arabia is on outdoor advertising.

Newspaper publishing

Background

The Saudi Arabian press first came to prominence in the late 1970s with the emergence of the first international Saudi Arabic language newspaper *Asharq Al Awsat*. Produced by Saudi Research and Publishing Company (SRPC) by simultaneous printing in different international locations, this publication has become well established following its debut in London in 1978. It was initially linked by satellite transmission with Saudi Arabia, through its three printing locations in Riyadh, Jeddah and Dammam, and then subsequently extended to other printing locations in North Africa, Europe and the United States. This Saudi publication was amongst the first to give Arab readers, in the midst of societies whose lingua franca was anything but Arabic, their first daily newspaper.

The success of *Asharq Al Awsat* and other pan-Arab titles, including *Al Hayat* published in Bahrain and the Egyptian title *Al Akram*, has led publishers to introduce other specialist pan-Arab publications, including both weeklies and monthlies to cater to diverse reader interests. Thus, magazines for general reading, as well as those for men, women, children, sports and motoring enthusiasts, have become established. The development of efficient international distribution networks has ensured that these publications have been made available to Arab populations internationally wherever a demand exists.

The globalization of the Arabic language print media will continue, almost certainly led by Saudi Arabian media groups such as SRPC, which already owns and publishes 18 titles including daily, weekly and monthly newspapers in three languages: Arabic, English and Urdu. Given the presence of large foreign communities in Saudi Arabia and the rest of the oil producing Gulf Cooperation Council (GCC) states, non-Arabic language dailies will continue to be significant for advertisers in the media planning process.

Main publishers and publications

The three key newspaper publishers in the Kingdom, together with the main titles published, are as follows.

1. Saudi Research and Publishing Company (SRPC):

- *Asharq Al Awsat* (leading Arab international daily) – www.aawsat.com;
- *Arriyadiyah* (daily sports newspaper) – www.arriyadiyah.com;
- *Al Eqtisadiah* (national business daily) – www.aleqtisadiah.com;
- *Arab News* (English language daily) – www.arabnews.com;
- *Urdu News* (daily newspaper and Urdu language colour weekly magazine);
- *Al Majalla Magazine* (international news) – www.al-majalla.com;
- *Sayidaty Magazine* (women's fashion) – www.sayidaty.net;
- *Al Jamila* (contemporary lifestyle magazine) – www.aljamila.com;
- *Hia* (glossy publication for the Arab lady) – www.hiamag.com;
- *Arrajol* (glossy publication for men);
- *Basim* (weekly magazine for children);
- *Malayalam* (daily newspaper in Malayalam language).

2. Al Yamama Press Establishment:

- *Al Riyadh;*
- *Al Yamama Magazine.*

3. Okaz Organization for Press and Publication:

- *Okaz;*
- *Saudi Gazette* (English language daily).

The industry publishes some 300 million items a year, of which an estimated 70 per cent are daily newspapers in Arabic, English and Urdu languages, with the remainder being magazines and commercial print items. Comparative circulation data for the main Saudi daily newspaper and weekly magazine titles is shown in Table 5.3.1.

Table 5.3.1 Main newspaper and magazine, titles, formats and circulation data

Publishers/ Titles	Type	Language	Format	Circulation
Arabic dailies:				
Asharq Al Awsat	Daily	Arabic	Broadsheet/ pan-Arab	235,000#
Al Riyadh	Daily	Arabic	Broadsheet	150,000
Okaz	Daily	Arabic	Broadsheet	110,000
Al Yaum	Daily	Arabic	Broadsheet	20,000
Al Madinah	Daily	Arabic	Broadsheet	25,000
Arriyadiyah	Daily	Arabic	Broadsheet/ sports	110,000*
Aalam Alriadah	Daily	Arabic	Broadsheet/ sports	66,000*
Al Jazirah	Daily	Arabic	Broadsheet	110,000
Al Bilad	Daily	Arabic	Broadsheet	15,000
Al Nadwaa	Daily	Arabic	Broadsheet	8,000
Al Eqtisadiah	Daily	Arabic	Broadsheet/ business	77,000*
Al Watan	Daily	Arabic	Broadsheet	n/a
Al Hayat	Daily	Arabic	Broadsheet/ pan-Arab/ Published in Bahrain	166,000
English dailies:				
Arab News	Daily	English	Broadsheet	110,000*
Saudi Gazette	Daily	English	Broadsheet	15,000
Other language dailies:				
Urdu News	Daily	Urdu	Broadsheet	55,000*
Malayalam	Daily	Malayalam	Broadsheet	35,000*

Publishers/ Titles	Type	Language	Format	Circulation
Magazines:				
Al Majalla	Weekly	Arabic	News/business magazine	92,800*
Sayidaty	Weekly	Arabic	Women's magazine	143,000*
Sayidaty Fashion	Weekly	Arabic	Women's fashion magazine	67,000*
Hia	Monthly	Arabic	Women's lifestyle magazine	45,000*
Asharq Al Awsat	Weekly	Arabic	General interest magazine	180,000*
Arrajol	Monthly	Arabic	Men's lifestyle magazine	36,000*
Assayarat	Monthly	Arabic	Motor magazine	35,000*
Al Jadeeda	Weekly	Arabic	Youth lifestyle magazine	153,000*
Basim	Weekly	Arabic	Children's magazine	32,000*
Al-Yamama	Weekly	Arabic	News/business magazine	20,000
Iqra'a	Weekly	Arabic	General interest magazine	52,000
Al Nadi	Weekly	Arabic	Sports magazine	30,000

total *Asharq Al Awsat* circulation of 235,000 includes some 60,000 international issues printed overseas

* includes overseas copies

Note: Circulation figures vary widely and few titles actually have ABC certification. All the titles of Saudi Research and Publishing Company (SRPC) have ABC certificates, while other publications use publisher's figures. All daily papers have government subsidies and benefit from daily bulk sales to government of up to 5,000 copies for distribution to ministries and government offices.

Source: ASA Consulting/SRPC/International media companies

The newspaper publishing industry in Saudi Arabia is characterized by a number of leading titles that offer the same basic political coverage. The main difference is one of presentation and local news coverage, with the leading indigenous titles exhibiting a particular regional orientation.

Asharq Al Awsat is the leading title in Saudi Arabia, with audited daily sales of 235,000 of which just over 170,000 copies are circulated within the Kingdom. Although *Asharq Al Awsat* is a Saudi title published by SRPC, it is now classified by media sources as a pan-Arab newspaper. This is because it is edited at its offices in London and transmitted via satellite to its in-Kingdom printing centres in Riyadh, Jeddah, Dammam, Abha and overseas printing centres in Frankfurt, Cairo, Casablanca and Kuwait City for simultaneous local printing and delivery. In most centres, the newspaper is printed on company-owned printing presses, although in Egypt it is printed with *Al Ahram*. While it is basically a pan-Arab title, *Asharq Al Awsat* is the closest of any of the daily Arabic language titles to being a national daily for the Saudi market. Distribution of *Asharq Al Awsat* in the Kingdom, together with the other SRPC titles, is through the in-house subsidiary company of Saudi Distribution Company.

Approximately 170,000 copies of *Asharq Al Awsat* are sold daily in Saudi Arabia on a single issue basis (excluding subscriptions and overseas copies) after returns, which are at a level of 20 to 25 per cent. *Asharq Al Awsat* is well supported by advertising, with space on some of its pages (front, second, third and fifth pages) selling out up to a year in advance. The title carries the same advertising content in both local and international editions. In recent years, a total advertising spend for *Asharq Al Awsat* of over SR200 million has constituted the highest level of advertising spend recorded in the local media analysis of all leading Gulf Arabic language daily newspapers. *Asharq Al Awsat* is published in broadsheet format in black and white, while the cover pages are printed on green newsprint giving the title a distinctive appearance.

Al Hayat, founded in 1946 by Kamal Marwa, is owned by Prince Khalid bin Sultan bin Abdul Aziz al-Saud. *Al-Hayat* describes itself as 'an independent international and Arab political daily paper'. As with *Asharq Al Awsat*, it is an influential Arab paper based in London. *Al Hayat* is targeted at Arab communities in about 30 countries in the Middle East, North Africa, Europe and North America, where it is available every morning through satellite printing.

Al Riyadh, published by Al Yamama Press Establishment in Riyadh since 1964, is a well-established Arabic daily. It is considered to be a leading Saudi newspaper in terms of editorial content and readership profile, although with a regional orientation to the Central Province. The political positioning of this title is considered to be indistinguishable from the competitive Arabic dailies, the main point of differentiation being its regional orientation. *Al Riyadh* is published in broadsheet format, with a typical edition consisting of 40 pages in both colour and black and white and an estimated circulation of 150,000 copies. The newspaper is one of the most respected for local and regional Arab Gulf affairs.

Okaz, founded in 1960 and based in Jeddah, is a strong indigenous Saudi newspaper with daily sales of about 110,000 copies. This publication is currently printed at the company's own printing presses in Jeddah and Riyadh simultaneously and has offices all over the Kingdom. *Okaz* is considered to be one of the leading Saudi dailies in terms of editorial content and readership profile, although with a regional orientation towards Jeddah and the rest of the Western Province.

Again the political positioning of this newspaper is considered to be indistinguishable from the competitive Arabic dailies, with the main point of differentiation being its regional orientation. *Okaz* is published in broadsheet format, with a typical edition consisting of 32 pages in both colour and black and white.

Al Yaum is a daily Arabic language newspaper published in Dammam by Al-Yaum Organization for Printing and Publishing, with a regional orientation to the Eastern Province and a circulation of some 20,000 copies. *Al Yaum* carries mainly local news and is published in broadsheet format with a typical edition consisting of 28 pages in both colour and black and white.

Al-Jazirah, published by Al-Jazirah Press of Jeddah, is a broadsheet format newspaper with a typical edition consisting of 28 pages in both colour and black and white. The paper is well known for its daily supplements, which cover the economy, sports, culture, computers, medicine and science. *Al-Jazirah* is one of the leading and most popular Arabic dailies and has branches in more than 30 cities inside and outside the Kingdom. This is a Western Province local daily newspaper published by an independent publishing group, with a circulation of some 110,000 copies.

Al-Watan, meaning 'the homeland' was founded in 2000 by Assir Establishment for Press and Publishing owned, by the governor of Assir Province, Prince Khalid Al-Faysal. *Al-Watan*, although based in Abha in western Saudi Arabia, is a national newspaper with international publishing facilities in London, New York, Amman and Cairo.

Al Bilad is very much a local newspaper with a regional orientation towards Jeddah. This title has an estimated circulation of some 15,000 copies and is not considered significant for media planning purposes, other than where local coverage is required.

Arriyadiyah is a popular sports daily newspaper published by Saudi Research and Publishing Company. *Arriyadiyah* is published in a broadsheet format, with a typical edition consisting of 12 pages with the front and back cover being printed on distinctive pink paper. *Arriyadiyah* enjoys a healthy circulation of some 110,000 copies.

Al Madinah is the local Arabic daily newspaper of Madinah, with an estimated circulation of some 25,000 copies. *Al Nadwaa* is very much a local title with a regional orientation towards Makkah. This daily has an estimated circulation of below 10,000 copies and is not considered significant for media planning purposes.

Newspaper distribution

The distribution of daily newspapers in the Kingdom is via a number of well-organized, specialist distribution companies, both newspaper publisher subsidiaries and independent newspaper and magazine distribution companies. Saudis prefer to buy their newspapers from the local newsstands every day, whereas companies tend to buy subscriptions. Street sales, which are a common form of daily newspaper distribution in some of the other Gulf states, are not permitted in the Kingdom.

Standard industry practice in the Kingdom is for the publisher to pay the distributor between 35 and 40 per cent of the cover price of actual copies sold, that is copies distributed less returns, to cover distribution costs. Publishers are paid 60 to 65 per cent of the cover price of sold copies by the distributor after 45 days.

Newspapers are supplied to retail outlets by the distributor on a sale or return basis. Retailers pay the distributor 90 per cent of the cover price for copies that they have sold, giving them a 10 per cent commission. Unsold copies are returned to the distributor for disposal or return, either in part or in full, to the publisher. Most local publishers elect to retain some returns, while most overseas publishers require distributors to destroy all returns.

Distributors collect the newspapers from print works in Riyadh, Jeddah and Dammam and then distribute locally by vehicle and by air to the main secondary cities of Abha, Jizan and Madinah for onward local distribution by road. A typical distribution network involves up to 200 routes serving some 8,000 outlets throughout the Kingdom.

Imported publications are received at distribution centres in the main cities of Riyadh, Jeddah and Dhahran. Distributors are obliged to send a total of 10 copies of each imported title to the Ministry of Information for instructions concerning censorship. The marking up of copies with a black pen or the application of stickers to publications takes place at the distributors premises prior to circulation of the publications.

The major newspaper distribution companies in Saudi Arabia include Saudi Distribution Company (Saudi Research and Marketing Group), Al Watania Consolidated Distribution Company and Tihama Distribution Company.

Saudi Distribution Company, a subsidiary of the Saudi Research and Marketing Group, is a pan-Gulf newspaper and magazine distribution company with its head office in Jeddah and branches in the United Arab Emirates, Kuwait, Bahrain, Qatar and Oman. The company's in-Kingdom network comprises 24 branches located throughout Saudi Arabia, including representation in all main cities. The company services more than 15,000 outlets via 180 distribution lines Kingdom-wide, with Riyadh alone accounting for some 2,700 outlets served by 60 distribution lines. The company handles some 1,500,000 copies or 20 tonnes of newspapers and magazines daily, covering over 1,000 titles including *Asharq Al Awsat* and four other daily newspapers.

Al Watania Consolidated Distribution Company is jointly owned by a number of the leading Saudi publishers, including *Al Yamamah, Okaz* and *Al-Jazirah*.

Tihama is a Jeddah-based group of advertising, public relations and marketing companies with advertising interests, as well as being involved in newspaper and magazine distribution. *Al Hayat* and some Egyptian titles are distributed exclusively by Tihama in Saudi Arabia.

Television

Saudi state-run TV consists of four channels: Saudi One, the main channel in Arabic; Saudi Two, an English language channel; a sports channel; and the more recent news channel *Al-Ikhbariya*. Prior to the introduction of satellite broadcasting, Saudi TV channels One and Two provided advertisers with good coverage of the Saudi consumer by providing access to 60 per cent of the adult population in the Kingdom. The exception was with regard to Eastern Province audiences who traditionally tuned in to Bahrain TV, with its popular terrestrial transmissions of BBC and other international programming.

The globalization of the Arabic language print media contributed greatly to the introduction and development of the first Arabic television channel based outside the Arab world and not subject to any form of official control. Middle East Broadcasting Centre – MBC TV, launched in September 1991, is the leading pan-Arab satellite channel. Based in London, MBC TV has proved a success due to its coverage of the entire Arab world and further afield. While owned by sources close to the Saudi royal family, the fact that it was established as a private venture, free from direct government control, somewhat enhanced its credibility as an independent broadcaster. MBC TV is able to provide added value services such as audience research information and programme packages targeted at varied audience profiles. While MBC is the leading satellite channel in Saudi Arabia, not all homes are equipped with receivers.

While some non-Saudi media companies have extended their TV transmissions via satellite throughout the Gulf region and further afield, the Saudis have tended to maintain their lead through the private sector that has witnessed the emergence of some very strong business rivals for MBC. They include ART (Arab Radio and Television Network), Orbit, LBC (Lebanese Broadcasting Corporation) and Future Television, which are privately owned and quite popular worldwide.

Qatar's government-owned Al-Jazeera satellite channel was established in 1996 and has gained rapid popularity with Arab viewers. This channel has distinguished itself by providing a broader cross-section of opinion than is available on the other television channels. Al-Jazeera satellite channel came to international prominence following the terrorist attacks on the United States of 11 September 2001, by broadcasting exclusive material received from the terrorist organizations.

In February 2003, Al-Arabiya TV news channel based in Dubai was launched as an all-news satellite channel to compete directly with Al-Jazeera TV. Saudi-controlled MBC and Lebanon's Hariri Group established Al-Arabiya with an investment of US$300 million. When Al-Arabiya went on the air, it promised its audience objectivity and accuracy. However, the US-installed Governing Council in Iraq banned the channel in November 2003, after it broadcast an audio tape purportedly made by deposed Iraqi President, Saddam Hussein.

Based on the increasing trend towards the globalization of television services and with the introduction of digital transmission, more developments of this kind are to be expected.

Radio

MBC FM, launched in 1994, is the leading broadcaster in the Saudi and wider Gulf market and is the main radio network in the Arab world. As the only pan-Arab FM station, it is now present in five Arab countries, namely, Saudi Arabia, Bahrain, Kuwait, UAE and Qatar. It broadcasts music entertainment, sports programming and news, and aims to provide advertisers with a medium giving them high frequency at low cost. MBC FM's policy of populist programming relies extensively on audience participation through celebrity phone-ins, competitions and request shows. The station offers split programming in Saudi Arabia, which is divided into two localized regions, providing more flexibility for advertisers. It has plans to extend its terrestrial coverage to other areas in the Middle East. It is also carried in stereo throughout the MBC satellite footprint on Arabsat and Eutelsat II.

Further information

For media research information contact the Pan Arab Research Centre (PARC), a member of the Gallup International organization. This is a well-established research and information services company with its head office located in Dubai, UAE. PARC also operates an independent branch office in Saudi Arabia. Contact details for PARC, Saudi Arabia, are as follows:

PARC Saudi Arabia
PO Box 50163
Jeddah 21523
Saudi Arabia
Tel: +966 2 651 7405
Fax: +966 2 651 8527
Email: parcjed@awalnet.net.sa

Further information about the activities of Saudi Research and Publishing Company can be found at website www.srpc.com.

ASA Consulting has conducted a number of media-related studies, including a feasibility study for the establishment of a new national daily newspaper in Saudi Arabia. For further information contact asaconsult@btinternet.com.

5.4

Exhibiting in Saudi Arabia

Al Harithy Company for Exhibitions Limited

Introduction

An area often overlooked when developing a marketing strategy for Saudi Arabia is participation in one of the many exhibitions that take place within the Kingdom.

As with any market, exhibitions in Saudi Arabia provide an ideal platform from which to launch a new product or simply promote brand awareness. Expertly organized, Saudi exhibitions provide an opportunity to showcase to a broad and high-volume targeted professional visitor audience.

Recent legislative changes by the Saudi government to actively encourage inward investment will assist and ease the way for companies looking at the market, but the question of how to launch a product, create awareness of a service or find a local partner remains. Exhibitions, particularly trade-orientated shows, provide one of the most effective ways of doing all three because they offer face-to-face negotiations on a one-to-one basis.

Exhibition organizers in Saudi Arabia

There are three principal exhibition organizers, providing worldclass facilities in purpose-built exhibition halls, each located in the heart of the Kingdom's three major business locations in the western, central and eastern regions (see Table 5.4.1).

Each of these organizers has a comprehensive programme of exhibitions, details of which can be found on their websites. When looking at the exhibitions on offer, the vast size of the Kingdom should be remembered, as should the business climate, which differs from region to region. So location is perhaps one of the most important considerations in determining participation.

- Riyadh, in the central region, is the legislative capital of the Kingdom and agricultural centre;
- Jeddah, in the western region, is considered the commercial and leisure centre;
- Dammam, in the eastern region, is dominated by the oil and gas industry.

Table 5.4.1 Saudi Arabia's principal exhibition organizers

Region	Name and address	Contact details
Western region	Al Harithy Company for Exhibitions Ltd, (ACE) PO Box 40740, Jeddah 21511	Tel: +966 2 654 6384 Fax: +966 2 654 6853 Email: ace@acexpos.com Web: www.acexpos.com
	International Office Al Harithy Company for Exhibitions UK Ltd, The Glassmill, 1 Battersea Bridge Road, London SW11 3BG	Tel: +44 20 7223 3431 Fax: +44 20 7228 4229 Email: international@acexpos.com
Central region	Riyadh Exhibition Company Ltd (REC), PO Box 56010, Riyadh 11554	Tel: +966 1 454 1448 Fax: +966 1 454 4846 Email: esales@recexpo.com Web: www.recexpo.com
Eastern region	Dhahran International Exhibition Centre, PO Box 7519, Dammam 31472	Tel: +966 3 859 1888 Fax: +966 3 859 0212 Email: info@dhahran-expo.com Web: www.dhahran-expo.com

With half the population located in the western region and some market sectors being quite polarized, selecting the right exhibition and venue is crucial to the success of any exhibition participation.

Market research will assist in identifying the region that is the most appropriate for a particular product or service and which exhibition is the most suitable.

Sources of information

For UK companies wishing to participate in exhibitions in Saudi Arabia, government departments such as UK Trade & Investment, Business Link, local British Business Groups in Saudi Arabia, as well as the commercial offices of the British Embassy and Consulate, all provide general market-based advice.

The exhibition organizers will also provide information, including visitor and exhibitor figures and profiles, much of which is available on their websites.

Preparatory groundwork

Exhibitions provide an extremely effective vehicle from which to approach the vast Saudi market. To ensure that the right product lines are exhibited, adequate preparatory market research is crucial.

However, in addition to researching and identifying the region and exhibition, it is equally important that the right products are exhibited. For example, in addition to the obvious climatic differences, Saudi families tend to be larger than their European counterparts and this impacts on their requirements. Everything from furnishings to vehicles must accommodate larger numbers of people, and visitors to an exhibition of furniture and furnishings would expect to see dining tables able to accommodate a larger number of diners than would be the case in Europe.

Selecting a suitable show is not difficult once the demographics have been considered but ensuring professional support from the organizer is important. Going it alone is possible but not advised. There are restrictions on what can be imported into the Kingdom, plus various legislative stipulations and procedures to be followed, so there is no substitute for having the professional support team of a large professional organizing company working for you behind the scenes and guiding you through the procedures.

Exhibition participation

As with participation at any exhibition, preparation is the key to a rewarding participation and a return on investment. It is highly advisable to follow the recommendations of the organizer set out in the show manual, as these include specific requirements for individual exhibitions and make participation as straightforward as possible.

The manual will cover in detail all aspects of exhibiting, including visa requirements, freight forwarding and legalities, as well as stand specifications, lighting, furnishings and special decoration.

Manuals include fax-back forms for most exhibitor requirements and some organizers also offer online forms that make the process even easier. For exhibitions in Jeddah, for example, Al-Harithy Company for Exhibitions Limited (ACE), members of AEO, provide a complete set of online forms on their website. These range from a simple request for information right through to stand fitting, freight forwarding and even visa applications.

Exhibition material, displays and exhibits need to arrive in the Kingdom at least three weeks before the exhibition. There must be no references to the State of Israel, alcohol or any religion other than Islam in any literature intended for use in the Kingdom, otherwise it may get no further than customs. Promotional material must conform to the Kingdom's moral code. Always check with either the organizer or preferred freight forwarder first.

It is advisable to work with the exhibition organizer to maximize publicity of your participation. The organizer will have a planned and targeted advertising campaign in place, and adding your advertisement to this will maximize return. Some exhibition organizers offer in-house design for print and pre-press facilities. It is worth considering taking advantage of these services by forwarding text, graphics or finished artwork, either on disk or via email, for design and production in Saudi Arabia and subsequent delivery to your exhibition stand.

Visas can be obtained for exhibition staff only and not for visitors. It is important to ensure that male staff can be made available for the exhibition as visa applications for females are rarely approved.

It is advisable to allow for additional time before and after the exhibition to conduct some market research. The exhibition opening times will invariably be from late afternoon to late evening, thus allowing for visits to potential clients during the day.

If in doubt, it is always advisable to consult the organizer, as they operate on the basis that your success is their success.

Post exhibition

Be prepared to make repeated visits, this will show commitment to the market and foster relations with clients. Also be prepared to consider further subsequent participation at exhibitions in the Kingdom.

Programme of recent and forthcoming events in Saudi Arabia

A selection of recent and forthcoming annual and biennial events in Saudi Arabia that are scheduled to take place during late 2005, 2006 and 2007 are shown in Table 5.4.2.

Table 5.4.2 Programme of recent and forthcoming exhibitions in Saudi Arabia

Exhibition Name	Description	Annual/ Biennial Event	Location	Date of Next Event
Saudi Computer 2005	The 21st Computer and IT Exhibition	Annual	Riyadh	11 Sept 2005
Saudi Office Technology 2005	The 16th Office Technology Show	Annual	Riyadh	11 Sept 2005
Saudi School and Training 2005	The 12th Student, Parent, Teacher and School Administrator Exhibition	Annual	Riyadh	11 Sept 2005
COMMTEL	Saudi Arabia's 20th International Event for Computing, the Internet, Office Equipment and Business Communications	Annual	Jeddah	12 Sept 2005
Saudi AGRICULTURE 2005	The 24th International Agriculture, Water and Agri-Industry Show	Annual	Riyadh	25–29 Sept 2005
Saudi GARDENTECH 2005	The 4th International Trade Show for Garden, Turf Products and Services	Annual	Riyadh	25–29 Sept 2005
Saudi Water Technology 2005	International Agriculture, Water and Agri-industry show	Annual	Riyadh	25–29 Sept 2005
Computer & Communication Exhibition (CCE)	Annual Information Technology Show	Annual	Dhahran	25 Sept 2005
Riyadh Motor Show 2005	The 24th International Exhibition for Motor Vehicles	Annual	Riyadh	27 Nov–1 Dec 2005
Saudi AUTOSHOP 2005	The 10th International Exhibition for Auto Repair Equipment, Tools, Parts, Accessories	Annual	Riyadh	27 Nov–1 Dec 2005

Exhibition Name	Description	Annual/ Biennial Event	Location	Date of Next Event
PLAST-PETRO-PACK 2005	Saudi International Plastic, Petrochemical, Packing and Packaging Products Exhibition	Annual	Dhahran	11–15 Dec 2005
Saudi BUILD 2005	The 17th International Building Construction Technology & Building Materials Show	Annual	Riyadh	11–15 Dec 2005
Saudi STONE 2005	The 8th International Stone and Stone Technology Exhibition	Annual	Riyadh	11–15 Dec 2005
Saudi Communications 2006	The 11th International Telecommunications Exhibition and Conference	Biennial	Riyadh	12–16 Feb 2006
ASTEX 2006	The 7th Arabian Security, Civil Defence & Life Safety Technology Exhibition	Biennial	Riyadh	12–16 Feb 2006
Middle East Education & Training Exhibition/ Symposium (MEETES)	Saudi Arabia's 12th International Event for Education, Training, Human Resources etc.	Annual	Jeddah	19–23 Feb 2006
Oil, Gas & Power Saudi Arabia Conference/ Exhibition	The International Oil, Gas & power Conference & Exhibition for the Middle East Region	Annual	Riyadh	15 Mar 2006
Saudi Arabia's International Trade Fair	24th Trade and Franchising Expo for Light Industries & Machinery, Consumer Goods, Giftware, Clothing, Textiles, Leather Goods, Fashion Accessories, Cosmetics & Perfumes	Annual	Jeddah	19–23 Mar 2006
LIFESTYLE	International Event for Furniture, Furnishings, Fabrics, Floor/Wall Coverings, Lighting, Exteriors	Annual	Jeddah	19–23 Mar 2006

Exhibition Name	Description	Annual/ Biennial Event	Location	Date of Next Event
Saudi World Trade Fair 2006	The 8th International Trade Fair for Consumer Goods, Industrial Products, Leisure and Services	Biennial	Riyadh	22–26 Mar 2006
Saudi Building Industries Exhibition	The 15th Building Industries Exhibition and Symposium incorporating Real Estate	Annual	Jeddah	2–6 April 2006
GITEX Saudi Arabia 2006	The 5th International Computer & Information Technology Exhibition	Annual	Riyadh	23–27 Apr 2006
Saudi HOMETEX 2006	The 2nd International Trade Show for Home Fabrics and Textiles	Biennial	Riyadh	7–11 May 2006
Saudi Fashion & Leather 2006	The 2nd International Trade Show for Fashion, Leather, Shoes and Accessories	Biennial	Riyadh	7–11 May 2006
Home, Décor & Garden 2006	The 3rd Interior Decoration & Garden Furniture Exhibition	Annual	Riyadh	7–11 May 2006
Saudi Furniture and Interiors 2006	The 10th International Trade Exhibition for Furniture and Interiors	Annual	Riyadh	7–11 May 2006
FOOD – ARABIA	Saudi Arabia's 11th International Event for Food and Beverages and Catering	Biennial	Jeddah	14–18 May 2006
HOTEL – ARABIA	Saudi Arabia's 8th International Event for Hotel Equipment Supplies and Services	Biennial	Jeddah	14–18 May 2006
PROPAC – ARABIA	Saudi Arabia's 11th International Event for Processing, Packaging, Canning, Bottling, Labelling and Plastics	Biennial	Jeddah	14–18 May 2006
Jeddah International Book Fair	Jeddah's 5th International Book Fair	Annual	Jeddah	10–18 June 2006

Exhibition Name	Description	Annual/ Biennial Event	Location	Date of Next Event
Recreation and Leisure Fair – RALF (Inc. Boat Show and LIVE)	Saudi Arabia's Second Event to Promote Tourism, Leisure and Sport	Annual	Jeddah	25–30 June
Saudi Agriculture 2006	The 25th International Agriculture, Water and Agri-Industry Show	Annual	Riyadh	17–21 Sept 2006
Saudi Water Technology 2006	The International Water Technology Conference and Exhibition	Annual	Riyadh	17–21 Sept 2006
Saudi GARDENTECH 2006	The 5th International Trade Show for Garden, Turf Products and Services	Annual	Riyadh	17–21 Sept 2006
Saudi BUILD 2006	The 18th International Building Construction Technology & Building Materials Show	Annual	Riyadh	12–16 Nov 2006
Saudi STONE 2006	International Stone and Stone Technology Exhibition	Annual	Riyadh	12–16 Nov 2006
Riyadh Motor Show 2006	The 25th International Exhibition for motor Vehicles, Showcasing 2007 Models	Annual	Riyadh	26–30 Nov 2006
Saudi AUTOSHOP 2006	The 11th International Exhibition for Auto Repair Equipment, Tools, Parts, Accessories	Annual	Riyadh	26–30 Nov 2006
Saudi International MOTOR SHOW	Saudi Arabia's 28th International Event for Motor Vehicles, Motor Cycles, Auto Parts, Accessories and Garage Equipment	Annual	Jeddah	5–0 Nov 2006
COMMTEL	Saudi Arabia's 21st International Event for Computing, the Internet, Office Equipment and Business Communications	Annual	Jeddah	3–7 December 2006

Exhibition Name	Description	Annual/ Biennial Event	Location	Date of Next Event
Saudi AIRCON	International Air-Conditioning, Ventilation, Heating & Refrigeration Show	Biennial	Riyadh	Feb 2007
Saudi ELENEX	International Electrical Engineering, Power Generation and Distribution Exhibition	Biennial	Riyadh	Feb 2007
Saudi LUMINEX	International Lighting Equipment Show	Biennial	Riyadh	Mar 2007
Saudi Furniture & Interiors	The International Trade Exhibition for Furniture & Interiors	Biennial	Riyadh	Mar 2007
Saudi SHOP	The International Shopfitting, Display and Signage Exhibition	Biennial	Riyadh	Mar 2007
Saudi PRINT	The International Pre-Press & Printing Technology Exhibition	Biennial	Riyadh	Mar 2007
Saudi PACK	The International Packaging Machinery & Materials Show	Biennial	Riyadh	Mar 2007
Saudi PLAS	The International Plastics Technology Show	Biennial	Riyadh	Mar 2007
Saudi CHEM	The International Exhibition for Chemicals and Chemical Technology Industry	Biennial	Riyadh	Mar 2007
Saudi FOOD	The International Food, Equipment & Catering Show	Biennial	Riyadh	May 2007
Saudi Hotel` & Restaurant	The Hotel, Restaurant, Catering Equipment & Supplies Exhibition	Biennial	Riyadh	May 2007
Saudi CLEAN	The International Cleaning, Maintenance & Property Management Exhibition	Biennial	Riyadh	May 2007

5.5

Research in Consumer and Real Estate Markets

David Green, ERAS Limited

Introduction

For market research in real estate and consumer markets, Saudi Arabia is quite unique, with its own set of frustrations and challenges. Any market researcher wishing to succeed in the Kingdom must understand and appreciate the factors that make the country special.

Many multinationals plan and control their market research from global or regional headquarters. Similar questionnaires are often used for a number of countries. Local research companies are then employed just to execute the survey. For the Saudi market this approach always causes problems.

Saudi-based market research organizations, such as SYRA House of Jeddah, receive numerous requests from multinationals to execute surveys. Typical requests specify the precise socio-income groups to be surveyed, give an exact percentage of the population of each group to be sampled and ask for video footage of sample interviews and focus group sessions. In general, none of this is possible in the context of Saudi Arabia, where a combination of the conservative nature of society and a lack of basic data requires a complete redesigning of the approach to such market survey work.

Availability of data

The key problem in Saudi Arabia is the lack of sound demographic and market data, a problem that cannot be overemphasized. In short, there is a distinct lack of reliable and detailed:

- demographic data by location, age or nationality;
- income data;
- consumer market data.

Demographic data

The Saudi market is characterized by a lack of accurate demographic data. For example, estimates of the population of Jeddah range from 2.4 million to 3.6 million. The situation is equally bad for the capital Riyadh and for other towns and cities. While some data is available, there is nothing comprehensive, because the detailed profiling of a market by postal code area, which researchers rely on in the West, is simply not yet available.

Furthermore, with a population growth rate of just under three per cent per annum and continued migration to the urban centres, what information is available rapidly becomes outdated. Another problem is the lack of data on the expatriate population. Estimated at around four million, expatriates are an important market in the Kingdom but can be difficult to survey effectively. Due to the number of different nationalities, a detailed breakdown by nationality and location is required for sampling purposes, but this is not available.

To build up a picture of a particular population, a mixed approach is generally undertaken, combining information from a range of sources, including:

- ad hoc published statistics;
- in-house databases;
- customer data from the utilities companies;
- map and ground surveys of housing density and housing types;
- statistics on services such as hospitals and schools;
- reports from embassies on numbers of registered nationals;
- reported births and deaths;
- population statistics (particularly age profiles) for neighbouring Arabian Gulf states.

Without accurate data on population size, it is usually impossible to provide meaningful estimates of the accuracy of any survey results. Fortunately, those commissioning work in the Kingdom are generally prepared to accept this situation.

A further problem is that results from surveys cannot be multiplied up to give accurate estimates for the whole market, as further checks on the total market size are required. For example, a recent survey for a canned food product included questions on frequency and volumes purchased. Annual consumption of the product in the Kingdom was then calculated using the available population estimates. The final figures were then checked with interviews with wholesalers.

It is common to work from both ends of the market in Saudi Arabia, and research will often combine surveys of consumers, retailers, wholesalers and manufacturers. Trade data is also often checked, but this can present additional problems.

Income data

A key focus of much market research at present is the young middle income Saudi population. While it is possible to define 'young', defining 'middle income' is far from easy.

There is no income expenditure survey in Saudi Arabia to provide a basis for segmenting households by income level. Furthermore, with no personal income tax and no reported national income surveys, it is not easy to construct effective income bands.

With the majority of Saudi males being employed by the government, it is possible to obtain a level of income segmentation from reported statistics on government employees by grade. However, many government employees have their own business interests, thus affecting the level of accuracy.

In these circumstances, indirect measures of wealth have to be used, but there is no simple formula and the approach will depend on the market sector or product being studied, as well as the location within the Kingdom. A further problem is that many Saudis live in fairly large extended households; consequently, any information on the earnings of one adult in the household may not be that meaningful.

To obtain an indication of income/wealth level, it is necessary to ask a series of questions concerning the number of cars, servants, bedrooms and adults in the household. Indexes can then be constructed combining simple ratios such as number of servants per adult and number of cars per adult. The resulting index is clearly meaningless as an objective measure of income or wealth. However, it does help to segment survey results and therefore facilitates analysis of relationships between survey responses and comparative income/wealth levels.

Industry and sales data

In general, competing companies are not inclined to share market data, either directly or through independent data auditors.

In Western markets, basic market data on sales volumes, price trends, activity levels etc, is often produced by industry groupings such as supermarket chains, high street retailers and car dealerships. In general, such groupings do not exist in Saudi Arabia, the prime exception being the hotel chains that do share data on occupancy rates.

A key reason for the general lack of willingness to share data is the fact that most companies are in private ownership and therefore have no reporting requirements. As more companies seek public share issues, it is likely that this situation will improve.

Trade data

With a limited production base it should be possible to use trade data as an estimate for the total Saudi consumption of a number of products. However, by setting a simple, single import tariff that covers almost all consumer products, there is little incentive to ensure that imports are correctly classified. As a result, import data is not that reliable. There can also be some considerable delays in reporting.

Data constraint

A serious constraint to the development of market research in Saudi Arabia is the lack of basic data. In many instances, a substantial amount of effort and money is required to provide a basic understanding of a market segment (for example, market size and growth trends) before effective research that provides actionable results can be undertaken.

Real estate

More so than in Western markets, real estate is a leading sector in the Saudi economy: it is difficult to find a Saudi business group that does not have real estate and construction interests. Rapid population growth, urban migration and economic development all mean that real estate will remain a leading sector for many years.

Although most parts of the real estate sector have shown strong growth, the leading markets are:

- housing in Jeddah and Riyadh;
- commercial developments in Riyadh;
- hotels and apartments in Jeddah and Makkah.

Indeed, developments in Makkah have been on an unprecedented scale and a package of major projects launched in 2004 (with budgets for the initial phases of over US$10 billion) will ensure that Makkah leads the Kingdom in construction activity for at least the next decade.

Market research in the real estate sector poses its own set of problems.

Housing

Surveys of both housing supply and demand are difficult. There is almost no secondary housing market: that is, very few houses are resold. Furthermore, many Saudis employ contractors directly to build their own homes. This means that market prices and take-up rates must be gathered from a relatively small number of multi-unit housing developments.

Direct housing demand surveys are difficult to undertake for all of the reasons discussed above. However, for trends in consumer tastes, surveys of architects and contractors are extremely effective. For estimates of housing demand numbers, econometric modelling of household formation, together with income (GDP) drivers, has proven effective.

Commercial and retail

'Build it and they will come' has been a guiding principle for many years in Saudi Arabia when developing shopping centres. Generally, this has worked as consumers have moved away from *bagalas* and open air markets to air-conditioned centres.

However, there are increasing signs of overcapacity in the retailing sector, and developers are commissioning surveys before building, and sometimes before designing, new shopping centres.

Surveying retailers is relatively straightforward, but consumers are more difficult. Furthermore, few shopping centres collect data on foot traffic.

Offices

The market for offices is highly fragmented and it is only in recent years that multi-tenant blocks have been developed. While these purpose-built office blocks have required market research, most offices are either built by and for one tenant, or as filler above a commercial development.

Researching the supply and demand side of the offices market therefore has similar problems to the housing market: it is a thin market with little turnover.

Hotels and apartments

Market information on hotels (occupancy by month, revenues per room, etc) can be readily obtained in Saudi Arabia. However, information on apartments is much harder to obtain. Normally this would not be a serious problem but in Saudi Arabia, as a result of large family size and a need for privacy, the hotel and apartment sectors compete directly for a large section of the market.

In Makkah, the situation is becoming more complex as an increasing number of mixed developments (hotel and apartment blocks with shared services) are being built. Furthermore, in several cases the apartments are being let on a long lease for renting out short term by private individuals or their agents. This makes obtaining information on occupancy rates and prices particularly difficult to obtain.

In general, good market data on the real estate sector requires building up a database over several years, combined with good contacts and 'pushy' surveyors.

Access and approach

The typical picture of market research in the West is of mature female enumerators interviewing strangers in a public place. This is not an image that will be seen in Saudi Arabia, where the conservative nature of Saudi society means that female enumerators cannot operate in public and women cannot be interviewed in public. Furthermore, women cannot be interviewed by men in private.

Men can be interviewed openly, but this is not that effective; the key place for doing so being shopping centres, where they are usually accompanied by their families.

A further problem is that door-to-door survey work is not possible. Permission for such work can be difficult to obtain and it rarely yields positive results. For this reason, locating suitable interview targets is a serious problem, particularly in finding Saudi women.

To solve this problem, local market research firms tend to develop their own network of Saudi female enumerators who will usually undertake the interviews in the home of the survey target, thus providing complete privacy. To identify the targets, the enumerators rely heavily on networking. Such networks are extensive and extremely effective at reaching all parts of Saudi society.

For locating men, a combined approach of networking and targeting places of work is usually effective. In addition, snowballing is used extensively (as there is less need to have a personal link to the target). Snowballing is where interviewees provide contacts to the enumerator for the next interview. Through this technique, long chains can be developed that give wide market coverage.

In general, people need to be interviewed in a comfortable environment, and this means either their home or their office.

Telephone surveys remain relatively new to the Kingdom. Although there is not the same resistance to these as there is in the West, people are usually not comfortable discussing many topics over the telephone.

Randomness

Clearly, without being able to undertake 'street' surveys, ensuring the randomness of a survey group becomes a serious problem. As the unchecked use of networking and snowballing may cause bias, several methods are used to limit this, such as:

- restricting the number of surveys undertaken by one enumerator – this is, of course, combined with using a large team of enumerators;
- standard checks for bias in results from individual enumerators (for example, is there any correlation between responses and enumerator) – where correlation is found to be significant, results from that enumerator are void;
- 'leapfrog-snowballing' – an odd-sounding metaphor that basically means using every other link in a snowballing chain.

Enumerators

There are very few professional and/or full-time enumerators in Saudi Arabia, and, in general, substantial effort is required for training and supervision. In particular, care must be taken with all enumerators to ensure that they fully understand the tasks to be undertaken.

Regarding quality control, experienced practitioners recheck at least 10 per cent of all surveys and a provision of +20 per cent on the sample size for potential voids is recommended.

Unless surveying non-Arabic speakers only, all surveys should be bilingual. Invariably clients require the results to be in English, and bilingual documents remove much of the ambiguity in the final analysis.

Consumer roles

The roles that consumers play in the Kingdom are not the same as they are in Western markets, and this is another factor that must be taken into account when structuring surveys. A key issue is that women do not drive in Saudi Arabia and, as a result, families undertake most shopping. This means that Saudi men play a dominant role in many purchase decisions, particularly for food items.

Scheduling of work

As with any market, there are good times and bad times for undertaking market surveys in the Kingdom. In general, the following times should be avoided, though this will depend on the target and market:

- Ramadan: hours for working and socializing alter during Ramadan with many people almost becoming nocturnal;
- *Hajj:* over two million pilgrims congregate in Makkah for the *Hajj*, and many of them also visit Madinah and Jeddah; as a result, logistics can be a serious problem and all three cities should be avoided during this period;
- Christmas: many European expatriates are on holiday during this period;
- school holidays: a substantial number of Saudis are on holiday at the same time as schools, particularly during the long summer vacation; this trend is most noticeable in Riyadh, which has some of the highest summer temperatures.

Saudi Arabia – an immature but expanding market

In the past, the benefits of market research were often not appreciated in Saudi Arabia. However, changes in the control of companies and market structure have increased the awareness and need for good research.

The founders of many of Saudi Arabia's leading businesses built their empires in the boom years, a period in which growth rates and profit margins were high. Market research was rarely used and investment decisions were often based on instinct alone. This generation of business leaders is being replaced by a new generation that is characterized by a good business school education and understanding of market research. At the same time, competition in the Saudi market has become more intense as economic stagnation and oversupply in some sectors has squeezed margins.

Furthermore, investors (including the commercial banks and the Saudi Investment Development Fund – SIDF) are imposing tougher requirements for market studies. Indeed, market research is increasingly being undertaken *before* the investment decisions are made.

However, while the requirement for market research has been increasing, problems remain – a key one being the credibility of the results obtained. Because of the lack of information, many companies have a serious misconception of their market position. This often leads to the results of market research surprising or even shocking the client. For example, in work for a food manufacturer, it was proved that the total market for the product was 10 times the client's estimate. While this should have been good news, it meant that the client's market share was one-tenth the level previously supposed. As this was not acceptable, the survey results were considered invalid.

Another problem concerns the investment ceiling, as in general there is a limit to what Saudi businessmen are willing to spend on intangibles such as market research or even advertising, with the limit likely to be much lower than in the West. In addition, the limit is not necessarily related to the total value of the investment at risk. It is not unusual, for example, for a market research budget ceiling of US$10,000 to be allocated for an investment project valued at US$500,000, while a similar research budget ceiling is established by the same company for another project valued at US$50 million.

Recommended approach for success

The key to successful consumer market research in Saudi Arabia is to remember not to treat the Kingdom as any other country. The nature of Saudi society and the lack of availability of basic market and demographic data means that considerable care is required in structuring survey work. Careful planning must go into all aspects of work, from instrument design to survey execution.

For success in undertaking consumer market research in Saudi Arabia, it has been found that the following approach helps:

- take professional advice;
- always test-run surveys;
- remain flexible;
- match surveyors to targets;
- avoid over-reaching;
- exploit in-house data.

It should be emphasized that while there are substantial problems with consumer market research in Saudi Arabia, the opportunities are great. The very lack of basic market data means that those companies that succeed with their market research will be well rewarded.

Part Six

The Business Environment

6.1

Manpower and Employment Issues

Anthony Shoult, ASA Consulting[1]

Introduction

For any organization considering an investment opportunity in Saudi Arabia over the next few years, a fundamental grasp of manpower-related issues is a prerequisite. In 2005, Saudi Arabia has, amongst the Gulf countries, the largest population of nationals, with some 60 per cent of this population under 25 years of age.

The growing issue of finding beneficial employment for the increasing number of young people is, therefore, a matter of the highest priority on the Kingdom's agenda.

Key manpower issues

Although estimates vary, the year 2005 finds Saudi Arabia with an expatriate labour force comprising around one third of the total population. Expatriates had traditionally filled the labour shortage experienced as a result of the economic boom of the 1970s following the discovery of oil. This trend continued as the number of job vacancies continued to be far greater than could be supplied by the indigenous labour pool. Only in the 1990s, with the drop in the price of oil and the resultant economic downturn, did the need for change arise. With less money flowing through the economy and, in particular, a decline in governmental handouts for sections of the population unable to support themselves, it quickly became evident that the anomaly would have to be addressed.

---

1 Sources of information include Saudi Development and Training Company Ltd and Hay Management Consultants.

As a result of the 'boom years', large sections of the Kingdom's population experienced increased levels of affluence. This, in turn, resulted in enormous population growth to the point where, in 2004, almost half of the population was under 20 years of age. When the economic slowdown began to take hold, the population issue became of primary importance. These young people were going to need to earn their living and whilst there are an abundance of jobs, most of them required skill levels that were above and beyond what the education system was able to provide.

Saudi nationals, who had needed to earn a living, had traditionally entered employment within the public sector. In this context, the various ministries and the armed forces provided a secure 'career for life' for those who needed it. Again, this situation changed with the economic downturn that resulted in a marked slowdown in public sector recruitment.

Meanwhile, the Saudi private sector had traditionally been seen as a less than desirable option when compared to the security and relative convenience of a government post.

Hence, apart from the Saudi nationals who owned the companies, expatriates staffed the majority of private sector organizations. This situation suited everyone in that expatriates performed the less desirable jobs, the private sector companies had a relatively stable and flexible workforce and the indigenous workforce was able to perform what they perceived as the higher status/shorter hours governmental jobs.

In turn and with no small amount of irony, many Saudi owners preferred to employ expatriate rather than local manpower. Saudi employees were often perceived as expensive and lacking in the areas of reliability and loyalty, both of which were desirable qualities from the perspective of an employer. In addition, it was thought by many that young Saudis had unrealistic expectations as to the kinds of employment they were prepared to undertake. Misperceptions, of course, happen from all sides.

The situation could be summarized as being how, on the one hand, to persuade private sector organizations to utilize local manpower in favour of expatriates and at the same time ensure that young people were coming out of the educational system with the requisite skills to enable them to begin productive careers within the private sector.

Manpower planning measures

A number of methods have been employed to address the manpower situation in Saudi Arabia. Most visibly, legislation to achieve 'Saudiization' of the workforce was put into effect in 1996, making it obligatory for all private sector organizations to increase their utilization of local manpower by five per cent compound per annum. This requirement is now being rigorously monitored and failure to comply has resulted in penalties, such as not being able to bid for government tenders or in some cases having visa applications for expatriate staff rejected. The Ministry of Labour was tasked with ensuring compliance and actively sought out those organizations failing to reach the required levels.

In addition, certain job categories have been classified as 'Saudi-only' positions, for example it is now obligatory for Government Relations Officers and Accounts Clerks to be Saudi nationals.

In addition, visa and residence permit charges for expatriates have been steadily increased over recent years. Some of the extra income earned as a result of this has been channelled into the Manpower Development Fund, which aims to assist young people to increase their marketability to the private sector by subsidizing both their training and initial periods of employment.

The success of manpower planning measures

There is no doubt that the manpower situation is now being redressed and there are now more nationals than ever before playing productive roles in the private sector. Employers are beginning to see, in practical terms, how local manpower can add value to their operations and, in turn, young people are coming out of the educational system with more realistic expectations in terms of career opportunities and remuneration. Stereotypes are being eroded as more companies experience success stories with their local labour. Some business sectors, most notably banking and insurance, have achieved commendable results. Utilization of local labour is well over 70 per cent in these areas and is still growing.

Estimates suggest, however, that local manpower still makes up less than 20 per cent of manpower in the private sector as a whole. The manufacturing sector, in particular, is still averaging single figure percentages of local manpower utilization. Broadly speaking, a 'clerical/technical divide' exists, which has yet to be successfully bridged. Technical training opportunities for young people do exist, with organizations such as Saudi Aramco, BAE Systems and Saudi Arabian Airlines (SV) leading the way, but there is still a long way to go before numbers of locals in technical positions are equivalent to those holding white collar posts.

Conclusion

The year 2005 sees Saudi Arabia in a unique economic and social position. Confidence in the economy has been greatly strengthened by the recent rises in oil and gas prices, while Saudi Arabia remains by far the largest consumer market in the Gulf. The Kingdom continues to attract substantial investment from overseas, and imminent entry into the World Trade Organization (WTO) has resulted in moves to facilitate increased participation in what has traditionally been a relatively difficult market to enter and operate in.

The fact remains, however, that organizations conducting business, or considering doing so, anywhere in the Kingdom need to have an understanding of the unique legal and social implications that this involves if their commercial aspirations are to be met.

6.2

Living and Working Conditions

Anthony Shoult, ASA Consulting[1]

Introduction

This chapter aims to provide information about life and conditions in Saudi Arabia in order to help those foreign nationals intending to work in the Kingdom to adjust more easily to a people, culture and climate that are very different from that of Western countries.

Until the 1950s, the Saudis lived in a relatively simple society, but the income derived from oil has since enabled the country to move very quickly towards a technological society, a world of computers and telecommunications.

The Saudis, generally, are very well aware of the longer-term benefits of the transformation, providing it takes place within an Islamic framework, but individual Saudi reactions to modernization are not always favourable. There are conservative, as well as progressive, elements in any society and it is understandable that sudden modernization will cause problems of adjustment. The expatriate's own adjustment to life in the Kingdom will depend upon their awareness and respect for the contradictions in this process.

While in Saudi Arabia, the expatriate is, of course, subject to the laws and moral standards of the authorities and people of the country. The expatriate will find that these are considerably stricter than those of Western society and that in certain cases, notably involving dress, drink and moral behaviour, what is not a crime in the West is treated as such in Saudi Arabia. The expatriate going to Saudi Arabia is therefore strongly advised to get to know the differences between Saudi law and that applicable to their own country and to abide by the laws of Saudi Arabia while they are there. Some of the important differences

[1] Sources of information include UK Trade and Investment.

in Saudi law and the judicial system are described in the following sections.

Security issues

With the rise in Islamic extremism following the terrorist attacks in the United States of 11 September 2001 and the subsequent invasion of Iraq by coalition forces in March 2003, living conditions for Western expatriate residents in Saudi Arabia have been subject to substantial change during the last two years. The greatly enhanced emphasis on security has resulted in the curtailment of many of the social activities that were previously a positive feature of expatriate life in the Kingdom. While some expatriates and businesses have left the Kingdom or relocated to neighbouring Gulf states, in particular Bahrain and the UAE, those that have chosen to remain now have a much greater awareness of security in going about their daily business.

This has mainly been as a result of the actions of militants linked to the Al-Qaeda network that have carried out a number of attacks in the Kingdom since May 2003. In Riyadh, suicide attacks took place in May and November 2003 resulting in the deaths of a number of Arabs and Muslims, while a number of more recent attacks appear to have been directed at Western expatriate interests. These included an assault on a residential compound in Al-Khobar and an attack in Yanbu in May 2004 that resulted in a number of casualties. Two further militant attacks occurred in December 2004, including an armed attack on the United States embassy in Jeddah.

Although recent security assessments suggest that the Saudi authorities are making headway against the militants, Western targets are expected to remain high risk due to strong anti-Western sentiment amongst some elements in the Kingdom.

In March 2005, British Airways suspended all its flights to Saudi Arabia. This decision was taken for commercial reasons, including the effect of rising fuel costs combined with weakening demand, making the routes increasingly expensive to operate. It was also reported in March 2005 that the airline management had become reluctant to ask its staff to stay overnight in the Kingdom.

Centres of population

Riyadh

Riyadh, located in the Central Province, is the capital of Saudi Arabia, with a population of three million. It is also a major centre for expatriates and is the location of all foreign embassies and Saudi government ministries. Outside of Riyadh and the other towns of the Central Province, the Nejd region is still inhabited by Bedouin nomads, although these are now becoming more and more settled in centres of population. The region is sprinkled with numerous oases, in many of which modern agricultural techniques have been introduced.

Jeddah

The major commercial city and port of Jeddah with a population of 1.3 million lies about halfway down the west coast of Saudi Arabia. It is an important centre of expatriate population and is the principal entry point for nearly two million foreign pilgrims to Makkah for the annual *Hajj*, as well as about three million pilgrims who visit Makkah throughout the year to perform *Umra*, the lesser pilgrimage.

The Eastern Province

The other main centre for Western expatriates in the country is the complex of communities on and near the Gulf coast, where the Kingdom's oil is extracted and exported. Several thousand expatriates live in the triangle of townships formed by Dhahran, Dammam and Al-Khobar.

Other centres of population

Other centres of expatriate population are Tabuk in the far north-west of the country, Taif in the mountains around Makkah, and Abha and Khamis Mushayt in the high mountains of the south-west. Newer centres of expatriate activity are the new industrial port cities of Jubail, located about 80 kilometres north of Dammam on the Gulf, and Yanbu, located 400 kilometres north of Jeddah.

Climate

In Riyadh, the humidity is much less and the extremes of temperature somewhat greater in winter, when temperatures occasionally drop to freezing point. There is a rather higher incidence of rainfall.

While Jeddah is hot and humid from April to October, from November to March the climate is pleasant. Average temperatures in Jeddah range from 19°C to 40°C, although temperatures of 52°C are not unknown. Some relief from the heat in the summer is provided by a moderate wind that blows off the sea. Jeddah's rainfall tends to consist of a few rainstorms that occur in the winter. Although there is the occasional day of patchy cloud, for the rest of the year the expatriate will generally enjoy sunshine from a clear sky.

In the Eastern Province the climate is similar to that of Jeddah. The humidity is high in the summer months. The temperature range is less than in Riyadh but greater than in Jeddah.

Working conditions and regulations

Working conditions will vary enormously depending upon what job the expatriate is going to do. Similarly, whether a spouse and family are able to accompany the expatriate will depend on the job and whether suitable academic or professional qualifications are held. Trade unions are illegal in Saudi Arabia and employees may have to negotiate their own working conditions. The 1969 Labour and Workmen Law is administered by the local labour offices, which adjudicate in any dispute between contracting parties. Western women entering Saudi Arabia can sometimes find suitable work at home, in embassies or in other foreign institutions.

Contractual disputes

In Saudi Arabia, foreign embassy representatives are unable to intervene in contractual or labour disputes. Aggrieved employees are generally advised to settle, if at all possible, direct with their employer without recourse to the Labour Office, where the procedures can be lengthy and legal costs high. (Direct settlement with the employer can also help in avoiding problems over the eventual exit visa, for which only the employer can apply, and over accommodation in the interim period.)

In signing a contract of employment, the expatriate employee should always bear in mind that conditions in Saudi Arabia may not be to their liking.

Termination of contract

The withdrawing of labour is against the law. It is therefore advisable to ensure that the contract contains some acceptable break clause. If a contract is broken for any reason, the expatriate may find that his employer will not provide the letter of rebase or 'no objection certificate', which is necessary to enable the expatriate to work for another organization in the country.

It should be borne in mind that the employee will probably have to pay their homeward fare (as well as recruitment and other related costs in some cases), so it is important to remain at work until sufficient funds have been earned to cover these eventualities.

Sponsorship

The employer also acts as sponsor and, as such, he is responsible for obtaining both work and residence permits and is legally responsible for the expatriate employee, provided that they do not offend against the local law. In such circumstances, the employer's responsibility ceases. Where the employee wishes to change employment, sponsorship must be transferred to another employer with the agreement of the first sponsor in the form of a letter of release. It would be unwise to assume that this will be forthcoming.

During the expatriate employee's stay in Saudi Arabia, the employer or sponsor will retain their passport. In return he should provide the employee with an identity document or *Iqama*, which should be carried at all times. Only the employer/sponsor can obtain the necessary exit and re-entry visa that will be entered into the employee's passport and returned to them prior to departure. It is not uncommon to encounter delays in the issue of exit or exit/re-entry visas, particularly at known holiday times. Exit-only visas are issued on satisfactory completion of the contract and normally the employer will be required to sign the employee out at the immigration counter on departure from the country.

If the expatriate is in Saudi Arabia as the employee of a foreign company that has won a contract there, it should be stressed that the need for sponsorship does still apply. The only difference is that the direct relationship of responsibility is between the foreign firm and its Saudi sponsor.

The expatriate and religion

Saudi Arabia is an exclusively Islamic (Muslim) country and Islam governs nearly every aspect of life. Islam means submission to the will of God (Allah). The practice of any form of religion other than Islam is prohibited in Saudi Arabia. Severe punishment (imprisonment and deportation) can result should such activities come to the attention of the authorities. In particular, this means that the authorities will stamp firmly on attempts at proselytization or conversion of Muslims to Christianity. (However, it should be added that meetings of Christians do take place, very privately and discreetly, in expatriates' homes.)

Islam recognizes many of the biblical patriarchs and prophets (among whom they count Jesus Christ); it proclaims that there is no

God but Allah and that Muhammad was his last and greatest prophet. God's will is said to be expressed in the *Qur'an* (Holy Book), as revealed to Muhammad at Makkah and Madinah in the 7th Century AD. Muhammad is buried at Madinah.

Makkah and Madinah are regarded as the two principal holy cities of Islam, the third being Jerusalem. Entry to Makkah and Madinah is strictly forbidden to all non-Muslims, though access to the outskirts of Madinah (eg the Sheraton Hotel) is possible. Millions of Muslims throughout the world face Makkah five times daily in prayer and it is a major expression of the faith for every Muslim to make the pilgrimage (*hajj*) to the shrine (*Ka'aba*) and other religious sites at Makkah once in his lifetime.

Every local community has a mosque in which Muslims pray and to which entry is barred for non-Muslims. The frequent calls to prayer from the towers (minarets) of mosques are a feature of life. It is common, however, to see people praying in the street, in offices, or any other public places, and service in shops, garages etc ceases during prayer time. Saudis live their religion and take their devotions very seriously indeed.

The Muslim calendar

The Muslim calendar consists of 12 lunar months and is 10 or 11 days shorter than the solar year. The calendar is also called '*Hijra*' or '*Hegira*' (flight) after the Prophet Muhammad's journey from Makkah to Madinah in 622 AD, the year from which the numbering of Muslim years starts. The start of each lunar month depends on a sighting of the new moon. While the date can be estimated in advance, this cannot be done with dependable precision.

The working week

The Muslim Holy Day is Friday; many offices are shut on Thursday as well as Friday, and the working week starts on Saturday.

Ramadan

The ninth month of the Muslim year is the month of fasting known as Ramadan. During Ramadan a Muslim must not let anything pass his lips between sunrise and sunset. The prohibition includes food, drink and cigarettes. Here, again, expatriates must be careful not to cause offence to Muslims by eating, drinking or smoking in public during the fasting hours, as strict penalties (possibly deportation) can be incurred for non-compliance.

Public holidays

The two major public holidays of the year are religious festivals. The first, the *Eid Al-Fitr*, lasts for about two weeks and celebrates the end of the month of fasting. The *Eid Al-Adha*, about two months later, lasts for about 10 days and celebrates the sacrifice during the pilgrimage to Makkah.

It should be pointed out that Christmas is not recognized in Saudi Arabia and most expatriates are expected to work on Christmas Day.

The expatriate and the law

The laws of Saudi Arabia are based largely on the *Qur'an*; the system is often known as *Shari'a*. Although punishments for some offences are harsh by Western standards, the Saudis claim to have a very low crime rate. The application of the law can sometimes be the source of much misunderstanding. The Saudis understand that the ways of non-Muslims are different from their own and they will not generally interfere with what foreigners do quietly, privately and discreetly.

However, foreigners who take advantage of this to break the law are running serious risks. Their offences can easily become known, if only by accident, and as soon as the breach of the law comes to public attention the perpetrator will find himself in trouble, possibly quite serious trouble. The Saudis are jealous of their reputation of having a well-ordered society. They will not allow foreigners to put it at risk.

There is generally no distinction in Saudi law between Muslims and non-Muslims, and expatriates in Saudi Arabia can expect to receive the full penalty for any offence. This might include a long prison sentence and strokes (lashes of the whip).

Assistance from embassy consular staff

Foreign embassy consular staff in Saudi Arabia will, naturally, do what is in their power to assist foreign nationals who are caught disobeying Saudi law. In most cases this has to be restricted to the giving of advice and to attempting to ensure that the normal correct Saudi legal processes are followed. It should be stressed that foreign embassy staff cannot save nationals from the consequences of their own actions or negligence – for example, the implementation of customary punishment.

Police procedures

The procedure upon arrest is usually as follows. The police will question the person arrested, carry out any relevant investigation and require the person to make a statement. The accused may not be allowed the benefit of any outside contact (with employers, friends, consul or lawyer) for as long as the investigation continues. If the police decide that there is a case to answer, the accused will be remanded in custody and probably moved from a police station to a prison until he/she can appear before a judge to confirm that the signed statement is accurate and was not made under actual physical duress. While in police custody, the foreign embassy official or consul will normally have unrestricted access to a prisoner. However, once the prisoner has been moved to prison, only limited access will be granted. There will then be a further remand in custody until the trial, which the judge will conduct in accordance with *Qur'anic* law. There is no jury and although the accused has no right to a lawyer or embassy representative, judges can (and sometimes do) permit consular attendance. The court provides an interpreter.

In the event of a conviction, the judge will normally impose a sentence and require the person convicted to sign acceptance of the sentence (unless there is to be an appeal against conviction to a higher court). The period from arrest to sentence can be three months or longer in difficult cases, partly because cases involving foreigners are dealt with particularly carefully.

The judge's sentence has to be confirmed (and can be increased) by a higher court, the Provincial Governor, the Ministry of Interior and, in serious cases, the Council of Ministers. An appeal can take up to a year to be heard. Inevitably, the movement of case files among the authorities concerned takes time, but a custodial sentence is generally reckoned to have started on the date of arrest. Deportation procedures at the end of the custodial sentence can add to the period spent in detention. Occasionally, expatriates who offend against the law may simply be deported after a few days or weeks in police detention, although this tends to happen rarely.

Serious offences

Murder and sexual immorality, such as adultery or homosexual acts, carry the death penalty in Saudi Arabia. So does apostasy (renunciation of the Muslim faith). The death penalty is carried out in public, usually by decapitation. Cutting off the thief's right hand punishes serious and/or persistent theft. This, too, is done in public, usually in front of the main Mosque after midday prayers on Friday.

Third party liability

Some cases have both criminal ('public right') and civil ('private right') aspects. For instance, after a theft or causing accidental injury or death, the person responsible is required first to make restitution or pay compensation. The question of punishment for any offence involved is usually only after private right claims have been settled. A driver who may be in no way to blame for the death or injury of another driver or pedestrian in a road accident will nonetheless have to pay 'blood money' on a varying scale to the injured party or relatives of the deceased person. The amount payable for the death of a Muslim man is now SR100,000 (for Christians the amount is half this).

Motor insurance

Motor insurance, including third party cover, is available in Saudi Arabia. However, it is not compulsory and some Muslims have scruples about the principle of insurance. An expatriate should not assume that he is covered for third party claims even when he is driving his employer's vehicle on business; he should check that he is adequately covered by insurance or otherwise. (Accidents can occur off the road too, and general personal liability insurance is worth considering.) The normal procedure after a road accident in which damage or injury has been caused is for the driver(s) held responsible to be imprisoned, possibly indefinitely.

Non-payment of debt

Under *Shari'a* law, non-payment of debt is considered a crime and sufficient reason for imprisonment. However, imprisonment does not in itself discharge debt and it is therefore important for the expatriate both to avoid getting into debt personally and to keep careful accounts of any employer's funds or goods for which he may have responsibility. The expatriate employee can be held personally responsible for company debts if considered the sole company representative responsible in Saudi Arabia. Experience has shown that debt cases can be the most difficult to resolve, particularly if Saudi citizens are involved, as their private rights are fundamental and not subject to royal or government intervention.

It is also necessary for the expatriate to take seriously any responsibility he or she may have for safeguarding company cash or property, whether in the safe or stores overnight or in transit. If it is stolen, negligence may be alleged and a severe penalty imposed.

Alcohol prohibition

For expatriates in Saudi Arabia it is the prohibition on alcohol that causes the most difficulty. Those who indulge are punished if their activities come to police attention, especially in the event of brawling, traffic accidents, noisy parties, or simply being out in the small hours. Sentences can vary from a few weeks or months in prison for consumption of alcohol to several years for smuggling, manufacture or distribution. For such offences, strokes are also part of the sentence, as well as a hefty customs fine if smuggled liquor is involved. Stiff penalties are handed out to those found in possession of equipment for manufacturing alcohol.

Drugs offences

The Saudi government takes a particularly serious view of drug offences. The death penalty is frequently imposed on drug smugglers, including foreigners, and sometimes also on minor traffickers guilty on second or subsequent charges. Possession of even the smallest quantity can lead to a two-year prison sentence, to which can be added strokes and a fine. To be found in possession of any drugs at an airport or border crossing may automatically incur a charge of smuggling and arrivals have been detained for three weeks while drugs (medication) have been analysed.

Prisons

Imprisonment in Saudi Arabia is a trying and uncomfortable experience; its purpose is punishment rather than rehabilitation. Prisons are generally overcrowded and, for much of the year, hot. Exercise, if any, is an occasional privilege. Visits are allowed regularly, though often under difficult conditions.

6.3

Practicalities of Doing Business

Anthony Shoult, ASA Consulting

Introduction

This chapter provides the business visitor intending to travel to Saudi Arabia or the expatriate planning to take up residence, with a few practical guidelines in order to help with the process of orientation or adjustment to life in a new country with a people, culture and climate very different from that to which they are likely to be accustomed. Table 6.3.1 provides some useful facts.

Travel to Saudi Arabia

Most business visitors to Saudi Arabia arrive by air to one of the country's three international airports, Riyadh, Dammam and Jeddah. The national carrier, Saudi Arabian Airlines, is the largest carrier in the Middle East. There are direct flights by Saudi Arabian Airlines and other international carriers from many European countries and neighbouring Gulf states to all of the country's international airports.

The major international airports are modern and well equipped. Riyadh King Khaled International Airport (RUH) has shops and car hire facilities. King Fahad Airport, Dammam (DMM) is some considerable way from Eastern Province cities but taxis and buses are available. For Jeddah, the King Abdul Aziz International Airport (JED) is located 18 kilometres north of the city and has a hotel, restaurant, bank, post office, shops, car hire and special pilgrimage facilities.

There is also road access to Saudi Arabia from all the countries with which it shares a land border, as well as Bahrain via the causeway, which levies a toll. It should be remembered that only Muslims are allowed to enter the holy cities of Makkah and central Madinah.

Passports, visas and work permits are required by all visitors to Saudi Arabia, except nationals of GCC states, certain seamen and pilgrims with passes. Therefore, prior to travelling to Saudi Arabia, it is absolutely essential to be in possession of a valid passport and a valid and appropriate visa. Failure to do so will most certainly result in the traveller being returned to their point of departure – sometimes after a few days of uncomfortable delay. In particular, it should be noted that the expiry date of passports must extend at least six months beyond the proposed stay. Also, visitors with passports containing evidence of a visit or an intended visit to Israel will not be admitted.

When applying for a visa, an original letter of invitation from a company or government department in Saudi Arabia must be submitted with the application to the appropriate Saudi embassy. No certificate of religion is required, but Judaism and atheism are not accepted as stated beliefs.

Upon arrival, all luggage is likely to be thoroughly searched and it is a good idea to have items arranged in such a way that they can be easily repacked. Items that cannot be brought into Saudi Arabia include narcotics, alcohol, pork products, religious books and material, obscene literature or videos or literature containing illustrations of scantily dressed women. Everyday pharmaceutical products may well be on the prescribed list of banned drugs in Saudi Arabia and travellers carrying them, even in good faith, are liable to detention.

Travellers should consider whether it is absolutely necessary to bring medicinal drugs with them; if they do bring them, they should not omit to carry the doctor's prescription. It is in the interests of the traveller not to arrive in Saudi Arabia under the influence of alcohol, as the consequences may be serious in that travellers who arrive obviously inebriated are liable to be arrested or deported. As soon as possible after arrival in Saudi Arabia, it is advisable to register with the appropriate embassy or consulate.

Table 6.3.1 Saudi Arabia: Useful facts

Official name:	Al-Mamlaka al-Arabiya as-Saudiya (The Kingdom of Saudi Arabia)
Land area:	2.250,000 square kilometres (868,730 square miles)
Population:	21.4 million – 77 per cent urban, 23 per cent rural
Capital:	Riyadh
Time zone:	GMT + 3 hours
Language:	Arabic (official), English (commercial)

International dialling code from overseas:	00 966 + area code and number (area codes: 1 for Riyadh, 2 for Jeddah and 3 for Dammam/Al-Khobar/Dhahran, 5 for mobiles)
Currency:	Saudi Riyal
Head of State and Prime Minister:	King Abdullah bin Abdul Aziz Al Saud, Custodian of the Two Holy Mosques
Business hours:	
Government:	Government offices are open from 7:30am till 2:30pm. They are closed for business on Thursdays and Fridays.
Private:	Private businesses generally operate from 8:00am until noon, and from 3.00pm to 6.00pm (split shifts) or from 8.00am until 2.00pm (single shift). They are closed for business on Thursday afternoons and Fridays.
Shops and other retail outlets:	Shops and garages are open from 8.00am until noon and from 3.00pm until 9.00pm or later. They are closed for business for approximately 20 minutes during morning, afternoon and evening prayer times, during which customers may be asked to leave the premises.
Restaurants and fast food outlets:	Restaurants and fast food outlet may be open throughout the day. Like shops, they close their doors for new business for approximately 20 minutes during morning, afternoon and evening prayer times, although diners that have already been admitted are not required to leave the premises.
Restrictions:	Forbidden items include alcohol, drugs, weapons, ammunition, pork, non-Islamic religious material and pornography. Prescription drugs must be documented. The cities of Makkah and Madinah hold special religious significance for Muslims and only persons of the Islamic faith are allowed entry.
Religion:	The official religion is Islam, which forms the basis of the nation's legal system. There are two major religious holidays: *Eid Al-Fitr*, celebrating of the annual Ramadan fast; and *Eid Al-Adha*, celebrating the pilgrimage to Makkah.
Calendar:	Saudi Arabia follows the Islamic Hijra calendar, which is based on lunar cycles. Thus, the year is 354 days long. Friday is the weekly day of rest and worship.

Accommodation

Whether or not the employee is obliged to find their own accommodation upon arrival in Saudi Arabia depends upon the terms of their contract. Their employer in this respect will almost invariably provide for blue-collar workers, but professional people may be given more choice. Saudis own all accommodation, and availability and cost fluctuate according to market demand.

The expatriate should not have any trouble finding somewhere to live but will have to agree with the employer about who meets the cost. In present circumstances, where security considerations are to the fore, the tendency is very much towards compound living, although villas and apartments in Saudi residential areas are also available.

The choice of accommodation will depend upon individual needs and means, but where a family accompanies employees, it is advisable not to be too distant from other expatriate families. As women are not allowed to drive in Saudi Arabia and taxis are neither readily available nor recommended to be used by women in the remoter suburbs, the employee may wish to live nearer the centre or to hire a reliable chauffeur. In circumstances where a spouse suffers from a sense of isolation, this may ultimately turn out to be a significant factor in the enjoyment of life in Saudi Arabia.

Recreation

Entertainment

Apart from restaurants, of which there is a good selection in the main centres and which have segregated family sections, there are virtually none of the facilities for entertainment normally found in Western cities. There are no cinemas, no theatres and no clubs as such. It follows that expatriates have to make their own entertainment, and exploit the natural facilities that abound. The expatriate communities in Riyadh, Jeddah and the Eastern Province are well organized and offer a wide range of communal activities. Elsewhere activities are organized privately.

There are hotels of good international standard in the major centres, although they tend to be expensive. Many hotels allow non-resident males to use their tennis and swimming facilities but mixed bathing in public pools is banned. Large organizations often provide recreation facilities for their employees living on a private compound. There are also some large housing compounds in which the villas or apartments are available for letting individually. It is important to remember that the expatriate's home is, in practice, not inviolable and they are responsible for what happens in it.

The expatriate can get into serious difficulties for behaviour in public that is deemed offensive to local customs and sensibilities. For example, accompanying a woman who is not a member of your immediate family (for example by simply driving her around) can lead to serious trouble with the authorities, even in the case of foreign nationals.

Water sports

The natural facilities available to the expatriate will depend upon where they are living. From Jeddah and Yanbu, the facilities for sea-water sports are superb. Sailing, fishing, water skiing and diving are all very popular pastimes. Diving and snorkelling are particularly so because the Red Sea coast is a coral reef and some of the most spectacular marine life in the world can be observed there.

Driving tours and desert expeditions

Driving tours and desert camping expeditions have always provided a pleasant leisure pastime for those living and working in the Kingdom. However, following a number of well-publicized incidents involving attacks on Westerners by Islamic militants, such excursions are now undertaken with a heightened awareness of one's personal security.

From Jeddah, particularly in the summer, it is pleasant to drive up to the mountains to Taif, where the air is cooler than on the coastal plain and where opportunities for camping and climbing are abundant. Indeed, simple camping is a pastime that can be indulged in anywhere in the Kingdom. The conditions are ideal and, as it rarely rains, a tent is not essential.

Desert expeditions are among the attractions available to expatriates living in Riyadh. It is not difficult to find an attractive oasis, to hunt for fossils in the landscape near Riyadh, or to venture with care into the pure sands of the southern extension of the Nefud Desert or the Empty Quarter. In the Eastern Province, the accent is, again, on aquatic activities, although there is no reef.

The air-conditioned comfort of a modern car can lull the expatriate into a false sense of security when travelling around. The deadliness of climatic conditions in Saudi Arabia will very quickly become apparent to those whose vehicle breaks down, or who get stuck in difficult terrain. The isolation and heat are such that, in those circumstances, death can result very quickly. It is essential for those venturing off the highway to let someone know where they are going, to travel in company (it is strongly recommended never to venture off the highway unless in the company of another four-wheel-drive vehicle), and to carry a large quantity of drinking water, spare fuel, a shovel, rope, some mats (to place under wheels if necessary), as well as some material for shade. Knowledge of mechanics and desert driving techniques is also useful.

Clothing and the dress code

There is no absolutely correct dress code for Saudi Arabia and the best way for both men and women to avoid getting into difficulties is to dress conservatively in public. For women this restriction is most conveniently observed by wearing loose ankle-length cotton dresses with sleeves and high neckbands. These dresses are relatively cheap and widely available in Saudi Arabia. Tight fitting clothes such as trousers or leggings are not recommended.

The Saudi government does not require non-Muslim women to wear the *abaya* or headscarf. However, some women do wear the *abaya*, and may also decide to cover their hair in order not to draw attention to themselves and to avoid being confronted by the *Mutawwa* (religious police) who are often in evidence patrolling the *souks* (marketplaces) and shopping centres and who frequently challenge women on this point. This is ultimately a matter for personal discretion and decision. No dress, however modest, can be taken as a guarantee against confrontation.

Men should not appear in public in shorts. Additionally, it is suggested that men either refrain from wearing, or cover up, gold chains and other jewellery (particularly crosses) in public. Restrictions on dress increasingly apply to the beach, particularly to those areas closest to the towns; and some embarrassment from roving voyeurs is always a risk.

Shopping facilities

In the three major centres there are Western-style shopping centres, supermarkets and other shops that carry a wide range of imported perishable and non-perishable food and other products. A very wide range of chemists' sundries and drugs are available without prescription. Electrical goods are generally much the same price in Saudi Arabia as in Europe and will be more suited to the local 60 cycles and 110 or 220 voltage requirements.

Local transport

Taxis are plentiful in the central area of major cities but difficult to find or call further out and away from trunk roads. There are limousine services in Riyadh, Jeddah and Dammam, and buses operate a good service on a limited route network in the major cities. A private car or good access to company transport is almost essential, since social life will otherwise be very limited (but remember, women are not allowed to drive).

For much of the year it is too hot to walk very far and distances between homes and shops are considerable. American and Japanese cars are readily available and are cheaper than in the UK. Buying a good second-hand car locally is quite possible and bargains are available; caution is obviously advisable, especially as standards of servicing are not always high. Although nowadays not essential, four-wheel-drive vehicles remain very popular.

Driving in Saudi Arabia

Those who are to drive while in Saudi Arabia as a resident must have a Saudi driving licence. An employer will usually help to obtain one, on the strength of a valid national licence, at the same time as he obtains your work and residence permits. Until the residence permit is obtained (or if on a visit to Saudi Arabia), the visitor may legally drive on a full national licence or international driving permit, preferably the former, for up to three months, provided the licence or permit is taken to the traffic police and a covering certificate (in Arabic) is obtained from them.

The visitor should carry a driving licence (with covering certificate if appropriate) at all times when driving, and may well be arrested if unable to produce it at a police checkpoint. Insurance is not compulsory but the visiting expatriate would be very unwise to drive without at least third party insurance cover, as accidents are frequent. As a general rule, never leave the scene of any serious accident until police permission has been given. Any trace of alcohol on the breath will lead to the driver being taken to a government hospital for a blood test, which, if proved positive, can lead to arrest and possible criminal charges being brought against the driver.

Mail and telephones

The postal and telephone facilities in Saudi Arabia work well and are improving, although there is currently a shortage of lines in some areas. All cities are on the direct dialling system, and it is possible to dial most numbers in Saudi Arabia from Europe or the United States. Letters to or from Europe can be received in five days but can take much longer and are subject to censorship.

Health and medical facilities

There should be no major risk of health problems for anyone who is thoroughly fit on arrival, likes an open-air life and takes the usual precautions necessary in any hot climate. Some areas of Saudi Arabia (notably the south-western coastal region of Jizan) are potentially malarial and anyone who is to live or visit one of those areas should consider taking a malaria prophylactic.

Except during the period of the *hajj*, when evidence of meningitis vaccination is required, vaccination certificates are not ordinarily necessary for entry to Saudi Arabia, but immunization against TB, polio, hepatitis and tetanus can be worthwhile health precautions. Although tap water in Saudi Arabia is drinkable, it is probably safer to drink bottled water available at local shops. Outdoors, it is advisable to wear something on the feet at all times, and certainly when bathing in the sea, where you may step on a stone fish, chicken fish or other venomous marine creatures, or simply cut the foot and get a coral infection. Serum for poisonous stings is not widely available in Saudi Arabia.

Medical facilities in the main centres are good, though not in all respects, and they are expensive. There are some Western doctors working in private clinics or hospitals, several of which are very well equipped. Before leaving for Saudi Arabia, it is advisable to find out what the arrangements are for access to hospitals and payment for medical treatment. If necessary, the arriving expatriate should arrange suitable overseas cover with a foreign medical insurance scheme.

Education

In the three main population centres there are international schools offering good British-style education for children up to 14 years of age; but all usually have waiting lists. There are also schools offering American-style education for children aged up to 16 years. School fees in Saudi Arabia are high, currently varying between US$7,000 and US$13,500 per year (see Table 6.3.2).

Table 6.3.2 Examples of structure of school fees 2005/06 (US$/term)

Name of School	Pre-School	Lower School (Year 1–2)	Middle School (Year 3–6)	Upper School (Year 7–11)	IB (IB1 and IB2)
British International School, Jeddah	1,545	2,343	2,370	3,009	4,447
American International School, Riyadh	2,379	3,964	4,103	4,506	-
British International School, Al Khobar	884	2,610	2,636	2,743	-

Note: Cost given is per term; there are three terms in the academic year

Language

It is a general principle that to get the most out of a stay in a foreign country, the visitor needs to know at least a little of the language. Although Arabic, with its formidable looking script, appears to be very difficult, expatriates can pick up the spoken language with a little effort. Courses are available locally. Saudis are delighted to come across an expatriate who has made the effort to learn a little of their language and, in a country where personal relationships are important, any such efforts will bring their reward. Although English is widely understood, many shopkeepers, taxi drivers and some officials do not understand a word of it.

Further information

Sources of further information on the practicalities of doing business in Saudi Arabia include UK Trade and Investment (www.uktradeinvest.gov.uk) and Council of Saudi Chambers of Commerce and Industry (www.saudichambers.org.sa)

Further reading

Saudi Arabia, Anthony Ham, Martha Brekhus Shams and Andrew Madden, Lonely Planet Publications (September 2004).

Understanding Saudi Arabia (The Complete Idiot's Guide), Colin Wells, Alpha Books (2003).

Living and Working in the Gulf States and Saudi Arabia, Robert Hughes, Survival Books Limited (April 2003).

Gorilla Guides: The Business Traveller's Guide to Saudi Arabia, Andrew Mead, Stacey International Publishers (October 2002).

Live and Work in Saudi and the Gulf, Louise Whetter, Vacation Work Publications (May 2000).

Riyadh Handbook, Ionis Thompson and Lisa Greeberg, Stacey International Publishers, (December 2000).

6.4

Business Culture

Dr Jehad Al-Omari, Trilateral Training Solutions

Introduction

The Arab population of Saudi Arabia is hospitable and courteous, and the perils of doing the wrong thing in the Middle East are much exaggerated. The style is more important than the act itself. While they do not expect outsiders to copy their way of doing things, Arabs will respect those who measure up to their standards of dignity. Nothing is said if one forgets this, but the atmosphere of a conversation can be spoiled by what local custom regards as bad manners. Courtesy, respect, patience and honour are very important in business.

Body language

Essentially, Arabs are a lot more tactile than most of their Western counterparts, although there are certain restrictions when one is dealing across gender. To start with, always shake hands on meeting and leaving, and expect the handshake to last longer than it would in the West. This is a sign of friendship. If you have made a good impression, the handshake on departure will be longer than that on arrival. It is normal for your host to hold your hand for few minutes whilst welcoming you or when showing you round the premises. The same goes for personal space, where Arabs will come too close for comfort for many Europeans. As in the case of long handshakes, this is a sign of warmth and friendship.

Furthermore, eye contact is important in that it should be both direct and continuous, but not staring. Good eye contact is a sign of both integrity and honesty, as the case is throughout Europe. Nevertheless, all of the rules regarding body language may change when one meets someone from the opposite sex. Handshakes will be significantly shorter, if they take place at all; personal space needs to be on the long side and eye contact may be broken occasionally as a sign of respect.

Continuing with body language, Arabs, especially the older generation, will avoid using their left hand when eating or when dealing with others. Try not to give and receive things with the left hand, and this is especially true for food. Another piece of advice is to avoid showing the soles of your feet to an Arab. This is a calculated insult, although the younger generation or those with plenty of exposure to the West are unlikely to take offence. Equally, do not sit rigidly – feet glued to the floor – and fear to move. The Arab will take to an easy outgoing personality. Finally, you may note your Arab colleagues pointing their fingers in your direction from time to time – this is not meant as an insult, so do not take offence.

Communicating with Arabs

Within cross-cultural literature, the Arab culture is generally known as 'high context' culture. This means that body language plays an important role in their communication and to the extent where body language can be more important than the spoken word. High context cultures are also characterized by their implicit style of communication, where the central message may be hidden and where people will frequently use idioms, proverbs, euphemisms and anecdotes to relay deeper meanings. Unfortunately, such a style can be confusing to outsiders and it may be misinterpreted as being vague or evasive. Suffice to say that high context communication is about politeness rather than evasiveness, and puts pressure on the listener to communicate with all their senses rather than concentrate on the explicit spoken word. It is worthwhile stating here that low context cultures, such as North American and German, can come across as being too direct, confrontational and adversarial.

Hospitality

When mixing with Arabs, you will quickly note that hospitality is their most endearing and prominent of characteristics. It is almost a way of life, where the guest is king, and he or she is pampered to a point where most Westerners could feel embarrassed. Hospitality begins with the offer of a drink as soon as the guest arrives, and to delay such offer for longer than few minutes verges on rudeness. The offer is frequently expressed several times, and to refuse such an offer can be interpreted as an insult to the host. This is especially true when you are still in the early stages of the relationship. Nevertheless, it is still traditional for the Arab host to extend invitations at least three times, and it is sometimes seen as the prerogative of the guest to decline the first two invitations by insisting on not troubling the host. Hospitality in the Arab world reaches its epitome when it is offered to complete strangers and when it is spontaneous. In respect of the latter, Arabs admire spontaneity as a personal trait, and you can expect invitations for 'now' rather than 'later'. Spontaneity in hospitality manifests itself most clearly when you admire personal belongings, where the Arab response would be to offer it immediately, whatever it may be. It is nevertheless traditional to decline such offers, unless your counterpart offers it repeatedly. As a rule of thumb, try not to admire personal belongings. Furthermore, you need to avoid 'going Dutch' when in the company of Arabs, and try and be spontaneous in terms of who pays. As far as gifts are concerned, it is worthwhile remembering that corporate gifts are big business in the Arab world, so try to be different and creative.

Coffee has a central place in traditional Arab life, and there are many rituals associated with it. There are two types of coffee that are normally served. The first type is what is often referred to as traditional, Bedouin or bitter coffee, which is served in handless china cups. You must always accept the first cup offered to you, and you must receive it with your right hand. If you would like another cup, simply hand it to the pourer and they will serve you again. If you do not want any more, simply shake the cup sideways as an indication that you have finished. It is an accepted tradition that you should never exceed three cups every time the coffee is served. The second type of coffee that is sometimes served is what is generally known as 'Turkish Coffee' in the West. This coffee is either served sweet or with no sugar, but unlike the previous type of coffee you are free to decline it, if you so wish. As a tip, wait a couple of minutes before you start drinking this coffee to allow the sediments to settle at the bottom, and whatever you do, do not try and finish the cup to the last drop. Tea may also be served after coffee, or sometimes instead of it, and it comes in many shapes and several flavours, but rarely with milk.

When you are invited to traditional meals, especially banquets that are held at someone's house or those held in the desert, do remember that Arabs will pamper their guests to the point of almost force-feeding them. In other words, your dish will always be full, but do not assume that you have to eat everything. Eat slowly, and do not assume that you have to eat everything your host places on your plate or in front of you. Do not accept food, or anything else, with your left hand. Sometimes, you may find that there is no cutlery, and you will be expected to wash your hands and eat with your right hand. (Don't knock it until you have tried it.)

If you are invited out to a Saudi household, you may well find yourself sitting cross-legged on the floor for the meal, which may take any form, but is usually very short; most of the talk and socializing goes on before the meal. Guests usually leave soon after it is over. The sexes dine separately, though non-Muslim Western women are sometimes allowed to eat with the men.

A traditional Muslim will usually say '*Bismillah ar-Rahman ar-Rahim*' ('In the name of God, the Merciful, the Compassionate') before he begins eating. He will not hurry to the table before everyone else, nor will he eat quickly or to excess. He will pay more attention to other people present than to his food. The fundamental virtue is self-discipline, hunger is preferable to gluttony and physical appetites must be controlled. At a traditional meal, it is polite for a host to select pieces of meat or other delicacies and put them on the guest's plate for him to eat. On some occasions, a host will not join in the meal but will hover around while it is being eaten, even serving a dish or two himself.

Doing business

When doing business, do not hurry; there is plenty of time for everything. Conversations begin slowly. Courtesies are important and fairly lengthy. You may find yourself engaged in pleasantries for longer than five minutes, and you may also find yourself returning to pleasantries throughout the meeting. Ask after your host's health and his family (never his wife). Normally, do not start talking business until coffee has been served. Do not be embarrassed by silence: a pause for reflection is common and considered as a sign of contemplation and seriousness. Nonetheless, do not be annoyed if you find yourself being interrupted, as this may mean that the conversation is going well, especially amongst friends. In this respect, and whilst Westerners tend conduct business in a linear way and try to follow agendas, Arabs tend to be more circular. The Western rush to structure is not something that the Arabs will warm towards, except during formal and important functions or meetings.

In the Arab context, although time is important, timing is of more importance. Cultures where time is important are generally characterized as being task-driven, whereas relationship-driven cultures are more prone to pay attention to timing or pacing. This is especially true for collective cultures such as the Arab culture. Remember that in the Arab world, your ability to do business is as much influenced by your network as it is influenced by your individual skills. Collective cultures such as Arab or Chinese also pay a lot of attention to face, and whatever you do, do not cause your Arab counterpart to lose face. In this respect, a direct and confrontational style is frowned upon. This is especially true when you are dealing with people for the first time or where your counterpart is senior to you in either position or age. Arabs tend to be deferential when it comes to power, age, position or background. You will notice that Arabs tend to use titles much more assertively and frequently than what is now the norm in most Western societies.

Take care of your personal appearance and wear well-pressed sober-coloured suits with shirt and tie. It is offensive to many Arabs for men to wear shorts or sleeveless vests without a shirt in public. Casual ware or dressing down is not a habit that has hit the Arab workplace, so always make sure that you are dressed smartly if you want to give the right impressions. Arabs will also frown on men wearing too much gold, such as bracelets or necklaces, and they will certainly look down on men wearing earrings or sporting ponytails. These are all considered as being feminine and unworthy of men.

Islam: A way of life

Islam plays a central role in the lives of most Saudi Arabians and sits at the heart of its political, judicial and commercial laws and systems. Visitors to the Kingdom of Saudi Arabia will do well to acquaint themselves with Islam, and there are many good books on this subject in most Western libraries. Ultimately, Islam is not just a religion divorced from real life but a way of life that encompasses every aspect and regulates Muslim attitudes and behaviours in all areas. The central belief system of Islam is about the belief in the Oneness of Allah (God) and that Mohammed is His messenger. Islam itself means submission to Allah and to free oneself from all tyrannies, whether they relate to other human beings or to material things or to vices.

Since present day Saudi Arabia is the birthplace of Islam, adherence to it is far more apparent than in many other Muslim countries. This is apparent in the overall emphasis on modesty in dress code and also in fact that prayers are observed in many public places. Muslims pray five times a day, at dawn, midday, mid-afternoon, sunset and about two hours after sunset. Shops will close three or four times during the day for half an hour of prayer, and work in offices is also interrupted. Do not be surprised if your host excuses himself during the meeting in order to attend prayers, and you will do well to arrange your meeting to avoid prayer times. Exact prayer times are given in local papers. The month of Ramadan is holy month in the Islamic lunar calendar, where Muslims will fast from dawn to dusk. Business during the month of Ramadan will inevitably be slower and working hours tend to be shorter. It would be more effective to try and get things done before the onset of Ramadan and if things could wait, to visit after Ramadan.

Out and about

Contrary to public belief, Saudi Arabia has a very varied topography ranging from empty deserts to mountainous areas and from rocky gorges to oases and so on. Visitors to Saudi Arabia tend to enjoy many outings and those who are interested in wildlife, camping and photography will find that Saudi Arabia has a lot to offer. However, do not take photographs of military installations, police stations, prisons, airports, government offices, power plants, embassies, mosques or Muslim women.

Although international tourism is not yet established in Saudi Arabia, internal tourism is a fast growing industry. There are, indeed, several government initiatives to promote this sector of the economy. Westerners living in Saudi Arabia tend to enjoy desert outings as well as visiting the mountainous areas to the west of Saudi Arabia and further south towards Yemen. There are a growing number of Red Sea resorts, which tend to cater for Westerners, and snorkelling is a particularly favourite activity.

As in most Arab countries, shopping in Saudi Arabia can be fun. There are now many shopping centres throughout the Kingdom, as well as traditional markets selling everything from the latest technology to spices and from traditional perfumes to rugs and from jewellery to antiques. Take your time to shop and remember that bargaining is not only acceptable but almost compulsory if you want to pay a fair price. On your first shopping trips, make sure that an experienced shopper accompanies you.

Hygiene

In the words of one Arab writer, Arabs and particularly Muslims are obsessive washers, and personal hygiene is central to Muslim life. In this respect, Westerners need to note that dogs are considered unclean in Arab society and their possession is limited to hunting, herding and guard duties. Beyond personal hygiene, visitors to the Kingdom will find that much effort is place on ensuring the highest standard of hygiene in public places, restaurants and shops. Nevertheless, due to the excessive heat, especially in the summer months, it is important to make sure that you wash fruit and vegetables repeatedly. There is no need to use chemicals for that purpose, but instead you may choose to soak such items. Where possible, avoid drinking water straight from the tap.

Making conversation

There are many subjects that Arabs will talk about, but you will find that there are certain sensitivities when it comes to politics whether it is local or regional, and you should tread carefully, especially in relation to the Palestinian issue. The same is true for the subject of religion, especially in view of recent events. As a rule of thumb, don't raise the subject yourself, and if you find yourself dragged into talking about these issues, make sure that you are asking the questions rather than the one who is passing judgements. As far as pleasantries are concerned, the Arab language is very flowery and you will find that Arab hosts will be happy to ask many questions and make many compliments. Nevertheless, by Western standards, Arabs are prone to ask too many private questions, so be prepared and do reciprocate. However, do not ask your colleagues about their wives, but rather about the family.

Muslim rules on diet

Every Westerner travelling to the Kingdom of Saudi Arabia must know that Muslims are prohibited from consuming alcohol and eating pork. It is a criminal offence to try to import both alcohol and pork into the Kingdom of Saudi Arabia. It follows that the law also forbids attempting to brew alcohol domestically. The prohibition on pork extends to its by-products such as lard and gelatine. The prohibition on alcohol extends to fermented liquids, such as pure vanilla and cider vinegar, and any food containing alcohol. Muslims are also forbidden from eating any blood products (eg black pudding) or animals that have died a natural death or that have been slaughtered as a sacrifice to a pagan deity or not slaughtered in the prescribed manner.

Arab names

Typically, Arab names will be composed of three or four names. The person's name (first name), his/her father's name and the family name. In some cases, the grandfather's name will follow the father's name. Arabs tend to use first names in every day transactions and the use of the family name is fairly limited. Arabs will sometimes use 'Bin' or 'Ibn' meaning 'son of' and 'Bint' meaning 'daughter of'. Many surnames will end with 'Al' or 'El' meaning 'the', and this often true for tribal names.

Common Arabic phrases

Knowledge of Arabic is not essential as English is widely used, though an ability to use the most common greetings and everyday phrases will be greatly appreciated by your host. Here are some useful phrases:

Hello	*Marhaba*
(Reply)	*Marhabtain*
Welcome	*Ahlan Wasahlan*
Good morning	*Sabah al khair*
(Reply)	*Sabah al noor*
Good evening	*Masa-al khair*
(Reply)	*Masa-al noor*
Peace be with you	*Assalam alaikum*
(Reply)	*Alaikum assalam*
How are you?	*Kaif halak* (male form), *Kaif halik* (female form)
(Reply) I'm fine, praise God goodbye	*Bikhayr, al-hamdu lillah*
(the one departing)	*Ma'essalama*
(the one remaining)	*Fi aman allah*
Yes	*Na'am*
No	*La*
Please	*Min Fadhlak* (male), *Min Fadhlik* (female)
Thank you	*Shokran*
If God is willing	*Inshallah*
Excuse me	*Afwan*
My name is	*Ismi*
How much? (cost)	*Bekam?*
Never mind	*Ma'laish*
Another time	*Marra thaniah*
How many?	*Kam?*

Further reading

The Arab Way: How to Work More Effectively with Arab Cultures, Jehad Al-Omari (April 2003).

Saudi Customs and Etiquette, Kathy Cuddihy, Stacey International Publishers, (October 2002).

Part Seven

Key Sectors of Trade and Investment

7.1

Oil and Gas Industry

Anthony Shoult, ASA Consulting [1]

Introduction

With one quarter of the world's proven oil reserves, the Kingdom is expected to retain its position as the world's largest oil producer for the foreseeable future. In addition, Saudi Arabia has four per cent of the world's gas reserves.

Oil and gas dominate the country's economy, representing up to 40 per cent of GDP. In any given year, 90 to 95 per cent of Saudi export revenues are derived from sales of crude oil, natural gas and refined products.

The national oil and gas company, Saudi Aramco, is continuing to invest heavily in production and is increasing the productivity of existing facilities. The thrust of this investment is concerned with the further development of Saudi's master gas system.

Saudi's proven gas reserves are estimated at over 220 trillion cubic feet and Saudi Aramco plans to increase annual natural gas production from three to five trillion cubic feet.

A number of new gas fields have already been discovered and the recent Hawiyah and Haradh projects will necessitate an expanded gas network, including an additional 3,000km of pipeline by 2006.

The Kingdom has reached agreement with Royal Dutch Shell on a gas exploration initiative and is in discussion with other international oil companies about other projects.

Oil industry

Saudi Arabia has the world's largest oil reserves, accounting for 25 per cent of world reserves. Proven crude oil reserves are at the level

---

[1] Sources of information include Saudi Aramco and UK Trade & Investment.

of 259.2 billion barrels. With production at a level in excess of nine million barrels a day in the first six months of 2004, the Kingdom accounts for just over 12 per cent of world oil production. There is sufficient oil for another 100 years' production at current rates.

Crude oil grades produced by Saudi Arabia are Arabian Heavy, Arabian Medium, Arabian Light, Arabian Extra Light and Arabian Super Light.

The key objective of the Saudi oil industry is to maintain sustained production capacity of around 10 million barrels per day (bpd). The key producing fields are Ghawar, the world's largest oil field (67 billion barrels), Safaniya, the world's largest offshore field (37 billion barrels), Hawtah (20,000 bpd of Arabian Super Light), and Shaybah (15 billion barrels, producing 500,000 bpd).

The Kingdom is also a major exporter of refined products, with 2,000 million bpd production capacity and 820 million bpd of exports planned for 2004. As such, the Kingdom ranks as one of the world's largest exporters of refined products and is the largest exporter to Asia.

Gas industry

Saudi Arabia has the world's fourth largest gas reserves after the Soviet Union, Iran and Qatar, accounting for four per cent of world reserves. Saudi's proven gas reserves are 224 trillion cubic feet, of which 77.4 trillion feet is non-associated. With production at the level of approximately 5.5 billion standard cubic feet per day in 2003, the Kingdom is the tenth largest world producer.

The key gas fields are Safaniya (5.36 trillion cubic feet) and Shaybah (25 trillion cubic feet). The Master Gas system processing capacity is 5.9 billion cubic feet per day (bcfpd). Processing plants are located at Shedgum (2.4 bcfpd), Uthmaniyah (2.5 bcfpd), Berri (1 bcfpd), Hawiyah (1.6 bcfpd) and Haradh (1.6 bcfpd). Hawiyah came on-stream in 2002 and Haradh in early 2003.

Expansion of the Saudi gas sector is urgently required to satisfy the Kingdom's growing domestic demand and to fuel the Kingdom's ambitious industrial development and economic diversification plans. It is estimated that by 2025, the demand for gas will reach more than 12 bcfpd, requiring an investment in excess of US$50 billion by 2020.

The need for gas for domestic energy is driven by an increasing demand for petrochemical production, the rapidly increasing demand for power (installed electric generation capacity is projected to increase from a current 20,000 MW to 60,000 MW by 2025), and expanding mining output.

International investment in the gas sector

A major recent development has been the opening up of Saudi Arabia's gas sector to international investment by involvement of the international oil companies.

Following the failed negotiations over the multi-billion Saudi Natural Gas Initiative between the Saudi government and the oil majors, Royal Dutch Shell and Total have agreed a form of joint venture with Saudi Aramco for the exploration of gas in an area of 200,000km^2 in the southern part of the Rub al-Khali.

The Southern Rub al-Khali (SRAK) Gas Upstream agreement, which is limited to natural gas exploration only, was signed in November 2003 between Shell (40 per cent), Total (30 per cent) and Saudi Aramco (30 per cent) and covers a total gas concession area of 210,000km^2.

Following on from this deal, in July 2003, 40 international oil companies attended a meeting in London at which Saudi Oil Minister, Ali Al-Naimi, invited tenders for a further three large natural gas exploration projects in the Rub al-Khali zone, an area that was originally designated to be developed under core venture 1 of the gas initiative.

As a result of this initiative, three further joint ventures were signed under the Gas Upstream Offering in March 2004:

- 30,000km^2 – 80 per cent Lukoil, 20 per cent Saudi Aramco;
- 39,000km^2 – 80 per cent Sinopec, 20 per cent Saudi Aramco;
- 51,000km^2 – 50 per cent ENI, 30 per cent Repsol, 20 per cent Saudi Aramco.

Saudi Aramco

Background

The Saudi Arabian Oil Company, or Saudi Aramco, was established in 1988, having previously operated as the Arabian American Oil Company since 1944. Between 1948 and 1973, the ownership structure comprised Standard Oil of California (now Chevron), Texas Company (now Texaco), and Standard Oil of New Jersey and Socony-Vacuum Oil (now ExxonMobil).

In 1973, the government of Saudi Arabia acquired a 25 per cent interest in Aramco, increasing in 1980 to a 100 per cent participation interest with the purchase of almost all of the company's assets.

The Master Gas System (MGS) project was launched in 1975. The aim was to enable Aramco to utilize associated gas (gas produced with oil production) and gas produced from deep natural reservoirs, known as Khuff non-associated gas. This was the largest industrial project in the world at that time.

In 1981, the East–West pipelines, built for Aramco's natural gas liquids (NGLs) and crude oil, linked the Eastern Province with Yanbu on the Red Sea. In 1993, Saudi Aramco took over responsibility from Petromin for the Kingdom's domestic refining, marketing and distribution and joint venture refining interests.

Current operations

Today, Saudi Aramco is the world's largest fully-integrated oil company, producing from more than 70 fields. As such, it will remain the world's largest oil exporter for many years to come. Crude oil production is currently running at nine million barrels a day.

Saudi Aramco employs more than 54,000 workers and is headquartered in Dhahran in the Eastern Province, with operations that span the Kingdom.

As well as world leader in crude oil production, Saudi Aramco owns and operates an extensive network of refining and distribution facilities and is responsible for the Kingdom's gas processing and oil and gas transportation installations.

Saudi Aramco has five domestic refineries at Ras Tanura (325,000 bpd), Riyadh (115,000 bpd), Jeddah (60,000 bpd), Yanbu (225,000 bpd) and Rabigh (400,000 bpd), with a combined capacity of 1.1 mbpd. There are two domestic 50:50 joint ventures, Sasref in Jubail with Royal Dutch Shell (305,000 bpd) and Samref in Yanbu with ExxonMobil (365,000 bpd). Refinery production from seven plants accounts for approximately 1.5 mbpd.

Saudi Aramco gas processing plants are located at Shedgum (2.4 bcfpd), Uthmaniyah (2.5 bcfpd), Berri (1 bcfpd), Hawiyah (1.6 bcfpd) and Haradh (1.6 bcfpd). Hawiyah came on-stream in 2001 and Haradh in early 2003.

Saudi Aramco also has an extensive pipeline network of more than 20,000km, which carries crude from wellhead to refinery. The major routes are:

- Trans–Arabian Pipeline (Tapline) completed in 1950 – 1,700km pipeline linking Eastern Province oil fields to Lebanon and the Mediterranean;
- Saudi Arabian–Bahrain Pipeline;
- East–West Crude Oil and Natural Gas Liquids (NGL) pipelines completed in 1981 – 1,200km pipeline from the Eastern Province to

Yanbu on the West coast (crude oil pipeline capacity five million bpd);

- NGL pipeline from Yanbu to Shedgum – at 1,170km long, the longest and most advanced gas line ever built.

Saudi Aramco also operates one of the world's largest fleets of crude carriers. Vela International Marine Limited is a wholly-owned subsidiary that operates 21 tankers and four product vessels. Saudi Aramco terminals handle more than 4,000 tankers a year. Terminals are located at Ras Tanura and Ju'aymah on the Arabian Gulf and at Jeddah, Rabigh, Jaizan, Yanbu and Duba on the Red Sea coast.

Saudi Aramco also controls a comprehensive petroleum product distribution system, which consists of delivery systems, storage facilities and air fueling operations. The company delivers approximately 700,000 barrels of refined products (gasoline, diesel fuel, jet fuel, kerosene, LPG fuel oil and asphalt) to some 5,000 bulk customers.

New oil and gas field discoveries

In April 2003, the Saudi Minister of Mineral Resources, Ali Bin Ibrahim Al-Naimi, announced the discovery by Aramco of the Yebrin field in the Eastern Province, some 50km south of Haradh on the southern edge of the Ghawar field. Production is estimated at 5,100 bpd of very light oil and 4.7 million cubic feet per day (mcfpd) of gas.

In July 2003, Mr Al-Naimi announced the discovery by Aramco of two new gas and oil wells in the central and southeastern regions. The main discovery of gas was made at a well in the Abqaiq field and the second discovery, including crude oil and gas, was made at Mazaleej field in the Gazal area. Estimated production is 45 mcfpd of sweet gas and 2,050 bpd of crude.

In September 2003, the Awtad gas field was discovered in Eastern Province. The estimated production capacity is 32 mcfpd.

Operational and capital expenditure

Saudi Aramco's day-to-day running costs are estimated to exceed US$2 billion a year, which does not take account of major projects. Around 85 per cent of all products and services are sourced through local agents/distributors, with 65 per cent of this figure sourced from abroad.

Saudi Aramco has carried out a programme of capital expenditure totalling US$34 billion over the 10 years to 2004. Combined Aramco capital and operating expenditure in 2000 alone amounted to US$6.2 billion, rising to US$6.7 billion in 2001. This included around

US$1 billion for drilling some 250 new wells. Similar levels of drilling activity are expected to continue.

Future Saudi Aramco developments

To meet future demand, Saudi Aramco has ambitious exploration and development plans. These include some US$20 billion expenditure over the next five years on new capital projects.

Saudi Aramco plans to increase annual natural gas production from three to five trillion cubic feet. As previously mentioned, in 2003 Aramco discovered four new fields, and the recent Hawiyah and Haradh projects necessitate an expanded gas network, with some additional 3,000km of pipeline by 2006 being planned.

Over the next five years (2005–09), Saudi Aramco plans to bring on-stream:

- five new crude increments;
- new NGL recovery plant and the expansion of the master gas system;
- the expansion and upgrade of refinery and distribution facilities.

These investments will require the design and construction of:

- in excess of 20 offshore platforms;
- gas/oil separation plants;
- process plants;
- some 2,300km of flow lines and long distance pipelines;
- infrastructure – roads, well sites and pipelines.

Because of the huge investment programme being implemented, Saudi Aramco represents the single largest market for materials and services in the Kingdom. This is estimated in the Saudi Aramco 2005/9 Business Plan at US$19.9 billion for the period 2005–09, out of a total Saudi market for materials and services of US$40.9 billion over the same period. Key areas of Saudi Aramco development will be at both Rabigh and Ras Tanura. With the planned expansion of Rabigh, Saudi Aramco is planning to make its first foray into the domestic petrochemical sector.

At Rabigh Saudi Aramco is seeking to maximize the value from its significant existing infrastructure investments by creating a platform for downstream industries, thereby attracting both local and international investors. Aramco wishes to integrate petrochemical and other industry with the existing 400 million bpd refinery as well as develop power, water and port facilities.

At Ras Tanura, Saudi Aramco is seeking to encourage investment opportunities, including mixed xylene, cumene, isobutene and nitrogen production.

For further information concerning Saudi Aramco, visit their website at www.saudiaramco.com.

7.2

Petrochemicals Industry

Anthony Shoult, ASA Consulting[1]

Introduction

There are currently 220 petrochemical plants of varying sizes in Saudi Arabia, representing an investment of US$29 billion and with an annual export value of US$3.2 billion.

The dominant player in the Saudi petrochemicals industry is Saudi Arabian Basic Industries Corporation (SABIC). This is one of the fastest growing petrochemical companies in the world, with a stated aim of becoming a truly global player in the world petrochemicals arena.

The SABIC manufacturing network in Saudi Arabia consists of a total of 18 world-scale industrial complexes, operated by 16 affiliates that produce petrochemicals, polymers, fertilizers and metals, as well as the industrial gases needed for their manufacture. Of these, 13 major SABIC industrial plants are located at Al Jubail industrial city on the Arabian Gulf. Of these, 11 plants are engaged in the production of petrochemicals and fertilizers. Two SABIC affiliate organizations are located at Yanbu industrial city on the Red Sea, and SABIC also partners in three regional ventures based in Bahrain.

SABIC is the world's 11th largest petrochemical producer and worlds largest exporter of fertilizers, polymers and chemicals. SABIC plants, together, represent US$24 billion in investments, with sales of US$9 billion in 2002. SABIC's total production of chemicals, plastics, fertilizers, steel and industrial gases reached the level of 42 million tonnes in 2004.

Private sector involvement in the Saudi petrochemicals sector started in 1996 and is taking an increasingly important role in its continued development, with over US$6 billion in major private sector petrochemicals projects currently in the planning and implementation stages.

---

[1] Sources of information include Yusuf Bin Ahmed Kanoo, Saudi Arabian Basic Industries Corporation (SABIC) and UK Trade & Investment.

Saudi Basic Industries Corporation (SABIC)

Background

SABIC was formed in 1976 to add value to Saudi Arabia's natural hydrocarbon resources. The earlier establishment of the Master Gas System (MGS) project in 1975 delivered the gases that were required for fuel and raw material to make value-added industrial commodities. SABIC was created in 1976 to develop a chain of basic large-scale industries to utilize these resources, which led to the downstream industrial diversification in Saudi Arabia.

The late 1970s and early 1980s saw the transformation of Al Jubail on the Gulf coast from a fishing village to a modern industrial city. A similar transformation followed at Yanbu on the Red Sea. The Royal Commission for Jubail and Yanbu built the infrastructure, while SABIC was responsible for creating the basic industries.

The first SABIC joint venture plant came on-stream in 1983, followed by a quick succession of several affiliates. In 1985, the total production capacity was about six million tonnes per year. By 2003, this had increased to 42 million tonnes per year. Total employment has increased from 5,400 employees in 1983 to 16,000 worldwide in 2003.

The net asset base of the Saudi Arabian hydrocarbon processing industry is increasing each year. SABIC's Saudi-based assets have increased at an accelerating rate over the last 15 years, from US$7.9 billion in 1989 to an estimated US$29.2 billion in 2004 (see Table 7.2.1).

Table 7.2.1 SABIC: Increase in Saudi-based asset values, 1989 to 2004

Year	Asset value (US$ millions)	Increase in assets over 15-year period (US$ millions)
1989	7,982	-
1992	9,278	1,296
1995	12,141	2,863
1998	19,841	7,700
2001	23,435	3,594
2004#	29,294	5,859

#estimated

Source: Saudi Basic Industries Corporation (SABIC)

SABIC operations

SABIC, established in 1976 to add value to Saudi Arabia's natural hydrocarbon resources, now accounts for about five per cent of world petrochemical production and is the main non-oil industrial enterprise in the country.

SABIC is also one of the Middle East's largest non-oil industrial companies. SABIC is 70 per cent owned by the state and 30 per cent by private investors. By 2003, total SABIC production (including European subsidiaries and steel) reached 42 million tonnes. By 2003, SABIC employees worldwide totalled 16,000.

SABIC's manufacturing network in Saudi Arabia consists of 18 affiliates. The majority of these are based in Al Jubail industrial city on the Arabian Gulf. Two are located in Yanbu industrial city on the Red Sea and one in the Eastern Province city of Dammam. The first plant to come on-stream was the Saudi Arabian Fertilizer Company (SAFCO) in 1969, the last being the Arabian Industrial Fibre Company (IBN RUSHD) at Yanbu in 1995 (see Table 7.2.2). SABIC is also partner in three regional ventures in Bahrain.

SABIC's business is grouped into six strategic business units. Five of these units cover the petrochemical and fertilizer interests and are:

- basic chemicals;
- intermediates;
- PVC and polyester
- polyolefins; and
- fertilizers

Basic chemicals

Basic chemicals, the building blocks for petrochemicals, are the basis of SABIC industries. They are produced from hydrocarbons that are by-products of crude oil. SABIC basic chemicals include methanol, ethylene, propylene, benzene, xylene, MTBE (methyl tertiary butyl ether), styrene, CIE (crude industrial ethanol), butadiene and butene-1.

SABIC business units in this sector are organized in three product management segments: olefins, aromatics and oxygenates.

Table 7.2.2 Existing SABIC petrochemicals plants, 2004

Operator and location	Joint venture partnership	Date on-stream	Capacity (t/y)
Saudi Arabian Fertilizer Company (SAFCO), Dammam and Al Jubail	SABIC 41%; SAFCO employees 10%; Saudi private shareholders 49%	1969 & 1993	600,000 urea, 500,000 ammonia, sulphuric acid melamine
Saudi Methanol Company (AR-RAZI), Al Jubail	SABIC 50%; Mitsubishi Gas Chemical Co 50%	1983	Chemical grade methanol
Al Jubail Fertilizer Company (SAMAD), Al Jubail	SABIC 50%; Taiwan Fertilizer Company 50%	1983	Ammonia, urea, 2-ethyl hexanol, DOP
National Industrial Gases Company (GAS), Al Jubail	SABIC 70%; Saudi gas producers 30%	1984	Oxygen, nitrogen, argon
Saudi Petrochemical Co (SADAF), Al Jubail	SABIC 50%; Shell Oil Co (Pecten Arabia) 50%	1985	1,100,000 ethylene, 300,000 ethanol 450,000 styrene, 840,000 ethylene dichloride, 670,000 NaOH, 700,000 MTBE
Saudi Petrochemical Co (SADAF II)			500,000 styrene, 550,000 paraxylene 115,000 O+M xylene, 400,000 benzene
Saudi Petrochemical Co (SADAF III)			800,000 ethylene, 170,000 propylene
Arabian Petrochemical Co (PETROKEMYA), Al Jubail Olefins I, II, III	SABIC 100%	1985	1,450,000 ethylene, 135,000 polystyrene 800,000 ethylene, 275,000 propylene, 25,000 benzene, 400,000 polyethylene, 100,000 polystyrene
Butane 1, II			butane
National Methanol Company (IBN SINA), Al Jubail	SABIC 50%; Hoechst-Celanese USA 25%; Pan Energy USA 25%	1985	700,000 MTBE, 1,000,000 methanol
Al Jubail Petrochemical Co (KEMYA I), Al Jubail	SABIC 50%; ExxonMobil 50%	1985	600,000 LLDPE/HDPE
Al Jubail Petrochemical Co (KEMYA II) Expansion, Al Jubail			700,000 ethylene, 200,000 propylene, 218,000 LDPE, 250,000 LLDPE

Operator and location	Joint venture partnership	Date on-stream	Capacity (t/y)
Saudi Yanbu Petrochemical Company (YANPET I)	SABIC 50%; ExxonMobil 50%	1985	600,000 ethylene, 335,000 MEG 205,000 LLDPE, 90,000 HDPE, 200,000 propylene
Saudi Yanbu Petrochemical Company (YANPET II), Yanbu			800,000 ethylene, 420,000 mono ethylene glycol (MEG), 535,000 LLDPE, 280,000 PP
Saudi Yanbu Petrochemical Company (YANPET III), Yanbu			800,000 ethylene, 260,000 polypropylene 450,000 ethylene glycol
Eastern Petrochemical Company (SHARQ), Al Jubail	SABIC 50%; Misubishi Corp. led consortium 50%	1985	130,000 LLDPE, 30,000 MEG, 1,500 TEG
Eastern Petrochemical Company (SHARQ) Expansion, Al Jubail			497,000 ethylene glycol, 300,000 LLDPE
National Chemical Fertilizer Company (IBN Al-BAYTAR), Al Jubail	SABIC 50%; SAFCO 50%	1987	Ammonia, granular urea, compound and phosphate fertilizers
National Plastics Company (IBN HAYYAN) Al Jubail	SABIC 86.5%; NIC 10%; others 3.5%	1987	Vinyl chloride monomer, polyvinyl chloride, PVC paste
Saudi European Petrochemical co (IBN-ZAHR), Al Jubail	SABIC 70%; Neste Oy-Finland 10%; Echofuel Italy 10%; APICORP 10%	1988	MTBE
Saudi European Petrochemical Co (IBN-ZAHR II), Al Jubail			320,000 PP, 60,000 PP additional
Arabian Industrial Fibre Company (IBN RUSHD)	Sabic 51.7%; Saudi/regional private sector partners 48.3%	1995	154,000 polyester – textile chips, textile staple, bottle grade chips, carpet staple
Arabian Industrial Fibre Company (IBN RUSHD III) Expansion, Yanbu			750,000 benzene, paraxylene, orthoxylene 350,000 PTA

Note: Excludes SABIC Bahrain affiliate companies Gulf Aluminium Rolling Mill Company (GARMCO), Gulf Petroleum Industries Company (GPIC) and Aluminium Bahrain (ALBA) and Saudi Iron and Steel Company (HADEED), Al Jubail

Source: Saudi Arabian Basic Industries Corporation (SABIC), ASA Consulting, based on industry enquiries

Intermediates

Intermediate chemicals, such as EG, EDC, VCM, 2-EH, caustic soda and DOP, are ingredients used by the petrochemical industry to manufacture other products. These are produced using basic chemicals as raw materials. SABIC's intermediates sector also produces a range of industrial gases, oxygen, nitrogen, argon and krypton-xenon.

The intermediates group's new business activities include downstream products such as plastic boards, wallpaper and artificial leather.

SABIC business units in this sector are organized in three management units: chemical intermediates, fibre intermediates and new business.

PVC and polyester

The PVC and polyester business unit of SABIC comprises polyester and melamine and PVC and polystyrene. Polyester and melamine includes many staple fibres used in textile and carpet manufacture and weaving and knitting, resins used to make bottles, trays and packaging and melamine adhesives, laminates, surface coatings and moulding compounds.

Polyolefins

SABIC is a world leader in the production of polyolefins – a family of polymers derived from propylene and ethylene. Applications range from rigid materials for refrigerators, computers and car components to soft flexible fibres for hygienic products.

The SABIC polyolefins business unit produces polyethylene (PE) and polypropylene. The PE range produced includes essential polymers such as linear low-density polyethylene (LLDPE), low-density polyethylene (LDPE) and high-density polyethylene (HDPE).

SABIC currently ranks as the third and fourth largest world polyethylene and polypropylene producer respectively.

Fertilizers

SABIC's fertilizer group produces ammonia and urea, and compound, phosphate and liquid fertilizers. SABIC is the world's largest exporter of urea. The three SABIC affiliates produce 5.5 million tonnes of fertilizer a year.

SABIC Europe

In July 2002, SABIC Europe came into being with the US$2 billion acquisition of the petrochemicals business of Dutch group DSM Petrochemicals. SABIC Europe employs 2,300 people and has two major manufacturing locations, in Geleen in the Netherlands and Gelsenkirchen in Germany.

SABIC, already the Middle East's largest petrochemical producer, has now moved to 11th position in the global petrochemical industry as a result of its acquisition of DSM Petrochemicals.

The acquisition of DSM Petrochemicals marks a sea change in SABIC's priorities. For the first 20 years of its existence, SABIC concentrated on investment at home and exports to the Asian market. Since then, concerns that feedstock availability will fail to keep pace with the company's ambitious growth targets, together with the company's dependence on the Asian market, has driven SABIC's global ambitions.

Future SABIC developments

By 2010, SABIC intends to be among the top industrial players, with a targeted capacity of 48 million tonnes a year.

SABIC's global aspirations lead it to continue to investigate acquisition of manufacturing capacity closer to its customers. The company, equally, supports a major development programme in Saudi Arabia, with new-build plants, catalyst improvements and de-bottlenecking, all designed to increase production capacity from the current 42 million tonnes to close to 50 million tonnes by 2010.

The current level of investment involved in SABIC projects, including new plants and existing plant upgrades and modernization that are in the planning and implementation stages (see Table 7.2.3), is almost US$3 billion.

In 2000, SABIC announced the go-ahead for its 17th affiliate in Saudi Arabia, Jubail United Petrochemical Company (UNITED), based in Al Jubail industrial city. The plant is scheduled to come on-stream in 2005 and will produce ethylene, ethylene glycol and linear alpha olefins (LAOs).

Also in 2000, SABIC announced the expansion of the Arabian Petrochemical Company (PETROKEMYA) with plans for an additional 800,000 tonnes per year of polyethylene capacity at two new plants.

Table 7.2.3 Current SABIC petrochemicals developments, 2004

Operator and location	Products/capacity (t/y)	Project value	Project status
Arabian Industrial Fibre Company	Acetic acid	US$70 million	Procurement, construction
(IBN RUSHD), Yanbu	PET plant	US$50 million	On hold
Jubail United Petrochemical Co. (UNITED), Al Jubail	1,000,000 ethylene (1), 450,000 ethylene glycol (2), 150,000 alpha olefins (3)	US$1,785 million	Construction
Arabian Petrochemical Company PETROKEMYA III, Al Jubail	800,000 polyethylene	US$176 million	Construction
BUTANE III	Butane	US$40 million	EPC
Saudi Petrochemical Co (SADAF), Al Jubail	Cogeneration, modernization etc	US$260 million	Contracts
Saudi Arabian Fertilizer Company (SAFCO), Al Jubail – SAFCO IV	Urea, ammonia	US$500 million	Construction
Al Jubail Fertilizer Company (SAMAD), Al Jubail	Pheptalic anhydride	US$90 million	Suspended

Source: ASA Consulting, based on industry enquiries

Private sector participation

The key drivers of private sector participation in the Saudi petrochemical industry may be summarized as:

- geographical advantage – Saudi Arabia is an ideal location to serve both European and Asian markets;
- feedstock price advantage, based on the world's largest oil reserves and top five gas reserves;
- government support to develop the petrochemical sector through loans, land costs and tax reforms;

- technology transfer, which has created a technocrat pool of qualified and experienced Saudi labour;
- substantial liquidity in the market, with an estimated Saudi net worth overseas of US$750 billion, combined with a reluctance of private investors to invest overseas due to poor stock market performance and concerns about asset freezing.

Private sector involvement in the Saudi petrochemicals sector began in 1996 with the formation of Saudi Chevron Phillips, a joint venture company between Chevron Texaco and Saudi Industrial Investment Group.

In 1999, the Saudi International Petrochemical Company was formed as a joint stock company with 65 per cent Saudi and 35 per cent Gulf Cooperation Council (GCC) ownership.

The year 2000 saw the formation of the National Petrochemical Industrialization Company. Its first joint venture, with Bassell, created the Saudi Polyolefins Company, which recently came on-stream with a 450,000 tonnes a year polypropylene plant. More recently, a joint venture with Acetex was formed to produce acetic acid, vinyl acetate monomer and methanol.

Table 7.2.4 Existing private sector petrochemicals plants in Saudi Arabia, 2004

Operator and location	Capacity (t/y)
Saudi European Petrochemical Co	MTBE
Duke Energy JV, Al Jubail	
Saudi Chevron Phillips Petrochemical, Al Jubail	222,000 cyclohexane, 480,000 benzene
Saudi Polyolefins Co. Petrochemical (National Petrochemical Industrialization Co/Bassell), Al Jubail	450,000 propylene(1), 450,000 polypropylene(2)
Jubail Chemical Industries Co (JANA), Al Jubail	320,000 polypropylene
National Polypropylene Co. (TELDENE), Yanbu	280,000 polypropylene
United Jubail Fertilizer Company, Al Jubail	Ammonia

Source: ASA Consulting, based on industry enquiries

The level of investment of major private sector projects that are in the planning and implementation stages (see Table 7.2.5) is in excess of US$6 billion. The challenges for new petrochemicals projects are:

- securing feedstock – Saudi Aramco gas joint ventures are critical to provide additional ethane volumes;
- finding a suitable joint venture partner who will bring the necessary licensing for the manufacturing technology.

Sahara Petrochemical Company recently launched its initial public offering (IPO) and was heavily over-subscribed, indicating the interest in the petrochemicals sector and the funding available for such projects.

The Project Management and Development Company has already commenced preliminary studies and has plans for a number of major projects. Further downstream diversification and the development of manufacturing facilities by small- and medium-sized enterprises (SMEs) will feed off the products that are being brought to the market by the major projects.

These smaller industries, which include plastics processing and non-woven fabrics, make up in excess of 200 plants already operating, with many more in the planning stages. The smaller end of the petrochemicals industry probably creates greater and more diverse opportunities than the major projects and should not be disregarded by potential investors.

Table 7.2.5 Planned private sector petrochemicals plants in Saudi Arabia, 2005–07

Operator	Products/capacity (t/y)	Project value	Project status
Gulf Farabi Petrochemical Company	n-paraffin LAB	US$325 million	Construction
Project Management & Development Company	Amines	US$600 million	Feasibility complete
Project Management & Development Company	Olefins	US$1,500 million	Preliminary study
Saudi International Petrochemical Co (SIPC), Al Jubail	800,000 ethylene, 170,000 propylene		Planned for 2007

Operator	Products/capacity (t/y)	Project value	Project status
	Acetic acid, BDO/MAN, methanol		Planning, contracts, construction
Saudi Carbon Company (AH Al-Zamil Group)	Carbon black	US$50 million	EPC contract awarded. On stream 2005
Sahara Petrochemical Company	Ethylene and polypropylene		PMC awarded
	Propane dehydrogenation and polypropylene	US$530 million	FEED
Saudi Chevron Phillips Petrochemical, Al Jubail	Aromatics expansion – ethylene	US$1,000 million	FEED awarded
Kanoo Propylene, Al Jubail	450,000 propylene 450,000 polypropylene		Planning stages
International Methanol Company (SIMC)	Methanol		Construction

Source: ASA Consulting, based on industry enquiries

Other petrochemicals developments

With the planned expansion of Rabigh and Ras Tanura, Saudi Aramco is planning to make its first foray into the domestic petrochemical sector. At Rabigh, Saudi Aramco is seeking to maximize the value from its significant existing infrastructure investments and by creating a platform for downstream industries, thereby attracting both local and international investors. Aramco wishes to integrate petrochemical and other industry with the existing 400 mbpd refinery, as well as develop power, water and port facilities.

At Ras Tanura, Saudi Aramco is seeking to encourage investment opportunities, including mixed xylene, cumene, isobutene and nitrogen production.

Further information

For information concerning the Saudi petrochemicals industry see the Saudi Arabian Basic Chemical Corporation (SABIC) website at www.sabic.com.

ASA Consulting has conducted a number of petrochemicals industry related market studies in Saudi Arabia and other Middle East countries, including most recently a study of utilization of molecular sieves zeolite products in the oil and gas industry in Saudi Arabia, other GCC and other Middle Eastern, North African and Central Asian countries (2002). For further information concerning the experience and activities of ASA Consulting, please contact asaconsult@btinternet.com.

7.3

Power and Water Industry

Anthony Shoult, ASA Consulting[1]

Introduction

Saudi Arabia has one of the largest per capita electricity consumption rates in the world. Its growing population means that demand is rising rapidly. According to current industry estimates, demand for power in the Kingdom is expected to increase from almost 30,000 MW in 2005 to approximately 60,000 MW by 2020.

In addition to the growing population, Saudi Arabia needs to expand its power capacity and network to support the Kingdom's ambitious industrialization plans.

Many power projects have been launched to achieve the desired expansion, including the upgrading of existing power plants and the building of new power facilities.

Saudi Arabia's demand for water is also growing rapidly. Saudi Arabia also needs to invest an estimated US$80 billion over the next 20 years in the expansion and maintenance of its existing water desalination plants and on the construction of new projects to meet the high water consumption levels caused by a rapid population rise and industrial growth.

In general, the government does not have the means to invest all the massive capital required for water sector development itself and is keen to attract private, largely foreign, investment.

In June 2002, Saudi Arabia announced its privatization strategy for the water and wastewater sector. Measures for the private sector participation in the water sector are under consideration by the Water Ministry.

---

[1] Sources of information include Yusuf Bin Ahmed Kanoo, Saudi Electricity Company (SEC), Saline Water Conversion Corporation (SWCC) and UK Trade & Investment.

Power industry

Background

Saudi Arabia has one of the largest per capita electricity consumption rates in the world. The Saudi population, at almost 23 million, is growing at a rate of 3.4 per cent, causing the number of electricity subscribers to increase from around 350,000 in 1975 to over 3.7 million at present. Between 1975 and 1995, power consumption per non-industrial consumer increased from 3.977KW/h per year to 21.775 KW/h per year.

According to the government's 25-year electricity plan, the growth in electricity demand between 1995 and 2020 will average 4.5 per cent. The Kingdom's 4.5 per cent annual growth has played a major role in boosting the demand for power. The demand for power has also dramatically increased because of the Kingdom's low tariff rates that are reported to have been the lowest in the world. Demand by 2005 was expected to reach almost 31,000 MW, approximately 2,000 MW above current capacity.

Since 1990, total electricity capacity has been increasing at a slower rate than consumption and peak load, mainly because of the need to maintain a reserve capacity of 17 per cent during periods of peak demand.

In addition to the growing population, Saudi Arabia needs to expand its power capacity and network to support the Kingdom's ambitious industrialization plan. The Ministry of Water and Electricity's 25-year electrification plan (1995) called for US$117 billion in capital investment to increase total capacity from about 17,000 MW per year at the beginning of the plan to 67,000 MW per year by the year 2020.

Additionally, the power network has not developed evenly throughout the Kingdom. In 1995, 85 per cent of the population had access to electricity, while the electrification rate in the northern region of Saudi Arabia was less than 50 per cent. There are some rural areas in the southern, central and western regions that are not yet connected to the power network and some rural areas in the south of the country not connected to the power network.

Many power projects have been launched to achieve the desired expansion, including the upgrading of existing power plants and the building of new power facilities. This tremendous growth potential makes the country one of the world's most attractive markets for power generation, as well as for power transmission and distribution equipment.

Apart from power generation, the country requires additional investment in power transmission. Currently, only two of the country's four power regions are connected. Creating a unified grid could require over 20,000 miles of additional power transmission lines.

Privatization

To encourage private sector investment in power generation, the Saudi government issued a decree in 1997 redefining power generation as an industrial activity. The new classification has brought power generation under the authority of the foreign investment code, allowing both domestic and foreign investors to freely invest in power generation.

Saudi Arabia has now taken further steps to liberalize the electricity sector through offering to the private sector a total of 11 power generation and desalination projects worth US$2.2 billion. The amount of investment required in power generation during the period from 2006 to 2010 has been estimated at about US$3.5 billion.

Project finance

Funding the required development is the biggest challenge and attracting investors is critical. The new classification redefining power generation as an industrial activity has brought new investment incentive benefits for private investors.

The benefits include a 10-year tax holiday, an exemption from customs duties, and concessionary financing by the Saudi Industrial Development Fund (SIDF) covering up to 50 per cent of the project's capital cost.

Private investment in the power sector is also a key component of the development plan of the two major industrial cities of Al Jubail and Yanbu. In 1999, the Saudi government officially approved the creation of the joint stock water and electricity utility company, Marafeq, with an initial capital investment of some US$530 million. The Public Investment Fund for the Royal Commission for Jubail and Yanbu, Saudi Aramco, SABIC and seven local investors jointly funded Marafeq.

A number of new power projects are financed by a finance regime totally new to Saudi Arabia's power sector. For example:

- Riyadh PP9 Power Station (1,200 MW) has been funded with extra revenues from a special tariff imposed on heavy electricity users since January 1995;

- Ghazlan II Power Station (2,400 MW) has been financed by an internationally syndicated loan of US$500 million – a first in Saudi history.

A programme has been announced for the construction, using private funding, of four major integrated water and power projects (IWPPs), with a combined estimated value in excess of US$5 billion and with a combined output of 5,000 MW. The bidding for these projects, which were originally to have been built as part of the gas initiative, commenced during 2004. A 50/50 joint venture company, Water Electricity Company (WEC) has been formed between SEC and SWCC to purchase power and water from the IWPPs.

A further programme is in place to construct seven integrated power projects (IPPs), with a combined estimated value in excess of US$7 billion and a combined output of over 14,000 MW.

The aim is to obtain 70 per cent of the required funding for the IPPs from the private sector. To provide the necessary incentives, sovereign guarantees are now in place for the purchase of power and water for a period of 20 years.

Regional power initiative

Seeking efficiency in the power sector on a regional level, the Saudi government has signed an agreement with its neighbours to set up the Gulf Cooperation Countries (GCC) interconnection authority (GCCIA). The grid is intended to cut the cost of electricity for all six GCC states and to achieve a more efficient use of the surplus power. The US$1.3 billion project will be constructed in three phases as follows:

- Phase I: interconnection of Kuwait, Saudi Arabia, Bahrain, Qatar;
- Phase II: interconnection of independent systems in United Arab Emirates (UAE) and Oman;
- Phase III: interconnection of Kuwait, Saudi Arabia, Bahrain, Qatar, UAE and Oman.

There is no single interconnected power system within the country, except the two large systems in the Eastern and Central Provinces, which are interconnected at 380 kV, the remaining regions have their own local transmission networks. However, the operation of small, stand-alone electric networks is still in practice in many parts of the country. The power transmission voltage is at 380, 230, 132, 115 and 110 kV. High voltage distribution networks operate at 69, 34.5, 33 and 13.8 kV. Electricity is delivered to households and small consumers at 380, 220 and 127 volts.

Saudi Electricity Company (SEC)

Background

In February 2000, Saudi Arabia's 10 regional power companies were consolidated into a single joint stock company, the Saudi Electricity Company (SEC), in order to expedite the streamlining of the sector's operations.

Capitalized at SR33.75 billion, the new electricity company is self-sufficient and independent from government. Accordingly, in April 2000 Saudi Arabia removed subsidies for electricity. The regional electricity companies had traditionally been operated at a loss, with electricity sold to customers at subsidized rates.

Future SEC developments

A programme of major generation and transmission projects is planned over the next 15 years. In addition to the four major IWPPs, with a combined estimated value in excess of US$5 billion and combined output of 5,000 MW, SEC will construct a total of seven IPPs, with a combined estimated value in excess of US$7 billion and a combined output of over 14,000 MW. The four proposed SEC IWPPs and seven IPPs are shown in Table 7.3.1.

In addition to the planned power generation developments, a total of 10 major power transmission projects are being proposed. These are necessary initially to create a Saudi national grid system and eventually a possible link to create a GCC grid.

A programme of major transmission projects is planned over the next 10 years with a combined estimated value in excess of US$2 billion and a combined length of 3,600km.

The 10 proposed SEC major power transmission projects are shown in Table 7.3.2.

Table 7.3.1 Proposed SEC power generation projects#

Project	Type of project	Location	Power capacity (MW)	Water capacity (mgd)	Project value (US$ million)	Projected completion
Shouaiba-III	IWPP	Western Province	700	176	1,330	2008
Shuqaiq-II	IWPP	Western Province	700	24	400	2008
Ras Al Zour	IWPP	Eastern Province	2,500	176	2,400	2008
Jubail-III	IWPP	Eastern Province	1,100	75	1,065	2008
Muzahimiyah Power Plant	IPP	Central Province	1,725	-	745	2011
Rabigh-II Power Plant	IPP	Western Province	2,400	-	1,330	2012
Qurayyah-II Power Plant	IPP	Eastern Province	3,600	-	1,920	2012
Sulbukh Power Plant	IPP	Central Province	1,725	-	745	2014
Yanbu-II Power Plant	IPP	Western Province	2,400	-	1,330	2015
Shuqaiq-II Power Plant	IPP	Southern Province	600	-	370	2016
Riyadh Power Plant-10 (Expansion)	IPP	Central Province	1,725	-	745	2017

Includes IWPPs to be constructed using private finance

Source: Saudi Electricity Company (SEC)

Table 7.3.2 Proposed SEC power transmission projects

Project	Location	Voltage (kV)	Length (km)	Project value (US$ million)	Projected completion
Shuqaiq-Sabya/ Asir	Southern Province	380	115	88	2007
Shuqaiq-Muhayil/Namera	Southern Province	380	140	112	2008

Project	Location	Voltage (kV)	Length (km)	Project value (US$ million)	Projected completion
Shouaiba-Namera	Southern/ Western Province	380	270	107	2010
Hail-Al-Jouf	Central/ Eastern Province	380	315	125	2010
Hawiyah-Muzahimiyah	Eastern/ Central Province	380	300	117	2011
Qasim-Madinah	Central/ Western Province	500	480	533	2012
Yanbu-Dhuba	Western Province	380	430	152	2013
Muhazimiyah-Bahra	Central/ Western Province	500	950	665	2013
Qaisumah-Rafah	Eastern Province	380	280	110	2014
Tabuk-Al Jouf	Eastern/ Western Province	380	330	128	2014

Source: Saudi Electricity Company (SEC)

Water industries

Background

Saudi Arabia is located in one of the most arid areas of the world, where average rainfall is less than 100mm per year, making the aquifer recharge inefficient and requiring many years to recover. With limited natural resources, the country has had no choice but to resort to well water and desalinated seawater to provide its rapidly increasing population with the water it needs.

Saudi Arabia accounts for 30 per cent of the world's total output of desalinated water. It also has more desalination plants than any other country. These plants produce up to one billion cubic metres annually from 30 desalination plants split between the two coasts.

Surface water is limited to 200 dams with a total capacity of about 800 million cubic metres used for drinking, irrigation and recharging ground water. Ground water is available from 18 aquifers with deep wells supplying water for municipal use, agriculture and industry. Water usage is split between irrigation (70 per cent), municipal supply (25 per cent) and industry (five per cent).

Sewage systems are the least available utilities in Saudi Arabia, as these exist in only 22 of the 106 municipal areas of the Kingdom. Treated sewage effluent is an important source of irrigation water and water for industrial use. The Ministry of Agriculture has operated a programme since 1982 to utilize treated sewage effluent from Riyadh Sewage Treatment Plant in the irrigation of ministry farms and the farms of King Saud University. A total of 200,000 cubic metres a day of treated sewage is pumped to the farms in the suburbs of Riyadh.

There is a growing need for Saudi water consumers to change their present patterns of water utilization. For example, in the farming sector, there is a move towards drip irrigation and greenhouse production, while domestic users are being encouraged to reduce their consumption from the current 230 litres per day to closer to 150 litres per day, in line with the European average. Also, greater use is to be made of recycled or treated water. New tariffs are being introduced to penalize heavy water users and a prohibition of the drilling of water wells has been introduced.

The agricultural sector is the Kingdom's biggest water consumer. This uses deep aquifer water, subject to a very low rate of replenishment (less than 100mm average annual rainfall) to the extent that it can be considered to be a non-renewable resource.

The need for investment

Many of the Kingdom's water and sewage treatment plants were built in the late 1970s and are nearing the end of their useful working life. In addition, the growing population is making the capacity of these plants insufficient to meet future demand.

The government has recognized that massive investment is needed to upgrade or replace the existing water desalination plants, water treatment plants and sewage treatment plants and to build new ones to meet the spiralling demand for drinking water and sewage treatment.

Contracts of about US$1.5 billion were awarded in 2002 for the construction of new water and waste treatment plants and to build water and sewer networks in various cities.

In 2002, a symposium held in Riyadh, entitled 'Future Strategy for Water Resources Management in Saudi Arabia', provided estimates of the level of investment required to expand water and wastewater treatment facilities up to 2040. The total expenditure envisaged was in the region of US$100 billion (see Table 7.3.3).

Table 7.3.3 Saudi Arabia's projected water sector investment requirements

Category of project	Projected investment requirement (US$ billions)	
	2005–2020	2021–2040
Desalination plants	2.1	16.0
Treatment plants and desalination of well water	0.8	6.6
Conveyance pipelines		3.4
Water distribution networks	2.4	17.8
Wastewater networks	3.4	19.4
Wastewater treatment plants	2.9	16.6
Strategic reservoirs and emergency distribution system	5.3	1.06

Source: 'Future Strategy of Water Resources Management in Saudi Arabia', Symposium, Riyadh, 19-23 October 2002

Privatization

The government does not have the means to invest or the massive capital required to meet the spiralling demand. The Kingdom has instituted progress of economic reform directed at attracting private local and foreign investment into key sectors.

The creation of the new Water Ministry and the appointment of a water minister in September 2002 were intended to speed up the process of opening the sector to private investors. The Council of Ministers resolved in November 2002 to privatize the water and wastewater sectors. This includes the planned privatization of the Saline Water Conversion Corporation (SWCC).

Saline Water Conversion Corporation (SWCC)

The Saline Water Conversation Corporation (SWCC) was established in 1974 as the primary producer and distributor of potable water. It now has a total installed capacity of over 2.8 million cubic metres per day, from 30 desalination plants of various sizes at 15 locations along the Arabian Gulf and Red Sea. As such, SWCC is responsible for providing all the Kingdom's desalinated water. Existing SWCC desalination plants are shown in Table 7.3.4.

Table 7.3.4 Existing SWCC desalination plants, 2004

Plant/ location	Phase	Date on-stream	Process	Desalinated water design capacity (m^3/day)	Electric power capacity (MW)	Cities served
Jeddah	2	1978	MSF	37,916	71	Jeddah
	3	1979	MSF	75,987	200	
	4	1981	MSF	190,555	500	
	RO1	1989	RO	48,848	-	
	RO2	1994	RO	48,848	-	
Al Shuaiba	1	1989	MSF	191,780	157	Makkah, Taif
	2	2002	MSF	390,909	340	Makkah, Taif, Jeddah
Yanbu	1	1981	MSF	94,625	250	Madinah, Yanbu
	2	1999	MSF	120,096	35	Madinah, Yanbu, adjacent cities
	RO	1999	RO++	106,904	-	Madinah, Yanbu, adjacent cities
Al Shuqaiq	1	1989	MSF	83,432	62	Abha, Khamis Mushait
Haql	2	1990	RO	3,784		Haql
Duba	3	1989	RO	3,784		Duba
Al Wajh	2	1979	MSF	473		Al-Wajh
	T1	1981	RH	825	-	
	T2	1983	RH	1,032	-	
	T3	1983	MSF	473	-	
Ummluj	RO	1986	RO	3,784	-	Ummluj
Rabigh	1	1982	MSF	1,204	-	Rabigh
	T1	1994	MSF	774	-	
Al Aziziyah	1	1987	RH	3,870	-	Al Aziziyah Island
Al Birk	1	1983	RO	1,952	-	Al Birk
Farasan	1	1979	MSF	430	-	Farasan Island
	T1	1990	MSF	1,075	-	
Al Khobar	2	1982	MSF	191,780	500	Al Khobar, Dammam, Dhahran, Qatif, Saihat, Safwa, Ras Tanourah
	3	2002	MSF	240,800	311	

Plant/ location	Phase	Date on-stream	Process	Desalinated water design capacity (m^3/day)	Electric power capacity (MW)	Cities served
Al Khafji	2	1986	MSF	19,682	-	Al Khafji
Al Jubail	1	1982	MSF	118,447	238	Riyadh, Al Jubail
	2	1983	MSF	815,185	762	
	RO	2002	RO			
Total				*2,877,436*	*3,426*	

Note: MSF = Multi-stage flash; RO = reverse osmosis, RH = reheat

++ the largest RO plant in the world

Source: Saline Water Conversion Corporation (SWCC)

Of the 30 desalination plants currently operated by SWCC, 12 are dual system and these represent approximately 12 per cent of the Kingdom's total power capacity.

The Al Jubail plant is the largest installation of its kind in the world and can supply approximately one million m^3/day of desalinated water, providing the primary water supply for Al Jubail and for Riyadh, some 900km to the west.

The second largest desalination plant in the Kingdom is the US$1 billion Al Shuaiba plant. The production capacity of this plant has been increased to 0.58 million m^3/day with the completion of the Phase II development in 2002.

SWCC allocated the sum of US$105 million in the budgets of 2001 and 2002 for the maintenance of desalination plants and to prolong their working life.

Future SWCC developments

SWCC is planning to establish 22 new desalination plants along the eastern and western coasts of the country, with a projected installed capacity of almost 3.7 million m^3/day. Some of these developments will be expansions of existing units.

It is estimated that investment of about US$16 billion is needed by 2020 to meet water demand at the current per capita consumption rate of 300 litres per day. SWCC currently lists 20 planned desalination projects as being under study (see Table 7.3.5).

Table 7.3.5 Projected SWCC desalination projects

Plant/location	Phase	Desalinated water design capacity (m^3/day)	Electric power capacity (MW)	Cities served
Qunfudah	1	9,000	-	Al Qunfudah
Rabigh	2	22,000	-	Rabigh
Al Laith	1	6,000	-	Al Laith
Al Wajh	3	20,000	-	Al Wajh
Al Jubail	3*	340,000	1,100	Eastern Province
Al Shuqaiq	2*	106,000	700	Aseer
Ras Al Zoor	1*	800,000	700	Riyadh
Shuaiba	3*	800,000	700	Makkah, Taif, Jeddah
Farasan	2	12,000	-	Farasan Island
Al Umlaj	3	9,000	-	Umjaj
Shuaiba	4	450,000	#	Makkah, Taif, Jeddah
Al Khafji	3	30,000	-	Al Kafji
Yanbu-Madinah	3	200,000	#	Madinah, Yanbu
Al Jubail	4	450,000	#	Riyadh
	5	100,000	#	Qasim
Al Bahah	1	182,000	#	Al Bahah
Al Birk	2	4,500	-	Al Birk
Tabuk	1	113,600	#	Tabuk
Haql	3	4,500	-	Haql
Duba	4	9,000	-	Duba
Total		*3,667,600*	*3,200*	-

power capacity still to be decided

* projects to be built with private sector participation

Source: Saline Water Conversion Corporation (SWCC)

SWCC has already issued tenders for a total of six desalination plants located on the west coast at Al Wajh Al Umlaj, Rabigh, Al Laith, Qunfudah and Farsan.

Saudi Arabia is planning to privatize SWCC as a step towards restructuring the power sector. There are plans for SWCC to divest itself of its operational facilities and become a holding company for the existing facilities.

Further information

For information concerning the Saudi power sector see the following:

- Saudi Electricity Company (SEC) website at www.se.com.sa;
- Saline Water Conversion Company (SWCC) website at www.swcc.gov.sa.

ASA Consulting has conducted a number power and water industry related market studies in Saudi Arabia and other Middle East countries including a market study for gas turbine filters in Saudi Arabia and a feasibility study for a water treatment plant and installations facility. For further information concerning the experience and activities of ASA Consulting please contact asaconsult@btinternet.com.

7.4

Minerals and Mining Industry

Anthony Shoult, ASA Consulting[1]

Introduction

Saudi Arabia is a vast country with a land area of over two million square kilometres; it is roughly the same size as Western Europe. It is located between the African Shield in the south and the more recent Alpine-Himalayan Zagros mountains of Iran to the north. This geological junction resulted in the formation of world-class mineral deposits during the past thousand million years.

It has the largest mineral deposits in the Gulf, including gold, copper, phosphate and a large spectrum of industrial minerals.

The Arabian Peninsula has ancient rocks, contains economically attractive metal deposits, and has extensive sedimentary successions of shallow water origin, hosting large deposits of industrial minerals.

The geology of the Kingdom can be divided into two main zones. These are:

- the Arabian Shield to the west adjacent to the Red Sea is the focus of gold and base metals exploration and mining; and
- the surrounding sedimentary rocks that dip gently toward the Arabian Gulf and contain industrial minerals as well as being the reservoir for the Kingdom's prolific oil and gas fields.

The Arabian Shield extends the length of the western Red Sea coastline, covers one-third of the Kingdom and spreads into the centre of the country. The Shield consists mainly of pre-Cambrian igneous and metamorphic rocks, covered in places by recent basalt. It contains

---

[1] Sources of information include Saudi Arabian Mining Company (Ma'aden)) and UK Trade & Investment.

numerous occurrences of precious and base metals, and a wide range of other mineral resources, many of which are undeveloped.

In the northern, eastern and southern parts of the country, the flat terrain is underlain by sedimentary rocks, which contain the largest known oil reserves in the world. Dipping gently north-east towards the Gulf, these younger formations are also important for their water reserves.

Minerals present in large quantities are bauxite and phosphate, while the coal potential remains untested. Other areas of interest for minerals include evaporate deposits of salt and potash along the Red Sea coastal plain and metalliferous brines in Red Sea Deeps.

The Saudi government is committed to the development of a mining industry and places major emphasis on the need to implement programmes of mineral exploration and mining development. They are keen that the Saudi private sector develops the mining industry in partnership with international companies, and the expansion of the mining sector is projected to be led by the private sector for the foreseeable future.

The government's objective for this sector includes reaching out to the private sector for foreign investors to establish industries for extracting and processing minerals, providing the Saudi manufacturing sector with its requirements in raw materials, as well as becoming an exporter of minerals. Despite the Kingdom's resources, annual imports of minerals are at the level of approximately US$1.4 billion.

Saudi Geological Survey

The formation of the Saudi Geological Survey was announced in November 1999 to take on the survey and exploration activities previously undertaken by the Deputy Ministry of Mineral Resources.

The establishment and organization of the Survey was completed in January 2001. According to their mission statement, they will use trained professionals to consult the government and the community on earth sciences, utilize advanced technology to produce geoscience information and develop sustainable mineral and water resources, and protect the environment and monitor geohazards.

The main activities of the Saudi Geological survey are geological mapping, mineral exploration, pre-feasibility studies and hydrogeology surveys, as well as research and consulting.

The Saudi Arabian Mining Company (Ma'aden)

The Saudi Arabian Mining Company (Ma'aden) was created in 1997 as a catalyst for private sector investment in the minerals and mining industry. Ma'aden is fully owned by the state and has an estimated capitalization value of more than US$1 billion. (Ma'aden is the Arabic word for 'minerals'.)

Ma'aden is responsible for consolidating the mining projects wholly or partly owned by the government and rebuilding them on a commercial basis in partnership with the private sector. The Saudi government is actively considering the partial privatization of Ma'aden by floating its shares within a five-year period.

Ma'aden has four operational gold mines, producing 260,000 ounces of gold annually. In addition, they also produce 300,000 ounces of silver, 900 tonnes of copper and 3,000 tonnes of zinc.

The largest of the four mines, in terms of gold output, is Mahad Ad Dahab, which is located near the centre of the Arabian Shield. It is estimated that more than one million ounces of gold have already been extracted from the mine. The Sukhaybarat open cast gold mine is located 250km north-west of Mahd Ad Dahab in the Nuqrah-As Safra area.

Ma'aden has two other gold mining projects, at Al Hajar and at Al Amar. The Al Hajar mine went into production in July 2001 and operations have also commenced at Al Amar. These gold/silver operations were scheduled to produce 182,000 ounces of gold in 2003. The Al Hajar mine is located in the Asir Region about 60km west of Bisha. The Al Amar gold mine is located on the eastern margin of the Arabian Shield, some 250km west of Riyadh.

Other key minerals and mining projects currently being undertaken by Ma'aden are:

- Az Zabirah aluminium project;
- phosphate project;
- Zarghat Magnesite project.

The Az Zabirah aluminium project

Ma'aden is undertaking the Az Zabirah aluminium project to exploit Saudi Arabia's extensive bauxite reserves and low-cost fuel supplies. The project involves the construction and operation of a 620,000 tonnes per year alumina smelter at Ras az Zawr located on the central east coast of Saudi Arabia, and a 3.5 million tonnes per year bauxite mine located at Az Zabirah in central northern Saudi Arabia.

Power, steam and desalinated water will be provided to the smelter and refinery by a captive 1.6 GW oil-fired power station that will also be constructed at Ras az Zawr. A fit-for-purpose port facility will also be constructed.

The Az Zabirah bauxite deposit is made up of three discreet zones, the north zone, the central zone and the south zone. Initial mining is earmarked around the south zone, where some 240 tonnes of mineral resources have been delineated at 57.3 per cent Al2O3 and 8.2 per cent SiO2.

Construction of the bauxite mine is being timed to coincide with the completion of the rail system linking the mine site and the refinery/smelter complex. The construction of the rail link is being undertaken as a separate project by the Saudi Arabian Ministry of Finance's Public Investment fund.

The alumina refinery is planned to operate continuously using two 700,000 tonnes per year independent process streams initially. A further 700,000 tonnes per year stream is envisaged following the successful operation of the first phase. Accordingly, to mitigate the risk associated with the timing of the completion of the rail link to the bauxite mine, the refinery will commence operations using imported bauxite.

The aluminium smelter will comprise two or more modern pre-bake high amperage technology potlines. All alumina requirements will be sourced from the project's dedicated alumina refinery.

A captive oil-fired power plant, desalination plant and steam generation facility will be built to provide dedicated capacity to the Az Zabirah project. Project planning allows for the doubling of plant output to take account of future expansions, the needs of downstream industries and the potential for sales both to the phosphate project and the national grid.

The project will also include the construction of a port facility at Ras az Zawr for the purpose of importing bauxite, process chemicals and other materials required during the construction and operating phases of the project. The facility will also permit the export of alumina and aluminium. Port construction will be a combination of a causeway and trestle construction to the quay, followed by a dredged channel to deeper water. In order to ensure alternative supply and export routes, it is expected that the railway construction from existing ports at Dammam and Al Jubail to the site will be given high priority.

Ma'aden is targeting first production of alumina and aluminium for mid-2007 based on imported bauxite. This timescale will reduce the railroad timetable risk to the project. The mining operations will commence as soon as the railway becomes available.

The phosphate project

Sedimentary phosphorite was first identified in Saudi Arabia in 1965, 70km east of Turayf, during water well drilling operations by Saudi Aramco. In the same year, a second discovery was made 250km southwest of Turayf. In 1988, the Sannan deposit was discovered by the US Geological Survey. Continued exploration indicates prospects for further resources in the Widyan Ar-Rushaydah, Amud and Al Fihah areas.

Sirhan-Turayf is part of a large phosphate-bearing sedimentary region that extends into Jordan, southern Iraq and Syria. Ma'aden's exploration programmes in the Al Jalamid and Umm Al Wu'al areas in the northern region indicate a total of 1.6 billion tonnes of indicated phosphate resource and 1.5 billion tones of inferred resource.

Based on detailed work, Ma'aden has estimated that a mineable resource of 313 tonnes exists at Al Jalamid and that Umm Al Wu'al contains a mineable resource of 208 tonnes.

Progress has been made in the project to mine and beneficiate phosphate rock at Al Jalamid and convert this into diammonium phosphate (DAP) fertilizer for export of up to 2.9 million tonnes a year within a period of six years. The phosphate rock will be transported by rail to a fertilizer complex at Al Jubail Industrial City for conversion into DAP fertilizer.

In addition to the DAP fertilizer complex, the project plan includes a rail link between the mine site and Al Jubail. The rail line will also be key to the development of the Az Zabirah bauxite project and for other general cargo.

Another resource prospect at Umm Al Wu'al, 70km west of the Al Jalamid deposit, has been under extensive exploration. The indicated resource is approximately 200 million tonnes. Feasibility study work is expected to lead to an offer of joint venture formation to national and international investors.

Zarghat magnesite project

A project to diversify Ma'aden's mining portfolio is the development of the Zarghat magnesite deposit in the north-central region of the country. The proven reserve at Zarghat is 2.7 million tonnes.

The magnesite deposit at Zarghat has been identified as a small but high-grade reserve that will provide feedstock for high-value refractory raw materials. The 3:1 lime/silica ratio of Zarghat magnesite makes it ideally suited to refractory magnesias production. The low iron content also gives the deposit a competitive edge over comparable products.

Further processing will occur at a state-of-the-art calcining, sintering and fusion plant to be built at Al Madinah Al Munawarah. The expected level of production is 160,000 tonnes of raw magnesite. This will be used to produce 20,000 tonnes of high-grade, high-value electrofused magnesia (EFM) and 20,000 tonnes of deadburned magnesia (DBM) for global and local refractories markets.

Future of the mining and minerals industry

By the year 2020, the mining sector and its downstream industries is expected to more than quadruple its contribution to the Saudi economy. This will primarily result from the multiplier effect associated with the phosphate and aluminium industries.

As far as privatization is concerned, it is likely that the government will own less that 50 per cent of Ma'aden's shares by the year 2010. By the year 2020, Ma'aden in its present form and structure will cease to exist, leaving leadership of the mining industry to the private sector.

Ma'aden's long-term strategy for the development and exploitation of the Kingdom's phosphate resources intends to position the Kingdom as a major supplier of fertilizers by the year 2020, making it the world's second or third ranked fertilizer exporter. Saudi Arabia will also put in place the first totally integrated aluminium production facility in the region and the Gulf will be among the largest regional producers by 2020.

On base and precious metals, Ma'aden is likely to more than quadruple its gold production through its ongoing exploration and development efforts.

The availability of minerals such as phosphate, calcite, magnesite, silica and dolomite will be an important spur to the development of the Saudi chemicals industry in synergy with the petrochemicals industry.

At a symposium in Riyadh in October 2002, The President and Chief Executive of Ma,aden, Dr A E Dabbagh, emphasized the potential for the Saudi minerals industry by describing the contribution of Ma'aden to the economy as 'the third leg of the stool', the others being Saudi Aramco and SABIC.

Further information

For information concerning the Saudi minerals and mining industry see the Ma'aden's website at www.maaden.com.sa.

ASA Consulting has conducted a number of market studies related to the minerals and mining industry including a world market study for barite used in the oil and gas drilling mud and other industrial applications and a study of the GCC market for basalt wool. For further information concerning the experience and activities of ASA Consulting please contact asaconsult@btinternet.com.

7.5

Agriculture, Horticulture and Fisheries

John Lawton, Green Vista and Anthony Shoult, ASA Consulting[1]

Introduction

The Saudi government is committed to further agricultural development, upgrading and expanding the existing infrastructure and to bring on new projects that will provide a dynamic market for manufacturers and suppliers of agricultural technology.

To put the size of the agriculture sector in perspective, less than one per cent of the whole surface area of Saudi Arabia is farmed. (This equates to about nine per cent of the farmed area of the UK.)

However, Saudi Arabia has imported no wheat since 1985 and is also self-sufficient in potatoes, fresh milk, eggs, watermelon and dates. Saudi is also more than 50 per cent self-sufficient in red meat, poultry meat, many vegetables, tomatoes, carrots and grapes.

Saudi dairy herds, ranging up to 25,000 milking cows on one site, out-perform all but a small number of herds worldwide, all of which are in much easier climates. No forage crops are imported and Saudi alfalfa (lucerne) yields over three times that in Europe.

The largest Saudi broiler chicken company produces over 300 million birds a year, while the second largest produces more than 130 million. Saudi broilers compete in an open market with both France and Brazil.

Saudi also has the largest number of centre pivot irrigators in the world, outside of the United States. Farming development is very

---

[1] Sources of information include Saudi Arabian General Investment Authority (SAGIA) and UK Trade & Investment.

recent; the first centre pivot irrigator was installed in 1976, two years before the first dairy cow was imported. A complete modern agriculture has therefore been developed in just 25 years.

Agriculture

Land area and climate

Saudi Arabia is 25 per cent of the size of the United States, 33 per cent of the size of Australia and bigger than the whole of Western Europe. It is one of the world's driest countries with less than 100mm of rainfall on average and no permanent surface water.

The Empty Quarter in the south-east is a desert of towering mobile sand dunes covering an area the size of France. There are other mobile sand areas, especially the Nafud in the north, but the remainder have large areas of gravel plain overlying sandy loam soils with some scrub vegetation around dry riverbeds.

In the south-west, the Asir mountains, towering over the coastal plains, reach 3,000 metres, almost 10,000 feet. The Asir area has reliable rainfall; up to 600mm annually at high elevations.

Water resources

All water is from underground aquifers. Wells vary from shallow at 150 metres to the deepest, which can be over 1,200 metres. Most are between 300 to 600 metres in depth. Almost all water is pumped by diesel engines using shaft driven turbine pumps.

The question of sustainability of the water supply is complicated by the many different aquifers underlying the country. Some, especially in the central region, are fossil water with minimal recharge, and are finite. There are other sustainable aquifers in the south-west (rain fed re-charge from the Asir mountains); the north (recharged from rainfall in Syria, Iraq, Jordan and possibly further north) and the western seaboard (recharged from the Tigris/Euphrates basin).

Agricultural areas

All agricultural areas are intensively irrigated, with a considerable climatic range from tropical in the far south, through extreme desert conditions in the central area, to hot summers and cold winters (30°C to 50°C to night-time frosts of –10°C) of almost Mediterranean type in the north.

The main agricultural regions of Saudi Arabia are as follows:

- Al-Ahsa in the eastern region;
- Hail and Gaseem in the north-central region;
- Tabuk and Al Jouf in the north-western region;
- Wadi Dawasir and Asir in the southern region.

It is estimated that the total value of investment in the agricultural sector is about US$28 billion. The sector directly employs about 5.5 per cent of all manpower in the country – with many more in the related supply and processing industries. The total area of farmed land is about five million hectares and the total suitable for farming is about 50 million hectares. According to Ministry of Agriculture statistics published in 2001, the open area producing grain and fodder is about 955,000 hectares, the area for vegetables is about 162,000 hectares, the area for fruits is about 162,000 hectares and the area for dates about 106,000 hectares.

Local chicken meat production is about 450,000 tonnes per annum, dairy production is almost 820,000 tonnes, red meat about 160,000 tonnes and fish about 45,000 tonnes per annum.

The structure of farming

The business structure of farming in Saudi Arabia is quite clearly stratified. The first group is the large farming companies, approximately 10 in number. These are huge operations by any standard. The largest is National Agricultural Development Company (NADEC) with 42,000 hectares. NADEC operations incorporate some 700 centre pivots and 500 wells. Watania agriculture now ranks alongside NADEC. The others are smaller and are in a size range of 10,000 to 20,000 hectares. The second group comprises large private companies with 1,000 to 10,000 hectares. The final group comprises the majority of farms that are owned by local Saudi businessmen and farmers that are mainly in the size range from 50 to 500 hectares.

The major players are joint stock agricultural development companies but there are a number of large privately-owned farms too. Some of the largest joint stock and privately-owned farming companies in the country are:

- National Agricultural Development Company (NADEC) – products include fresh milk and dairy products and fruit and vegetables;

- Al Watania Farms – poultry (live and slaughtered), eggs, fresh fruits and vegetables and fish farms;
- Tabuk Agricultural Development Company (TADCO) – products include fresh fruit, vegetables and honey;
- Hail Agricultural Development Company (HADCO) – products include fresh fruits, vegetables and poultry;
- Astra Agricultural Company Limited (ASTRA) – products include fresh fruits, and vegatables, quail, flowers and honey, jams and frozen vegetables;
- Al-Jouf Agricultural Development Company (JADCO) – products include fresh fruit and vegetables, olives, olive oil and grains;
- Al Safi Dairy – the largest integrated dairy farm in the world;
- Al Marai Dairy – fresh milk and processed dairy products and juices;
- Al Othman Agricultural Produce and Processing Establishment (NADA) – a leading dairy farm with more than 14,000 cows and a leading producer of juices and tomato paste.

Arable agriculture

During the past 10 years, arable farming has diversified away from dependence on wheat and is now a much broader based and balanced system. The current cropping pattern is dominated by wheat, alfalfa and summer forage. The other main crops are Rhodes grass, water-melon, onions, other vegetables and barley.

Field crops

The major field crops farmed in Saudi Arabia are wheat, barley, maize, potatoes, onions and watermelons.

- *Wheat:* Wheat seems likely to stay as a cornerstone of the agricultural sector at around 1.4 to 1.8 million tonnes. The national average yield is around 4.5 tonnes per hectare and this implies around 400,000 hectares. A key reason for wheat remaining as a major crop is the national requirement for hard red wheat as source of bread flour.
- *Barley and maize:* Saudi is the world's largest importer of barley at around four million tonnes a year. Saudi also imports a significant quantity of maize (between 800,000 and 1.2 million tonnes). Barley is widely used in the poultry industry and the dairy sector. There is also a requirement from the traditional Bedouin sheepherders.

Barley and maize are currently subsidized at SR160 per tonne. This subsidy is likely to be reduced in the short term, with the intention to eliminate it completely in the longer term.

- *Potatoes:* These can be harvested year round. The north will produce good quality harvests from May to December and the south (Wadi Dewasir) from January to May. This allows processors to use potatoes of suitable varieties direct from the field, year round.
- *Onions:* These could increase considerably to displace imported onions from India, Pakistan and Egypt, because high-yielding hybrid varieties make it economic to produce under Saudi conditions, especially in the north.
- *Watermelon, tomatoes, etc:* These are completely dependent on the local market and cannot increase significantly above population growth. Watermelons have a significant export market during the high summer and Ramadan periods.
- *Beans, peanuts and lentils:* These can be grown and achieve high yields.

Forage crops

It is likely that forage crops will match the continued rapid growth of the livestock sectors, particularly dairy. Most of the large dairies now have long-term contracts with the forage producers, especially in the north.

- *Alfalfa:* This is much the largest forage crop and all the intensive livestock producers depend on it as their main forage crop. The cutting cycle is 12 times a year and hay yields of 25 tonnes or more are now being achieved by all of the serious growers.
- *Rhodes grass:* Hay yields of 35 tonnes per hectare are achieved in five to six cuts.

Commercial seed

All wheat seed is produced locally and is processed to the best international standards using state-of-the-art equipment. There could be potential for foreign seed companies to use Saudi for the production of commercial seed such as maize and other crops, especially those sensitive to GM contamination.

Saudi Arabia does not allow the importation of GM seed and is, therefore, currently clean of any potential contamination.

Livestock

The major features of the livestock sector in Saudi Arabia are huge dairy herds, with some farms being among the largest in the world with world-class performance, a major poultry sector and traditional sheep, goat and camel producers.

- *Dairy:* This has evolved as an industry over the past 25 years into huge industrialized units. Al Safi, with 25,000 milking cows on one site, is the biggest integrated dairy farm in the world. Al Marai farms have approaching 45,000 cows, split into a number of units of 5,000 to 10,000 cows. Al Marai is now achieving 13,000 litres rolling average annual yields, which positions it amongst the elite of dairy herds worldwide.
- *Poultry:* This is very big business in Saudi Arabia, as chicken is much the most popular meat for daily consumption. Per capita consumption in Saudi Arabia is approximately 33 kilos compared to 29 kilos in the UK and 51 kilos in the United States. The main producers are Watania at Gassim, HADCO in Hail and Al-Fakieh in Taif.
- *Sheep:* Local production is based on two main breeds, Najdi and Nayomi, both extremely heat-acclimatized, fat tail breeds. The meat of young male lambs is highly valued and especially in demand for the *Hajj*.

Horticulture

The major features of the horticulture sector in Saudi Arabia are established long-stem flower production and export and the cultivation of open field vegetables, ornamentals, fruits and tropical plants.

- *Flowers:* Production is now well established, especially in the more temperate north. ASTRA has developed an export market in Europe and annually exports around 10 million long-stem flowers, mainly roses and carnations.
- *Ornamentals:* All types are grown and production is now well established, even in the Riyadh area. The production of high-quality turf grass has also become big business and exports are now made all over the GCC states.
- *Open field vegetables:* Careful planting can result in excellent quality and good yields of crops as diverse as garlic, salad onions, sweet melon, okra, peas, broccoli and cauliflower.

- *Fruit:* Production has become a very well-developed business. The main crops are stone fruit – apricots, nectarines, peaches as well as plums and cherries. Grapes are grown in very large areas in the north, and citrus fruits, mainly oranges, are produced in Najran. Dates are produced in the Hofuf oasis – at over 45,000 hectares this is the largest production area for dates in the world. Total date production in 2004 approached one million tonnes and is expected to exceed two million tonnes by 2010. Also grown are pomegranates and olives.
- *Tropical:* The Jizan area produces a wide range of tropical and temperate fruit and vegetable crops. These include bananas, paw-paw, guava, figs and mango.

Fishing and aquaculture

Fish production and consumption

Fish production using modern techniques is a recent innovation. There has always been traditional inshore fishing on the 2,400km of the Gulf and Red Sea coasts. The first modern fishing commenced in 1981, with the establishment of the Saudi Fisheries Company. This has grown from an operation with one leased boat to a fleet of 14 modern trawlers fishing in Saudi and international waters, supplemented by 35 traditional boats.

The total annual production from sea fishing has tended to stabilize at around 50,000 tonnes over the past few years. Consumption has risen consistently, starting from a low figure of three kilos per capita in 1977 to nine kilos per capita in 1999. The demand for fresh and frozen fish has, therefore, increased to around 110,000 tonnes per year and is projected to increase to 140,000 tonnes by 2005.

Aquaculture

Fish farming is a more recent introduction to Saudi Arabia. The first fish farm started in 1983 and there are now about 150, most established recently to produce freshwater Tilapia. They are located in the central agricultural areas where the water used by the fish farm can be reused for irrigation.

Marine fish farming

Marine fish farming is a much more recent innovation and the current production is small but set to grow rapidly. The Red Sea coastline, which is around 1,800km long, is particularly attractive due to suitable temperatures ranging from 21 to 35°C, good water quality, low pollution and a protective reef along much of the shoreline, which forms lagoons protected from the open sea. The gulf coast has cooler winter temperatures, rendering it somewhat less suitable for aquaculture.

The Tihama coastal plain is well suited to onshore production, especially of shrimps. The protected inshore waters are ideal for many production systems, such as cages and pens.

Agronomic advantages in Saudi Arabia

Climate

All crops must be irrigated and therefore fertigation and chemigation can be easily incorporated. Weather damage during harvest is almost eliminated and field drying is usually quick and reliable. Drought can be used as a most effective, non-chemical herbicide.

The large range of climates makes it possible to supply crops such as potatoes fresh from the field year round by exploiting the relatively cool summers of the extreme north and the completely frost-free winters of the south.

Other agronomic advantages

Other agronomic advantages relate to factors including rotation, chemical residues, alternate hosts for insects and diseases and the cleanliness of the water supply as follows.

- *Rotation:* Long rotations are easy for most crops, thereby reducing the need for crop protection chemicals.
- *Chemical residues:* All chemicals utilized in the Saudi agricultural sector are subject to the same approvals required in the United States and Europe. Saudi residue levels are very low and, where they exist at all, are of safer, more modern, less toxic chemicals.
- *Alternate hosts for insects and diseases:* There is almost no natural vegetation between cropped areas. This eliminates the potential host plants for insects and fungal diseases.
- *Clean water:* Irrigation water is from deep aquifers and therefore free from pesticides and fertilizer residues and from pathogens, such as brown rot in potatoes.

Trading and other business opportunities

Saudi Arabia's main imports in the agricultural sector are irrigation equipment including pumps, agricultural equipment and machinery, veterinary products, livestock handling machinery, agrochemicals and seeds.

Machinery imports

Many specialized niche markets exist in:

- specialized crop production machinery – for example large air-seeders have replaced conventional planting machines, while large, high-density square balers are replacing all conventional balers;
- self-propelled sprayers and similar equipment with large daily work rate potential;
- specialized vegetable production, harvesting, post-harvest (especially field heat removal), cleaning, grading and packing;
- cool chain technology, including pack-houses;.
- spare parts and engine re-build packages for some 30,000 large diesel engines;
- animal food processing and handling equipment;
- livestock feeding equipment.

The main exporting nations for agricultural machinery to Saudi Arabia are the United States, Germany, the UK, France and the Netherlands.

Specialized livestock technology

With very large units, many management techniques that might have only a marginal impact on a few hundred animals can have significant benefits and considerable markets.

This can be in almost any sector, from bio-security, disease prevention and control, husbandry improvements (heat detection in cows, etc), and sophisticated housing technology related to improved environmental control, either by ventilation, insulation or reduction of heat load, stress reduction by better airflow, etc.

Organic farming

Very low or non-existent soil residues of chemicals, coupled with many agronomic advantages, could make organic field scale vegetable and other crop production easy and very high quality. There is a significant local market and high export potential.

Processing of crops for industrial, snack and primary food

There are considered to be business opportunities in the following areas:

- innovative process technology in meat preparation, pre-cooked and other prepared meals – the convenience food and packaged meals market is not exploited at present, while the introduction of Western-style eating habits is accelerating the trend towards fast food;
- snack foods based on 'healthy alternatives' – nuts, popped corn, potato chips etc, with low oil or salt or similar;
- breeding and production of broiler chicken – approximately 35 per cent of this rapidly increasing market is imported at present;
- preparation and freezing of pre-fried chicken nuggets – at present there is no Saudi-based production of frozen chicken pieces or nuggets or any other form of pre-cooked shaped chicken meat;
- olive oil manufacturing and olive preservation – while there is rapidly developing Saudi oil production, there is little organized manufacturing of olive oil, preserved olives or speciality products;
- preparation, grading and packaging of citrus;
- preparation and freezing of French fries and the preparation and drying of potato flour and potato starch;
- manufacturing of dried apricot slices, dried grapes and other dried fruit;
- manufacturing of tomato paste and tomato juice.

Crop and ornamental seed production

A rare combination of a GM-free environment, clean land, clean environment, very large separation distances, counter-season production potential and significant financial incentives would favour crop and ornamental seed production in Saudi Arabia.

Fish farming

There are considered to be business opportunities in the following areas:

- marine fish farming, especially of high-value shrimp such as Tiger prawn, Indian white prawn and Greek prawn;
- production of fin fish, such as groupers, mullet, sea bream and sea bass;
- preparation and freezing of fish and fish canning;
- fish feed production;
- fish breeding and commercial seed supply.

Other business opportunities

There are considered to be other business opportunities in the following areas:

- intensification of sheep production – management techniques, both fundamental and advanced, could be combined as a package for the production of premium quality fat lamb using already established crosses;
- irrigation technology – soil water monitoring and irrigation scheduling to maximize water use and water conservation, without reducing economic production levels;
- tropical fruit and vegetable production – based on Jizan in the south, there are opportunities to produce tropical fruit during the spring and summer and temperate vegetables during the winter, as water is from rainfall and therefore permanently sustainable from an increasing number of dams;
- marketing in all sectors including arable and horticultural crops – marketing and downstream processing of all categories of agricultural products including milk, red meat, chicken meat, eggs, fish and fruit, as well as export of a wide range of vegetables, fruit, especially dates, and food products.

Government support for project funding

The Saudi Arabian Agricultural Bank advances loans to arable crop farms, livestock farms (dairy cows, sheep and poultry), horticulture and fish farming. Lending can be short, for inputs up to one year, medium term for equipment and infrastructure over 10 years, or long term up to 25 years for capital projects.

For investments that fall outside the rules of the agricultural bank, the Saudi Industrial Development Fund (SIDF) provides soft-, medium- and long-term loans to industrial establishments for up to 50 per cent of the total cost of the project for up to 15 years.

Further information

Green Vista Agriculture Specialists is a firm of management consultants specializing in the agricultural sector of Saudi Arabia (email: info@greenmountain.com.sa).

Anthony Shoult of ASA Consulting has conducted a number of market and techno-economic feasibility studies related to agricultural production in Saudi Arabia and other Middle East countries, including a review of the marketing operation of a major Saudi agricultural products producer and a feasibility study for a food processing plant. For further information concerning the experience and activities of ASA Consulting please contact asaconsult@btinternet.com.

7.6

Manufacturing Industry

Anthony Shoult, ASA Consulting[1]

Introduction

To date, the Saudi government has spent in excess of SR2 billion on the development of eight industrial cities, which cover a total of 35 million square metres. The Kingdom has some 3,200 factories, with a total capital investment of over US$70 billion and employing around 250,000 people.

These factories are engaged in a wide variety of activities for various industry sectors, ranging from foodstuffs and beverages, through textiles and leather, to chemicals and plastics, metals, paper and mineral products and machinery and equipment. A breakdown of operating factories in 1974 and 1999 is shown in Table 7.6.1.

Table 7.6.1 Number of operating factories and their size of investments, 1974–1999 (SR millions)

Sector	1974	1999	1974	1999
Food and beverages	73	529	1,144	16,919
Textiles, readymade clothes and leather	12	156	66	3,786
Wood, wooden products and furniture	25	155	232	2,324
Paper, printing and publishing	46	205	338	6,116
Chemical industries and plastic products	63	670	1,460	151,462

[1] Sources of information include Saudi Industrial Development Fund (SIDF) and UK Trade & Investment.

Sector	1974	1999	1974	1999
Building materials, glass, ceramic and non-metal basic industries	91	571	4,359	29,619
Manufactured metals, machines and equipment	159	915	2,159	23,221
Other industries	3	79	121	1,374
Total	*472*	*3,280*	*9,879*	*234,821*

Source: Ministry of Industry and Electricity 2000

Over 350 of the factories that have been established are joint ventures, involving a total investment of SR100 billion, the majority of which are profitable and productive.

Saudi Arabia has a strong and expanding manufacturing base, and the manufacturing sector grew by 8.6 per cent in 1997. In 1996, Saudi industrial exports totalled SR27.7 billion, while imports of electrical machinery, equipment and tools were worth US$5.8 billion.

Role of Saudi Industrial Development Fund (SIDF)

The Saudi Industrial Development Fund (SIDF), established in 1974, has made a substantial contribution to the industrial development of the Kingdom through the provision of soft loans and consultative services in the technical, financial, administrative and marketing fields to borrower projects.

Since its inception in 1974 up to the end of fiscal year 2002, SIDF had extended a total of 2,483 loans amounting to over SR42 billion. These loans assisted in the building of over 1,800 industrial projects throughout the Kingdom.

In 2002 alone, SIDF commitments to industrial projects amounted to SR1,815 million, a 16 per cent increase over 2001. During 2002, SIDF approved 90 loans committed in support of 40 new industrial projects and 50 expansions of existing industrial plants.

SIDF is particularly active in encouraging joint venture projects involving the transfer of modern technology and professional administrative expertise for emerging projects. The number of joint ventures approved by SIDF up to 2002 was in excess of 520, almost 30 per cent of all projects approved for support by the Fund. Loans committed to joint ventures amount to SR16 billion, 38 per cent of all SIDF loans. The foreign partners' share in these projects accounted for 34 per cent of their capital.

Key industry sectors

Metals processing industries

The principal metal processing industries in Saudi Arabia, including those with large rolling mill operations, are shown in Table 7.6.2. The major player in the metals processing sector in Saudi Arabia is the Saudi Iron and Steel Company (HADEED). This is a wholly-owned affiliate of the Saudi Basic Industries Corporation (SABIC).

Table 7.6.2 Major metal processing industries, 2004

Company	Location	Capacity (tonnes)	Sector
Basic steel industries			
Saudi Iron and Steel Company (HADEED)	Al Jubail	2,800,000 (long products) 850,000 (flat products)	Rolled steel long products – rods and bars. Flat steel products
United Gulf Steel Mill	Al Jubail	350,000	Medium section steel rolling mill
Al-Ittifaq Iron Industries	Dammam	150,000	Reinforcement steel rods, sections
Steel pipe producers			
Saudi Steel Pipe Company	Dammam	220,000	Galvanised and ungalvanized steel pipes
National Pipe Company	Dhahran	180,000	Spiral welded steel pipes
Arabian Pipes Company	Riyadh	160,000	Steel pipes – longitudinal welded
Steel coil coating companies			
BHP Universal Metal Coating Company Ltd	Al Jubail	120,000	Pre-painted galvanized steel and aluminium coils
(UNICOIL)			
Saudi Metal Coating Company (SMC)	Jeddah	120,000	Pre-painted galvanized steel and aluminium coils

Company	Location	Capacity (tonnes)	Sector
Major metal products processing companies			
Yamama Iron Industries	Jeddah	300,000	Steel pipes, corrugated sheet, structural steel frames etc
Al Jazeera Steel Products Factory	Jeddah	160,000	Steel pipes, sheet, hollow profiles
Baghlaf Al Zafer Factory	Jeddah, Dammam	160,000	Pipes and profiles, galvanized and coloured black sheets etc
Rashed A Al Rashed Steel Products Factory	Dammam	130,000	Galvanized fence netting, wire, corrugated sheet, reinforcement wire mesh etc
Al-Usaimi Factory for Industrial Steel	Dammam	120,000	Corrugated galvanized sheet, drawn wire
Saudi Steel Products Company (STEPCO)	Riyadh	120,000	Reinforcement wire and rod, wire mesh
Wire Drawing and Related Products Factory (ASLAK)	Al Jubail	33,000	
Steel containers			
Saudi Can Company	Jeddah	25,000	Tin cans, pails, other containers
Aluminium processing companies			
Aluminium Product Company Ltd (ALUPCO)	Dammam, Jeddah	60,000	Extruded aluminium profiles

Source: ASA Consulting

Saudi Iron and Steel Company (HADEED)

Saudi Iron and Steel Company (HADEED), located at Al Jubail, was the first integrated iron and steel plant to be established in Saudi Arabia. HADEED commenced steel production in December 1982.

The original design capacity of 850,000 tonnes was increased to 2.8 million tonnes of finished long products in 1997. The flat products expansion added a further 850,000 tonnes of capacity from 2000. HADEED is a wholly-owned subsidiary of Saudi Arabian Basic Industries Corporation (SABIC).

The HADEED steel complex includes rolling mills consisting of three separate plants with a combined capacity of 2.6 million tonnes that convert 130×130mm billets:

- bar mill with a capacity of 1.2 million tonnes a year, producing plain and deformed reinforcing bar from 12mm to 40mm;
- rod and bar mill with a capacity of 700,000 tonnes a year, producing wire rod in coils (350,000 tonnes) and rebar in coils from 5.5mm to 14mm (350,000 tonnes);
- section and bar mill with a capacity of 600,000 tonnes a year, producing rebar from 10mm to 32mm (575,000 tonnes) and light sections – channels, angles, square and flat bars (25,000 tonnes).

The actual product mix produced by HADEED includes rebar, wire rod and light sections with a capacity of 2.8 million tonnes a year.

In 1999, HADEED carried out a SR4.7 billion expansion project that provided a capacity of 850,000 tonnes of hot and cold rolled flat products. The facilities of the flat products expansion include a hot strip mill and cold rolling mill complex.

The range of HADEED flat products is as follows:

- hot rolled flat products:
  - mill edge coils in widths from 900mm to 1,650mm;
  - edge trimmed coils in widths from 75mm to 1,650mm;
  - slit coils in widths from 75mm to 1,650 mm;
  - cut to length plates in widths from 850mm to 1,600mm;
- cold rolled flat products:
  - pickled and oiled coils in widths from 850mm to 1,650mm;
  - cold reduced, annealed and tempered coils in widths from 850mm to 1,650mm;
  - cold reduced, annealed and tempered slit coils in widths from 75mm to 800mm;
  - cold rolled galvanized coils in widths from 850mm to 1,400mm;
  - cold rolled galvanized slit coils in widths from 75mm to 800mm.

BHP Universal Metal Coating Company Ltd (UNICOIL)
BHP Universal Metal Coating Company (UNICOIL), located at Al Jubail, is one of two Saudi companies engaged in the manufacture of pre-painted galvanized steel and aluminium coils. It is a joint venture between BHP Steel Middle East Investment Pty Ltd of Australia and the Al-Zamil and Al-Rashed Groups of Saudi Arabia. UNICOIL, established in 1998, has an installed capacity of 120,000 tonnes and is capable of painting the full range of coil strip products, including galvanized steel, zinc-aluminium coated steel, aluminium and cold rolled steel. It is one of the market leaders in the supply of pre-painted steel and aluminium to the pre-engineered buildings sector. Current output is estimated at 80,000 tonnes a year.

The UNICOIL processing line is a twin coater configuration for single pass production with a steel throughput capacity of 120,000 tonnes per year. The facilities include prime and finish coaters.

Saudi Steel Products Company (STEPCO)
The Saudi Steel Products Company (STEPCO), of Riyadh, which was established in 1979, is an important end user of HADEED wire rod. This is a secondary steel production or wire drawing manufacturing unit, with a nominal annual capacity of 120,000 tonnes.

STEPCO commenced its operations as a welded wire mesh producer but is now effectively operating as a wire drawing company. The company produces high tensile cold drawn wire in a range of sizes from 5.5mm to 14mm and welded wire mesh up to 14mm in diameter. STEPCO also has an operation for cutting and bending rebar, which utilizes some 30,000 tonnes a year of HADEED rebar in coil form.

Wire Drawing and Related Products Factory (ASLAK)
The Wire Drawing and Related Products Factory (ASLAK), part of the National Metal Manufacturing and Casting Company (MAADANIYAH) of Al Jubail, is a secondary steel production or wire drawing manufacturing unit, with a nominal annual capacity of 33,000 tonnes. ASLAK's production facilities include wire rod pickling, wire drawing, galvanizing, fastener manufacturing, heat treatment, electroplating and annealing.

The following are the main products for ferrous wire consuming industries currently produced by ASLAK:

- low relaxation pre-stressed concrete (PC) strand to ASTM 416-80/ BS 5896–1980;
- spring wire to DIN 17223;
- galvanized high and low carbon galvanized wires to ASTM B498/500, BS 443/1442, IEC209, DIN 1548 and BS 4565;

- copper coated welding wires to DIN 8559-SG2, ANSI/AWS A5.17, AWS/ASME A5 18 and AWS ER 70S-6;
- a metric range of fasteners (nuts and bolts) to DIN 931/933, DIN 601/558 grade 8.8 and 4.8;
- electroplated and black concrete nails (Grip Tight brand).

Aluminium Products Company Ltd (ALUPCO)
Aluminium Products Company (ALUPCO), located at Dammam and Jeddah, is the largest manufacturer of extruded aluminium profiles in the Middle East. ALUPCO has an installed capacity of 60,000 tonnes and output is estimated at 40,000 tonnes a year.

Chemicals industries

The principal chemicals industries, excluding SABIC joint ventures (see Chapter 7.2), in Saudi Arabia are shown in Table 7.6.3.

Saudi Arabia has a growing number of private sector specialized chemicals companies. Many of these have become established in the main industrial centres of the Eastern Province. The most prominent companies include Basic Chemical Industries (BCI), Dammam; Saudi Formaldehyde Chemicals Company Limited (SFCCL), Al Jubail; and Arab Pesticide Industries (MOBEED), Al Jubail.

Basic Chemical Industries (BCI)
Basic Chemical Arabia Industries (BCI) Ltd is Saudi's largest private sector chemical company. BCI, established in 1975, is 100 per cent Saudi owned and employs over 250 at its production facility located at Dammam First Industrial City.

BCI produces chlorine, caustic soda, hydrochloric acid and sodium hypochlorite. Subsidiary companies have been established to produce industrial aqueous emulsion and hot melt adhesives, rigid polyurethane systems and a range of water treatment chemical products.

Saudi Formaldehyde Chemicals Company Limited (SFCCL)
Saudi Formaldehyde Chemicals Company Limited (SFCCL) at Al Jubail, is a private sector enterprise established in 1992 and has an annual capacity of over 260,000 tonnes of aqueous formaldehyde solutions, urea formaldehyde concentrate, hexa methylene tetramine, paraformaldehyde and urea/melamine formaldehyde resins.

Table 7.6.3 Saudi Arabian chemicals industries, 2004

Company	Location	Capacity (tonnes)	Sector
Arabian Saudi Fertilizer Company (SAFCO)	Dammam	450,000	Urea, sulphuric acid, melamin
Saudi Formaldehyde Chemicals Company (SFCC)	Al Jubail	265,000	Aqueous formaldehyde solutions, urea formaldehyde concentrate, hexa methylene tetramine, paraformaldehyde, urea/ melamine formaldehyde resins
Basic Chemical Industries	Dammam	80,000 (various chemicals) 12,000 (chlorine gas)	Hydraulic acid, calcium chloride, sodium hypochlorite, chlorine gas etc
National Fertilizer Company (NAFCO)	Riyadh	50,000	Granulated and liquid compound chemical fertilizers, insecticides
Saudi Industrial Resins Company	Jeddah	30,000	Alkide resins, phenolic formaldehyde resins, polyvinyl ester, polyester
Dhahran Harco Chemical Industries	Dammam	24,000 (various chemicals)	Polymethyl methacrylate, styrene acrylic, adhesives
Saudi Industrial Gas Company	Al Khobar	12,000 (various industrial gases)	Oxygen, nitrogen, hydrogen, carbon dioxide, acetylene, argon etc
Arab Pesticide Industries Co (MOBEED)	Al Jubail	7,000	Insecticides, fungicides, herbicides, aerosols

Source: ASA Consulting

Arab Pesticide Industries (MOBEED)

Arab Pesticide Industries (MOBEED) at Al Jubail, established in 1995 is a joint venture between the Dallah Al-Baraka Group, Alujain and the National Industrialization Company. The company has an annual capacity of 7,000 tonnes and produces a range of pesticides (insecticides, fungicides, herbicides, aerosols) for both agricultural and domestic use.

Building materials industries

The principal cement and other building materials industries in Saudi Arabia are shown in Table 7.6.4.

Table 7.6.4 Major building materials industries, 2004

Company	Location	Capacity	Sector
Cement industries			
Yamama Saudi Cement Company Company	Riyadh	3.5 million tonnes	Cement of all kinds
The Qasim Cement Company	Buraydah	1.5 million tonnes	Portland cement, pozzolana
Arabian Cement Company	Rabigh	2.5 million tonnes	Portland cement
Yanbu Cement Company	Yanbu	3.5 million tonnes	Portland cement
Eastern Province Cement Company	Dammam	4.5 million tonnes	Cement of all kinds
Saudi Cement Company	Dammam	4.5 million tonnes	Cement of all kinds
Southern Province Cement Company	Jizan	1.5 million tonnes	Cement of all kinds
Basic building materials industries			
Al-Rashid A Betong Company	Riyadh	160,000m^2 (precast 143,000m^3 (pre-mix)	Precast concrete components, pre-mixed concrete
Saif Noman Said & Partners	Riyadh, Jeddah	220 million m^2 pre-cast panels	Precast concrete components, hollow core tiles
Qanbar Dywidag Precast Concrete Co	Al Jubail	130,000m^3 (precast)	Precast concrete components
National Marble & Granite Company	Jeddah	430,000m^2	Marble and granite panels
National Gypsum Company	Riyadh, Yanbu	250,000 tonnes	Gypsum

Source: ASA Consulting

Cement industry

The cement industry is one of the most important in the building materials sector. At present there are seven companies producing normal grey Portland cement, with an aggregate annual production capacity of 21.5 million tonnes. Additionally there are two further companies, one producing white cement and the other crushing clinker into white cement, with an aggregate annual capacity of 370,000 tonnes.

Total investment in the cement industry by 2001 reached SR12 billion, representing five per cent of the total investment in processing industries in the Kingdom.

Paper and printing industries

Paper and printing industries in Saudi Arabia include the following:

- newspaper publishing (newsprint);
- packaging industries;
- corrugated cardboard.

The principal newsprint, packaging and corrugated cardboard industries in Saudi Arabia are shown in Table 7.6.5.

Table 7.6.5 Major newspaper publishing, printing and packaging and corrugated cardboard industries, 2004

Company	Location	Capacity (tonnes)	Sector
Newspaper publishing			
Al Yamamah Printing & Publishing Company	Riyadh	22,000 <100,000 (circulation)	Newspapers and periodicals: (*Al Riyadh*, *Riyadh Daily*, *Al Yamamah Magazine*), books
Dar Okaz Organization for Press and Publication	Jeddah	6,000 <100,000 (circulation)	Newspapers and periodicals: (*Okaz*, *Saudi Gazette*)
Saudi Research and Publishing Company/Al Madinah Printing and Publishing	Jeddah	40,000 >500,000 (circulation)	Newspapers and periodicals: *Asharq Al Awsat*, *Arriyadiyah*, *Al Eqtisadiah*, *Arab News* etc
Al Jazerah Corporation Press	Riyadh	11,000	Newspapers, books and magazines

Company	Location	Capacity (tonnes)	Sector
Al-Attar Printing Press Co	Riyadh	30,000	School books
Printing and packaging industries			
Obeikan Group:	Riyadh		
Commercial Printing		15,000	Commercial printing – mainly school books
Obeikan Duplex		20,000	Duplex – food packaging
Obeikan Elopak		30,000	Elopak – liquid packaging
Obeikan Flexible Packaging		5,000	Flexible packaging
Obeikan Combibloc			Combibloc long-life packaging
Obeikan Packaging Film			Polypropylene/PE film
National Paper Company (NAPCO) Group	Jeddah	25,000	Tissue and disposables
United Plastic Products Co (UPPC)`	Jeddah		Flexible plastic packaging
Paper and corrugated cardboard industries			
Arab Paper Manufacturing Company (WARAQ)	Riyadh	70,000	Carton paper rolls
National Packaging Products Company (WATAN PAC)	Riyadh	50,000	Corrugated cardboard
Riyadh Carton Factory	Riyadh	40,000	Corrugated cardboard
Safaripak	Jeddah	40,000	Corrugated cardboard
Saudi Carton Factory	Jeddah	50,000	Corrugated cardboard
Badypak	Dammam	24,000	Corrugated cardboard

Source: ASA Consulting

Obeikan Group

Obeikan is a large Riyadh-based printing and packaging products company. The individual group companies are involved in the following products:

- book printing and publishing;
- food products packaging (Obeikan Duplex);
- liquid packaging (Obeikan Elopak);
- flexible packaging for food and pharmaceuticals and foil lids;
- long life packaging for food and drinks (Obeikan Combibloc);
- technical fabrics – weaving and coating;
- polypropylene and polyethylene film.

National Paper Company (NAPCO) Group of Companies
The National Paper Company (NAPCO) is a large Jeddah-based printing and packaging products company. The NAPCO Group comprises 10 operating plants, manufacturing a range of paper and plastic packaging products located in Jeddah, Riyadh and Dammam, and is organized in three divisions as follows:

- tissue and disposables;
- flexible packaging;
- corrugated carton.

National Packing Products Co (WATAN PAC)
The National Packing Products Company (WATAN PAC) is a large Riyadh-based corrugated cardboard company. WATAN PAC's annual production is at the level of 50,000 tonnes.

Water treatment installation manufacturing industries

The principal potable water and waste wastewater treatment installation manufacturing and contracting companies in Saudi Arabia, with plant construction and maintenance requirements giving rise to potential requirements for polyurethane coating services and wear parts, are shown in Table 7.6.6.

Table 7.6.6 Main water treatment installation manufacturing and contracting companies, 2004

Company	Location	Sector
Metito Arabia Industries	Riyadh	Packaged extended aeration wastewater treatment plants from 100m^3/day to 500m^3/day
Al Kawther Industries	Jeddah	Extended aeration wastewater treatment plants. Large municipal wastewater projects
General Enterprises & Trading Company (GETCO)	Riyadh	Supply and installation of packaged wastewater treatment plants
EMCO	Riyadh	EMCO markets a range of packaged water and sewage treatment systems, much of which is directly imported from the United States
Reza Environmental Engineering Division	Jeddah	Water and wastewater treatment engineering contracting company

Source: ASA Consulting

Recent developments in key industry sectors

Chemical products

During 2002, SIDF approved 28 loans in the chemical products sector with a total commitment of approximately SR330 million. This was in respect of 17 new industrial establishments and the expansion of 11 existing projects.

New projects approved by SIDF for this sector in 2002 include:

- a thermal carbon black production facility at Al Jubail (loan value of SR95 million);
- a chlorine and caustic soda production facility at Dammam (loan value of SR61 million);
- a HDPE and PP pipes production plant in Jeddah (loan value of SR30 million).

Major project expansions approved by SIDF in 2002 include:

- formaldehyde liquid, urea formaldehyde and melamine resins for an established Al Jubail-based producer (loan value of SR33 million);
- plastic bottles, barrels and caps for a Jeddah plant expansion (loan value of SR7 million).

A total of 10 new plants and 11 factory expansions commenced production during 2002, including manufacturing facilities for the production of pharmaceuticals, perfumes, cosmetics, calcium phosphate, polyester resins, printing inks, adhesives, antioxidants, printing and lamination of polypropylene sheets and plastic packaging materials.

Engineered products

During 2002, SIDF approved 25 loans in the chemical products sector with a total commitment of approximately SR408 million. This was in respect of 13 new industrial establishments and the expansion of 12 existing projects.

New projects approved by SIDF for this sector in 2002 include:

- a steel scrap conversion facility at Bahra, Jeddah (loan value of SR103 million);
- a reinforcement bars production facility at Bahra, Jeddah (loan value of SR90 million);
- a spirally welded pipe production plant in Dammam (loan value of SR22 million).

Major project expansions approved by SIDF in 2002 include:

- extruded aluminium sections for an established Dammam-based producer (loan value of SR44 million);
- hot drawn steel sections and cold drawn steel reinforcement bars and sheet steels for a Kharj plant expansion (loan value of SR32 million).

A total of 11 new plants and 11 factory expansions commenced production during 2002, including manufacturing facilities for the production of electric power and telephone line poles, scrap steel billets, flanges, pipe fittings, suspended ceilings, steel scaffoldings, freon air-conditioning systems, mechanical spare parts, digital consoles, water desalination units and fibre optics.

Consumer products

During 2002, SIDF approved 23 loans in the consumer products sector with a total commitment of approximately SR840 million. This was in respect of seven new industrial establishments and the expansion of 16 existing projects.

New projects approved by SIDF for this sector in 2002 include:

- a soya oil, oil cakes and seed husk production facility at Yanbu (loan value of SR200 million);
- a duplex cardboard production facility in Riyadh (loan value of SR150 million);
- a seawater desalination plant in Jeddah (loan value of SR66 million).

Major project expansions approved by SIDF in 2002 include:

- dairy products for an established Kharj-based producer (loan value of SR100 million).
- carton paper rolls processing plant expansion (loan value of SR84 million).

A total of 12 new plants and factory expansions commenced production during 2002, including manufacturing facilities for the production of dairy products, juice, olive oil, ready-made garments, non-woven fabrics, cotton yarns, animal feed, phenol impregnated paper, formica and other sheets and craft paper.

Cement and other building materials

During 2002, SIDF approved 13 loans in the building materials sector, with a total commitment of approximately SR230 million. This was in respect of two new industrial establishments and the expansion of 10 existing projects.

New projects approved by SIDF for this sector in 2002 include:

- a red bricks production facility at Bahra (loan value of SR80 million);
- reinforced fibreglass pipes production facility in Jeddah (loan value of SR29 million).

Major project expansions approved by SIDF in 2002 include:

- granite slabs and tiles for an established Riyadh-based producer (loan value of SR23 million);
- a gypsum powder plant expansion (loan value of SR12 million);
- modernizing and upgrading of the Southern Province Cement Company (loan value of SR11 million).

A total of two new plants and factory expansions commenced production during 2002, including manufacturing facilities for ceramic sanitary ware and fibreglass pipes.

Further information

ASA Consulting has conducted a large number of manufacturing industry-related market and techno-economic feasibility studies in Saudi Arabia and other Middle East countries including the following:

- a market study for industrial polyurethane products manufacturing in Saudi Arabia (2004);
- a feasibility study for industrial valve refurbishment services in Saudi Arabia (2004);
- a market study for specialist vehicle manufacturing plant in Saudi Arabia (2003);
- a feasibility study for steel industrial flooring manufacturing plant in Saudi Arabia (2001).

For further information concerning the experience and activities of ASA Consulting please contact asaconsult@btinternet.com.

7.7

Construction Industry

Anthony Shoult, ASA Consulting[1]

Introduction

Saudi Arabia has long been the largest construction market in the Middle East. As oil revenues constitute around 80 per cent of the Kingdom's total revenues, the direction of Saudi Arabia's economy is predominantly governed by the value of its natural resources. Therefore, the level of construction activity in the Kingdom has, over the years, tended to have a direct correlation with the movement of oil prices.

Level of construction activity

The link between the oil price and level of construction activity in the Kingdom has been particularly evident in recent years. When, for example, the average price of Brent crude increased from US$17.7 per barrel in 1999 to US$28.31 per barrel in 2000, the annual value of total publicly awarded contracts increased by 26 per cent from SR9.95 billion (US$2.65 billion) to SR12.56 billion (US$3.34 billion) (see Table 7.7.1).

Between 1997 and 2002, construction investment in Saudi Arabia was estimated at US$19.5 billion per year and peaked at around US$20.8 billion in 2000. Following the 9/11 economic slowdown, the government curbed its planned expenditure for 2002 by 20.8 per cent to US$54 billion, compared to US$68 billion in 2001. However, after a surge of construction and industrial and urban developments in 2002, the total value of contracts awarded rose considerably.

---

[1] Sources of information include National Commercial Bank (NCB) and UK Trade & Investment.

Table 7.7.1 Construction contracts awarded by sector, 1997–2003, (SR million)

Sector	1997	1998	1999	2000	2001	2002	2003
Hotels	228.00	1,593.00	1,001.76	131.25	7.77	52.00	-
Urban development	3,500.17	2,539.28	2,748.68	3,151.39	3,963.66	5,707.70	5.154.00
Social, hospitals and philanthropic	1,215.65	4,695.60	896.89	1,061.95	240.40	1,012.40	4,204.00
Industrial	3,554.88	1,407.05	1,220.23	4,741.95	2,919.40	5,232.00	1,741.00
Power	301.26	1,149.44	633.90	268.80	607.24	45.00	2,177.00
Roads	5,205.68	1,560.51	523.67	2,356.58	3,740.27	3,412.10	2,992.00
Commercial	1,450.00	1,274.32	1,971.44	278.30	0.00	92.30	3,504.00
Other	590.00	393.89	956.55	574.00	330.51	5.00	71.00
Total contracts[1]	*16,045.64*	*14,613.09*	*9,953.12*	*12,564.22*	*11,809.25*	*15,558.50*	*19,843.00*
Total construction investment[2]	53,774.00	54,099.00	50,532.00	55,081.00	56,500.00	61,500.00	63,468.00
% change	n/a	0.6%	-6.6%	9.0%	2.6%	8.8%	3.2%
Brent crude US$/ barrel	*19.12*	*12.72*	*17.70*	*28.31*	*24.20*	*25.10*	*27.00*

[1] Relates to contracts that have been announced only

[2] Includes National Commercial Bank estimates for 2002 and ASA Consulting estimates for 2003. Also included are the 15 per cent of power contracts that are considered as construction

Source: SAMA, MEED, Saudi Economic Survey

In 2003, the Saudi construction industry continued to exhibit the excellent performance that had been exhibited in 2002. Strong investment in the construction sector, as measured by the gross fixed capital formation, was estimated to have jumped by 8.8 per cent to SR61.5 billion in 2002, compared to SR56.5 billion in 2001 (see Table 7.7.2).

Table 7.7.2 Construction sector: Gross fixed capital formation, 1990–2002 (SR million)

Year	Residential buildings	Other construction	Total construction	Change %
1990	6,951	47,450	54,401	-
1991	9,459	53,713	63,172	16.1
1992	14,038	54,137	68,175	7.9
1993	15,510	55,434	70,944	4.1
1994	13,260	47,017	60,277	-15.0
1995	13,764	49,065	62,829	4.2
1996	25,081	26,070	51,151	-18.6
1997	25,675	28,099	53,774	5.1
1998	25,455	28,644	54,099	0.6
1999	25,712	24,820	50,532	-6.6
2000	28,236	26,845	55,081	9.0
2001[#]	29,500	27,000	56,500	2.6
2002[#]	30,300	31,200	61,500	8.8

[#] NCB estimates

Source: Saudi Arabian Monetary Agency (SAMA)

In value terms, the demand for residential buildings grew by 2.7 per cent, to an estimated SR30.3 billion, on the back of a rapidly growing population and the availability of long-term credit from the Real Estate Development Fund.

Type of construction activity

In 2000, the total of construction activity in Saudi Arabia, as measured by the issue of building permits, represented 25.86 million square metres of floor space with a construction value of SR40.5 billion (US$10.8 billion) (see Table 7.7.3).

The level of Saudi construction activity indicated in 2000 by the issue of building permits of 25.86 million square metres compares to a level of 21.30 million square metres in 1993. This suggests a consolidated average annual growth of the Saudi construction industry between 1993 and 2000 of approximately three per cent. By 2004, the annual level of building construction is likely to have risen to the level of 30 million square metres of building floor space, valued at approximately SR45 billion.

Table 7.7.3 Construction of buildings,[1] 2000

Type of building development	Percentage of construction (%)	Total floor area (million m^2)	Total number of floors	Construction value (building)[2] (SR billion)	Construction value (site)[3] (SR billion)	Total construction value[4] (SR billion)
Residential and commercial	87	22.52	63,411	33.8	1.57	35.37
Industrial and commercial	9	2.31	2,209	3.47	0.09	3.56
Education, health, mosques	3	0.80	999	1.21	0.05	1.26
Social and government	1	0.23	96	0.35	0.01	0.36
Total	*100*	*25.86*	*66,715*	*38.83*	*1.72*	*40.55*

[1] as measured by the issue of building permits

[2] building only (assumes average construction cost of SR1,500 per m^2 of floor area)

[3] site related (assumes average construction cost of SR500 per linear metre of boundary wall)

[4] excludes road construction by government, valued at SR12.6 billion in 2000

Source: Ministry of Municipalities and Rural Affairs/NCB Economics Department

Construction methods

In Saudi Arabia, an estimated 90 per cent of all building construction utilizes concrete structures or framing systems comprising slabs, beams, columns and walls. Based on statistics published by the Ministry of Municipalities and Rural Affairs concerning the issue of building permits, ASA Consulting estimates that this represents some 27 million square metres of construction of floor space in 2004.

The types of structural concrete flooring system commonly utilized in Saudi Arabia are in-situ concrete construction and pre-cast hollow core floor slab construction. In Saudi Arabia, in-situ solid flat slab concrete construction dominates the market for building construction, with 90 per cent penetration of concrete building construction. The dominance of in-situ solid flat slab concrete construction is due to the preference of traditional engineering consultant practices in the Saudi construction industry, opting for traditional methods of construction that they are familiar with for the majority of projects that are small domestic and commercial developments.

Pre-cast hollow core floor slab construction is increasingly important for in-Kingdom concrete frame structures in Saudi Arabia. Saudi Arabia has a well-established pre-cast hollow core industry that was first established in the mid-1970s and now boasts an annual production capacity of over 2.5 million square metres.

Construction industry outlook

In 2005, a combination of robust oil prices and a dynamic budget are serving to propel the construction sector forward, with a string of projects involving real estate, oil and gas and infrastructure development.

While government spending has always powered the Kingdom's growth, an unprecedented level of investment activity in the private sector is also playing a major role in driving the construction sector to new heights.

The 2005 fiscal budget has doubled the spending on new projects in Saudi Arabia, with allocations set at SR75.5 billion. The 2005 budget has made allocations for:

- the establishment and renovation of 1,420 schools, 22 colleges, four university hospitals, and 61 training colleges and centres;
- the construction and renovation of 420 primary healthcare centres in various parts of the Kingdom;
- the setting up of 23 new hospitals with a total of 3,150 beds;
- the construction of 6,700 kilometres of roads.

State spending for 2005 includes SR17.2 billion for new water, sewage and desalination projects and dams, SR15.6 billion for roads and ports, SR14.7 billion to build schools and universities and SR4.6 billion for new hospitals and healthcare centres. Allocations have also been made for new infrastructure projects in the industrial cities of Jubail and Yanbu. In addition, the Kingdom has just allocated SR2 billion from its budget surplus to build low-cost housing units for the poor and needy in various parts of Saudi Arabia.

The stimulative budget for 2005, combined with the Saudi Aramco expansion plans, major power and water projects, numerous planned IPOs and other capital market developments and robust construction and real estate sectors, is expected to contribute towards strong economic growth. In particular, two key initiatives made recently will provide a considerable boost to development in the Kingdom, namely:

- the go-ahead for projects worth SR30 billion (US$8 billion) in Makkah; and
- the launch of a major new industrial city in Al Jubail.

New construction industry developments

Development of Makkah and Madinah

In 2004, Crown Prince Abdullah gave the green light to massive development projects in Makkah, including a plan to expand part of the Grand Mosque, to enable the built prayer areas to accommodate 200,000 worshippers. In addition, the construction of hotels, residential towers and commercial centres was sanctioned. This initiative will provide a major impetus to the already-booming real estate construction market in Makkah and Madinah, currently witnessing the construction of such major projects as the SR12 billion Jabal Al Omar residential tower development and the Al Bait Towers, the first Islamic time-share property.

Saudi Landbridge project

Saudi Arabia is increasingly looking at the private sector to further its growth in a number of areas. A landmark scheme in this regard is the Saudi Landbridge project. This is the first ever rail link between the Red Sea and the Arabian Gulf. This project is believed to be one of the longest railway lines and the largest build-operate-transfer (BOT) project ever undertaken in the Middle East.

Al Jubail II

Under the second initiative, Saudi Arabia launched work on a new multi-billion riyal industrial city when Crown Prince Abdullah laid the cornerstone of Al Jubail II, to be built near the existing Al Jubail Industrial City on the Kingdom's east coast. The government has allocated SR14 billion towards the 16 square kilometre industrial zone and expects it to attract a further SR210 billion of private money over the next two decades.

Other new industrial developments

In addition, the Kingdom has laid out ambitious plans for establishing an exclusive industrial zone at Ras Al Zour situated about 60 kilometres north of Al Jubail. Work on the new zone will start with the setting up of a major aluminium and fertilizer export plant. The 640,000 tonnes capacity aluminium smelter and three million tonnes per year di-ammonium phosphate plant are estimated to cost SR22 billion.

Saudi Aramco and Saudi Basic Industries Corporation (SABIC) will continue to spearhead major growth in the oil and industrial sectors. Saudi Aramco moved forward in early 2005 on two new major projects, the Khursaniyah Oil and Gas Programme and the Hawiyah Natural Gas Liquids (NGL) Recovery Programme.

The estimated US$2–3 billion Khursaniyah Programme will develop oil and gas production facilities for the onshore Abu Hadriya, Fadhili and Khursaniyah oil fields near Jubail Industrial City, with capacity reaching 500,000 barrels of crude oil daily by the end of 2007. The Hawiyah NGL Recovery Programme will produce an additional 310,000 barrels of ethane and NGL products daily through the Hawiyah NGL plant near the Ghawar Field and an expansion of the Ju'aymah Gas Fractionation Plant not far from Ras Tanura. Italy's Snamprogetti was selected for the execution of the Khursaniyah production facilities, while a consortium of Bechtel Overseas of London and Technip of Rome was selected for the Khursaniyah gas plant.

Saudi Aramco also awarded five contracts to build the world's largest NGL processing plant at Hawiyah to recover ethane and NGL from approximately four bcf/d of sales gas. Aramco is also considering revamping its Ras Tanura refinery at a cost of around US$4–5 billion and adding a petrochemical complex. Other plans include setting up a 400,000 barrel-per-day export refinery in the Red Sea city of Yanbu.

SABIC, the Middle East's largest petrochemicals company, recently commenced work on a 150,000 tonne per year alpha olefins plant, which is being developed by its subsidiary the Jubail United Petrochemical Company (JUPC).

Many of SABIC's other subsidiaries have launched expansion plans. These include the Saudi Arabian Fertilizer Company (SAFCO), which is building its fourth fertilizer plant in Al Jubail Industrial City. Also, the Saudi Iron and Steel Company (HADEED) is doubling its capacity for flat products among other developments, and the Eastern Petrochemical Company (SHARQ) has launched its third expansion project.

Private sector power and water projects

Another major project that is expected to draw private sector participation is the US$1.5 billion Shoaiba independent water and power project (IWPP). The Water and Electricity Company (WEC) has opened bids to build, own and operate (BOO) the project. The 650 MW to 900 MW and 880,000 cubic metre-per-day IWPP is believed to be the world's first oil-fired IWPP and will be the world's largest private desalination plant when complete. The project is intended to form the template for WEC's future IWPP developments in the Kingdom.

Roads

The Ministry of Transport is currently working on 264 projects, with a total length of 10,728 kilometres and with a total value of SR11 billion. These include the recently commenced SR600 million Taif–Baha–Abha Road. The first phase covers the expansion of the road up to Baljurashi in the Baha region with a length of 200km.

Among the other major road projects that have recently been tendered are the Riyadh Ring Road (northern–western leg) and the upgrading of the 113km Taif to Abha road into a dual carriageway.

Real estate

A large number of private developers are spearheading projects in the Kingdom. While the focus of interest is undoubtedly the holy cities of Makkah and Madinah – where Makkah Construction and Development Company and Jabal Omar Development Company are leaders in the sector – Jeddah, Riyadh, and Dammam/Dhahran are also seeing a surge in real estate projects, including commercial, residential and shopping complexes.

In early 2005, Rikaz Developers, a leading real estate development company, launched its Royal Amwaj project in the Eastern Province. The company initiated its flagship project, City Fanar, early in 2004. Other major developers include Oula Development Company, Al Hokair Group and the Saudi Real Estate Development Company (SREDCO), which has a large number of ongoing projects in Jeddah.

Tourism

While Saudi Arabia's primary focus in the tourism sector has traditionally been on catering to the domestic tourist and providing family-oriented recreational opportunities, the Kingdom has drawn up tourism projects worth SR50 billion. The Supreme Commission for Tourism (SCT), which is promoting this sector, intends to carry out a number of projects on the Red Sea coast. Apart from coastal resorts on the Red Sea, the government also plans tourist centres in the Kingdom's rural areas to ensure continuous development of urban and rural areas.

A large number of investment opportunities are being opened up for private participation, including the Higher Commission for Arriyadh Development's Thumamah Park and Saleh Al Doribe Group's Al Bundoquiya Island project.

Several hotel properties are taking shape in the Kingdom – the highest density being in Makkah – which will be managed by some of the leading hotel chains in the world. A showpiece hotel set to open later this year is the Hilton Palace (Qasr Al Sharq), which will be the only seven-star luxury property in Saudi Arabia.

Current construction projects

Examples of major construction projects that were in the planning and implementation stages in the Kingdom in 2004/2005 include the following:

- the Jebel Omar Complex, Makkah, consisting of 11 high-rise residential towers valued at US$0.53 billion;
- the General Organization for Social Insurance Granada Shopping Centre Project, Riyadh, valued at US$107 million;
- the Arcade Commercial Centre, Riyadh, valued at US$13.9 million;
- the Al Moqren Trading complex in Riyadh, valued at US$37.3 million;
- at King Abdulaziz International Airport, Jeddah: the construction of two new terminals for domestic and international flights and additional parking facilities, valued at SR3.80 billion (US$1.01 billion);
- the east–west railway expansion: a commercial line connecting the Red Sea and Gulf coasts and rail links connecting Jeddah to the Dammam–Riyadh line and a line linking Jeddah to Makkah and Madinah;
- minerals railways for the transportation of phosphate and bauxite from Al Jalamid in the North to processing facilities at Al Jubail via Riyadh and Dammam;
- power projects valued at US$1.60 billion, with a construction component of US$242 million, including Shouaiba Phase II comprising three 350 MW turbines;

- the Zamzam Tower residential building in Makkah, comprising 31 floors with 1,457 residential units at a cost of US$389 million;
- Ministry of Education schools building contracts for 134 schools – in Riyadh (46), Makkah (38), Northern Border (29), Madinah and Al Qassim (21) at a total cost of US$290 million;
- four dams in the Makkah area at a combined cost of US$191 million.

Further information

For construction industry research information see the National Commercial Bank's *Market Review and Outlook* publication. Copies of reports can be obtained by visiting www.alahli.com.

ASA Consulting has conducted a number of construction industry-related market studies in Saudi Arabia and other Middle East countries including, most recently, a study of utilization of thermal energy storage air conditioning systems in the Saudi construction industry (2005). For further information concerning Anthony Shoult and the experience and activities of ASA Consulting please contact asaconsult@btinternet.com.

7.8

The Medical and Healthcare Sector

Anthony Shoult, ASA Consulting[1]

Introduction

The Saudi health sector is facing new challenges as the government continues to finance health services for a rapidly growing population of over 23 million, which is growing at three per cent a year. Saudi Arabia is the largest market for medical equipment and healthcare products in the Gulf, with the Ministry of Health (MOH) the largest buyer, representing around 60 per cent of sales. In its 2003 budget, the Saudi government allocated US$6.2 billion for health and social care. In the same year, the Saudi Ministry of Health's expenditure budget stood at US$4 billion.

While healthcare has traditionally been provided by the MOH, it is increasingly being shared with other public and private agencies. In 2001, the total number of hospitals in the Saudi health sector stood at 320 (45,700 beds). Of these, the MOH accounted for 60 per cent of beds, while the private sector accounted for 28 per cent. The remaining 12 per cent of beds is accounted for by specialist government agencies that operate separate hospitals for their employees. These include the Ministry of Defence and Aviation (MODA), the National Guard, the Ministry of Interior and King Faisal Specialist Hospital and Research Centre (KFSH).

The growing need for medical staff at all levels has meant that local medical training programmes have not been able to keep up with demand. The Kingdom's health services are, therefore, heavily dependent on expatriates, who provide around 80 per cent of physicians and nurses.

---

[1] Sources of information include National Commercial Bank (NCB) and UK Trade & Investment.

The rapidly increasing demand for health services has created renewed concerns for the government. In order to reduce the burden on their budget, the MOH has privatized some government hospitals, while encouraging and creating more opportunities for private sector participation in the health sector in general.

In 1999, the Saudi government passed a number of regulations restricting resident expatriate access to public hospitals, with the intention of passing on the cost to private insurance companies in the form of new cooperative medical insurance. Medical insurance for the estimated six million expatriates in the Kingdom has now been introduced, with a number of foreign and local insurance companies providing coverage.

Healthcare provision

Healthcare in Saudi Arabia is under the general policy control of the MOH. The delivery of healthcare is provided by state-owned facilities on the one hand and by the private sector on the other.

The MOH is not the sole provider of healthcare and there are a number of other ministries, commissions and quasi-governmental bodies that also provide healthcare services through their own facilities, as follows:

- MOH hospitals;
- other government agency hospitals including:
  - Ministry of Defence and Aviation (MODA);
  - National Guard;
  - Ministry of Interior;
  - Royal Commission for Jubail and Yanbu;
- Ministry of Education;
- private sector hospitals.

MOH and other government agency hospitals

The state provides the bulk of its healthcare through units of the MOH; however, the National Guard, the MODA and the Ministry of Interior provide primary, secondary and advanced levels of healthcare for their employees and segments of the general population. The

General Organization for Social Insurance (GOSI) also provides treatment for a specialized clientele.

In addition to these, the Red Crescent Society provides emergency services and assists pilgrims during the *Hajj*. Specialist hospitals, including those provided by the Royal Commission and those associated with the universities have a high degree of autonomy from the MOH. The Royal Commission for Jubail and Yanbu provides health facilities for employees of these two industrial cities. The Ministry of Education provides medical coverage through boy's schools, and the Presidency of Girls Education through girl's schools.

Thus, the organizational structure of state healthcare facilities is fragmented and not wholly under the direct operational control of the MOH. Standards vary widely within the state system, tending to be lowest in some MOH outlets and highest in outlets of the National Guard, MODA, the university hospitals and the Royal Commission for Jubail and Yanbu.

MOH hospitals

The MOH is the mainstream provider of healthcare to the population of Saudi Arabia, operating a primary healthcare network comprising hospitals and primary healthcare centres throughout the Kingdom. The first level of healthcare is provided by Primary Healthcare Centres (PHCs) of which, in 2000, there were approximately 1,750 distributed throughout 20 MOH regions. PHCs refer four per cent of patients to some 190 MOH hospitals, comprising over 28,000 beds located throughout the Kingdom.

All of the Saudi population has access to medical services through the Saudi primary healthcare network, which is funded in full by the Saudi government through its health budget. Through the primary healthcare network, the MOH is responsible for ensuring that Saudi citizens can obtain primary and further medical care anywhere in the Kingdom. However, expatriates are not normally eligible for treatment in MOH hospitals.

Other government-funded hospitals

Other government-funded hospitals include the following:

- teaching hospitals, such as King Khalid University Hospital (KKUHR), Riyadh;
- military and security hospitals, such as the Armed Forces Hospital, Riyadh, Security Forces Hospital and National Guard Hospital;
- specialist hospitals, such as King Faisal Specialist Hospital and King Khalid Eye Hospital;

- quasi-governmental hospitals, such as those operated by the GOSI, Saudi Aramco and the Royal Commission for Jubail and Yanbu.

Approximately 40 government-funded hospitals outside the MOH comprised some 9,500 beds in 2001. The leading institutions in this group include Riyadh Armed Services (Military) Hospital, King Faisal Specialist Hospital, King Khalid University Hospital and King Fahad National Guard Hospital in Riyadh, King Fahad Armed Forces Hospital, King Khaled National Guard Hospital and King Abdulaziz University Hospital in Jeddah and King Fahad Military Medical Complex and King Fahad University Hospital in the Eastern Province.

Private hospitals

Approximately 90 Saudi private hospitals comprised approximately 10,600 beds in 2001. The private sector is becoming increasingly important in comparison with the total government sector, now accounting for over 22 per cent of all hospital beds in the Kingdom.

The rapid growth of the private sector (up from 16 per cent of all Saudi hospital beds in 1994/95) is driven by the following factors:

- Saudi's requirement for a higher standard of medical services;
- demand by expatriates who are not eligible for treatment in MOH and other government sector hospitals.

The private healthcare sector has grown from a nucleus of single doctor clinics into a network of specialist hospitals and multi-doctor clinics. The state, now wary of ever increasing healthcare costs, is encouraging the private sector to provide medical insurance and services to foreigners and an increasing proportion of Saudis.

Major organizations, such as Saudi Aramco and Saudi Arabian Airlines (SAUDIA), provide medical services to employees, which they contract out to the private hospitals. Saudi Aramco has entered into direct five-year agreements with five private hospitals in Jeddah and three private hospitals in Riyadh to treat its staff, thus bypassing the insurance companies. Private hospitals are having to increase the specialist medical services they provide in order to meet the increasing needs of the population and of companies like Saudi Aramco and SAUDIA.

Leading Saudi private hospitals include Dallah and Al Hammadi Hospitals in Riyadh, Saudi German, Bugshan and Dr Sulaiman Fakeih Hospitals in Jeddah, Al Salamah Hospital in Al-Khobar and Saad Medical Centre in Dammam.

Local manufacturing of pharmaceuticals

Currently, the local manufacturers of pharmaceuticals are involved mainly in production of generic expired patent medicines. In 2000, local manufacturers accounted for less than 20 per cent of Saudi market demand.

GlaxoSmithKline Saudi Arabia of Jeddah was established in 1997, under the Al-Yamamah Economic Offset Programme, as a joint venture with Banaja and is now one of the largest pharmaceutical companies in Saudi Arabia. The range of products manufactured and marketed include Zantac, Ventolin, Becotide, Becloforte, Flixonase, Fortum, Zinnat, Zinacef, Betnovate, Dermovate, Eumovate, Eltroxin and Imigran. The therapeutic areas covered include respiratory, bacterial infections, viral infections, CNS disorders, metabolic, gastrointestinal, vaccines, cancer, dermatology, anesthesia, rhinitis and analgesics. Sales of GlaxoSmithKline Saudi Arabia were reported to be over US$125 million in 2001. The company is distributing its products through a number of local distributors, including Saudi Import Company (Banaja) (Glaxo, Allen & Hanbury's), SITCO Pharma (Wellcome, SKF & Sterling Health), Al-Haya Medical Co. (Beecham) and Al-Naghy Brothers (SB).

Saudi Pharmaceutical Industries and Medical Appliances Corporation (SPIMACO) is the other large pharmaceutical firm in Saudi Arabia. This company was established in 1986 and its main manufacturing facility is the Al-Qassim Pharmaceutical Plant, located 320 kilometres north of Riyadh. This plant has facilities for liquid and oral solids, cream and ointment, penicillin and aseptic manufacturing. Products include antibiotics (Zimax), anti-acids (Proton), steroid creams (Cortimax), anti-diabetic agents (Formit) and analgesics (Sapofen).

Pharmaceutical Solutions Industries (PSI) commenced production in Jeddah in 1982 as a subsidiary of Fresenius AG of Germany. The company produces some 30 million units of intravenous solutions and related products.

Imports of pharmaceuticals

The Saudi pharmaceutical industry relies mostly on imported prescription drugs and medicines (85 per cent), with local producers supplying the remaining requirements. In 2001, imports of drugs and medicines were at the level of approximately SR3.5 billion (US$0.93 billion). Imports are dominated by European manufacturers, which account for some 70 per cent of the imported medicines market.

Imported pharmaceuticals fall in to two categories, namely, retail products for pharmacies and non-retail products for private and government hospitals. At present, the main types of imported medicines are penicillin (33 per cent), hormones (14 per cent) and vitamins (7 per cent).

Purchasing of healthcare and medical products

MOH purchasing

The MOH purchases medical supplies by two methods, namely:

- competitive tendering through the Gulf Cooperation Council (GCC) annual tender;
- direct MOH tenders.

Secretariat Gulf-wide Purchasing Agreement (SGH)
The GCC created the Gulf tender in order to reduce the overall cost of medical supplies by consolidating individual country demand. The tender is placed on an annual basis and the Saudi MOH share is estimated to be at least 80 per cent. The tender is estimated to account for 70 to 80 per cent of the MOH's demand for medical supplies.

MOH direct tenders
Demand not covered by the GCC tender process is accommodated by the MOH's issue of direct tenders. This practice can now account for up to 20 to 30 per cent of the MOH's total demand. The MOH prefers to place direct tenders with local formulators, if the products are available. Local manufacturers' agents representing the large international players also participate in MOH direct tenders.

Other government institution purchasing

Other government hospitals have a significant degree of purchasing independence, with medical supplies acquired mainly by direct tendering and local purchase orders. They also engage in competitive tendering through the appropriate government body. For example, the Riyadh Armed Forces (Military) Hospital participates in the MODA Medical Service Department tendering process. Some institutions, such as Riyadh Kharj Hospital, King Saud University Hospital and National Guard King Khaled Hospital, also engage in the Gulf-wide tendering process to procure a percentage of their requirements of medical supplies.

Private hospital purchasing

In general, private hospitals obtain their medical supplies by direct purchase from the local manufacturers' agents at wholesale prices or slightly less. Large private hospitals have annual tenders for their medical supply requirements.

The future of Saudi healthcare

With a rapidly increasing population, together with a high bed dependency ratio, investment by both government and the private sector is required to meet the rapidly growing demand for medical care in Saudi Arabia. In particular, educational health facilities are in need of upgrading and expansion.

The government has established the Higher Council for Health with a brief to restructure the health sector. The council, which includes representatives from private hospitals and foreign agencies, aims to develop strategic proposals to improve the efficiency of the Kingdom's health sector. Suggestions include a privatization scheme for a number of public hospitals.

As part of the government's efforts to diversify its sources of revenue to finance the growing demand for health services, selected government-run specialist institutions have started to provide treatment for patients holding health insurance. For example, the King Faisal Specialist Hospital in Jeddah and the King Khaled Specialist Eye Hospital in Riyadh are now both used by insurance holders.

Despite competition from specialist government hospitals, opportunities for private investment in health remain very attractive, especially in the major cities where the bed dependency ratio exceeds national averages and where population growth is concentrated. With the population growing by 2.75 per cent annually, or 600,000, the Saudi health sector requires at least six new 200-bed hospitals per year just to keep up.

Assuming that the Saudi government shares the necessary incremental investment with the private sector, then there are opportunities for new private hospitals in the most populated cities, Riyadh, Jeddah and Dammam/Al-Khobar, which account for two thirds of the Saudi population.

Further information

For further information concerning Saudi healthcare and medical products manufacturers see the following:

- GlaxoSmithKline Saudi Arabia (www.glaxowellcome.com.sa);
- Saudi Pharmaceutical Industries & Medical Appliances (SPIMACO) (www.spimaco.com.sa).

ASA Consulting has conducted a number of healthcare and medical industry-related market and feasibility studies in Saudi Arabia including a market, techno-economic and financial feasibility study for the establishment of an intravenous solutions manufacturing facility (2001). For further information concerning Anthony Shoult and the experience and activities of ASA Consulting in the health and medical sector please contact asaconsult@btinternet.com.

7.9

Telecommunications and Information Technology

Anthony Shoult, ASA Consulting[1]

Introduction

Saudi Arabia's telecommunications and information technology sector is one of the largest and fastest growing in the Middle East. A major investment has been made in recent years in developing a modern telecommunications and IT infrastructure capable of supporting e-commerce and the demands of a growing information conscious society.

Saudi Arabia is committed to developing an information-based economy. The government announced in November 2002 that the Saudi Computer Society would formulate a five-year national information technology plan by the end of 2003, as part of a strategy to develop the IT sector. The main objectives of the plan are to support the economy by establishing and empowering the IT industry and stimulating activities such as e-commerce and distance work.

Other goals are to promote a national IT culture through projects of e-education, e-government and distance medicine; educate and train national individuals in IT fields; protect Arabian and Islamic culture in the digital world; raise productivity and efficiency in the most cost-effective manner and support national security through judicious investment in the IT sector.

In 2005, the Saudi Information and Communications Technology (ICT) market is estimated by industry sources at just under US$5 billion. This comprises computer equipment (22 per cent), software

---

[1] Sources of information include UK Trade & Investment and US-Saudi Arabian Business Council.

(28 per cent), IT services (34 per cent) and data communications (16 per cent).

Growth of information technology has been projected at in excess of eight per cent in recent years, with the fastest growing segment being data communications, driven by developments related to the internet and mobile networks.

Telecommunications

The expansion and subsequent privatization of telephone services have been important objectives in Saudi Arabia's five-year development plans, with particular emphasis placed on the telecommunications sector during the Seventh Development Plan (2000–05). The plan called for increasing line density rates from 10 lines per 100 people in 1996 to 25 lines per 100 people by 2005. By 2003, line density rates were in excess of 15.5 lines per 100 people, with a 450,000 fixed line expansion being carried out by four telecommunications companies.

The expansion of telecommunications services began in 1994 with the Telephone Expansion Project (TEP-6), awarded to Lucent Technologies. In 2003, the Kingdom completed an expansion of its GSM network, which doubled capacity of the network to 5.8 million lines.

In 1998, Saudi Arabia began the privatization process by passing control of telecommunications services to a joint stock company called the Saudi Telecom Company (STC). With a starting capital of over SR12 billion, STC was formed as a major holding company that will eventually consist of several subsidiaries. In January 2003, STC sold 60 million shares, or 30 per cent of the company, through an initial public offering (IPO) raising nearly US$4 billion for the Saudi government.

Fixed network

In 2003, the Kingdom operated more than 3.5 million telephone lines, representing a 62 per cent increase from 1998. By the end of 2004, STC had targeted to provide some 12 million fixed and mobile phone connections. The increase in capacity has been the result of the advancement in telecommunications technology as well as pressures of a rapidly expanding Saudi population.

Saudi Arabia began updating its telephone lines from analog to state-of-the-art digital lines in the mid-1990s. Lucent Technologies, under the US$4 billion TEP-6 project, installed digital telephone lines in the Kingdom, effectively doubling the existing phone lines. Similar projects have followed, resulting in a four million line expansion of the fixed system. The new lines have a standard industry capacity of

65,000 bits per second (bps), and enable subscribers to access the internet.

Additional projects include the TEP-7 project awarded to Siemens and Lucent Technologies, involving the installation of 1.1 million fixed lines, a further 2.2 million fixed lines, 900 switches, long haul fibre optic connections, wireless loop systems, intelligent networks and microwave transmission systems.

The backbone of the Saudi Arabia cable network consists of 76,700km of cabling, including 16,700km of fibre optic cable. In addition, Saudi Arabia is a member of SEA-ME-WE submarine coaxial cable, complementing the country's international communications capabilities.

Mobile network

The introduction of mobile phones has dramatically altered the telecommunications market in Saudi Arabia. Since 1994, when the Kingdom launched the Global System for Mobiles (GSM), known locally as 'Al-Jawal', Ericsson, Nokia and Lucent have been involved in the transformation of the Kingdom's mobile infrastructure.

By April 2003, the number of mobile telephone subscribers had reached 5.8 million, more than double the amount in 2001. Despite this dramatic rise in subscribers, Saudi Arabia still maintains the lowest number of fixed and mobile lines in the GCC, with market penetration of 22 per cent. However, recent industry forecasts suggest that revenues in the Kingdom's GSM market are set to rise from US$3.4 billion in 2002 to US$7.9 billion by 2007. This is, in part, due to the privatization of STC and to increased competition in the market.

In recent years, the Kingdom has attempted to meet increased demand by rolling out a new cellular GSM licence. This was awarded, in late 2004, to the Etisalat-led consortium and this has now become the second GSM service provider in the Kingdom.

Internet and data services

The internet has been available in the Kingdom since February 1999. King Abdul Aziz City for Science and Technology (KACST) was responsible for the management of the Kingdom's initial internet services until January 2003 when the Saudi Telecommunications and Information Technology Commission (STITC) took over all regulatory control.

There are currently over 20 operational ISPs providing internet access to an estimated 4.5 million users, with an internet penetration of 17.5 per cent compared to an estimated Arab world average of eight per cent penetration. The five largest ISPs control 65 per cent of the subscriber market, with the trend having been for the smaller ISPs to merge into large companies. The Saudi Network Information Centre (SaudiNIC) is responsible for the administration of the domain name space for the country code of Saudi Arabia.

The average bandwidth for ISPs is 6mbps. A dedicated data network system is being installed to improve the capacity of the network. Monthly subscription fees range between US$13 and US$75, depending on limited or unlimited usage.

In July 2001, STC introduced asymmetric digital subscriber lines (ADSL) services to the Kingdom, significantly reducing the cost of internet services. STC is also expanding digital subscriber line (DSL) services to cover Jeddah, Makkah, Taif and Dammam. The new service enables subscribers to contact ISPs at a high speed without the need for special connections.

Computer hardware and software

With the rise in popularity of information technology, Saudi Arabia has developed a significant market for networking and related software as well as for computer hardware and software products. In 2003, there were over three million PCs in the Kingdom, representing 13.7 per 100 inhabitants. Growth is being driven by the increased use of the internet and e-commerce as well as the growing use of Voice Over Internet Protocol for long distance calls.

The top international players are all represented in the market, including HP, Compaq, IBM, Dell and Apple. In 2003, HP was in the lead across all personal systems products including desktops, notebooks and tablets. With the introduction of more sophisticated computer systems, demand is expected to increase for products such as Unix-based systems, Net Ware and NT.

In 2003, Dell installed its largest high-performance computing cluster in the region at Saudi Aramco in order to accelerate its oil and gas exploration programme.

In 2000, the Microsoft Corporation and Intel participated with the Al-Faisaliah Group of Riyadh in the country's first factory to fully manufacture computers. The ZAI computer facility has a capacity to assemble 15,000 units a year.

Most of the key players in software and integration are active in the Kingdom. Oracle is close to the e-government agenda and Microsoft has a US$800 million project to modernize the education sector. Also, in late 2002, Microsoft was awarded a contract by the Ministry of Interior to provide its .NET software to the ministry.

Saudi Aramco has moved its systems to SAP and is developing a network storage infrastructure that will allow Saudi Aramco's Exploration & Petroleum Engineering Centre to protect, manage and analyse exploration and field development activities. EMC, IBM and Sun Microsystems all maintain a strong presence across both the public and private sectors.

E-commerce

Business via e-commerce is practised in the Kingdom. However the lack of regulations and security measures, among other things, continue to limit its use. The government and various agencies are now addressing the issues towards the establishment of a robust e-commerce structure.

Saudi Arabia's business-to-business (B2B) and business-to-consumer (B2C) e-commerce are both expected to see major growth, with levels in 2005 projected at US$8 billion for B2B e-commerce and US$0.5 billion for B2C e-commerce. Projected annual rates of growth are extremely high, ranging from 40 per cent for B2C e-commerce to 75 per cent for B2B e-commerce.

Several major international companies require in-Kingdom dealers and distributors to use the internet for ordering through their B2B private exchanges. The two largest Saudi corporations, Saudi Aramco and Saudi Arabian Basic Industries Corporation (SABIC), now require their local suppliers to deal with them on the internet.

Saudi Aramco, which holds more than one million items on its supplier catalogue, is encouraging its partners and suppliers to join B2B exchange. The company has 900 partner agreements in place and has a target of 1,200 to transfer to a full e-commerce process. SABIC is also following a B2B exchange strategy. Between them, these important exchange-based supply chain initiatives are seen as acting as a powerful incentive for Saudi companies to become very quickly e-capable in business-to-business dealings.

In June 2004, Saudi Arabian Airlines launched its e-business centre, which uses IBM's Websphere technology to allow the development, deployment and hosting of the airline's e-business solutions, while providing integration with its existing core enterprise systems and applications.

The new regulatory framework

In May 2001, Saudi Arabia approved a bill liberalizing the telecommunications sector and opening up the sector to foreign investment and competition. The Saudi Cabinet passed new laws on the regulation of the sale of stakes in the telecommunications sector to the private sector, and created the Saudi Communications Commission (SCC), which was renamed the Saudi Telecommunications and Information Technology Commission (STITC) in April 2003. This coincided with the renaming of the Ministry of Post, Telegraph and Telephone (PTT) as the Ministry of Telecommunications and Information Technology.

The STITC is responsible for granting licences to private investors, and for regulating telephone and internet services as well as other media.

In mid-2003, the STITC issued new by-laws that will provide for the deregulation of the Saudi telecommunications sector. The new by-laws cover issues such as licensing, interconnectivity, tariffs, anti-trust regulations and standards for telecommunications equipment. By 2005, the STITC will supervise a step-by-step liberalization of the data and GSM sectors, and then the fixed line network. The plan provides for one in three Saudis to own a mobile phone by 2006. The STITC has initiated the process of introducing competition into the Saudi market by tendering new GSM, data and VSAT licences.

E-commerce

A large number of existing laws (up to 30) need to be revised in order to support the mechanics of e-commerce in the Kingdom. The new regulations will be based on guidelines set out by the United Nations Commission on International Trade Law (UNCITRAL).

The Ministry of Finance and the Saudi Arabian Monetary Agency (SAMA) are responsible for the development of the new regulatory framework. New laws and changes to legislation will mirror other countries in addressing authentication, center of access/security, litigation and validation of data. Much like in Europe, a principal feature of the new regulations will involve the recognition of electronic signatures. Other provisions relate to the security of financial transactions, confidentiality of operations and systems security.

The future of online financial services in the Kingdom is the responsibility of SAMA and this agency is overseeing five projects under the control of its e-Working Group. These are PKI infrastructure, the provision of common route certificate for the financial sector, building a secure facility to host all certificates; e-payment and business-to-business (B2B) infrastructure development; and a new payment system to support business-to-consumer (B2C) transactions.

Further information

For further information concerning Saudi telecommunications and information technology sector see the following:

- Saudi Telecom Company (STC) (www.stc.com.sa);
- King Abdul Aziz City for Science & Technology (KACST) (www.kacst.edu.sa);
- Saudi Communications and Information Technology Commission (www.citc.gov.sa/citc).

7.10

Education and Training

Anthony Shoult, ASA Consulting[1]

Introduction

With its rapidly growing population estimated to reach 39 million by 2020, Saudi Arabia needs to find work for its rapidly growing number of unemployed graduates. The answers to the problem are seen in better education and training to increase the number of suitably qualified graduates.

A measure of the Saudi government's substantial commitment to this sector is the allocation of nearly 25 per cent of the total budget for fiscal 2005 for human resource development, encompassing education and vocational training, an amount totalling almost US$18.7 billion. The Kingdom's budgetary provision for education in 2005 included increased funding for three new universities, the construction of 1,420 schools, 10 technical colleges and 32 vocational training centres, and an increased budget for the General Organization for Technical Education and Vocational Training (GOTEVOT).

The Kingdom's educational system now comprises some 28,000 schools, eight universities, over 200 colleges and other educational and training institutions. The Saudi educational system provides free education, books and health services to some five million students, one in every four people in the Kingdom, from kindergarten through to university and from adult education to vocational training. An estimated five million students are enrolled in the Kingdom's education system.

In 2001, Saudi Arabia implemented measures to improve the quality of education. One is a school computer project that seeks to provide computers to every student and also to establish a network that connects all schools and universities to facilitate teaching and research. Implemented with the active support and participation of the private

---

[1] Sources of information include UK Trade & Investment, Hay Management Consultants and the Saudi Arabian Information Service.

sector, the project also provides computer training for more than 100,000 teachers.

The education and training market in the Kingdom consists of a mix of public and private sector interests, but given the population factors that prevail, the government is increasingly looking to the private sector to provide appropriate education to young Saudis.

Private sector education covers schools, with separate institutions for Saudi and expatriate children, technical colleges and institutions, private academies and private universities.

The United States, Canada and Australia all have a strong presence in the Saudi education and training market, with the United States, in particular, enjoying strong education links.

General education

The current objectives of Saudi educational policy are that education becomes more efficient, meets the religious, economic and social needs of the country, and eradicates illiteracy among Saudi adults.

General education in the Kingdom consists of kindergarten, six years of primary school and three years each of intermediate and high school. The Ministry of Education sets overall standards for the country's educational system, whether in government schools or private institutions, and also oversees special education for the handicapped.

After elementary education, students can attend either high schools offering programmes in both the arts and sciences, or vocational schools. The progress of students through high school is determined by comprehensive exams conducted twice a year and supervised by the Ministry of Education.

The Kingdom's ratio of 12.5 students to every teacher is one of the lowest in the world. The government is working to improve educational standards by raising the quality of teacher training programmes, improving standards for evaluation of students and increasing the use of educational technology, principally by introducing computer science at the secondary level. In 2000, the Ministry launched a project to make computers available in all classrooms.

The school curriculum is designed with a view to preparing students for the future. In grade school, students take nine to 11 subjects in the arts and sciences, and English is taught as a second language starting in the fifth grade. High school students are taught calculus, physics, chemistry, biology, psychology and sociology, in courses that compare with those in first year colleges abroad.

During the 2001/02 academic year, the Saudi Ministry of Education operated over 11,300 primary, intermediate and secondary schools for boys, enrolling 1.19 million students. There were also more than

1.64 million girls in 16,600 schools previously run by the General Presidency for Girls' Education, which are now under the jurisdiction of the Ministry of Education. The number of teachers employed in both boys and girls schools in 2001/02 was approximately 335,000.

Another 1.5 million boys and girls are enrolled in private schools that are run under the supervision and guidelines of the Ministry of Education.

As part of its efforts to make education available to Saudi students residing abroad, the Kingdom has, over the past two decades, established educational institutions throughout the world. Overseas, there are 16 academies (in the United States, the UK, Germany, Russia, France, Spain, Indonesia, Malaysia, Austria, Turkey, Morocco and Djibouti) that cater to the educational needs of Saudi, Arab and Muslim students.

A major evolution of the Saudi educational system occurred in 2002, when King Fahd issued a Royal Decree directing that the General Presidency for Girls' Education be fully merged into the Ministry of Education, which traditionally had dealt only with the schooling of boys.

Higher education

The first modern university was established in Riyadh in 1957. Now known as King Saud University, the complex is the largest in the country and has some 30,000 students. By 2002, more than half a million students were enrolled in higher education in Saudi Arabia. There are eight universities, with a total of 72 university colleges, offering more than 400 degree courses (see Table 7.10.1).

In June 2004, King Fahd approved plans to create three new universities from existing university branches in Qasim, Taif and Madinah. Regional branches of Imam Muhammad ibn Saud Islamic University (IMSIU) and King Saud University will be merged to form the new Qasim University. Branches of IMSIU and King Abdul Aziz University in Madinah will be merged to form Taiba University, while the branch of Umm Al-Qura University in Taif will form the nucleus of the new Taif University.

There are also well over 200 colleges in the Kingdom, of which some 70 are for girls, offering post-secondary education. Plans are under way for four more community colleges, one technical institute, and a number of non-profit making private colleges, of which there are already six, in Jeddah, Riyadh, Abha and Al-Baha. In the medical institutes alone, there are more than 66,000 students.

Table 7.10.1 Saudi Arabian Universities*

University	Location	Founded	Website
King Saud University	Riyadh	1957 (1377/77 AH)	www.ksu.edu.sa
Islamic University	Madinah	1961 (1380/81 AH)	www.iu.edu.sa
King Abdul Aziz University	Jeddah	1967 (1386/87 AH)	www.kaau.edu.sa
Imam Muhammad bin Saud Islamic University (IMSIU)	Riyadh	1953 (1372/73 AH)	www.imamu.edu.sa
King Faisal University	Dammam and Hofuf	1975 (1395 AH)	www.kfu.edu.sa
King Fahd University of Petroleum and Minerals	Dhahran	1963 (1382/83 AH)	www.kfupm.edu.sa
Umm Al-Qura University	Makkah	1979 (1399/1400 AH)	www.uqu.edu.sa
King Khaled bin Abdul Aziz University	Abha	1988	www.kku.edu.sa

* Three new universities are to be established at Al Madinah, Al Qasim and Al Taif

In 2003, 38 new colleges opened in various parts of the country, focusing on specializations required by the job market and each able to admit some 4,000 students. Approximately 20 of the new institutions are owned and operated by the private sector.

In 2004, the government announced the setting up a further 36 private colleges expected to attract SR3 billion in investment. These are to be located in Riyadh, Jeddah, Tabuk, Hail, the Eastern Province, Buraidah, Madinah, Qassim and Taif.

Also in 2004, the government announced the setting up of two new private universities, one of which is an affiliate of Riyadh Charitable Foundation for Sciences, which owns Prince Sultan Private College for Boys and Prince Sultan Private College for Girls in Riyadh, as well as Prince Sultan Private College for Dentistry in Riyadh. The other, Dar Al-Faisal, is affiliated with the King Faisal Charitable Foundation that owns Effat College in Jeddah and Prince Sultan College for Tourism and Hotel Management in Abha.

In 2002, the Majlis Al-Shura (Consultative Council) called on the Higher Education Council to prepare a long-term plan for university education for at least 25 years, defining its goals, quality requirements and financial sources. The Council also called for opening new specializations for girls at universities and colleges. The recommendations were made after the Council completed studies that indicated the education sector will need an annual budget allocation of some SR90 billion by the year 2020, when the Kingdom's population is expected to reach in excess of 30 million and the number of students will exceed eight million.

Special and adult education

The Special Education Department of the Ministry of Education operates schools for the blind, deaf, and the physically and mentally handicapped. By 2002, there were 180 such schools in the Kingdom, with more than 8,000 students and 2,000 teachers.

Several institutes for handicapped children have been established and more are under construction. Other institutes care for older handicapped people. The special schools are part of the Kingdom's effort to encourage every individual to reach his or her full potential.

Another important sector of Saudi Arabia's educational programme is adult education. In isolated rural areas, the government conducts intensive three-month adult education courses during the summer. The Kingdom's literacy rate is 90.9 per cent for men and 70.2 per cent for women. The Ministry of Education now runs about 2,200 adult education centres for male students and more than 2,000 for female students, which enrol a total of 110,000 students.

National system for joint training (Saudiization)

In common with all Gulf countries, Saudi Arabia has a growing issue in finding beneficial employment for the increasing number of young people coming into the labour market. With the largest population of nationals and some 60 per cent of this population under 25 years of age, the issue is more pressing for the Kingdom than for any other country in the Gulf region.

At present approximately one-third of the country's 25 million inhabitants are foreigners. Reducing dependence on foreign labour and increasing the numbers of Saudi nationals in all types of jobs has been on the agenda for some time, but in recent years the government has been showing increasing determination to make the programme work.

After many years of discussion on this issue, in 1996 the government introduced a requirement for all businesses to set a target to increase the numbers of Saudi nationals in the workforce by five per cent compound per annum. This requirement is now being rigorously monitored and has been backed up by the stipulation of a number of penalties for companies that fail to meet their targets, including refusal of applications for new expatriate employment visas, and being barred from competing for government contracts.

In the last three years, there are clear signs of these sanctions being enacted. Companies failing to meet their targets are finding it increasingly difficult to secure new visas for foreign employees and there is a growing list of occupational groups for which visas for foreign employees will not be issued, except, perhaps, in very exceptional circumstances. Even outside these groups, applications for visas for foreign workers are being scrutinized increasingly rigorously.

Alongside the policy of Saudiization there has been a significant expansion in training programmes to equip young nationals coming into the labour market to secure jobs and replace skill sets historically sourced from abroad, and it is gratifying to see the increased numbers of nationals working successfully in a wide range of organizations.

Far-sighted organizations are now moving to select the best talent from the local market and establish comprehensive training and career development programmes to ensure nationals are equipped with the skills they need to be successful.

While large sums are now being invested in training, much of this has gone on sending individuals on expensive broad-based courses overseas. It has become increasingly apparent that the training of broad-based employees needs to be much more focused on addressing specific gaps between an individual's present capabilities (both vocational knowledge and skills and behavioural competencies) and the requirements of their present job and identified likely career path.

A number of initiatives are now emerging to provide high-quality, focused training within the Kingdom, both in companies and through bodies such as the Chambers of Commerce. Forward-thinking organizations are also talking actively of opening these in-house training facilities to staff from other organizations

Vocational training

To help further train technicians and workers to fill the many positions available in factories, workshops and commercial enterprises now operating in the Kingdom, the Saudi government has placed special emphasis on technical and administrative training as an essential sector of education. These facilities, as well as private training centres supported by the government, turn out thousands of graduates in technical and mechanical sciences, healthcare, agriculture, teaching and other areas every year, who are steadily filling positions at industrial, agricultural and social institutions throughout the country.

The General Organization for Technical Education and Vocational Training (GOTEVT), along with the Ministry of Labour and Social Affairs, operates most of the Kingdom's vocational training centres and higher institutes of technical education, while other government agencies run institutes or training centres in their particular specialties.

The Royal Technical Institute in Riyadh, the Hofuf Technical Training School, and centres in Jeddah, Madinah, Abha, Taif, Unaizah, Dammam and other cities, train thousands of young Saudis every year in a variety of fields, including machine tooling, metalworking, electromechanics, auto mechanics, electronics and maintenance of industrial machinery.

Another important institution, designed to address the country's shortage of administrative personnel, is the Institute for Public Administration, established in Riyadh in 1961 as a semi-independent public agency. The institute provides basic as well as in-service training for civil servants, carries out research, and assists government agencies in administration, communication and computer sciences. Today, it has branches in Dammam and Jeddah, and a special branch in Riyadh for training women. It offers students courses in administration, law, accounting, computer science, maintenance, personnel management, secretarial skills and management planning.

General Organization for Technical Education & Vocational Training (GOTEVOT)

The General Organization for Technical Education and Vocational Training (GOTEVOT), based in Riyadh, plays a crucial role in the development of the Kingdom's national workforce. It is in charge of the autonomous Technical and Vocational Education and Training (TVET) system, which is integrated within the general education system of the country.

The TVET system includes technical colleges, secondary institutes and vocational training centres located all over the Kingdom, together with private institutes accredited by GOTEVOT serving over 21 million residents.

A government review revealed three main reasons why GOVEVOT needed to reassess the scope and capacity of its programmes and facilities. These are:

- the Kingdom has one of the fastest growing populations in the world, necessitating extra buildings and more places for students and trainees;
- changes in technology, which make it necessary to upgrade the system's laboratories and workshop training centres;

- the requirement to Saudiize the workforce in order to sustain development.

In addressing these areas for redevelopment, GOTEVOT has established a partnership with the private sector, part of which involved International Training Australia (ITA) being engaged to work on various assignments such as safety in industrial systems and computer centre development, as well as study tours for Saudi students to Australia and elsewhere.

Saudi Development and Training Company Ltd (SDT)

Saudi Development and Training Company Ltd (SDT), a joint venture between Al Gosaibi Group and BAe Systems, is an example of an international joint venture that has been established to assist the manpower development and technology transfer in the Kingdom by offering a broad range of high-quality training products and services. SDT is in a unique position to provide total training solutions for its customers in the core lines of business outlined below. The organization works in partnerships to deliver Saudiization through:

- the provision of totally integrated practical training and academic educational training solutions;
- efficiently and profitably increasing Saudi Arabian levels of manpower;
- transferring technology through vocational and educational training.

SDT operates by the provision of a curriculum in line with the latest and best practices as adopted by leading industrial countries. SDT has an in-house capability to provide integrated training solutions to its clients, while its core capabilities allow it to deliver bespoke services in all areas of human resource consultancy, human resource management training, English language training and technical training.

The Saudi British Electronics Institute (SBEI) is the technical training division of SDT. SBEI is committed to the transfer of technology through Saudiization, and offers some of the best-appointed training facilities in the Kingdom to deliver a host of professional vocational, educational and technical training programmes at its Riyadh training centre. This is a 'state-of-art' learning college offering numerous course options for Saudi nationals.

The SDT Professional Engineers Programme (PEP) covers a wide range of technical skills and English language training. It covers six main choices of specialization:

- electrical engineering;
- computer technology;
- telecommunications;
- electronic manufacture;
- mechatronics.

The programme is flexible in delivery, offering additional studies where necessary to ensure students are provided with maximum opportunity to achieve the Professional Engineers Qualification.

The PEP is normally a three-year programme leading to a UK Higher National Diploma and following successful completion of the programme, students are eligible to study for a further one to two years in leading universities to achieve the Bachelor of Engineering Degree.

BAe Systems Education Programme

The BAe Systems Education Programme in Saudi Arabia involves sponsorship, scholarships and academic exchanges, training and skills transfer. As already mentioned, BAe Systems' training arm in Saudi Arabia, Saudi Development and Training, provides training and skills transfer in engineering and electronics to other companies and government organizations within the Kingdom. The company is also involved in specific projects and programmes that include:

- Al Faisal University – in 2002, BAe Systems became a founder of the new Al Faisal University, pledging funds and offering training expertise from the BAe Systems joint venture company, Saudi Development and Training. The university will provide Saudi students with an international education in science, engineering and technology.
- Chevening Scholarships – operated by the British Council in over 100 countries around the world and given to young people who have a bachelor's degree and a minimum of three years' work experience. The scholarships fund a year's study in the UK. The intention is for scholars to return with skills that will contribute to the development and wealth of their home country. BAe Systems funded 15 such scholarships for Saudi students in 2002, up from seven in 2001.
- Post Doctoral Research Programme. BAe Systems is a corporate sponsor of this British Council-run programme that provides Saudi academics with grants to conduct research in British universities. Twenty-four Saudi academics received grants in 2002.

Further information

For further information concerning education and training in Saudi Arabia see the following:

- Saudi Development and Training Company Ltd (SDT), Riyadh. Tel: +966 1 293 3166, Fax: +966 1 293 3352, Website: www.dwalej.com.sa.
- International Training Australia (ITA), Level 10, 636 St Kilda Road, Melbourne, Victoria 3004, Australia. Tel: +613 9533 2600, Fax: +613 9533 2911, Email: headoffice@ita.edu.au.
- Hay Management Consultants, Middle East Office, Oud Metha Towers (101), PO Box 30987, Dubai, UAE. Tel: +971 4 324 73960, Fax: +971 4 324 7395, Email: haygroup@emirates.net.ae.

7.11

Real Estate

Cluttons Middle East

Real estate market conditions

Introduction

Inflated oil prices and the repatriation of funds by Arab nationals from Western economies have resulted in a construction boom in Saudi Arabia and elsewhere throughout the Middle East. This has had implications for a number of sectors – not only has it stimulated supply growth but demand increases have also been witnessed from the rapidly increasing population and from the business community.

Office space

The office space market in Saudi Arabia has, historically, consisted of buildings that, by international standards, would be considered to be of 'secondary' standard. International firms, local firms and government agencies have occupied these buildings. However, more recently there has been a trend towards the development of 'landmark' buildings in all of the major cities of the Middle East, with Riyadh boasting two of the most spectacular. By international standards these would be considered to be 'prime' office space, setting new standards of design, construction and layout.

However, in Saudi Arabia terrorist attacks on Western interests throughout the Kingdom have coincided with the development of these landmark properties and demand from international companies has entered a period of decline, with the likely consequence that there will be downward pressure on both rates and occupancy.

Retail space

Similar to office space, the retail sector has, historically, consisted of medium quality malls. However, the retail mall sector is undergoing a period of rapid change with the development of numerous high-quality malls across almost all of the main cities of Saudi Arabia. These malls are typically owned and financed by firms with existing retail interests, but it is likely that the sheer number of new retail malls will result in some pressure on rental rates and/or occupancy.

Residential property

Private ownership

Saudi Arabia, in common with the entire Middle East region, is faced with pressing demographic problems and a consequent need for more housing. In Saudi Arabia, most of the nationals in the population are under 20 years old and with such rapid annual population growth, the provision of housing will increasingly become a critical issue.

With Saudi Arabia increasingly in danger of slipping further into a housing deficit position and the costs of government housing becoming increasingly onerous, it is clear that private sector real estate developers have a key role to play in meeting the future housing needs of the people. However, the lack of financial products in Saudi Arabia means that citizens are unable to buy property over an extended period of, say, 20 years.

This has caused major cash flow problems for private developers, who are unable to bear the costs of long-term credit arrangements and, as a consequence, most properties are bought over a short period of typically two to three years. This has historically suppressed private house building activity and prices.

However, in many of the Middle East countries this has been overcome. In particular, Bahrain, Kuwait and the UAE have had financial products enabling Arab nationals to buy villa products for some time. Islamic-compliant financial products have recently been devised in Saudi Arabia that will allow extended payment periods to be arranged for the purchase of property, and it likely that when these are introduced over the next year or so, this will revolutionize the Kingdom's huge housing market, prompting a surge in prices and residential development activity.

Rental property

Residential compounds

The presence and style of compounds are not uniform across the Middle East. In Saudi Arabia every major city has numerous compounds, as do Bahrain and Doha, Qatar, whilst the UAE and Kuwait have few, if any, compounds as upper-income expatriates live in apartments or villas. The range of compound sizes is extremely varied, ranging from single employer 'mini-cities' such as Saudi Aramco in Dhahran, to small villa groups located in virtually every major city. When properly managed, these compound projects have, historically, proved to be extremely profitable revenue generating assets. The compound villas and apartments have been constructed at low cost on relatively cheap land and yet have been rented by Western nationals at premium rates.

However, the situation in Saudi Arabia has changed substantially over the last two years, with terrorist attacks targeting Westerners living on compounds in Riyadh and Al Khobar. Heightened concern for safety in Saudi Arabia has meant that Western nationals are increasingly working on single visas, leaving their families either in their home countries or commuting from neighbouring countries such as Bahrain. Despite the tightening of security arrangements on compounds in Saudi Arabia, demand for residential compound accommodation has fallen off from family groups but much of this has been replaced by expatriates on single visas, necessitating a shift in the design, layout and services offered by such compounds.

Rental apartment buildings

Rental apartment buildings are typically rented by expatriates working throughout Saudi Arabia and can range from upper-income fully-furnished apartments with sea views to lower-income apartments in ageing buildings in central city locations.

Commonhold and leasehold ownership laws are not sufficiently developed in Saudi Arabia to encourage purchases of individual apartments, and Arab nationals have, historically, preferred villa housing for reasons of privacy and family size, and this preference is likely to remain into the foreseeable future.

Apartment rentals are strong in all the major cities of Saudi Arabia due to the rapid growth of both national and expatriate populations, which remains unmatched by growth in housing supply.

Land

Residential land

The strong demand for villa housing by Arab nationals throughout Saudi Arabia is forecast to continue at least into the medium-term future as demographic pressures intensify throughout the region. 'Urban sprawl' is occurring in most major population centres and there will, in future, need to be much thought given to public transport solutions or suburban mixed-use centres offering housing, employment, retail, leisure and so on.

There are two main types of residential land, namely those suitable for:

- primary home (principal place of residence) developments, typically as close as possible to the centres of the major population centres; and
- secondary home (holiday/weekend homes) developments, such as Jeddah Corniche and the coastal areas of Al Khobar.

Real estate investment opportunities

Introduction

In the booming Saudi economy there are strong opportunities for real estate investment. Given the desire to moderate asset risk and investment returns across the portfolio, an investment strategy should:

- invest in low-risk, commercial and residential property that is already generating income;
- acquire and re-develop or re-position existing real estate assets on an opportunistic basis to improve revenue generation and therefore capital values;
- identify and invest in land plots with likely value growth potential;
- utilize leverage to maximize returns;
- invest in off-plan real estate projects in order to benefit from capital growth;
- invest primarily in existing major population centres;
- focus on two main property types:
  - commercial (office, retail and residential); and
  - land and development properties.

Each potential asset acquisition should be subjected to a detailed assessment, focusing on:

- supply and demand dynamics for that type of asset in that location;
- occupancy rates, length of leases and tenant quality;

- age, quality and condition of the asset;
- valuation relative to market comparables; and
- liquidity of market, particularly the ability to exit investments.

Real estate investment strategy issues

Introduction

Real estate as an asset class is not as volatile as equities and provides more income and more upsides than bank deposits. With no taxation in Saudi Arabia on revenues or capital gains, no transactional tax and a stable and current income, real estate can represent an attractive option as part of a balanced corporate strategy.

There are two components to an investment strategy, namely current income and capital appreciation. Current income from commercial property typically provides stable returns and with current market dynamics in Saudi Arabia, it is likely that capital appreciation will be positive.

The objective for real estate investment is to achieve above-average, risk-adjusted rates of return through income and realized capital gains.

Investment in real estate

In a balanced investment portfolio, real estate in the form of direct property holdings might comprise between 15 and 35 per cent. For many years, this has been a preferred asset class for many Middle Eastern investors, which is now attracting even wider interest. There has been a dramatic global increase from both private and institutional investors over the last five years, as low returns on equities and deposits has highlighted the appeal of real estate.

Most real estate investment is risk averse and has the advantage of relatively secure income flows with the opportunity for capital appreciation. More speculative real estate includes the development sector and portfolios tend to be customized and balanced to match the investor's objectives.

A conservative portfolio would invest primarily in institutional standard income-producing properties, with only a modest exposure to the development and land sector.

Real estate sectors

As mentioned above, investment in real estate is broken down between income-producing and development properties. The former include a wide range of mainly commercial and residential properties that are leased out to independent occupiers to produce a rental return, which is frequently enhanced by capital appreciation. In each sector, there are prime, secondary and tertiary investment grade properties that are analyzed for their relative rates of income return and capital appreciation.

Development properties are acquired primarily to exploit a capital return from a construction and development project, and involve management participation as well as capital investment. These are usually finite term projects that may give the equivalent of a lump sum return, even where the project life is several years. Land holdings are viewed in this way.

In terms of investment characteristics, each asset class has its own attributes, ranging from positive through neutral to negative (see Table 7.11.1).

Table 7.11.1 Characteristics of real estate investments

	Land	**Residential**	**Office**	**Retail**
Liquidity	Neutral	Neutral	Negative	Negative
Management time	Positive	Negative	Neutral	Neutral
Maintenance costs	Positive	Negative	Positive	Positive
Tenant turnover	n/a	Negative	Positive	Positive
Revenue generation	Negative	Positive	Positive	Positive
Capital growth	Positive	Neutral	Neutral	Neutral

Geographic distribution

The Middle East real estate market offers an array of investment opportunities and ranges of yields. The major population centres offer mature investment markets. The real estate market in Saudi Arabia, and throughout the Middle East, is extremely dynamic at present, with key factors being:

- the repatriation of substantial Arab monies from Western economies;
- the activity of real estate funds in the market;
- new financial products (mortgages), enabling purchase of residential property on extended repayment terms.

Other factors affecting the market include high oil prices, demographic considerations, macroeconomic conditions and the present uncertainty due to terrorist activity.

In terms of opportunities for investment in various products in the major Saudi cities, these are summarized in Table 7.11.2.

Table 7.11.2 Opportunities for investment in major Saudi cities

	Capital growth		Revenue generation	
	Historic	**Future**	**Historic**	**Future**
Riyadh				
Residential				
Apartments for rent	→	↗	→	↗
Compounds	↗	↘	↗	↘
Villas for sale	→	↗	n/a	n/a
Prime office space	→	→	→	→
Retail space	→	↗	→	↗
Land speculation & development property	↗	↗	n/a	n/a
Jeddah				
Residential				
Apartments for rent	→	↗	→	↗
Compounds	↗	↘	↗	↘
Villas for sale	→	↗	n/a	n/a
Prime office space	→	→	→	→
Retail space	→	↗	→	↗
Land speculation & development property	↗	↗	n/a	n/a
Al Khobar				
Residential				
Apartments for rent	→	↗	→	↗
Compounds	↗	↘	↗	↘
Villas for sale	→	↗	n/a	n/a
Prime office space	→	→	→	→
Retail space	→	↗	→	↗
Land speculation & development property	↗	↗	n/a	n/a

7.12

Travel, Tourism and Transport

Anthony Shoult, ASA Consulting[1]

Introduction

The travel market in Saudi Arabia is dominated by business or work-related travel and religious pilgrimage, with little or no inbound international tourism. This is because in the past Saudi Arabia has discouraged international tourists and it is only recently that travel from neighbouring countries has been promoted.

Statistical information submitted to tourism monitoring organizations, such as the World Tourism Organization (WTO), is limited, although some official data is now published. Despite making little effort to encourage non-Arab tourism, Saudi Arabia has been involved for many years in the massive annual pilgrimage to Makkah.

While religious and leisure tourism and business travel account for some 7.5 million overseas visitors annually, religious pilgrimage accounts for the vast majority of overseas visitors, with over six million pilgrims from overseas each year going to the holy places. This compares to a level of some six million overseas visitors in 1993, of which an estimated 4.8 million were engaged in pilgrimage-related travel.

Approximately 50 per cent of non-resident overseas visitors entering and leaving the Kingdom do so via air travel, while almost as many travel via land ports, of which the most important is King Fahd Bridge linking the Eastern Province with Bahrain. Only some five per cent of non-residents travelling to and from the Kingdom do so via seaports, nearly all travelling via Jeddah Islamic Port, which handles up to 400,000 foreign traveller arrivals a year.

---

[1] Sources of information include the Supreme Council for Tourism, Civil Aviation Presidency and Saudi Government Railroad Organization.

Business and work-related travel

Inland and outbound travel by foreigners is dominated by business and work-related travel, with the market characterized by volume labour traffic business. In 2003, of a total of 7.33 million non-resident visitors of foreign nationality entered the Kingdom, an estimated 800,000 were travelling for work, business or professional reasons. As such, business and work-related travel accounts for a little over 10 per cent of all inbound travel by non-resident visitors to the Kingdom.

Historically, 70 per cent of room nights in the Riyadh market have been generated from government-related business but, today, the figure has now decreased to about 30 per cent. The majority of room nights in Riyadh are now sold to business travellers and demand from the commercial sector has replaced some of the lost government-related business demand.

According to the WTO, occupancy rates for hotels and similar establishments in the Kingdom stood at 42 per cent in 2003, with an average length of stay of 2.7 nights.

Pilgrimage-related travel

Each year the Kingdom attracts over six million visitors; the majority of visitors are Muslims coming to the Kingdom to take part in the *Hajj* and *Umrah* pilgrimages. In addition to those coming from abroad, each year up to 1.5 million pilgrims travel to the holy cities from within the Kingdom.

Improved transportation and accommodation have dramatically increased the number of visitors who enter the Kingdom for pilgrimage. In 1965, approximately 300,000 Muslims came from abroad to perform the rites of pilgrimage, primarily from other Arab and Asian countries. In 2004, an estimated two million Muslim pilgrims gathered in Makkah for the annual *Hajj* to perform the circumambulation of Kaaba ritual. At this time, Jeddah International Airport, located 80 kilometres from Madinah, operates at full capacity with a plane landing or taking off every two minutes. The *Hajj*, or pilgrimage to Makkah, occurs annually between the eighth and thirteenth days of the last month of the Muslim year, *Dhu al Hijjah*. The *Hajj* represents the culmination of the Muslim's spiritual life and, for many, is a lifelong ambition.

The Ministry of Pilgrimage Affairs and Religious Trusts handles the immense logistical and administrative problems generated by such a huge international gathering. The government issues special pilgrimage visas that permit the pilgrim to visit Makkah and to make the customary excursion to Madinah to visit the Prophet's tomb. Care is taken to assure that pilgrims do not remain in the Kingdom after the *Hajj* to search for work.

In 2004, Saudi Arabia allowed foreign airlines to fly to the Holy City of Madinah during the *Hajj* pilgrimmage in early February for the first time.

Certain rites of pilgrimage may be performed at any time, and although meritorious, these constitute a lesser pilgrimage, known as *Umrah*.

During the 2004 *Umrah* season to the end of Ramadan, some 2.5 million visitors performed the *Umrah* pilgrimage. During this period alone, Saudi Arabian Airlines claims to have transported 1.5 million travellers through 65 locations. In total, some six million people perform *Umrah* every year.

To further develop this important segment of the tourism trade, Saudi Arabia is now promoting a pilgrimmage and tourism package called 'Umrah-plus' to the regional and Islamic tourism market into the Kingdom. Since 2002, Saudi Arabia has allowed *Umrah* pilgrims to travel across the Kingdom, rather than restricting them to the Holy Cities of Makkah and Madinah. Also, consideration is being given to extending the validity of the 30-day *Umrah* visa to 60 days, to better facilitate travel by pilgrims to other parts of the Kingdom.

The rite of pilgrimage not only has special significance in the life of Muslims but also has profound political significance for the Saudi monarchy. The King has claimed for himself the title Khadim al Haramayn, or 'custodian of the two holy mosques', a title that complements the Saudi claim to legitimacy. To prove themselves worthy of the title, Saudi monarchs must show that they are not only capable of defending the interests of Arabian Muslims but also of defending the holy sites of Islam for the benefit of Muslims the world over. The Saudis have, therefore, invested heavily over the years in facilitating the arrival, transportation, feeding and accommodation of pilgrims arriving annually for the rites of the *Hajj*. New airport buildings, road networks, water supplies, and public health facilities have been provided.

Much publicity has accompanied government contributions to the comfort of pilgrims. The government distributes bottled water, juices, and boxed lunches during the climbing of Mount Arafat; stations ambulances staffed with first-aid teams in strategic locations; shows health education videos on aircraft and ships bringing pilgrims; and relieves pilgrims of the task of having to slaughter their sacrificial animal. The Islamic Development Bank now sells vouchers for sacrificial animals, which are chosen by the pilgrim and then slaughtered, processed, and frozen for distribution and sale at slaughterhouses in Mina Valley outside the holy city of Makkah.

Holidays and leisure tourism

Saudi Arabia wishes foreign visitors to enjoy its cultural heritage, environmental attractions, and take full advantage of conference locations, shopping facilities and adventure holidays. There are a variety of desert landscapes to enjoy, including the vast Empty Quarter in the south of the country, as well as attractive mountain and Red Sea beach resorts.

According to the WTO, the Kingdom had recorded visitor arrivals for purposes of leisure, recreation and holidays numbering just over 260,000 in 2000. This is well below the highest tourism destination in the Middle East, Egypt, with some five million recorded arrivals, but above such countries as Kuwait and Yemen.

As far as the Kingdom is concerned, the principal in-Kingdom business and leisure tourist destinations are Riyadh, the commercial city of Jeddah, and the Holy Cities of Makkah and Madinah. Jeddah is both the financial and commercial centre, as well as the main leisure destination, in Saudi Arabia.

In the hotel industry, average occupancy levels in Riyadh's leading hotels have historically averaged less than 60 per cent. However, in Jeddah, occupancy levels had been amongst the highest in the Middle East, with average levels of 75 per cent being usual throughout the 1990s.

In 2004, Saudi Arabia's hotel industry had been struggling to regain levels achieved in 2000, as a reduction in business travel to the Kingdom due to security concerns has led to occupancy levels of around 28 per cent, the lowest recorded by any market in the Middle East. Even in Jeddah, room occupancy rates in the top five-star hotels have fallen steeply to levels well below 40 per cent during some months in 2004. However, in 2005 Saudi Arabian destinations such as Makkah and Jeddah have shown improvement, with occupancy levels returning to those of 2000.

As far as local leisure tourism is concerned, a new pattern of summer travel emerged in 2003, as Saudi families continued to avoid travel to the United States and also became averse to travelling to the Far East because of Severe Acute Respiratory Syndrome (SARS). This has led to an increase in travel within the Kingdom or elsewhere in the Gulf or wider Middle East region, as well as to parts of Europe, in particular Spain. In this context, Saudi Arabia estimates that up to 4.5 million Saudis go abroad every year.

Travel demand, other than that related to religious pilgrimages, is expected to continue to be dominated by business travellers rather than tourists, while Saudi Arabia is expected to follow the Middle East trend of attracting more intra-regional travellers.

Development of the tourism industry

Saudi Arabia is developing its tourism industry under an ambitious plan that will create up to 2.3 million jobs for Saudi nationals and raise the current annual number of visitors from just over 20 million to 45 million by 2020. The Kingdom's tourism industry, worth an estimated US$9.6 billion in 2003, is estimated to rise to US$22 billion by 2025, when at least 44 million tourists a year are expected to visit the Kingdom.

For the development of its tourism industry, the Kingdom has targeted local Saudi tourists, *Hajj* and *Umrah* pilgrims, GCC and Arab nationals as well as foreign tourists. Each year the Kingdom attracts over six million visitors, the majority being Muslims coming for pilgrimage to Makkah.

In 2004, the Secretary-General of the Supreme Commission for Tourism, Prince Sultan bin Salman, announced that Saudi Arabia intends to spend US$350 million over the period to 2010 to develop non-religious tourism. The Supreme Commission for Tourism has also stated that is working to remove all obstacles to visas for tourists by 2008.

Saudi Arabia is building an infrastructure that will cater for all the needs of visitors without contravening Islamic teachings. A tourism charter is being developed that contains regulations governing the industry, including licences, tourist security and visas. An e-visa system is also being developed.

As part of its plans to develop tourism, the Kingdom has identified some 38 tourism development areas and 175 designated tourist sites. Also, 50 tourism development authorities are to be developed by 2020, with the government playing the role of regulator and facilitator rather than investor and owner.

The Kingdom's tourism industry development plans include the building of an extra 50,000 hotel rooms over a period to 2015 to add to the 95,000 already in the country. To cope with the expected demands of tourists, the industry is also projected to need 74,000 more apartments by 2015. Certain areas are receiving special attention. For example, some US$250 million is being invested annually in the hill resort of Taif in western Saudi Arabia, in an attempt to fully develop its tourism potential. The southern Saudi Arabian resort of Abha is also being developed. Abha is reported to have earned up to US$50 million in tourism revenues in 2004 due to an annual festival that attracts up to 450,000 visitors, mainly from elsewhere in Saudi Arabia.

Air travel

Air travel accounts for some 50 per cent of all travel to or from the Kingdom, the largest number travelling through King Abdul Aziz International Airport (KAAIA), Jeddah.

In 2004, Jeddah's King Abdul Aziz International Airport accounted for over 52 per cent of travellers arriving or leaving the Kingdom by air, a total of 14.1 million passengers. In the same year, Riyadh's King Khalid International Airport (KKIA) accounted for a further 37 per cent of travellers, a total of 9.9 million passengers.

Total passenger traffic at the Kingdom's international and domestic airports in 2004 was 34.26 million (see Table 7.12.1). This represents an increase of over 7.5 per cent on the 2003 level of 31.84 million passengers.

The total number of flights operated to and from the Kingdom's airports in 2004 stands at approximately 272,000 compared to 262,364 in 2003, an increase of some four per cent.

Table 7.12.1 Breakdown of airline passenger traffic in Saudi Arabia, 2002– 2004) #

Year/airport	Scheduled/ non-scheduled domestic	Scheduled/ non-scheduled international	General aviation	*Hajj* pilgrims	Total arrivals and departures
2002					
King Khalid, Riyadh	5,578,000	3,443,000	33,000	-	9,054,000
King Abdul Aziz, Jeddah	5,050,000	5,799,000	76,000	1,713,000	12,638,000
King Fahd, Dammam	1,563,000	1,015,000	169,000	-	2,747,000
Total international airports	12,191,000	10,257,000	278,000	1,713,000	24,439,000
Total domestic airports	6,630,500	-	-	-	6,630,500
Total all airports	*18,821,500*	*10,257,000*	*278,000*	*1,713,000*	*31,069,500*

Year/airport	Scheduled/ non-scheduled domestic	Scheduled/ non-scheduled international	General aviation	*Hajj* pilgrims	Total arrivals and departures
2003					
King Khalid, Riyadh	5,657,000	3,481,000	30,000	-	9,168,000
King Abdul Aziz, Jeddah	5,102,000	6,146,000	77,000	1,818,000	13,143,000
King Fahd, Dammam	1,560,000	1,053,000	173,000	-	2,786,000
Total international airports	12,319,000	10,680,000	280,000	1,818,000	25,097,000
Total domestic airports	6,747,500	-	-	-	6,747,500
Total all airports	*19,066,500*	*10,680,000*	*280,000*	*1,818,000*	*31,844,500*
2004					
King Khalid, Riyadh	6,082,000	3,799,000	30,000	-	9,911,000
King Abdul Aziz, Jeddah	5,504,000	6,753,000	83,000	1,762,000	14,102,000
King Fahd, Dammam	1,637,000	1,145,000	220,000	-	3,002,000
Total international airports	13,223,000	11,697,000	333,000	1,762,000	27,015,000
Total domestic airports	7,246,400	-	-	-	7,246,400
Total all airports	*20,469,400*	*11,697,000*	*333,000*	*1,762,000*	*34,261,400*

Note: Arriving and departing passengers at Saudi international and domestic airports

Source: Civil Aviation Presidency

Saudi Arabian Airlines (SV)

The national carrier, Saudi Arabian Airlines (SV), operates approximately one third of flights, with the balance operated by foreign airlines. Of all SV flights, just over 30 per cent are operated to or from King Khalid International Airport, Riyadh.

In 2005, SV will carry approximately 16 million passengers on over 90,000 domestic and international flights. This represents a decline in activity since 1993, when SV operated almost 176,000 flights from in-Kingdom airports, involving the handling of almost 21 million arriving and departing passengers at all Saudi airports.

In 2000, HRH Prince Sultan Bin Abdul Aziz, Minister of Defence and Aviation, announced that studies for the privatization of SV were to be undertaken. By 2005, the planning for this programme of privatization has reached an advanced stage.

In 2004, the Prince Sultan Aviation Academy was opened at SAUDIA City in Jeddah. This is reported to be one of the largest aviation training centres in the Middle East.

Private sector aviation

Since 1945, Saudi Arabian Airlines (SV) has been the only carrier to fly to and from Saudi destinations. However, in recent years, there have been a number of private aviation companies that lease aircraft and provide chartered flights, especially for business people. One of these companies is National Aviation Services (NAS), which is one of the largest and fastest growing private aviation companies.

As part of its privatization efforts, the Saudi government has now passed a resolution sanctioning private companies to operate domestic flights. However, the government is still to release information pertaining to the rules and regulations for establishing a private domestic carrier.

Private companies are expected to compete with the national carrier, breaking the SV monopoly in this vital sector. Industry analysts predict that private companies will be able to capture close to 30 per cent of the domestic passenger load.

In addition to the government announcing an end to the SV monopoly, plans to privatize the airports are also being rolled out.

Road travel

With the rapid increase in traffic that has accompanied the Kingdom's industrial and agricultural development, it has been necessary to upgrade many of the inter-city roads to expressways that can accommodate up to eight lanes of traffic.

Some of the more important inter-city highways are:

- Dammam–Abu Hadriya–Ras Tanura (257km);
- Khaybar–Al Ola (175km);
- Makkah–Madinah (421km);
- Riyadh–Dammam (383km);
- Riyadh–Sedir–Al Qasim (317km);
- Riyadh–Taif (750km);
- Taif–Abha–Gizan (750km).

As the main Saudi cities have become congested by the growth in traffic, modern ring roads have been constructed in an attempt to reduce congestion and pollution. By 2002, over 110,000 kilometres of road had been constructed in the Kingdom.

Probably the most spectacular road construction project has been the building of the King Fahd Causeway – a 25 metre-wide, 26 kilometre-long, four-lane highway that connects the Saudi Arabian mainland with the island of Bahrain. The cornerstone of the bridge was jointly placed by King Fahd and the then ruler of Bahrain, Sheikh Isa bin Salman Al-Khalifa in November 1982 and the Causeway was opened to traffic at the end of 1986. The project cost was reported to be US$1.2 billion.

Car rental

The in-Kingdom market is dominated in the Kingdom by the top five international car hire firms operating out of the Middle East and the rest of the world, namely Budget, Hertz, Europcar, Avis and Thrifty.

In addition, a large number of local car hire firms generate much of the local car hire business from both city centre outlets and their car rental counterparts at in-Kingdom airports. The larger of the national companies, such as Abu Dyab, Hanco and Halla, operate national networks and have Gulf link-ups.

The five international major car hire companies that operate in over 50 countries and maintain international networks are all represented in Riyadh. An enormous amount of business is generated in the Kingdom by these companies in connection with international travel, with many Saudi residents travelling for three to four weeks a year to Gulf countries, Europe and other destinations. This almost always involves a requirement to hire a car and Saudis prefer to reserve and pay for this facility in-Kingdom rather than at the overseas location.

Bus and coach

There is a single bus/coach operator in the Kingdom, The Saudi Arabian Public Transport Company (SAPTCO). This company operates nationally between all the major cities and also provides international routes serving the Arabian Peninsula and whole Gulf area. This form of transport is popular with large families, where economy and safety are the main considerations.

The Saudi Arabian Public Transport Company (SAPTCO)
SAPTCO, established in 1979, is a national bus service providing inexpensive public transport within and between major population centres. Every year, SAPTCO assigns approximately 2,000 buses in response to the arrival of pilgrims from all over the Kingdom and overseas to perform the annual *Hajj* pilgrimage to the Holy Cities of Makkah and Madinah.

SAPTCO also operates regular international passenger services between the Kingdom and Egypt, Jordan, Syria, the United Arab Emirates, Qatar, Kuwait, Bahrain and Turkey. In 2005, SAPTCO introduced a new route between Saudi Arabia and Yemen.

Rail travel

Rail travel remains the least developed means of transportation in the Kingdom. With vast distances to cover across difficult terrain and often in adverse environmental conditions, airline services have developed as the more practical mode of transportation.

The Kingdom's railways currently consist primarily of a single track, standard-gauge line, running for 570 kilometres from Riyadh to Dammam in the eastern region. This line, which was opened in 1951 and operates from the eastern commercial centre of Dammam, passes through Dhahran, Abqaiq, Hofuf, Harad and Al-Kharj, and has benefited from substantial renovation over the years. An additional line joining Hofuf and Riyadh was opened in 1985.

The Kingdom's railways are managed by the Saudi Arabian Railway Organization (SRO), which was established as an independent public utility called the Saudi Arabian Railway Corporation in 1976.

SRO reported revenues of SR194.8 million in 2003, up from SR164.7 million in 2002. Revenue from passenger transport rose to SR29 million and the company transported a total of 913,000 passengers and handled 1.9 million tonnes of cargo.

This form of transport is cheaper than air travel, is considered to be extremely safe and is widely used by students. In 2004, Saudi Arabia's railways operator, SRO, started offering a 50 per cent discount for both private and state university students, effective on all SRO routes. The discount is a part of SRO's efforts to increase its client base and offer quality services.

Saudi 'Landbridge' project

In early 2005, plans for Saudi Arabia's rail 'Landbridge' project, which aims to link the Red Sea with the Arabian Gulf, were unveiled. A 950 kilometre railway line will link Saudi Arabia's three major ports: the Jeddah Islamic Port, Riyadh's Dry Port and Dammam's King Abdul Aziz Port.

The line will allow for cost savings in cargo transportation between the Gulf and United States and Europe and provide a major passenger network across the Kingdom.

According to the SRO, the line will be funded through a build-operate-transfer (BOT) agreement. Under this type of contractual arrangement, the successful bidder, which is expected to be a consortium that demonstrates a wide variety of expertise, will design, build and operate the line for a set period of time.

The 'Landbridge' project will be one of the largest BOT projects ever undertaken in the Middle East and is a key initiative in the Railway Expansion Programme approved by the Kingdom's Supreme Economic Council. As such, the project is a key part of the Kingdom of Saudi Arabia's privatization strategy.

Riyadh railway network project

In August 2004, the proposed Saudi rail network, which includes a 950 kilometre link between Riyadh and Jeddah, moved a step closer to reality after the Saudi General Investment Fund signed a legal consultancy agreement with several partners. These included the General Railway Establishment and the UK International Office of Riyad-based Abdulaziz Alfahd Law Office.

In September 2004, the French consulting firm, Semaly, was awarded a US$2.2 million contract to prepare preliminary plans for an electric railway network in Riyadh. Semaly won the contract jointly with local engineering firm Dar Al-Handasah. The studies will assess the social, economic and environmental impact of the project on the Saudi capital.

Shipping and ports

The Kingdom has five major commercial ports and two major industrial ports. The commercial ports are at Jeddah, Dammam, Jizan, Jubail and Yanbu.

The industrial ports are King Fahd Industrial Port at Jubail and the King Fahd Industrial Port at Yanbu. There is also the oil port of Ras Tanura, the Dhiba Port, as well as a number of minor ports. In 2004, the main industrial ports handled 120 million tonnes of cargo.

Approximately 10,200 ships called at Saudi seaports in 2000. Of these over 80 per cent were cargo ships, tankers and tugs. Just over 50 per cent of all ships call at Jeddah Islamic Port, with the other main ports being King Abdul Aziz and Ras Tanura for tanker traffic. Sailboats, launches and other types of vessel, such as cruise liners, account for approximately 15 per cent of ships calling at Saudi ports. The number of arriving and departing passengers using Saudi seaports in 2004 was just over two million.

Jeddah Islamic Port

Jeddah Islamic Port is the busiest of all the Kingdom's ports. It is the principal commercial port and the main port of entry for pilgrims on their way to the Holy Cities of Makkah and Madinah. In 1975, Jeddah imported 2.8 million tonnes of cargo, which represented almost half of all imports to the Kingdom in that year. By 2001, the volume of imports reached a peak of 23 million tonnes. As well as providing the main point of entry for industrial and consumer goods, Jeddah Islamic Port is the Kingdom's main port for the importation of livestock.

King Abdul Aziz Port, Dammam

King Abdul Aziz Port at Dammam ranks second to Jeddah as a commercial port. Like Jeddah, it boasts a fully equipped repair yard. In 1975, Dammam imported 2.4 million tonnes of cargo (approximately 40 per cent of the total entering the Kingdom that year). In 2001, King Abdul Aziz Port handled 13.7 million tonnes.

Sea cruise travel

The cruise travel market in the Gulf is very small at present but is growing rapidly. The size of the entire Gulf market is estimated at between 750 and 1,000 individual cruise bookings a year. Of this total, Saudi Arabia accounts for an estimated 50 per cent, ie some 500 individual bookings a year. A typical package sold in the region would be a three to four-day Bahamas cruise from Orlando in Florida.

The very small market for cruising in the region is a reflection of the nature of the cruise market, which is not generally well promoted to, or well known by, the majority of the population. Apart from cruising, there is little related to leisure boating in the Kingdom.

Further information

Contact details for key organizations involved in the field of travel and tourism are as follows:

- Supreme Commission for Tourism, PO Box 61355, Riyadh 11565. Tel: +966 1 480 8855, Fax: +966 1 480 1008, Website: www.sauditourism.gov.sa;
- Presidency of Civil Aviation, PO Box 887, Jeddah 21165. Tel: +966 2 640 5000;
- Saudi Ports Authority, PO Box 5162, Riyadh 11422. Tel: +966 1 405 0005, Fax: +966 1 405 3508, Email: info@ports.gov.sa, Webite: www.ports.gov.sa.

ASA Consulting has conducted a number of travel industry-related market and feasibility studies in Saudi Arabia, including a market study for the establishment of an integrated travel and tourism centre in Riyadh. For further information concerning Anthony Shoult and the experience and activities of ASA Consulting in the travel and tourism sector, please contact asaconsult@btinternet.com.

Part Eight

Profiles of Leading Saudi Companies

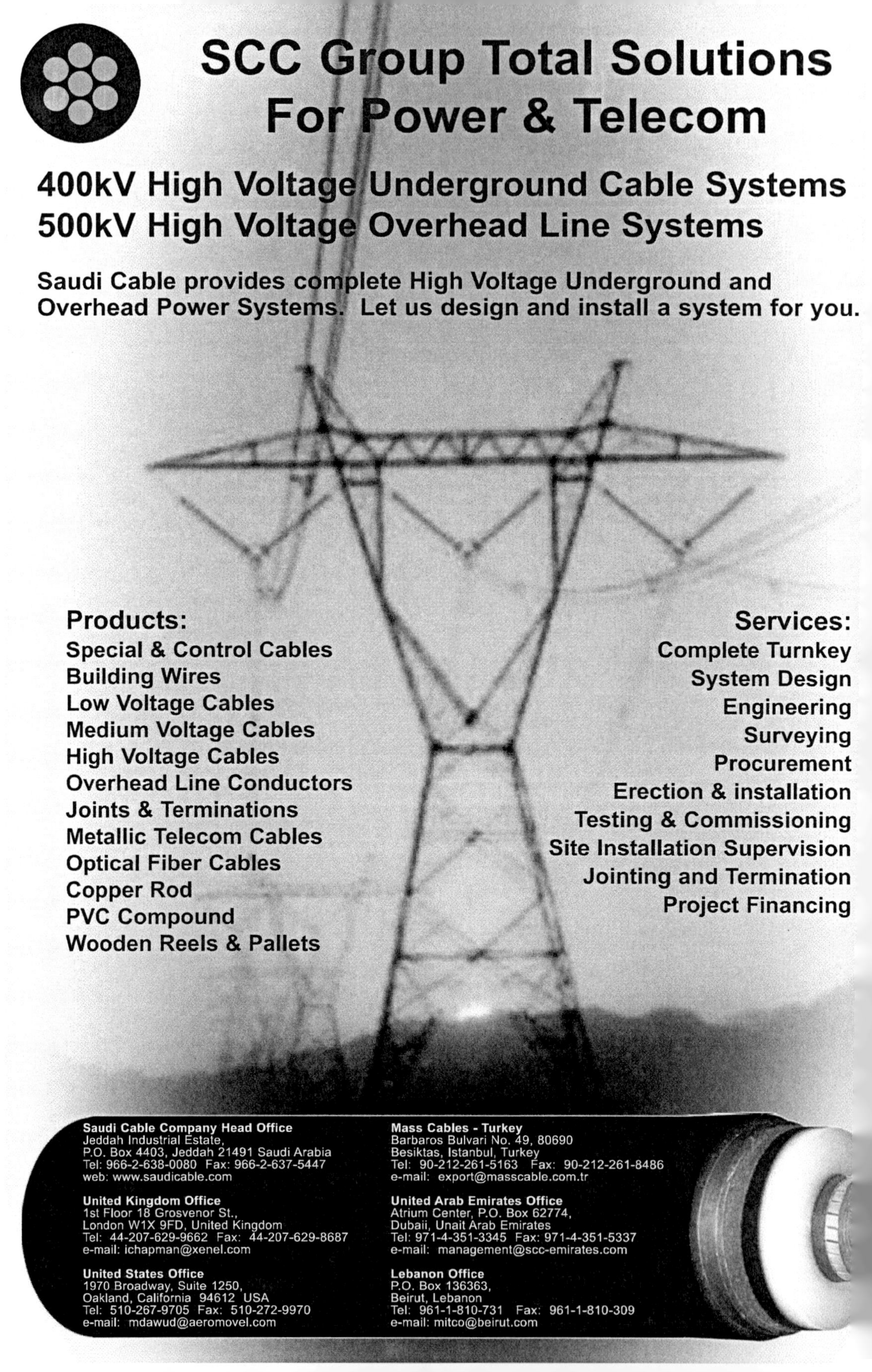
SCC Group Total Solutions
For Power & Telecom
400kV High Voltage Underground Cable Systems
500kV High Voltage Overhead Line Systems
Saudi Cable provides complete High Voltage Underground and Overhead Power Systems. Let us design and install a system for you.
Products:
Special & Control Cables
Building Wires
Low Voltage Cables
Medium Voltage Cables
High Voltage Cables
Overhead Line Conductors
Joints & Terminations
Metallic Telecom Cables
Optical Fiber Cables
Copper Rod
PVC Compound
Wooden Reels & Pallets
Services:
Complete Turnkey
System Design
Engineering
Surveying
Procurement
Erection & installation
Testing & Commissioning
Site Installation Supervision
Jointing and Termination
Project Financing
Saudi Cable Company Head Office
Jeddah Industrial Estate,
P.O. Box 4403, Jeddah 21491 Saudi Arabia
Tel: 966-2-638-0080 Fax: 966-2-637-5447
web: www.saudicable.com
United Kingdom Office
1st Floor 18 Grosvenor St.,
London W1X 9FD, United Kingdom
Tel: 44-207-629-9662 Fax: 44-207-629-8687
e-mail: ichapman@xenel.com
United States Office
1970 Broadway, Suite 1250,
Oakland, California 94612 USA
Tel: 510-267-9705 Fax: 510-272-9970
e-mail: mdawud@aeromovel.com
Mass Cables - Turkey
Barbaros Bulvari No. 49, 80690
Besiktas, Istanbul, Turkey
Tel: 90-212-261-5163 Fax: 90-212-261-8486
e-mail: export@masscable.com.tr
United Arab Emirates Office
Atrium Center, P.O. Box 62774,
Dubaii, Unait Arab Emirates
Tel: 971-4-351-3345 Fax: 971-4-351-5337
e-mail: management@scc-emirates.com
Lebanon Office
P.O. Box 136363,
Beirut, Lebanon
Tel: 961-1-810-731 Fax: 961-1-810-309
e-mail: mitco@beirut.com

8.1

Saudi Cable Company

Introduction

Saudi Cable Company (SCC) is the Middle East's foremost provider of technologically advanced energy and telecommunications solutions and services. Conceived in 1975, the company has now come to be globally recognized by various governmental agencies and public utilities worldwide for its excellence in product design and engineering, as well as world-class total solutions services.

Production facilities

Saudi Cable production facilities are located in Jeddah, Kingdom of Saudi Arabia; in Bursa, Turkey; and Manama, Kingdom of Bahrain; with a total world-class manufacturing capacity of 140,000 tonnes of copper and aluminium rod; 85,000 tonnes of insulated power cables and conductors, six million core kilometres of metallic telephone cable and 20,000 kilometres of optical fibre communications cable.

Each manufacturing facility has its specialization: the insulated energy cables product range is complete to 400 kV, including specialized cables – fire resistant, low smoke halogen free, control, pilot, signal, instrument, airfield lightening cables and lead sheathed for the oil and petrochemical industry; for the telecommunications range, production is also world-class for metallic telephone cable complete to 3,800 pairs and 288 fibre count optical fibre cables, in either loose tube or 'light pack' constructions.

With regard to technology, all manufacturing facilities are ISO 9001:2000 certified. In fact, Saudi Cable was the first manufacturing plant in the entire Middle East to be ISO 9001:2000 certified. The ISO 9001 certification is for design. Saudi Cable's basic technology comes from Krupp and Nokia. Saudi Cable has made significant investments in state-of-the-art machinery in order to manufacture the latest designs and specifications. Saudi Cable is capable of manufacturing to all major recognized specifications and standards and has supplied cables to over 60 countries worldwide. Saudi Cable also has major alliances and partnerships with other leading manufacturers in high voltage and optical fibre systems, in order to offer its customers complete 'System Solutions'.

SCC Group products

The backbone of every cable industry is low voltage and bare conductors, providing as much as 35 per cent of Saudi Cable production. Low voltage cables are used for all electrical applications up to 1,000 volts. Medium and high voltage cables provide another 35 per cent of production: medium and high voltage cables and conductors are the means of power distribution and transmission of electrical utilities, power plants and sub-stations, major industrial plants, sea ports and airports, water distribution and agriculture, as well as the oil and petrochemical industries. Speciality cable accounts for approximately five per cent of SCC production, having various important system control applications. Metallic and optical fibre telecommunications cables for the transmission and distribution of telecommunications provide for 25 per cent of production.

Total Solution Services

With regard to unique products, Saudi Cable claims to be the Middle East's only provider of 'Total Solution Services'. For customers, this means that Saudi Cable, with 27 years' manufacturing experience, is capable of designing the right energy or telecommunications system, being very familiar with the climate and terrain and knowing how to find the best solutions for customers. More than just designing and engineering a system, Saudi Cable manufactures, installs, tests and commissions the system. The company has invested in high voltage and optical fibre mobile site testing equipment, whereby it can take the facility to the site and make sure that the system is in proper working order before it is turned over to the customer. Also where customers do not have the financial resources to complete their project, Saudi Cable is able to provide financial engineering services for a complete turnkey total solution package.

Rehabilitation of Kuwait transmission grid after the Gulf war

Saudi Cable has provided Total Solution Services in many countries and in all kinds of situation including emergencies. Saudi Cable's first major project was the restoration of power to Kuwait City in 1991, immediately following the evacuation of the occupying force, where, by

Figure 8.1.1 Saudi Cable's 1991 restoration of the electrical power to Kuwait City in an environmental disaster immediately following the evacuation of the occupation forces

working around the clock in an environment of oil fires, unexploded ordinance and dense smoke, Saudi Cable was able to restore power to Kuwait City within 17 days. Saudi Cable further continued to reconstruct the entire transmission grid of Kuwait, replacing 7,400 kilometres of conductors and providing 94 tonnes of steel for damaged towers.

Supplying 25 per cent of Pakistan's electrical power – 500 kV overhead transmission lines

Another Saudi Cable major Total Solution Service was sponsoring the first 1,200 megawatt independent power plant in Pakistan, whereby Saudi Cable established two parallel 200 kilometre 500 kV overhead transmission lines to bring 25 per cent of the entire electrical energy to Pakistan's main grid station at Jamshoro. The first line was completed and energized ahead of schedule in June 1996, and the second in October 1996. Saudi Cable also arranged the US$110 million finance necessary to undertake the project.

Establishing 225 kV underground and overhead transmission systems – Lebanon

Saudi Cable designed, engineered and tested a 225 kV underground feeder cable network, as well as an optical fibre communications network for the newly established downtown area of central Beirut. The network was completed in 18 months and energized in February 2000. Saudi Cable was able to arrange for the necessary US$7 million in project finance. Further, Saudi Cable also established an entirely new 225 kV backbone overhead transmission line, thereby providing electrical power throughout the country. Saudi Cable was able to provide the US$23 million required to undertake the project.

Clients and projects

The main clients of Saudi Cable are the electrical utilities and telecommunications network providers, as well as the oil and petrochemical industries in the GCC and North Africa and their contractors. Saudi Cable has forged alliances and is well known by all the major world contractors from the United States and South America, through Europe across to Japan and Korea. Saudi Cable has installed high voltage cable systems, not only in the United States and Europe, but also in India, Australia and New Zealand.

Shaoiba 380 kV overhead transmission lines – Jeddah, Saudi Arabia

In Saudi Arabia, one of Saudi Cable's major projects was the establishment of two parallel 200 kilometre 380 kV overhead transmissions lines from the new Shaoiba Power Plant to Jeddah South Main Grid Station. This project was undertaken on a turnkey basis, which was entirely designed and engineered, manufactured, erected, tested and commissioned in 2002 by Saudi Cable.

High voltage underground cable systems in Saudi Arabia

Other major projects involving underground high voltage cable systems in the Kingdom are the 13 projects in the western region for Makkah (132 kV), Madinah (132 kV), Jeddah (110 kV), Taif (132 kV), Jizan (132 kV), Abha (132 kV) and Najran (132 kV); nine projects for the expansion of the main 132 kV City Grid of Riyadh in the Central Region; and various 69 and 115 kV networks in the Eastern Province, including major HV underground connections for industries in both

Jubail and Yanbu, as well as Saudi Aramco gas producing facilities in Qatif.

High voltage underground cable systems in overseas markets

Major overseas projects include Cairo and the Suez Canal in Egypt (1992); main 110 kV feeder network for Damascus (1991); 63 kV network for Algiers, and 90 kV for Casablanca, Morocco (1995); 132 kV feeder cables for the city of Abu Dhabi (2000).

Saudi Cable's Turkish subsidiary, Demirer Kablo, has installed 138 kV cables in Atlanta, Georgia and Sacramento, California. In Europe, 40 kV cables have been supplied to London Underground and the Channel Tunnel. Currently, Demirer Kablo is involved in various 110 kV underground projects in Germany, Austria, Italy and Spain.

Saudi Cable 220 kV underground network extension – Kingdom of Bahrain

In 2005, Saudi Cable is expanding the 220 kV underground networks for the Ministry of Electricity, Kingdom of Bahrain. This project was awarded against strong competition from six major world

Figure 8.1.2 The jointing of 230 kV underground cable, Kingdom of Bahrain

manufacturers of high voltage cable systems. Major circuits for this network have already been installed and energized and the Ministry of Electricity has awarded Saudi Cable two additional extensions totalling some 260 kilometres of 220 kV underground high voltage cable, including the associated optical fibre network. This project is scheduled for completion in 2007.

Asia's first 'multi-circuit' 380 kV overhead transmission line – Saudi Arabia

Saudi Electricity Company (SEC) has contracted Saudi Cable to design and install a 'multi-circuit' 380 kV overhead transmission line that will encircle the City of Jeddah, thus bringing electrical power directly from Shoiba Power Station to Jeddah North Station at King Abdul Aziz Airport. This turnkey project covers the design, engineering, manufacture, erection, testing and commissioning of two parallel 380 kV 'multi-circuit' overhead transmission lines. As such, it is the first of its kind, not only in the Kingdom and the wider GCC, but also in Asia.

Product innovation

The world's first watertight pilot cable

One very important product solution taken up by Saudi Cable was the requirement for a completely watertight 'pilot cable". This cable is used to control high voltage circuits in Jeddah and other cities in the western region. The need arose due to SEC having difficulties with water penetration of existing pilot cables. Saudi Cable designed a completely new and unique watertight pilot cable to match SEC requirements. This is now being utilized to replace old water damaged pilot cables.

400 kV underground cable production

Saudi Cable's newest solution is the successful testing of 400 kV underground cable. This cable is used in power stations and connections between sub stations where gas insulated bus bars or overhead lines are not practical. Saudi Cable has now become one of only 10 manufacturers worldwide manufacturing such cable. This is a significant achievement for a GCC and Middle East manufacturer, providing Saudi Cable's customers with a complete product line and 'Total Solution Service'.

Total Quality Management System

Saudi Cable Company has put into place a Total Quality Management System, for which it has received ISO 9001:2000 certification from two certification bodies, namely Germanischer Lloyd Quality Management Systems, Germany and accreditation by the Dutch Accreditation Council RvA, Netherlands. Saudi Cable was the first company in the Middle East to receive ISO 9001:2000 Certification. ISO 9001 includes Design and Engineering as well as Manufacturing, Testing and Commissioning.

8.2

National Commercial Bank

Introduction

Established in 1953 as the first Saudi bank, the National Commercial Bank (NCB) has grown to become the largest and leading bank in the Arab world. NCB has pioneered the introduction of numerous conventional and *Shar'ia*-compliant financial services that now meet the needs of over one million customers. Today, over 65 per cent of all transactions are conducted electronically. The Bank is represented in the major international financial centres, while its domestic network exceeds 250 branches. Throughout its long history, NCB has always taken great pride in its support for the economic and social development of the Kingdom of Saudi Arabia.

NCB's vision is to be the premier consumer bank in Saudi Arabia; the preferred provider of financial services to selected corporate clients; the innovator of Islamic banking; and the leading regional bank. The core purpose of NCB is to maximize shareholder value and serve society, while the Bank's values are focused on people, customers and performance. In this connection, the Bank is proud of its role in supporting charitable and other organizations, as well as its contribution to the Kingdom's infrastructure development and economic growth.

Background

In 1953, Saudi Arabia's largest currency exchange house, Saleh and Abdulaziz Kaki and Salem bin Mahfouz Company of Jeddah became the first officially recognized bank, known as The National Commercial Bank. The balance sheet for 1953/54 shows total assets of SR111 million, customer deposits of SR31 million, and loans of SR52 million. The Bank had nine domestic branches and two overseas – in Beirut and Damascus. In addition to serving the leading merchant families, NCB acted as the receiver of the government's oil revenues, and the paymaster of public employees.

NCB was initially established in 1953 as a general partnership by Royal Decree, and was converted in 1997 into a joint stock company. Since 1999, shareholding has been divided between two major government institutions – the Public Investment Fund (PIF) and the General Organization for Social Insurance (GOSI) – and a number of individual investors. The government's current shareholding, which stands at 80 per cent, reflects confidence in the Bank and will help to create a transparent market for NCB shares when the general public are invited to invest in the Bank's capital.

Current size and standing

In 2003, NCB's net income exceeded SR3 billion for the first time, the highest of any regional bank, while customer deposits rose by over SR5 billion to over SR90 billion, representing more than 22 per cent of all customer deposits in the Saudi banking sector. Total assets stood at SR11.7 billion, while shareholders' equity was SR10.3 billion. Return on average equity was in excess of 31 per cent, the highest in the Saudi banking sector, compared with the industry average of less than 24 per cent.

Today, NCB provides retail, private, commercial, corporate and Islamic banking, together with a range of investment and treasury services to more than one million customers. The Bank's distribution network in the Kingdom comprises 252 branches, 873 ATMs and 4,636 point-of-sale terminals. NCB's international operations comprise branch offices in Bahrain and Beirut, plus representative offices in the UK, Japan, Singapore and South Korea. The Bank's staff totals almost 4,300 people, of whom over 80 per cent are Saudi nationals. In particular, Saudi nationals comprise over 90 per cent of NCB's executive management.

Product innovation

Over the past 50 years NCB has been a leader in the introduction of new banking products and services in the Kingdom. These include the first credit cards, ATMs, special savings schemes for students, and exclusive branches for ladies. In 1979, NCB was the first bank in Saudi Arabia to launch a mutual fund, and has followed this with numerous other innovations in real estate, healthcare, and auto finance funds. Most recently, NCB led the way with the introduction of the first collateralized loan obligation (CLO), and the first hedge fund.

The Bank also enjoys a reputation for technological innovation and leadership, and is a pioneer in internet-based banking, with e-services for retail, commercial and corporate customers. NCB launched the Kingdom's first mobile phone banking and SMS services, while its telephone banking service is the largest of its kind, handling over 2.5 million transactions annually. More than 65 per cent of all banking transactions are now conducted electronically.

NCB has also played a leading role in the development of *Shari'a*-compliant products and services in the Kingdom, including the first Islamic credit card and commercial facilitation based on the *Tawarruq* principle. NCB has over 20 Islamic mutual funds across a wide range of asset classes and investment styles, including the world's largest *Shari'a*-compliant equity fund, and the world's largest *Murabaha* fund. Nearly 50 per cent of NCB branches in the Kingdom now exclusively offer *Shari'a*-compliant products and services, including all branches in the Southern Province. By the end of 2005, it is planned for all branches to be converted to exclusively offering *Shari'a*-compliant products and services, with the exception of corporate and private banking.

NCB's leading position in the Kingdom's banking industry has been recognized by a number of international industry awards from leading institutions and publications, including Moody's and *Euromoney*. Areas of the Bank's operations that have been recognized by such awards include retail, private and corporate banking, Islamic banking and asset management and e-banking.

Further information

For further information please contact: Mr Abdullah Salem Bahamdan, Chairman and Managing Director, PO Box 3555 Jeddah 21481, Saudi Arabia. Tel: +966 2 644 1100/649 3333; Fax: +966 2 643 9595/644 6468; Email: alahli.com@alahli.com or a.bahamdan@alahli.com; Website: www.alahli.com.

Saudi European Petrochemical Company
US$ 400,000,000
Term Loan Facility
Arranger & Book Runner
May 1998
Saudi Telecom Company
SR 2,250,000,000
Medium Term Loan Facility
As one of the Arranger banks
March 1999
Saudi Petrochemical Company
US$ 300,000,000
Term Loan Facility
Arranger
May 1999
Al Jubail Fertilizer Company
US$ 105,000,000
Term Loan Facility
Arranger & Agent
April 2000
Al Mabani General Contractors
SR 335,000,000
Various Facilities
Arranger
December 2000
Aziz Company Limited
SR 304,120,778
Various Credit Facilities
Arranger & Agent
April 2002
Jubail United Petrochemical Company
US$ 1,154,000,000
Term Loan Facility
Arranger
August 2002
Saudi Petrochemical Company
US$ 650,000,000
Term & Revolving Facilities
Arranger & Agent
February 2003
Saudi Oger
US$ 260,000,000
Term Loan & Revolving Credit Facilities
Arranger
January 2004
The Banker
DEALS OF THE YEAR 2004
Ettihad Etisalat
Islamic Bridge Financing Facility
US$ 2,350,000,000
Lead Arranger, Escrow Agent, Modareb & Local Book Runner
September 2004
Saudi Electricity Company
SR 6,000,000,000
Term Loan Facility
Mandated Lead Arranger & Account Bank
May 2004
NCB الأهلي

8.3

Al-Faisaliah Group

Introduction

Al-Faisaliah Group (AFG) is a major diversified enterprise based in Saudi Arabia and operating across the Middle East. Established in 1970 by HRH Prince Abdullah Al-Faisal, the eldest son of late King Faisal, the Group has grown to become one of the top 20 Saudi companies with over 5,000 employees, and is also one of the fastest-growing organizations in the country. Today, AFG has 13 subsidiaries involved in five business sectors and an annual turnover of approximately SR2billion (US$533 million).

Through its subsidiaries, and in partnership with major international groups, AFG has established a dominant position in six major sectors: food and beverages; consumer electronics; medical equipment, measurement and media equipment; IT and communications; entertainment and multimedia; and speciality chemicals.

Known in Saudi Arabia as a leading 'brand builder', AFG has successfully utilized partnerships with leading companies to develop international and local brands for the local and regional markets. This includes the Group's own brands such as Al Safi dairy, ZAI computers, Areen juices and Al-Wasmi meats.

Group strategy

The Group's strategy, directed by the present Group Chairman, HRH Prince Mohammed Al-Abdullah Al-Faisal, is to ensure sustainable and profitable growth. This will be achieved through organic and external development of its core businesses as well as development of new businesses in prime growth sectors. A key element of this strategy is to work with leading international companies to develop markets in the Middle East. This entails growing existing business partnerships while actively seeking new strategic alliances with other leading international players.

AFG has ambitious revenue, profitability and cash flow targets, and deploys substantial ongoing investment in research and development, people and information technology. This supports its goal of becoming the leading Saudi-based multinational organization, operating in selected prime growth sectors.

Sectors of group activity

Supply chain management

PWC Logistics is the leading provider of supply chain solutions to companies and governmental organizations throughout the Middle East. Through its integrated network of warehouse facilities and transportation options, PWC provides its customers with flexible logistics solutions tailored to meet their business needs.

PWC provides third and fourth-party logistics services to a wide range of industries, including food and grocery, consumer packaged goods, apparel and footwear, consumer and industrial electronics, oil field services and governmental and military organizations. In addition to traditional warehousing services, PWC offers inventory management and order processing and fulfilment. PWC's value-added services include product labelling, packing, co-packing, bundling, kitting, light assembly, and returns processing. PWC's customers can view and actively manage their inventories through a web-based portal.

Both customers and industry experts have praised PWC's strong focus on customer service. During 2004, the Global Institute of Logistics named PWC the best company of its kind in the GCC. PWC Logistics is traded on the Kuwaiti Stock Exchange.

Speciality chemicals

AFG is a leading supplier of speciality chemicals to the Saudi oil and gas and petrochemical sectors and to the downstream plastics processing industry.

Established in 1983, Modern Petrochemicals, supplies fuel additives, lubricating oil additives, bulk active pharmaceuticals, additives to the polymer and composites industries, catalysts and hydrocarbons. The Company is also specialized in the handling of IMCO classified hazardous chemicals.

Modern Petrochemicals acts as the sole distributor in Saudi Arabia for a number of major international chemical manufacturers including ETHYL Corporation, AFTON Chemicals, Albemarle Corporation, BP Chemicals, Tessenderlo, Grace Davison and TANFAC. It has also established business alliances with other leading manufacturers such as Dow Chemicals and ATOFINA.

Entertainment and multimedia

AFG is also a major regional entertainment and multimedia company. Established in 1992, AFG subsidiary company, Megastar, imports, wholesales, distributes and retails a wide range of entertainment software such as music, video films and programmes, multimedia software, accessories and hardware. It represents major audio and visual labels such as Sony, Universal, Twentieth Century Fox, Columbia TriStar and MGM. In recent years, Megastar has enjoyed strong growth, with an annual growth rate in 2004 exceeding 40 per cent.

Megastar's independent distribution network now has more than 650 dealers throughout the Middle East, together with its own retail outlets in the GCC. It also has a highly sophisticated music and videocassette replicating facility. In addition, it has established its own Artist and Repertoire division to promote the development of Arabic music.

IT and communications

AFG is the dominant IT networking company and primary internet access provider in Saudi Arabia. The leading provider of integrated IT solutions and services in the Kingdom of Saudi Arabia, Ebttikar Technology Company is also the first local company in the Middle East to receive Cisco 'Gold Partner' certification.

AFG subsidiary Arabian Internet and Communications Services Company (AWALNET) is the premier ISP in the Kingdom, with a large client base comprising corporate and individual customers.

Another AFG subsidiary, Al-Faisaliah Business and Technology Services Company (FBTC), leads the way in ERP, SAP, corporate treasury, mobile sales and content management solutions.

Medical, measurement and media equipment

AFG is a major supplier of medical equipment, pharmaceutical supplies, chemical analysis systems, telecommunications products, and test and measurement equipment, to the public and private sectors.

A market leader in medical equipment, Al-Faisaliah Medical and Measurement Systems (FMMS) has long-established relationships with international partners that include Agilent Technologies (previously HP), Bausch and Lomb, Philips, Leica, Sony and Canon.

Al-Faisaliah Telecom and Measurement Systems (ATMS) provides test and measurement equipment, and complete test solutions, for the defence, telecommunications, oil and gas, and education sectors. It represents leading international partners that include Aethra, Sumitumo, Wave Wireless Networking, and Sofrecom.

Modern Media Systems (MMS) is a leading player in the field of professional electronics, specializing in audio-visual media equipment, video broadcast systems, and security systems. MMS has been the exclusive distributor for Sony since 1971, and also represents Canon, Tektronix and Quantel.

Consumer electronics

AFG is a leading distributor of consumer electronics, computers and related products, as well as a manufacturer of personal computers.

Modern Electronics Company has acted as the exclusive distributor for Sony Corporation for over 30 years, and today enjoys a market share approaching 40 per cent, with annual sales exceeding US$200 million, and a network of more than 800 dealers in Saudi Arabia.

The ZAI personal computer produced by the Al-Faisaliah PC Factory is the only personal computer entirely assembled in Saudi Arabia, and the only local brand certified by Microsoft and Intel in the Middle East. In just three years, ZAI has achieved a market share in Saudi Arabia estimated at five per cent in 2004.

Food and beverages

AFG is also a major producer and distributor of dairy products, fresh meat and fruit juices. Al Safi-Danone, a joint venture between Danone Group, France and AFG, is a market leader in Saudi Arabia for fresh dairy products. Around 200,000 tonnes of dairy, meat and juice products are produced annually, and distributed daily to more than 27,000 retail outlets via 26 main distribution centres in Saudi Arabia, Kuwait and Qatar, with further expansion planned in the near future. With annual sales of over US$200 million, Al Safi accounts for an estimated 33 per cent of the Kingdom's market for dairy products.

Al Safi Dairy is the largest integrated dairy farm in the world, with a herd of over 32,000 Holstein cattle, and this provides Al Safi-Danone with an exclusive source of high-quality milk. Al Safi produces 450,000 litres of milk daily and 6,000 kilos of boneless meat annually.

Al Safi-Danone further benefits from the global R&D and training facilities of Groupe Danone, a global leader in dairy products. Al Safi owns a fleet of more than 450 refrigerated trucks, delivering directly to 18,000 retail outlets every day.

AFG also provides fresh red meat (Wasmi Meat), and a range of fruit juices (Areen Juice), and has plans to diversify further into the non-dairy food sector. The Group recently expanded its food retail services with the acquisition of the prestigious Kingdom-wide chain known as Steakhouse Restaurants.

Further information

For further information on the activities of the Al-Faisaliah Group visit www.alfaisaliah.com. In addition, information on specific AFG subsidiaries can be found as follows:

- Al Faisaliah Medical & Measurement Systems: www.alfaisaliah-medical.com;
- Al Safi-Danone: www.Alsafi.com;
- Awalnet: www.Awalnet.net.sa;
- Modern Electronics: www.mee.com.sa;
- Al Faisaliah PC Factory: www.zai.com.sa;
- Megastar: www.megastar.com.sa;
- PWC Logistics: www.pwclogistics.com.

8.4

HIDADA

Introduction

HIDADA was established in Jeddah in 1982 to support the Kingdom's ambition to be self-sufficient in steel fabrication. Since then, HIDADA has grown rapidly to become a leader in the engineering and fabrication of quality steel products, both as a major player in the Kingdom's steel fabrication industry and for global markets.

Since its establishment, HIDADA has grown, as a wholly-owned subsidiary of XENEL Industries Group, through measured expansion and diversification to become a leading supplier of steel products to the GCC, Middle East and international markets, with a total of 1,200 employees.

The company increased its capacity from 2,000 tonnes per year of structural steel fabrication to more than 184,000 tonnes of diversified and specialized steel products (see Figure 8.4.1), catering for the requirements of power, oil and gas, petrochemicals, airports, seaports, high-rise buildings, cement plants, metal smelters, water desalination plants and other industries.

HIDADA's Jeddah-based manufacturing facilities are geared up to produce a broadly diversified range of products. The company's services range from basic structural fabrication to the design, supply and installation of the most complex structural steelwork based on a broad range of international standards (ASTM, BS, DIN, JIS).

The main areas of HIDADA's business are the fabrication, construction and erection of heavy steel structures. HIDADA's steel fabrication includes boilers, pressure vessels, light poles, masts, pylons, tanks, gratings and transmission towers. The company's activities also cover design engineering and surface treatment of structures.

HIDADA is recognized for the supply of good quality products and services to many countries in Africa, Asia and Europe and the United States. The company is known for its policy of investing in human skills optimization, the latest technology, work process improvement and other resources required to enable it to compete in a global marketplace.

Clients are offered design, engineering, fabrication and on-site erection services, supported by qualified skilled engineers and technicians.

Computer-aided design and manufacturing facilities are employed by the company to fulfil orders that suit specific requirements. HIDADA's Central Engineering and Operation System (CEOS) is an in-house developed software that constantly monitors design, engineering, production and treatment to assure sequential deliveries meeting customers' needs.

HIDADA is also looking to enhance the level of cooperation with its clients by offering a 'Total Solutions' approach that, according to the company, may take the form of alliances and joint ventures with other global organizations. This approach aims to identify areas where the company can expand its range of value-added services offered to potential clients and diversify this range to serve different sectors. The 'Total Solutions' approach will cover, but will not necessarily be limited to, project management services, design, engineering, manufacturing and on-site erection. This is complemented by HIDADA's Total Quality Management environment, which aims to ensure that projects are completed in accordance with agreed budgets and schedules.

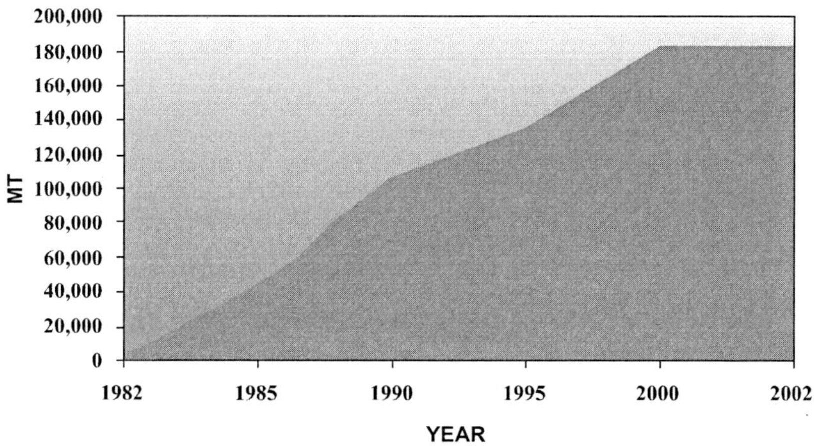

MT = metric tonnes

Figure 8.4.1 HIDADA capacity growth 1982–2002

Products and services

HIDADA is a diversified organization carrying out the design and fabrication of specialized products for power transmission and distribution, lighting, telecommunications, petrochemical plants, seaport container handling cranes, airports, power plants, desalination plants, high-rise buildings, and other industries. Key product and service areas of HIDADA's business are as follows:

- lattice steel towers for national and international telecommunication and power transmission (33kV to 500kV);
- high masts, wind turbine masts, lighting poles, power distribution poles, and power transmission poles;
- various types of crane, ranging from the largest lifting capacity of 50 tonnes, seaport container handling cranes, straddle cranes, rubber-tyred gantry cranes (RTGs) and overhead travelling cranes (OTCs);
- cable support systems, including cable trays and cable ladders of different heights and thickness in steel and aluminium as well as steel cable trays and cable ladders;
- bulk storage tanks manufactured to international codes API650, API620, BS2654, either in carbon or stainless steel for power and water desalination plants, oil and gas installations, petrochemical plants, chemical and other industrial plants;
- steel grating panels for platforms for open steel walkways and stair treads that are installed in power stations, desalination plants, petrochemical complexes, cement factories and industrial manufacturing bases;
- heaters, pressure vessels, boilers, steel chimneys;
- aircraft hangars or shelters, blast-proof doors (measuring up to 60 metres in length and weighing 150 tonnes);
- in-house anti-corrosion treatment, including dry process hot dip galvanizing to provide long lasting protection against the harshest environmental conditions.

HIDADA offers specialist fabrication and related services that include:

- design, detailing, fabrication, supply and on-site erection of structural steelworks for the power generation, water desalination, oil and gas, petrochemical, defence and aviation, seaports, commercial/high-rise buildings, cement plants, metal smelters industries;
- surface treatment including hot-dip galvanizing.

Turnkey jobs include the preparation of detailed design as per specification, material supply, installation and pre-commissioning. Under the 'Total Solutions' approach, HIDADA will also aim to introduce new products such as Complete Heaters, Heat Recovery Steam Generators (HRSG) and Specialized Tanks.

Production facilities

HIDADA has six specialist plants and associated warehouse facilities located at Jeddah Industrial Estate. The company's production and warehouse facilities cover over 120,000m^2 as follows:

- Production Plant 1 – towers, poles, high masts and galvanizing plant (15,000m^2);
- Production Plant 2 – medium and heavy structural steelworks, blast-proof doors, gratings, pressure vessels, container handling cranes, EOT cranes and surface treatment (42,000m^2);
- Production Plant 3 – cable support systems and light and medium structure steel (10,000m^2);
- Production Plant 4 – production of gratings and cable support systems (5,000m^2);
- Production Plant 5 – storage tanks and boilers (2,650m^2);
- Production Plant 6 – bolts and nuts (7,500m^2);
- warehouses for storage of materials, finished products and trial assembly.

Quality standards

HIDADA's product range complies with all Saudi Arabian and international standards for industrial and commercial applications. The company's processes are also certified in accordance to ISO9001 for quality assurance (see Figure 8.4.2).

Complete vertical integration means that design engineering, fabrication and treatment facilities at HIDADA are carried out in-house, offering clients total control through the company's state-of-the-art monitoring Centralized Engineering and Operation System (CEOS), which allows constant detailed monitoring of the progress of a job by a customer from any location via the internet. All of HIDADA's production facilities are linked by fibre optic cable for the CEOS.

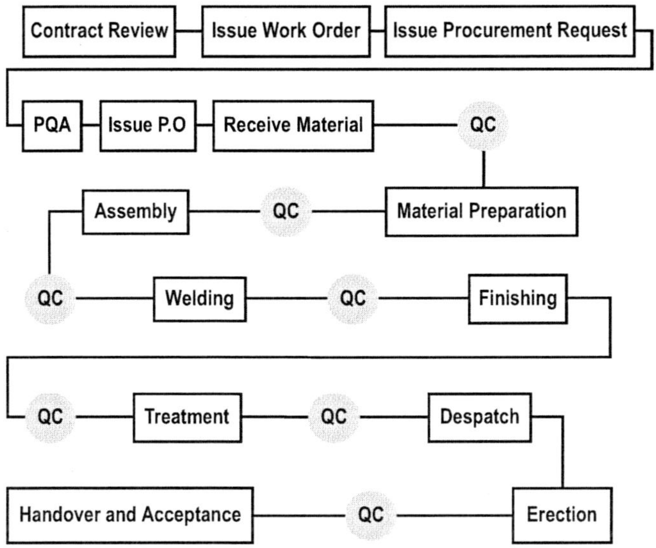

Figure 8.4.2 HIDADA quality assurance and quality control

Domestic and international markets

In Saudi Arabia, HIDADA has forged a close working relationship with Saudi Aramco, SABIC affiliate companies and the Saudi Electricity Company (SEC), having worked on many of their prestigious projects (see Table 8.4.1).

It has also worked extensively with SEC on overhead transmission line towers and distribution lighting poles. Bulk storage tanks are manufactured in carbon or stainless steel to international codes API650, API620, BS2654 for customers that include both Saudi Aramco and SEC.

HIDADA's products and services are also provided throughout the GCC and Middle East region. The company has also been successful in penetrating markets in many parts of the world, including the United States, Central and South America, Caribbean, Western Europe, Africa and Asia. In particular, high masts, wind turbine masts, lighting poles, power distribution poles, and power transmission poles have been supplied to the Far East, the Arabian Gulf, and North African markets.

Table 8.4.1 Examples of HIDADA clients by product group 1992–2002

Year	Structural steel work	Towers and poles	Storage tanks and cranes
2002	Cinergy	Gecol, Libya	Shuweihat Power Generation, Abu Dhabi
	Electricity De France	NEPA, Nigeria	
2001	SEC (West) Saudi Aramco	MEW, Kuwait WAPDA, Pakistan SEC (West)	Saudi Aramco
2000	ABB	SEC (West)	
1999	American National Power	SCECO (Central)	Qatar Vinyl Corporation Electricity Corporation
1998	Petrokemya Yanpet Ministry of Public Works and Housing SAFCO	SAFCO (South) Etisalat, UAE Egyptian Electricity Authority	
1997	SCECO (East) KNPC Kuwait Chekka Cement Plant, Lebanon	PLN, Indonesia Ministry of PTT	
1996	SCECO (Central) Ibn Rushd, Yanbu Saudi Iron & Steel (HADEED)		
1995	SWCC	Electricite Du Liban, Lebanon	Saudi Cable Company
	Tabuk Cement Plant United Sugar Co	MEW, Oman	Mansour Al Dakhil
1994	Southern Province Cement Co Mahmood Saeed	Electricity Corporation	Saudi Iron and Steel Company (HADEED)
1992	Ibn Zahr		Jeddah Islamic Port

Further information

For further information concerning HIDADA contact: Sheikh Khalid Ali Reza, Managing Director, HIDADA, PO Box 11809, Jeddah 21463, Saudi Arabia. Tel: +966 2 637 4450, Fax: +966 2 637 5428, Website: www.hidada.com.sa.

HIDADA

Since its establishment in 1982, Jeddah-based Hidada has grown through measured expansion to become a leading supplier of steel products to the GCC, Middle East and international markets.

Such growth has mirrored the economic development of Saudi Arabia and has seen the company - a wholly Saudi-owned subsidiary of Xenel Industries - expand to a total annual fabrication capacity of more than 160,000 tonnes, making it the cornerstone of the steel fabrication industry in the Kingdom.

Hidada continues to invest in human resource development, the latest technologies and process improvements to stay ahead of the competition and help meet the varied and stringent needs of its customers.

To enhance its reputation for innovation and quality, Hidada has been actively seeking new ways to maintain its competitive edge. A major recent restructuring programme, for instance, saw the introduction of a balanced scorecard system as well as a process-centred organisation programme and process renewal for major processes.

Hidada is also looking to enhance cooperation with its clients by offering a 'total solutions' approach which, according to the company, may take the form of alliances and joint ventures with other global organisations.

The approach will aim to identify areas where the company can expand its range of value added services offered to potential clients and diversify this range to serve different sectors.

This approach will cover, but will not necessarily be limited to, project management services, design, engineering, manufacturing and on-site erection.

At present, Hidada has five specialist plants in Industrial Estate next to Jeddah Islamic Port. From these, Hidada offers specialist fabrication and related services which includes:

1) Design, Detailing, Fabrication, Surface Treatment, Supply, Delivery and Erection of Structural Steelworks for the Power Generation, Water Desalination, Oil & Gas, Petrochemical, Defense & Aviation, Seaports, Commercial / High-rise Buildings, Cement Plants, Metal Smelters Industries.

2) Design, Detailing, Fabrication, Galvanizing (hot-dip), Supply and Delivery of Power Transmission & Telecommunication Towers, Transmission/Distribution & Lighting Poles.

3) Turnkey job for Storage Tanks catering for Power Plants, Water Desalination Plants, Oil & Gas Sector, Petrochemical Plants, Chemical and Other Industrial Plants. Our scope involves Preparation of Detailed Design as per Specification, Material Supply, Installation and Pre-commissioning.

4) Other Activities / Products include Gratings, Cable Support Systems, Heaters, Pressure Vessels, Air Ducts, Steel Chimneys, Boilers, Container Handling / Seaport / E.O.T. Cranes and Blast Proof Doors.

Under the 'Total Solutions' approach, Hidada will also aim to introduce new products such as Complete Heaters, Heat Recovery Steam Generators (HRSG) and Specialised Tanks.

Hidada's product range complies with all Saudi and international standards for industrial and commercial applications. The company's processes are also certified in accordance to ISO9001 for quality assurance. These standards are backed by a highly qualified workforce of approximately 1000.

Complete vertical integration means that design engineering, fabrication and treatment facilities at Hidada are carried out in-house, offering clients total control through the company's state-of-the-art, unique monitoring Centralized Engineering & Operation System (CEOS), which allows constant detailed monitoring of the progress of a job by a customer from anywhere on earth via the Internet. All Hidada's factories are linked by fibre-optic cable for the CEOS.

In Saudi Arabia, Hidada has forged a close relationship with Saudi Aramco and Sabic companies, having worked on many of their prestigious projects. It has also worked with the Saudi Electricity Company for overhead transmission line towers and distribution/lighting poles.

As well as being renowned in Saudi Arabia, Hidada's services are provided through the GCC and Middle East. The company has also penetrated projects in different parts of the world, including the US, Mexico, Chile, Peuroto Rico, Denmark, Spain, Africa and Asia, often against stiff competition, proof then that Hidada is a truly world-class operator.

8.5

Saudi Arabian Amiantit Group

Introduction

The Saudi Arabian Amiantit Group is a leading industrial organization that manufactures high quality pipe systems, supplies advanced pipe technologies, and provides water management services. The Group delivers to municipal, industrial, agricultural and energy markets worldwide – supporting global infrastructure development.

Since the establishment of the parent company, The Saudi Arabian Amiantit Company (SAAC) in 1968 in Dammam, Amiantit has developed an extensive global sales and service network that ensures customers in some 70 countries have access to the wide range of pipe systems, technologies and services offered by the Group. The company's range of pipe systems and products include concrete, GRP, glass reinforced epoxy (GRE), polyolefin and ductile iron. Amiantit is a major player in all market segments and now ranks as the world's biggest manufacturer of GRP pipes.

SAAC is a Saudi joint stock company, listed on the Saudi Stock Exchange. The other members of the Group are mainly limited liability companies – owned by the Amiantit Group in varying percentages and operating under individual commercial registrations.

In 2003, the Amiantit Group's turnover was US$432 million, the paid up share capital US$187million[1] and the market capitalization US$800 million. In August 2005, the Amiantit Group announced that it had secured contracts in the GCC totalling US$211 million for the first half of 2005 to supply various industrial and infrastructure projects in Saudi Arabia, other GCC countries and Yemen.

---

[1] In 2005, Amiantit obtained approval from the Capital Money Authority (CMA) to increase its capital from SR770 million to SR1,155 billion through issuance of 7.7 million rights issues that represent 50 per cent of the circulated shares. Subscription in the new shares was limited to current shareholders registered at July 2005.

The Amiantit Group is comprised of 34 pipe and other manufacturing facilities (majority owned or joint ventures), 11 pipe technology companies, and a number of trading and service companies operating in 16 countries around the world. A total of 31 of Amiantit's production plants manufacture a comprehensive range of pipe products whereas the rest produces rubber products for seals and air conditioning applications, fibreglass insulation products for thermal and acoustical applications, fibreglass products, fibreglass reinforced plastic products, sizing and agents, lining materials against corrosion, and polyurethane products for pipes and tanks, flooring and insulation. In addition, the Group's technology division, consisting of 11 technology companies, makes the Amiantit Group a global leader in pipe technology.

The mission of the Amiantit Group is to be a global leader in the fields of pipe manufacture and pipe technology and to deliver superior quality services to customers worldwide, providing pipe systems for water, sewage, gas, oil and industrial applications and expertise in the latest pipe technologies. The Group vision is to be the world leader in pipe and technology solutions.

Amiantit Pipe Systems Division

Amiantit Group's 31 pipe production plants produce pipes and pipe systems of concrete, GRP, GRE and ductile iron, with brand names like Amidip, Amiplas, Amipol, Amipol Mobile, Amipox, Budaplast, Flowtite, Meyer Polycrete, Sarplast, Speedmark, SwedePipe and Vectus that are marketed in 18 countries around the world.

Concrete pipe systems

The main applications of concrete pipe systems are storm water, drainage, wastewater and sewage systems. The Amiantit Group companies involved in GRP pipe industries are: Ameron Saudi Arabia Ltd (ASAL) of Dammam and Al Jubail and Saudi Arabia Concrete Products Ltd (SACOP) of Jeddah.

ASAL was founded in 1978 as a joint venture between Amiantit (70 per cent) and Ameron International (USA). ASAL's five production plants in Dammam and Al Jubail have the capacity to make a total of 1,100 kilometres a year of high quality concrete cylinder pipes, reinforced and pre-stressed concrete cylinder pipes and reinforced concrete pipes in diameters ranging from 300mm to 4,000mm. ASAL also carries out cement mortar lining of steel pipes and fittings in diameters ranging from 75mm to 100mm (in lengths of 12m to 16m). Ameron pipes are used for most water and sewage system requirements. ASAL and Ameron also operate the joint venture company, Ameron Egypt Ltd, to produce concrete pipes for the Egyptian market.

SACOP was formed in 1978 in Jeddah as a joint venture between Amiantit, Ameron Saudi Arabia Ltd (79 per cent) and Ameron International. SACOP produces reinforced concrete pipes in diameters ranging from 300mm to 3,000mm for storm water and drainage systems, reinforced concrete pipes (with T-Lock or PVC lining) in diameters ranging from 700mm to 3,000mm for waste water and sewer systems and reinforced concrete jacking pipes with diameters of 1,800mm. The company also produces reinforced concrete manholes (with T-Lock or FRP lining) and inspection chambers in diameters ranging from 1,000mm to 1,800mm and 750mm to 3,000mm respectively. SACOP has the capacity to manufacture 56,000 tonnes of quality products per annum.

GRP pipe industries

The main applications of GRP pipe systems are water, gravity and forced main sewer lines, water transmission, irrigation, and municipal storm water lines. The Amiantit Group companies involved in GRP pipe industries are Amiantit Fibreglass Industries (AFIL), Fibreglass Company (FPC) and Amitech Saudi Arabia Limited.

AFIL is located in Dammam, Saudi Arabia. Since its establishment in 1977, AFIL has become a global leader in the design and manufacture of GRP pipes. The company has, to date, produced over 6,000 kilometres of GRP pipes and fittings. AFIL produces pipes up to 3,700mm in diameter with a wall thickness of 53mm, as well as tanks, manholes and inspection chambers. AFIL overseas subsidiary companies include:

- Amiantit Fibreglass Egypt Company Ltd – a producer of GRP pipes in Egypt, where AFIL owns 50 per cent;
- Amiantit Fibreglass Industries India Pvt. Ltd (AMITECH) – a joint venture in India established in 2002 between Amiantit (70 per cent) and the Salgaocar Group to produce GRP pipes in diameters ranging from 300mm to 3,000mm and tanks.

FPC was established in 2001 in Dammam as a joint venture between Amiantit and a local investor. FPC uses the helical-winding process to produce fibreglass pipes and fittings in diameters ranging from 25mm to 3,000mm. FPC also produces structural manholes, manhole liners and aboveground tanks. FPC pipes are used for water, seawater, sewer and chemical applications.

Amitech Saudi Arabia Ltd, wholly owned by Amiantit, began production in 2002 in Jeddah. The ultramodern factory employs both the Flowtite continuous mandrel production technology and the C-Tech centrifugal casting technology to produce GRP pipes in diameters ranging from 300mm to 3,000mm. Amitech and other Amiantit Group overseas subsidiaries include:

- Amitech USA LLC – formed in 2001 to cater to the demands of the huge North American market. To date, it is the greatest international greenfield investment of the Group. The factory, situated in Baton Rouge, Louisiana, uses the Flowtite technology to produce GRP pipe systems in diameters ranging from 300mm to 2,400mm. The yearly benchmark capacity is 200km of DN 600 pipes;
- Amitech Industrial South Africa (Pty) Ltd, located in Krugersdorp, is a joint venture between Amiantit (51 per cent) and South African partners. The company has been designing, manufacturing and supplying GRP pipes, vessels, chimney stacks and related thermoplastic products for the mining and chemical industries since 1979;
- Amitech South Africa (Pty) Ltd was established in 2001 in Alrode, south of Johannesburg. The company, which is fully owned by Amiantit, produces GRP and GRV pipes in diameters ranging from 300mm to 1,200mm and 150mm to 2,200mm respectively. The plant is also equipped with three lines for un-elasticised (uPVC) and modified polyvinyl chloride (mPVC) pipes in diameters ranging from 50mm to 500mm and four lines for solid wall high density polyethylene (HDPE) pipes in diameters ranging from 16mm to 630mm.
- Amitech Spain SA was formed in Camarles in 1994 to manufacture GRP pipes in diameters ranging from 300mm to 3,000mm. The annual benchmark capacity of the two machines is in excess of 400km of DN 600 pipes;
- Amitech Poland SP, established in 1991 in Gdansk, Poland, is a joint venture between Amiantit (78 per cent) and a local partner. Amitech employs the Flowtite technology to manufacture GRP pipes and fittings in diameters ranging from 500mm to 2,400mm (the benchmark capacity is 140km of DN 600 pipes per annum);
- Amitech Brazil Tubos SA (formerly G-Tec Tubos), located in São Paulo, began its activities in 2000 as the first company to produce centrifugally-cast GRP pipe systems in Latin America. The company has a yearly benchmark capacity of 200km of DN 600 pipes and produces pipes in diameters ranging from 350mm to 2,400mm.
- Chongqing Tianli Amiantit Materials Engineering Joint Stock Co. Ltd (TLA) was formed in 2003 in Chongqing by Amiantit (who owns

25 per cent) and two Chinese partners. TLA produces GRP pipes in diameters ranging from 900mm to 4,000mm;

- Sarplast Iniziative Industriali SpA was established in Santa Luce, Italy in 1973, with Amiantit as minority shareholder. The company offers design, manufacture and supply of cross-winded GRP pipes/ accessories in diameters ranging from 25mm to 3,000mm;
- Subor Boru Sanayi ve Ticaret AS was founded in 1996 in Adapazari with Yapi Merkezi and Amiantit as equal partners. In 2000, Subor Boru and Fernas Insaat formed the 80/20 joint venture Subor Gap Boru Sanayi ve Ticaret AS in Sanliurfa. The two plants, employing the Flowtite technology, manufacture GRP pipe systems in diameters ranging from 300mm to 2,400mm;
- Dubai Pipe Factory Ltd was established in 2001 and is located in Dubai, United Arab Emirates. It manufactures GRP pipes, tanks, manholes, fittings and accessories. Relatively new on the scene, the company is trying to make a name for itself using Flowtite technology, provided by Amiantit.

Glass reinforced epoxy (GRE) pipes

Glass reinforced epoxy (GRE) pipe systems are well suited for environments where corrosion resistance is required at a reasonable price – petrochemical process lines, oil and gas systems, offshore and onshore systems, as well as ship and marine systems. One of the many advantages of GRE systems is that, once installed, they are virtually maintenance free. The Amiantit Group companies involved in GRE pipe industries are Bondstrand Ltd (BSL) and Amitech Industrial Saudi Arabia.

BSL, formed in Dammam, Saudi Arabia in 1982, is a joint venture between Amiantit (60 per cent) and Ameron BV. BSL produces GRE pipes, fittings, flanges and spools in diameters ranging from 25mm to 1,000mm. Bondstrand Kuwait Ltd, founded in 1999, is a joint venture between BSL (49 per cent) and the Kuwaiti Al-Watani Factory and Nouri Industrial Est. The company produces and sells fibreglass pipes in Kuwait.

Amitech Industrial Saudi Arabia Ltd was established in Dammam in 2003 as a fully-owned subsidiary of Amiantit. The plant uses state-of-the-art technology to produce lightweight, high-quality GRE pipes in diameters ranging from 80mm to 600mm in a fully automated process. The company also manufacture fittings, flanges and spools. The products, marketed under the brand name Amipox, have a wide range of applications – petrochemical process lines, oil and gas systems, fire fighting systems, offshore and onshore systems, as well as marine systems – where fire and corrosion-resistant materials are required at reasonable prices.

One Amiantit Group overseas subsidiary is Composite Pipe Industries LLC (CPI). This company was established in Sohar, Sultanate of Oman in 1998. In late 2001, Amiantit acquired the majority of the shares in CPI (51 per cent). The company, which obtained its expertise by a technology transfer from the former French company SEPMA, manufactures GRE, GRP and GRV pipes, fittings, flanges and spools in diameters ranging from 25mm to 2,400mm.

Polyolefin piping systems

The main applications of polyolefin pipe systems are drinking water transmission pipelines, irrigation, industrial and municipal sewage networks, and in electrical, telecommunication and fibre optic cable systems. They are also used in gas distribution networks and industrial outfalls. The Amiantit Group companies involved in polyolefin pipe industries are Saudi Plastic Products Company (SAPPCO) and Amiantit Polyolefin Piping Systems Company Ltd (APPSCO).

SAPPCO, in which Amiantit holds 48 per cent, was formed in the early 1980s in Dammam. Its integrated plant produces a wide range of PVC and PE pipe products for sale on the domestic and international markets. (SAPPCO's affiliated company APLACO in Riyadh makes fittings designed for use with its pipes.) The SAPPCO plant is ISO 9002, EN ISO 9002, ANSI, AQSC Q9002, SASO and GS ISO 9002 certified.

APPSCO was founded in 2000 in Jeddah. The hi-tech 80,000m^2 facility is equipped with three lines for the production of solid wall high density polyethylene (HDPE) pipes in diameters ranging from 25mm to 630mm and one line for the production of corrugated double wall polypropylene (PP) pipes in diameters ranging from 200mm to 1,000mm. Using the latest developments in equipment and technology, APPSCO has the capacity to produce 15,000 tonnes per year of superior quality pipes and fittings.

Ductile iron (DI) piping systems

The main applications of ductile iron pipe systems are transporting potable water, industrial water, irrigation water, pressure sewage, natural gas, high temperature liquids and chemicals and in industrial heating and fire extinguishing systems.

The Amiantit Group companies involved in ductile iron pipe industries are Saudi Arabian Ductile Iron Pipes Company Ltd (SADIP) and DIFAV Amiantit Ltd.

SADIP, founded in 1988 in Dammam, is a joint venture between Amiantit (70 per cent), Pont-A-Mousson and a local partner and is the largest ductile iron pipe factory in the Middle East. Four centrifugal casting machines with a yearly capacity of 130,000 tonnes produce ductile iron pipes and fittings in diameters ranging from 100mm to 700mm for use in irrigation, forced sewer lines, and transmission of water, natural gas and high temperature liquids. A wide range of linings and external coatings ensures that pipes can withstand the harshest of environments. In due course, SADIP will open a plant in Jeddah where two centrifugal casting machines with an annual capacity of 85,000 tonnes will produce ductile iron pipes and fittings in diameters ranging from 800mm to 2,000mm.

DIFAV Amiantit Ltd was established in 2000 and is located in Dammam. The company, which is fully owned by Amiantit, manufactures flanged ductile iron pipes, fittings and valve assemblies. The main purchaser of the company's products is SADIP. Amiantit's recent overseas joint venture company in ductile iron pipes is Amidip SA, located in Calan, Romania. The plant consists of a blast furnace and a modern equipped foundry with state-of-the-art centrifugal casting machines that will produce high-quality ductile iron pipes from 100mm to 700mm from 2005.

Amiantit Materials Division

Amiantit Materials Division is comprised of six enterprises that manufacture rubber products for seals and air-conditioning applications, fibreglass insulation products for thermal and acoustical applications, fibreglass products, fibreglass reinforced plastic products, sizing and agents, lining materials that are used to protect pipes and structures against corrosion, and polyurethane products for pipes and tanks, flooring and insulation.

Amiantit Rubber Industries Ltd (ARIL) established in 1977, produces quality rubber seals to match the Group's pipe products. The company, which is 80 per cent owned by Amiantit and located in Dammam, is also engaged in the manufacture of products for air-conditioning applications and the industrial, building and construction sectors.

Arabian Fibreglass Insulation Company (AFICO) was established in Dammam in 1980. The company, with an annual capacity of 9,000 tonnes, manufactures fibreglass insulation products for thermal and acoustical applications for the commercial, industrial and residential sectors. The product range comprises acoustical ceiling panels, blanket, board and roof insulation, faced duct wrap, duct liner, mechanical board insulation, heavy density pipe and pipe wrap insulation, thermal insulation wool, and cavity wall and metal building insulation.

Chongqing Polycom International Corporation Ltd (CPIC) and Chongqing Techfibre New Materials Company Ltd (Techfibre) are located in Chongqing, China. The companies (of which Amiantit owns 17 per cent and 25 per cent respectively) manufacture fibreglass products, fibreglass reinforced plastic products, sizing and agents. Both companies have been channelling huge resources into research and development and have thus become experts in industrial fibreglass manufacturing technology. CPIC and Techfibre have a total annual production capacity of 65,000 tonnes – a number that will increase to 100,000 tonnes when a second furnace at Techfibre commences production in 2005. The Amiantit Group is a main purchaser of the high-quality fibreglass produced by the plants.

Saudi Arabian Amiantit Plastic Products Manufacturing Company Ltd (AmPlas) was formed in 2002 as a 100 per cent subsidiary of Amiantit. AmPlas produces lining materials that are used to protect pipes and structures against corrosion. AmPlas is the first company in the world to produce such lining material with a width of 2,000mm. The company boasts an impressive integrated plant that consists of an entirely automated production line – from the compounding to the actual production of the primary lining material – used to manufacture the T-Lining from PVC and PE polymers. PVC lining material is jointed by high frequency welding machines, which ensure uniform jointing and strength.

Ya-Coat Amiantit Ltd was established in 2001 in Dammam. The company, fully owned by Amiantit, produces 100 per cent solid polyurethane coating systems for pipes and tanks – suitable for both metallic and non-metallic surfaces. The company also manufactures elastomeric polyurethane for flooring and polyurethane foams for insulation. The company's products are distinguished by high resistance to abrasion, corrosion, erosion, chemicals, gases, diluted acids, water suspended materials, sea water, crude oil, sewage petroleum, radiation and high temperatures.

Amiantit Services Division

In addition to providing a wide range of pipe systems and technologies, the Amiantit Group also offers its customers a range of supply and engineering services, through a number of international subsidiary companies. The Amiantit Services Division specializes in supply and engineering activities, concentrating on turnkey water supply projects and the supply of capital goods for industry, infrastructure, agriculture, health and educational institutions. Wide-ranging expertise and international experience guarantee competence and reliability from companies such as Engineering and Consulting Services (ECS).

Engineering & Consulting Services (ECS) is a newly organized department under the Amiantit Corporate Division. ECSD offers consulting services and pipeline engineering activities. The products covered by these services are mainly Amiantit Pipe Systems products, ie concrete and steel, GRE, GRP, DI and PE. ECSD is responsible for assisting clients in specifying appropriate Amiantit pipe products for required applications by providing them with engineering and technical support, as well as seminars and presentations to familiarize the clients with Amiantit pipe products. With the latest engineering and technical tools, ECSD can provide stress analysis, as well as hydrostatic and surge analysis, and any other engineering calculations requested by their clients.

Amiantit Group Technology Division

The Amiantit Technology Division is comprised of 11 technology companies – making the Amiantit Group a worldwide leader in pipe technology. This vast array of expertise benefits not only the Group's production companies but also its customers. Key companies within the group include the following:

- Amiantit Technology Services (ATS) – was founded in Velden, Austria, in 2002. ATS provides specialized services to all the technology companies in the Amiantit Group. These services include the design, procurement and installation of most of the machinery marketed and sold by the various technology companies in the Group. ATS plays an important part in the 'Central Engineering Concept' within the Technology Division (see Figure 8.5.1);
- Amipox Technology Ltd supports the manufacturing of Amipox GRE (Glass Reinforced Epoxy) pipes that are ideal in all applications where high mechanical properties, reliability and an economic service life are required. Amipox products are rated using ASTM-D-2992 and conform to ASTM-D-2996 specification for machine-made products;
- Ductech supplies the technology to companies within the Amiantit Group that manufacture ductile iron (DI) pipes and fittings. The outer surface of DI-pipes is coated with zinc and a layer of bitumen to ensure maximum protection against the harsh environment, whereas the inner one is coated with cement liner, making the pipes highly corrosion-resistant and guaranteeing low friction and longevity. Other advantages of pipes produced with the Ductech

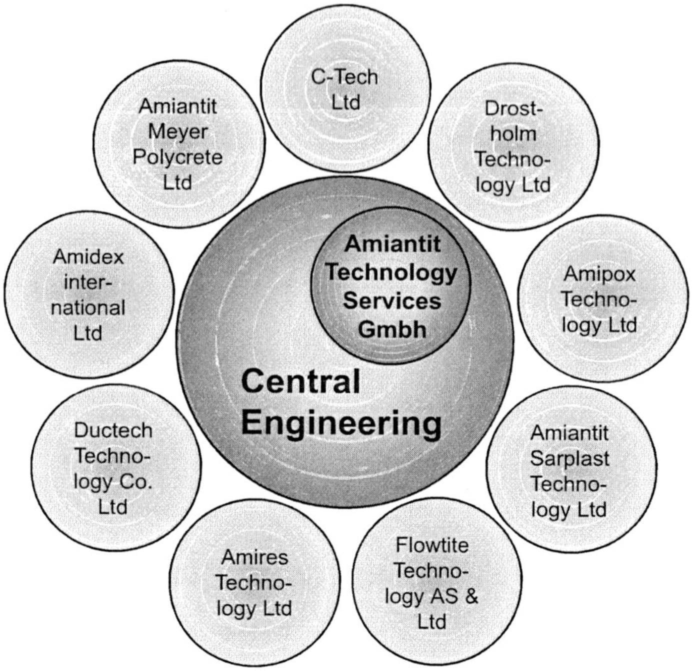

Figure 8.5.1 Amiantit's 'Central Engineering Concept'

technology are their good elastic qualities and high level of flexibility, making the pipes well-suited for high pressure applications.

The 'Central Engineering Concept' – with the objectives to direct R&D developments and plant start-ups and to pool the individual companies' know-how and equipment resources – involves a centralization of all non-core functions in each of the 11 technology companies. This process will lead to an optimal utilization of all available resources within the Group, thereby achieving higher efficiency and lower costs as well as the possibility of employing high-calibre professionals to perform these tasks.

Further information

For further information on the activities of the Saudi Arabian Amiantit Group contact: Fareed Yousef Al-Khalawi, Group CEO and Managing Director, Amiantit Group Corporate Office, PO Box 589, Dammam 31421. Tel: +966 3 847 1500; Fax: +966 3 847 1645; Website: www.amiantitgroup.com.

In addition, information on specific Amiantit Group subsidiaries can be found as follows:

- Ameron Saudi Arabia Ltd (ASAC), PO Box 589, Dammam 31421. Tel: +966 3 847 1500; Fax: +966 3 847 1311; Website: www.ameronsal.com.
- Saudi Arabia Concrete Products Ltd (SACOP), PO Box 7727, Jeddah 21472. Tel: +966 2 637 4406; Fax: +966 2 637 4551.
- Amiantit Fibreglass Industries Ltd (AFIL), PO Box 589, Dammam 31421. Tel: +966 3 847 1500; Fax: +966 3 847 2133; Website: www.afilpipe.com.
- Fibreglass Pipe Company Ltd (FPC), PO Box 589, Dammam 31421. Tel: +966 3 812 1289; Fax: +966 3 812 1272.
- Bondstrand Ltd (BSL), PO Box 589, Dammam 31421. Tel: +966 3 847 1955; Fax: +966 3 847 1955.
- Amitech Industrial Saudi Arabia Ltd, PO Box 589, Dammam 31421. Tel: +966 3 847 1500; Fax: +966 3 847 2916.
- Saudi Plastic Products Company Ltd (SAPPCO), PO Box 4916, Dammam 31412. Tel: +966 3 847 1703; Fax: +966 3 847 1969; Website: www.sappco-dammam.com.
- Amiantit Polyolefin Piping Systems Company Ltd (APPSCO), PO Box 2140, Jeddah 21451. Tel: +966 2 236 3362; Fax: +966 2 236 3494.
- Saudi Arabian Ductile Iron Pipes Company Ltd (SADIP), PO Box 3430, Dammam 31471. Tel: +966 3 812 1001; Fax: +966 3 812 1131; Website: www.amiantitductile.com.
- DIFAV Amiantit Ltd, PO Box 3430, Dammam 31471. Tel: +966 3 812 1001; Fax: +966 3 812 1131; Website: www.amiantitductile.com.
- Amitech Saudi Arabia Ltd, PO Box 32262, Jeddah 21428. Tel: +966 2 236 1568; Fax: +966 2 236 3494.
- Amiantit Rubber Industries Ltd (ARIL), PO Box 589, Dammam 31421. Tel: +966 3 847 1500; Fax: +966 3 847 3200; Website: www.aril.com.sa.
- Arabian Fibreglass Insulation Company Ltd (AFICO), PO Box 589, Dammam 31421. Tel: +966 3 847 1500; Fax: +966 3 847 2133; Website: www.afico.com.sa.
- Saudi Arabian Amiantit Plastic Products Manufacturing Company Ltd (AmPlas), PO Box 589, Dammam 31421. Tel: +966 3 847 1500; Fax: +966 3 847 3200.

- Ya-Coat Amiantit Ltd, PO Box 3430, Dammam 31471. Tel: +966 3 812 1001; Fax: +966 3 812 1131.
- Engineering & Consulting Services, PO Box 589, Dammam 31421. Tel: +966 3 847 1500; Fax: +966 3 847 3550.

8.6

AH Al-Zamil Group of Companies

Introduction

The Al-Zamil Group is an internationally known and respected Dammam-based conglomerate with diversified industrial and commercial interests including steel fabrication, air-conditioning products manufacture, food processing, plastics, petrochemicals, chemicals, paint, fencing and security systems, packaging and glass industries. The Group is also involved in banking and industrial investment and the provision of travel and other services through joint venture affiliations with numerous international organizations as well as through strategic acquisitions.

By 2005, the Al-Zamil Group, founded by the late Sheikh Abdullah Al-Hamad Al-Zamil (1897–1960), had grown from its inception in the 1930s as a trading house to a company that comprises 23 managed and 35 associate companies that together employ almost 8,000 people of 40 nationalities. As such, it offers a wide range of industrial, commercial and consumer solutions and services, all of which contribute to its market leading positions at local, regional and international levels spanning six continents.

The current Al-Zamil Group Board of Directors comprises 12 sons of the late Sheikh Abdullah Al-Hamad Al-Zamil who are actively involved in managing the strategic expansion and international presence of the Al-Zamil Group under the leadership of Group Chairman, Mohammed Al-Zamil. Annual capital investments by the Group exceeded SR150 million in both 2001 and 2002, while exports accounted for just under 30 per cent of Al-Zamil Group turnover in 2002.

Industrial and building products

Steel buildings and fabrications

Zamil Steel Industries (ZSI) is a global leader in the manufacture of pre-engineered steel buildings and is the Middle East's premier supplier of steel structures, transmission and telecommunications towers, open web steel joists and floor deckings.

Founded in 1977, ZSI's main factories are located in Dammam First and Second Industrial Cities, with additional factories now located in Egypt and Vietnam. More than 400 engineers are employed in its engineering departments in Saudi Arabia, Jordan, Egypt, Vietnam and India.

Pre-engineered steel buildings
As the oldest and largest ZSI business unit, the ISO 9001:2000 certified PEB unit designs, fabricates and supplies low-rise, pre-engineered steel buildings for commercial, industrial, agricultural and military premises, eg factories, aircraft hangars, shopping malls, supermarkets and showrooms. Products are sold in more than 70 countries through a network of 50 sales offices, 59 certified builders and 27 agents and distributors. In 2002, its 'eZ-Build' – Electronic Zamil Steel Buildings System – proprietary software solution was launched, which enables sales teams worldwide to estimate and design many buildings and to submit detailed proposals and drawings within hours of receiving client requests. Allied to this, the new Project Information System provides web-based sharing of project information for estimating and engineering purposes. Together, the two systems have significantly accelerated customer response times, while reducing operating costs.

Structural steel
Al-Zamil is the leader in steel fabrication in Saudi Arabia and the region. It fabricates high-rise steel buildings, air and gas ducting and other support structures. Activities include engineering design, estimation, project management, planning, preparation, fabrication and blasting/painting. Applications include power, desalination, fertilizer and petrochemical plants, refineries and high-rise commercial buildings. In addition to clear market leadership in Saudi Arabia, in 2002 Al-Zamil serviced orders from Qatar, the UAE, Sudan, Cyprus, Portugal and Bangladesh. It is ISO 9001:2000 certified and holds AISC certification for the fabrication of Complex Steel Structures (CBD) Category, and ASME certification for the design and fabrication of pressure vessels, boilers and heat exchanges. However, Al-Zamil constantly seeks the highest possible certification and has commenced the

process to attain ISO 14001 & OHSAS 18001 certifications that will result in improvements in process efficiencies, safety of the workforce and response to the environment and community.

Towers and galvanizing
Al-Zamil produces premium galvanized steel towers for electrical transmission projects, telecommunications projects and various other specialized lattice steel structures, servicing markets in Saudi Arabia and the GCC countries and across the Middle East, Asia, Latin America and Africa. As well as being ISO 9001:2000 certified, the T&G Unit's tower designs employ GTSTRUDL computer planning; drawings utilize 'BOCAD' computer software, enabling rapid drawing and the automatic generation of Bill of Material; and the entire manufacturing process is managed through computer control.

Steel joists and floor decking
CanAm Asia, founded in 2002 as a joint venture between Zamil Industrial Investment Company (ZIIC) and Steel Plus Ltd, a subsidiary of CanAm Manac Group (Canada), CanAm Asia is the only company in the region that custom designs, fabricates and supplies open-web steel joists and floor decking for the markets of Saudi Arabia and the GCC countries as well as Africa, Europe and Asia.

Air-conditioning systems

Zamil Air Conditioners (ZAC) is a leading international manufacturer of air-conditioning systems and is market leader in the Middle East. One of the first air-conditioning businesses to be established in the Kingdom of Saudi Arabia, in 1974, ZAC designs, manufactures, tests, markets and services a comprehensive range of air-conditioning products, which range from compact room air-conditioners and mini-splits to large-scale, central air-conditioners, chillers and air handling units for highly specialized applications. These are marketed under various brand names including 'Classic' (within Saudi Arabia), 'Cooline' (exported products), 'Cool Care' (service and maintenance within Saudi Arabia) and 'Clima Tech' (air handling units) and 'Geoclima' (chillers). ZAC also produces branded air-conditioners under its original equipment manufacturer (OEM) programme for world leading air-conditioning manufacturers including include Sanyo, Trane, Luxaire, Philco, Admiral, Siemens, Bosch and Frigidaire.

The primary manufacturing takes place in Saudi Arabia and is supported by subsidiaries in Italy and Austria. ZAC is divided into the following business units:

- *Consumer Products* – Classic, Cooline, MEAC and OEM branded consumer range, mainly window air conditioners up to two tonnes cooling capacity and mini-splits up to 2.5 tonnes;
- *Unitary and Applied Products* – Classic, Cooline and OEM branded commercial range with unitary products offer cooling capacities of three to 30 tonnes and applied products of 20 to 500 tonnes;
- *Cooline Products* – marketing and distribution for export markets based in Dammam with regional sales offices in the United States, UAE, Australia, Morocco and Lebanon;
- *Zamil Cool Care* – air-conditioning equipment service and maintenance provider, with over 500 qualified technicians at 11 branches in Saudi Arabia and one in the UAE;
- *Clima Tech Air Conditioners GmbH* – based in Grunbach, Austria, develops and manufactures air handling units and related components for hygiene climate and clean room applications;
- *Geoclima srl* – based in Trieste, Italy, manufactures chillers (air and water cooled) and fan coil units for regular commercial applications;
- *Middle East Air Conditioners (MEAC)* – a joint venture between ZAC and General Electric (GE) provides a range of GE branded air-conditioning consumer products manufactured by ZAC for Saudi Arabia and the other Gulf countries.

Glass products

Zamil Glass Industries (ZGI), established in 1983 in Dammam, is a fabricator and processor of architectural glass, including tempered, heat strengthened, laminated, insulating, heat mirror high performance and fire resistant glass. Its products serve the requirements of the construction industry and end users in Saudi Arabia, the GCC countries and in selected international markets. Production of a new range of safety and security glass commenced in 2003 following the introduction of the latest laminated glass production technology.

Saudi Guardian International Float Glass Company Limited (Gulf Guard) produces float and patterned figure glass as well as mirrors. It is the first plant of its type in the Middle East region and exports to markets in the Gulf countries, Middle East, Africa and Far East. The company is a joint venture between the National Company for Glass Industries 'Zoujaj' (45 per cent), Guardian Middle East & Africa (45 per cent) and The Eastern Company for Industrial Investments (10 per cent).

Architectural products

Zamil Architectural Industries (ZAI) serves the requirements of the construction and architecture sectors, with products manufactured through its various divisions:

- Zamil Doors – roll-a-doors, sectional doors, industrial doors and fast-action doors, in collaboration with international suppliers such as B&D (Australia);
- Gates and Operators – traffic barriers (boom gates), sliding/swing gates and wardrobe sliding doors, in collaboration with Serai (Italy);
- Shades - Shade Guard and PVC-membrane structures, offering controlled shade blocking for swimming pools, motor vehicle parking and public recreational areas;
- Art Glass – stained glass, surface-decorated glass (sand blasting/ acid etching), and fused glass for doors, windows, floors, ceilings, skylights and building facades;
- Metal Works – balustrades, handrails, stairs, doors, column claddings, canopies and screens for use in private villas and palaces, government offices, commercial centres, offices and showrooms;
- Skylights – skylight domes made from aluminium or stainless steel that are commonly decorated with a combination of plain, stained and fused glass.

Partitions

Zamil Partition Industries (ZPI), established in 1985, provides solutions for flexible office space. Its product offering includes demountable partitions – solid, full or semi-glazed of aluminium and laminated gypsum panel, toilet partitions – made from Formica-finished plywood or high-pressure laminated panels, moveable walls, work stations, hygienic clean rooms and radiation-proof partitions for hospitals and laboratories, ceiling walls with suspension and wooden works and internal decoration.

Technical seals

Technical Seal Company Limited, based in Dammam, produces synthetic rubber weather seal gaskets to international standards for a wide range of building applications. The company manufactures ethylene propylene dyne monomer (EPDM), one of only two products to retain its mechanical properties in the extreme climate of the Middle

East. The company also produces polypropylene (PP) yarn in various deniers, for use in both the packaging and carpet industries, as well as PVC gaskets, used in windows, kitchens and for decorative and other purposes.

Ladders

Zamil Ladder Factory, established in 1978 in Dammam, produces aluminium and steel ladders for Saudi Arabia, GCC countries and other Middle East markets. The manufacture of a wide product range meets international safety standards and includes low-cost, ultra-light step-ladders; extension, mobile platform, mobile telescopic and loft ladders; as well as special safety cage and fire escape ladders, which are used in, among others, towers, minarets, water tanks and underground pumping wait rooms.

Paints

Sigma Paints is one of the largest producers of paint in Saudi Arabia. The company manufactures a wide range of products created from a formula specifically designed to provide optimum durability and longevity against harsh climactic conditions in the Middle East. Paint production commenced in 1981 at Dammam and, in 1999, a second production facility was established.

Bricks

Yamama Factories for Red Bricks and Clay Products Company Limited, established in 1979, manufactures more than 100 varieties of red clay bricks conforming to Saudi Arabian, European and or US technical standards. Production capacity stands at 1,000 tonnes per day with a product range including load bearing, hollow, ceiling, facing and paving bricks, as well as insulation and roofing products.

Metal sheets

Universal Metal Coating Company Limited (UNICOIL), established in 1998, is the first Saudi Company to manufacture pre-painted steel products in Saudi Arabia and the largest producer of pre-painted steel in the Middle East. The company is joint venture between by AH Al-Zamil and Rashed Al-Rashed Group of Companies. UNICOIL is located at Al Jubail and has an installed capacity of 120,000 tonnes per annum, capable of coating the full range of coil strip products, including galvanized steel, zinc-coated steel, aluminium and cold rolled steel. UNICOIL supplies pre-painted steel and aluminium to the pre-engineered builders sector, roll-formers, door manufacturers, lighting fixtures, sandwich panel and refrigeration and cold stores. Also a slitting/cut-to-length line and strippable film application unit has been installed in order to provide full service to its customer requirements. UNICOIL achieved ISO 9001:2000 certification for manufacturing of pre-painted metal coils in March 2003 and is a frequent member of European Coil Coating Association (ECCA).

Fencing

Guardian Fencing and Security Systems Company Limited (GFSS) commenced manufacturing in Dammam in 1978 and is now a market leader in high security fencing and vehicle access control systems. Other fabricated products include steel gratings and handrails, shade cover structures and steel security doors.

Nails and screws

Zamil Nails and Screws Factory, located in Bahrain, manufactures nails and screws to international standards. Products include common, headless, twisted, threaded and concrete nails and mild steel brass and stainless steel screws in metric and inch sizes with various head configurations. The company also produces self-drilling screws for sheet and steel structural applications, and products for refrigeration, air-conditioner manufacturing and electrical lighting companies.

Cranes

Eastern Morris Crane Company Limited supplies the Morris brand of cranes to customers in Saudi Arabia and surrounding countries. A workforce of mobile technicians offers after-sales crane testing, servicing and inspection services. The company also supplies spare parts for all types of cranes and undertakes refurbishment work.

Doors

Dorma Arabia Automatic Doors Limited (Dorma Arabia), established in 2000, manufactures automatic sliding, circular sliding, revolving and swing doors, as well as manual revolving doors according to German standards, using German components. Its technologically advanced products are marketed through a network of distributors located throughout the Middle East. Dorma Arabia is a joint venture between the Group, which provides logistical and marketing strength, and Dorma GmbH, a global leader in door automation technologies.

Petrochemicals, chemicals and plastics

Methanol

Saudi International Petrochemical Company (SIPC), located at Al Jubail, will, in 2005, commence production of maleic anhydride (MAN), butanediol (BDO) and methanol, through three limited liability companies being established through joint venture agreements with international partners. The company's initial venture involves the manufacture 75,000 tonnes a year of MAN/BDO and one million tonnes a year of methanol. As a Saudi joint stock company, SIPC has a fully paid up capital of SR500 million (US$133 million). The International Methanol Company, which uses ICI technology, is 35 per cent owned by a Japanese consortium and 65 per cent owned by SIPC.

Maleic anhydride/butanediol

Gulf Advanced Chemical Industries Company Limited (GACIC) will be the first plant in the Middle East and Asia to produce maleic anhydride/butanediol (BDO) and derivatives, with an initial capacity of 75,000 tonnes per annum. The majority of shares are owned by SIPC, while other shareholders include Al-Babtain Group, Astra Group, Huntsman Corporation and Davy Process Technologies Limited.

Formaldehyde

Saudi Formaldehyde Chemical Company Limited (SFCCL), established in 1989, is a world-class producer of petrochemicals and derivatives, which are used as conditioning and anti-caking agents in the urea fertilizer industry; intermediate chemicals for oilfield formulation, raw materials for insulation and resin industries, fumigants for poultry farms and pharmaceutical agents. More than 70 per cent of its production capacity of in excess of 200,000 tonnes per annum is exported to more than 45 countries in the Middle East, Indian subcontinent, Africa, Europe, Asia, Australia and North America. SFCCL's current product range comprises aqueous formaldehyde solutions, urea formaldehyde concentrate, hexa methylene tetramine, paraformaldehyde, melamine and urea formaldehyde resins, glazing powder, methanolic/butanolic solutions of formaldehyde and sulphonated naphthalene and melamine based superplasticizers.

Stabilizers

Gulf Stabilizers Industries (GSI) is a joint venture with Great Lakes Chemical Corporation of the United States, and is the first entity of its type in the Middle East. Its Al Jubail plant, with a capacity of 5,700 tonnes a year, commenced production activities in 2002 to meet the regional demand for economical antioxidant additives and NDB. GSI produces antioxidant polymer additives, which enhance polymer longevity by preventing oxidization and polymer degradation in the polymer manufacturing process; and non-dusting blend (NDB) products, which minimize atmospheric powder pollution to facilitate storage and handling requirements.

Woven sacks

Al Tawfiq Company for Plastic & Woven Sacks Industries Limited of Jeddah is a manufacturer of polypropylene woven bags for the food, animal feed, fertilizer, chemical and fuel packing industries. Products include jumbo bags for bulk packing, valve bags for fertilizers and chemicals, laminated bags and plain and laminated sheets for lumber, textiles and cotton as well as special order heavy-duty bags and sheets also produced at the Jeddah-based facility.

Coating products

Zamil Industrial Coatings (ZINDCO), located in Dammam First Industrial City, provides powder coating for all materials, from mill finish aluminium extrusions to hot dip galvanized steel, using powder coating technology, including chemical pre-treatment systems. The company's state-of-the-art technology enables ZINDCO to meet all relevant international specifications for powder coating ranging from 60 to 1,000 microns. Powder coating applications offered by ZINDCO include cable trays, ladders, electrical and switch gear panels, aluminium profiles, handrails, sheets and steel, electrical conducts, fittings and accessories, fence posts and accessories, welded wire mesh and electrical bus bars.

Non-woven products

Saudi German Company for Non-woven Products (SGN) produces a range of SMS (spun bond, melt blown, spun bond) and SS (spun bond, spun bond) non-woven fabrics for hygiene, medical, agricultural and industrial markets. The capacity of the factory, equipped with German technology spinning equipment, is 13,500 tonnes per annum. The joint venture was established in 1997 with Saudi Arabia's Al Rajhi House

Enterprises and international non-woven manufacturer, BBA Non-Wovens.

Polyethylene blown tube film

Bischof and Klein Middle East Company produces heavy-duty bags and pallet-wrap using polyethylene blown tube film. Its finished products (which are composed of co-extruded polyethylene tube film) are used by chemical industries located throughout the Middle East, Indian subcontinent, Africa and Asia, and include form fill seal film (FFS film), shrink film and Smartflex film. The company was established in 2000 as a joint venture with Al-Rajhi House Enterprise and A Al-Ohaly Establishment, with the technical backing of Bischof + Klein GmbH & Company of Germany. It was the first company in the Kingdom of Saudi Arabia to introduce the chemical and physical advantages of co-extruded film over monolayer film to the local market.

Caustic soda

Arabian Alkali Company (SODA), established in 1998, is one of the largest chlor-alkali manufactures of caustic soda in the Middle East, with an annual capacity of 50,000 tonnes a year. Its various forms of anhydrous caustic soda (ACS) – prills, pearl and solid/fused – serve domestic and international markets.

Epoxy resins

Al Jubail Chemical Industries Company (JANA) manufactures epoxy resins using CIBA technology and epichlorohydrin using Showa Denko technology for markets in the Middle East, Central Asia and Africa. Epoxy resins are among the most versatile of polymers, with uses in the aircraft and aerospace, automotive, construction, heavy and light engineering, chemical, electrical, electronic, food and beverage, leisure and marine industries. The JANA plant, which uses Swiss technology, is situated in Al Jubail. Plant capacity is 20,000 tonnes of epoxy resin and 30,000 tonnes of epichlorohydrin.

Plastics

Zamil Plastics Industries Limited (ZPI), established in 1980, is now one of the largest manufacturers of integrated plastic products in the Gulf Region. Its commodity speciality and engineering-grade plastics are processed into custom moulded products, such as electrical appliance parts, as well as containers for chemicals, paints and adhesives; and consumer products for household applications, including disposable cups for food and drink items. Clients include reputed dairy companies, beverage and juice bottlers, electrical appliance manufacturers, automotive component factories, as well as chemical, paint and adhesive manufacturers.

Consumer and automotive products

Food products

Zamil Food Industries Limited, located in Al Jubail, produces a wide range of food products for institutional, commercial and catering industries, as well as for retail markets throughout the Gulf region. It also commands a prime position in the frozen foods market. Zamil Food's processed meat division produces meat products in bulk and retail packs, while its dairy department produces a range of products under the 'Blue Ribbon' trademark for retail markets and the catering industry. A van sale division also serves rural and metropolitan areas of Saudi Arabia, while the company is also active in the importation of a wide variety of frozen food products for resale in the Kingdom.

Corrugated cartons

United Carton Industries Company is the largest and most technologically advanced corrugated packaging factory in the Middle East. A wide product range, incorporating distinctive graphic and structural design and accommodating artwork, tooling preparation, maintenance and transportation services, ensures complete customer service provision to a worldwide supply chain from its 18,000m^2 manufacturing plant located in Jeddah.

Auto glass

Saudi Lamino Company Limited is the Kingdom's leading manufacturer of laminated safety glass featuring PVB (poly-vinyl-butyral) inter-layers; laminated curved glass; bullet resistant glass (comprising several layers of clear float glass, PVB and polycarbonate layers); and tempered glass, amongst others. It supplies government departments, military installations, major construction companies and windscreen glass dealers throughout Saudi Arabia and the Middle East region.

Packaging materials

Gulf Packaging Industries Limited (Gulf Pack) produces biaxially oriented polypropylene (BOPP) film, which is used in a wide variety of applications including, among others, flexible packaging of food items, adhesive tapes, cigarette and flower wrapping. Gulf Pack was the first BOPP film producer in the Arabian Gulf region when it was established in 1989.

Car batteries

Middle East Battery Company manufactures, markets and sells maintenance-free batteries for automotive, commercial, marine and speciality markets. It is a joint venture with Delphi Automotive Systems of the United States, and its manufacturing base in Saudi Arabia is the world's first Delphi Battery plant to specialize in serving the after sales market.

Contracting and services

Operations and maintenance

Zamil Operations & Maintenance Company Limited (ZOMCO), established in 1977, is now the largest company of its type in Saudi Arabia, offering turnkey operations and maintenance (O&M) services for the private, public and defence sectors. ZOMCO employs more than 2,000 managers, engineers and technicians to offer O&M services that include marine vessel chartering, ship repair and dry docking, shipbuilding, stevedoring, navigation and pilotage services, maintaining domestic Saudi airports, seaports and military bases. ZOMCO also supplies potable water to townships, is involved in sea water cooling systems, utilities (power, HVAC and sanitation), desalination plants, housing complexes and accommodation camps, landscaping activities, institutional and military catering, as well as the complete management of hospital and healthcare services.

Contracting and engineering

Arabian Gulf Construction Company Limited is a general contracting company that undertakes civil, mechanical and electrical projects throughout Saudi Arabia. Completed projects range from turnkey industrial complexes to multi-storey reinforced structures that include factories and industrial plants, housing and recreational complexes, luxurious residential multi-storey buildings and accommodation camps.

Delta Catalytic Limited (DCSA) is a joint venture company between Delta Catalytic Limited (a wholly-owned subsidiary of Jacobs Engineering Corporation) and the Al-Zamil Group. DCSA provides services in the field of project evaluation, engineering, procurement, construction management and plant maintenance to the oil, gas and petrochemical industry. DCSA offers the capabilities of Jacobs Engineering Corporation (JEC), a large and diversified professional and technical services provider. DCSA offers the capabilities of its sister companies in the United States, Canada and Europe.

Information technology

Zamil CONECT, established in 1994, provides security and complete technology solutions in the form of IT consulting and services, application development and maintenance, package implementation, system integration, outsourcing and training, hardware and software services, networking and communications and VPN and security solutions. Zamil CONECT is in partnership with Tata International, the largest software solutions provider in Asia. Areas of business and expertise include finance and insurance, manufacturing, public sector, transportation, retail and distribution, telecommunications, healthcare, energy and utilities, engineering automation, system integration and application development and maintenance, business intelligence, E-business, architecture and technology consulting, ERP and E-security. The company's business partners include Microsoft, HP, Oracle and Compaq.

Zamil Birla Technical Services (ZABITS), a joint venture between the Zamil Group and Birla Group of India, was established in 1987 and includes Birlasoft and Intelligroup as its strategic alliance partners. The company provides the following software consultancy, development, implementation and support solutions and services:

- Management Consultancy – business process re-engineering, change management, project and programme management, project recovery and strategic system planning and software selection;
- Business Application Software – development and customization services;
- Business Intelligence – SAP and Oracle-based enterprise resource planning solutions, supply chain management solutions, customer relationship management and data warehousing solutions and onsite software services.

Travel and tourism

Zamil Travel of Al-Khobar is a well-established travel agency in the Eastern Province of Saudi Arabia. Its services include reserving and issuing international and domestic tickets, planning tourism services, making international and domestic hotel and car reservations and issuing international driving licences. It is a member of the International Air Transport Association (IATA), and is the General Sales Agent for both Saudi Arabian Airlines and KLM (Royal Dutch Airlines).

Utilities

Industrial power plant

National Power Company (NPC) was established as a joint venture with El Seif Group in 2003 with the objective of participating in investment opportunities created by the privatization of the industrial infrastructure of Saudi Arabia and other Middle East countries, with particular emphasis on the power and water sectors. NPC aims to provide power by means of build, own, operate and other schemes, using co-generation technology based on natural gas. Working in alliance with international technology providers, NPC's first power plant will supply a chemical installation in Al Jubail with 250 MWH when it becomes operational in 2006. NPC is a Saudi joint stock company with a capital of SR200 million.

Commercial services

Real estate

Zamil Real Estate provides accommodation and recreational facilities through Zamil Resorts, Zamil Village and Zamil Group Camps:

- Zamil Resorts – high quality standards at competitive rates;.
- Zamil Village – a high standard of accommodation and wide range of services, including full maintenance, security and recreation and leisure outlets;
- Zamil Group Camps – economical furnished accommodation for expatriate bachelors. Camps for more than 1,000 people are located in Riyadh, Dammam, Al Jubail and elsewhere.

Further information

For further information on the activities of AH Al-Zamil Group of Companies contact: Khaled A Al-Zamil, President, PO Box 9, Al-Khobar,

31952. Tel: +966 3 882 4888; Fax: +966 3 882 2509; Website: www.zamil.com.

In addition, information on specific AH Al-Zamil Group subsidiaries and affiliates can be found as follows:

- Zamil Steel Industries (ZSI), PO Box 877, Dammam 31421. Tel: +966 3 847 1840 Fax: +966 3 847 1291 Website: www.zamilsteel.com.
- Zamil Air Conditioners (ZAC), PO Box 1440, Dammam 31424. Tel: +966 3 847 3333; Fax: +966 3 847 1904; Website: www.zamilac.com.
- Zamil Industrial Investment Company (ZIIC), PO Box 14441, Dammam 31424. Tel: +966 3 847 1840; Fax: +966 3 847 2574; Website: www.ziic.com.

8.7

The National Bank of Dubai

Founded in 1963, NBD is the oldest locally incorporated bank in the southern Gulf. From its imposing new Headquarters, depicting a ship in full sail, it operates 40 branches in the UAE in addition to one branch in London and a representative office in Teheran.

Business Activities

Corporate Banking

A key division of the National Bank of Dubai, Corporate Banking offers a comprehensive suite of products and services that support the requirements of its corporate clientele and include a full range of trade finance, treasury, lending and deposit taking services, which are offered to all UAE-based customers. NBD works with a broad range of transportation, tourism and government client segments, serving as a leader in providing professional and responsive relationship banking to all its customers.

Treasury Products & Services

The National Bank of Dubai enjoys a pre-eminent position in the Dirham Money Market, being an active market maker. The Bank is also active on the Foreign Exchange markets. Its dealers actively track the global markets and provide advice to customers on exchange markets and interest rate outlook.

'The Private Office'– NBD Private Banking Services

'The Private Office' of The National Bank of Dubai has been established with the commitment to preserve and protect the personal wealth of its customers, offering highly responsive tailored solutions emphasizing a total relationship management approach.

The primary objective of 'The Private Office' is to provide the customers with world-class solutions for three of their most important requirements: wealth preservation and growth, investment management and succession and estate planning.

Retail Banking & Card Services

Complementing its Branch Network are the bank's off-site ATMs, consisting of a network of more than 100 ATMs as well as Point of Sale Terminals installed at a large number of hotels and stores.

The Bank also hosts a range of automated banking services, which comprise of an internet service (NBD Online), a telebanking facility (NBD Telebank), the SMS based service (NBD Mobile). Moreover, National Bank of Dubai offers a suite of choices including exclusive service based products for special customer segments, secured facilities, personal loans auto loans and home loans, as well as a comprehensive card portfolio, in addition to a host of card benefits.

NBD, also recently launched Suhail Priority Banking Services, a premier banking service offering customers personalized relationship management and a host of exclusive products and services.

Investing in Technology

The National Bank of Dubai has been at the forefront of identifying and investing in new banking technology to support its operations and to respond to the needs of the community services. The Bank, together with other UAE banking institutions, played a leading role in introducing SWIFT. It was also among the first banks to join the UAE Switch, linking the ATMs of major UAE banks. The Bank launched its Web Site in June 1998.

Investing in People

Whilst the Bank employs staff drawn from 29 countries, the Bank is proud that more than 32% of its workforce are UAE nationals.

The bank has an ongoing commitment to providing training and development opportunities, to enable UAE Nationals to build banking careers and help the development of the UAE. Specially designed and developed training programmes underpin the Bank's desire to Emiratization and preservation of its traditional values of quality and service. NBD received the 'Dubai Human Development Award' for 2002 in the financial sector and the 'Human Resources Development Award' in the Banking Sector for the year 2003 in recognition of its efforts in the field of Emiratization.

Awards Received

Throughout the years, National Bank of Dubai has received a number of awards culminating the Bank's high-quality performance.

For two consecutive years, National Bank of Dubai was chosen the Best Bank in UAE by Global Finance Magazine. The Bank was also named Best Foreign Exchange

National Bank of Dubai received for the seventh time the 'Quality Recognition Award' from JP Morgan Chase Bank. The Bank was also ranked the fourth best bank and the first local bank in the UAE for private banking services by EuroMoney Magazine.

Further information

For further information see: www.nbd.com Or contact: National Bank of Dubai, P.O. Box 777, Dubai, United Arab Emirates; Tel:+971 4 222 2111; Fax:+44 971 4 228 3000.

8.8

The SKAB Group

The SKAB Group has earned an enviable reputation with a variety of interconnected business enterprises, spanning such disciplines as environment protection & recycling, power generation, water treatment and desalination, contracting, real estate, hospitality industry, shopping malls, travel & tourism, dairy farming, food products and construction and maintenance. The Group strives to expand its business with partners who share its vision and commitment to expertise that has made SKAB one of the largest and most diversified groups operating in the Kingdom of Saudi Arabia.

The Group seeks to employ the right people, processes, skills and technologies to deliver tangible benefits. The SKAB Group believes that it represents today's realities and is structured to perform in today's dynamic marketplace.

The SKAB group says its core values are:

- Proven Expertise – to constantly apply extensive industry expertise to refine and improve its business to delver best practices.
- Performance Driven – to maintain relentless focus on attaining the objectives of its customers.
- Proactive Spirit – to anticipate challenges and translate them into actionable business opportunities to deliver best results.
- Culturally Attuned – to offer unwavering local market focus by listening and fully understanding each customer 's unique combination of business culture.

SKAB had strategic association with such international organizations as the US Airforce, GE, AT&T with whom SKAB co-operated in the expansion of the telecommunication network in Saudi Arabia. Further, its association with Boeing Industrial Technology Group Corporation (BITG), the flagship of the Peace Shield Offset Program, gave it the opportunity to be involved with the Offset Companies formed to date; Al Salaam Aircraft Company, Aircraft Accessories and Components Company, Advanced Electronic Company and International Systems Engineering Company.

The SKAB Group is an entity proud of its heritage of innovation and achievement. Each group company has been carefully structured to add a new dimension that complements and expands the group's horizon to a brighter, more secure future.

Companies in the SKAB Group

SADACA O&M

SADACA embodies all the technical expertise necessary to handle large scale projects such as airports and cities to the smallest scale operations such as private swimming pools. From the construction, development and continued maintenance of such substantial communities, as SAUDIA CITY for Saudi Arabian Airlines, a self sufficient and complete community of 3,700 housing units, with all the amenities of a modern municipality to power generation, desalination, environment protection & recycling, telecommunications, city cleaning projects and construction.

SADACA ENVIRONMENT

In tune with SKAB's expansion plans, about 20 years ago, it established a new strategic business unit SADACA Environmental Company, which is presently ranked as the only company in Saudi Arabia to provide comprehensive solutions for Environment protection. It was awarded by the Ministry of Municipal & Rural Affairs a contract to recycle Municipal Solid Waste in the different parts of the Kingdom of Saudi Arabia. Further, the Royal Commission Of Jubail & Yanbu has given it the contract to maintain their Compost factory and Landfill at Yanbu Industrial City.

Through exhaustive research in the areas of plastic, compost and steel the company is increasingly playing an important role in the management of recyclable resources from waste material for a more harmonious existence with the environment.

Its future plans include to establish recycling plants in Riyadh and Makkah and to establish a plant to process plastics recovered from Municipal Solid Waste and to work with other environmental activities such as waste fluids treatment.

ACE TRAVEL GROUP

ACE TRAVEL GROUP made a modest beginning over 50 years ago, and over the years has grown to be ranked among the top three travel agencies in the Kingdom of Saudi Arabia. Its hallmark of success is its founding principles of providing customer service excellence and understanding customer needs.

Its ability to reach globally and respond locally through its extensive network of partnerships help it to create the best solutions for business travel and leisure travel. Today, ACE TRAVEL Group has more than twenty five travel offices and Cargo Offices in the Kingdom and an IATA registered Corporate & Leisure Travel Management Company, Caravan Travel with the network of offices all across Saudi Arabia. Additionally it has network of partnership associates in over 100 countries, through our partnership agreement with Carlson Wagonlit Travel, a global travel management company.

ACE Travel Group has interwoven its business processes with its teams and technology providing continuous, seamless operations so that every client gets comprehensively tailored solutions.

Range Of Services

- Comprehensive Corporate Travel Management Services
- Incentive Travel
- Air Charters
- Leisure & Personal Travel
- Global Car Rental Reservations
- Cargo
- Online Fulfillment Centers
- Emergency Service Centers
- Travel Insurance

NATIONAL FOODSTUFFS MANUFACTURING COMPANY LTD.

The National Food Stuff Manufacturing Co. Ltd is one of the oldest and biggest food companies in the Kingdom of Saudi Arabia. The factory was established in Jeddah in 1971, and is the first factory specialized in the production of different types and shapes of macaroni. In addition to manufacturing Macaroni, its other manufacturing product range includes cakes, rusks, sweets dry powders, jelly and cream caramel.

The company has branches and sales offices all over the Kingdom and exports its products to all the countries of the Cooperation Council for the Arabian Gulf States and Yemen, Eastern European Countries,

Jordan, Canada and the African Countries and exploring business opportunities in the Western Europe.

The phase one expansion of the factory is in progress on an area of 2,500 sq. meters in the Industrial City (Stage five) equipped with the state of the art machinery and equipment.

AYAN UTILITY VEHICLES DIVISION

AYAN Utility Vehicles Division (AYAN - UVD) is one of the strategic business units of AYAN COMMERCE & INDUSTRY, which was established in 1997 to cater to the specialized transportation needs of the Industrial, Leisure, and Recreational market in Saudi Arabia. It is a pioneer in offering, locally, the diverse specialized transportation requirements.

Today, AYAN – UVD boasts the largest sales and service network of its kind in Saudi Arabia, with showrooms and service centers located in Jeddah and Riyadh with planned expansion in Al Khobar. Its client portfolio in Saudi Arabia includes but not limited to large corporate giants in their respective fields and to name a few; ARAMCO, SAUDI BINLADEN GROUP, SAUDI ARABIAN AIRLINES and other core sectors in the leisure industry.

AYAN's product range includes:

- Industrial utility vehicles from the simplest task to parking jumbo jets!
- Hotel and resort service vehicles-from back of the house to guest shuttles!
- Refresher vehicles for resorts and parks
- Full range of Industrial and Golf cars.
- Customized cars adding fun to your resort, Golf course or compound.
- Exterior sweepers - Maintain your property with a full range of sweepers.
- Landscaping - Full range of tools to maintain and improve your parks, gardens, resorts or clubs.

AYAN's business partners include:

- E-Z-GO, which is part of Textron, companies such as Cushmaan, Jacobsen, Bell Helicopter, Cessna Aircraft, Kautex, Lycoming and Greenlee make up this multi billion dollar publicly held corporation.

- Columbia ParCar Corporation, the successor to Harley-Davidson Golf Car Company. Today, Columbia produces the broadest line of electric and gaspowered golf, industrial and low speed vehicles on the market.

NAJRAN DAIRY & JUICE CO.

Najran Dairy & Juice Company is one of the leading companies in the Southern region of Kingdom of Saudi Arabia. The Plant is located in Najran.

It has been in business since 1981 and have branches all across Saudi Arabia. Its product range includes variety of Milk and its byproducts, Breakfast items and Fresh Fruit Juices.

HERAA INTERNATIONAL MALL

With a name from Arabic Legends that symbolizes the joy of discovery, HERAA INTERNATIONAL MALL" is the premiere shopping and recreation center in Jeddah, Saudi Arabia hosting over 240 International and Local retailers. It is a member of Middle East Council of Shopping Centers and International Council of Shopping Centers.

Since its opening in 1994 Heraa Int'l Mall has strived to maintain its position as the premiere shopping and recreation centre in Jeddah. The leasing team prides itself in having established an in-depth relationship with its local and international retailers and has created a strong and solid foundation for continued growth into the future. Heraa Int'l Mall is located on the intersection of Madina Road and Heraa Street, Jeddah. It has one of the largest cars parking area that can accommodate 1,500 cars at any given time.

- A recent survey revealed that approx. 10,000 footfall each evening in Heraa Int'l Mall resulting in an average 100,000 people each week, and increases by around 20% during peak season, i.e. Ramadan, Haj and Summer Festival.
- Heraa Int'l Mall total area is 112,000 Sq. Meters.
- Has over 240 International and Local Retailers.
- Anchor store for Mango, Zara, Danube 24Hr Supermarket.
- International brands include: Mothercare, BHS, Miss Selfridges, Benetton, Diesel, Lacoste, Bata, Clarks, Sony, Laura Ashley, Samsung.
- Restaurants: Fuddruckers, Pizza Hut, McDonalds, Burger King, Baskin Robbins, Joffreys.

DHIAFAH

DHIAFAH is a leading real estate development company with interests in hotels, housing units, seaside resorts, buyer & seller and developer of real estate, contracting work for residential and public buildings, amusement parks and catering services. Some of its leading properties are the Movenpick Hotel located on a commercial area, off Madina Road in Jeddah, Al Baia Hotel in the downtown Jeddah and an exclusive self contained seaside resort Les Sablon, completely equipped with modern facilities.

To keep pace with the rapid economic development of the Kingdom Of Saudi Arabia, DHIAFAH is expanding our real estate development activities with substantial investment in constructing large housing units, shopping malls and recreational centers.

Further information

For further information see: www.skabco.net or contact: SKAB Group, P.O. Box 13271, Jeddah 21493, Kingdom of Saudi Arabia.
Tel: +966-2-606 0608
Fax: +966-2-606 1702 / 606 0940
E-mail: info@skabco.net

8.9

Financial Transaction House

Financial Transaction House is an investment banking firm based in Saudi Arabia. It provides a wide range of corporate finance advisory services to a diversified client base in the Middle East and offers we offer our clients a complete and integrated solution from structuring the transaction, providing negotiation and legal support to closing the deal.

The Firm's focus on the Middle East and its knowledge of the local business context and culture has helped it establish close relationships with the senior management of top companies, as it helps them address the challenges they face in an increasingly complex, global and competitive business environment. Financial Transaction House's extensive network of local and regional contacts, which includes high net-worth individuals, financial institutions and governments, is of immense value to its clients.

The investment banking advisory services provided by Financial Transaction House:

- **Private Placements** – Advising on structuring private placements of debt and equity and assisting management in obtaining capital from a wide array of institutional investors such as insurance companies, pension funds, commercial banks, and venture capital firms;
- **Mergers & Acquisitions** – Assisting with all phases of M&A transactions, including structuring and raising capital and negotiating and closing the transaction. In sales & divestiture deals, conducting extensive investor searches;
- **Public Offerings** – Advising companies on the considerations and risk associated initial public offering and secondary offerings. Advising companies on how to position themselves, assess their market value, select an underwriter and structure an underwriting agreement;

- **Debt Capital Raising** – Assisting companies with identifying and approaching potential lenders and subsequent negotiations and review of financial terms;
- **Valuations (brand and business) and Fairness Opinions** – Providing fairness opinions on transactions, valuations of the fair market value of an entity, its minority interests, its restricted securities, and other assets;
- **Capital and Financial Restructuring** – Assisting companies in refinancing their debt and capital and in raising new credit facilities;
- **Strategic Financial Consulting** – Advising on the financial and strategic aspects of privatizations, analyzing capital structures, renegotiating loan agreements, and formulating takeover defence strategies.

Further information

For further information visit www.fthgulf.com or contact: Financial Transaction House, PO Box 24368, Jeddah 21446, Saudi Arabia; Tel: +966 2 657 3030; Fax: +966 2 657 3366

Appendices

Appendix I

Further Sources of Information

Government offices

Ministry of Agriculture
Airport Road, PO Box 2639, Riyadh 11195
Tel: +966 1 401 6666; Fax: +966 1 403 1415
Website: www.agrwat.gov.sa

Ministry of Commerce and Industry
Omar bin Al-Khatab Road, PO Box 5729, Riyadh 11127
Tel: +966 1 477 2722/477 6666; Fax: +966 1 477 5451
Website: www.commerce.gov.sa

Ministry of Defence and Aviation
Airport Road, PO Box 26731, Riyadh 11165
Tel: +966 1 441 6055; Fax: +966 1 406 2146

Ministry of Finance
King Abdulaziz Road, Riyadh 11177
Tel: +966 1 405 0000; Fax: +966 1 405 9202
Website: www.mof.gov.sa

Ministry of Foreign Affairs
Nasseriya Street, Riyadh 11124
Tel: +966 1 406 7777; Fax: +966 1 403 0159
Website: www.mofa.gov.sa

Ministry of Health
PO Box 21217, Riyadh 11176
Tel: +966 1 401 2220; Fax: +966 1 402 9876

Ministry of the Interior
PO Box 2933, Riyadh 11134
Tel: +966 1 401 1944; Fax: +966 1 403 1185
Website: www.passport.gov.sa (Directorate of Passports)

Ministry of Labour and Social Affairs
Omar bin Al-Khatab Street, PO Box 1182, Riyadh 11157
Tel: +966 1 477 1480/478 7166; Fax: +966 1 477 7336
Website: www.mol.gov.sa

Ministry of Petroleum and Minerals
Maather Street, PO Box 757, Riyadh 11189
Directorate-General for Mineral Resources (Jeddah)
Tel: +966 1 478 1661/1133; Fax: +966 1 479 3596
Website: www.mopm.gov.sa

Ministry of Telecom and IT
Riyadh 11112
Tel: +966 1 452 2222; Fax: +966 1 452 2601

Autonomous government agencies and state-owned corporations

Central Department of Statistics
PO Box 3735, Riyadh 11118
Tel: +966 1 401 4138; Fax: +966 1 405 9493
Website: www.planning.gov.sa/statistic

Department of Customs
PO Box 3483, Riyadh 11197
Tel: +966 1 401 3333
Website: www.customs.gov.sa

Directorate General of Zakat and Income Tax (DZIT)
PO Box 6898, Riyadh 11187
Tel: +966 1 401 0182 /404 1537; Fax: +966 1 404 1495

Economic Offset Secretariat
PO Box 27040, Riyadh 11417
Tel: +966 1 478 4330; Fax: +966 1 478 4123

General Organization for Grain Silos and Flour Mills
PO Box 3402, Riyadh 11471
Tel: +966 1 464 3500; Fax: +966 1 477 9958
Website: www.gosi.com.sa

General Organization for Social Insurance
PO Box 878, Riyadh 11421
Tel: +966 1 477 7735; Fax: +966 1 477 9958

General Organization for Technical Education and Vocational Training
PO Box 7823, Riyadh 11472
Tel: +966 1 405 2770; Fax: +966 1 406 5876
Website: www.gotevot.edu.sa

Majlis Al Shura (Consultative Council)
Riyadh 11212
Tel: +966 1 482 1666
Website: www.shura.gov.sa

Meteorology and Environmental Protection Agency (MEPA)
PO Box 35662, Jeddah 21583
Tel: +966 2 651 8887; Fax: +966 2 651 1424
Website: www.mepa.org.sa

Real Estate Development Fund (REDF)
PO Box 5591, Riyadh 11433
Tel: +966 1 477 5120/403 3817; Fax: +966 1 479 0148

Royal Commission for Jubail and Yanbu
PO Box 5864, Riyadh 11432
Tel: +966 1 479 4444 Fax: +966 1 477 5404
Website: www.royalcommission.com

Royal Commission for Jubail
PO Box 10001, Jubail Industrial City 31961
Tel: +966 3 341 3000; Fax: +966 3 341 9891
Website: www.rcjubail.gov.sa

Royal Commission for Yanbu
PO Box 30031,Yanbu Industrial City
Tel: +966 4 321 6116; Fax: +966 4 396 8001
Website: www.rcyanbu.gov.sa

Saline Water Conversion Corporation (SWCC)
PO Box 5968, Riyadh 11432
Tel: +966 1 463 0503/463 0501; Fax: +966 1 463 1952/465 0852

Saudi Arabian Agricultural Bank (SAAB)
PO Box 1811, Riyadh 11126
Tel: +966 1 402 3911/3934; Fax: +966 1 402 2359

Saudi Arabian Basic Industries Corporation (SABIC)
PO Box 5101, Riyadh 11422
Tel: +966 1 225 8000; Fax: +966 1 225 9000
Website: www.sabic.com

Saudi Arabian Monetary Agency (SAMA)
PO Box 2992, Riyadh 11461
Tel: +966 1 463 3000; Fax: +966 1 441 1384
Website: www.sama-ksa.org

Saudi Arabian Standards Organization (SASO)
PO Box 3437, Riyadh 11471
Tel: +966 1 479 3332/452 0101; Fax: +966 1 479 3063
Website: www.saso.gov.sa

Saudi Industrial Development Fund (SIDF)
PO Box 4143, Riyadh 11149
Tel: +966 1 477 4002; Fax: +966 1 479 0165

Saudi Arabian General Investment Authority (SAGIA)
Investment Services Agency
PO Box 1267, Riyadh 11431
Tel: +966 1 448 4533; Fax: +966 1 448 1234
Website: www.sagia.gov.sa

Saudi Arabian Oil Company (Saudi Aramco)
Corporate Headquarters, PO Box 5000, Dhahran 31311
Tel: +966 3 872 0115; Fax: +966 3 873 8190
Website: www.saudiaramco.com

Saudi Ports Authority
PO Box 5162, Riyadh 11422
Tel: +966 1 405 0005; Fax: +966 1 405 3508
Website: www.ports.gov.sa

General Organization for Social Insurance (GOSI)
PO Box 878, Riyadh 11421
Tel: +966 1 477 7735; Fax: +966 1 477 9958

Saudi Telecommunications Commission
Riyadh 11231
Tel: +966 1 452 2099; Fax: +966 1 452 2625

Supreme Commission for Tourism
PO Box 66680; Riyadh 11586
Tel: +966 1 480 8855; Fax: +966 1 480 8844

Supreme Council for Petroleum and Mineral Affairs
Riyadh 11272
Tel: +966 1 483 1444; Fax: +966 1 483 3085

Supreme Economic Council
PO Box 94737, Riyadh 11614
Tel: +966 1 483 4037; Fax: +966 1 483 4035

Chambers of commerce and industry

Council of Saudi Chambers of Commerce and Industry
PO Box 16683, Riyadh 11474
Tel: +966 1 405 3200/7502; Fax: +966 1 402 4747
Website: www.saudichambers.org.sa

Riyadh Chamber of Commerce and Industry
Dabab Street, PO Box 596, Riyadh 11421
Tel: +966 1 404 0044/0300; Fax: +966 1 440 1103
Website: www.riyadh-chamber.org.sa

Jeddah Chamber of Commerce and Industry
King Khalid Street, PO Box 1264, Jeddah 21431
Tel: +966 2 651 5111; Fax: +966 2 651 7373/647 3026
Website: www.jeddah-chamber.org

Eastern Province Chamber of Commerce and Industry
PO Box 719, Dammam 31421
Tel: +966 3 857 1155; Fax: +966 3 857 0607
Website: www.chamber-ep.org.sa

Foreign embassies and diplomatic missions in Saudi Arabia

European countries

Belgium
PO Box 94396, Riyadh 11693
Tel: +966 1 488 2888; Fax: +966 1 488 2033

Denmark
PO Box 94398, Riyadh 11693
Tel: +966 1 488 0101; Fax: +966 1 488 1366

Finland
PO Box 94363, Riyadh 11693
Tel: +966 1 488 0515; Fax: +966 1 488 2520

France
PO Box 94367, Riyadh 11693
Tel: +966 1 488 1255; Fax: +966 1 488 2882

Germany
PO Box 94001, Riyadh 11693
Tel: +966 1 488 0700; Fax: +966 1 488 0660

Greece
PO Box 94375, Riyadh 11693
Tel: +966 1 480 1974; Fax: +966 1 488 0927

Ireland (Eire)
PO Box 94349, Riyadh 11693
Tel: +966 1 488 2300; Fax: +966 1 488 0927

Italy
PO Box 94389, Riyadh 11693
Tel: +966 1 488 1212; Fax: +966 1 488 0590

Netherlands
PO Box 94307, Riyadh 11693
Tel: +966 1 488 0011; Fax: +966 1 488 0544

Norway
PO Box 94380, Riyadh 11693
Tel: +966 1 488 1904; Fax: +966 1 488 0854
Email: emb.Riyadh@mfa.no

Portugal
PO Box 94328, Riyadh 11693
Tel: +966 1 464 4688; Fax: +966 1 464 4419

Spain
PO Box 94347, Riyadh 11693
Tel: +966 1 488 0606; Fax: +966 1 488 4741

Sweden
PO Box 94382, Riyadh 11693
Tel: +966 1 488 3100; Fax: +966 1 488 0604

Switzerland
PO Box 94311, Riyadh 11693
Tel: +966 1 488 1291; Fax: +966 1 488 0632

United Kingdom
PO Box 94351, Riyadh 11693
Tel: +966 1 488 0077; Fax: +966 1 488 2373
Jeddah Consulate: Tel: +966 2 622 5550; Fax: +966 2 622 6249

North and Latin American countries

Argentina
PO Box 94369, Riyadh 11693
Tel: +966 1 465 2600; Fax: +966 1 465 3057

Brazil
PO Box 94348, Riyadh 11693
Tel: +966 1 488 0025; Fax: +966 1 488 1073

Canada
PO Box 94321, Riyadh 11693
Tel: +966 1 488 2288; Fax: +966 1 488 0997

Mexico
PO Box 94391, Riyadh 11693
Tel: +966 1 482 8218; Fax: +966 1 482 8379

United States of America
PO Box 9041, Riyadh 11693
Tel: +966 1 488 3800; Fax: +966 1 488 3278/482 4364

Venezuela
PO Box 94364, Riyadh 11693
Tel: +966 1 476 7867; Fax: +966 1 476 8200

Middle Eastern and North African countries

Bahrain
PO Box 94371, Riyadh 11693
Tel: +966 1 488 0044; Fax: +966 1 488 0208

Egypt
PO Box 94333, Riyadh 11693
Tel: +966 1 465 8425; Fax: +966 1 465 2800

Iran
PO Box 94394, Riyadh 11693
Tel: +966 1 488 1916; Fax: +966 1 488 1890

Jordan
PO Box 94316, Riyadh 11693
Tel: +966 1 488 0039; Fax: +966 1 488 0072

Kuwait
PO Box 94304, Riyadh 11693
Tel: +966 1 488 3500; Fax: +966 1 488 3682

Lebanon
PO Box 94350, Riyadh 11693
Tel: +966 1 419 7000; Fax: +966 1 419 2767

Morocco
PO Box 94392, Riyadh 11693
Tel: +966 1 482 8941; Fax: +966 1 482 7016

Oman
PO Box 94381, Riyadh 11693
Tel: +966 1 482 3120/3067; Fax: +966 1 482 3738

Qatar
PO Box 94353, Riyadh 11693
Tel: +966 1 482 5685; Fax: +966 1 482 5694

Syria
PO Box 94323, Riyadh 11693
Tel: +966 1 482 6191; Fax: +966 1 482 6196

Turkey
PO Box 94390, Riyadh 11693
Tel: +966 1 482 0101; Fax: +966 1 488 7823

Tunisia
PO Box 94368, Riyadh 11693
Tel: +966 1 488 7900; Fax: +966 1 488 7641

United Arab Emirates
PO Box 94385, Riyadh 11693
Tel: +966 1 482 6803; Fax: +966 1 482 7504

Yemen Republic
PO Box 94356, Riyadh 11693
Tel: +966 1 488 1769; Fax: +966 1 488 1562

Asian/Far Eastern countries

China, People's Republic of
PO Box 75231, Riyadh 11578
Tel: +966 1 482 4246; Fax: +966 1 456 3315

China, Republic of (Taiwan)
PO Box 94393, Riyadh 11693
Tel: +966 1 488 1900; Fax: +966 1 488 1716

India
PO Box 94387, Riyadh 11693
Tel: +966 1 488 0144; Fax: +966 1 488 4750

Indonesia
PO Box 94343, Riyadh 11693
Tel: +966 1 488 2800; Fax: +966 1 488 2966

Japan
PO Box 4095, Riyadh 11491
Tel: +966 1 488 1100; Fax: +966 1 488 0189

Korea, Republic of
PO Box 94399, Riyadh 11693
Tel: +966 1 488 2211; Fax: +966 1 488 1317

Malaysia
PO Box 94335, Riyadh, 11693
Tel: +966 1 488 7100; Fax: +966 1 482 4177

Pakistan
PO Box 94007, Riyadh 11693
Tel: +966 1 488 4111; Fax: +966 1 488 7953

Philippines
PO Box 94366, Riyadh 11693
Tel: +966 1 488 0835; Fax: +966 1 488 3945

Singapore
PO Box 94378, Riyadh 11693
Tel: +966 1 465 7007; Fax: +966 1 465 2224

Sri Lanka
PO Box 94360, Riyadh 11693
Tel: +966 1 460 6906; Fax: +966 1 460 8846

Thailand
PO Box 94359, Riyadh 11693
Tel: +966 1 488 1174; Fax: +966 1 488 1179

Australasian countries

Australia
PO Box 94400, Riyadh 11693
Tel: +966 1 488 7788; Fax: +966 1 488 7973

New Zealand
PO Box 94397, Riyadh 11693
Tel: +966 1 488 7988; Fax: +966 1 488 7912

African countries

Ghana
PO Box 94339, Riyadh 11693
Tel: +966 1 454 5122; Fax: +966 1 450 9819

Nigeria
PO Box 94386, Riyadh 11693
Tel: +966 1 482 3024; Fax: +966 1 482 4134

South Africa
PO Box 94006, Riyadh 11693
Tel: +966 1 456 2983; Fax: +966 1 454 3727

Saudi overseas commercial offices/diplomatic representation

European countries

Austria
PO Box 126, Formanekgasse 38, A-1190 Vienna
Tel: +431 368 2316/368 2317; Fax: + 431 368 2560
Email: atemb@mofa.gov.sa

Belgium
45 Avenue Franklin Roosevelt, 1050 Brussels
Tel: +322 649 2044; Fax: +322 646 8538
Email: beemb@mofa.gov.sa

Denmark
27 Lille Strandvej, 2900 Helrup, Copenhagen
Tel: +45 3962 1200/1370; Fax: +45 3962 6009
Email: dkemb@mofa.gov.sa

France
5 Avenue Hoche, 75008 Paris
Tel: +33 1 56 79 4000; Fax: +33 1 56 79 4002
Email: fremb@mofa.gov.sa

Germany
Godesberger Allee 40–42, 5300 Bonn 2
Tel: +49 8892 5030; Fax: +49 8892 5102
Email: deemb@mofa.gov.sa

Italy
9 Via GB Pergolesi, Rome 00198
Tel: +39 6 844 5851; Fax: +39 6 855 1781
Email: itemb@mofa.gov.sa

Netherlands
19 Alexanderstraat, 2514 JM The Hague
Tel: +31 70 360 0877/361 4391; Fax: +31 70 363 0348
Email: saudiembassy@wanadoo.nl

Spain
C/Dr. Alvarez Sierra 3, Madrid
Tel: +34 913 832 229; Fax: +34 913 021 212
Email: esemb@mofa.gov.sa

Sweden
PO Box 26073, Koldungagatan 5, S-10041 Stockholm
Tel: +468 238800; Fax: +468 4113849
Email: seemb@mofa.gov.sa

Switzerland
Kramburgstrasse 12, 3006 Berne
Tel: +41 31 352 1555/1567; Fax: +41 31 3514581
Email: chemb@mofa.gov.sa

United Kingdom
30 Charles Street, London WIJ 5DZ
Tel: +44 20 7917 3000; Fax: +44 20 7917 3113
Email: ukemb@mofa.gov.sa
Website: www.saudiembassy.org.uk

North and Latin American countries

Argentina
Alejandro Maria de Aguado 2881, CP 1452 Buenos Aires
Tel: +54 11 4802 4303; Fax: +54 11 4806 1581
Email: consaudi@fibertel.com.ar

Brazil
Shis Q1 10 Conjunto Casa 20 Brasilia
Tel: +55 61 248 3525; Fax: +55 61 248 2905
Email: bremb@mofa.gov.sa

Canada
99 Bank Street, Suite 901, Ottawa, Ontario K1P 6B9
Tel: +1 613 237 4100/4101; Fax: +1 613 237 0567
Email: caemb@mofa.gov.sa

Mexico
Av. Pasco de las Palmas No 2075, Col. Lomas de Chapultepec, Mexico DF 11000
Tel: +52 251 0789; Fax: +52 251 8587
Email: mxemb@mofa.gov.sa

United States of America
601 New Hampshire Avenue NW, Washington DC 20037
Tel: +1 202 342 3800; Fax: +1 202 944 3140
Email: info@saudiembassy.net
Website: www.saudiembassy.net

Venezuela
Calle Andres Pietri Quinta Makkah Urbanizacion Los Chorros 1071, Caracas
Tel: +582 12 239 0290; Fax: +582 12 239 6494
Email: veemb@mofa.gov.sa

Middle Eastern and North African countries

Bahrain
Road 1702, Building 317, Diplomatic Area, Manama
Tel: +973 537 722; Fax: +973 533 261
Email: bhemb@mofa.gov.sa

Egypt
2 Ahmed Naseem Street, Giza, Cairo
Tel: +202 761 4308; Fax: +202 749 3495
Email: egemb@mofa.gov.sa

Iran
1 Niloufar Street, Boustan Street, Pasdaran Avenue, Tehran
Tel: +98 21 228 8543; Fax: +98 21 229 4691
Email: iremb@mofa.gov.sa

Jordan
6th Floor, Zahrat Altahoni Building, Jabal Ammam, Amman
Tel: + 96 26 592 4154; Fax: +96 26 592 1154
Email: joemb@mofa.gov.sa

Kuwait
Arabian Gulf Street, East Dasman Qasma 9 Kuwait
Tel: +965 240 0250; Fax: +965 242 0654
Email: kwemb@mofa.gov.sa

Lebanon
Kuraitem Area, Beirut
Tel: +961 860 351; Fax: +961 861 524
Email: lbemb@mofa.gov.sa

Morocco
43 Al Wehdah Al Afrequiah Square, Rabat
Tel: +212 37 730 171; Fax: +212 37 768 587
Email: maemb@mofa.gov.sa

Oman
PO Box 1411, Ruwi PC 112, Muscat
Tel: +968 601744/601791; Fax: +968 603540
Email: omemb@mofa.gov.sa

Qatar
Dafrah, Diplomatic Area, Doha
Tel: +974 483 2030; Fax: +974 483 2720
Email: qaemb@mofa.gov.sa

Syria
Alglaa Street, Abu Romanah, Damascus
Tel: +963 11 333 4914; Fax: +963 11 333 7383
Email: syemb@mofa.gov.sa

Tunisia
Yougartah Nahg Al Riyadh Mewal Fel, Tunis
Tel: +216 784 075; Fax: +216 783 225
Email: tnemb@mofa.gov.sa

Turkey
Turan Emeksiz Sok 6 Gaziosmanpsa, Ankara
Tel: +90 312 427 4886; Fax: +90 312 427 4886
Email: tremb@mofa.gov.sa

United Arab Emirates
Diplomatic Quarter, Abu Dhabi
Tel: +971 2 444 5700; Fax: +971 2 444 8491
Email: aeemb@mofa.gov.sa

Yemen Republic
Quds Street, Building 1, Sana'a
Tel: +967 1 240 429; Fax: +967 1 240 859
Email: yeemb@mofa.gov.sa

Asian/Far Eastern countries

India
D12 ND South Extension Part II, New Delhi 110049
Tel: +911 625 2470; Fax: +911 625 9333
Email: inemb@mofa.gov.sa

Indonesia
Ji MT Hargano Kav 27, Cawang Jakarta-timur, Jakarta
Tel: +62 21 801 1533; Fax: +62 21 390 5864
Email: idemb@mofa.gov.sa

Japan
1-4-8 Roppongi, Minato-Ku, Tokyo 106-0032
Tel: +813 3589 5241/5242; Fax: +813 3589 5200
Email: jpemb@mofa.gov.sa

Korea, Republic of
1–112 Shinmoonro, 2-KA Chongro-Ku Seoul
Tel: +82 2 739 0631/0635; Fax: +82 2 732 3110
Email: kremb@mofa.gov.sa

Malaysia
7 Jalan Kedondong, Off Jalan Ampang Hilir, 55000 Kuala Lumpur
Tel: +603 4257 9825/9433; Fax: +603 4256 1303
Email: myemb@mofa.gov.sa

Pakistan
14 Hill Road, Sector F-6/3, Islamabad
Tel: + 925 1 282 0150; Fax: + 925 1 227 8816
Email: pkemb@mofa.gov.sa

Philippines
389 Sen. Gil Puyat Avenue, Ext. Malkati City, Manila
Tel: +632 2 890 9735; Fax: +632 2 895 3493
Email: phemb@mofa.gov.sa

Singapore
10 Nassim Road, Singapore 1025
Tel: +65 734 5478/5479; Fax: +65 738 5291/0624

Thailand
Seng Thong Thani Building, 23rd/24th Floor 28, North Sathorn Road, Bangkok 10500
Tel: +662 639 2999; Fax: +662 639 2950
Email: themb@mofa.gov.sa

Australasian countries

Australia
38 Guilfoyle Street, Yarralumla ACT 2600, Canberra
Tel: +61 2 6282 6999; Fax: +61 2 6286 8911
Email: auemb@mofa.gov.sa

African countries

Nigeria
Plot 347H, Abuja 11
Tel: +234 9 413 1880; Fax: +234 9 413 4906
Email: ngemb@mofa.gov.sa

Appendix II

Business Services

Advertising services

Akeel Saatchi & Saatchi
Abanumay Commercial Centre, Building 1, PO Box 26532, Riyadh
Tel: +966 1 473 1413; Fax: +966 1 476 9512
Website: www.saatchi-saatchi.com
Contact: Nizar Nakfoor

Memac Ogilvy & Mather
PO Box 54062, Riyadh
Tel: +966 1 460 4484/3499; Fax: +966 1 460 4474
Website: www.ogilvy.co.ae

Target Leo Burnett Advertising
PO Box 295797, Riyadh
Tel: +966 1 273 7070; Fax: +966 1 273 7071
Website: www.leoburnett.com

Audit and accountancy services

Al Juraid & Company (PricewaterhouseCoopers)
King Faisal Foundation Building, North Tower, 10th Floor, PO Box 8282, Riyadh 11482
Tel: +966 1 465 4240 Fax: +966 1 465 1663
Email: info@alijuraid.com and djohnson@aljuraid.com
Website: www.aljuraid.com
Contact: David Johnson, Audit Partner

Ernst & Young
Level 6, Al Faisaliah Office Tower, King Fahad Road, PO Box 2732, Riyadh 11461
Tel: +966 1 273 4740; Fax: +966 1 273 4730
Website: www.eyme.com
Contact: Abdulaziz A Al-Sowailim or Kevin O'Brien

Exhibition and trade fair services

Riyadh Exhibition Company Ltd (REC)
PO Box 56010, Riyadh 11554
Tel: +966 1 454 1448; Fax: +966 1 454 4846
Email: esales@recexpo.com
Website: www.recexpo.com

Al Harithy Company for Exhibitions Ltd
PO Box 40740, Jeddah 21511
Tel: +966 2 654 6384; Fax: +966 2 654 6853
Email: acejedxpos@zajil.net
Website: www.alharithy.com
Contact: Mohieddin Saadieh or Khaled Maqbool

Dhahran International Exhibition Centre
PO Box 7519, Dammam 31472
Tel: +966 3 859 1888; Fax: +966 3 859 0212
Email: info@dhahran-expo.com
Website: www.dhahran-expo.com

Financial advisory services

GIB Financial Advisory Services
Abraj Atta'awuneya, King Fahd Road, PO Box 93413, Riyadh 11673
Tel: +966 1 218 0555; Fax: +966 1 218 0055
Contact: Salman M Al-Deghaither

Gulf International Bank BSC (Head Office)
Al-Dowali Building, 3 Palace Avenue, PO Box 1017, Manama, Bahrain
Tel: +973 17 534 000; Fax: +973 17 522 633
Email: info@gibbah.com
Website: www.gibonline.com

Management consultancy (industrial/business to business marketing)

ASA Consulting
PO Box 238, Cobham Surrey KT11 2WP, UK
Tel: +44 1372 844317; Fax: +44 1372 844437
Email: asaconsult@btinternet.com
Contact: Anthony Shoult

Ernst & Young
Al Faisaliah Office Tower, King Fahd Road, PO Box 2732, Riyadh 11461
Tel: +966 1 273 4740; Fax: +966 1 273 4730
Website: www.eyme.com
Contact: Phil Gandier, Management consultancy (consumer marketing)

ERAS Limited
4/6 Canfield Place, London NW6 3BT, UK
Tel: +44 207 625 1455; Fax: +44 207 625 1246
Email: david@erasuk.com
Contact: David Green

Management consultancy (human resources/ training)

Hay Management Consultants Ltd
Middle East Office, Oud Metha Towers (101), PO Box 3098, Dubai, UAE
Tel: +971 4 324 7396; Fax: +971 4 324 7395
Email: haygroup@emirates.net
Contact: Mark Eaton or Martin Mankowski

Saudi Development and Training Company Ltd (SDT)
King Fahd Road, PO Box 67775, Riyadh 11517
Tel: +966 1 293 3166; Fax: +966 1 293 3169
Website: www.sdt.com.sa
Contact: Ron Ross

Insurance services

Royal & Sun Alliance Insurance (Middle East) Limited
2nd Floor Al Rajhi Commercial Exchange Building, Palestine Street, PO Box 2374, Jeddah 21451
Tel: +966 2 672 1461; Fax: +966 2 617 8408
Website: www.royalsun-me.com
Contact: Philip Head or John Davies

BUPA Middle East
PO Box 23807, Jeddah 21436
Tel: +966 2 663 6936; Fax: +966 2 663 3156

Email: sales@bupame.com
Contact: David Maltby

Norwich Union Insurance
3rd Floor, Kanoo Building, Kilo 7 Madinah Road, PO Box 812, Jeddah 21421
Tel: +966 2 664 6655/667 3759; Fax: +966 2 660 9505/669 5801
Email: nuisa-jed@saudionline.com.sa
Website: www.nu-me.com
Contact: Paul Adamson

Investment advice (Al Yamamah Economic Offset Programme)

British Offset Office
Al Bilad Building, King Fahd Road, PO Box 1003, Riyadh 11431
Tel: +966 1 419 5957; Fax: +966 1 419 5957 ext 4214
Contact: Steve Kelly or Saud Al Fozan

British Offset Office
5th (N) Castlewood House, 77–91 New Oxford Street, London WC1A 1DS, UK
Tel: +44 (0) 20 7829 8556; Fax: +44 (0) 20 7829 8116
Contact: Gary Bonsall

Investment advice (general)

Saudi Arabian General Investment Authority (SAGIA)
Governor's Office, PO Box 59277, Riyadh 11432
Tel: +966 1 263 5010; Fax: +966 1 263 5020
Email: info@sagia.org
Website: www.sagia.gov.sa
Contact: HE Amr Abdullah Al-Dabbagh

Legal services

Legal Advisors (Baker & McKenzie)
Olayan Complex Tower 11, Al-Ahsa Street, PO Box 4288 Malaz, Riyadh 11491
Tel: +966 1 291 5561; Fax: +966 1 291 5571
Website: www.bakernet.com
Contact: John E Xefos

The Law Firm of Saleh Al-Hejailan
PO Box 1454, Riyadh 11431
Tel: +966 1 479 2200; Fax: +966 1 479 1717
Email: lfshriyadh@naseej.com.sa
Website: www.hejailannet.com
Contact: Jean-Benoit Zegers

Property and facilities management services

PMDC Cluttons
PO Box 4843; Jeddah 21472
Tel: +966 2 698 0145; Fax: +966 2 698 0146
Contact: Keith Procter

Public relations services

Gulf Hill & Knowlton
Azwal Plaza 1st Floor, PO Box 12651, Jeddah 21483
Tel: +966 2 652 3232; Fax: +966 2 652 3131
Email: ghk@hillandknowlton.com.sa
Contact: Damian James

Travel services

Al-Tayyar Travel Group
PO Box 52660, Riyadh 11573
Tel: +966 1 463 3133; Fax: +966 1 465 6049
Email: altayyar@attayyargroup.com
Website: www.altayyargroup.com
Contact: Nasser A Al-Tayyar

Attar Travel Co
PO Box 18600, Jeddah 21425
Tel: +966 2 661 1222; Fax: +966 2 667 4663
Email: johnm@attar.com.sa
Contact: Sheikh Ghassan Attar or John Marshall

YBA Kanoo Travel
PO Box 37, Dammam 31411
Tel: +966 3 835 5633/5793; Fax: +966 3 835 4743
Email: ktd@kanoosa.com
Contact: Abdulla Abo Khamseen or Timothy Casey

Hotel accommodation

Riyadh

Hotel Al Khozama
Olaya Street, PO Box 4148, Riyadh 11491
Tel: +966 1 465 4650; Fax: +966 1 464 8576
Website: www.rosewoodhotels.com

Al Faisaliah Hotel
King Fahd Road, PO Box 4148, Riyadh 11491
Tel: +966 1 273 2000/1; Fax: +966 1 273 2704
Website: www.rosewoodhotels.com

Hyatt Regency Riyadh
Airport Road, PO Box 18006, Riyadh 11415
Tel: +966 1 479 1234; Fax: +966 1 477 5373

Minhal Holiday Inn
Old Airport Road, PO Box 17058, Riyadh 11484
Tel: +966 1 478 2500; Fax: +966 1 477 2819

Inter-Continental Riyadh
Mather Street, PO Box 3636, Riyadh 11481
Tel: +966 1 465 5000; Fax: +966 1 405 3697

Marriott Riyadh Hotel
PO Box 16294, Riyadh 11464
Tel: +966 1 477 9300; Fax: +966 1 477 9089

Sheraton Riyadh Hotel & Towers
King Fahd Street, PO Box 90807, Riyadh 11623
Tel: +966 1 454 3300; Fax: +966 1 454 1889
Website: www.sheraton.com/riyadh

Jeddah

Albilad Hotel Jeddah (Golden Tulip)
Al Corniche Highway, PO Box 6788, Jeddah 21452
Tel: +966 2 694 4777; Fax: +966 2 694 3737

Au Fau Holiday Inn (Crowne Plaza)
PO Box 10924, Jeddah 21443
Tel: +966 2 661 1000; Fax: +966 2 660 6326

Jeddah Inter-Continental Hotel
Al-Hamra Corniche, PO Box 41855, Jeddah 21531
Tel: +966 2 661 1800; Fax: +966 2 661 1145
Email: Jeddah@interconti.com

Marriott Jeddah Hotel
Palestine Road, PO Box 6448, Jeddah 21442
Tel: +966 2 671 4000; Fax: +966 2 671 5990

Red Sea Palace Hotel
King Abdul Aziz Street, PO Box 824, Al-Balad, Jeddah 21421
Tel: +966 2 642 8555; Fax: +966 2 642 2395

Sofitel Alhamra Hotel
Palestine Road, PO Box 7375, Jeddah 21462
Tel: +966 2 660 2000; Fax: +966 2 660 4145

Hyatt Regency Jeddah
Madinah Road, PO Box 8483, Jeddah 21482
Tel: +966 2 652 1234; Fax: +966 2 651 6260
Email: Jeddah_reservations@hytmiddle-east.co.ae

Sheraton Jeddah Hotel & Villas
North Corniche, PO Box 14315, Jeddah 21424
Tel: +966 2 699 2212; Fax: +966 2 699 2660

Makkah

Inter-Continental Makkah
PO Box 1496, Makkah Al Mukharramah
Tel: +966 2 560 1000; Fax: +966 2 543 4054

Sheraton Makkah Hotel & Tower
Al Ghaza Street, PO Box 4009, Makkah
Tel: +966 2 576 6000; Fax: + 966 2 575 5560

Taif

Taif Inter-Continental
Hawiyah Street, PO Box 827, Taif
Tel: +966 2 750 5050; Fax: +966 2 750 5040

Sheraton Al Hada Hotel
PO Box 999, Taif
Tel: +966 2 754 1400; Fax: +966 2 754 4831

Dammam/Al Khobar/Dhahran

Alhamra Holiday Inn
PO Box 1411, Dammam 31431
Tel: +966 3 833 3444; Fax: +966 3 833 0944

Dhahran International Hotel
Dhahran Airport 31932, PO Box 428, Dhahran
Tel: +966 3 330 5000; Fax: +966 3 891 8559

Le Gulf Meridien Al Khobar
Prince Turki Street, PO Box 1266, Al Khobar 31952
Tel: +966 3 864 6000; Fax: +966 3 898 1651

Sheraton Dammam Hotel and Towers
First Street, PO Box 5397, Dammam 31422
Tel: +966 3 834 5555; Fax: +966 3 834 9872

Al Jubail

Hotel Inter-Continental Hotel Al Jubail
Tareeq 101, PO Box 10167, Al Jubail 31961
Tel: +966 3 341 7000; Fax: +966 3 341 2212

Madinah

Sheraton Medina Hotel
Khalid Ibn El-Waleed Street, PO Box 1735, Madinah
Tel: +966 4 846 0777 Fax: +966 4 846 0385

Dar Al Hijra Inter-Continental Madinah
King Fahd Street, PO Box 20201, Madinah
Tel: +966 4 820 7777; Fax: +966 4 820 7788
Email: hijramadinah@interconti.com

Dar Al Iman Inter-Continental Madinah
Off Sitteen Street, PO Box 20205, Madinah
Tel: +966 4 820 6666; Fax: +966 4 820 6677

Dar Al Taqwa Inter-Continental
PO Box 20944, Madinah
Tel: +966 4 829 1111; Fax: +966 4 829 0611

Yanbu
Rahdwa Holiday Inn Yanbu

PO Box 452, Yanbu 51888
Tel: +966 4 322 3767; Fax: +966 4 322 7281
Email: radhwa@holidayinn-sa.com
Website: www.holiday-inn.com/yanbu

Abha

Inter-Continental Abha
PO Box 1447, Abha
Tel: +966 7 224 7777; Fax: +966 7 224 4113

Appendix III

Leading Companies and Organizations (Listing by Sector)[1]

Note: For those companies/organizations marked with an asterisk, further information can be found in the alphabetical listings in Appendix IV.

Agribusiness

Almarai Company Ltd
PO Box 8524, Riyadh 11492
Tel: +966 1 470 0005; Fax: +966 1 470 1555
Website: www.almarai.com
Chief Executive: Abdulrahman bin Abdulaziz Al Muhanna

Arab Supply and Trading Corp (ASTRA)
Tel: +966 4 422 0400; Fax: +966 4 423 7649
Website: www.astra.com.sa
Chief Executive: Kamil A Saaddin

Hail Agricultural Development Company (HADCO)
Tel: +966 6 520 0011; Fax: +966 6 520 0022
Website: www.hadco.com.sa
Chief Executive: HE Ibrahim Bin Fahad

National Agricultural Development Company (NADEC)
Tel: +966 1 404 0000; Fax: +966 1 405 5522
Website: www.nadec.com.sa
Chief Executive: Abdulaziz Al-Babtain

---

[1] Sources of information include Arab News Top 100 Saudi Companies, December 2004.

Saudi Fisheries Company
Tel: +966 3 859 1919; Fax: +966 3 859 3090
Website: www.saudi-fisheries.com
Chief Executive: Eng Essam Abdulghani

Banking and financial services

Al Bank Al Saudi Al Fransi*
Tel: +966 1 404 2222; Fax: +966 1 404 2311
Website: www.alfransi.com
Chief Executive: Jean Marion

Al-Rajhi Banking and Investment Corporation*
Tel: +966 1 460 1000/2015; Fax: +966 1 460 0922/2040
Website: www.alrajhibank.com.sa
Chief Executive: Abdullah Sulaiman Al-Rajhi

Arab National Bank*
PO Box 56921, Riyadh 11564
Tel: +966 1 402 9000; Fax: +966 1 402 7747
Website: www.anb.com.sa
Chief Executive: Abdulaziz Al Sugaire

Financial Transaction House
PO Box 24368, Jeddah 21446
Tel: +966 2 657 3030; Fax: +966 2 657 3366
Website: www.fthgulf.com
President & CEO: Faisal Al-Sayrafi

National Company for Cooperative Insurance
PO Box 86959, Riyadh 11632
Tel: +966 1 218 0100; Fax: +966 1 218 0102
Website: www.ncci.com/En
Chief Executive Officer: Mousa Al Rubaian

National Bank of Dubai*
P.O. Box 777 Dubai, United Arab Emirates
Tel: 00-971-4-222 2111; Fax: 00-971-4-228 3000
Website: www.nbd.com
Chairman: Abdullah Mohamed Saleh

The National Commercial Bank*
PO Box 355, Jeddah
Tel: +966 2 644 0377

Website: www.alahli.com
Chairman: Abdullah S Bahamdan

The Saudi British Bank*
PO Box 9084, Riyadh 11413
Tel: +966 1 405 0677; Fax: +966 1 405 0660
Website: www.sabb.com.sa
Chairman: Abdullah Mohamed Al-Hugail

Riyadh Bank*
PO Box 22622, Riyadh 11416
Tel: +966 1 401 3030; Fax: +966 1 404 2707
Website: www.riyadbank.com.sa
Chairman: Rashed Abdulaziz Al-Rashed

Samba Financial Group (SAMBA)*
PO Box 833, Riyadh 11421
Tel: +966 1 477 5200; Fax: +966 1 479 9676
Website: www.samba.com
Chief Executive Officer: Eisa Al-Eisa

Al Jazira Bank*
Khalid Bin Al Walid Street, PO Box 6277, Jeddah 21442
Tel: +966 2 651 8070; Fax: +966 2 653 2478
Website: www.baj.com.sa
Chairman: Abdul Monem R Al-Rashed

Saudi Hollandi Bank*
Al-Dhabab Street, PO Box 1467, Riyadh 11431
Tel: +966 1 401 0288; Fax: +966 1 403 1104
Website: www.saudihollandibank.com
Chairman: Sulaiman AR Al-Suhaimi

The Saudi Investment Bank*
PO Box 3533, Riyadh 11481
Tel: +966 1 478 6000; Fax: +966 1 477 6781
Website: www.saib.com.sa
Chairman: Dr Abdulaziz Al-Abdullah O'Hali

Construction/contracting

Al Abdulkarim Trading Group
9th Floor, Khashoggi Building, Dhahran Street, PO Box 31377,
Al-Khobar 31952

Tel: +966 3 889 2085; Fax: +966 3 889 2086
Website: www.akte.com.sa
Executive Director: Khalid Al Abdulkarim

Consolidated Contractors International Co WLL
PO Box 234, Riyadh 11411
Tel: +966 1 465 0311/5; Fax: +966 1 464 5963/465 5647
Website: www.ccc.gr
President: Said Tawfiq Khoury

Saad Trading and Contracting Company*
PO Box 3250, Al Khobar 31952
Tel: +966 3 882 2220/887 0999; Fax: +966 3 882 8699/7989
Website: www.saadgroup.com
Chief Executive: Maan A Al-Sanea

MS Al Suwaidi Est for Contracting
King Saud Street, PO Box 12, Ras Tanura 31941
Tel: +966 3 667 3746; Fax: +966 3 667 1044
Website: www.suwaidi.com
Chairman: Salem Al-Suwaidi

Makkah Construction & Development Company
Tel: +966 2 557 0037; Fax: +966 2 558 3086
Chief Executive: Rahman Faqeeh

Manufacturing industry (leading companies)

ABB Saudi Arabia
Al-Ahsa Street, PO Box 4441, Riyadh 11491
Tel: +966 1 476 2644; Fax: +966 1 476 3547
Website: www.abb.com.sa
Country Manager: Mahmoud Shaban

Aluminium Products Company Ltd (ALUPCO)
PO Box 2080, Dammam 31451
Tel: +966 3 847 1300; Fax: +966 3 847 3010
Website: www.alupco.com
Managing Director: Waleed H Al-Soggaf

Arabian Pipe Company Ltd
PO Box 42734, Riyadh 11551
Tel: +966 1 265 0123; Fax: +966 1 265 0311

Website: www.arabian-pipes.com
Chief Executive: Saud Al-Fayze

National Gas & Industry Company (GASCO)
PO Box 564, Riyadh 11421
Tel: +966 1 466 4999; Fax: +966 1 466 4888
Website: www.gasco.com.sa
Chief Executive: Abdul Aziz Al Hodaithi

National Paper Products Company (NAPCO) Group
PO Box 538, Dammam 31421
Tel: +966 3 847 3111; Fax: +966 3 847 1435
Website: www.napcopaper.com
Chief Executive: Jamal Al-Moaibed

Riyadh Cables Group of Companies*
PO Box 26862, Riyadh 11496
Tel: +966 1 265 0850; Fax: +966 1 265 1423
Website: www.riyadh-cables.com
Chief Executive: Hamdi S Zaim

Saudi Arabian Amiantit Company*
PO Box 589, Dammam 31421
Tel: +966 3 847 1500; Fax: +966 3 847 1645
Website: www.amiantit.com
Chief Executive Officer: Fareed Yousef Al-Khalawi

Saudi Cement Company
PO Box 306, Dammam 31411
Tel: +966 3 834 0407; Fax: +966 3 834 3091
Website: www.saudicement.com.sa
Chief Executive: Khaled Al-Olayan

Saudi Cable Company*
PO Box 4403, Jeddah 21491
Tel: +966 2 638 0080; Fax: +966 2 635 2220
Website: www.xenel.com/site/industrial
Chief Executive: Khalid Alireza

Saudi Ceramic Company
PO Box 3893, Riyadh 11481
Tel: +966 1 464 4244; Fax: +966 1 465 2124
Website: www.saudiceramics.com
General Manager: Abdul Karim

Savola Group
8th Floor, Saudi Business Centre, Madinah Road, PO Box 14455, Jeddah 21424
Tel: +966 2 657 3333; Fax: +966 2 648 4119
Website: www.savola.com
Chairman: Eng Adel Fakeeh
Chief Executive Officer: Dr Abdulraouf Mannaa

Saudi Pharmaceutical Industries & Medical Appliances Corp (SPIMACO)
PO Box 20001, Riyadh 11455
Tel: +966 1 477 4481; Fax: +966 1 477 3961
Website: www.spimaco.com.sa
Chief Executive: Dr Abdullah Abdulkader

Yamama Saudi Cement Company
PO Box 293, Riyadh 11411
Tel: +966 1 405 8288; Fax: +966 1 403 3292
Website: www.yamamacement.com
Chief Executive: Saud Al Dablan

Yanbu Cement Company
PO Box 5330, Jeddah 21422
Tel: +966 2 653 1555; Fax: +966 2 653 1420
Website: www.yanbucement.com
Director General: Dr Saud S Islam

Heavy industry (SABIC affiliates/petrochemicals/steel)

Saudi Basic Industries Corporation (SABIC)*
(Headquarters) PO Box 5101, Riyadh 11422
Tel: +966 1 225 8000; Fax: +966 1 225 9000
Website: www.sabic.com
Chief Executive Officer: Eng Mohammad H Al-Mady

Al Jubail Fertilizer Company (SAMAD)
PO Box 10046, Al Jubail 31961
Tel: +966 3 341 6487/88; Fax: +966 3 341 7122
Website: www.sabic.com

Arabian Industrial Fibre Company (IBN RUSHD)
PO Box 30701, Yanbu 21441

Tel: +966 4 396 0965; Fax: +966 4 321 8008
Website: www.sabic.com

Al Jubail Petrochemical Company (KEMYA)
PO Box 10084, Al Jubail 31961
Tel: +966 3 357 6000; Fax: +966 3 358 7858
Website: www.sabic.com

Arabian Petrochemical Company (PETROKEMYA)
PO Box 10002, Al Jubail 31961
Tel: +966 3 358 7000; Fax: +966 3 358 4480
Website: www.sabic.com

Eastern Petrochemical Company (SHARQ)
PO Box 10035, Al Jubail 31961
Tel: +966 3 357 5000; Fax: +966 3 358 0383
Website: www.sabic.com

National Chemical Fertilizer Company (IBN AL-BAYTAR)
PO Box 10283, Al Jubail 31961
Tel: +966 3 341 9988; Fax: +966 3 341 5894
Website: www.sabic.com

National Industrial Gases Company (GAS)
PO Box 10110, Al Jubail 31961
Tel: +966 3 357 5700; Fax: +966 3 358 5542
Website: www.sabic.com

National Methanol Company (IBN SINA)
PO Box 10003, Al Jubail 31961
Tel: +966 3 340 5500; Fax: +966 3 340 5604
Website: www.sabic.com

National Plastic Company (IBN HAYYAN)
PO Box 10002, Al Jubail 31961
Tel: +966 3 358 600; Fax: +966 3 358 4736
Website: www.sabic.com

Saudi Arabian Fertilizer Company (SAFCO)
PO Box 553, Dammam 31421
Tel: +966 3 857 5011; Fax: +966 3 857 4311
Website: www.sabic.com

Saudi European Petrochemical Company (IBN ZAHR)
PO Box 10330, Al Jubail 31961

Tel: +966 3 341 5060; Fax: +966 3 341 2966
Website: www.sabic.com

Saudi Iron and Steel Company (HADEED)
PO Box 10053, Al Jubail 31961
Tel: +966 3 357 1100; Fax: +966 3 358 7385
Website: www.sabic.com

Saudi Methanol Company (AR-RAZI)
PO Box 10065, Al Jubail 31961
Tel: +966 3 357 7800; Fax: +966 3 358 5552
Website: www.sabic.com

Saudi Petrochemical Company (SADAF)
PO Box 10025, Al Jubail 31961
Tel: +966 3 357 3000; Fax: +966 3 357 3343
Website: www.sabic.com

Saudi-Yanbu Petrochemical Company (YANPET)
PO Box 30333, Yanbu 21441
Tel: +966 4 396 5000; Fax: +966 4 396 3236
Website: www.sabic.com

Ibn Hayyan Plastic Production Company (TAYF)
PO Box 10273, Al Jubail 31961
Tel: +966 3 358 4000; Fax: +966 3 358 7577
Website: www.sabic.com

Oil and gas industry

Saudi Arabian Oil Company (Saudi Aramco)*
PO Box 5000, Dhahran 31311
Tel: +966 3 875 6385/873 7607; Fax: +966 3 873 8708
Website: www.saudiaramco.com
President and Chief Executive Officer: Abdallah S Jum'ah

Saudi Arabian Lubricating Oil Company (PETROLUBE)
PO Box 1432, Jeddah
Tel: +966 2 661 3333; Fax: +966 2 661 3322
Chief Executive: Mou'tasam Abdul Aziz Al Ma'shouk

Saudi Aramco Mobil Refinery Company (SAMREF)
PO Box 30078, Yanbu

Tel: +966 4 396 4000; Fax: +966 4 396 0942
Chief Executive: Muhammad Saib Al Gosaibi

Saudi Aramco Shell Refinery Company (SASREF)
PO Box 10088, Al Jubail Industrial City 31961
Tel: +966 3 357 2000; Fax: +966 3 357 2235
Chairman: Abdel Aziz Bin Mohammad Al Haqil

Publishing and marketing

Saudi Research and Marketing Group
Tel: +966 1 441 0101; Fax: +966 1 441 9569
Website: www.srmg.com
Chairman: HRH Prince Faisal Bin Salman Bin Abdul Aziz Al Saud

Tihama for Advertising, Public Relations & Marketing
Tihama Building, Al Andalus Street, PO Box 5455, Jeddah 21422
Tel: +966 2 651 1100; Fax: +966 2 651 2228/9990
Website: www.tihama.com
Chief Executive: Fahad Bakhaidher

Trading and diversified companies

Alessayi Trading Corporation (Mitsubishi)
Makkah Road Kilo-11, PO Box 1342, Jeddah 21431
Tel: +966 2 620 2000; Fax: +966 2 620 6469
Website: www.alesayi.com.sa
Chief Executive: Omar Alessayi

Al Faisaliah Group Company
PO Box 16460, Riyadh 11464
Tel: +966 1 463 6103; Fax: +966 1 273 1119
Website: www.alfaisaliah.com
Chief Executive: Muhammad Al-Ariefy

Alhamrani Group of Companies*
PO Box 1229, Jeddah 21431
Tel: +966 2 606 5555; Fax: +966 1 606 0265
Website: www.alhamranigroup.com
Chairman and Chief Executive Officer: Sheikh Mohamed A Alhamrani

El Seif Group*
PO Box 15665, Riyadh 11461

Tel: +966 1 454 5996; Fax: +966 1 454 0863
Website: www.el-seif.com.sa
President: Faisal Musaed El-Seif

Al Suwaiket Trading and Contracting Group
PO Box 691, Dhahran Airport 31932
Tel: +966 3 857 9780/84; Fax: +966 3 857 2904
Website: www.alsuwaiket.com
Chairman: Mobarak Al Suwaiket

Marei Bin Mahfouz Group & Co Ltd*
Mohammad Bin Abdul Aziz Street, PO Box 4100, Jeddah 21491
Tel: +966 2 668 5656; Fax: +966 2 668 5959
Website: www.binmahfouz.net
Chairman: Sheikh Marei Bin Mahfouz

Dallah Albaraka Group*
PO Box 430, Jeddah 21411
Tel: +966 2 671 0000; Fax: +966 2 617 7056
Website: www.dallah.com
Chief Executive Officer: Abdullah Saleh Kamel

Haji Hussein Alireza & Co Ltd (Mazda)
PO Box 40; Jeddah 21411
Tel: +966 2 642 3509; Fax: +966 2 642 6435
Website: www.hhalireza.com.sa
Chief Executive: Hussein Alireza

Isam Kabbani Group of Companies
Tel: +966 2 667 2000; Fax: +966 2 665 8079
Website: www.ikkgroup.com
Chairman: Isam Khairy Kabbani

Kingdom Holding Company*
PO Box 2, Riyadh 11321
Tel: +966 1 211 1111; Fax: +966 1 211 1112
Website: www.kingdom.net
Chief Executive: HRH Prince Al-Waleed Bin Talal Bin Abdulaziz Al Saud

Mohammed Saad Aldrees & Sons Company*
PO Box 609, Riyadh 11421
Tel: +966 1 206 3333/6333; Fax: +966 1 206 7777
Website: www.aldrees.com
Chief Executive: Eng Abdulmohsen M Aldrees

The Olayan Group*
PO Box 1520, Al-Khobar 31952
Tel: +966 3 887 1000; Fax: +966 3 887 2000
Website: www.olayangroup.com
Chairman: Khaled S Olayan

SKAB Group
P.O. Box 13271, Jeddah 21493
Tel: +966-2-606 0608 Fax: +966-2-606 1702 / 606 0940
Website: skabco.net
President & C.E.O: Sheikh Ibrahim Bin Ali Bin Musallam

Transportation, travel and tourism

Al Tayyar Travel Group
Takassusi Street, Olaya, PO Box 52660, Riyadh
Tel: +966 1 463 3133; Fax: +966 1 465 6049
Website: www.altayyargroup.com
Chief Executive: Dr Nasser A Al-Tayyar

Fursan Travel and Tourism
King Fahd Highway, Riyadh 54854
Tel: +966 1 293 1160; Fax: +966 1 461 1743
Website: www.fursan.com.sa
Chief Executive: Abdullah Al-Rajhi

National Shipping Company of Saudi Arabia
Siteen Street, PO Box 8931, Riyadh 11492
Tel: +966 1 478 5454; Fax: +966 1 477 8036/7478
Website: www.nscsa.com
Chairman: Abdullah Saleh Nojaidi

Saudi Arabian Airlines*
PO Box 620, Jeddah 21231
Tel: +966 2 686 0000; Fax: +966 2 686 2112
Website: www.saudiairlines.com
Director General: Dr Khaled A Ben-Bakr

Saudi Public Transport Company (SAPTCO)
PO Box 10667, Riyadh 11443
Tel: +966 1 454 5000; Fax: +966 1 454 2100
Website: www.saptco.com.sa
Chief Executive: Abdullah Fayez

Saudi Hotels and Resort Areas Company
PO Box 5500, Riyadh 11422
Tel: +966 1 481 6666; Fax: +966 1 480 1666
Website: www.saudi-hotels.com.sa
Chief Executive: Abdul Aziz Al Ambar

Utilities

Saudi Electricity Company (SEC)
PO Box 57, Riyadh
Tel: +966 1 403 1033/403 2222; Fax: +966 1 408 2647
Website: www.se.com.sa
Chief Executive: Suleiman Al Qadi

Appendix IV

Details of Leading Companies and Organizations[1]

Abdel Hadi Abdullah Al-Qahtani & Sons Group of Companies (Tariq Abdel Hadi & Brothers Co)

Founded in 1948, the Al-Qahtani Group of Companies (AHQ) is one of the largest conglomerates in Saudi Arabia. AHQ is committed to serving the petrochemical, power generation and oil and gas industries in Saudi Arabia and other countries throughout the Middle East. One of the Company's subsidiaries, Al-Qahtani IT Division, is involved in wireless network solutions, video-conferencing solutions, mobile computing solutions, SAP end-user training, software development, networking services and electronic publishing management systems. AHQ is interested in meeting US firms in the following fields: wireless networking technology; video conferencing; oil field equipment and heavy industrial machinery; cooling water treatment chemicals; VoIP technology (IP Telephony); mobile computing solutions; VSAT technology; ATM networks; network services; switching and transmission systems; software applications; network management; multimedia applications; travel; insurance; customs clearance and transportation services; and farming.

Contact: Mr Tariq Abdel Hadi A Al-Qahtani, Chairman of the Board, PO Box 20, Dammam 31411, Saudi Arabia. Tel: +966 3 826 1477; Fax: +966 3 826 9894; Email: info@ahqsons.com and info@abdelhadialqahtanisons.com; Website: www.ahqsons.com.

Abdulali Al-Ajmi Co Ltd

Established in 1980 by Mr Abdul Ali Mohamed Al-Ajmi, the company has extensive experience in engineering, construction and management projects for Saudi Arabia's public and private sectors. Abdul Ali Al-Ajmi Company is primarily involved in the construction and maintenance of Saudi Arabia's

[1] Member Companies of the US-Saudi Arabian Business Council.

transportation network including the maintenance of streets, roads, highways and bridges; installation of street lights and irrigation system; slurry sealing, micro surfacing and road marking paintwork; mass earth moving and site preparation; bulk supply of hot mix asphalt and paving.

The company also owns asphalt batching plants and distribution centres. Abdul Ali Al-Ajmi Co has primarily worked with the Ministry of Communication, Saudi Aramco, SCECO East, the Mohammad Al-Mojil Group, Saudi Arabian Saipern Ltd, ABB, Raymond Saudi Arabia Ltd, C.C.C. WLL, Saudi Technit Ltd. and Arabian Drilling Co. The company employs a total workforce of 1,184 and has annual sales of more than US$39 million.

Contact: Mr Awiadah Abdulali Al-Ajmi, General Manager, PO Box 447, Al-Hasa 31982, Saudi Arabia. Tel: +966 3 592 2672; Fax: +966 3 592 8704. Company address and contact details: PO Box 86059, Riyadh 11622, Saudi Arabia. Tel: +966 1 215 2848/460 5626; Fax: +966 1 460 6315; Email: ajmi@ogertel.com and alajmico@saudionline.com.sa and info@alajmicompany.com; Website: www.alajmicompany.com.

Abdul Latif Jameel Group of Companies

Established in 1955, the Abdul Latif Jameel (ALJ) Company is a multi-billion dollar international enterprise, geographically diversified in the Middle East, UK, US and Asia. ALJ Company is involved in automobile sales and service, real estate, financing, advertising, consumer electronics and durables, hotels, and shipping. Headquartered in Jeddah, ALJ Company is the world's largest independent Toyota distributor.

Contact: Mr Mohammed Abdul Latif Jameel, President, PO Box 248, Jeddah 21411, Saudi Arabia. Tel: +966 2 693 0000 ext 250; Fax: +966 2 678 1000/628 3937; Email: contact@alj.com; Website: www.alj.com.

Abdullah A.M. Al-Khodari Sons Co.

Abdullah A.M. Al-Khodari Sons Co. (Al-Khodari Contracting), of the Al-Khodari Group, is one of the largest general contracting entities in the Middle East. Its expertise includes operation and maintenance of public buildings and projects, earthworks, site development, landscaping, airports, marine works, sanitary engineering projects, water desalination and treatment facilities, pipelines, highways and bridges, HVAC, oil, gas and petrochemicals support projects, and power stations. Other activities include, industrial projects, city cleaning and waste collection, transportation, sorting, disposal and management of industrial and hazardous waste, land transportation, travel and tourism, trading, and other specialized industrial services.

Contact: Mr Fawwaz A Al-Khodari, President, PO Box 3589, Al-Khobar 31952, Saudi Arabia. Tel: +966 3 895 2840/865-3403; Fax: +966 3 898 6856/865 3454; Email: president@alkhodari.com; Website: www.alkhodari.com.

Abdullah Abbar & Ahmed Zainy Company

Jeddah-based Abdullah Abbar & Ahmed Zainy Company was established in 1956. It is a highly diversified trading and manufacturing group whose activities include trade in foods, marine transport, petroleum products, agriculture, cold storage facilities, shipping, catering and meat processing, and aviation service. It is also a major investor in the oil business.

Contact: Ossama Ahmed Zainy, Executive Director, PO Box 17956, Jeddah 21494, Saudi Arabia. Tel: +966 2 647 0038; Fax: +966 2 647 8853; Email: ossama@zainy.net.

Abdulla Fouad Holding Co.

Established in 1947, the Abdulla Fouad Holding Co. is involved in civil construction, commercial trading, computers and software, travel and tourism, medical supplies, electro-mechanical services, cathodic protection services, and industrial material supply and services. Other activities include super computers, high-tech services to the petrochemical and power generation industries, and telecommunications.

Contact: Mr Fouad A. Fouad, President, PO Box 257, Dammam 31411, Saudi Arabia. Tel: +966 3 832 4400/833 2600; Fax: +966 3 834 5722/834 0320; Email: fouad.fouad@abdulla-fouad.com or info@abdullafouad.com. Website: www.abdulla-fouad.com.

Abdul Mohsen A. Al-Swailem Est.

Abdul Mohsen A. Al-Swailem's activities include household appliance stores, electric and gas retail, space heating, air conditioning, ventilation and humidifying plants. The company is also focused in the home electronics industry, specializing in television sets, video recorders and camcorders. Abdul Mohsen A. Al-Swailem is headquartered in Riyadh.

Contact: Mr Saad A. Al-Swailem, Vice President, PO Box 544, Riyadh 11421, Saudi Arabia. Tel: +966 1 465 8100; Fax: +966 1 464 8783/464 4108; Email: saad@alswailem.com; Website: www.alswailem.com.

Abdul Rahman S. Al-Rashid Est. for Contracting

Founded in 1957, Abdul Rahman S. Al-Rashid Company has grown to become one of the leading Saudi contracting companies. The company's activities include contracting, real estate and development.

Contact: Mr Saad Abdul Rahman Al-Rashid, General Manager, PO Box 9102, Riyadh 11413, Saudi Arabia. Tel: +966 1 419 1574/419 1691/419 1892; Fax: +966 1 419 1734; Email: artar@artar.ws or info@artar.ws; Website: www.artar.ws.

Abdullah Said Bugshan & Bros.

Abdullah Said Bughsan & Bros. was established in 1923 as a trading company. Its activities include civil, electrical, mechanical and telecommunication construction, sales, installation, operation and maintenance of power generation, telecommunication networks, air-conditioning equipment and heavy construction equipment. Some of the major companies Bughsan represents in the Kingdom include Lucent Technologies, Inc., Stone & Webster Engineering Corporation, Komatsu Ltd., Bridgestone Ltd., Rockwell-Collins, and Deutz MWM.

Contact: Mr. Marei Abdullah Bugshan, Vice President, PO Box 80, Riyadh 11411, Saudi Arabia. Tel: +966 1 478 7711; Fax: +966 1 477 0189/477 4225; Email: info@abugshan.com; Website: www.abugshan.com.

Advanced Electronics Company Limited

Advanced Electronics Company, established in 1986, manufactures sophisticated military and commercial components. AEC is MIL-I-45208A and ISO 9001 certified and its manufacturing programmes include M1 A2 tank electronics, F-15S and F-16 avionics, Panther V tactical radio, Paveway laser-guided bomb, CDU-800 avionics for military aircraft, Smart card pay phones, and telecommunication switches.

Contact: Dr Ghassan A Al Shibl, President and CEO, PO Box 90916, Riyadh 11623, Saudi Arabia. Tel: +966 1 220 1340/220 1350; Fax: +966-1-220-1355/220-1356; Email: info@aecl.com and shiblg@aecl.com Website: www.aecl.com.

Aggad Investment Company (AICO)

Aggad Investment Company was formed in 1975. The company has expanded into a group of 27 companies engaged in the manufacturing, contracting, distribution, service and consumer product sectors. Three of AICO's companies enjoy a product monopoly in the Kingdom, while a majority of the remainder are either the biggest in their market or enjoy a dominant market share, in competition with international brand names. A list of AICO member companies is provided below.

Contact: Mr Omar A Aggad, Chairman, PO Box 2256, Riyadh 11451, Saudi Arabia. Tel: +966 1 476-7911; Fax: +966 1 476 7895; Email: info@aico.com.sa; Website: www.aico.com.sa

AICO Member Companies

Industrial manufacturing

Aluminum Products Ltd (ALUPCO), PO Box 2080, Dammam 31451. Tel: +966 3 857 0184 Fax: +966 3 857 8311.
Products: Extruded aluminium products, anodized, painted or mill finished profiles, aluminium architectural products. Authorized capital: SR100 million.

Aluminum Manufacturing Company Ltd. (ALUMACO), PO Box 7661, Jeddah 21472. Tel: +966 2 691 3173; Fax: +966 2 691 5722.
Products: High performance aluminium architectural products. Authorized capital: SR16 million.

Arabian Plastic Compounds Company Ltd (APC), PO Box 27507, Riyadh 11427. Tel: +966 1 490 0909; Fax: +966 1 490 0153.
Products: PVC compounds for manufacturing plastic containers and bottles. Authorized capital: SR12 million.

Arabian Tile Company Ltd (ARTIC), PO Box 55993, Riyadh 11544. Tel: +966 1 456 7714; Fax: +966 1 455 0672.
Products: Cement-based and terrazzo tiles curbstones and pavers; conglomerate marble products. Authorized capital: SR10 million.

National Pigment Masterbatch Company Ltd (MULAWINAT), PO Box 5882, Riyadh 11432. Tel: +966 1 498 6125; Fax: +966 1 498 6129.
Products: Pigment master batches for use in colouring polyolefin based products. Authorized capital: SR6 million.

Saudi Plastic Products Company Ltd (SAPPCO), PO Box 2838, Riyadh 11461. Tel: +966 1 448 0448; Fax: +966 1 446 1392.
Products: PVC pipes, bends, couplings and associated fittings. Authorized capital: SR75 million.

Arabian Plastic Manufacturing Company Ltd (APLACO), PO Box 6193, Riyadh 11442. Tel: +966 1 448 0250; Fax: +966 1 448 0543.
Products: A wide range of pressure and non-pressure plastic fittings. Authorized capital: SR18 million.

Saudi Plastics Products Company Ltd (SAPPCO) Dammam, PO Box 4916, Dammam 31412. Tel: +966 3 857 5748; Fax: +966 3 857 1969.
Products: PVC pipes, high and low-density polyethylene piping. Authorized capital: SR20 million.

SAPPCO-Texaco Insulation Company Ltd (SAPTEX). PO Box 40042. Riyadh 11499. Tel: +966 1 498 4676; Fax: +966 1 498 0443.
Products: Polystyrene and polyurethane thermal insulation products. Authorized capital: SR30 million.

Saudi Industries for Desalination Membranes and Systems Ltd (SIDMAS), PO Box 52816, Riyadh 11573. Tel: +966 1 498 2727; Fax: +966 1 498 0902.
Products: Thin-film, spiral wound membrane elements for ultra filtration and reverse osmosis. Authorized capital: SR6 million.

Steel Products Company Ltd (STEPCO). PO Box 4930, Riyadh 11412. Tel: +966 1 498 1888; Fax: +966 1 498 2600.
Products: Wire rod and ribbed tensile wire mesh, distribution of cut-to-length rebar. Authorized capital: SR12 million.

Saudi Coating Company Ltd (SACCO), PO Box 8331, Jeddah 21482. Tel: +966 2 665 7502; Fax: +966 2 661 0373.
Products: Fusion-bonded, epoxy-coated reinforcing bars. Authorized capital: SR14 million.

National Packing Products Company Ltd (WATAN PAC), PO Box 25817, Riyadh 11476. Tel: +966 1 498 2211; Fax: +966 1 498 2483.
Products: Corrugated cardboard containers. Authorized capital: SR12 million.

Contracting, distribution and services

Arabian Elevator and Escalator Company Ltd (AREECO), PO Box 14326, Jeddah 21424. Tel: +966 2 665 7502; Fax: +966 2 661 0373.
Products: Supply, installation and maintenance of elevators, escalators and auto walks. Authorized capital: SR4 million.

Arabian Technical Contracting Company Ltd (ARTEC), PO Box 1387, Jeddah 21431. Tel: +966 2 671 1171; Fax: +966 2 672 5470.
Products: Construction/maintenance and associated electrical/mechanical requirements of roads, bridges, tunnels and expressways. Authorized capital: SR15 million.

Aggad Medical Supplies & Services Company Ltd (MEDISERV), PO Box 17550, Riyadh 11494. Tel: +966 1 477 1234; Fax: +966 1 477 7109.
Products: Supply of medical, laboratory and hospital equipment and supplies through medical diagnostics division. Sole distributor of Abbot Diagnostic products. Authorized capital: SR10 million.

National Advanced Systems Company Ltd (NASCO), PO Box 50009, Riyadh 11523. Tel: +966 1 477 1307; Fax: +966 1 477 4913.
Products: Supply and distribution of Fujitsu digital EPBX and key systems, Lanier copiers and facsimiles, QMS printers and Siemens Nixdorf computer systems. Authorized capital: SR5 million.

National Industrial Services Company Ltd (NISCO), PO Box 2821, Riyadh 11461. Tel: +966 1 477 2004; Fax: +966 1 477 6418.
Products: Electrical, mechanical and plumbing contracting, and project operation maintenance. Authorized capital: SR1.5 million.

Saudi Continental Insurance Company Ltd (SCINCO), PO Box 2940, Riyadh 11461. Tel: +966 1 476 6903; Fax: +966 1 476 9310.
Products: Full range of insurance services. Authorized capital: US$3 million.

United Arab Motors (UAM), PO Box 58310, Riyadh 11494. Tel: +966 1 233 2222; Fax: +966 1 233 2996.
Products: Supply and distribution of Chrysler, Dodge, Jeep and LIAZ vehicles, plus associated back-up service. Authorized capital: SR60 million.

Gulf Motor Company Ltd (GMC), PO Box 58310, Riyadh 11494. Tel: +966 1 493 1117.
Products: Supply and distribution of Asian motors, commercial and military vehicles, and ALKEO passenger cars. Authorized capital: SR5 million.

National Marketing Company Ltd (NMC), PO Box 20830, Riyadh 11465. Tel: +966 1 477 4050; Fax: +966 1 477 3279.
Products: Supply and distribution of Daewoo cars and commercial vehicles. Authorized capital: SR10 million.

Consumer products

Arabian Confectionery Company Ltd (ACP), PO Box 25356, Riyadh 11466. Tel: +966 1 498 0800; Fax: +966 1 498 3051.
Products: A wide range of wafers, biscuits, candy bars and toffees. Authorized capital: SR20 million.

Almultaka Trading Establishment Ltd (ALMULTAKA), PO Box 16301, Riyadh 11464. Tel: +966 1 478 3388; Fax: +966 1 478 9608.
Products: Fashion design and related retail outlets. Authorized capital: SR6 million.

Hygienic Paper Company Ltd (FINE), PO Box 8160, Jeddah 21482. Tel: +966 2 637 0090; Fax: +966 2 637 6343.
Products: Facial tissues, handkerchiefs, infant diapers, sanitary pads, toilet tissues, kitchen towels and napkins. Authorized capital: SR25 million.

Health Water Bottling Company Ltd (NISSAH), PO Box 2948, Riyadh 11461. Tel: +966 1 490 0244; Fax: +966 1 490 0153.
Products: Nissah and Alrawda brands of bottled drinking water. Authorized capital: SR25 million.

Refreshments Manufacturing Company Ltd (REMACO), PO Box 20615, Jeddah 21465. Tel: +966 2 594 0451; Fax: +966 2 594 0104.
Products: Al-Wadi bottled drinking water, a range of soft drinks and juices including the beverage Orangina. Authorized capital: SR18 million.

A.H. Al-Zamil Group of Companies

A.H. Al-Zamil Group of Companies is one of the leading diversified industrial and commercial groups in Saudi Arabia and the Gulf states. The Company's operations range from air-conditioner manufacturing to food processing, plastic and steel fabrication, operations and maintenance.

Contact: Mr Khaled A. Al-Zamil, President, PO Box 9, Al Khobar 31952, Saudi Arabia. Tel: +966 3 882 4888; Fax: +966 3 882 2509/847 1291; Email: webmaster@zamil-group.com; Website: www.zamil.com.

Ahmad Hamad Algosaibi & Bros.

Headquartered in Al Khobar, Ahmad Hamad Algosaibi & Bros. is involved in manufacturing, powder coating, hotel, insurance, trading services, pipecoating, oil field chemicals, agriculture, shipping, commercial and industrial agents, travel and tourism, and banking and investment.

Contact: Mr Saud Abdulaziz Algosaibi, Vice President and Director, PO Box 106, Al-Khobar 31952, Saudi Arabia. Tel: +966 3 882 2666 ext 100; Fax: +966 3 882 2470/882 2624/882 0857; Email: ahalgosaibi@hotmail.com or mailbox@ahalgosaibi.com; Website: www.ahalgosaibi.com/home.htm.

A.K. Al-Muhaidib & Sons Group of Companies

A.K. Al-Muhaidib & Sons Group of Companies was founded in 1946 with the name Abdulatif and Abdulkadir Al-Muhaidib Company, and was focused on building materials and wholesale foodstuffs. In 1959, the company name changed to Al-Muhaidib and Al-Nafea Company and again in 1979 to Abdul Kadir Al-Muhaidib and Sons Company. This subsidiary undertakes large contracting projects including sewer and water lines, school facilities, banks, housing projects, shopping malls, warehouses, and office facilities.

Contact: Mr Sulaiman Abdul Kadir Al-Muhaidib, Chairman, PO Box 245030, Riyadh 11312, Saudi Arabia. Tel: +966 1 472 4411; Fax: +966 1 472 4422. Company address and contact: PO Box 30, Dammam 31411, Saudi Arabia. Tel: +966 3 832 2033; Fax: +966 3 833 6065; Email: ch@muhaidib.com and mail@muhaidib.com; Website: www.muhaidib.com.

Al Abdulkarim Group

The Al Abdulkarim Group is Saudi Arabia's leading wholesale and retail supplier of electrical, telecommunication, instrumentation and oilfield components and equipment. The Group is headquartered in Dammam with branches, showrooms, and warehouses in Al Khobar, Jubail, Riyadh, Jeddah, Yanbu, Dubai and Doha. The Group carries large inventories of electrical, instrumentation, and communication products, as well as pipes, valves and fittings. These stocks supply projects for many key contractors engaged in the development of Saudi Arabia's oil, gas, petrochemical, and industrial sectors.

Contact: Mr Khalid A Al Abdulkarim, Executive Director, PO Box 5777, Dammam 31432, Saudi Arabia. Tel: +966 3 889 2085/833 7110; Fax: +966 3 889 2086/833 8242; Email: akte@akte.com.sa and khalid@akte.com.sa; Website: www.akte.com.sa.

Al-Afandi Est. for Trade, Industry & Contracting

Al-Afandi Est. for Trading, Industry & Contracting is involved in marketing and international trade, environment, cement factories, medical equipment and solar energy. The company is located in the city of Jeddah in the Eastern Province.

Contact: Mr Ibrahim Mohammed Afandi, General Manager, PO Box 452, Jeddah 21411, Saudi Arabia. Tel: +966 2 663 3580/665 7438/663 4443; Fax: +966 2 660 8580/665 7428; Email: ibrahim@al-afandi.com and afandim@zajil.net.

Al Alamiah Electronics Company

Since its founding in 1972, Al Alamiah Electronics Company has become one of the leading Saudi companies in the computer industry. Al Alamiah operates in the fields of computers, electronics, networking, training, maintenance, office equipment, Photofast, Arabic computational linguistics, Arabic software development, and intranet/internet. Al Alamiah has trading partners in the US, Japan and Taiwan. The company has diversified its business activities and formed seven separate business divisions, namely Computer Systems Division, Projects Division, Electronics Division, Networking Division, Training Division, Maintenance Division and Intranet/Internet Solutions Division.

Al Alamiah Electronics Company has more than 1,000 professionals to assist the needs of its customers and to support its technologies worldwide. The company ranks 300th among Saudi Arabia's top 1,000 companies, and has annual sales of SR375 million (US$100 million). Al Alamiah has sold more than 600,000 computers and more than three million software titles since 1985. It is the largest PC desktop supplier, holding 11 per cent of the market, in the Kingdom.

Contact: Mr Hamed Abdullah Al-Sharekh, President, PO Box 5954, Riyadh 11432, Saudi Arabia. Tel: +966 1 477 0106; Fax: +966 1 478 4893; Email: alalamiah1@anet.net.sa and hs@anet.net.sa; Website: www.al-alamiah.com.

Al-Bayan Group Holding Company

Established in 1980, Al-Bayan Group Holding Company's activities include medical supplies and services, computer and electronic equipment, and media and investment.

Contact: Mr Mohammed Obeid Al-Hammad, President, PO Box 42589, Riyadh 11551, Saudi Arabia. Tel: +966 1 477 2440; Fax: +966 1 476 5777; Email: al-bayan@concept.net.sa; Website: www.albayan.com.sa.

Albuldan Int'l Trading Co. Ltd

Founded in 1998, Albuldan Int'l Trading Co. Ltd. is engaged in the wholesale and retail trade of medical furniture and equipment; communications, cleaning and laundry equipment; ready-made garments; imitation jewellery; perfumes; food products and general contracting. Albuldan also undertakes electrical and mechanical works; operation and maintenance of hospitals; installation and operation of computer programs, systems and networks; and exploration and excavation of minerals. Albuldan also runs the Institute of Science for Telecom & Technology (IST&T), recognized by the General Organization for Technical Education & Vocational Training (GOTEVOT). The Institute awards diplomas in communication systems, such as microwave, mobile, satellite, optical fibre, distribution and networking systems, as well as in computer networking and programming, electronics, accounting and marketing. The Institute is affiliated with other international and Arab universities, such as Oman National University and Applied Sciences University in Jordan.

Contact: Mr Almas H Al-Faisal, General Manager, PO Box 69006, Riyadh 11547, Saudi Arabia. Tel: +966 1 487 1980/487 1981/275 3072; Fax: +966 1 275 3072/275 3081/275 3072; Email: albuldan@istt.edu.sa; Website: www.istt.edu.sa.

Al-Busaili Co. Elect. Mechanical Works

Al-Busaili Co. Elect. Mechanical Works was established in 1961. Since its inception, the company has provided specialized technical services mainly in the areas of design, testing, installation and maintenance in the field of electric works, air-conditioning systems and flight fuelling equipment systems. Since 1961, the company has undertaken 417 technical projects and is currently engaged on projects in 31 cities in the Kingdom. Some of the prominent clients of the company are the Ministry of Defence and Civil Aviation, the Ministry of Finance and National Economy, Saudi Aramco, Al-Yamamah Cement Factory, King Saud University, and the Institute for Public Administration. The company registered annual sales revenue of SR7 million (US$1.9 million approximately) in 1999 and has a staff of 384 people.

Contact: Mr Ali A Al-Busaili, General Director, PO Box 4173, Riyadh 11491, Saudi Arabia. Tel: +966 1 491 2605; Fax: +966 1 491 2602; Email: albusailico@hotmail.com.

The Al Dhahry Group

The Al Dhahry Group is one the leading companies in the Gulf region. Since its establishment in 1983, Al Dhahry has conducted over US$2 billion worth of business in the region and now maintains a staff of more than 4,000 employees. The Group has diversified its business portfolio to include: catering; general contracting; commercial transactions and agencies; military and security installations; supermarket and restaurant management; restaurant equipment; and the Al Qaqaa Security and Guarding Services, the Group's most prominent subsidiary.

Contact: Mohammed Bin Saleh Al Dhahry, Chairman, PO Box 56272, Riyadh 11554, Saudi Arabia. Tel: +966 1 232 0242; Fax: +966 1 231 5317; Email: hala@al-dhahry-group.com; Website: www.al-dhahry-group.com.

Al-Dhoheyan Consultant Office for Finance & Administration

Al-Dhoheyan Consultant Office for Finance & Administration is the parent establishment of a number of organizations. The company activities include import and trade in sanitary ware, building materials, plumbing accessories, tiles, ceramic goods, wholesale and retail, and agriculture and allied activities.

Contact: Mr Mohammed Dhoheyan A Al-Dhoheyan, President, PO Box 59683, Riyadh 11535, Saudi Arabia. Tel: +966 1 478 8471/477 2879; Fax: +966 1 206 1559; Email: dhoheyan@awalnet.net.sa.

Al-Emtiaz Establishment

Al-Emtiaz Establishment was founded in December 1977, and began its first commercial activities from the capital city of Riyadh. The company specializes in undergarments. Al-Emtiaz's other activities include garments and textiles.

Contact: Mr Fahad Abdulaziz Al-Ajlan, Proprietor & Manager, PO Box 1802, Riyadh 11441, Saudi Arabia. Tel: +966 1 411 6566; Fax: +966 1 411 0800; Email: fahad@alemtiaz.com; Website: www.alemtiaz.com.

Alfanar Co.

Alfanar Co. is based in Riyadh with branches in Jeddah and Dammam. It runs a wide range of activities related to the manufacturing, marketing and sales of low voltage (LV) and medium voltage (MV) electrical distribution, installation and protection equipment. Alfanar is active as a turnkey contractor for the construction of power houses, substation and transmission lines, including design, interface, supply of equipment, construction at site, testing, commissioning and warranty coverage. The company is supplied by Alstom, ABB, GE, and Foxboro. The Alfanar Co. is interested in meeting companies specializing in the following activities or products: gas turbines, power generation, auxiliaries, filet handling and fuel treatment systems; switch gears, circuit breakers and substation equipment up to 400 kV; power control and protection equipment; design and engineering for power house and electrification schemes; and scada, telecontrol and telecommunication systems.

Contact: Mr Hisham M Al-Mutlaq, Managing Director, PO Box 301, Riyadh 11411, Saudi Arabia. Tel: +966 1 275 5999; Fax: +966 1 274 0888 (MD Office)/ 966 1 275 6699; Email: baalbaki@alf.com.sa or hisham@alfanar.com; Website: www.alfanartrading.com and www. alfelectric.com

Al Foadia General Trading & Contracting

Al Foadia General Trading and Contracting, established in 1977, had annual sales of more than SR30 million (US$8 million) in 1999 and employs 1,050 people. The Riyadh-based company is involved in the operation and maintenance of buildings, janitorial and allied services, renovation and refurbishment, and general trading and garments manufacturing. Al Foadia is interested in forming joint ventures with companies in the fields of duct cleaning, environmentally-friendly cleaning products, hotel and catering equipment and supplies, and export of garments from Saudi Arabia.

Contact: Mr Ahmed F. Jizawi, Chairman & Owner, PO Box 1650, Riyadh 11441, Saudi Arabia. Tel: +966 1 402 7557; Fax: +966 1 404 2312; Email: contracting@alfoadia.com.sa; Website: www.alfoadia.com.sa.

Al-Hamdan Trading Est.

The Al-Hamdan Trading Est. and its subsidiaries offer a variety of trading and consulting services, mainly in the aviation sector and in the plastics and textiles industries.

Contact: Mr Abdullah A Al-Hamdan, Executive Director, PO Box 53874, Riyadh 11593, Saudi Arabia. Tel: +966 1 464 1995/464 0239; Fax: +966 1 463 1068.

Alhamrani Group of Companies

Alhamrani Group of Companies was established in 1965. The Alhamrani Group's activities include sales and distribution of Nissan cars and spare parts, automatic banking tellers, security systems, production and distribution of steel drums, red bricks, ceilings, wall panels, lubricating and glass fibre.

Contact: Mr Mohamed A Alhamrani, Chairman, PO Box 1229, Jeddah 21431, Saudi Arabia. Tel: +966 2 606 5555/669 6690; Fax: +966 2 606 0265/667 4394; Email: chairman@alhamranigroup.com or info@alhamranigroup.com; Website: www.alhamranigroup.com.

Al-Hobayb Group of Companies

Al-Hobayb Group has many subsidiaries in various fields. One subsidiary, ABB Contracting Co. Ltd., was established for contracting in the electrical works field, power generation and allied activities on a turnkey basis. Their projects consist of mechanical and engineering contracting and supply in the field of industry, installation, high voltage substations and power transformers. ABB Contracting has branches in Dammam, Jeddah, and Al-Khobar and its head office in Riyadh. Another subsidiary, ABB Electrical Industries Co. Ltd., was established as a joint venture in 1985 but was later reorganized into a fully owned Saudi enterprise. The company is involved in the manufacturing of electro-mechanical equipment, transmission covering products, distribution equipment, transformers, distribution boards and relay and control equipment. The principal activity of the company is to manufacture low and medium voltage switchgears, compact substations and other related items. The ABB Electrical Industries Co. Ltd. is located in Riyadh and has branches in Dammam, Jeddah, Jubail and Al-Khobar.

Contact: Eng. Abdullah I Al-Hobayb, President, PO Box 556, Riyadh 11421, Saudi Arabia. Tel: +966 1 479 0100; Fax: +966 1 479 0171; Email: abdullah@al-hobayb.com.

Al-Hudaithy Attorneys at Law

Al-Hudaithy Attorneys at Law, founded in 1983, has long-standing experience in the fields of *Shari'a* and Islamic jurisprudence, as well as Saudi Arabian law, to meet the comprehensive legal needs of domestic and international corporate clients. Al-Hudaithy's specialty areas include corporate services, family business counselling, electronic commerce and telecommunications, assets protection, wills, trusts and probate, labour and employment, mergers and acquisitions, litigation, mediation, commercial arbitration, bankruptcy, liquidation, copyright law, trade mark law, patents and industrial rights, domestic and international real estate disposition, mortgage, taxation, and criminal cases.

Contact: Mr Abdulaziz Ibrahim Al-Hudaithy, Chairman, PO Box 365, Riyadh 11351, Saudi Arabia. Tel: +966 1 279 1337/279 1338; Fax: +966 1 279 1335; Email: alhudaithy@yahoo.com or alqatatsha@hotmail.com; Website: www.hudaithylaw.com.

Ali Abalkhail Real Estate Investment & Trading Group

Ali Fahad Aba-Alkhail Trading and Real Estate Group was established in 1987. The group's main activities include: marketing and home management ownership; investment in industrial projects such as marble industries; trading gold and jewellery with a huge share in the local and international market; hotel towers; resorts villas; and rental car services.

Contact: Mr Ali Bin Fahad Abalkhail, CEO and Chairman, PO Box 53980, Riyadh 11593, Saudi Arabia. Tel: +966 1 461 4377; Fax: +966 1 462 6315; Email: A1@ali-abalkhail.com; Website: www.ali-abalkhail.com.

Ali Zaid Al-Quraishi & Brothers Co.

Ali Zaid Al-Quraishi & Brothers Co. was founded in 1958 and has grown to become one of the leading commercial groups in Saudi Arabia. It has long-established associations with a number of major corporations in the United States, Europe and Japan, and distributes their world recognized brands throughout the Kingdom. Ali Zaid Al-Quraishi & Brothers Co. is involved in marketing and distribution of brand names in leisure goods, cigarettes, toiletries, office furniture and equipment, motor vehicles, telecommunications and electronics. It is also involved in the manufacturing of electrical products and high voltage oil-insulated and low voltage dry-type transformers, ranging from 15 to 1,500 KVA and has a joint venture with Taylor Woodwork in the construction field.

Contact: H.E. Abdulaziz Z Al-Quraishi, Executive Director and Co-Chairman, PO Box 1848, Riyadh 11441, Saudi Arabia. Tel: +966 1 479 3195/477 1618/479 2409; Fax: +966 1 478 6947; Email: azaq@alquraishi.com; Website: www.alquraishi.com.

Al-Jazirah Vehicles Agencies Co. Ltd.

Al-Jazirah Vehicles Agencies Co. Ltd. was established in 1987. Al-Jazirah is the sole distributor of Ford and Lincoln vehicles and after sales service in the Kingdom of Saudi Arabia.

Contact: Mr Abdullah Fahd Al-Kraidees, President, PO Box 4416, Riyadh 11491, Saudi Arabia. Tel: +966 1 231 9944; Fax: +966 1 231 1811/233 3531;

Email: mkt@ryd.aljazirahford.com.sa or akraidees@ryd.aljazirahford.com.sa; Website: www. aljazirahford.com.sa.

Aljomaih Holding Company

Founded in 1956, Abdulaziz & Mohammed Al-Jomaih Company activities include import and distribution of automobiles, spare parts, tyres, lubricating oil, earth moving equipment, construction and agricultural equipment, and soft drinks bottling. The company has branches in all major cities in the Kingdom.

Contact: Mr Ibrahim Mohammed A Al-Jomaih, General Manager, Al-Jomaih Building, Kilo 6 Madinah Road, PO Box 467, Jeddah 21411, Saudi Arabia. Tel: +966 2 660 5111; Fax: +966 2 667 0802/663 5260/667 6692; Email: ibrahim.aljomaih@aljomaihmail.com or aljomaih@aljomaih.com.sa; Website: www.aljomaih.com.sa.

Al Kuhaimi Metal Industrial Ltd.

Al Kuhaimi Metal Industries Ltd., established in Dammam in1975, manufactures various types of doors for industrial, commercial, residential, and security purposes as well as for other special needs and applications. Al Kuhaimi Metal Industries Ltd is divided into four divisions: hollow metal doors, rolling doors, highly specialized doors, and installation and maintenance. The hollow metal doors division manufactures fire-rated and ordinary hollow metal doors, soundproof doors, airtight doors, and variety of other types of doors. The rolling doors division manufactures industrial, commercial and such residential supplies applications as rolling and sectional doors. The highly specialized doors division manufactures blast resistant doors and gates, aircraft hangar doors, and other similar highly specialized products. The installation and maintenance division is involved in the installation and maintenance of different types of doors in addition to the execution of long-term maintenance contracts for major clients throughout the Kingdom. The company employs 550 people and has clients in the United States and Europe.

Contact: Mr Mohammed A Al Kuhaimi, Chairman, PO Box 545, Dammam 31421, Saudi Arabia. Tel: +966 3 847 2777; Fax: +966 3 847 2591; Email: alkuhaimi@alkuhaimi.com; Website: www.alkuhaimi.com.

Al Moaibed Group Co. Ltd.

The Al Moaibed Group's activities include trading, first-class hotels, dental clinics, travel, and contracting. The company is headquartered in Dammam.

Contact: Mr Jamal A Al Moaibed, President, PO Box 4701, Dammam 31412, Saudi Arabia. Tel: +966 3 847 2288/847 3040/857 7740; Fax: +966 3 857 9993/847 1504; Email: info@napcogroup.com; Website: www.napcogroup.com.

Al-Murjan Trading and Industrial Co. Ltd.

Headquartered in Jeddah, Al-Murjan's 18 companies are involved in activities that include trading, industry, franchising, mining, manufacturing, manufacturing of baby diapers, facial tissues, wipes, water treatment, sewage, medical equipment, real estate, computer software, furniture and home accessories, food and hazardous waste treatment.
Contact: Mr Othman M. Bafagih, CEO, PO Box 52558, Jeddah 21573, Saudi Arabia. Tel: +966 2 699 5555 ext 604; Fax: +966 2 699 2222; Email: obafagih@hotmail.com.

Al-Qahtani Maritime

Al-Qahtani Marine is a subsidiary of Abdel Hadi A. Al-Qahtani Sons Group of Companies. Established in 1971, Al-Qahtani Maritime (AQM) has three main activities: tyres, marine products, and oilfields. AQM's tyre division provides tyre-related services and accessories, including performance-rated US tyres and high quality RIKEN brand Japanese tyres for all passenger cars and light trucks. Its marine division is trading as the International Enzyme Company and manufactures environmentally-friendly enzymes, chemicals, and enzyme catalytic products for earth surface preparation and compacting. The activities of AQM's oilfield division include the services of cementing, fracturing, sand control, coiled tubing, drilling engineering, directional drilling systems, completion systems, surface logging systems, mud engineering and management construction and laying of onshore and offshore oil and gas pipelines, and related services. The oilfield division also supplies all the related tools, equipment, and accessories used in its oil and gas exploration. AQM is the sole agent for many US companies, some of which include Cooper Tire and Rubber Company; Myers Tire Supply, Inc.; and Reed Tool Company of Houston, Texas.

Contact: Mr Abdel Aziz Abdel Hadi A Al-Qahtani, Chairman, PO Box 2224, Dammam 31451, Saudi Arabia. Tel: +966 3 857 5156/858 0909 ext 109; Fax: +966 3 857 6460/857 7184; Email: azizqahtani@yahoo.com or aqm@q3group.com; Website: www.q3group.com.

Al-Qussie International Contracting Establishment

Al-Qussie International has been serving the government and private sectors in the Kingdom of Saudi Arabia since 1981. It is one of the top government maintenance service contractors in the Kingdom.

Contact: Mr Abdulaziz MS Al-Athel, President, PO Box 53172, Riyadh 11583, Saudi Arabia. Tel: +966 1 488 1177; Fax: +966 1 482 6685; Email: amsa@alqussie.com.sa; Website: www.alqussie.com.sa

Al Rajhi Banking & Investment Corporation

Al Rajhi Banking & Investment Corporation, a Saudi joint stock company, was formed in 1988. Al Rajhi Banking & Investment Corporation is engaged in banking and investment activities inside and outside the Kingdom, both on its own account and on behalf of others. It is a well-established commercial bank, with 365 branches in Saudi Arabia. In addition, the Corporation has established wholly or substantially owned subsidiaries outside Saudi Arabia.

Contact: Mr Abdullah Sulaiman Al Rajhi, Director and General Manager, PO Box 28, Riyadh 11411, Saudi Arabia. Tel: +966 1 460 1000/460 2015; Fax: +966 1 460 2040/460 0922; Email: asalrajhi@alrajhibank.com.sa; Website: www.alrajhibank.com.sa.

Al-Rashid Trading & Contracting Co.

Al-Rashid Trading & Contracting Co., established in 1957, is a leading general contractor in Saudi Arabia. The company's activities include civil and electro-mechanical works, real estate investment in Saudi Arabia and abroad, establishing and managing shopping malls; and the cement industry (precast and prestressed).

Contact: Mr Abdullah S Al-Rashid, General Manager, PO Box 307, Riyadh 11411, Saudi Arabia. Tel: +966 1 401 1134/401 2550/401 1478; Fax: +966 1 402 2055; Email: gmrtcc@awalnet.net.sa.

Al Rushaid Investment Company

The Al Rushaid Investment Company was founded in 1977. Its activities include manufacturing and trading in oilfield equipment and related products, real estate, hotel, construction, and electro-mechanical. The Company is one of the premier trading and industrial conglomerates in the Kingdom and the region.

Contact: Mr Abdullah R Al Rushaid, Chairman, PO Box 31685, Al-Khobar 31952, Saudi Arabia. Tel: +966 3 893 3333; Fax: +966 3 864 7320/898 3551; Email: sh.abdullah@al-rushaid.com or corporate@al-rushaid.com; Website: www.al-rushaid.com.

Al Sanie Holding & Trading Company

Al Sanie Holding & Trading Company's core activities are drilling wells, agricultural investment, and such agricultural related activities as poultry and egg tray manufacturing. The company is the sole agent and distributor for many world famous agricultural equipment and tractor companies, such as FENDT tractors and MVM diesel engines from Germany, NORDSTEN seed drill from Denmark, NEMITSAS water pumps from Cyprus, and MARZIA agricultural implements from Italy. Al Sanie, established in 1982, presently employs 700 people and has registered annual sales of SR300 million (US$80 million).

Contact: Dr Abdullah M Al Sanie, Chairman and General Manager, PO Box 4186, Riyadh 11491, Saudi Arabia. Tel: +966 1 498 3900/498 6107; Fax: +966 1 498 6123/282 1345; Email: info@alsanie.com or doctor@alsanie.com Website: www.al-yamama.com.sa.

Al-Sulaiman Group (Rolaco)

Established in 1968, Al-Sulaiman Group is a pioneer in supplying various building materials to many key projects. The company imports and sells transportation and construction equipment, cables and electrical accessories, industrial machinery, building materials, construction chemicals, medical and hotel supplies, animal feed, industrial adhesives, surveying instruments, and weighing equipment.

Abdulaziz A Al-Sulaiman, Chairman, PO Box 222, Jeddah 21411, Saudi Arabia. Tel: +966 2 651 8028; Fax: +966 2 653 4280; Email: info@rolaco.net or asulaiman@rolaco.net; Website: www.rolaco.net

Al Taher Group

The Taher Group of Companies, based in Jeddah, is 58th among the top 100 companies in Saudi Arabia. Since its inception in 1975, the Group has diversified rapidly into a variety of national markets. Activities cover high technology maintenance, chemical manufacturing, poultry raising and food processing, hotels and property management, industry, oil additives and lubricants, construction, contracting, services, insurance and general trading.

Contact: Mr Tarek Abdulhadi Taher, President and CEO, PO Box 1178, Jeddah 21431, Saudi Arabia. Tel: +966 2 284 3333; Fax: +966 2 284 4488; Email: desertfalcon@earthlink.net or tat@aaltaher.com; Website: www.aaltaher.com.

Alujain Corporation

Established in 1991 as a closed joint stock company, the corporation went public in 1997. It retains close ties with the Xenel Group, the Jeddah-based company that created Alujain. It is one of the Kingdom's leading business families, having traded throughout the GCC countries in various industries. Alujain's activities include mining, metals and petrochemicals.

Contact: Eng. Sami M Eid President & COO, PO Box 50575, Jeddah 21533, Saudi Arabia. Tel: +966 2 669 5140/669 5956; Fax: +966 2 669 3986; Email: alujaincorp@xenel.com.

AMA Group

Established in 1975, the AMA Group had annual sales of about SR12 million (US$3.2 million) in 1999 and employs about 300 people. AMA's core activities are real estate/compounds leasing, operation and maintenance, home and office furniture manufacturing and retailing, interior designing and decoration. They are interested in an American partner in the fields of home and office furniture, investment, franchising and industrial manufacturing. A subsidiary of AMA, Al-Abdulkader Furniture Co is one of the leading companies for furniture in Saudi Arabia. They also manufacture curtains and trade in wall and ceiling panelling as well as decorative items.

Contact: Mr Abdul Aziz M Al-Abdulkader, President, PO Box 2468, Riyadh 11451, Saudi Arabia. Tel: +966 1 465 7929; Fax: +966 1 463 0456; Email: amagroup@anet.net.sa and office@akfc.com.sa; Website: www.akfc.com.sa.

Amir H. El-Hoshan Est.

Amir H. El-Hoshan Est. is the only company in the field of stationery that has warehousing, sales and marketing centres in all GCC countries, in addition to branches in Yemen, Jordan, Syria, Lebanon, and Australia. An established network of over 2,000 retailers and wholesalers in these countries are serviced on a daily basis through a team of dedicated and specialized sales and marketing professionals. El-Hoshan trades in office automation and furniture, graphic arts, stationary, construction, agriculture and landscaping, postal equipment and supplies, industrial and contracting.

Contact: Mr Amir H M Al-Hoshan, Chairman, PO Box 509, Riyadh 11421, Saudi Arabia. Tel: +966 1 217 0000/217 0070/217 0071/466 1643; Fax: +966 1 465 6248; Email: info@hoshangroup.com or hoshanco@hoshanco.com.sa; Website: www.hoshangroup.com.

Arab National Bank

Arab National Bank (ANB), headquartered in Riyadh, was formed in 1979 and has been operating in the Kingdom for over 30 years. ANB owns 40 per cent of the shares, while the other 60 per cent are held by Saudi nationals. It has over 117 branches and is a pioneer in internet banking in the Kingdom with the launch of alarabi-ebank, the first of its kind in Saudi Arabia.

Contact: Mr Nemeh Sabbagh, Managing Director and CEO, PO Box 56921, Riyadh 11564, Saudi Arabia. Tel: +966 1 401 0928/402 9000 ext 1700; Fax: +966 1 402 7747/403 0052; Email: nemehes@anb.com.sa Website: www.anb.com.sa.

Arabian Auto Agency Company Ltd.

Founded in 1965, the Arabian Auto Agency is a distributor of commercial vehicles and heavy equipment, representing known international brands. The company has 13 branches in the Kingdom and its activities include construction equipment, cranes, forklifts, agriculture and irrigation equipment, spare parts and farming equipment.

Contact: Mr Ziyad Bin Zaid Mohammed Al-Sidairi, Partner and General Manager, PO Box 2223, Jeddah 21451, Saudi Arabia. Tel: +966 2 660 6988/669 5595; Fax: +966 2 669 2359; Email: equipment@aaa.com.sa; Website: www.arabian-auto-agency.com.

Aujan Industries Company

Abdul Wahab Al-Aojan & Brothers Co. for Trading and Industry was established in 1981. The company is involved in beverages, foodstuff distributors, soft drink canning and bottling, manufacture of kitchen cabinets and industrial safety products.

Contact: Mr Adel Abdulrahman Al-Aujan, Board Chairman, PO Box 990, Dammam 31421, Saudi Arabia. Tel: +966 3 857 0777; Fax: +966 3 857 7923/966 3 857 3226; Email: adel@aujan.com.sa or aujan@aujan.com.sa; Website: www.aujan.com.

Bank Al Jazira

Bank Al Jazira was founded in 1975 and is the first of the foreign banking operations converted into local joint stock entities. Jazira's activities include banking services, investments and financing.

Contact: Mr Mishari Ibrahim Al-Mishari, General Manager, PO Box 6277, Jeddah 21442, Saudi Arabia. Tel: +966 2 651 8070; Fax: +966 2 653 2478; Email: info@baj.com.sa; Website: www.baj.com.sa.

Bassam Trading Establishment

Al Bassam Group was started in 1955 in Saudi Arabia. In the past four and a half decades, the group has grown into a major regional conglomerate. Their offices are located in Dammam, Riyadh, Jubail and Dubai, United Arab Emirates. Several joint ventures are located in United States, Switzerland, France and Oman. Areas of activities are supplies to oil and gas, utilities, and petrochemical industries; heavy engineering fabrication; engineering services; healthcare and hospital management services; real estate development and investments; projects and joint ventures.

Contact: Mr Bassam R Hamadeh, President and CEO, PO Box 4611, Riyadh 11412, Saudi Arabia. Tel: +966 1 463 3059/462 3846; Fax: +966 1 464

4014; Email: info@bte-hds.com or management@bte-hds.com; Website: www.bte-hds.com.

Beit Binzagr

Beit Binzagr was established in 1978 and provides such services as supplying materials to the oil and gas industries throughout the Kingdom, and the manufacture and supply of safety matches. The Group is located in Jeddah.

Contact: Mr Wahib Said Binzagr, Chairman, PO Box 209, Jeddah 21411, Saudi Arabia. Tel: +966 2 643 8235/643 9901; Fax: +966 2 643 8983; Email: abuobeid@binzagr.com.sa; Website: www.binzagr.com and www.binzagr.com.sa.

Dabbagh Group Holding Company Ltd.

Sheikh Abdullah Dabbagh, former Saudi Arabian Minister of Agriculture, founded the Dabbagh Group of Companies in 1962, with an initial focus on the agricultural and engineering sectors. The Dabbagh Group comprises 30 autonomous companies grouped into five portfolios, which operate in 30 countries. The food and agriculture portfolio involves the production and marketing of food products, processed livestock, veterinary medicines, animal feed, and the distribution of agricultural equipment. The energy portfolio represents various businesses involved in major projects in the oil, power, chemicals, and infrastructure sectors. The information technology (IT) portfolio of Dabbagh Group helps obtain electronic information technology, arranges exhibitions and conferences, provides IT network solutions, and offers consultancy and training services. The real estate portfolio handles property management and turnkey project construction and development. The trade and financial services portfolio promotes trade and extends general and life insurance services to the community. Some of the Group's strategic partners are Lucent Technologies; Ziff-Davis Publishing Company, New York; ALSTOM Engines, Ruston Division, UK; Normandy International Holdings Ptv. Ltd., Australia; Nissho-Iwai Corporation, Japan; Ross Breeders Ltd., Scotland; etc.

Contact: Mr Mohammed Husnee Jazeel, Chief Financial Officer, PO Box 1039, Jeddah 21431, Saudi Arabia. Tel: +966 2 669 7220; Fax: +966 2 669 6184; Email: info@dabbagh.com or jazeel@dabbagh.com; Website: www.dabbagh-group.com and www.dabbagh.com.

Dallah Albaraka Holding Co.

The Dallah Albaraka Holding Co. was established in 1969 and its activities include trading; finance and banking; industrial investment; agriculture; real estate development; tourism; transportation; media production; communications; insurance; medical services; construction and maintenance and operations.

Contact: Mr Abdullah Saleh Kamel, CEO and Executive Director, PO Box 430, Jeddah 21411, Saudi Arabia. Tel: +966 2 671 0000; Fax: +966 2 671 7056; Email: irshad@dallah.com; Website: www.albaraka.com.

Delmon Co. Ltd.

Delmon Co. Ltd. was formed in 1981 with its main activities in such industries as chemicals, petrochemicals, trading, processing minerals, travel, transportation, and advertising. The company has annual sales of SR100 million (US$26.7 million) and employs 200 people. Delmon Company Ltd. is currently interested in locating partners in the following areas: producing oil-related speciality chemicals, transportation, travel, and tourism.

Contact: Mr Ahmed S Al-Ghunaim, Managing Director, PO Box 6800, Dammam 31452, Saudi Arabia. Tel: +966 3 847 1777/847 1700 ext 221; Fax: +966 3 847 1683; Email: info@delmon.com.sa; Website: www.delmon.com.sa.

E.A. Juffali & Brothers

The activities of E.A. Juffali & Brothers include passenger cars, commercial vehicles, trucks, and accessories; household appliances and equipment, including all types of air-conditioning equipment; chemicals and petrochemicals industries; and information technology. The company is based in the capital city of Riyadh.

Contact: Mr Khaled Ahmed Juffali, Vice Chairman and Managing Partner, PO Box 1049, Riyadh 21431, Saudi Arabia. Tel: +966 2 667 2222; Fax: +966 2 669 4010; Email: juffali@eajb.com.sa; Website: www.eajb.com.

Eamar Albyader Development & Trading Co.

The Eamar Albyader Development & Trading Company, established in 1993, is an affiliate of Eamar Albyader Holding Company, a major commercial and development conglomerate in Saudi Arabia. Eamar Albyader is 100 per cent Saudi-owned and is based in Riyadh. Eamar Albyader Holding Company has 23 affiliated companies operating in a wide range of economic activities including real estate development, building and construction, real estate finance, building materials, consultancy, Islamic investment banking, promotional services, and technology and computers. The company employs a highly experienced and qualified workforce of nearly 2,500 people.

Contact: Mr Yousef bin Abdullah Al-Shelash, Chairman of the Board, PO Box 90671, Riyadh 11623, Saudi Arabia. Tel: +966 1 225 4888; Fax: +966 1 263 7788; Email: yousef.alshelash@ebyader.com

Elaf Travel, Tourism & Hotels Group

Founded in 1981, Elaf Travel, Tourism & Hotels Group (ETT&H) is a subsidiary of the Saudi Economic and Development Company (SEDCO) – one of the largest privately owned conglomerates in Saudi Arabia. SEDCO is involved in investing in world financial markets and real estate, and direct investment in travel and tourism, information technology, e-commerce, healthcare, family entertainment and fast food franchising. ETT&H represents a fully integrated business covering hotels, travel services and inclusive religious tours. Its core activities include hotel management in partnership with Accor, a world leader in the field, travel agency services incorporating business travel and cargo, and incoming tours of the Kingdom's holy sites. Elaf is the sole franchiser of Accor hotel brands – Sofitel, Novatel, and Mercure – in Saudi Arabia. Elaf/Accor's hotel portfolio has grown from three in 1999 to six in 2000, which are located in Jeddah, Makkah and Madinah. ETT&H has six outlets in Jeddah and branches in Riyadh, Al-Khobar and Makkah.

Contact: Mr Moutaz Fouad Kayal, President and General Manager, PO Box 13541, Jeddah 21414, Saudi Arabia. Tel: +966 2 664 1233; Fax: +966 2 664 0838/665 2830; Email: mfkayal@sedcogroup.com.

El Seif Group

The El Seif Group is ranked 25th out of the top 100 companies in Saudi Arabia. Its major activities are power plant construction, hospital management, medical equipment, pharmaceuticals and construction machinery, security and defence systems, commercial representation and investment. The Group represents major US corporations in Saudi Arabia such as GE Medical Systems, Becton Dickinson, Space Lab, and Beckman.

Contact: Mr Faisal Musaed El Seif, President, PO Box 15665, Riyadh 11461, Saudi Arabia. Tel: +966 1 454 5996; Fax: +966 1 454 0863; Email: fes@elseif.com.sa.

Enany Group of Companies (FAMCO)

FAMCO is involved in building contracting including construction by assembling prefabricated components, restoring buildings and monuments, hospitals, laboratories, schools, apartment buildings, office blocks, hotels, housing estate building and municipal housing schemes, basement garages, agricultural buildings and petrol stations.

Contact: Mr Hassan Mohammad Khalil Enany, President, PO Box 5865, Riyadh 11432, Saudi Arabia. Tel: +966 1 478 0038; Fax: +966 1 478 9773.

Fakieh Poultry Farms

Fakieh Poultry Farms, owned by Sheikh Abdulrahman Fakieh and established in 1965, is one of the largest poultry producers in Saudi Arabia. In 2001, Fakieh Poultry ranked as the 34th largest company is Saudi Arabia, with more than US$480 million in assets and over 6,000 employees. The company is the exclusive daily supplier of fresh chicken to the Al Taza restaurants in Saudi Arabia. Poultry is part of the Fakieh Group of Companies, which has several branches, among them, Fakieh Feed Industries, Fakieh New Projects, Fakieh Tourism Projects and Al Tazaj.

Contact: Mr Abdul Rahman Abdul Gader Fakieh, Chairman and CEO, PO Box 2621, Makkah, Saudi Arabia. Tel: +966 2 556 2946/557 1011/557 2225; Fax: +966 2 557 1592/558 2985; Email: ak19@hotmail.com or poultry@fakiehgroup.com; Website: www.fakiehgroup.com.

Financial Transaction House

Financial Transaction House is an investment banking firm based in Saudi Arabia. It provides a wide range of corporate finance advisory services to a diversified client base in the Middle East and offers clients a complete and integrated solution from structuring the transaction, providing negotiation and legal support to closing the deal.

Its focus on the Middle East and its knowledge of the local business context and culture has helped it establish close relationships with senior management of top companies, helping them address the challenges they face in an increasingly complex, global and competitive business environment. Its extensive network of local and regional contacts, which includes high net-worth individuals, financial institutions and governments, is of immense value to its clients.

Contact: Financial Transaction House, PO Box 24368, Jeddah 21446, Saudi Arabia. Tel: +966 2 657 3030; Fax: +966 2 657 3366.

Hajjan Trading Establishment (HATCON)

Hajjan Trading Establishment (HATCON) is headquartered in Al-Khobar, with full branch offices in Riyadh, Jeddah and Yanbu. The company has been in the trading business for over 20 years, specializing in equipment and materials for the oil, gas and petrochemical industries, power and desalination plants, and offshore and marine sectors. HATCON also specializes in surface coatings and linings, sandblasting and painting, and the supply of blasting abrasives. The company represents numerous US and European manufacturers including Belzona Polymerics Ltd., UK/USA; Pauli Systems Co. Inc., USA; J. Wagner GmbH, Germany; Eurogrit BV, The Netherlands; Clestra Hauserman Overseas Co., France; Thejo Engineering Services (P) Ltd., India; Unaflex Inc., USA, Butterworth Jetting Systems Inc., Sponge-Jet Inc., KCC/Koch Corrosion Control Company, and Technical Urethanes Co. HATCON's clientele in the Kingdom include Saudi Aramco, SABIC, the Royal Commission for Jubail and Yanbu, the Royal Saudi Naval Force, Saudi Electricity Company, and the Saline Water Conversion Corporation.

Contact: Mr Ayad Y Noueyhed, General Manager, PO Box 991, Al-Khobar 31952, Saudi Arabia. Tel: +966 3 882 2058/882 3569/882 2846; Fax: +966 3 882 1709; Email: hatcon@hatcon.com.sa; Website: www.hatcon.com.sa.

Hamad M. Bin Saedan & Sons (HASCO)

Since its founding in 1967, Hamad M. Bin Saedan & Sons (HASCO) has developed into one of the largest commercial groups in Saudi Arabia. HASCO is now engaged in the manufacturing and marketing of centre pivot and linear irrigation systems, ERW steel pipes, wrought iron products, plastics, and furniture. HASCO also maintains prominent portfolios in the areas of galvanization, mechanical and electrical engineering, and real estate. In addition, HASCO maintains investment interests in Tunisia, Sudan, Syria, Geneva, Turkey, Egypt and Bahrain. HASCO is interested in meeting US companies specializing in the following activities or products: high quality and low cost construction materials; medical equipment; mechanical and electrical engineering contracting.

Contact: Hamad Bin Mohamed bin Saedan, Chairman or Mohammed I A bin Khamis, Adviser, P.O Box 2879, Riyadh 11461, Saudi Arabia. Tel: +966 1 454 3321; Fax: +966 1 454 0565; Email: hamad@h-saedan.com or mibk1948@hotmail.com; Website: www.h-saedan.com and www.saedan.com.

Hassan A. Karim Algahtani Sons Group of Companies

Hassan A. Karim Algahtani Sons Group of Companies was founded in 1967 with a capital of SR5,000. It consists of four branches in Dammam and one in Jubail and is headquartered in Al Khobar. Its activities include trade in electronics; household appliances; communication systems and accessories; and real estate. The Group has experience in real estate development, insurance, tourism, investment, manufacturing of dairy and confectionery products, fishing, printing, transportation, shipping, customs clearance, cargo handling, import and trade of industrial and consumer products, fire fighting trucks, industrial pumps, emergency vehicles, computer and accessories, office systems and furniture, US security and other uniforms, and wall finished natural stone. It also extends its services to supplying technical and administrative manpower, email, internet and parcel express delivery services. The company employs more than 1,500 people and has annual sales of SR750 million (US$200 million). The Group is looking for alliances with small- and medium-sized companies with expertise in oil and gas exploration, well site preparation, tubing, casing on oil wells, cementing services, logging, drilling fluids (mud), drilling equipment transportation, drilling equipment maintenance, supply and maintenance of high pressure valves, marine services, chemical supply, pipeline construction, seismic services, environmental protection system supply and tank cleaning. It would like to start manufacturing such products as valves, chemicals, generators, instrumentation, and automotive spare parts.

Contact: Mr Khalid Hassan A Karim Algahtani, President and CEO, PO Box 195, Al-Khobar 31952, Saudi Arabia. Tel: +966 3 882 0222; Fax: +966 3 882 2111; Email: info@hakgroup.com or khalidg@hakgroup.com or ceo@hakgroup.com; Website: www.hakgroup.com.

HIDADA

Since its establishment in 1982, Jeddah-based HIDADA has grown through measured expansion to become a leading supplier of steel products to the GCC, Middle East and international markets. Such growth has mirrored the economic development of Saudi Arabia and has seen the company – a wholly Saudi-owned subsidiary of Xenel Industries – expand to a total annual fabrication capacity of more than 160,000 tonnes, making it the cornerstone of the steel fabrication industry in the Kingdom.

HIDADA continues to invest in human resource development, the latest technologies and process improvements to stay ahead of the competition and help meet the varied and stringent needs of its customers. To enhance its reputation for innovation and quality, HIDADA has been actively seeking new ways to maintain its competitive edge. A major recent restructuring programme, for instance, saw the introduction of a balanced scorecard system as well as a process-centred organization programme and process renewal for major processes.

HIDADA is also looking to enhance cooperation with its clients by offering a 'total solutions' approach which, according to the company, may take the form of alliances and joint ventures with other global organizations.

Contact: Sheikh Khalid Ali Reza, Managing Director, HIDADA, PO Box 11809, Jeddah 21463, Saudi Arabia. Tel: +966 2 637 4450, Fax: +966 2 637 5428, Website: www.hidada.com.sa.

Jadawel International

Jadawel International, based in Riyadh, is involved in building materials and supplies (wholesale).

Contact: Mr Mohamed Bin Issa Al-Jaber, Chairman, PO Box 61539, Riyadh 11575, Saudi Arabia. Tel: +966 1 463 1760/464 4679; Fax: +966 1 465 1013; Email: info@jadawelinternational.com; Website: www.jadawelinternational.com.

Jeraisy Group

Established in 1958, the Jeraisy Group is a leading business group in the Kingdom of Saudi Arabia. Its subsidiaries collectively specialize in computers and communications equipment, office automation, office furnishing products, manufacture of plastic cards, computer paper products, high-grade office and home wooden and metal furniture.

Contact: Mr Abdul Rahman A Al-Jeraisy, Chairman, PO Box 317, Riyadh 11411, Saudi Arabia. Tel: +966 1 419 6005/419 8000; Fax: +966 1 419 2651/419 5171; Email: cm@jeraisy.com or chairman@jeraisy.com; Website: www.jeraisy.com.

Kingdom Holding Company

Founded in 1997, the Kingdom Holding Company invests in banks, hotels, amusement parks, computer companies, and real estate development.

Contact: H.R.H. Prince Al-Waleed Bin Talal Bin Abdulaziz Al Saud, Chairman, PO Box 2, Riyadh 11321, Saudi Arabia. Tel: +966 1 211 1111; Fax: +966 1 211 1112; Email: info@kingdom.net or alwaleed@kingdom.net or mhm@kingdom.net; Website: www.kingdom.net (under construction).

The Law Firm of Yousef & Mohammed Al-Jadaan

The law firm of Yousef & Mohammed Al-Jadaan is a Saudi Arabian professional partnership established by Yousef Al-Jadaan and Mohammed Al-Jadaan. The firm is one of the largest law firms in Saudi Arabia, giving it the resources to be attentive to its clients. Al-Jadaan has a close relationship with the leading UK law firm of Clifford Chance, LLP. For the past seven years, Al-Jadaan and Clifford Chance have worked together on a number of projects. They have been recently appointed as legal advisers in connection with the privatization of Saudi Arabian Airlines. Al-Jadaan maintains a select group of legal experts with years of experience in the fields of both *Sharia'a*/Islamic jurisprudence and Saudi Arabian law to meet the comprehensive legal needs of domestic and international corporate clients. The firm specializes in corporate services, business counselling, electronic commerce, assets protection, labour and employment, liaison, mergers and acquisitions, corporate restructuring and privatization, litigation, mediation, arbitration and disputes, copyright, trade marks, patents and industrial rights, real estate acquisitions, dispositions, and mortgages. The Al-Jadaan law firm has a special expertise in litigation and court representation, banking and finance, corporate law, intellectual property, foreign investment, commercial arrangements, and property.

Contact: Mr Yousef A Al-Jadaan, Partner or Mr Mohammed A Al-Jadaan, Partner, PO Box 3515, Riyadh 11481, Saudi Arabia. Tel: +966 1 478 0220; Fax: +966 1 476 9332/472 6606; Email: info@aljadaan.com or yousef@aljadaan.com; Website: www.aljadaan.com.

M. & A. Albawardi Group of Companies

M. & A. Albawardi Group of Companies provides consultancy services for power plants, electrical transmission lines up to 380 kV, GIS substations up to 380 kV for SCECO, and desalination plants in the Kingdom. Other company activities include building materials, steel industries, tools and hardware, warehousing, cargo, bagging grain terminals and metal alloying.

Contact: Mr Khaled M Albawardi, President, PO Box 112, Dammam 31411, Saudi Arabia. Tel: +966 3 834 4422/833 5555; Fax: +966 3 833 6666/832 8500/833 4122; Email: info@albawardi.com or khaled@albawardi.com; Website: www.albawardi.com.

M.H. Sherbiny for Commerce

M.H. Sherbiny for Commerce was established in 1986 and acts as a representative for numerous US and European companies by marketing their products and providing technical solutions and service support. The company provides such services as electrical instrumentation, mechanical training, service and spare parts products and services to oil refineries and companies in the oil, gas, petrochemical, power, desalination, and sewage industries in Saudi Arabia and other Gulf states. M.H. Sherbiny consists of four divisions including electrical, instrumentation, mechanical and training. M.H. Sherbiny for Commerce is headquartered in Al-Khobar and also has an office in Jeddah.

Contact: Mr Mohammad H Sherbiny, President, PO Box 3082, Al-Khobar 31952, Saudi Arabia. Tel: +966 3 894 4298; Fax: +966 3 864 7278; Email: sales@sherbinyforcommerce.com or mohds@sherbinyforcommerce.com; Website: www.sherbinyforcommerce.com.

Mahmood Saleh Abbar Company

Established in 1960 in the Western Province of Saudi Arabia, Mahmood Saleh Abbar Company is among the top Saudi 100 companies. Mahmood Saleh Abbar's activities include electrical appliances for the home; audio; and supply and installation of air-conditioning systems, commercial laundry and kitchen equipment.

Contact: Mr Ridha Mahmood Saleh Abbar, General Manager, PO Box 461, Jeddah 21411, Saudi Arabia. Tel: +966 2 651 2768/651 2940/651 2764; Fax: +966 2 651 4032/651 2750; Email: abbar@abbar-sa.com; Website: www.abbar-sa.com.

Marei Bin Mahfouz Group & Co., Ltd.

The Marei Bin Mahfouz Group & Co. Ltd., established in 1970, is involved in the trade of construction materials and equipment, and sanitary wares. The activities of the company include trading, contracting, investments, and real estate.

Contact: Mr Abdullah Marei Bin Mahfouz, Vice Chairman and CEO, PO Box 32703, Jeddah 21438, Saudi Arabia. Tel: +966 2 674 0402; Fax: +966 2 676 1274; Email: info@binmahfouz.net or bmahfouz@zajil.net; Website: www.binmahfouz.net.

Mohamed Al-Awadi Company

Mohamed Al-Awadi is involved in investing and trading of companies, banks and real estate.

Contact: H.E. Mohamed Mohamed Ali Al-Awadi, President, PO Box 601, Jeddah 21421, Saudi Arabia. Tel: +966-2-651 8042/651 2366/651 0962; Fax: +966 2 651 0970/651 5704.

Mohammed Saad Aldrees & Sons Co.

Mohammed Saad Aldrees & Sons Co. was founded in 1938. It is a diversified company with activities in trade and contracting for equipment, supplies, automobile spare parts, oil and petrochemical equipment as well as inland transportation services, gas stations, engineering, automobile workshops. The Company also manufactures all types of glass, hollow metal doors, scrap metal and is involved in farming and agriculture.

Contact: Eng. Abdulmohsen M Aldrees, Managing Director, PO Box 609, Riyadh 11421, Saudi Arabia. Tel: +966 1 206 3333/206 4115/206 6333/206 0964/206 1542; Fax: +966 1 206 7777; Email: info@aldrees.com; Website: www.aldrees.com.

The National Commercial Bank

The National Commercial Bank (NCB) was the first Saudi bank established in the Kingdom of Saudi Arabia and is now the largest in the Arab world. The bank was established in 1953 and was converted to a joint stock company in 1997. A pioneer in private banking, it ranks among the top Saudi 100 companies and is a leader in its field. It has made vast strides and set up branches in every major city to augment its services to the private and public sectors. Company activities include all aspects of commercial banking.

Contact: Mr Abdullah Salem Bahamdan, Chairman and Managing Director, PO Box 3555 Jeddah 21481, Saudi Arabia. Tel: +966 2 644 1100/649 3333; Fax: +966 2 643 9595/644 6468; Email: alahli.com@alahli.com or a.bahamdan@alahli.com; Website: www.alahli.com.

National Industrialization Co. (NIC)

Established in 1985 to promote industrial development in Saudi Arabia, National Industrialization Company acquired, in the early 1990s, a portfolio of investments that included minority stakes in manufacturing firms across the Kingdom. NIC is a diversified industrial company with investments in chemicals, glass, metals, consumer products, industrial and environmental services. It promotes many industrial investments in Saudi Arabia with local, US and European partners.

Contact: Dr Moayyed I Al-Qurtas, Chief Executive, PO Box 26707, Riyadh 11496, Saudi Arabia. Tel: +966 1 476 7166/476 9910; Fax: +966 1 477 0898; Email: general@nic.com.sa; Website: www.nic.com.sa/english.

The National Shipping Company of Saudi Arabia (NSCSA)

The National Shipping Company of Saudi Arabia (NSCSA) was established in 1979 to meet the transportation needs of importers and exporters in the Kingdom of Saudi Arabia and other countries in the Middle East. In 1991, NSCSA America Inc., was established to serve as the general agent in North America for the liner service between the United States, Canada and the Middle East/Indian Subcontinent/East Mediterranean regions. NSCSA specializes in heavy lift and Ro-Ro cargoes, as well as containers. In 1997, NSCSA began services between North America and Italy, Greece and Turkey.

Contact: Eng. Khalil I Al Gannas, CEO, PO Box 8931, Riyadh 11492, Saudi Arabia. Tel: +966 1 477 4982/478 5454; Fax: +966 1 477 7478/477 8036/478 5454 ext 111; Email: kgannas@nscsa.com.sa or ceomail@nscsa.com.sa; Website: www.nscsa.com.

The Olayan Group

Established in 1947 by Suliman S Olayan, the Olayan Group is a multinational commercial, industrial, financial and investment enterprise, consisting of more than 40 companies conducting business in the Middle East, the United States and Europe. In Saudi Arabia, the Group is extensively engaged in joint ventures, manufacturing, and exclusive distributorship for heavy equipment and consumer goods, franchise operations, construction and services. The Group, today, is among the world's largest privately held entities.

Contact: Mr Khaled S Olayan, Chairman, PO Box 1520, Al-Khobar 31952, Saudi Arabia. Tel: +966 3 887 1000; Fax: +966 3 887 2000/882 7074; Email: ofc@olayangroup.com or k.manna@oshco.com; Website: www.olayangroup.com.

Omar K. Al-Esayi & Co. Ltd.

Since its establishment in 1962, Omar K. Al-Esayi & Co. has grown significantly and holds the exclusive agency for Mitsubishi vehicles in the Kingdom. Company activities include heavy and agricultural equipment; motor technical inspection systems; food; petrochemicals, plastic and carton industry; and traffic control systems.

Contact: Mr Aidroos Hassan Al-Esayi, General Manager, PO Box 6456, Riyadh 11442, Saudi Arabia. Tel: +966 1 477 3660/477 3656; Fax: +966 1 478 5015.

Omran M. Al Omran Corporation

Al Omran Trading Company (AOTC), owned by Abdul Rahman and Abdul Karim Saleh Al Omran, has been in operation for over 20 years and is considered one of the largest and most popular companies in the sanitary wares and accessories field in the country. Additionally, it specializes in the industrial sectors of plastic pipes fittings, floor and wall ceramic tiles, and electric water heaters.

Contact: Mr Omran Mohammed Al Omran, President, PO Box 91929, Riyadh 11643, Saudi Arabia. Tel: +966 1 478 2278/479 1500; Fax: +966 1 477 7521; Email: omran@omrancorp.com.

Prima International Company Ltd.

Prima International Company, established in 2000, is under the guidance of H.H. Prince Abdul Rahman Bin Saud Al-Kabier, as Chairman of the organization. Prima engages in exporting and importing, company representation, commercial and industrial projects, trading in food stuffs, paper products, communications, computers, electronic and electrical equipment, agricultural systems, plastic products, building materials, medical equipment, providing marketing services and real estate management and investment. The company is interested in partnerships to establish commercial and industrial projects and to foster an export and import trade relationship.

Contact: H.H. Prince Abdul Rahman Bin Saud Al-Kabier, Chairman, PO Box 66971, Riyadh 11586, Saudi Arabia. Tel: +966 1 470 5323/1 279 0328/1 279 0327; Fax: +966 1 279 0331; Email: prima@prima.com.sa.

Raka Holding Co. Ltd.

Raka Holding Company was founded in 1982 in Riyadh, Saudi Arabia. Raka Trading Company began supplying the Saudi Armed Forces with equipment, spare parts and uniforms. It is now the holding company for more than six Saudi companies and represents many companies worldwide. It is one of the major suppliers to the Saudi government. Raka provides maintenance, repair and services.

Contact: Mr Musa Hamad Al-Malik, Chief Executive Officer, PO Box 16010, Riyadh 11464, Saudi Arabia. Tel: +966 1 464 6767/464 3962; Fax: +966 1 463 1639; Email: rakaa@ae.net.sa.

Rana Investment Company

Rana Investment Company, based in Riyadh, is involved in mergers and acquisitions, private investment, placement opportunities, corporate services and venture capital.

Contact: Dr Mazen Ibrahim Hassounah, General Manager, PO Box 60148, Riyadh 11545, Saudi Arabia. Tel: +966 1 462 6262; Fax: +966 1 462 6056; Email: rana@ranainvestment.com or mhassounah@ranainvestment.com; Website: www.ranainvestment.com.

Rashed A. Al Rashed & Sons Company

Rashed A. Al Rashed & Sons Company was established in 1989 and has grown steadily as a reputed supplier of fasteners in the Kingdom as well as neighbouring GCC countries. The company is the integrated source of trading, manufacturing, services, construction, contracting and development. Moreover, the company is a major investor in projects and entities globally, delivering on its promise to perform to the highest standard of quality.

Contact: Mr Abdulaziz Rashed Al Rashed, Chairman, PO Box 550, Riyadh 11421, Saudi Arabia. Tel: +966 1 276 7676, ext. 853; Fax: +966 1 276 6827/276 7378 or Mr Abdulrahman Rashed Al Rashed, Executive Director, PO Box 99, Al Khobar 31952, Saudi Arabia. Tel: +966 3 857 4991; Fax: +966 3 857 2370/857 3918; Email: rarinvest@alrashed-group.com; Website: www.alrashed-group.com.

Rezayat Co. Ltd.

Rezayat Co. Ltd. has long-standing expertise in the fields of oil, gas, petrochemicals, public utilities, engineering and construction sectors in Saudi Arabia. The company offers turnkey engineering/construction; mechanical/electrical services and maintenance; transportation and freight logistics; marine services; catering/accommodation and life support services; crane hire; scaffolding services; drilling; fabrication of spiral welded pipe; brake linings; steel rebar; steel fabrication; catalyst regeneration; desalination systems; medical support management; product testing and insurance services.

Contact: Mr Teymour Abdulla Alireza, President and Vice Chairman, PO Box 996, Riyadh 11421, Saudi Arabia. Tel: +966 1 477 2630/477 7061; Fax: +966 1 477 4969; Email: taalireza@rezayat.net or rtclcomriy@rezayat.com.sa or hqr@rezayat.com.sa; Website: www.rezayat-commercial.com.

Riyadh Bank

Riyadh Bank was established in 1957 as a full service commercial bank and is one of the three 100 per cent Saudi-owned banks in the Kingdom. Riyadh Bank is the second largest bank, in terms of capital, both in the Kingdom and in the Arab World, and ranks 172 in the world. It is headquartered in Riyadh and has a network of 177 branches in Saudi Arabia, overseas branches as well as a wholly owned subsidiary in London and an agency office in Houston, Texas, United States.

Contact: Mr Basel Algadhib, Executive Vice President, International Banking Division, PO Box 22615, Riyadh 11416, Saudi Arabia. Tel: +966 1 401 3030 ext 2556; Fax: +966 1 404 1255; Email: baselmg@riyadbank.com.sa; Website: www.riyadbank.com.sa.

Riyadh Cables Group of Companies

Riyadh Cables Group of Companies was founded in 1984 and has branches in the major cities in the Kingdom. Company activities include the manufacture and distribution of electrical cables, copper rods, telecommunications and fibre optic cables.

Contact: Mr Hamdi S Zaim, Chairman, PO Box 26862, Riyadh 11496, Saudi Arabia. Tel: +966 1 265 0850/265 1415; Fax: +966 1 265 1423; Email: rcgc@riyadh-cables.com; Website: www.riyadh-cables.com.

Saad Group of Companies

The Saad Group, established in the 1980s, employs over 6,000 people in the fields of building design and construction, medicine, education, transportation, agriculture, civil engineering, finance, investment, information technology and property development. The Saad Group is comprised of the following companies: Saad Medical Services, Oasis Residential Resorts, Saad Travel & Tourism, Saad Information Technology, Saad National Schools, Saad Al-Sanea Centre, Saad Recruitment and Saad Investments.

Contact: Mr Maan A Al-Sanea Chairman, PO Box 3250, Al-Khobar 31952, Saudi Arabia. Tel: +966 3 882 2220/882 9998; Fax: +966 3 882 8699/882 7989/887 3557; Email: chairman@saad.com.sa or sohail@saad.com.sa; Website: www.saadtrading.com.

Safari Company Ltd.

The Safari Company's expertise includes O&M of military bases and international and local airports and the O&M and cleaning of water-desalination plants and water networks; water treatment and sewage treatment plants. Safari is also actively engaged in O&M of hospitals, provision of food supply, importation and sale of cars and tyres, trade in and retail of foodstuffs, leather luggage and light equipment, exclusive distributorship of cellular phones, and travel and tourism agencies.

Contact: Mr Saleh Ali Al-Sagri, Chairman and CEO, PO 7710, Riyadh 11472, Saudi Arabia. Tel: +966 1 231 5577/232 9487; Fax: +966 1 230 0010/232 6438; Email: saleh@safari.com.sa; Website: www.safari-e.com.

Salehiya Trading Establishment

Salehiya Trading Establishment was founded in 1967. The company activities include hospital equipment (wholesale), pharmaceuticals (wholesale), hospital furniture (wholesale), hospital management, operation, maintenance, medical, surgical equipment (wholesale) and retail pharmacies.

Contact: Mr Sultan Mohamad Bin Saleh Bin Sultan, President, PO Box 991, Riyadh 11421, Saudi Arabia. Tel: +966 1 463 3205; Fax: +966 1 463 4362; Email: genmail@salehiya.com; Website: www.salehiya.com

Samba Financial Group (Samba)

Samba (formerly Saudi American Bank) is one of the largest banks in Saudi Arabia and the Middle East. It offers an extensive range of banking and investment products and services to corporate, institutional and government customers, high net worth individuals and retail customers. The bank has an extensive network of branches Kingdom-wide, and has an overseas branch in London, a subsidiary in Geneva and a representative office in Beirut.

Contact: Mr Abdulrahman Saad Al-Sadhan, Chief of Staff and Corporate Secretary, PO Box 833, Riyadh 11421, Saudi Arabia. Tel: +966 1 477 4770 exts 1292 and 1662; Fax: +966 1 479 9428; Email: abdulrahman. sadhan@citicorp.com; Website: www.samba.com.sa.

Saudi Advanced Industries Company (SAIC)

Saudi Advanced Industries Company was established in 1987 and its activities include, but are not limited to, transfer of technology through participation in technically oriented ventures with technology holders, as well as the promotion and development of industrial projects. SAIC had an active role in developing and establishing most of the peace shield offset programme ventures and is active in AlSalam Aircraft Company, Aircraft Accessories & Components Company, Middle East Propulsion Co. and Intl Systems Engineering Company. SAIC is continuously seeking new investment opportunities through promoting and developing its own projects or participating with others who have projects under development, whether within the economic offset programme concept or not.

Contact: Mr Abdullah Ibrahim Al-Hudaithy, Chairman, PO Box 51743, Riyadh 11553, Saudi Arabia. Tel: +966 1 461 4121/478 9840; Fax: +966 1 464

8520/477 6193; Email: info@saic.com.sa or ahcecorp@cecorp-sa.com; Website: www.saic.com.sa.

Saudi Arabian Mining Company (Ma'aden)

The Saudi Arabian Mining Company (Ma'aden) currently employs 523 people. Ma'aden's objectives are to explore, develop, and extract mineral resources; develop associated processing industries in the Kingdom; and to train Saudi nationals for mineral industries. The company annually produces 150,000 ounces of gold from its Mahd Ad Dahab and Sukhaybarat mines, with production expected to reach 270,000 ounces when the Al Hajar and Al Amar mines are added. In addition, by-products of silver, copper, and zinc have projected yields of 560,000 ounces, 1,700 tonnes and 17,000 tonnes respectively, which will double the value of metals production from approximately US$50 million annually to more than US$100 million. The company also plans to produce 5,000 tonnes of electro-fused magnesia per year, eventually increasing to 20,000 tonnes from its Zarghat magnesite deposits. Ma'aden's Al Jalamid project will begin exporting in seven years, providing more than three million tonnes per year of di-ammonium phosphate (DAP). As a diverse, export-oriented company, Ma'aden is ready for equity partnerships, joint ventures, technology transfer, and feasibility and marketing studies with a foreign partner.

Contact: Dr Abdallah E Dabbagh, President and CEO, PO Box 68861, Riyadh 11537, Saudi Arabia. Tel: +966 1 479 3825/472 1222; Fax: +966 1 477 0495; Email: maaden@maaden.com.sa; Website: www.maaden.com.sa.

Saudi Arabian Airlines

Saudi Arabian Airlines, the country's national commercial airline, was established in 1945 with a single DC-3. In 1963, Saudi Arabian Airlines became the foremost airline in the Middle East to operate commercial jets. Saudi Arabian Airlines currently carries over 12.3 million passengers annually.

Contact: Mr Thomas B Quinn, Manager Marketing and Sales, North and South America, 725 Fifth Avenue, 18th Floor New York, NY 10022, USA. Tel: 212 751 7000; Fax: 212 751 7270; Email: svmktg@aol.com; Website: www.saudiairlines.com.

Saudi Arabian Amiantit Co

Founded in 1968, Saudi Arabian Amiantit Co produces rubber rings for all types of pipes and fittings, rubber sheets, cable duct sealing units, refrigeration and air-conditioning parts, insulation tubes, continuous profiles, and other moulded and extruded rubber products.

Contact: Eng. Fareed Y Khalawi, CEO and Managing Director, PO Box 589, Dammam 31421, Saudi Arabia. Tel: +966 3 847 1399/847 1500 ext 112;

Fax: +966 3 847 2307/847 1645 or PO Box 2140, Jeddah 21451, Saudi Arabia. Tel: +966 2 606 4271; Fax: +966 2 606 4257; Email: fykhalawi@amiantit.com or info@amiantit.com; Website: www.amiantitgroup.com.

Saudi Arabian Oil Company (Saudi Aramco)

Saudi Aramco is responsible for the operation of all aspects of the Kingdom's petroleum industry, including exploration, production, processing, refining and distribution, as well as shipping. Saudi Aramco is the world's largest oil company.

Contact: Dr Ibrahim Saud Mishari, Vice President, Information Technology, PO Box 5000, Dhahran 31311, Saudi Arabia. Tel: +966 3 875 6385/873 7607; Fax: +966 3 873 8708; Email: misharis@aramco.com.sa or webmaster@aramco.com.sa; Website: www.saudiaramco.com.

Saudi Basic Industries Corporation (SABIC)

Saudi Basic Industries Corporation, established in 1976, is one of the largest petrochemical producers in the world and is the largest non-oil industrial company in the Middle East. SABIC is a manufacturer and marketer of petrochemicals, fertilizers, and iron and steel products, through its 19 manufacturing companies. In 2003, SABIC's production capacity reached 42.3 million tonnes.

Contact: Eng. Mohamed H Al-Mady, Vice Chairman and CEO, PO Box 5101, Riyadh 11422, Saudi Arabia. Tel: +966 1 225 9655/225 8000 ext 9688; Fax: +966 1 225 9660/225 9000; Email: almady@sabic.com; Website: www.sabic.com.

Saudi Binladin Group

The Saudi Binladin Group, founded in 1931, is focused on engineering, design, and construction of large-scale turnkey projects involving highways, bridges, tunnels, airports, buildings, industrial and power plants, high-rise structures, petrochemicals and mining, real estate development, and maintenance and operation. The Binladin Group has in-house capabilities for the production of a wide range of construction and building finishing materials, as well as research and development.

Contact: Eng. Yahia Mohammed Binladin, Managing Director and Deputy Chairman of the Board, PO Box 8918, Jeddah 21492, Saudi Arabia. Tel: +966 2 664 3033; Fax: +966 2 664 3261/664 2987/664 3221; Email: ymb@sbg.com.sa or yjyehia@sbg.com.sa; Website: www.sbg.com.sa (under construction) and www.sbguae.com.

The Saudi British Bank (SABB)

The Saudi British Bank (SABB), an associated company of the HSBC Group, is a full-service commercial bank that operates through a network of 73 branches. With total assets of more than US$15.4 billion, SABB is one of the leading banks in the Kingdom and was rated as the 'Best Bank in Saudi Arabia for 2004' for the second consecutive year by *Euromoney Magazine*. In 2004, SABB recorded a net profit of US$436 million, while customer deposits increased to US$11.9 billion, a 24 per cent increase from the previous year. Established in 1978, SABB is a leader in offering its customers a full range of banking services such as: personal, commercial, corporate, private and Islamic banking; investment, treasury, trade service; and electronic, internet and telephone banking. SABB VISA and MasterCard credit cards are welcomed in more than 18 million commercial outlets within the Kingdom and around the world. In addition, SABB ATM and credit cards can access more than 350,000 ATMs in the Kingdom and around the world. SABB has also made headlines in the area of public subscriptions, managing the US$4 billion Initial Public Offering (IPO) of Saudi Telecom Company (STC) in January 2003 and the US $4.4 billion IPO for the National Company for Cooperative Insurance (NCCI) in December 2004.

Contact: Geoff Calvert, Managing Director, PO Box 9084, Riyadh 11413, Saudi Arabia. Tel: +966 1 405 0677/405 4607; Fax: +966 1 405 0677/405 0069; Email: johnrichards@sabb.com; Website: www.sabb.com.

Saudi Brothers Commercial Company

Established in 1978, the Saudi Brothers Commercial Company is a multinational company with a diversified industrial and commercial business portfolio, including theme parks, amusement parks, livestock, grazing farms and construction. Saudi Brothers Commercial Company established the first and the largest theme park project in the Arab World in Jeddah. In addition, Saudi Brothers Commercial Company is focused on hotel and leisure, amusement and recreational services, tourism, commercial real estate development and operation, marina development and operation, air transportation and services, canning, processed foods, retail trade, wholesale trade, manufacturing, agriculture production (with livestock and animal specialities), and printing.

Contact: Mr Khalid Mohammed Al-Nowaiser, Vice Chairman and General Manager, PO Box 5604, Jeddah 21432, Saudi Arabia. Tel: +966 2 660 6802/660 6925; Fax: +966 2 660 8140; Email: info@saudibrothers.com; Website: www.saudibrothers.com.

Saudi Business Insight Group

Since its inception in 1999, Saudi Business Insight, Ltd. (SBIT) has dealt in numerous products and services in the local market, including showrooms for mobile phones and accessories in the main shopping centres of Jeddah. The goal of SBIT is to manufacture, market, and install desalination and water treatment equipment in Saudi Arabia. SBIT plans to offer *Hajj* and *Umrah* services to pilgrims and VIP travel services in the Kingdom's expanding tourism industry. The company is interested in joint ventures, representative offices, and agency relationships with overseas companies. SBIT seeks a partner to implement an advanced waste-recycling technology for conversion into such products as fertilizers, metal and paper in Saudi Arabia.

Contact: Mr Turki bin Ibrahim bin Abdulaziz Al-Ibrahim, Chairman, PO Box 14069, Jeddah 21424, Saudi Arabia. Tel: +966 2 669 1881/644 8802; Fax: +966 2 668 0866/644 8721; Email: habiss@yahoo.com or turki666@aol.com.

Saudi Cable Company

Saudi Cable Company, a joint stock company established in 1975, has recorded continuous growth to become one of the leading companies in its field worldwide. The company is engaged in the manufacture and supply of electrical and telecommunications cables, copper and aluminium rods, PVC compounds, wooden reels and pallets, and other related products. Over the years, strategic partnerships have been formed with such leading companies as Anaconda Wire & Cable, Philips/NKF, Hitachi Cables, and Cable Cortaillod. The company comprises three local and eight international subsidiaries, and three associated companies. The SCC Group is engaged in the manufacturing, contracting, trading, distribution and supply of power, and telecommunications cables, including optical fibre cable, electronic products, information technology products and related accessories. The total annual sales of SCC were SR1.2 billion (US$343 million) for 1999. The company employs 1,600 professionals to conduct its business activities. The SCC Group ranks 31st among Saudi Arabia's top 100 companies.

Contact: Mr Mohammad Hadoun Al Attas, Group Vice President, Finance and Corporate Affairs, PO Box 4403, Jeddah 21491, Saudi Arabia. Tel: +966 2 638 0080 ext 1410; Fax: +966 2 637 5447/635 2220; Email: saudi_cable@hotmail.com or mattas.scc@xenel.com; Website: www.xenel.com/site/industrial.

Saudi Consulting Services

Founded in 1965 by its Chairman, Dr Shawaf, Saudi Consulting Services is a sole proprietorship and 100 per cent Saudi owned. It has branches located in major cities in the Kingdom, including Jeddah, Riyadh, Madinah, Jubail, and Al Khobar. Saudi Consulting Services is a multidisciplinary engineering/architectural firm, engaged in all phases of design and construction, which range from preparing feasibility studies, programming and conceptual planning, to detailed design of diverse kinds of projects.

Contact: Eng. Dr Tarek M A Al-Shawaf, Chairman of the Board and President, PO Box 2341, Riyadh 11451, Saudi Arabia. Tel: +966 1 465 9975; Fax: +966 1 465 0530/464 7540; Email: scr@zajil.net or sc@saudconsult.com; Website: www.saudconsult.com.

Saudi German Hospitals Group

The Batterjee family established the country's first pharmaceutical distribution network with international companies in the 1940s. In 1988, they created the Saudi German Hospitals Group and opened the first of its hospitals in Jeddah. The Saudi German Hospitals Group is the first hospital group in Saudi Arabia to introduce helicopter rescue services. Specialities include orthopedics and traumatology. They currently have hospitals in Jeddah and Abha with Riyadh, Madinah and Qasim openings in the very near future.

Contact: Engr. Sobhi A Batterjee, CEO and President, PO Box 2550, Jeddah 21461, Saudi Arabia. Tel: +966 2 682 9000; Fax: +966 2 683 5874/690 5038; Email: sgh@sghgroup.com; Website: www.sghgroup.com.

Saudi Hollandi Bank

Saudi Hollandi Bank, the first bank in Saudi Arabia, was founded in 1926 and became a joint stock company in 1976 with capital of SR630 million (US$168 million). Saudi Hollandi Bank is headquartered in Riyadh with regional offices in Jeddah and Al-Khobar and has relationships with 500 banks in 52 countries. Saudi Hollandi Bank provides its customers with more than 381,000 cash access points worldwide through the Bank's affiliation with Saudi Payment Network's (SPAN) 1,600 ATMs nationwide and its own arrangements with VISA and PLUS networks. Saudi Hollandi Bank offers a wide array of banking products for personal and business purposes, backed by advanced technological systems for maximum accuracy and enhanced customer and information service. Its state-of-the-art data processing ensures accurate and fast processing to make funds available when and where they are needed. Saudi Hollandi Bank has maintained growth in profits for six consecutive years. Net profit in 1999 increased to SR302.9 million (US$80.8 million), a 20 percent increase from the previous year. The Saudi Hollandi Bank's credit portfolio remains sound as stated in rating reports issued during 1999 by Bank Watch, Capital Intelligence, Moody's, and Standard and Poor's.

Contact: Mr Giel-Jan van der Tol, Managing Director, PO Box 1467, Riyadh 11431, Saudi Arabia. Tel: +966 1 406 7888 ext 522; Fax: +966 401 0968; Email: gvandertol@shb.com.sa; Website: www.shb.com.sa.

Saudi Industrial Export Company

Saudi Industrial Export Company, the leading export house of Saudi Arabia, deals in a variety of Saudi-made industrial commodities. Their marketing network consists of five product groups, namely raw materials (cement, sulphur, etc), building materials, food and consumer products, electrical and engineering products, and plastic and chemicals products.

Contact: Mr Abdullah M Al Khenaifer, Executive President, PO Box 21977, Riyadh 11485, Saudi Arabia. Tel: +966 1 405 8080/408 3734; Fax: +966 1 402 2854/401 2622; Email: siec@siec.com.sa; Website: www.siec.com.sa.

Saudi International Petrochemical Company

Saudi International Petrochemical Company (SIPC), capitalized at SR500 million (US$133 million), is a joint stock company incorporated on 22 December 1999. SIPC initially formed three limited liability companies in joint venture with foreign partners to produce and market 50,000 tonnes of maleic anhydride (MAN) and butanedial (BDO), 850,000 tonnes of methanol and 300,000 tonnes of acetic acid in Jubail Industrial City. SIPC's goal is to grow into a major petrochemical manufacturer in the basic and downstream petrochemical industries within 10 years. In addition, SIPC seeks new investors for its project integration projects. The projects are capital intensive, export-oriented and value-added to generate foreign exchange and enhanced opportunities for Saudi professionals.

Contact: H.E. Eng. Abdulaziz A Al-Zamil, Chairman and CEO, PO Box 251, Riyadh 11411, Saudi Arabia. Tel: +966 1 476 3127; Fax: +966 1 472 4115. Company contact details: PO Box 130, Al-Khobar 31952, Saudi Arabia. Tel: +966 3 801 0109/801 0110/801 0111; Fax: +966 3 801 0222; Email: yahya@sipc.com.sa; Website: www.sipc.com.sa (under construction).

The Saudi Investment Bank

The Saudi Investment Bank (SAIB) is a Saudi Arabian joint stock company that began operations in April 1977. It provides personalized and professional banking services to financial institutions, corporations and individuals. The Saudi Investment Bank is 90 per cent owned by Saudi shareholders. The foreign shareholders are Chase Manhattan with 7.5 per cent and the Industrial Bank of Japan with 2.5 per cent. The Bank offers traditional wholesale, retail and commercial banking products and services in addition to investment banking. In particular, it arranges financing of the quasi-government enterprises and private industrial sectors and trade finance products for imports.

Contact: Dr Abdulaziz O'Hali, Chairman, PO Box 3533, Riyadh 11481, Saudi Arabia. Tel: +966 1 477 8433; Fax: +966 1 478 1557; Email: info@saib.com.sa or aohali@saib.com.sa; Website: www.saib.com.sa.

Saudi Logistics & Technical Support (SALTS)

Saudi Logistics & Technical Support was founded by the owner of Dallah AlBarakah Group as an affiliate of Dallah Group in 1986. Some 70 per

cent of this firm's dealings is to supply equipment and material to the parent company and its group companies, and 30 per cent to the local market. SALTS' activities include human resources support, trade in electronics, mechanical and electrical equipment and its spare parts, filtration systems, corrosion control coating, computer services, training, systems and logistical support for defence, industrial and commercial projects, and procurement.
Contact: Mr Saleh Mohammed Al-Hajaj, President, PO Box 57085, Riyadh 11574, Saudi Arabia. Tel: +966 1 465 0138; Fax: +966 1 465 5712; Email: sales@salts.com.sa; Website: www.salts.com.sa.

Saudi Pharmaceutical Industries & Medical Appliances Corporation (SPIMACO)

Saudi Pharmaceutical Industries and Medical Appliances Corporation is a Saudi joint stock company with a fully paid-up capital of SR600 million. It was established in January 1986, with the main objective of creating an advanced pharmaceutical industry in the Kingdom for the local production of medicines and medical appliances and to market these products inside the Kingdom and for export.

Contact: Dr Abdullah A Abdulkader, Managing Director, PO Box 20001, Riyadh 11455, Saudi Arabia. Tel: +966 1 477 4481; Fax: +966 1 477 3961; Email: general@spimaco.com.sa or drabdullah@spimaco.com.sa; Website: www.spimaco.com.sa.

The SKAB Group

SKAB is one of the largest and most diversified groups in the Kingdom of Saudi Arabia. Its companies operate in a variety of interconnected and mutually compatible business sectors and its activities cover areas such as real estate development and construction, power generation, environmental protection, tourism, food products and dairy farming.

Contact: The SKAB Group, P.O. Box 13271, Jeddah 21493, Kingdom of Saudi Arabia. Tel: +966-2-606 0608; Fax: +966-2-606 1702 / 606 0940; E-mail: info@skabco.net Website: www.skabco.net

Seder Group

The Seder Group was founded in 1981 as a small, family establishment providing operation and maintenance services to both the government and private sectors in Saudi Arabia. Seder has since become one of the largest conglomerates and professional group of companies in Saudi Arabia, with a broad range of businesses and services. The primary areas of company activities include operation and maintenance, construction, technical building services, telecommunications, direct mail services, housing compound management, catering, travel and tourism, water supply, janitorial and housekeeping services, pest control services, solid and liquid waste management, metal scrap collection and environmental services. The Seder Group employs over 5,000 people, ranging from highly trained managers, engineers and technicians to labourers, in many different areas. The company is headquartered in Riyadh with offices in Jeddah and Dubai. The Group's subsidiary concerns are Seder Operation & Maintenance; Seder Construction; Technical Building Services; Seder Village; Seder Telecom; Seder Water Supply; Metals Corner; Seder Crown; Maxim Restaurant; Maxim Oasis; Elite Oasis; Seder Travel & Tourism; and Kerdah for Civil Security.

Contact: Dr Mohammed Saud Al-Blehed, Vice President and CEO ,PO Box 8896, Riyadh 11492, Saudi Arabia. Tel: +966 1 460 6666; Fax: +966 1 460 7588/460 5897; Email: info@sedergroup.com; Website: www.sedergroup.com.

Solar Energy Trading Est.

Solar Energy Trading Est. (SETE), which began operations in 1990, deals in all types of equipment and materials in the field of mechanical, electrical, power plants equipment and spare parts, and industrial supplies. Solar Energy also maintains an office in Houston, Texas. SETE is the sole representative of Ceramic Cooling Tower Corporation (CCTC), USA; Furmanite International, UK; and Indumar Products Inc., USA. CCTC, founded in 1947, manufactures heat transfer and thermal energy equipment for the air-conditioning, refrigeration and petrochemical industries and all industrial process cooling. The company is known for high quality cooling tower design and construction of concrete and fibreglass towers and services for all cooling towers. Furmanite International specializes in hot tapping, line plugging, line freezing, under pressure leak sealing, on-site machining, inspection services, steam trap inspection programmes, and valves and safety valves repair. Indumar Products Inc. produces problem-solving products for the industry, including 'Stop It Pipe Repair Systems' for repairing leaks in all metal and plastic pipes, repairing conduit and reinforced pipe joints.

Contact: Mr Saleh Abdul Azeez Al-Namleh, General Manager, PO Box 40968, Riyadh 11511, Saudi Arabia. Tel: +966 1 206 0622/206 0662; Fax: +966 1 472 7024; Email: solar@awalnet.net.sa.

Suhayl Bin Abdul Mohsin Al Shoaibi & Sons Holding Co. Ltd

Suhayl Bin Abdul Mohsin Al Shoaibi & Sons Holding Co. is a fully owned subsidiary of Shoaibi Group, which was established in 1977. The company was established to develop and carry out commercial and industrial activities in the Middle East, United States and Europe. Its primary areas of activity since 1992 have been in the oil, gas and petrochemical industries in the Middle East. Other areas of long-term experience for the group are information technology,

HVAC manufacturing, and the installation, service and manufacturing of oilfield service products. The Shoaibi Group's joint venture partners are J. Ray McDermott, Technipetrol/TPL, Western Geophysical, Forasol Foramer, Carlo Gavazzi, BEA, OMB, and Halliburton Energy Services. Shoaibi Group is also the sole agent of such well-known equipment manufacturers and suppliers as GE Nuovo Pignone, Daniel Industries, Alcatel Telecom, Harris Corp, Aspen Tech, Control Systems International, and Origin. Shoaibi Group's sales exceeded SR900 million (US$240 million) in 1998, and Shoaibi Contracting Est. has total sales of more than SR562.5 million (US$150 million) and employs 100 people.

Contact: Mr Walid S Al Shoaibi, General Manager, PO Box 1280, Al Khobar 31952, Saudi Arabia. Tel: +966 3 894 1700; Fax: +966 3 895 2597; Email: enquiries@shoaibigroup.com; Website: www.shoaibigroup.com.

Tamimi Group of Companies

One of the leading companies in Saudi Arabia, the Tamimi Group of Companies is specialized in electrical, mechanical and civil contracting, pipeline construction, industrial works, general trading and real estate development.

Contact: Mr Tariq Ali Al-Tamimi, President, PO Box 172, Dammam 31411, Saudi Arabia. Tel: +966 3 847 4050/847 4130; Fax: +966 3 847 1592/847 1725; Email: tamimi-ho@al-tamimi.com; Website: www.al-tamimi.com.

Trading and Development Partnership Co.

The Trading and Development Partnership of Riyadh is involved in electrical power stations, sub-stations, and overhead transmission lines (33 kV up to 132 kV); turnkey contracting for supply, delivery and water installation; trading and marketing of electrical materials; water proofing works specialized in geosynthetic liners; supply and installation of other products.

Contact: Mr Abdullah M Al-Hugail, President, PO Box 1327, Riyadh 11431, Saudi Arabia. Tel: +966 1 419 4444; Fax: +966 1 488 9035; Email: faiz@tdpco.com; Website: www.tdpco.com.

United Saudis

United Saudis was established in 1976. The company is involved in import and trade in agriculture and providing technical know-how to farmers. Other company activities include oil and gas field machinery and equipment manufacturing.

Contact: Mr Saleh Al Ali Al-Rashed, Managing Director, PO Box 572, Al-Khobar 31952, Saudi Arabia. Tel: +966 3 887 6000/887 4863/887 4946/882 1531; Fax: +966 3 887 4945; Email: info@alrashedtower.com or saleh@alrashedtower.com; Website: www.alrashedtower.com.

Wallan Group

Established in 1976 in Riyadh, the Wallan Group's activities include importing, spare parts, beverages, equipment, cosmetics, tyres and tubes, motor vehicle dealerships, and new and used cars retail. Wallan is a distributor of Hyundai vehicles.

Contact: Mr Saad F Wallan, Chairman, PO Box 3176, Riyadh 11471, Saudi Arabia. Tel: +966 1 493 3331/491 0808; Fax: +966 1 493 2238; Email: saad@wallan.com or saad@wallanaviation.com; Website: www.hyundai.com.sa.

Xenel Industries Limited

Founded in 1973, Xenel is one of the leading Saudi companies. Xenel Industries is a holding company whose activities include medical, industrial, petrochemicals, oil and gas, electricity, water, power, construction, operation, maintenance and investment.

Contact: Mr Khalid Ahmed Yousuf Xenel Alireza, CEO and Executive Director, PO Box 2824, Jeddah 21461, Saudi Arabia. Tel: +966 2 643 7619/645 5555/644 7776; Fax: +966 2 643 8405/644 4651; Email: khalidaalireza@xenel.com; Website: www.xenel.com.

Yusuf Bin Ahmed Kanoo

Founded in 1890 as an importer of consumer goods and natural pearls, Yusuf Bin Ahmed Kanoo was initially established as a shipping agency and port and cargo services business. Kanoo's present-day activities include shipping; travel; aircraft handling; machinery sales and services; oil field supplies and services; air freight and cargo services; insurance; industry; and banking and investments.

Contact: Mr Abdulla Ali Kanoo, Group Chairman and CEO, PO Box 37, King Saud Road, Dammam 31411, Saudi Arabia. Tel: +966 3 835 5700/835 6000/835 5744; Fax: +966 3 835 5747/835 5710; Email: info@ybakanoo.com or abdullakanoo@kanoosa.com or info@kanoogroup.com; Website: www.ybakanoo.com and www.kanoogroup.com.

Appendix V

Contributor Contact Details

Al Harithy Company for Exhibitions UK Limited
The Glassmill
1 Battersea Bridge Road
London SW11 3BG
United Kingdom
Tel: +44 (0)20 7223 3431
Fax: +44 (0)20 7228 4229
Email: international@acexpos.com
Website: www.acexpos.com

Al Yaqoub Legal Advisers
PO Box 57288
Riyadh 11574
Kingdom of Saudi Arabia
Tel: +966 1 211 0600
Fax: +966 1 211 0601
Website: www.alyaqoub.com
Contact: Kamal K. Mahjoub, Legal Counsel
Email: kkmahjoub@alyaqoub.com

ASA Consulting
PO Box 238
Cobham
Surrey KT11 2WP
United Kingdom
Tel: +44 (0)1372 844317
Fax: +44 (0)1372 844437
Contact: Anthony Shoult
Email: asaconsult@btinternet.com

The British Offset Office

London
Castlewood House
77–91 New Oxford Street
London WC1A 1DT
United Kingdom
Tel: +44 (0)207 829 8556
Fax: +44 (0)207 829 8116
Email: AYOffset@aol.com

Riyadh
UK MoD Team
PO Box 1003
Riyadh 11431
Kingdom of Saudi Arabia
Tel: +966 1 419 5957 ext 4210
Fax: +966 1 419 5957 ext 4214
Website: www.britishoffset.com

Cluttons Middle East/PMDC Cluttons
PO Box 4843
Jeddah 21412
Kingdom of Saudi Arabia
Tel: +966 2 698 0145
Fax: +966 2 698 0146
Website: www.cluttons-me.com
Contact: Keith Procter, Project Manager
Email: keith_p@pmdccluttons.com

ERAS Limited
4/6 Canfield Place
London NW6 3BT
United Kingdom
Tel: +44 (0)207 625 1455
Fax: +44 (0)207 625 1246
Contact: David Green, Senior Consultant
Email: david@erasuk.com

Ernst & Young
PO Box 2732
Level 6, Al Faisaliah Office Tower
Riyadh 11461
Kingdom of Saudi Arabia
Tel: +966 1 273 4740

Fax: +966 1 273 4730
Email: kevin.obrien@sa.eyi.com
Website: www.ey.com/me

Green Vista Agriculture Specialists

PO Box 5133
Riyadh 11422
Kingdom of Saudi Arabia
Tel: +966 1 403 0302
Mobile: +966 5 326 3599
Fax: +966 1 406 8307
Email: info@greenmountain.com.sa
Contact: John Lawton, Director

Gulf International Bank BSC

Head Office

Al-Dowali Building
3 Palace Avenue
PO Box 1017
Manama
Bahrain
Tel: +973 17 534 000
Fax: +973 17 522 633
Email: info@gibbah.com

Riyadh Branch

Abraj Atta'Awuneya
King Fahad Road
PO Box 93413
Riyadh 11673
Kingdom of Saudi Arabia
Tel: +966 1 218 0555
Fax: +966 1 218 0055
Website: www.gibonline.com

Islamic Development Bank

PO Box 5925
Jeddah 21432
Kingdom of Saudi Arabia
Tel: +966 2 636 1400
Fax: +966 2 636 6871
Contact: Dr Bashir Fadlalla
Email: bfadlall@isdb.org.sa

The Law Firm of Saleh Al-Hejailan
PO Box 1454
Riyadh 11431
Kingdom of Saudi Arabia
Tel: +966 1 479 2200
Fax: +966 1 479 1717
Email: lfshriyadh@naseej.com.sa
Website: www.hejailannet.com

Legal Advisors
Baker & McKenzie
Olayan Complex, Tower II
Al-Ahsa Street, Malaz
PO Box 4288
Riyadh, 11491
Kingdom of Saudi Arabia
Tel: +966 1 291 5561
Fax: +966 1 291 5571
Website: www.bakernet.com

Riyadh Bank
P O Box 22622
Riyadh 11416
Saudi Arabia
Contact: Dr H Khan Zahid, Chief Economist and Vice President
Tel: +966 1 401 3030 ext 2534
Email: khan.zahid@riyadbank.com

The Saudi Arabian Business Information and Economic Research Centre (SABIERC)
Station Farm
Station Road
Melbourne
Derby DE73 1BQ
United Kingdom
Tel/Fax: +44 1332 865380
Contact: Professor John Presley
Email: j.r.presley@lboro.ac.uk

The Saudi Arabian General Investment Authority (SAGIA)

Head Office, Riyadh
PO Box 5927
Riyadh 11432
Kingdom of Saudi Arabia

Tel: +966 1 263 5010
Fax: +966 1 263 5020
Email: info@sagia.gov.sa

Investor Service Centre, Riyadh
PO Box 1267
Riyadh 11431
Kingdom of Saudi Arabia
Tel: +966 1 447 0031
Fax: +966 1 447 3697

Investor Service Centre, Jeddah
PO Box 1001
Jeddah 21431
Tel: +966 2 657 1580
Fax: +966 2 657 2097
Kingdom of Saudi Arabia

Investor Service Centre, Dammam
PO Box 1234
Dammam 31431
Kingdom of Saudi Arabia
Tel: +966 3 858 1110
Fax: +966 3 858 8177

Trilateral Training Solutions
PO Box 191
Abu Dhabi
United Arab Emirates
Tel: +971 2 6324631
Fax: +971 2 6211058
Contact: Dr Jehad Al-Omari
Email: omaritrd@emirates.net.ae

Yusuf Bin Ahmed Kanoo
PO Box 37
Dammam 31411
Kingdom of Saudi Arabia
Tel: +966 3 835 5768
Fax: +966 3 835 5662
Email: colin@kanoosa.com